VOICE OF THE LEOPARD

■ ■ ■

CARIBBEAN STUDIES SERIES
Anton L. Allahar and Shona N. Jackson
Series Editors

Voice of the Leopard

AFRICAN SECRET SOCIETIES AND CUBA

■ ■ ■

IVOR L. MILLER

University Press of Mississippi / *Jackson*

www.upress.state.ms.us

Publication of this book is sponsored by InterAmericas®/Society of
Arts and Letters of the Americas, a program of The Reed Foundation.

The University Press of Mississippi is a member
of the Association of American University Presses.

First printing 2009
∞
Library of Congress Cataloging-in-Publication Data

Miller, Ivor.
   Voice of the leopard : African secret societies and Cuba / Ivor L. Miller.
      p. cm. — (Carribean studies series)
   Includes bibliographical references and index.
   ISBN 978-1-934110-83-6 (cloth : alk. paper) 1. Sociedad Abakuá
(Cuba) 2. Secret societies—Cuba. 3. Blacks—Cuba—Social life and
customs. I. Title.
   HS1355.S64C845   2008
   369.097291—dc22

                                                2008033971

British Library Cataloging-in-Publication Data available

Ñañiguism [Abakuá] is not a masquerade, nor a
fearsome society: it is an ethnic re-importation: it
is an African country that plays, chants, and dances
things that in Africa must have meaning. What does
it mean? Like Hamlet, I said, *That is the question.*
—SPANISH PENAL AUTHORITY (Salillas 1901: 342)

History has two parts: that which happens
and that which is written.
—CUBAN ABAKUÁ LEADER, 2001

To all who struggle to
defend historical memory of
family and community

■ ■ ■

CONTENTS

∎ ∎ ∎

ACKNOWLEDGMENTS

...

For their help with my research in Cuba, I gratefully thank the following individuals: Natalia Bolívar, Luisa Campuzano (Casa de las Américas), Luis Carbonel, Osvaldo Cárdenas-Villamil (Efí Kunanbére), Niudys Cruz-Zamora, Idania Díaz-González, Pedro-Michel Díaz, Jorge and Norma Enriquez, José-Antonio Fernández, Tomás Fernández-Robaina (Biblioteca Nacional "José Martí"), Radamés Giro (musicologist), Gregorio "El Goyo" Hernández (musician), Lázaro Herrera (Septeto Nacional de Ignacio Piñeiro), Mercedes Herrera Sorzano (Museo del Ferrocarril de Cuba), Mirta González-Fernández, Eusebio Leal (Historian of the City of Havana), Zoila Lapique Becall (historian), Dra. María-Terésa Lináres, Jorge Macle-Cruz (Archivo Nacional de Cuba), Ibraim Malleri, Rogelio Martínez-Furé (Conjunto Folklórico Nacional), Maria-Elena Mendiola, Frank Oropesa (Septeto Nacional), Pablo Pacheco-López (ICAIC), Carmen Pasqual (Museo de Guanabacoa), Guillermo Pasos-González, Francisco Peñalver-Sánchez "El Chino" (Awana Mokóko Efó), Alfredo Prieto (Centro Martin Luther King, Jr.), Rafael Queneditt, "Tato" Quiñones, Jorge Reyes (bassist), Roberto Sanchez-Ferrer (composer), Ernesto Soto-Rodríguez "El Sambo" (Itia Mukandá), Pedro-Alberto Suarez Gonzáles "Pedrito el yuma" (Moruá Eribó Engomo de Betongó Naróko Efó), Margarita Ugarte (Conjunto Folkórico Nacional), Oscar Valdés, Jr. (Irakere), Sergio Vitier (composer), and Francisco "Minini" Zamora (Grupo AfroCuba).

My work in Nigeria was made possible by the gracious help of the following: Sunday Adaka (curator, National Museum, Calabar), Nath Mayo Adediran (director of museums, National Commission for Museums and Monuments), Engineer Bassey Efiong Bassey, Etubom Bassey Ekpo Bassey (Efe Ékpè Eyo Ema, Ekoretonko), Donald Duke (former governor, Cross River State), Edidem Atakpor-Obong (Dr.) E.B.A. Ekanem (Nsomm the 3rd and Paramount Ruler of Uruan Inyang Atakpo), H.R.M. Obong (Dr.) Essien U. Ekidem (Ntisong Ibibio, Ntison III, Obom Ibibio), Liza A. Gadsby and Peter D. Jenkins Jr. (Pandrillus). H.R.M. Edidem (Prof.) Nta Elijah Henshaw IV (the late Obong of Calabar), Prince Etim Ika (Efut Ifako), H.R.M. Ndidem (Dr.) Thomas

Ika Ika Oqua III (Ndidem of the Qua Nation), Jill Salmons, Professor Eno-Abasi Urua (UniUyo), and Okon E. Uya (UniCal).

For their help in Cameroon, I extend my sincere gratitude to the following: J.B.C. Foe-Atangana (Minister Plenipotentiary, Consulate of the republic of Cameroon), Dr. Enoh Richard Agbor (University of Buea), Chief Esoh Itoh (Paramount Ruler of the Balondo people of Cameroon), Fongot Kinni (University of Buea), Roland Ndip (University of Buea), Victor Julius Ngoh (University of Buea), Edmond Nofuru, and Francis Nyamnjoh (CODESRIA).

My research in Spain was aided by Juan Carrete (Centro Conde/Duque), Octavio Di Leo, and Maya García de Vinuesa.

I thank the following for their help and support during my work in the United States: John Aubry (Newberry Library), José-Juan Arrom, Antonio Benítez-Rojo, Kenneth Bilby, George Brandon, Amanda Carlson, David Cantrell, Alvaro Carraro-Delgado, Bruce Connell, Jill Cutler, C. Daniel Dawson, Ogduardo "Román" Díaz (Ekueri Tongó Ápapa Umoni), Cristóbal Díaz-Ayala, Alejandro de la Fuente, David Easterbrook (Herskovits Library), Joseph Edem, Orok Edem, David Eltis, Luis "El Pelón" Fernández-Peñalber (Amiabón Brandí Masóngo), Raul A. Fernández, Robert Glover, Michael Gomez, John Gray, Ángel Guerrero-Vecino (Itia Mukandá Efó), James de Jongh (IRADAC), Joseph Inikori, Callixtus E. Ita, Reynold Kerr, Chester King, Christopher Krantz, Diana Lachatenere (the Schomburg Center), Jayne Lovett, Victor Manfredi, Nancy Mikelsons, Craig Miller, Jean Miller, Lynn Miller, Robin Moore, Patricia Ogedengbe (Herskovits Library), Colin Palmer (the Schomburg Center), Julio "Tito" Rafael–Díaz (Munandibá Efó), Enid Schildkrout, Alfonso Serrano (Grand Lodge of New York, F & AM), Ilan Stavans, Ned Sublette, Helen Hornbeck Tanner (Newberry Library), Robert Farris Thompson, Asuquo Ukpong (Ekoretonko), and Grete Viddal. Thanks to my copyeditor, Lisa DiDonato Brousseau, and to Craig Gill, Anne Stascavage, and Todd Lape at the University Press of Mississippi for their support and contributions to this project.

Finally, I extend my thanks to the many Abakuá members who wish to remain anonymous.

These following libraries and their staff were instrumental to research: Amherst College Library Special Collections, Amherst, MA; Archivo Nacional de Cuba, La Habana; Biblioteca Nacional "José Martí", Cuba; Boston University African Studies Library; Center for Black Music Research. Columbia College, Chicago (Suzanne Flandreau); The Center for Cuban Studies in New York City; DePaul University, The Richardson Library (Margaret Powers); Díaz-Ayala Cuban and Latin American Popular Music Collection, Florida International University; Harvard University Libraries, Cambridge, MA; Hemeroteca Municipal, Ayuntamiento de Madrid, España; Melville J. Herskovits Library of African Studies, Northwestern University Library; Museo de la Música, La Habana; Pritzker Legal Research Center, Northwestern University

School of Law (Jim McMasters); and The Schomburg Center for Research in Black Culture of the New York City Public Library.

Research for this book was supported by the following grants and institutions: the National Endowment for the Humanities, Samuel I. Newhouse, and the Schomburg Center for Research in Black Culture's Scholars-in-Residence Program (2007–2008; any views, findings, conclusions, or recommendations expressed in this publication do not necessarily represent those of the National Endowment for the Humanities); Calabar Mgbè (2007–2008), an association of Ékpè lodges from Èfik, Efut, Qua, Okoyong, and Umon; Council for the Development of Social Science Research in Africa (2006–2007), Transnational Working Group on Africa and Its Diaspora; Rockefeller Resident Fellow (2005–2006), Center for Black Music Research, Columbia College, Chicago; Summer Research in West Africa (2004), West African Research Association, African Studies Center, Boston University; Cultural Grant (2003), City of Chicago Department of Cultural Affairs; Visiting Faculty (2002–2004), DePaul University, Chicago, Center for the History and Culture of Black Diaspora; The Copeland Fellowship (2001–2002), Amherst College; Rockefeller Resident Fellow (2000–2001), The City College of New York; The Institute for Research in the African Diaspora in the Caribbean and the Americas, a Rockefeller Foundation Humanities Fellowship Program; Cuba Exchange Program Fellowship for Study in Cuba (2000). Johns Hopkins University; Scholar-in-Residence (1999–2000), Schomburg Center for Research in Black Culture, funded by the National Endowment for the Humanities; and an H. H. Rice Foreign Residence Fellowship (1990), Yale University, for twelve months of residency in Cuba.

Profound thanks to Jane Gregory Rubin for her assistance in arranging a publication grant from InterAmericas®/Society of Arts and Letters of the Americas, a program of The Reed Foundation.

Research materials from this book are located in the Ivor Miller Collection, Amherst College Archives and Special Collections, Amherst College Library.

A NOTE ON THE TYPOGRAPHY
AND WORD USAGE

■ ■ ■

The font used for Èfìk orthography is PanKwa. Èfìk has two tones: high and low.[1] Starting in the 1860s, the standard writing system of Èfìk has been based on the Roman
alphabet, now modified by the addition of diacritic marks above the letter. Accent
marks over vowels and nasal consonants indicate tone: acute ['] for high tone and
grave [`] for low tone. The umlaut (two dots over a vowel) as used by Goldie in the old
Èfìk orthography has been replaced with the subdot (ẹ and ọ), as used in the current
official orthography for Èfìk, as well as Ìgbo and Yorùbá (cf. Essien c. 1982, 1985). Without such diacritics, Roman spellings of Èfìk words would be either ambiguous (out of
context) or meaningless. One would be unable to distinguish the Ékpè chieftaincy title
Mbàkàrà and the Èfìk term *Mbàkárá*, meaning "those who govern" (popularly used to
mean "white man"); to distinguish between *úyò* meaning "voice" from *ùyó* meaning
"biscuit" (Aye 1991) or the Ékpè leopard club of the Cross River region from the Èkpè
religious ritual among neighboring Ìgbo of Ngwa, Umuahia, and Owerri (Amankulor
1972). Or, in Ejagham, between *nsí* meaning "earth" and *nsí* meaning "fish" (P. O. E.
Bassey, 2005, pers. comm.). Because diacritics have not become standard in Èfìk publications, I have used them when possible, in other cases, more research is required.

Several comparisons are made in this volume between words derived from Cross
River languages as used in contemporary Cuba and words used in contemporary West
Africa. When introducing Abakuá words, their Hispanicized spelling as commonly
written in Cuba has been altered to be phonetic in English, so that ñáñigo becomes
nyányigo; Usaguaré becomes Usagaré; Aguana becomes Awana; Bacocó becomes
Bakokó, Embácara becomes Mbákara, and so on. In this way, I intend to make the
terms easy to pronounce by readers from both sides of the Atlantic, leaving evident to
the critical reader any conclusions about their similarities or sources.

FOREWORD

■ ■ ■

Engineer Chief Bassey Efiong Bassey is highly regarded in the Calabar community for his knowledge of the history and practice of the Ékpè system and for sharing some of his wisdom in the book *Ékpè Èfik* (2001). He was among several Ékpè title-holders who actively supported my research in southeastern Nigeria and southwestern Cameroon. My study was completed only after learning from Bassey's insights into the Cuban materials. Thanks to his generosity, we have made great advances in the interpretation of Abakuá through Ékpè consciousness and symbols.

—IVOR MILLER

Trans-Atlantic trade in slaves involved mostly Africans of the tropical forest region of what is popularly referred to as the Dark Continent. The main ports of embarkation of the slaves were in the geographical zone of West Africa, more precisely the Gulf of Guinea. Calabar, an inland port with access to the Atlantic Ocean and beyond, played the ignominious role, among a few others, of facilitating the trade promoted and funded by Europeans and white Americans who did not think much of black Africans. The trade was premised on the belief that black Africans were not worth more than preferred beasts of burden. Being beasts, they were not entitled to human rights and privileges. Consequently they were said to be devoid of culture, tradition of note, and civilization. Even though the principles of human rights were not well accepted in the world, the slaves were exposed to more inhuman treatment in their new abodes than they ever experienced in their original homes of purchase. The black procurers and sellers, not realizing the attendant insults to their persons, fell for the immediate monetary gains. Soon afterward, stories filtered through to slave masters in the land of purchase, causing a few to regret the part they had played, especially when the status of some of those sold out came to mind. Some of those sold had claims to royalty in their original homes. After a while the world came round to recognize the dehumanizing practices and stamped them out. Action taken was limited to the protection and prevention of abuses to the body. The psyche was left unattended and has continued to receive bashings ever until today.

Primordial culture, tradition, and civilization are endowments to man from birth. Some are more conscious of their psyche than others. Background and environment bestow form and color. Black Africans are perhaps more conscious of their psyche than the white race. They had from birth been exposed to vehicles for bringing them into conscious rapport with their psyche. The vehicles are music, dance forms, incantations, variety of equipment, to mention but a few. They are employed discriminatingly, in a synthesis named culture, to bring one into contact with his psyche. To a black African, culture is the food that nourishes his psyche. It is the dynamic body-cleansing agent that facilitates conscious contact with the psyche. It is exportable in the hands of experts of the culture, and because psyche is involved, differences that occur between the same culture in different lands, far and near, are not significant. Tradition is sedentary. It is localized.

Without a firm cultural base, tradition is subject to changes brought about by external forces and time. Civilization has become a discriminating tool in the hands of the white race. Those not educated in the ways of the white race are looked upon as uncivilized. No one asks what those who are not educated in the ways of black African should be called. In the context of black African, no one is accepted into a cultural school unless he is humble, submits, and acknowledges the culture. Appreciation comes later, and the outpouring of civilization comes much later. There is first the desire to know and a belief that a school for learning exists, even though it may be informal. Despite these conditionalities, commentators were in the habit of pouring scorn on African practices. They wrote copiously after fleeting visits to Africa, where they were joined by religious pundits and governments to blot out belief in indigenous culture, tradition, and civilization. It was an attempt to rubbish black African self-esteem.

A trained black African is conscious of his psyche and invests to nurse it. He is not at home in an environment that is not conducive for his cultural practices. So he tries to make room for it. The much-heralded abolition of slavery had limited benefits for black African slaves. Even after emancipation they had little or no freedom to practice their culture or to be involved in their civilization. The Cuban situation narrated by Dr. Ivor Miller points clearly to that. Freedom was peripheral. The psyche was still in bondage. Under the guise of prevention of budding rebellion, Africans in Diaspora were denied the freedom of involvement in their indigenous culture, religion, and other psyche-searching activities. Here again Dr. Miller's experience in Cuba is relevant. To further firm their grip on blacks, the white masters and their supporters took to peddling of contentious stories about imagined powers of cultism, black magic, and witchcraft. Of all the practices, cultism was the most feared. This was partly because witchcraft and black magic were well-established practices among the white race, whereas cultism, which the whites were advised to avoid in their own interest, was supposedly the preserve of blacks. It is not unnatural for practices that are unfamiliar to a foreigner to be looked upon with awe. The engagement of black African communication techniques may cause spasm of shivering on the unenlightened. The whites were generally afraid when their imagination went rioting out of ignorance. It was not long before they felt insecure, to the point of conjecturing a possible overrun of constituted authority by the blacks engaged in cultism. The Cuban experience is relevant.

Denial of the existence of black culture, tradition, and civilization had its adherents among some blacks brow-beaten to accept the humiliation as a fact of life. Those who knew they had something of value resisted, and these were those whose investment had brought them into conscious contact with their psyche. The Cuban experience of Dr. Miller is supportive. That was why the attempt to effectively prohibit the more worthy practices of the blacks failed. Aside from fear, occasioned by lack of knowledge of the psyche as perceived by an African trained in his culture, Christian religious attempts to reach psyche knowledge through circumlocutious routes and practices caused problems. By this, Christianity introduced profound bias into the matter. It may well be that some blacks do not posses any culture of note. Certainly not those of the Cross River basin of Nigeria, where some of the slaves came from. In Cuba, the popular belief among the white population was that black culture practiced in the country is home grown, and therefore lacking in the depth of a culture of note. If that were true, it meant the black culture of Cuba is as old as the blacks in Cuba. Being of recent origin, the claim to culture could not be sustained. That was also the position of various commentators, governments, and the white race generally.

The situation remained the same until Dr. Ivor Miller buried the white man's pride, humbled, and submitted himself to be admitted into black culture at its roots in Calabar. Having lived in Cuba studying the Abakuá culture, he was amazed to find a striking similarity between Abakuá and Ékpè/Mgbè Society of Calabar and beyond. This confirmed the oral tradition of Abakuá that traced its origin to Calabar. Dr. Miller learned from his travels in the Cross River region of West African and neighboring sovereign countries. He experienced the benefits of humility and submission to black culture and learned from the custodians of Ékpè/Mgbè culture. After his initiation into the culture, benefits of the system are dawning on him, and if he is patient, he may discover in time that a civilization exists. In the short term, what he saw and learned are similar if not identical with his experience of Cuban Abakuá. The proof of relationship came when he brought Abakuá exponents to Calabar. The spontaneous reactions of the Cubans to Ékpè/Mgbè music, dance forms, acclamations, and others proved beyond doubt to the Cubans and Ékpè/Mgbè exponents that Abakuá and Ékpè/Mgbè are sister organizations with the same root. All are employing the same techniques to bring man into conscious contact with his psyche and enable him to know himself.

There is much talk about cultism—not only in Cuba. The initial instinct of a man about the things he does not understand is the attempt to exterminate or get away from it. Extermination may be through deliberate wrong labeling, blackmailing, and the assignment of spurious supernatural powers of destruction. Attitudes of the white race of Cuba are not unusual. It had been the practice the world over. But are Abakuá, Ékpè, and Mgbè cults? Certainly not. A cult is usually a small body of persons engaged in spurious intellectual or religious pursuits. The most important determining factors are purity of purpose, size of group, coverage, and area of influence. Abakuá, Ékpè, and Mgbè do not fit into the definition. With at least 15 million adherents in many sovereign countries, the practice could not adequately be labeled cultism. Second, its teachings are not spurious. If they were, the groups would not have existed longer than Christianity in the area of its adherence, despite Christian attitude. Third, the teachings for bringing man into conscious contact with his psyche have been tried, tested, and proven to be efficacious. Its purity of purpose is a precondition for membership. If Freemasons, Roscicrucians, and others have a system for bringing man into conscious contact with his psyche and are not called cultists, why should a black African, home-grown system not earn respectability? Is it because anything black lacks credibility? P. Amaury Talbot and others found it difficult to accept black African origin of Ékpè/Mgbè but elected to assign Ékpè/Mgbè audio and written communication techniques to Egypt, where such a system does not exist.

The Abakuá system of Cuba was exported from Calabar, the area endemic with Ékpè/Mgbè. The Abakuá account of how the system came into Cuba is in concert with Ékpè/Mgbè practice. Only those who have attained a certain minimum grade have the spiritual authority to effect a transfer of Ékpè/Mgbè from one territory to another. Ordinarily Ékpè/Mgbè or Abakuá is sedentary until energized into action by a spiritual authority. Perhaps the words *secret* or *brotherhood* more appropriately describe Abakuá and Ékpè/Mgbè groups. Secret, not because they are sinister. Down memory lane all the early groups dedicated to the study of man and his potentials have been secret groups. Even Nazarene, of which Jesus was supposed to have been a member, was a secret group. In Calabar of old, only Ékpè initiates were trusted with community assignment requiring steadfastness, secrecy, and valor. They made good in soldiering. Military commanders were ranked members. Contrary to modern belief, they were not selfish, but public-spirited. It is not surprising that Abakuá members took risks in the overall interest of Cubans. Public service is a basic teaching in Ékpè/Mgbè. Abakuá is not different. As it was in the days of old, Ékpè/Mgbè was the moving spirit of the community. It regulated community life for the overall good and defended community rights even at the point of death. Abakuá, a child of Ékpè/Mgbè, could not have performed less in Cuba.

VOICE OF THE LEOPARD

■ ■ ■

INTRODUCTION

...

Òbúb mbùmè ókùp ùsèm.
He who asks questions hears (or learns) the language, or gets interpretations.
—ÈFÌK SAYING[1]

The Abakuá mutual aid society of Cuba, recreated in the 1830s from several local variants of the Ékpè leopard society of West Africa's Cross River basin, is a richly detailed example of African cultural transmission to the Americas. The Abakuá is a male initiation society, and its masquerades and drum construction, as well as musical structures, are largely based on Ékpè models.[2] Its ritual language is expressed through hundreds of chants that identify source regions and historical events[3]; several of them have already been interpreted by speakers of Èfìk, the precolonial lingua franca of the Cross River region.[4] The term Abakuá itself is likely derived from the Àbàkpà community of Calabar, the historical capital of the Cross River basin of southeastern Nigeria and southwestern Cameroon.[5] The social life of the Àbàkpà (Qua Ejagham), Èfìk, and Efut peoples of the Cross River basin in the eighteenth and nineteenth centuries was organized not in kingdoms but in dispersed, sovereign communities united by networks of obligation and prestige. In the absence of a state, each autonomous community had its own lodge of the leopard society, known throughout this region is as Ékpè or Ǹgbè, literally meaning "leopard."[6] In West Africa, as in Cuba, the societies are organized into a hierarchy of grades, each with a specific function. With the help of both African Ékpè members and Cuban Abakuá, I have been able to reconstruct fundamental aspects of how and why Ékpè was recreated in Cuba, and how Abakuá presence formed an important strand of identity and artistry in the emerging Cuban nation.

Those privileged to have participated in Abakuá ceremonies, as the yellow moon slides across the sky to the sound of chanting, bells, and a mystic Voice in the temple, or as the sun rises over the temple grounds to the chant and dance of men beneath the canopy of a ceiba tree, will understand the awesome energy of this tradition. Abakuá is the product of its African sources, the Cuban history it helped shape, and the fortressed cities within which it emerged. In what follows, I present the essentials of this story, with the hope of enabling others to appreciate the foundations laid by Africans in Cuba, the fidelity of those creoles who followed their teachings, and the sublime music created to express them. My research began the process of confirming the Cuban narratives, but among the unexpected results was the commencement of a dialogue among West Africans and Cubans.

This book tells the story of how several generations of West Africans who were enslaved and forced to migrate to the Caribbean were able to regroup and reestablish an important homeland institution in the process of their self-liberation. The Africans recreated their homeland society, a form of government, in order to instill its values in their Caribbean-born offspring. This achievement occurred not in a marginal backwater, but in Havana, a fortified city at the heart of Spain's maritime empire. It did not involve a few people, but hundreds and later thousands working collectively, as it became foundational to the future nation-state.

Only with the help of contemporary members of this society have I been able to understand details of this history. Abakuá leaders have aided my research because, as their counterparts in West Africa have initiated me as an unofficial ambassador to Cuba, they hope that my activities will facilitate communication across the Atlantic, enabling related cultural groups, separated through the forces of the European global expansion nearly 200 years ago, to reconvene.[7] With the help of both Cuban Abakuá and Cross River Ékpè, the material here has been carefully selected to identify historical and cultural continuities, as well as some aspects unique to the Cuban variant.

Ékpè and Abakuá leaders speaking about their cultural systems often use the sun as a metaphor for its teachings (see examples from Cuba in Plates 6 and 7).[8] As the Earth revolves around the sun that radiates light and heat to give life, so too the cultural and economic lives of Cross River communities revolved around Ékpè, its teachings radiated insights into correct living. The epicenter of Ékpè and its Abakuá variant, the mystic Voice that issues from a center, is likened to a sun, a giver of life. The teachings required to maintain it are passed from one generation to the next in the form of philosophical insight, moral values, and aesthetic mastery.[9] The ceremonies were often symbolic reenactments of cultural history, a form of theater used to teach participants past events and bring their meanings to the present. Like the Homeric epics, the legends were understood as historical events by their most gifted performers.[10] Across the African continent, ritual performances proceeded in various ways, each with ultimate goal of "opening the eyes" of initiates, of giving them a "second birth," so that they could be taught incrementally the esoteric mysteries of their civilization, to prepare them for community leadership. In the Cross River region, the mysteries of creation were shared, over a long process, from one autonomous community to another, through a club called Ékpè (leopard), whose defining symbol was a sound representing the voice of this beast.[11]

Thrown into the vortex of the trans-Atlantic slave system, Africans in the Western Hemisphere were in many cases able to regroup to form communities in which their specific philosophies and lifeways could be taught to their offspring. This information was so valuable in the process of adaptation and defense in the new environment that it has been passed on for many generations. For those who practice them, for example, the Cross River Ékpè society and its Cuban Abakuá variant are equated with "life." This is why Abakuá say, "el hombre muere, pero el Abakuá no" (man dies, but Abakuá does not).

This process has been almost totally misunderstood by outsiders because it occurs in initiation societies, where only members are taught. In the Cuban case, it was common in the nineteenth century that family members were unaware that their father or brother was an Abakuá member until his funeral, when rites were performed by his ritual brothers. Being Abakuá was illegal in the colony, and continuity was assured through invisibility.

Contemporary Abakuá leadership base their practice on knowledge taught by Africans to their Cuban creole apprentices throughout the nineteenth century. Those not initiated into Abakuá are called *ndisimi*; in Ékpè practice, ndisimi means literally "ignorant," those who do not know.[12] Ékpè and Abakuá are popularly known as "secret societies," but in fact their existence is well known. Technically, they are initiation societies. What is genuinely secret in them is mainly procedural, ritual knowledge, taught incrementally in stages, as members rise in status to become community leaders.[13] In the case of Abakuá, the psychological barriers members raise to outsiders, combined with their marginal status vis-à-vis the larger society, makes them effectively an "invisible society."[14] As boxer Muhammad Ali observed, "You cannot hit what you cannot see."

Abakuá practice is a form of history, as well as politics, because its teachings counter the misguided notion that black history began with slavery. Instead, Abakuá builds confidence by training members in the details of their precolonial history, beginning with the foundation of Ékpè in Africa through contact with divine creation.[15] In the 200 years since the founding of Abakuá to the present, there has been no significant communication between West African Ékpè and Cuban Abakuá. Although Abakuá practice adapted to the Cuban context was enriched through its encounters with other cultural ideas there, its fundamental mechanisms are clearly recognizable to West African members of Ékpè.

THE ÉKPÈ IMPERIUM

In the Cross River basin of Nigeria and Cameroon of the eighteenth and nineteenth centuries, social life was organized through separate initiate societies for men and women. In the absence of a state system, regional trade networks were sustained through membership in a titled society, with each autonomous community having its own lodge.[16] The leopard society of the Cross River basin is known variously as Ékpè,

Ǹgbè, and Obè, after the local terms for leopard.[17] Being among the most diverse linguistic regions in the world, to simplify, I will hereafter use Ékpè, the Èfìk term most common in the existing literature.

Hundreds of Cross River settlements each possessed their own Ékpè lodge, a symbol of their autonomy, where matters concerning local governance were settled in councils until colonial rule at the end of the nineteenth century.[18] In Old Calabar in 1847, the Reverend Hope Waddell wrote, "The towns of Calabar are, in fact, a number of small republics, each with its own chief and council, united only by the Egbo [Ékpè] confraternity, so far as they have joined it for mutual defense."[19] Few details are known about early Ékpè history, but indications are that after continuous contact with European merchants was established in the early 1600s, Ékpè was transformed by the Èfìk-speaking traders whose beachhead settlements on the Calabar River received European cargo ships.[20] Based upon a mercantile and educational relationship with British port cities, Èfìk Ékpè in Calabar developed an eclectic tradition reflecting the reach of their trade networks. As the European demand for slaves grew (from the 1630s to the 1840s), Èfìk traders extended these networks throughout the entire Cross River basin, eastward into present-day Cameroon and northward to the Árù (Arochukwu) trading oligarchy,[21] encompassing all the Cross River settlements mentioned in this study, where languages such as Balondo (Efut), Ejagham, and Ìbìbìò, Ìgbo, Oron, and Umon were (and still are) spoken.[22] Many settlements in the reach of the expanding Èfìk trading zone, like Àbàkpà (Qua Ejagham), Oban, and Uruan, may have already possessed forms of Ékpè (as many of their contemporary leaders claim). Nevertheless, Èfìk merchants shared their own forms of Ékpè with many settlements with the aim of solidifying trade relationships.[23] The result, according to one Cross River historian, was an Ékpè Imperium.[24] Being the dominant form of interethnic communication, the ceremonial practices of Ékpè reflect a rich variety of languages, costumes, music, and dance from the entire region.[25] As the European demand for slaves increased, competition among dominant Èfìk settlements for access to the cargo ships intensified, resulting in several battles where some Ékpè members were enslaved and carried to the Caribbean.[26] Peoples from the hinterlands who may not have been Ékpè members, but who stayed in Ékpè regions while passing down the Cross River from Cameroon or while passing through Arochukwu en route to Bonny or Calabar, would have learned about Ékpè's importance as a political system, enabling them to have contributed to its recreation if they reached Cuba.[27]

CARABALÍ DIASPORA

The trans-Atlantic slave trade transferred many thousands of people from southeastern Nigeria and southwestern Cameroon throughout the Americas, where they were known as *Calabarí* or *Carabalí*, after the port city of Calabar from which many departed.[28] From the well-known Calabarí presence in Florida, Louisiana, and South Carolina to the neighborhood of Calabar in Salvador, Brazil, to the Calabar High School in Kingston, Jamaica, to the Carabalí nation-groups of colonial Cuba, Calabarí presence was nearly ubiquitous.[29] The island of Cuba received significant Cross River influence in the form of oral historical narratives that continue to be communicated in apprenticeship systems. Many narratives memorializing places and ethnic terms of the Calabar region are maintained by the Cuban Abakuá.[30]

Approaching Ékpè and Abakuá History

On the west coast of Africa, "Someone said at independence: 'the principal victory of colonization was to have perpetuated a real cultural genocide.' "[31] In the Caribbean, however, some African descendants claim to have very specific information about their African heritage. With regard to their collective ceremonies, Cuban Abakuá say, "Nothing is done which is not based on knowledge of what was done in the beginning."[32]

Abakuá was formed in the nineteenth century, mainly by free urban black workers in the port zones of Havana and Matanzas. African knowledge was taught to Cubans and then maintained through ceremonies that included the recitation of chants called *tratados* (mythic histories) in African-derived languages.[33] These tratados are taught in apprenticeship systems within initiation families and are often maintained in manuscript form. In a narrative about how aspects of Abakuá philosophy and instruments were passed on from a master to an apprentice who developed into a leading twentieth-century musician, the manuscripts are described as key. As a young man, Esteban "Chachá" Bacallao, founding member of Los Muñequitos de Matanzas (a famous rumba percussion ensemble), inherited the manuscripts and drums of his late teacher: "There were kept the secrets of his life, the mysteries, prayers, and chants of Abakuá.... The notations by [master drummer] Carlos Alfonso throughout his lifetime were as important as those century-old drums that so often had moaned in his hands."[34]

Only the lack of access to these texts by earlier scholars of Cuba and the Caribbean can explain the dearth of detailed knowledge about African-based philosophies in the literature.[35] The communities organized around these philosophies were active forces in resistance movements throughout Caribbean history; they produced the arts that best express the national experience. In the course of conversations among non-Cuban anthropologists and historians over the years, I have generally been met with blank stares when asking them about the oral texts of the Kongo/Yorùbá/Arará/Abakuá groups they studied, whether historically or in the anthropological present. Not housed in libraries, these texts are maintained within the minds and manuscripts of the leaders of these traditions. Access to them, and, equally important, their interpretations, requires a meaningful relationship with these leaders. These unpublished and coded texts depict Africans in the role of protagonists using their own cultural systems, quite distinctly from the usual portrayal in the published literature of Africans as protagonists—itself a rare phenomenon—in the quest of assimilation into the norms of the dominant culture. During my research, I was instructed to document several foundational Abakuá treaties. Since these form the basis of ceremonial practice, I had privileged access into the mechanics of Abakuá history. Without the approval of Abakuá leaders, and until we have furthered the process of their interpretation through Cross River languages, these Abakuá tratados will not be published (a portion of one treaty is transcribed in the discussion of the Ékuéri Tongó lodge, in chapter 3). In cases where segments of Abakuá tratados have been recorded commercially by Abakuá musicians, I refer to those topically in the following chapters.

Reflecting the topic of study, my research became trans-Atlantic through the aid of Nigerians and Cameroonians who began to interpret phrases of the Cuban Abakuá into Cross River languages. Evidence was gathered to show that the oral historical memories of slave descendants in Cuba are relevant to Cross River social history, itself largely synonymous with Ékpè history, of the nineteenth and eighteenth centuries and earlier. In what follows, I document and discuss the recreation of Cross River Ékpè into nineteenth-century Cuba and its impact in the cultural history of the island, particularly Havana and Matanzas.

The first studies of Cross River life were conducted by missionaries and colonial officers. In 1862 Scottish Presbyterian the Reverend Hugh Goldie published *A Dictionary of the Efik Language*; in 1863 the Reverend Hope Waddell published his memoirs *Twenty-Nine Years in the West Indies and Central Africa*; in 1912 District Commissioner Percy Talbot published the first of his voluminous studies, *In the Shadow of the Bush*. Regarding these and other works, Cross River specialist Keith Nicklin observed that studies of the history of southeastern Nigeria have "tended to concentrate upon the coastal zone, especially the trading settlements of the Niger Delta and Calabar. Large groups like the Ìbìbìò, Ejagham, and Bokyi have been virtually ignored."[36] Later critics charged that some classic texts about the region, like "the much quoted works of Amaury Talbot (1926) are in parts at best organized and educated guesswork."[37]

Given the lack of information about this region during the trans-Atlantic slave trade, Cuban Abakuá is a totally new source, freed from the colonial and contemporary ethnic politics often imposed upon historical studies of the region. The use of Abakuá chants as historical narratives is nothing more than an extension of African oral literary methods. In the West African kingdome of Dahomey, anthropologist Melville Herskovits observed that "songs were and are the prime carriers of history."[38] When a Dahomean specialist "at one point could not recall the sequence of important names in the series he was giving[,] under his breath, to the accompaniment of clicking fingernails, he began to sing, continuing his song for some moments. When he stopped he had the names clearly in mind once more, and in explanation of his song stated that this was the Dahomean method of remembering historic facts. The role of the singer as the 'keeper of records' has been remarked by those who visited the kingdom in the days of its autonomy."[39]

I witnessed such a scenario repeatedly in conversations with Abakuá leaders, whose lore is largely embedded within responsorial chants. This kind of historical dialogue is comparable to other traditions in which elders use chants as mnemonic devices for historical and geographical information. Central Australian song lines, for example, express origin stories related to "the travels of a Dreaming ancestor through a particular landscape."[40] The songs were created by founding ancestors as they journeyed through a region, naming and creating features of the land. Their performance creates a map of that original journey.[41] Other examples are found in the navigational chants of the Pacific South Sea islanders or the Norse sagas including geographical information that helped people travel from place to place.[42]

Cuban Abakuá narratives are vehicles for travel through time and space. Their chant lines reach across the Atlantic ocean to evoke specific places and historical figures in the Cross River and, in rare cases, actually map out physical journeys through Cross River geographical zones.[43] Through performances of chanting with the corresponding ritual actions, Abakuá recreate the mythic history of their society, reenacting the original sequence of events in the creation of Ékpè. By doing so, they recreate them in the present.

Leading Cuban scholar Fernando Ortiz identified this process through two books in the 1950s, La "tragedia" de los ñáñigos (The "Tragedy" of the Ñáñigos [Abakuá])and Los bailes y el teatro de los negros en el folklore de Cuba (The Dance and Theater of the Blacks in the Folklore of Cuba). In both cases, Ortiz compared the structures and meanings of Abakuá initiation to the Eleusinian Mysteries and to ancient Greek drama.[44]

Fernando Ortiz and Abakuá Studies in Cuba

In the nineteenth century, the study of African-based communities in Cuba began with police arresting black people, taking their possessions, and writing about it. As a consequence, many confiscated African-centered sacred objects became artifacts in anthropological museums. Rodríguez Batista, who ended his term as civil governor of the Province of Havana in 1890, donated many items to the Museo de Ultramar (Overseas Museum) in Madrid, including Abakuá Íreme costumes and instruments.[45] In the early twentieth century, Fernando Ortiz (1881–1969) began his life long-interest in African-Cuban studies after seeing Abakuá objects in this museum.[46] Ortiz later recounted to his friends, "I returned to Cuba with the Abakuá on my mind."[47] Don Ortiz came to be regarded as the "third discoverer" of Cuba, largely for his pivotal and voluminous studies of Cuba's African influences. Being an inspiration to his formation as a scholar and writer, Abakuá became a constant theme in his work.[48] While reflecting upon his initial interest, Ortiz described Abakuá as,

> the most characteristic of the colored element in Cuba, that is the mystery of the secret societies of African origin which still survive in our land. Everyone talked about this, but no one really knew the truth. It seemed to be a shady business, about which there were many macabre fables and bloody tales, all of which served to spur my own interest. I even offered to a publisher, a friend of mine, a book I was to write within a year. Forty years have elapsed and the book is not yet written, notwithstanding the wealth of facts and observation I have accumulated. I began my investigations but soon realized that I, like most Cubans, was utterly confused. For it was not only the curious phenomenon of Negro Masonry [Abakuá] that I encountered, but also a most complex mélange of religious survivals of remote cultural origin. All this with a variety of societal origins, languages, music, instruments, dances, songs, traditions, legends, arts, games, and folkways; in other words, I found that the whole conglomeration of different African cultures—then virtually unknown to men of science—had been transplanted to Cuba."[49]

Throughout his life, Ortiz referred to his work in progress.[50] He wrote a letter in 1956 to Dr. Vera Rubin in New York City regarding his project on the Abakuá: "I have all the necessary materials to write this book, gathered laboriously through my fifty years of research into the origin of the ñáñigo society in Africa and Cuba, its history, activities, organization, personages, rites, music, chants, dances, its expanse in Cuba, its functions and future. I think the work of writing will be complete in one year."[51] This volume never materialized.[52] Fortunately, Ortiz did publish materials about Abakuá in many of his later works, as indispensable as the studies by Lydia Cabrera to any researcher on this theme. I refer to the work of Cabrera throughout this study.

Calabar

"If I did not know that you are a chief, I would not allow you to wear that cloth you have on," announced Chief Joe Bassey through the microphone in the filled auditorium.[53] As the crowd applauded, a mischievous smile appeared on his face, leading him on to other remarks about my presentation to the community of Calabar, Nigeria.

In the lecture hall were many men and women in traditional attire, among them leaders of the indigenous government of the entire region, known as the Ékpè or Mgbè (leopard) society in the local languages of Èfìk, Ejagham, and Efut (Balondo). As did

I, they wore ceremonial hats, carried walking sticks, and wore loin cloth wrappers tied around the waist. The type I wore, called Ukara, was an indigo dyed cotton that only Èkpè members may wear, since they display symbols and signs related to the mystic workings of the society.

We were in the Old Residence of the former colonial District Officer overlooking the Calabar River, now home to the National Museum. Down the hill from us to the west sprawled Atakpa, an ancient Èfìk settlement with a beachhead that served as the port to embark thousands of enslaved locals to the Americas. In the distance upriver (to the east) lay the port of Creek Town, the first Èfìk settlement before Calabar became a metropolis and the place from where the majority of enslaved humans were loaded onto canoes that placed them on the European ships that carried them to their fates.[54]

During my first trip to Calabar, the museum curator invited me to speak about the Cuban Abakuá founded by enslaved Èkpè members taken from these shores.[55] I called my talk "Okóbio Enyenisón Èfìk Obutong: Cross River History and Language in the Cuban Èkpè Society," based on a Cuban chant memorializing those who founded the first Cuban lodge (see chapter 1). With the help of speakers of Cross River languages in the United States and now in Calabar, we had made great strides in interpreting many of the Cuban chants, in the belief that these are important links to the history of the region. We confirmed that Obutong was an Èfìk settlement, some of whose leaders were enslaved during conflicts in the eighteenth century, and that all terms in this Cuban phrase are coherent in the Èfìk language (see the appendix of songs).

Local personages were taking this topic very seriously, since—as the depth of the cultural transmission to Cuba becomes apparent—they have learned that Cuban Èkpè is a direct link to their own past as a people(s), an issue with contemporary ramifications. Several other scholars have worked on the links between Calabar and Cuba, but I was particularly well received, perhaps because for the first time we were organizing a trip of leading Cuban members to visit Calabar.

With me at the presenters' table in the lecture hall were several leading intellectuals and traditionalists.[56] In the front row sat a dozen Èkpè leaders in regalia, with many others present discretely wearing street clothes. Among those dressed to the nines, Joseph Bassey was the Muri (clan leader) of the Efut Ekondo lodge in Calabar.[57] Representing the Èkpè lodge of Big Qua Town in Calabar was Chief Imona, whose father had been the Ndidem (paramount ruler) of the Qua Ejagham of Calabar.[58] A week earlier the Qua Ndidem had received me in their lodge with Èkpè masquerades, drumming and chanting, food and drink; afterward Imona told me that, due to my recent initiation by another lodge, I was the first foreign researcher they had allowed past their portal. Imona had worked with many foreign Èkpè researchers in Calabar over the years[59]; the privilege I enjoyed was a sign of their interest in communicating with Cuban Abakuá.[60]

FIGURE 1. First encounter between Cuban Abakuá and Nigerian Ékpè, in Brooklyn, New York, 2001. Cuban Abakuá members Vicente Sánchez (standing, with drum and white hat) and "Román" Díaz (shaved head, on tall lead drum) play to Íreme masker. Photo by I. Miller.

My interaction with West African Ékpè members began in 2000, after I published samples of Abakuá phrases from a commercially recorded album. Soon afterward, Nigerian members of the Cross River Ékpè society living in the United States informed me that they had recognized these texts—particularly the phrase "Efí Kebú-ton"—as part of their own history. Thus began a process of interpretation that led to what was perhaps the first meeting between both groups, at the Èfìk National Association meeting in Brooklyn in 2001, then at the 2003 meeting in Michigan with the Obong (paramount ruler) of the Èfìks. This process culminated in the first official visit to Calabar of Cuban Abakuá during the Third Annual International Ékpè Festival in December 2004, a trip organized by myself and paid for by the government of Cross River State (see the epilogue). Fittingly, one of the two Abakuá was "Román" Díaz, a professional musician from whose 1997 recording I transcribed the chant identified by Nigerians (this recording is found on the accompanying CD).[61]

The key to my facilitation of these meetings was presenting myself as a historian, that is, a scholar not interested in secrets, but in using Abakuá chants to identify African source languages and regions, a project of great interest to Abakuá themselves. As a North American scholar, I had access to information about Africa that Abakuá did not have. By sharing this with Abakuá intellectuals, we became colleagues, helping each other unlock the coded history contained in the chants.

During three months in Calabar in the summer of 2004, I met Ékpè/Mgbè leaders from many lodges, first in Calabar and then throughout the entire Cross River region.

Once initiated, I was accompanied by one Èkpè brother or another to the communities of Akpabuyo, Creek Town, Efut Ibonda, Abijang and Nsofan in southern Etung, Oban, Oron, Umon, and Uruan, all in the Akwa Ibom and Cross River States of Nigeria.[62] I also traveled to southwestern Cameroon, to present a lecture at the University of Buea at the foothills of Mt. Cameroon and to meet with M̀gbè elders in Ekondo Titi, Dibonda-Balondo, Bekura, and other villages.[63] All these regions were connected during the eighteenth and nineteenth centuries through the Calabar trading network, and all of them are reflected in the Cuban Abakuá narratives. Because I traveled alone to Cameroon, the Iyámba, or head, of my lodge gave me an "Èkpè passport" that identified me as a member.[64]

I shared an English translation of my Cuban manuscript with selected Èkpè leaders who were formally educated and who grasped the significance of the work. One of them, Engineer Bassey Efiong Bassey, was able to interpret large portions of the Cuban material into the Èfìk language, the nineteenth-century lingua franca of the region. He was able to make sense of how the language was transformed using an Èkpè system of communication known as *nsìbìdì*, which consists of signs and symbols that are expressed through recitation, playing instruments, gesture, or drawn images.[65] Like Abakuá language, nsìbìdì was designed to keep outsiders away, as this Èkpè chant makes clear:

Ùsèm Èkpè ékèrè nsìbìdì	Nsìbìdì is the language of Èkpè
àbànékpè ìkpòng ódiòngó ùsèm émì	only members understand the language
úkèméké ndídiòngó ké múbànké	you can't know unless you are initiated
Èkpè Èfìk ímèmké; dá nsàn-nsàn![66]	Èfìk Èkpè is complex; keep off![67]

Engineer Bassey and I speculated that in addition to using coded Èkpè terms, Cuban Abakuá may have phrases from Èfìk, Ejagham, and other Cross River languages that were intentionally transformed to disguise their meanings. The purpose was to block the understanding of Cross River language speakers in Cuba who were not initiated. This type of camouflage is consistent with nsìbìdì practice in West Africa.

During the process of interpretation in West Africa, I read Cuban terms aloud or played recordings of Abakuá chanting, then described their meanings to many Èkpè leaders who helped me identify the Cross River sources. In this way, I began to map out the likely sources for scores of Cuban lodges founded in the nineteenth century.

New York City

My research in Africa was the logical conclusion of a process that began in 1987 in New York City, where I first witnessed a rendition of an Abakuá signature by Cuban artist Juan Boza. Cross River nsìbìdì was adapted to the Cuban context in many ways, one of them being an immense vocabulary of signs called *firmas, gandó*, or *anaforuana* (signatures).[68] From our first meeting in 1987, we began a profound friendship that included his teaching me about Santería (Yorùbá-derived Ocha), of which he was a full initiate. Portentously, Juan presented me with his print of an Abakuá initiation signature (called Aráka Suáka). Although not Abakuá, Juan was one of several twentieth-century Cuban artists who used its symbolism in the fine arts as a means of expressing a Cuban identity. Many Cubans who are not members identify with and defend Abakuá. As my teacher, Juan led me through my first consecrations in the Ocha tradition, and with his support, I was awarded a fellowship from Yale University to travel to Cuba to learn more.[69]

Cuba

I arrived in Havana in 1991 as a student of the Cuba's National Folklore Ensemble (Conjunto Folklórico Nacional, CFN). Already a performer of various West African and modern dance styles, I had begun to learn about the three major African-derived religions of Cuba, Santería (Ocha), Palo Monte, and Abakuá, through Cuban initiates living in New York City.[70] Because African influences in the Americas are maintained most prominently through religious practice, this is the logical place for students to begin. After the CFN workshop, I remained in Havana and Matanzas to apprentice with elders in Santería houses (ilé Ocha), learning about the overflow from ritual music, dance, and symbolism into popular culture. Some of this material, including interviews with singers Celina González and Merceditas Valdés, was later published.[71]

When in Havana, I stayed at the home of my wife Idania Díaz, whose family gave immeasurable guidance to my work. Supporting my interest in learning from elders of the Cuban religions, Guillermo Pazos, a family member, located a group of elderly men who frequented the nearby Parque de la Fraternidad in Centro Havana. These men happened to be Abakuá, and they recommended we speak with Andrés "el Ñáñigo."

In June 1993 we met Andrés on the street corner of La Parque Curita, where he sold printed sheets of Catholic prayers. He agreed to talk with us. The next day, at Andrés' request, we crossed Havana's harbor to el Castillo del Morro, a seventeenth-century fortress overlooking the city. Facing the sea, with his back to the limestone bulwark, Andrés began to evoke the memory of the first Carabalí who entered Havana, in "tiempo de España" (the colonial days), as if he could see them arriving on ships. Reciting portions of Abakuá history in Abakuá with interpretations in Spanish, he recounted how they arrived, regrouped, and recreated their leopard society. That Andrés was a master storyteller became obvious to all; that Andrés also had rare information to convey became increasingly obvious to me as a scholar.

While revising my transcriptions, Andrés used a technique common in Abakuá manuscripts of creating a border between the sacred Abakuá phrases and the profane Spanish interpretations by inserting the symbol XXX. Respecting this solution arrived at by nineteenth-century Abakuá scribes, I have left the marks as integral to the texts whenever possible. In Calabar, I found a parallel attitude toward the formal use of Ékpè and other Cross River languages: During ceremony inside the Efe Ékpès (Ékpè temples), only indigenous languages are used. English, the official language of government, is kept separate.[72]

During our first meeting, Andrés was reserved and soft-spoken. Upon reflection, this was an awkward occasion. Being a repository for privileged knowledge about the Abakuá, Andrés wanted his testimony to be documented and preserved. That this information was normally to be shared with members only made this a delicate issue. Because Abakuá was very marginal to Cuban societal values, however, research on this topic was nearly impossible for a Cuban scholar, for several reasons.[73] It was not surprising then, that Andrés would work with a foreign scholar like me, who was not formed by or involved in local concerns.

When I look back at my photos of Andrés that first day, his face was pinched, hard, and impenetrable. This is not the tender and generous man I came to know. As we began to work regularly, this face would soften, becoming dramatically expressive as Andrés went deeper into the subject. When parting that first day, I presented Andrés with a frozen chicken to cook at home. This was a time when many elderly people, especially those with no family to help them, were starving in Cuba. With the end of funding for Cuba by the Soviet Union in 1989, and the tightening of the United States embargo against Cuba, the situation was desperate. To paraphrase a family member, this period was "worse than slavery. At least then, a master was required to feed slaves. But today. . . ." In spite of Andrés' hunger, he took a long time in accepting my offer. When Guillermo accompanied Andrés home, he attempted to share the chicken with him. This kind of nobility, I learned, exemplifies Abakuá values. That it survived even when Andrés had not eaten meat in months (as I later learned), demonstrated his motives for teaching Abakuá history were not primarily economic.

I had come to Cuba to learn about Yorùbá influences. Being far more developed than studies of other African migrations at the time, there were several opportunities in the United States to study Yorùbá cultural aesthetics; thus this was the obvious place to begin.[74] I had not intended to study Abakuá, but having been presented with this rare opportunity through Andrés, I began to read all I could find about the society. For the next four years, we worked intensively as I documented all he wanted to tell me.

Born and raised in the solares (tenements) of Centro and Old Havana, Andrés Flores Casanova (1891[?]–2001) had been an involuntary lifelong member of the Havana underground. He was a self-taught reader with an incredibly agile mind, but his dark skin and lack of formal schooling determined that he would move from one unskilled job to another (Plate 1). Andrés utilized his intelligence by becoming an unofficial historian of the Abakuá.

Andrés was descendant of the Cross River region. His great-grandfather, grandfather, father, and several brothers were Abakuá members. Andrés learned the language and history from within his own family, from manuscripts left by his great-grandfather, who was born in Africa. He also learned from his elder brother Julian "Planta Firme," a title-holder in the Isún Efó lodge. Considered by many as an important teacher of Abakuá language and traditions, Andrés shared his knowledge with many young members. A living connection to ancestral Abakuá practices, Andrés was a repository of the perspective of black Abakuá members at the turn of the last century. Because many historical barrios (neighborhoods) have at least one lodge, its activities are of great symbolic importance to the local populations.

There is no standard written text for Abakuá practice—most elders have personal versions of handwritten vocabularies and passages they inherited from their elders. To learn, each initiate must seek out a teacher. Those few who learn from a Basaibéke (an elder with vast knowledge) and who assimilate all they are taught may become title-holders.[75] In any communal practice, one person cannot embody all knowledge, but as I was taught in The Gambia, "Every elder is a burning library." Until the end of his life, Andrés was continually visited by younger Abakuá seeking to learn about the past.

From 1993 to 1996, Andrés trekked—hat on head and walking staff in hand—from Old Havana to our apartment in el barrio de Colón, where we worked in the comfort of a familial atmosphere.[76] By 1997 his legs would no longer carry him. I began to visit Andrés, riding my bicycle through the narrow, cobbled streets of Old Havana, to the wharf area of the barrio de Belén where he lived. Once inside his small, dark apartment in a centuries-old building, we would clear off a space at the table and continue to work. I would begin by presenting my list of questions, which were geared toward interpreting Abakuá phrases and clarifying chronologies. Having exhausted my questions, Andrés would often quiz me in Abakuá, as he was quizzed in his youth by elders, about the interpretation of phrases or the order of historical events. Unlike the youthful Andrés, I had our manuscript to refer to. In this way we tested its contents. He often emphasized that I should not change anything he told me, because he told it as he had learned it, and because he felt that the present generation was poorly informed about the history of their brotherhood.

During this last phase of our research, Andrés introduced me to many of the Abakuá brothers who lived on his block, as well as others who worked on the docks or who visited him from other parts of the city and from Matanzas. By this time, Andrés was very proud of our manuscript and talked openly about it. He would tell those who came to him for information, "Wait till the book comes out, it's all in there."

As I learned over time, Andrés was not bound by an oath of secrecy, as are Abakuá members. For his own personal reasons, he was never initiated. This gave him the freedom to speak with me and convey the history as he understood it in Abakuá language, with translations in Spanish. According to local legend, Andrés was not initiated because he knew too much and in his youth criticized his elders for their lack of knowledge. In the early twentieth century, when Abakuá temples were made of wood, a person standing in the patio of a temple could hear the liturgical phrases emanating from in the inner sanctum. Having already learned Abakuá lore from his grandfather, father, and brothers, all of whom were Abakuá, Andrés would attend ceremonies. On one occasion as he listened from outside the temple, he disagreed with the chanting of a ritual leader and criticized him vocally, interrupting the ceremony. Andrés was not forgiven for this ostentatious transgression. Being barred from initiation into his favorite lodge, he chose not to enter any other. This anecdote indicates that Andrés lived with high ideals about the way Abakuá should be performed and narrated, according to the inherited teachings. He remained critical of contemporary practice throughout his life and chanted with a remarkable emotional depth and authority.[77]

I felt no reason to question Andrés about his membership status, because much of his information was proven accurate when compared to the earlier work of Fernando Ortiz and Lydia Cabrera. I also knew that many initiates of this society know as little about its esoteric teachings as does the rank and file of any religion. Furthermore, on the African continent, many traditions require a long process of apprenticeship before initiation; neophytes are tested on their knowledge before allowed entry. Initiation, then, is a confirmation of the training undergone by a neophyte. About one initiation society in Nigeria, Yorùbá scholar and diviner Wándé Abímbólá wrote, "The Ifá cult is semi-secret. The literary corpus used for divination is regarded and held up as a great secret which the uninitiated should not know about. . . . There are also public and semi-public divination ceremonies in most towns in connection with public ceremonies and rituals. In this way, many Yorùbá men and women get to know a good many of the 'secrets' of Ifá divination, so that these secrets are, in fact, no more than open secrets."[78]

In the context of Caribbean slave societies, the rules of initiation societies were altered for protection; one learned Cuban Abakuá, Kongo, or Lukumí traditions only after making a commitment to them through initiation. In other words, while few disputed Andrés' narrative, many challenged his authorization to speak it. Another factor was one that Pierre Bourdieu called "rites of Institution," where ritual is used to consecrate and reify differences, such as gender and class, between people. Bourdieu wrote that consecration transforms initiates by transforming the way others in their community perceive and behave toward them and simultaneously transforms the way that initiates view themselves.[79]

But in the case of Andrés, who seemed to consider himself an African in exile, he rejected offers of consecration from several Abakuá lodges (his first choice being unavailable to him), because as a descendant of Calabar with deep knowledge of the traditions, he rejected the contemporary Cuban practice of his day. A repository of the perspective of black Abakuá members at the turn of the nineteenth century (quite distinct from a person using inherited materials creatively to transform them), Andrés was an idealist who loved the practice so much that he did not practice.

The Interview Process

Because details of Abakuá history are contained in oral narratives, I was faced with the task of documenting them. In the process, I created a technique that enabled me to do a comparative study of their variants. I prepare for interviews by reading about the topic and by making a list of open-ended questions related to its major themes. I approach the initial interview as an opportunity for the teller and I to become acquainted and as an informal brainstorming session. I usually begin by switching on the recording device, asking the teller to state his or her name, a brief summary of their background, and then to deliver his or her most important story. My job is then to listen, in an active and supportive way, resorting to the prepared questions only if the teller asks for guidance. When the teller finishes the immediate story or reaches a point of fatigue we stop. I later transcribe this material, then formulate questions intended to elicit responses that will fill in gaps or resolve contradictions in the testimony.[80] Conducting interviews without strict adherence to a list of formal questions is less orderly, but it allows the speaker to free associate, letting linkages between events emerge in the telling that may not be chronological, but that may reveal meaning or give insight. Chronology can always be established later in the editing process.

This type of interviewing requires building relationships. One day Andrés arrived to tell me that the night before his late brother, an Abakuá title-holder, had spoken to him in a dream, asking Andrés to reveal to me the circumstances of his death and the ensuing ceremonies. Had I insisted on following a rigid agenda of my own design, there may not have been room for such spontaneity. Supportive listening by the researcher allows the teller to explore hidden areas of experience. In the case of Andrés, who had experienced a life of poverty, the drama was sometimes raw and terrifying, and his stance against it hard. The patience and support I tried to demonstrate while recording testimony, as well as my consistency in transcribing and editing, elicited a trust in our working relationship. In turn, his feelings for the grandeur of the history and practice of his ancestral traditions made him an ideal teacher.

In June 1994 Andrés came almost daily to our home in Centro Habana. We often sat for several hours throwing out questions, which he answered profoundly, usually without hesitation. Often when ours were exhausted, Andrés—whose Herculean mind seemed to be just warming up—asked for more questions. By continually expanding upon earlier themes he had presented, Andrés recreated a world that may have been otherwise lost to history. Being that Abakuá ritual performances are structured upon the question and response method, our interview sessions were, according to Andrés, modeled on Abakuá debates, which have their maximum expression in *la valla* (the cock-fighting pit), where the performance of responsorial chanting is accompanied by a percussion ensemble and dancing during ceremonies.[81] When the results of our sessions were transcribed, Andrés would read them, point to areas that needed reworking, and dictate corrections. As the body of material grew, I began to organize it into thematic chapters.

Writing a public document on an initiatory society is a delicate matter, and I was guided by the recommendations of Andrés at all times. His first condition was that I not speak about this project with others. This was apparently for his own safety, because he felt a local person might become jealous of our collaboration and try to disrupt it. After we had worked for a year, Andrés introduced me to several Abakuá title-holders, bringing them to the house for interviews. In this way Andrés demonstrated generosity as well as confidence in his own position, unafraid that others might take center stage in our work. All whom I met, including the late Luis Salinas, a title-holder in the group Abarakó Sisi, readily acknowledged that Andrés was a highly knowledgeable person on Abakuá lore.[82]

Later I tape-recorded several interviews with Salinas about his life as a foreman on the Havana docks, where Abakuá had long been a major labor force. Salinas spoke with a distant sadness in his eyes about the respect and camaraderie Abakuá gave each other in his youth, when they were united as a labor force. He brought me to a ceremony of his Abakuá lodge in Regla, across the harbor from Havana. The experience of participating in a crowd of hundreds of men performing an initiation, with Íreme masquerades, dance, drum, and chant, was awe-inspiring. I particularly appreciated the affection and respect given to elders like Salinas, who received intimate embraces from his brothers and whose voice, low and cracked with age, was listened to attentively, the younger men straining to hear his chanting.

Several other title-holders I met shied away from contributing to this project, fearful of being associated with a published work. In the past, many Abakuá have been suspended or banished from their lodges for divulging information to non-Abakuá. By struggling to see the completion of this volume, Andrés continually demonstrated his generous character and extraordinary willpower. He wished to record his great-grandfather's knowledge so it could be shared. He also wanted the achievements of his elders and contemporaries to be remembered. Andrés actively conducted research by asking other Abakuá elders for their anecdotes and versions of Abakuá history. He began to clarify issues that were often deliberately enmeshed in esoteric labyrinths in order to confound inquisitive outsiders. He recalled urban rebels who risked their lives to defend the Abakuá from authorities. His joy in this intellectual pursuit fueled his desire to document this history, making it more difficult for those who would come later to distort it for their own purposes.

In 1996, after three years of this work, Andrés continued to deepen his revelations of Abakuá lore. At first I found this confusing, because several things he said at the start of the project did not jibe with what he said later. I learned to scrap earlier versions, often sparse and superficial in comparison, replacing them with later versions that were usually accompanied by long passages of Abakuá as well as logical explanations as to why they existed. It became clear that because of the success of our relationship, where Andrés may have earlier treaded lightly, he was now reaching into the depths of his intellectual resources. After three years of tape-recording and transcribing, we began to work exclusively from the written text. Over the ensuing months and years, Andrés revised the manuscript repeatedly, until his eyes grew too dim with age, at which point I began to read aloud to him. In our more than thirty revisions of the entire manuscript, it was rare that a new phrase, a new organization, or clarity to this material did not result.

By working with one voice relating an overarching narrative, I had hoped to give the reader a coherent and dramatic tale. In order to expand upon its overarching themes with greater detail, however, I began to review my manuscript with several Abakuá masters interested in the historical work I had done. Their scrutiny of Andrés' narrative gave them many exciting points to debate; their responses offered insightful interpretations of the ritual language, a process reflecting the living practice, where no one person has the entire picture. This collective tradition exists within a multi-centered conversation.

El Chino Mokóngo, Abelardo Empegó, and the Interpretation of Abakuá Lore

In 1998, a friend and Abakuá title-holder brought me to the home of Gerardo Pazos "El Chino" (1925–2002), a title-holder of the Kamaroró Efó lodge.[83] Known as "El Chino Mokóngo" since he was Mokóngo (a leader) of his lodge, his lineage directly descends from the first white Abakuá lodge, created in the 1860s. His grandfather, father, and other family were Abakuá leaders, and El Chino was reputed to be an orthodox master. Housebound by a debilitating illness, El Chino welcomed my regular visits to document his own experiences, as well as his responses to Andrés' text. Over a period of two years, he helped me reconstruct the historical material I had already gathered on the controversial lineage of Mukarará (white Abakuá).

After several months reviewing Andrés' text with El Chino, I integrated parts of his dialogue into the final version. Because it is not possible to obtain the totality of knowledge of any tradition, I avoided firm conclusions as I began to comprehend the collective, democratic implications embedded in the unfolding dialogue.

Following standard Cuban logic about the importance of initiation as a means of access to esoteric knowledge, one would suppose that El Chino knew more than

FIGURE 2. El Chino Mokóngo with the Mokóngo sign on his hat. Photo by I. Miller.

Andrés about Abakuá, but this was not necessarily the case. Some passages rejected by El Chino as bogus, for example, had been documented in the 1950s by Ortiz.[84] On the one hand, Ortiz wrote, "These differences can be explained at times by the concurrence of various African languages and dialects in the formation of the Abakuá jargon."[85] On the other, interpretations may differ because of the interpreters' access to information about the language and its use in ritual.

After reading aspects of Andrés' narrative to El Chino, he remarked that he had learned from it. The reason why a practicing Abakuá leader with sixty years of experience would find something new is twofold. First, Abakuá practice could be compared to that of medicine, with specialists for each branch of knowledge. El Chino knew the facets of his own responsibilities as Mokóngo very well, but about those of other dignitaries he knew much less. Second, the noninstitutional nature of African-derived traditions in the Caribbean makes them vehicles for constant reinterpretation within each group of practitioners, explaining their dynamic adaptability to the context of each new generation. Had I worked intensively with five Abakuá masters from five different branches of the society, I may have received as many more varieties in the interpretation of inherited lore. Thoughtful humans do not passively consume monotonously repeated received traditions. Instead, they creatively reinterpret and renew received practices in ways that give them meaning in the present.[86]

During this time another friend and Abakuá title-holder guided me to the home of Abelardo, a title-holder (Empegó) in the Munyánga Efó lodge (Plate 2). Abelardo had grown up with Andrés in the same barrio, where they were schoolmates. I reviewed the manuscript with Abelardo, who related that since a young man, Andrés spoke in a manner reminiscent of a nineteenth-century *bozal* (a person born in Africa). He confirmed Andrés' extensive knowledge and related to me the story of why he was not initiated.[87]

Thus, in the course of my research, Andrés set the terms and then El Chino, Abelardo, and others responded with sometimes different and sometimes coinciding interpretations of Abakuá lore. The dialogue among them reflects the living dynamic of African-derived orality in Cuba. Each had differing perspectives. Andrés, a descendant of Calabar but not an initiate, seemed to live in the nineteenth century, hardly discussing the ongoing revolution in Cuba. El Chino, I learned after he passed away in 2002, was a chief of police on the Havana wharves in the 1950s during the Batista regime. A descendant of Spaniards, he was from a white Abakuá lineage. Abelardo, an enthusiast of Castro's regime, became a member of the Communist Party of Cuba (PCC) after receiving his title in 1963. Soon afterward, belonging to both the PCC and a religion was prohibited, so Abelardo stopped attending reunions of his lodge.[88] He was a descendant of Africans, a former dockworker, and finally a construction engineer who, as a representative of Castro's regime, built structures for Cuba's allies throughout the world, including the Republic of Congo and Angola. I found that the political orientation of the speaker made little or no difference in the information diffused about Abakuá, an indication that the ritual material exists at a level beneath the machinations of everyday public life in the national sphere, giving members a particular group and individual identity within their barrio.

Critiquing the Literature

From the first publication in 1881 to the 1930s, all studies of Abakuá—as virtually all ethnographic studies of African-Americans—were written by police and criminologists.[89] Andrés was acutely aware of this. I brought copies of these early publications from libraries in the United States, and Andrés critiqued them. Because Abakuá was established to liberate men destined to die as slaves, Andrés was shocked by intellectuals who viewed as primitive and unholy a society whose aim was mutual aid among workers. He told me:

> Much has been written about the Abakuá religion. Many writers have been misinformed and others augmented their writings based on speculations. In order to rectify what has already been written, I can only speak about what I have been taught by the elders and what I have experienced, and I hope that you will publish this accordingly.
>
> Some writers have profaned the Abakuá religion by stating that after a man is initiated he must commit a bloody deed. This is false, and if a man is known to be problematic or violent, it is highly unlikely he would be accepted into a juego [lodge], because the other members would not want this responsibility.[90]
>
> During the colonial period many writers launched works that censured our religion, stating that we ate children's hearts. All those things have been denied

and have been demonstrated to be propaganda against us because all beliefs and people deriving from Africa were discriminated against by the government and the wealthy social class.

In response to this prejudice, Andrés felt that only a work based upon the African treaties could accurately tell the story:

> There are many legends written about the origins of Abakuá in Africa, but none of them are based on the treaties and their concepts. Each writer tells it their own way, based on their imagination, but until now no one has written anything that the Basaibékes [wise men] of Abakuá can reaffirm. The Abakuá never told the truth to those who came despotically seeking for information. Even the *plazas* [title-holders] would send the *obonékues* [first-level initiates] away on errands in order to do their works in secrecy. Due to these facts, some fear that our truth cannot be known. I don't mean to say that some books don't have some good qualities and should be forgotten—I feel that a serious researcher will be able to understand and justify our reality.
>
> To speak of the origins of Abakuá in Africa, one must first speak of Sikán [the female founder]; when one speaks of our origins in Cuba, one must begin with the first *baróko* [ceremony] performed by the king Efík Ebúton.[91]

Beginning with the first publications, Andrés read and commented. In 1882 the book *Los criminales de Cuba y D. José Trujillo* (The Criminals of Cuba and Don José Trujillo) was published.[92] About it, Andrés told me: "The chief of police of Havana, José Trujillo, never had the opportunity to acquire firsthand knowledge of this religion. Because of his position he was able to gather some information, but his prisoners never told him the truth. For example, he mentions a confrontation involving a juego called Umorice in the barrio of Los Sitios.[93] This is false, since the first juego created in Los Sitios was Ntáti Machecheré, later Usagaré Mutánga Efó was founded, and still later Ororó Mayambéke Efó. To this day these juegos control this zone, and a juego called Umorice has never existed."

Through his arsenal of knowledge, Andrés challenged the published literature on Abakuá, literature often considered "authoritative" to outsiders, but that is in fact often hostile. Reading propaganda written against his ancestral practice made Andrés even more determined to document Abakuá history. It also served an important methodological purpose: By responding to the literature, he recalled anecdotes and phrases he otherwise may not have.

Andrés told me, "There are many errors in Trujillo's vocabulary, as well as in the names of the juegos. For example, he published this chant, but didn't know what it meant: 'Bani, Bani, nyampe eyeneká makua sakon minombaira apofene ke atebere atamundira abore keron abecekuenyon heyey bario sanaribó ekué.'[94] This is a poorly written funerary chant. It contains the phrase 'heyéy bário,' used only in the context of a celebration." Abelardo agreed, "He is right; in the funerary rites one chants: 'jimí jimí nankuéo,' instead of 'heyéy bário,' which is for a feast." In Nigerian Ékpè contexts, the phrase "heyéy bário!" is a standard way to begin evoking Ékpè.[95]

As scholars of their tradition, Andrés, El Chino, and Abelardo consistently brought clarity to themes that were often incoherent in the earlier literature. In 1916 Israel Castellanos' *La Brujería y el ñáñiguismo en Cuba* (Sorcery and Ñáñiguism in Cuba) was published. Andrés reported, "This is pure propaganda. The majority of its information was acquired in the prison archives and among prisoners. He posits a relationship among assassins, men who wear tattoos, and Abakuás, which is absurd. In this era many people who were not prisoners wore tattoos, for example, sailors, who were not Abakuá." El Chino Mokóngo added, "There were sailors who were Abakuá, like nowadays there are policemen who are Abakuá. In my juego there have always been sailors. Most of the Abakuá were dockworkers. They were also owners of schooners or worked on schooners or ships. They were persons who traveled to different countries and spoke several languages; they must have had contact with Africa." Again and again through our discussions, I was able to document rare perspectives absent from the published literature, such as the maritime Abakuá, a topic with exciting possibilities for trans-Atlantic studies (see chapter 2).

Three editions of Rafael Roche y Monteagudo's *La policía y sus misterios en Cuba* (The Police and Their Mysteries in Cuba) were published in the early twentieth century.[96] Andrés apparently knew many of the people documented therein, commenting, "This book is one of the greatest abuses ever published by the author. He did not know the theme of this religion profoundly. The Abakuá was progressing and expanding in this period. The government and the Christian religions saw the Abakuá as monsters, thus people began to speak badly about the Abakuá—they went to the point of comparing them to cannibals. Almost all the men mentioned in his book had criminal records, but this does not mean they were Abakuá. They were simply evil-doing men. It is true that some of the men he mentions, like Rapisún, Emilio Larrazaba, Eusebio Enipopo were sworn-in, but 'Mula Ciega' and many others were not Abakuá." Abelardo agreed, "It is true what he says." El Chino Mokóngo added, "Police chief Roche's book mentioned some true facts, but the aim of the book was to attack the criminals, and as they thought that all the criminals were Abakuá, they attacked the Abakuá."[97]

As is described in chapter 5, Abakuá was declared illegal in 1875, with its members treated like criminals. Following its Ékpè model, Abakuá were autonomous communities who policed their own members. Colonists recognized the threat to their claims over the territory. While confrontations occur wherever competing judicial systems coexist, the conflict was disguised by official propaganda that would have the public confuse Abakuá activities with murder and cannibalism. Abakuá became scapegoats, the boogiemen of Cuba; anything they were accused of that was outside the norms of polite society seemed possible to the propertied class. Andrés noted, "Roche compared this religion with the Mafia, which is false.[98] In the Mafia when a man is removed from his group, he is executed, and when an Abakuá member is separated from his juego, he is respected, there is no statute to punish him. Moreover, we are not smugglers, and during ceremonies there are no business transactions, only rites of brotherhood and fraternity."[99] The prejudices have run so deep that in all periods of Cuban history, the colonial, republican, and revolutionary authorities, with some exceptions, have consistently expressed hostile attitudes toward Abakuá. A recent example is found in a book of police testimonies published in Cuba in 1980, when one author claimed that "another strategy often employed by the Abakuá mafia is 'to make the bed' (prepare an aggression of many against one)."[100]

Despite the hostile stance toward Cuban Abakuá in the work of Trujillo and Roche, some of their documentation was useful. For example, several Abakuá explained to me that some treaties (mythic histories) reproduced in Roche's work reflected their language and history (see examples in chapter 3). While turned off by condescending speculations, Andrés would carefully read an author demonstrating a solid understanding of Abakuá history and precepts. By the 1940s and 1950s, vocabularies and monographs—by Lydia Cabrera, Juan Martín, and Fernando Ortiz—began to appear that recognized Abakuá as a system to be studied on its own terms.[101] For example, Andrés read Cabrera's 1958 *La Sociedad Secreta* in its entirety. We were fortunate to have Cabrera's pioneering work as a springboard, although her fieldwork conducted primarily in Matanzas, and my own was largely in Havana.[102]

Cabrera's works were based on years of conversations with Abakuá members who relayed fragmented and contradictory versions of Abakuá mythology to her. In her earliest work on the Abakuá, Cabrera expressed her frustration with the obscurity of the material, "regarding the first consecrations of the 'fundament,' the Abakuá texts speak with a prolixity as entangled as it is detailed."[103] She concluded—somewhat tongue in cheek—that the "Foundational sacred histories of the brotherhood . . . appeared without any order in these dirty librettos, manuals of the ocobios [brothers], worn with use, composed with the same sincere dis-preoccupation of syntax and written at times with ink of two colors, that various initiates have put in my hands as crystal-clear keys that would guide me through the obscure labyrinth of their traditions."[104] Eight laborious years later, she had come to appreciate the labyrinth of Abakuá mythology, "Los ñáñigos [Abakuá], like the Greeks . . . were not usually in agreement about a single mythic event. But we don't complain at the amount of versions and disparities about any of these themes . . . since with such variance their traditions are nobly enriched."[105]

The literature on Abakuá is vast and cited throughout this book. Generally speaking, all earlier works published in Cuba treat Abakuá as an important national sociological phenomenon, with little preoccupation for the international implications of its continuities with Cross River Ékpè (even though Ortiz, Cabrera, and Martín had pondered the origins of many terms and concepts). A paradigm shift occurred with the publications of Robert Farris Thompson, perhaps the first scholar to conduct research among both Cross River Ékpè and Cuban Abakuá. As a young student I was inspired by his work to embark on my own career. While building on early works by W. E. B. DuBois, Melville J. Herskovits, Lorenzo Turner, Pierre Verger, and others, Thompson's *African Art in Motion* (1974) and *Flash of the Spirit* (1983), mapped out the field of trans-Atlantic studies by identifying a variety of regional and ethnic African transmissions. My own contribution has been to follow up these leads by sustained research in a particular region, while using language and performance as major sources of evidence.

In the process of comparative research, I found that the hostility toward Ékpè in the literature about West Africa was comparable to that toward Abakuá in Cuba. In one of many other examples, contemporary historians have compared Ékpè to the Mafia: "By the 1790s, virtually all males at Old Calabar were being forced to purchase membership in Ékpè, if they did not join willingly. Those individuals who were not members of the society but were in the streets when ekpe was being 'run' were punished, usually by whipping. In 'running ekpe' through the different wards, the 'grand council' turned the Ékpè society into a type of protection racket, akin in its operation to organizations like the Mafia, and with its religious functions seemingly subordinated to commercial and political ends."[106]

This description may not be incorrect, but it portrays Ékpè in a sinister light. One could alternatively make the case that belonging to Ékpè in Calabar was like belonging to a university in a society where education is highly valued. Education may be expensive, but without a title or a degree, one has few chances of survival and protection from menial jobs. Nevertheless, some young adults reject this institution, but truant officers are hired to punish them. Although the colonial literature contains many references to "whippings" by Ékpè masks, few of these were eyewitness accounts.[107] On the one hand, Ékpè masks could and still do carry sticks to beat noninitiates who fail to make way for members in procession. On the other, the Ékpè bells around their waists were a warning to nonmembers to stay away.[108]

The comparison of Ékpè to the Mafia is indeed provocative. Was Ékpè run like organized crime in North America? Thanks to the analysis of Eric Hobsbawm, we know that "the Mafia" is not one thing, but an umbrella term for several institutions with various functions and tendencies, first emerging in mid-nineteenth-century Sicily in order to defend landowners from emerging capitalism. Its later development as organized crime in twentieth-century North America is quite a different matter.[109] Since these historians failed to distinguish one form of Mafia from another in time and space, they seem to use the term for shock value. If from a perspective of European colonization Ékpè and Abakuá were criminal, one can also say that from a perspective of West African traditionalists, colonialism was organized crime.[110] But this kind of dialogue takes us nowhere. Instead, it would be much more interesting to understand why Èkpè was created in West Africa and the important functions it carried out. Likewise, why was Abakuá created in Cuba, and how did its leadership adapt it to respond to the issues facing their communities in different periods of history?

The Èfìks of nineteenth-century Calabar certainly transformed Èkpè to maintain their position as middlemen in the trade with Europeans, but this extreme use of the society did not define it for all times or places.[111] Other Cross River communities with Èkpè that were marginal to the trade routes seem to have continued their earlier practices.[112] One academic observed that Èkpè membership lost its affiliation with ethnic lineage and "revolved around the sheer economic power to buy the esoteric knowledge and titles."[113] Primary sources in Calabar confirm this trend for the leading lodges of Calabar, but these were aberrations that neither defined the practice nor its philosophic insights for the entire region. Undoubtedly, as settlements grew into heterogeneous towns and cities, club membership became open to the wealthy who met other requirements; entry fees were a form of social security for the elders.[114] But prices of entry fluctuate, then as now, depending on one's relationship to the community. If purchasing power became definitive to leadership in Èkpè, why then is the following Èkpè phrase still chanted in Calabar?

Ebonko mfon emana	Ebonko is a birthright [a royal inheritance]
Ete ama eyen aban eyen esie Èkpè	Father initiates only the son he loves.[115]

Even missionaries, who competed with Èkpè for influence in the community and who therefore viewed it as a negative force, understood the importance of family lineage in Èkpè. The Rev. William James Ward, who spent many years in Oron in the early 1900s, noted, "To become a member of Egbo [Èkpè] is the dearest wish of nearly every youth, and a fond father feels that his money, hardly won, is well spent in securing the fulfillment of his son's desire. It is by no means easy to become an Egbo [Èkpè] member."[116] Reports from the same period in Usaghade (Isangele), a source region for Èkpè in present-day Cameroon, also maintain that "membership of Èkpè was usually acquired in the first instance for a youth by his father."[117]

Facile condemnations of Èkpè and Abakuá systems reflect hostile attitudes best understood in the context of Euro-centric assumptions. How could Èkpè be both a spiritual practice and a social security system? How could titles be inherited within families, yet nonindigenes could become members? The multiple facets of Èkpè continue to mystify. The first missionaries who settled in Calabar were invited by Èkpè leaders who sought the education of their children, while British sought to create a literate elite who could help run the palm oil trade.[118] The Rev. Hope Waddell, who was originally invited by Èkpè leaders into Calabar, later wrote, "the Egbo [Èkpè] Society was originated and maintained, not to repress crime, but to render its members absolutely irresponsible for their conduct toward their dependents."[119] An invited guest, Waddell became exasperated when he realized he could not act in Calabar society without the permission of an Ékpè council. Statements like these were used to garner military force to suppress Ékpè and install British law.

Missionary arrogance resulted in crimes against the laws of the land. In 1855 the town of Obutong was bombarded and burnt down by a British naval ship "at the request of European traders," with the excuse that a treaty was violated.[120] The conflict began six years earlier when the Reverend Edgerley purposely broke a drum inside the Ékpè temple, then in 1854 broke a symbolic egg at the shrine of Ndem, the water divinity.[121] In the aftermath, the Mission House in Atakpa (Duke Town), Calabar's economic center, declared itself independent from Ékpè law, with naval support.[122]

In retrospect, observers have argued that southeastern Nigerian communities experienced little crime before the arrival of Europeans. Colonists justified their presence to keep law and order, yet Nigerians have responded that "a false picture of African lawlessness and disorder" was created.[123] Traditional law was apparently very effective, as it evoked the presence of the living and the ancestors in crime detection. In Calabar, Ékpè was dreaded as "no respecter of persons."[124] But once locals learned that the new Christian authorities pardoned offenses and that they could escape local law by running to the Mission House, a dramatic rise in crime resulted.[125]

Countering the myths of Ékpè as a purely commercial enterprise, several anecdotes demonstrate the judicious use of power by Ékpè leaders to resist subjugation. From the 1820s to 1830s, when Atakpa (Duke Town) was at the height of its power, their leader did not allow European traders to create settlements in the region.[126] In the 1850s, his successor "had on many occasions refused to blow Egbo [evoke Ékpè] on anyone the supercargoes requested, who was indebted to them."[127] Calabar historian Monday Efiong Noah wrote that Ékpè "was the most fair and effective instrument of government that was ever devised in the region. European traders often times resorted to the use of Ékpè laws for orderly conduct of their business."[128] In 1851 British Consul for the Bight of Biafra John Beecroft "argued that Ékpè was the only government that could effectively rule Calabar."[129]

The Ékpè and Abakuá systems, while certainly modified from their nineteenth-century models, continue to share important strands of philosophy, values, and aesthetics, some of which are described in the following chapters. The persistence of these values indicates how flexible these systems are in adapting to local conditions and pressures, while maintaining their basic structure and teachings.

A dramatic advance in my own learning began with the support of Victor Manfredi, a linguist specializing in Ìgbo and Yorùbá who has extensive contacts in the global Nigerian community. I began to communicate with his colleagues, linguists and historians from southeastern Nigeria, sending them audio and visual recordings of Cuban Abakuá for analysis. Once the linguistic continuities with Cross River Ékpè became obvious, I searched in vain for several years to find Èfìk speakers in Chicago, Boston, and New York City. Only when Nigerians themselves contacted me after reading my work did the process of trans-Atlantic interpretation began in earnest.

Mutual recognition between the Ékpè and Abakuá provokes many questions about West African cultural continuities in the Caribbean. That both Ékpè and Abakuá perceive themselves in the other's language and ritual practice points to the vitality of oral history and performance as sources for new evidence in the African Diaspora. To identify continuities is to create a platform, for the implications of this knowledge are not lost upon members of both communities, since Ékpè and Abakuá currently struggle to use traditional practices as a means of responding to contemporary issues.[130]

The Talmudic Spirit

As Max Weber noted, "the intellectual seeks in various ways, the casuistry of which extends into infinity, to endow his life with pervasive meaning, and thus to find unity with himself, with his fellow men and with the cosmos."[131] Abakuá practice is nonauthoritarian, and lore is parceled throughout the society. No single person has a total view of its practice or the authority to decide for the group. Following Ékpè protocol, Abakuá lodges are run by councils following very clear inherited guidelines.[132] In a rare public expression of the nonauthoritarian tendencies of Abakuá and other African-derived systems, a Cuban percussion ensemble with Abakuá members recorded "La plegaria" (The Prayer) in the 1950s. This elegant song uses codes to express the profundity of their collective, inherited traditions, while distinguishing them from would-be authoritarians seeking to impose their will.[133] One cannot enter these systems or learn about their teachings willfully, one must be invited, after undergoing a series of tests.[134]

Regarding the interpretations of their inherited texts and traditions, Abakuá leaders recognize the existence of variants. This is easily said, but when one is face to face with a learned initiate convinced that his version is the truth, the sway of charisma can be powerful. Working with El Chino, Abelardo Empegó, and other Abakuá titleholders in Havana and Matanzas, broadened my view of Abakuá history and practice. I learned to keep variations of liturgy and historical anecdotes integral, placing them side by side (versus displacing one for another). Early on, I sought the common denominators in variations, attempting to create an overarching narrative by blending all the materials. Experience taught me that the diversity of narratives is interesting in itself, because the narratives sustain a rich debate centered on the interpretation of the origin myths, a sign of a vibrant intellectual tradition. By traveling to various villages in West Africa where Ékpè/Mgbè exists, I learned that there never was a master narrative about the society's origins, but confirmed that each group has their own perspective.

If there were merely one published narrative, then anyone could purchase and read it. Instead, access to Abakuá information has a rigorous protocol. Members demonstrate their commitment to the tradition by actively seeking information from their elders, by critically observing ceremonial action, and then making their own conclusions. The study and interpretation of Abakuá lore can be compared to the "reasonings" of Rastafari elders, whose theological debates seek to reveal the Truth of their history and received divine messages. Both approach their traditions in an almost Talmudic spirit. The Judaic Talmudic tradition is believed to have originated in the Revelation granted to Moses; a small portion was delivered in writing, a larger one orally. Since Moses, the "Oral Torah" was passed on in apprenticeships from generation to generation to the third century C.E., when it was transcribed.[135] This "core document of Talmudic tradition" has been the subject of study and interpretation ever since.

Abakuá narratives are not divine revelation, but mythic histories recounting how Calabarí ancestors received contact with the divine, then maintained it through the formation of the Ékpè society in historical stages. Parallels with the Talmud are found in the original orality of the material and especially in the lack of preoccupation for a single interpretation. In some Talmudic passages, one finds unresolved disagreement, where "no single answer is ever declared authoritative, and in fact several of them are couched in extremely vague or exotic terms and never clarified at all."[136] In the Talmud's argumentative style, some passages contradict others. In rare passages, "the Talmud admits that two different versions of a master's teaching are inconsistent, but then leaves both standing."[137] Torah study has such a detailed protocol that it has become "a religious ritual in its own right . . . [perhaps] the most sacred ritual that Jewish life had to offer."[138] So too the most respected Abakuá leaders are dedicated students of the inherited lore, much of it contained in a myriad of small chants and longer treaties. These erudite spend a lifetime receiving, memorizing, and interpreting them, then demonstrating mastery of them in ceremony. In the process, they are trained as intellectuals, critically engaged in the history and philosophy contained in the passages. In a society with few avenues for social advancement, Abakuá practice enables working-class males to express their intelligence and artistry as well as any artist in any other form.

Because they are coded, the narratives are labyrinthine. In Cuban Abakuá, as in West African Ékpè, "there are things that [the elders] should never articulate clearly," not even to initiates.[139] Abakuá treaties are fixed in writing, although variations exist. These hand-written texts are treated like oral passages: divulged piecemeal to apprentices who, after memorizing, then reciting them correctly, are given more. Abakuá narratives have many branches, there is no single book or codified text.[140] Little is known about the process of reducing African oral knowledge into writing in Cuba. It may be relevant that literacy has a long history in Calabar: since the eighteenth century the sons of Èfìk elites were educated in England.[141] The narrative told by Abakuá leaders is that in the process of Africans initiating the first Cubans into the society, the ritual texts were written down. Since Cuban creoles were not native speakers of the language(s), and since the Cuban context did not easily allow for the lengthy process of oral transmission, the Cuban initiates could study the written fragments and pass them on.

Methods of selection and interpretation used by Abakuá leaders include applying their own logic to received texts and then comparing these with actual practice by participating in *plantes* (ceremonies). That is, one cannot function without the theory, but if that is all one has, one cannot function. During ceremony, a percussion ensemble with chanters performs outside in the patio as rites proceed inside the temple. Those who chant take turns demonstrating their knowledge, challenging others to respond to their questions. If other participants can follow, they also participate in a dialogue exploring the vast terrain of Abakuá epics.

Reconstructing Abakuá History

The traditions of each lodge may be distinct but should be legitimized by reference to a passage in the Abakuá language. Though the texts may have divergent interpretations, being written, they are not likely to have been altered much since the nineteenth century, making them sources of information for Cross River history.

This book documents those lodges established in nineteenth-century Cuba, a period when Ékpè from Africa were present and participating in the dissemination of knowledge. The process of identifying the lodges, their foundation dates, titles, and sponsoring lineages required the reconstruction Abakuá history. By examining the oral *tratados* (mythic histories), the published literature, and by interviewing knowledgeable elders, I constructed a general picture of important Potencies (lodges) and their lineages. Fieldwork taught me, however, that many initiates are uninformed about the history of their own group, such that I had to find the right elder to discover a particular piece of the oral tradition.

The historical reconstruction of Abakuá lineages requires multiple methods of verification. By speaking to dignitaries such as El Chino, Abelardo, and others in Havana and Matanzas, I verified the testimony of Andrés, always returning for his evaluation of what I was learning. Andrés' advanced age and his declining health motivated me to investigate incessantly the oral traditions of Abakuá history, believing that with his passing away there would be little hope for completing this task.[142]

Andrés was my Calabarí Homer, and to him I am eternally grateful. But in fact, after being initiated in Calabar and charged with being an ambassador, my relationship to Abakuá shifted, as I was able to offer information to its leadership, who in turn sent messages to Calabar through me. My subsequent learning enabled me to understand Abakuá history in deeper ways. Although I am obliged not to reveal these teachings, they have allowed me to grasp the essential elements in the story, as well as to reduce speculation.

Historical Anthropology of the African Diaspora

My own approach to understanding the contributions of Africans to American history and society is a historical anthropological one that considers the perspectives of contemporary Africans and their indigenous philosophies as necessary participants in a dialogue. An example of this approach is found in *Black Rice: The African Origins of Rice Cultivation in the Americas* (2001) by historian Judith Carney, who convincingly documented the agency of "Rice Coast" African men and women in recreating "an entire cultural system" in the production of rice from the onset of European colonization of the Americas. This kind of work allows us to "see Africa through the Americas," that is, to understand aspects of African technologies that were foundational to American societies, in this case the diversity of West African rice producing methods and the "domestication of a separate species of rice in West Africa" that was not fully understood until the twentieth century.[143]

James Sweet's study *Recreating Africa: Culture, Kinship, and Religion in the African-Portuguese World, 1441–1770* (2003) is a model of comparative trans-Atlantic research in the archives. Using the records of the Portuguese Inquisition in Brazil as a primary source, Sweet's findings "challenge widely held notions that African slaves were unable to replicate specific African institutions in the Americas."[144] He detailed how divination practices brought by Africans were continued, even if their imperatives were transformed because of the condition of slavery, but that these transformations were "made in much the same way that acclimations were made for wars, droughts, and famines that periodically occurred in African societies. In all cases, the driving force behind divination was the restoration of communal balance and harmony."[145]

In 1948 Melville Herskovits created an important model in his essay "The Contribution of Afroamerican Studies to Africanist Research." Herskovits observed that because the study of cultural elements taught by Africans to members of American societies can help scholars better understand their African source regions, a trans-Atlantic dialogue can only be a win-win situation.[146] He suggested that collaborative exchanges with communities of international scholars could transcend linguistic and ideological borders.

The colonial project of erasing African history and presence has been countered by dialogues between West Africa and the Americas and the work of earlier scholars/ participants such as Wáñdé Abímbọ́lá, William Bascom, Maureen Warner-Lewis, and Pierre Verger, and it was exemplified in a collection of essays called *Rethinking the African Diaspora* (2001).[147] More recently, Professor J. Lorand Matory has demonstrated in *Black Atlantic Religion* (2005) that trans-Atlantic dialogues have been ongoing for hundreds of years within communities of African descent. Many examples of such dialogues have been documented in the Yorùbá-derived Diaspora between the Republic of Benin and Nigeria and Brazil.

In the case of the Cross River Diaspora, there is little evidence for an ongoing dialogue between Ékpè and Abakuá; instead, there is much evidence that Ékpè members in eighteenth- and nineteenth-century Cuba were able to reorganize their homeland institution in Havana and Matanzas, a creative process of adaptation to this Caribbean society that became foundational to its urban social networks and music culture. Being a hermetic group that does not proselytize, Cuban Abakuá do not want to be studied. When I learned of their strong interest in confirming their West African sources, however, I began to share information about the Cross River Ékpè with them, to their great satisfaction. As one Abakuá title-holder told me, "After learning about Ékpè in Africa, we understand that we are not alone in the world." That many Cross River Ékpè have a similar interest in the Abakuá is a signal of the political use of inherited cultural systems on both sides of the Atlantic.

My own experience of becoming an initiate of a Calabar Ékpè lodge and receiving a title therein was important to the process of identifying continuities between Cuba and Calabar.[148] For example, the lodge to which I belong, Ekoretonko (Efe Ékpè Eyo Ema), has a namesake in Cuba, the Ekuéri Tonkó lodge of Havana.[149] The title I received, Mbàkàrà, is also an important title in Cuban Abakuá lodges, with a similar function.[150] In all Ékpè lodges, Iyámba is a title of great importance; this title is also preeminent in Abakuá.[151] In M̀gbè lodges of the Ejagham, the equivalent of Iyámba is Musungu; in Cuba, the grade Mosóngo is fundamental.[152] There are many, many other examples.

It is remarkable that the Abakuá cultural movement has been able to maintain some degree of intelligibility of its texts to current Cross River practitioners of Ékpè— the source tradition from which it was separated some 200 years ago. As with other cases of oral transmission across long time and space intervals, such as the Vedic and Homeric poems, the Abakuá example combines intensive artistic discipline with a ritualized guild framework. Since the revolution in 1959 information about the Abakuá has been inaccessible to most non-Cuban scholars. By documenting the nineteenth-century transmission of Ékpè to Cuban receivers, I hope to contribute to a contemporary dialogue in the Cross River Diaspora, an awareness by Cross River peoples of the contributions of their ancestors to Cuban society, and the ability of Cuban Abakuá to confirm the sources of their inherited traditions.

As the present moment of history is witnessing the reconnection of the two ends of this vast Diasporal arc, the impact of this encounter on the local communities of participants will be fascinating to observe. At the same time, the public nature of the new encounter is eliciting unprecedented openness from all sides to scholarly access, which promises to enrich the description of each of the local traditions that were heretofore so closely guarded from outside view. Eventually the global Ékpè-Abakuá network may develop its own scholarship from within, such has happened already to an extent with the Yorùbá-Lukumí tradition.

The Chapters

In Cuba, the persistence of the myths of docile slaves and the contentment of the impoverished with their condition was such that historians José Luciano Franco and Pedro Deschamps-Chappeaux devoted much of their writing to demonstrate the continual resistance to enslavement. In the 1980s, Deschamps-Chappeaux wrote, "never did a year pass in the Americas that was not marked by a rebellion against the slavery system."[153] The vast majority of Cuban rebellions, as well as communities of fugitives, were multi-ethnic, involving the descendants of Africans, American Indians, Asians, and Europeans. In other words, where the colonists tried to divide and conquer, their subjects organized across every imaginable barrier to fight back. The story of the Abakuá society is a narrative within this larger picture, one with all the elements of an epic: the slave commerce on the African coast, the forced migration to the Caribbean, the incredible ability to regroup in order to recreate the indigenous leopard societies of the homeland, and then the infusion of African traditional values into creole populations of all backgrounds by bringing them into this society of prestige. I doubt there is a better example than this of the inclusive inclination of African systems, although similar examples are found in Brazil, Haiti, and other places. Instead of working within the limitations of race—what Europeans imposed upon them—Carabalí migrants used their indigenous systems to maintain group solidarity by teaching initiates the responsibilities inherent in the privileges of membership.

Chapter 1 is based largely upon Abakuá narratives about the arrival of Carabalí Ékpè members and the many stages in their process of recreating Ékpè in Cuba, creating the first Abakuá lodges, and establishing the three major "ethnic" lineages: Efí, Efó, and Orú. Although not readily apparent to the reader, most of the Abakuá language used to tell this story is contained in chants used even today in ceremonies. Comparative research shows that symbols, objects, and concepts fundamental to Cross River Ékpè were reproduced in Cuba.

The significance of Abakuá is evident in the history of Havana, where enslaved people built the city and renamed its barrios on their own terms. Chapter 2 describes the roles of free urban blacks, urban cabildos de nación (African nation-groups), fugitives from slavery living in Havana, workers on the wharves of Havana, battalions of blacks and mulattos who worked there also, Hispanicized free urban blacks known as *black curros*, as well as the multiple anticolonial movements in the early 1800s, and how all of these strands impacted the emergence of Abakuá in the 1830s.

Abakuá leaders resisted even the harshest periods of colonial oppression by continuously creating lodges based upon their Calabarí homeland traditions. Chapter 3 uses the concept of planting, of activating the brotherhood—shared by Ékpè and Abakuá—to describe how Abakuá expanded from the 1830s to 1860s in a cosmopolitan urban environment and in the face of barbaric repression as experienced in the wake of the infamous Conspiracy of La Escalera in the 1840s. Documenting the process of the transmission of Ékpè into Cuba, this chapter lists the major lodges founded and identifies their possible Cross River precedents. In the 1860s, Abakuá expanded into the nearby port city of Matanzas, with the sponsorship of Havana lodges.

Chapter 4 describes the process by which creoles, or Cuban-born initiates, were assimilated into Cross River traditions through Abakuá practice, focusing on how an Abakuá title-holder in Havana named Andrés Petit created the first lodge of white men, thereby founding an entire lineage that continues today. This process was related to general conditions in Cuba at the time, including economic crises and tensions with the colonial regime. The creative responses of Abakuá leadership made it the first integrated institution in Cuba, before the Wars of Independence began and before the rebel leaders such as Antonio Maceo and José Martí proclaimed that an independent Cuba would be an integrated one.

Integration threatened the structure of colonial rule. Chapter 5 describes how Abakuá was made illegal in 1875, with its members (as well as other anticolonials) dispersed to Spanish penal colonies in North and West Africa. Those who could escaped from Cuba to Florida to join the emerging cigar industry. Responding to scholarship that argues for the recreation of Abakuá lodges in exile, having learned otherwise from Abakuá leaders, I discuss issues basic to the process, which serve to highlight the extraordinary achievements of Abakuá's foundation in Cuba.

Chapter 6 reviews the last two decades of colonial rule, including the official termination of the African cabildos de nación, as well as their Three Kings' Day processions in Havana, and the attempts by police to destroy Abakuá by confiscating their sacred objects. Meanwhile, in the emergent Cuban popular theater and music there is evidence of Abakuá used as a symbol of cubanía (Cuban-ness). To understand contemporary anecdotes I gathered about Abakuá and African-descended General Antonio Maceo, I review the significance of Maceo, whose mother is regarded as the "mother of the Cuban nation."

Because music is fundamental to the expression of Abakuá and because many Abakuá have been professional musicians, there is a profound relationship between Abakuá and Cuban popular music, itself a globally popular form since the 1920s, if not earlier. Chapter 7 lays out evidence for Calabarí presence in the formation of rumba music in the nineteenth century and the use of clave sticks in the rumba and son genres. In addition, it describes how Abakuá composers have consistently recorded their social and ritual history using Abakuá language as well as rhythms and distinctive sounds in commercial recordings.

The epilogue describes an encounter of Abakuá and Ékpè in Calabar at the International Ékpè Festival in 2004. This event created waves of repercussions throughout Abakuá and Ékpè groups, who are confirming their local history through the practice of their counterparts.

The three appendices contain additional data for a comprehensive view of nineteenth-century Abakuá. The first is a list of lodges founded from the 1870s to the end of the century, the second has detailed interpretations of Abakuá chants mentioned throughout the book, and the third discusses issues that arose in the comparison of masking practices in Calabar and Cuba.

The glossary contains Ékpè, Abakuá, and Spanish terms. Many key Abakuá terms are slightly transformed from those still used in the Calabar region (particularly in the Èfìk language) and in Ékpè ritual phrases. For example, the word *Ékue* (the Voice of the leopard) derives from *ékpè* (leopard);[154] the word *íreme* (masquerade) derives from *ídèm* (masquerade).[155] Used to evoke ancestral and other mystic energies, Abakuá words are believed to motivate inanimate forces into action. The Abakuá language has influenced Cuban popular speech.[156] Most famously, the term *chébere* (or *chévere*) used in Cuban popular speech to mean "valiant, wonderful, excellent" derives from *Ma' chébere*, a title of the Abakuá dignitary Mokóngo.[157] Mokóngo is an Ékpè title in southwestern Cameroon.[158] Through the global expansion of Cuban popular music, from the first son craze in the 1920s and 1930s, the word *chébere* became widespread throughout Latin America as an affirmation of "something positive."

1. Arrival

...

Bóto kenbóto engrinerón awarumba moropo íreme.
My body is in Cuba but my mind is in Africa.
—ABAKUÁ PHRASE[1]

Ninety-seven-year-old Andrés Flores, a descendant of Calabar, born and raised in Old Havana, told the story as he learned it from his ancestors and immediate family of how the founders of Abakuá came to Cuba. For him the story of their migration began with the Europeans: "To speak of slavery one should mention Bartolomé de las Casas, who suggested to Queen Isabel that Africans be brought to the Americas.[2] The first Africans arrived in Cuba in the early 1500s didn't come directly from Africa, they came from Spain and spoke Spanish.[3] In 1513 the Spaniards brought the first four slaves directly from Africa with the authorization of the government in Cuba.[4] In 1557 the first shipment of African slaves arrived directly from Africa; they were 1400. The English sent 1100 to Jamaica and 300 remained in Cuba."[5]

Andrés mentioned the participation of a representative of the Church, a Spanish ruler, and West African slave traders to reveal his class position of absolute distrust in the rulers and leaders of powerful institutions. In his experience, and in that of members of his race and class, all had failed him and his ancestors. Most histories begin and end with the Europeans. But Andrés and other descendants of Africans in the Caribbean know a very different history, one that begins in Africa and does not have Europe at the center.

Founding Fathers

Andrés noted, "It is well known that many Africans were sold into slavery by other Africans. Most of them were warriors captured in battle.[6] All were from different tribes and regions of Africa known in Cuba as Gangá, Kongo, Kongo-Real, Mandinga, Lukumí, Bríkamo, and Carabalí."[7] Enslaved Africans brought their languages and cultures. Among them were members of the Ékpè (leopard) society of the Cross River region (Calabar), known in Cuba as Calabarí or Carabalí. "Around 1800 they brought a cargo of Bríkamo Carabalí to Cuba, represented by a sovereign king named Efík Ebúton from Efí territory belonging to Calabar. With him came a prince from Efó territory named Anamerúto Ápapa Efó and nine wise men.[8] They all belonged to the same Abakuá religion, but were representatives of different tribes."[9]

Indeed, many of their names are clearly recognizable as Cross River terms for various places and ethnic groups.[10] In Cuba, Ékpè became known as Abakuá after an ethnic term used in Calabar. As Andrés indicated, Ékpè was multi-ethnic and practiced throughout this region where many languages were spoken. "Although they spoke different languages, like Bibí, Ápapa, Bríkamo, and Suáma, they could understand one another.[11] They came on a secret mission to guide the Carabalís, because many men in that region had disappeared and their destiny was unknown." Many languages of the lower Cross River are indeed mutually intelligible. Furthermore, by the late 1700s, Èfìk traders of Calabar had extended networks throughout the entire region, making Èfìk the lingua franca.[12]

Although Andrés' story has a mythic ring, there is evidence that some African royalty did travel as free persons to the Caribbean and back.[13] In Calabar, Eyo Honesty II was "crowned king of Creek Town in either 1835 or 1837." As a young man in the late 1700s, Eyo had traveled the triangular trade route between Calabar, the Caribbean, and England by working as a cabin boy on an English ship.[14] Eyo was one of several children of Èfìk elites who learned to read and write in English; many were schooled in England, having intimate and sustained contact with British captains and merchants.[15] Eyo's travels confirm the possibility of contact by him or other Cross River sailors with Ékpè members in Havana, many of whom worked along its wharves from the 1760s onward.[16]

Some Èfìk princes may have traveled freely, but most Calabar people came in chains. Ebúton, the "Èfìk king" of Andrés' narrative is a reference to the town of Obutong in precolonial Old Calabar.[17] In 1767 leaders of this town and their retinues were captured by British ships and transported to the Caribbean, an incident well documented in written sources. Known as the "Massacre of Old Calabar," this tragedy resulted from a power struggle between the neighboring Old Town (Obutong) and Duke Town (Atakpa) over foreign trade.[18] Duke Town leaders made a secret pact with captains of British slave ships anchored in the Old Calabar River. These, in turn, invited Obutong leaders aboard their vessels to "mediate" the dispute. Once on board, three brothers of Obutong Chief Ephraim Robin John were held captive, and an estimated 300 of their townspeople were slaughtered. One brother, released to the Duke Town leaders, was beheaded, and the other two, along with several of their retinue, were sold as slaves in the West Indies.[19]

The rivalries among Èfik settlements on the Calabar River lasted for decades, almost certainly leading to the capture of several Ékpè masters who participated in the establishment of Abakuá in Havana.[20] "Grandy King George" (Ephraim Robin John) described the loss of four of his sons "gone allredy with [captain] Jackson and I don't want any more of them caried of by any other vausell" [sic].[21] Meanwhile, hundreds of Africans embarked from Calabar were transported on British ships directly to Havana.[22] There, in spite of linguistic and ethnic diversity, they would have been known generally as Calabarí and participated in the formation of cabildos de nación (nation-groups), many of which included Ékpè members who guided the emerging Abakuá.[23]

The forced migration of Cross River peoples coincided with the success of the Haitian Revolution in the early 1800s, when Africans in Haiti ceased sugar production there by ending European domination. An unintended consequence was that in Cuba the wealthy class seized this opportunity to increase sugar production. Cuba emerged as a leading sugar producer in the world only by increasing the numbers of African laborers there.[24] After the 1807 British abolition of the trans-Atlantic slave trade, Cuban-based slavers dominated the illegal trade in the Calabar region.[25]

Andrés picks up his story on the Cuban docks, "The African Abakuá told that when they arrived in Cuba, they disembarked on the wharves of Casablanca [in Havana's port]. Today we ask the apprentices: 'Éntre enyúge ororó amána semé unkayo Núnkue néwe amanisón erieron?' At what part of Cuba did the first Carabalís land? 'Itiá Ororó Kande.' This means: 'At the wharves in Regla.' They renamed Havana as Núnkue; the phrase 'Núnkue ítiá ororó kánde' means 'the part of the harbor belonging to Regla'" (Plate 3).[26]

As Andrés told me this history, he often began in the Abakuá language, then translated this to Cuban Spanish. After traveling to Calabar, I found that many Abakuá terms are standard usage in the Cross River region, whereas some are used only by Ékpè members. Being an initiation society, Ékpè has its own coded terms and phrases, as do other initiation groups around the world. Linguist Ken Hale called these systems "auxiliary languages," because they are often created by relexifying the language of the larger community.[27] Cuban Abakuá is also an auxiliary language that includes many terms from Èfik and Ejagham, as well as purely Ékpè phrases.[28]

Cross River peoples exported to the Caribbean region became known as Calabarí, (and later in Cuba, Carabalí, reversing the *l* and *r*). The port many departed from was called Old Calabar, and the language of many others (from the Niger Delta) was Kalabari. A similar process of regrouping occurred in Cuba when various Yorùbá subgroups became known collectively as Lukumí, and various Bantu groups became known as Kongo.[29] As Africans arrived in the urban areas of Cuba during the slave trade, they formed cabildos, or nation-groups.[30] Andrés continued, "Anayúgue besun kányo anawe kório Abakuá? How was the Abakuá created in Cuba?[31] The Africans were preparing to unify with the Cubans in order to resist their common enemies, the Spaniards; as everything was done in secret, they carried many details of this history to their tombs. The Africans, organized into cabildos, began to celebrate their feasts on Three Kings' Day, when they wore their ceremonial clothes and were allowed to collect *aguinaldos* (gratuities) from the merchants and the wealthy of that period.[32] The money they collected was used to buy the freedom of those enslaved who had brought knowledge and titles of the Abakuá from Africa."

The Three Kings' Day, or the Three Magi, procession in Havana was one day of the year when African cabildos were allowed to publicly display the dances, music, and costumes of their homelands (see Plate 4). The purpose was that each cabildo, led by a king and queen, would march through the streets of Old Havana to the palace of the governor general to salute him and swear their loyalty, after which he would present them with a gratuity (see descriptions in chapter 4).[33] The account of Andrés suggests another subversive use of this official event: to gather money to support the establishment and perpetuation of Abakuá by buying the freedom of its African sponsors.[34]

Andrés explained, "Many sympathetic Spaniards served as intermediaries to purchase their freedom. The aim of the Africans was to develop their religion and to keep performing their rituals without the knowledge of overseers and owners. They said: 'Kúsón kúsón' (silence), and the owners never knew that they were practicing their religion, only that they celebrated their feasts."[35] With these words, Andrés describes what Bajan historian E. K. Brathwaite called "the art and philosophy of camouflage," in itself an "aesthetic response to the environment."[36] Abakuá also used culturally specific methods of camouflaged communication taught to them by Cross River Ékpè, whose nsìbìdì "language" in both visual and audio forms is still used in West Africa and in Cuba (a discussion of some of their key signs is given ahead).[37]

"With the blessings of the king Efík Ebúton they were able to organize themselves; they began to practice their Abakuá religion with the same devotion and traditions they had observed in their own land. They kept the same name they had in Africa: Ápapa Efó.[38] An Abakuá leader reported that the Ápapa Efó cabildo, made up exclusively of Africans, waited more than twenty years before creating the first lodge of creoles in Cuba: "The Creoles, my grandfather said, deformed everything, and the Africans did not want their religion to become distorted."[39] Carabalí cabildos had existed in Havana since at least the 1750s, some eighty years before the foundation of Abakuá. Like Ápapa Efó then, other Carabalí cabildos waited decades before sharing forms of Ékpè with their Cuban offspring in a concerted effort.[40] The hesitation of African Ékpè leaders lay in the tension between a desire to maintain Ékpè among themselves, knowing it would die out with them, and the realization that this system could serve a purpose in Cuba, therefore their duty was to share it with the creoles.[41] In the end, Abakuá was recreated from Ékpè models and perpetuated because it functioned to protect and liberate Africans.

Andrés told me, "In 1836, some Africans realized that some creoles met the conditions of belonging to the religion. To unify the Carabalís and the black creoles, who were culturally divided (but as 'negroes' received the same treatment from the Spaniards), they decided to create the first juego [lodge] presided over by creoles and some Carabalís who were not Abakuá.[42] Many of the Africans did not agree, but the prince Ápapa Efí Ákamaró decided to give the transmission to these men, based on a treaty of his land, which was Efí territory."[43]

What Abakuá call treaties are ritual passages that convey mythic history about the origins of their society in West Africa. *Tratado* translates as "treaty," as in "pact" or "alliance treaty." In most cases, the Cuban treaties express the sharing of cultural ideas from one settlement to another, reflecting the multi-ethnic nature of Cross River Ékpè. Each Abakuá lineage is based on a treaty evoking specific places in the Cross River region; the treaties are usually held to be the original phrases uttered by the founding members of the society in West Africa.[44] Abakuá lodges are named from phrases in the treaties. By examining them, Abakuá scholars can trace the sources of their lineage and lodge, hence their authority as representatives of ancestral tradition. In Calabar, the concern with genealogy is a prominent feature of the "whole political structure," because the head of lineage must be able to trace his descent from a founding figure.[45] Thus, the Abakuá preoccupation with lineage is continuous with Cross River social history.

The First Lodge (Efí Territory)

The first Carabalí in Cuba uttered the phrase "Mi botán botán ékue enyenisón" (a good heart is the best fundamento).[46] Andrés described the formation of the first Abakuá group in Cuba, "The first juego [lodge] they made here was from Efí territory. The phrase 'Bóto kenbóto akama enyéne Efó, Ápapa Efí Akamaró, erendió Efík Ebúton' refers to the meeting where the creation of this juego was proposed.[47] The first baróko [ceremony] to create the Efík Ebúton lodge was held in the municipality of Regla in 1836. Regla was renamed Itiá Ororó Kandé, which means: 'a land at the other side of the harbor.'" In fact, this phrase was interpreted by an Ékpè authority in Calabar as a proclamation of Ékpè's foundation in Cuba (see the appendix of chants for details). To enact the birth of the first Cuban lodge, Ékpè leaders entered a cave, a symbolic womb in the earth.[48] Andrés continued, "They performed the baróko to consecrate the Obónes [dignitaries] of the juego Efík Ebúton, in a cave called Itiá mbóko Nékre Ákamaró." This name can be interpreted as "the foundation of the Voice by prince Ákamaró." In Èfìk Ékpè, *itiat* is the foundation stone that every lodge must have.[49] Mbọ̀kọ̀ is a leading Ékpè grade linked to the sound of the Divine Voice.[50] "They gave the cave this name because the Africans who acted as godparents belonged to a lodge in Africa of the same name. Anasakó enkrúkoro enchemiyá mbóko Nékre Ákamaró. This means 'The diviner Nasakó is working inside the cave with the treaty' [origin myth/incantation].[51] The Africans who created Efík Ebúton were initiated in Calabar; they possessed the fundamento [ritual authority] to give birth to Efík Ebúton."[52]

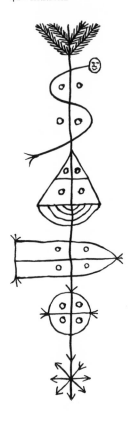

FIGURE 3. Èfìk Obutong firma from a nineteenth-century Abakuá manuscript. The arrow points downward, signifying birth. The circles represent Efó, whose representatives founded this lodge. This form of communication is derived from the nsìbìdì ritual communication of Cross River Èkpè. Reproduced by Leandro Soto, 2006.

For obvious reasons, those who brought knowledge of Èkpè could not carry ritual implements across the Atlantic, but they possessed the authority to fabricate new ones. Some Cuban narratives argue that the African founders of Abakuá created the first fundamento objects in Cuba in 1836. Others—based upon the mechanics of Èkpè practice—argue that African Èkpè created their own ritual implements from within their cabildos, then used them to authorize the first creole lodge.[53] All Cuban narratives agree that Abakuá's foundation was guided by Èkpè specialists who regrouped in Cuba. The demographic density of Cross River people in Cuba was important, but this process also required the presence of Èkpè masters who could teach and organize their communities.[54] The creation of Èfìk Ebúton in Cuba, when the Africans authorized the creoles to continue their Cross River practices, was a watershed moment whose ramifications changed the course of Cuban history.

Andrés told me,

The prince Ápapa Efí Ákamaró sponsored Efík Ebúton, naming it in honor of the African king who brought the Voice of Abakuá. Other Africans from the Ápapa Efó lodge served as witnesses.[55] They agreed that the first lodge of creoles should carry the name of the king. Efík Ebúton Efí Méremo wafatá baróko Núnkue. This means, "Efík Ebúton was the first lodge to perform baróko in Cuba."[56]

When the Africans witnessed this ceremony, they said: "Asarorí beson kányo," meaning "Well done, very good."[57]

To perform the ceremony, the Africans used the Cuban equivalents of their offerings and attributes. In order to differentiate the two countries [Cuba and Calabar], the Africans said, "Embára Núnkue Ororó Amurámo."[58] This means that the main fundamento is in Africa and we are its representatives in Cuba. The first initiates were called: Núnkue Amanisón Bióráma, meaning "those in Havana were consecrated in the African way."[59]

This narrative indicates a central theme of Abakuá history that continues to guide its contemporary leadership: Abakuá was established in Cuba in accordance with the protocol of West African Ékpè. During conversations with Ékpè and Abakuá leaders, I found that both agreed that the Efí Ebúton lodge was an extension of the Obutong settlement's Ékpè lodge in Calabar. This perspective has been documented by Abakuá musicians who commercially recorded tratados narrating the birth of Èfìk Obutong in Cuba. In the 1950s, the first Abakuá composition was recorded in Matanzas and included this phrase:

Asére núnkue itiá ororó kánde   We greet Havana and Regla
Erendió Èfìk Obutong   birthplace of Èfìk Obutong.[60]

This tratado is merely one of scores extolling the 'birth' of Obutong in Cuba.[61]

Creation of the Fundamento

Andrés explained, "As part of the baróko in the cave, the prince Ápapa Efí Akamaró led the members of the Efík Ebúton lodge to the river to create the first fundamento. This was the ekoriantán baróko [first baróko] of the Efík Ebúton lodge." According to narratives in both Cuba and Calabar, because the "perfection" of Ékpè was achieved in an estuary zone, foundational rituals should be performed there. The procession to a river to establish a lodge has been memorialized by Abakuá musicians in commercial recordings.[62]

Because it is a collective tradition, knowledge of Abakuá is shared by many elders. I reviewed Andrés' narration with several leading Abakuá, who generally confirmed its veracity. El Chino Mokóngo told me, "Ekoriantán baróko means the first baróko made in Cuba; it is correctly pronounced 'ekoria otan baróko.'"[63] Throughout this work, the commentaries of El Chino give insight into obscure issues raised by Andrés.

Describing an aspect of the ceremony at the river, Andrés continued, "To perform the ceremony to bring the 'Divine Voice,' they chanted 'Ndíbó, díbo, makáró mofé.'"[64] In both Cuba and the Cross River, the resonant sound of the Divine Voice confirms the presence of Ékpè. Through this and other chants, performed to choreographed ritual actions, the African sponsors reenacted the mythical first time that the Voice emerged from a river in West Africa and was used to perfect Ékpè. In this way, on the bank of a river in Regla, ritual authority was channeled into the new lodge, infusing its implements and members.[65] In Cuba, *dibo* is a chant to call the Voice. In Cross River Ékpè, Dibo is a reference to the spirit of Ékpè.[66]

Continuing his description of the ceremony at the river, Andrés told me, "The Africans also said, 'My body is here but my head is in Africa. We brought the Abakuá in our minds. We have come with much sacrifice to continue the religion with the men on our expedition. We have achieved unity with the creoles, and this is their first fundamento to follow the laws of Efí territory.' This was the authorization given by Efík Ebúton to constitute the first Abakuá fundamento on the banks of the river."

There exist many versions of the process of founding the first Cuban lodge. Abakuá leaders practice with the faith that their inherited lore is what it proclaims to be: the teachings of African Ékpè who shared their esoteric knowledge with the Cubans. Being a foundational moment for the organization of African-descendant communities in the Caribbean, it was a very important act. Various strands of evidence indicate that this narrative has a historical basis. One would be a chant performed after the baróko of Èfìk Ebúton on the banks of the river in Regla. According to Andrés: "To celebrate the foundation of Efík Ebúton, they chanted Okóbio, okóbio enyenisón (repeat), Awana bekura mendó, Núnkue Itiá Ororó Kánde, Efík Ebúton ooo Ékue.[67] This means: 'Our brothers from Africa founded the first Cuban *juego* in Regla; we praise Ékpè.'"

After I published a transcription of this chant in 2000, the response by Nigerian Ékpè members led to the ongoing process of trans-Atlantic interpretation of Abakuá lore (see details in the appendix of chants).[68] More research brought me to early maps of the Cross River region, where I could confirm some of the indigenous names memorialized in Cuba, including the Èfìk settlement of Obutong.[69] Whereas European presence along the West African coast transformed the names of many settlements on maps, I found that local, indigenous names are maintained within communities on the Cross River. Therefore, I was fortunate to meet an expert mapmaker and Ékpè initiate in Calabar, Chief Aniyom, who created a map of Cross River settlements using indigenous terms as maintained on both sides of the Atlantic.

El Chino Mokóngo offered more evidence in the form of a chant,

During an initiation, Abakuá chant the following in the temple's patio to remember those who came from Africa to create Efík Ebúton:

Ékue asanga abiá epó nípó	Ékue came to the land of white people
Endafia awereké Abasí obón Efí	We thank Abasí [God] and the Obongs [Chiefs] from Efí
Afotán konomí Ékue Enyemiyá	I came from Enyemiyá land
Jura Natakuá	I was consecrated in Natakuá
Abasí akuárirú	with the blessing of Abasí
Ékue ita munanguí monína manyóngo umpabio	The first Ékue was activated in Cuba with medicines [nyóngo]

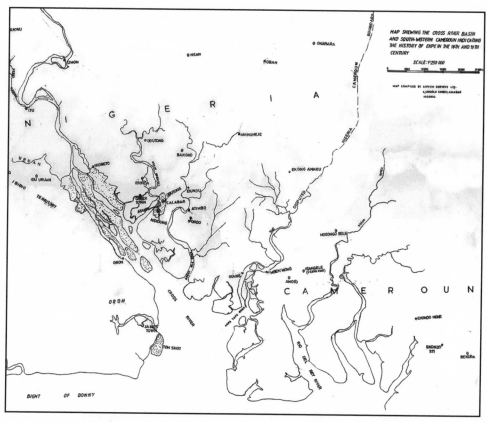

FIGURE 4. Map showing the Cross River basin and southwestern Cameroon indicating the history of Ékpè in the eighteenth and nineteenth centuries as memorialized through Abakuá practice. Drawing by Chief Aniyom, Calabar, 2005.

Piti Naroko Efí obonékue	The other African initiates were named Piti
masongo esísí Abarako	Naroko and Efí Abarakó.[70]

    There were four men from Efí who came to Cuba and made the transmissions. When they founded the potency and gave it the Voice they named it Efík Ebúton, meaning "the Voice from Efí." They left a manuscript and we do not know if it is true or not, but these are the ceremonies performed in Cuba when a new potency is created.

    Confirming the message of the African founders, many terms and phrases in this chant were interpreted by speakers of Èfìk and other Cross River languages (see details in the appendix of chants). The terms Natakuá (line 4) and Abarakó (line 7) are mentioned. These are likely the Calabar settlements of Atakpa and Mbarakom (as discussed in chapter 3). The second phrase of this chant: 'We thank Abasí [God] and the Obongs [Chiefs] from Efi' may be a literal indication of the founders of Èfìk Obú-tong in Cuba. In Calabar, Ékpè remained in the hands of elite Èfìks, who generally barred the enslaved and the poor from membership.[71] These indicators point to the presence of Ékpè leaders—the ruling class of many Cross River settlements—in Cuba during the process of Abakuá's foundation. As I mentioned earlier, during a series of conflicts between Calabar communities for domination of the trade with Europeans, several Ékpè leaders indeed were enslaved and banished from the region. Another source of evidence is a historically based myth I learned from contemporary Ékpè lead-ers of the Obutong settlement in Calabar.

THE LEGEND OF OBUTONG

In Nigeria, when contemporary leaders of Obutong learned how their settlement was memorialized in Cuba, their explanation of why Obutong Ékpè would have reached the Caribbean and become rooted there was liked to the origin story of Ékpè. The Efe Ékpè (Ékpè shrine) of Obutong is named after Asibong Ekondo, a founding ancestor whose wife is credited with the discovery of Ékpè in Usaghade centuries ago.[72] The Iyámba of Obutong recounted a legend from the history of his settlement,

> Since Asibong made a sacrifice that entered the rivers and sea, it became the world's. Asibong was married to Mbang, a woman from Usaghade [the legend-ary source of Ékpè's discovery].[73] After filling his canoe with offerings for his wife's father, Asibong was en route to Usaghade when his boat capsized, and all the offerings went into the water, flowing to the four directions.[74] Some things were rescued by people downriver, who were not a party to his trip. Some people from his boat were carried by the river, then captured by foreign ships and taken far away. Mbang's father said to Asibong, "You did not bring your property to me, you brought it to the whole world." We in Obutong have the belief that those people who were missing, who were rescued by foreign ships, were taken to other nations like Cuba. Some people left because of their belief in Ékpè, so they would establish it there. Some people were sent away because of their misbehavior according to Ékpè law, and the Europeans used to take them. These people were very powerful, and they could have disrupted society. These people would want to recreate Ékpè wherever they went. They would have established Obutong in Cuba. What we call Ekondo in English means "world," the whole world.[75] Since Asibong made a sacrifice that went to the rivers and sea, it became the world's.[76]

In Ékpè practice, a tribute paid to the river, the abode of ancestors, is a method of communication.[77] In this case, the tribute was believed to have carried the authorization of Obutong, through the flow of water, to the four corners of the world. Some offerings were picked up by locals who were later carried to the Caribbean. The Obutong legend of Asibong Ekondo's offering to the river in Usaghade resonates deeply with Cuban narratives (more on Usaghade/Usagaré is ahead).[78]

Cuban narratives tell that the African sponsors of Abakuá used Cross River techniques to evoke the power of Mother Nature with words, actions, and offerings. Many symbols used by Cross River Ékpè are shared among other initiation societies in the region, including those for females. This observation suggests why, in spite of exclusively initiating males, Abakuá has been consistently defended by the larger community of male and female noninitiates.[79] Cross River female societies were not established in Cuba, apparently because more males were enslaved than females, and because within Cuban slave society, males had different kinds of social space within which to move than did females.[80] A comparative study of the shared symbols of Ékpè and Abakuá evokes a broad discussion of indigenous values and their persistence on both sides of the Atlantic.

Ndèm

In many Cross River settlements, the Ékpè leopard society and the Ndèm mermaid society are separate but interdependent.[81] While Ékpè rules the land and Ndèm rules the water, both share key symbols. Both regard "living" water as the realm of the ancestors and a symbol of regeneration.[82] Ritual correspondence between Ékpè and Ndèm seems to mirror the complimentary roles of males and females in society.[83] During Ékpè ceremonies, a portion of offerings are customarily reserved for Ndèm and taken to the river. Meanwhile, Ndèm priestesses are ordinarily initiated into Ékpè in order to be "fully effective."[84] Not merely a gendered society, Ndèm was described as a "tribal deity."[85] Ndèm is a source for Ékpè's authority, as well as for that of the paramount ruler of a community.[86] The famous Calabar folktale "Mutanda" revolves around Ndèm's powers, as identified in the phrase "Ndèm Èfik ete mi," meaning "Ndèm is the goddess that the Èfiks, my parents, worship."[87]

In Cuba, Abakuá use the term Ndèm to name the spiritual base of their system. The common Abakuá phrase, "Ndèm Efí, Ndèm Efó," is a reference to the "spirit of the consecration of Efí and of Efó."[88] As in Calabar, this spirit emerges from the river and is feminine.[89] During the foundation of Èfik Obutong, Ndèm was evoked and an offering sent to the river.[90] The process was memorialized in the phrase "Èfik Obutong Ékue anameruton bongo Ndèm Efi," meaning "the Ékpè lodge Èfik Obutong and its Voice were established through the power of Ndèm."[91]

The Ndèm priesthood remains important in Calabar. In the 1960s, during an investigation into the traditional procedure for crowning an Èfik paramount ruler, the only female witness was a Ndèm priestess, whose position gave her the authority

Cuadro que simboliza el nacimiento del ñañiguismo en el Africa Occidental, junto al río "Oldan-Ororó", donde se descubrió el misterio de Ecue.

FIGURE 5. Drawing of Abakuá mythic history published by Roche y Monteagudo (1925: 99–101), who reported that the eighty-six-year-old "native" who drew it to depict the foundation of Ékpè in Calabar also included brief explanations of the symbols. The caption beneath the image reads, "Drawing symbolizing the birth of nyanyiguismo in West Africa, next to the 'Oldan-Ororó' river, where the mystery of Ekue was discovered."

to speak about Èfìk history and traditions.[92] The investigation confirmed that an Èfìk paramount ruler, who must have a high title in Ékpè, is considered crowned only after participating in a ceremony at the Ndèm shrine, known as the Efe Asabo (python shrine).[93] In Calabar, the Efe Asabo is a component of the Ékpè lodge named Efe Ékpè Eyo Ema, after a founding ancestor of the Èfìks, who was both the custodian of Ndèm and the head of Ékpè.[94] Eyo Ema led migrating Èfìks from Uruan into the Calabar region. Uruan was an important place in Ékpè history, where the same interdependence between Ékpè and Ndèm was found.[95] *Ndèm* is a regional term for "water deity," but the shrine of each settlement has a distinct name.[96] In Uruan settlements, Ndèm is known as Atakpo.[97] As in Calabar, where a paramount ruler is crowned on the Asabo (Ndèm) shrine, the leaders of Uruan villages were crowned at the Atakpo shrine. Narratives of Èfìk migration from Uruan to Creek Town agree that Uruan's Atakpo shrine was the basis for the Asabo shrine of Creek Town and Calabar.[98] In Cuban Abakuá narratives, Atakpo is memorialized as Natacho, a water deity at the foundation of Ékpè.[99]

During the foundation of the Èfìk Obutong lodge in Cuba, when the African sponsors led the creoles to the river, they evoked a complex of symbols related to

Ndèm. These shared symbols of Ékpè and Abakuá form important strands of evidence for the historical basis of Abakuá narratives. They are found in material culture, including the construction of drums and techniques for using them, the construction and use of masquerade suits, as well as the visual representation of symbols, both figurative and abstract. In both traditions, their uses and interpretations coincide in large part.

Cross River Ékpè use visual symbols to identify the mechanics of their system. These can be compared to representations made in Cuba—one by a Cross River descendant, others by Abakuá title-holders—that depict the foundation of Ékpè in Africa. Because Cuban treaties report that the "birth" of Abakuá was achieved by recreating the "perfection" of Ékpè in Africa, these visualizations represent simultaneously the essential elements of both processes.[100] The earliest known Cuban image, published in 1925, was described as depicting, "The first consecration in West Africa. A graphic drawing by a Calabar native, eighty-six years old, who before dying explained the foundation of Abakuá, the only such drawing by an African in Cuba" (see Figure 5).[101] In addition to this original, I documented other derivative paintings in the homes of Abakuá leaders. What follows is an examination of the key symbols in these paintings.

THE CROCODILE

In the Ékpè/Ndèm systems, water beings are associated with Ndèm.[102] The crocodile symbol ubiquitous in Cross River cultural systems represents Ndèm's power.[103] Percy Amaury Talbot, who lived in Oban for nearly a decade in the early 1900s as the first District Officer of Southern Nigeria, began his study of Ejagham culture with reference to the river, the crocodile, and Nimm (the Ejagham equivalent to Ndèm): "Nimm is, above all, the object of the women's devotion. She manifests herself sometimes as a huge snake, sometimes as a crocodile. Her priestesses have more power than those of any other cult, and the society which bears her name is strong enough to hold its own against the dreaded 'Egbo [Ékpè] Club.'"[104]

In Oban and other Ejagham communities, royal women used ceremonial coiffures symbolizing the crocodile as an aspect of Ndèm.[105] Talbot visited a sacred lake in Ejagham territory, where the "crocodile are regarded as manifestations of the guardian spirits of the place, and therefore as specially sacred."[106] He observed that, "In many of the Egbo [Ékpè] houses a representation of... the crocodile is usually found carved on the principal pillar."[107] During my own visit to Oban's Mgbè lodge in 2004, a crocodile skin hung prominently on a central post.[108]

A Cuban Abakuá leader who viewed my photograph of this lodge immediately recognized the symbol and responded with an inherited phrase about the use of the crocodile in Oban Ékpè: "Korokó menanko erufia aweremi? Erombe Obane amakuminyan? The head of the first nyányago was made of what material, and what

FIGURE 6. Photo on the left from Nigeria by Talbot (1969/1926: vol. 2, 230–231); photo on the right by Pierre Verger, 1950s, Havana. Compare the use of plumed rods on the headpieces. The Cuban mask has seven plumed rods as well as crocodile teeth.

ceremony was made in Obane? Obane Efí mendo urakabia mokondo efí kondo Iremo Iya berakabia Isué anaraguí. In Obane it was adored as a divinity. It was made of crocodile skin with shells. [The title-holder] Isué used it to make a fundamento."[109]

The crocodile played a fundamental role in Abakuá mythology.[110] It was visually represented in the drawing by a Carabalí man in Cuba (see Figure 5), as well as on a rare Íreme mask (see Figure 6, right).[111] Andrés recited a variant phrase regarding the Ndèm aspects of the first masquerade to appear in Ubáne (Oban, a Cross River settlement): "Korópo mekondó unpón awaremí erómbe Ubáne newe ákua eromísón? How was the first íreme who appeared in the consecration in Ubáne?[112] Awára kábia Íreme Ísunáka. His head was made of sea-shells and his name was Isunáka."[113] In turn, El Chino Mokóngo responded with this related phrase and its interpretation:

> Íreme iya iya isún Anarukíe erukábia abesumbí. The first íreme of Ubáne was made with the leaves of trees like palms. On its hat was a crocodile head that represented the head of Tánsi; it was adorned with seashells. Its title was Íreme Isun Anarukíe.[114]
>
> I remember the masquerade with the crocodile head, based on the treaty of Isún Anarukíe, that I saw in 1963 in the potency Amiabón.[115] It was worn by [the title-holder] Nkóboro with a headpiece adorned with a crocodile head and full of seashells. It was a gift of their late Iyámba who had commissioned it in Matanzas. I was very impressed, because the elders did everything based on the treaties.[116]

The Nkóboro mask is a guardian of the brotherhood, so the crocodile represents a force against invaders. The crocodile appeared when the divine fish Tánsi of Abakuá lore entered the water pot of the founding female.[117] This woman is represented in the Cuban drawing, standing next to the river with a ceramic jar over her head (Figure 5). Crocodiles were represented in Abakuá practice consistently with Cross River models. In Oban, Talbot described a crocodile masquerade: "The image was robed in a long gown of dark blue cloth, daubed with mud from the river-bed. . . . On its head it bore a crocodile mask, carved in wood, perhaps a representation of Nimm [Ndèm] herself."[118]

THE SERPENT

The long, winding form of the serpent is that of the river itself. Like the crocodile, the serpent as symbol extends deeply into Ékpè and Ndèm.[119] It is sufficient to observe that the Ndèm shrine used to coronate the Obong of the Èfìks is called Efe Asabo (python shrine).[120] Abakuá treaties describe the serpent at the foundation of Abakuá in Africa, when "an enormous serpent . . . entangled itself in the feet of Sikán" (the founding woman) as she carried the Fish from the river in a gourd.[121] The symbols of the gourd, the woman, the serpent, the water, all reverberated during the "perfection" of Abakuá in Usagaré.[122]

Cuban firmas (nsìbìdì) used during the birth of the Èfìk Obutong lodge in the 1830s contain the symbol of the serpent (see Figure 7),[123] evoking the ancestors and Ndèm in this process. In Abakuá mythology, the serpent and the crocodile are guardians of the oracle and the healing arts. The title-holder responsible for these functions is Nasakó, a diviner who organized the birth of Ékpè.[124] The fundamento

FIGURE 7. This *firma*, or a variation of it, was used in the foundation of Èfik Obutong. The perpendicular and horizontal lines signal death and rebirth, as used in cosmograms throughout West-Central Africa. Originally published with the caption "Regla" in Rodríguez (1881: 17), it was later reproduced in Trujillo y Monagas (1882: 371), Cabrera (1975: 497), Thompson (1983: 250). Reproduced by Leandro Soto, 2006.

(or prenda) that Nasakó works with is known as *nyóngo-empabio*, or simply *nyóngo*.[125] Abakuá treaties place the figure of Nasakó in Usagaré, in southwestern Cameroon, where nyongo was a form of traditional medicine.[126]

In the Cuban drawing (Figure 5), the serpent wrapped around the palm tree symbolizes the healing arts and divination.[127] The serpent is associated with Nasakó, known in Abakuá mythology as a Kongo diviner who organized the society centuries ago in Cameroon, when the Voice resonated from the water.[128] In twentieth-century Cuba, Abakuá selected to receive the title of Nasakó were often Tata Nkisi (leading practitioners of Palo Monte, a Cuban-Kongo system).[129] In both Cuban systems (Abakuá and Kongo), the serpent is regarded as a protector of fundamentos.[130] Given the closely related philosophies from regions of the Cross River to the Congo River, it was obvious that in Cuba the Abakuá and the Kongo healing systems would have led to their cross fertilization (an example is discussed in chapter 4, "Transforming the Eribo Drum").[131]

THE MANATEE

The mysterious Voice of Ékpè and Abakuá practice may sound like a leopard, but its mythic source was a river. Some aquatic animals do vocalize, and the West African manatee (*Trichechus senegalensis*) was central to mythology in coastal Nigeria and Cameroon.[132] These mammals lived in shallow coastal waters and freshwater rivers of Cameroon and Nigeria. They remain understudied, but like their Caribbean variant they seem to communicate with high-pitched vocalizations.[133] The manatee is also known in Abakuá mythology.[134] In a painting by and for Abakuá use, this mammal was depicted beneath the tree at the riverbank, the source of the Voice (see Plate 6).

Some Ékpè implements were made with manatee skin, and the hunter who caught one was highly rewarded.[135] A report from the early 1900s in Oron confirms this: "Initiation is costly, though an exception is made when a man catches the famous Egbo [Ékpè] fish–the manitee [sic]. If he is not a member he is initiated free of cost, but if a member already, he is promoted to a higher grade on the same terms. Otherwise every step upward is only possible by the payment of heavy fees."[136] Another report from 1805 in Old Calabar indicated the same scenario.[137] The English explorer Peter Nicholls observed, "If any person kills a tiger, a large snake, or a manatea, he is obliged to take it to the king of Calabar, from whom he receives a reward for killing it; but should he apply it to his own use, without sending it to the king, he pays a very heavy fine to the king."[138]

THE FISH

The divine Fish of Abakuá mythology was the source of the Voice that "perfected" the Ékpè system.[139] Legends tell that the Fish was encountered in the Odán River of Usagaré. In southwestern Cameroon, along the Ndian River of the Usaghade community, leaders of the Bateka village reported that the sister of the village founder had "landed a fish which started vibrating and making the voice of the leopard," leading to the founding of the "leopard spirit cult, which they call Butamu."[140] In Abakuá, the term *Butamú* refers to the temple from which the Voice emerges.[141]

Biologists have confirmed the existence of sound-producing fishes in the Cross River region. Several species of freshwater fish are known to produce sounds when taken from the water, some easily heard at a distance of 100 feet,[142] although research on this topic remains in the early stages.[143] It may be relevant that a nineteenth-century traveler noted the extraordinary echo effects in the region of the Calabar River and its mangrove forests, which seem to funnel sound along the water.[144]

The Trees

Large trees are beholden as sacred throughout Africa, and the Cross River region is no exception.[145] In nineteenth-century Calabar a visitor observed, "Every large tree and every remarkable spot in their noble river is supposed to be the residence of an [n]dem, to which the people of the locality pay their worship, the rites being prayer, offering, and sacrifice."[146] During Talbot's visit to the sacred lake of the Ejagham, he noted, "at the point most near to the Sacred Lake, stands a huge cotton tree, hung round with strips of cloth and other votive offerings. This is the special Juju [medicine] tree for the town of Nsan."[147]

Throughout the Calabar region, large silk-cotton trees along rivers are used as shrines to Ndèm.[148] Outside Creek Town, a huge silk-cotton tree Ndèm shrine stands near an Ékpè lodge, because Ékpè and Ndèm "go hand in hand."[149] This relationship is reflected in Abakuá practice, because every Cuban lodge that is able to plants a ceiba (the silk-cotton tree of Cuba) in its patio, a living symbol of the birth of Abakuá.[150]

El Chino Mokóngo described the significance of trees in Abakuá history and practice: "The palm represents the birth of Abakuá by the river and the ceiba next to it. According to the legend, the ceiba is the mother of the palm. This is why in all the juegos in Cuba, if they can, plant a ceiba and a palm in their patio. When the baróko in Usagaré was made [in Africa], Nasakó buried the fees, and then planted the ceiba in the same spot.[151] When Efí Butón was founded in Cuba, they planted a ceiba that is still on the hill of Regla.[152] In that time that zone was forested. The Abakuá still take care of this ceiba. Whenever a potency performs a plante [ceremony], they go there to greet the ceiba."

As expressed by El Chino and as depicted in the Cuban paintings by Abakuá, the palm tree is also integral to Abakuá practice, in ways consistent with Cross River mythology.[153] In Abakuá, the term for tree is *úkano*; in Èfìk, it is *ùkánà*.[154]

THE GOAT

A favorite food throughout West Africa, the goat is required for Ékpè and Abakuá ceremonies in which initiates receive titles. As depicted in the 1925 drawing from Cuba (Figure 5), the goat stands next to the tree at the riverbank, as an offering. In Abakuá, goat is *mbóri*; it is *mboi* in the Qua (Ejagham) of Calabar, as well as related languages in southwestern Cameroon.[155] The goat is extolled in Abakuá chants, some of them recorded commercially.[156]

THE ROOSTER

The rooster is a favorite sacrificial bird throughout the Caribbean. In Abakuá, the rooster is known by the Ìbìbìò term *nkíko*. An Abakuá phrase describes one use of the rooster in consecrations: "Obonékue efión enkíko, obonékue efión bongo," meaning "Initiates were cleansed; rooster blood was given to the bongó." This entire phrase has meaning in Cross River usage (see appendix of chants for details).[157]

THE LEOPARD

Throughout West and Central Africa, leopard symbols are used to represent social power.[158] For example, in the Grassfields region of Cameroon, the rulers are known as "children of the leopard," and as such are believed to have special protection from danger.[159] Considered an animal of the night, leopards are believed to possess "dark knowledge," meaning that the obscurity or the mystery holds no secrets from them. Historian Jan Vansina summed it up, "The trail of the leopard is the trail of power. Among all peoples of the rainforests, without exception, the leopard was a major emblem of political power and apparently always had been. Hence the disposition of the spoils of the leopard, from hunter to highest authority, is the best indicator of the political structure."[160] A hunter was obligated to bring a captured leopard to the highest local authority, who would then elevate the hunter's status.[161] In nineteenth-century Calabar, the Èfìk Obong received "as a tribute the skins of all leopards killed."[162]

Cuban Abakuá revere the leopard through the sound of its mystic Voice, which they call Ékue, after Ékpè, leopard in Èfìk (Plate 7). In Cuban mythology, a founding title-holder in Africa was a hunter who brought a leopard as a tribute; its skin was used to wrap the Eribó drum (more on Eribó ahead).[163] In Cuba, this title-holder is called Ekuenyón, whose function is to summon the Voice from the forest to the temple.

In the Oron community near Calabar, Ékpényǫng was an Ékpè title.[164] Throughout the Cross River region Ékpènyòng is a reference to Ndèm, the water divinity.[165] Ékpéyóng is a popular personal name, and several nineteenth-century leaders of Atakpa (Duke Town) in Old Calabar were called Ékpéyóng.[166] In Ékpè practice, a killed leopard was brought to the Ékpè shrine, shared with the Iyamba, and then offered to the water.[167] This process is consistent with the balance of land and water, male and female, addressed by Cross River ceremonies.

THE VOICE

The primary sound-symbol of Ékpè and Abakuá culture is the mystic Voice of the leopard, known as *úyò Ékpè* in Èfìk, and *uyó Ékue* in Abakuá.[168] The source of this Voice is the primary secret shared by members, and those who break the taboo by discussing it with outsiders will be repulsed. Initiation societies throughout Africa have a variety of secret instruments that may not be seen by nonmembers.[169] In the case of Ékpè, the sound is held sacred; its source is immaterial. Ékpè liken the sound to that of a trumpet that magnifies the thoughts of the musician who is in a meditative state.[170]

The mythology of both Cross River Ékpè and Cuban Abakuá concur that the Voice originally emerged from a river.[171] In both regions, the mystic Voice is a symbol of political authority in an autonomous community. Each lodge in West Africa and in Cuba may reproduce this sound as a sign of their authority; it is heard but not seen.[172] Ortiz called it an "*instrumentum regni.*"[173] What Abakuá call el Bongó and Ékpè call Ebonko is associated with "the Voice of Ékpè," whose regenerative powers are essential for protection and healing.[174] The Abakuá phrase "Bongó Itá," meaning "one voice," is used to mean that all lodges in the brotherhood are equal, since the Bongó of each defines their autonomy.[175] When the Voice of the Èfìk Obutong lodge sounded in Cuba, a phrase was created to confirm its legitimacy: "Abasí lorí Èfìke Butón Bongó Ita," meaning essentially "the Divine Voice of Èfìk Obutong is one with Ékpè."[176] This same concept structures Cross River Ékpè practice. Among Ejagham of the upper Cross River, I learned the phrase "Eyom Mbǫ́kǫ̀ na mmutami eri jit" (the sound from the inner sanctum is one).[177] Èfìk and Efut of the Calabar region have their own version: "Úyòm Mbǫ́kǫ̀ kpúkpùrù édì kièt" (the sound in all the Ékpè lodges is only one).[178]

In Havana, after Abakuá leaders viewed my video footage of Cross River Ékpè ceremonies, including the Voice emerging from those inner sanctums, they concluded that this was the determining evidence that the African and Cuban traditions are intimately related.[179]

FIGURE 8. Masquerade at Efut Ibon-da, Calabar. Photo by Keith Nicklin, 1975 (Nicklin and Salmons 1988: fig. 9), used with permission. Compare with Abakuá Eribó plumes (Plate 26) and the Íreme photographed by Verger (Figure 6).

MBỌ́KỌ̀

As seen in the two Cross River phrases above, the Ékpè term for the Voice is *Mbọ́kọ̀*. In West Africa, as in Cuba, there is a grade with this name.[180] In both regions, the titles and their functions are directly related to this mystic Voice.[181] The term *Mboko* is also used in KiKongo and no doubt other West-Central African languages, to mean "voice, roar, law."[182] This is not surprising, because similar resonant sounds are reproduced in other initiation clubs throughout West-Central Africa.[183] Some of these variants were also reproduced in Cuba.[184] More research is required to understand the scope and philosophical meanings of this phenomenon. In southwestern Cameroon, for example, locals pay tribute to a water spirit called Mboko, in a place where the souls of their ancestors dwell.[185]

THE ERIBÓ DRUM

Drums are central to African-derived traditions, and the Abakuá have several types. Andrés presented a key theme of West African culture in the Americas when he told me that among the fundamentos "created in Cuba by the juego Efík Ebúton was the Eribó drum" (see Plates 8 and 26). A drum is much more than the sum of its materials. When fabricated by authorized people representing complex social organizations, it can be a mechanism for activating powers that can maintain and defend communities. In the Calabar region, an Ékpè origin myth depicts the first masquerades as emerging from a drum given by the ancestors to a human.[186] Similarly, Abakuá could not fully function until specific drums were "born" as consecrated objects, and to do that the people had to become organized.[187]

In Uruan settlements on the Cross River, Ékpè elders claimed the Cuban Eribó drum as part of their own history; their traditions regard Edibo as a mythic hero who founded their Ékpè.[188] Uruan legend tells that in the distant past, Edibo miraculously returned from the forest with several leopards he had tamed.[189] Contemporary Uruan title-holders evoke their Ékpè with the phrase: "Bap Edibo!, dibó, dibó!" (Arise

Edibo!).[190] They interpreted the Cuban Eribó drum as a monument to their epony-
mous ancestor.[191] Ékpè leaders in Calabar, however, understand "Edibo" as "Dibo," a
reference to the spirituality of their institution and not tied specifically to Uruan.

THE PLUMED RODS

In Cuba the Eribó is referred to as the "mother" of the Abakuá, being associated with
the founding female and having powers to "rebirth" men as members.[192] Around its
rim are inserted a set of munyón (plumed rods; Plates 8, 9, 26) placed upright, each
of which represents a founding ancestor.[193] Andrés narrated, "During the creation of
the juego Efík Ebúton, they constructed the Sése [sacred] Eribó drum. Before placing
the plumes on this drum, they said: 'Sése Ekoi efórí Ibondá,' then placed the plumes
on the drum."[194] El Chino Mokóngo responded that this phrase derived from a treaty
describing the African foundation: "After the plumes were made . . . they took them
to Usagaré, to consecrate the Eribó on Ibondá hill, during the first baróko in Africa."
(Early Abakuá lodges were established following Cross River history and geography
as taught by their African founders. *Ekoi* is an Èfik term for Ejagham peoples, Ibondá
is an Efut settlement near Creek Town, and Usaghade is a community in the estuary
southeast of Calabar.[195])

The plumed rods of the Eribó drum are essential to Cross River Ékpè and Ndèm
performances. In a famous Calabar folktale, as villagers search for a person captured by
river beings, a maiden performed a dance called Abang: "The hair on her head resem-
bled that of a mermaid."[196] The Abang headdress, with its mermaid and crocodile symbolism, often includes plumed rods placed upright.[197] A masquerade from Efut Ibondá,
near Calabar, that represents this female headdress includes the plumed rods (Figure
8). Ékpè masks representing high titles like Ebongó and Nyámkpè used them in various
ways, held in the hand, or placed on the head. So too Abakuá title-holders have plumed
rods that they use in procession, including those seen on the Eribó drum.[198]

THE COCONUT ORACLE

During the baróko of Èfik Obutong in Regla in the 1830s, all the elements discussed
above played a role. Many other items were used as tributes, as foods, and as divination tools. In the foundation of Abakuá, the supplicants who paid tribute to the river
gained the support and protection of the ancestors and divine forces.[199] Neophytes of
Ékpè and Abakuá use a wicker basket to carry their offerings. The symbol of the basket
is found the Ukara cloth used by Ékpè title-holders. In Cuba, the tributes offered by
Abakuá neophytes include nkíko (rooster), a plantain, a yam, mimbo (liquor), and
other materials used in precolonial West Africa, some of whose Abakuá names are
comparable to their Èfik counterparts.[200]

While comparing Èkpè and Abakuá symbols is a source of evidence for a historical trans-Atlantic relationship, it is also a method for critiquing the literature. Some sources indicated that a coconut was used as the source of the Voice during the creation of Èfìk Obutong in the 1830s. Others claim a calabash was used. This debate is not taken seriously by Abakuá leaders, who know the internal mechanics of their system.

In the 1920s, Havana criminologist Roche wrote, "Anáwe kamanba Èfíke búton? Tell me who is the mother of Èfìk Ebúton? Kambito Eribó, the coconut."[201] Roche then cited a treaty, giving this interpretation: "The African slaves who came to the land of the whites brought the memory of the voice of Ekué. They gathered in Havana and performed a consecration, with rooster blood over a coconut and a goat skin, so that Efibuton would sound."[202]

The theme of the coconut fundamento at the birth of Abakuá has been consistently repeated in the literature.[203] A comparison with the mechanics of Èkpè in Africa, however, suggests that this theme is a red herring, an example of how Abakuá have intentionally misguided inquisitive outsiders since their first interrogations by police in the nineteenth century. Instead, the coconut is better understood as a symbol of the oracle and of purity, as it is in the Cuban Lukumí and Kongo systems.[204] The water of the coconut is used to prepare the mokúba (ritual drink) that all initiates swallow.[205] In the process of creating the Èfìk Obutong lodge in Cuba, the coconut was used as a metaphor for purity, discretion, and clairvoyance, and it is still used as such by contemporary Abakuá (Plate 10).[206]

Efí Akuaráyo, the Treaty of Efí Territory

Andrés noted, "In Cuba all the lodges born from Efí territory were ruled by the treaty Efí Akuaráyo. This treaty was used when the first juego made was made in Cuba." Efí akuaráyo speaks of the beachhead of Efí Abakuá in Africa, where an offering was given to the sea to authorize the birth of Abakuá in Efí territory. As a representative of the ancestors, an Íreme (masquerade dancer) present at this event was given the title Efí akuaráyo.[207]

In the Cross River estuary beachheads are not only physical ports, but also symbolic shrines. Èkpè scholar Engineer Bassey wrote: "In Èfìk land, the journey to deliver Èkpè to a purchaser was often a riverine affair. A fleet of dug-out canoes appropriately adorned for the purpose set sail from the Èkpè beach, a beach so designated by the fraternity, for a predetermined beach of the purchaser. . . . Should the purchaser be land-locked, delivery was effected using an improvised vehicle adequately camouflaged to resemble a canoe. It was mandatory for Ídèm Nyámkpè [a masquerade] to provide security for the fleet. Consequently, it was on the bow of the leading canoe on departure from and arrival at the ports."[208]

The transfer of Ékpè along the river is depicted in the seal of the Efut community in Calabar (see Plate 11). In Cuba, the Ékpè sponsors of Abakuá followed their home-land protocol by creating the first lodge on a beachhead. From the creation of the first lodge in Regla in the nineteenth century to the later expansion of Abakuá activities into Havana, Guanabacoa, Marianao, Matanzas, and Cárdenas, most lodges were cre-ated and continue to exist near rivers and ports.[209] Engineer Bassey explained the Ékpè rationale for this process in Calabar: "There exists the strong belief that the temple should face a natural body of water. . . . Closeness to a natural body of water aids evoca-tion and invocation of elemental spirits of water."[210] In those cases where Abakuá lodges were founded in a land-locked place, they were still considered "beachheads" for that lodge. To the present, Abakuá processions follow Ékpè practice by including an Íreme masker at the lead to provide security.

Ékpè Patterns of Independent Settlement

In the history of many Cross River settlements, an Ékpè lodge was the first structure raised in the new site, since it established the autonomy of the future community.[211] Cross River migrants in nineteenth-century Cuba could not physically establish Ékpè lodges, but they regrouped using Ékpè systems, then taught their essentials to others in their Cuban communities. In the process, the consecration of land and trees that accompanied the creation of fundamentos by Calabarí immigrants effectively trans-planted Abakuá in Cuban soil, where it has been maintained ever since. Because their primary allegiance is to their lodge and lineage, Abakuá consider their society to exist as a separate state within the nation, with their own language and laws.[212] There is no coincidence that Abakuá lodges are also called *tierras* (lands), nor that many lodges represent West African territories important to Abakuá history. The *tierra* Èfik Obu-tong, the first lodge of creoles, was recreated as an extension of the Calabar settlement of Obutong in Cuba. According to Èfik Ékpè tradition, "Initiation of an Èfik man is normally done on Èfik soil. Initiation done outside the boundaries of Èfik land is supposedly wrong in tradition."[213] Following this, Cuban Abakuá call their potencies tierras, with the implication that they could legitimately initiate members.

The founding of Cuban lodges follows a pattern of independent settlement closely resembling the social organization of precolonial southeastern Nigeria. All Abakuá groups share a common mythology and organizing structure. The foundational tratado (origin myth) of each lodge identifies it with a Cross River ethnic group—Efí (Èfik), Efó (Efut), and Orú (Uruan), whose ancestors interacted in the development of Ékpè in West Africa. While relatively independent, the leaders of each lodge are bound to protocols of etiquette toward brother lodges in their immediate lineage and to con-sult with leaders of fellow lodges before sponsoring a new lodge. When necessary, problems are solved by an informal council of elders (recognized for their mastery of Abakuá lore) who represent various lodges.

The First Lodge from Efó Territory (Baróko of Eforisún)

Andrés explained, "Four years after Efík Ebúton had been created, the prince of Efó and the king of Efí founded Eforisún, the first lodge of Efó territory. The night of January 5, 1840, under the Arco de Belén [in Old Havana] the Africans of the cabildo Ápapa Efó initiated the first juego of creoles belonging to Efó territory." With these clues, Andrés revealed how in the middle of Havana's fortified city, Africans used a Catholic holiday to initiate neophytes next to a Catholic Convent. Africans and their descendants outnumbered the European-derived population inside Havana, enabling Carabalí to diminish attention to their activities.[214] An American traveler in the 1840s described the context: "The next day being *el día de los Reyes*, twelfth-day, almost unlimited liberty was given to the negroes. . . . Havana is on this day in a perfect hubbub, and the confusion that seems to reign among its colored population is indescribable."[215]

The fifth of January, the vespers of Three Kings' Day (el día de los Reyes), was a bustling time for the city's inhabitants, including the African cabildos preparing for the next day's processions, which commemorate the arrival of the Three Magi at the manger. The authorized cabildo meetings of this evening were used as a cover for the organization of a new lodge.[216] This kind of camouflage led to a famous Cuban expression: "¡En el cuarto de fondo hay rumba!" (There's a rumba party in the back room!). Musicologist María-Terésa Linóres explained, "In the nineteenth century, drum ceremonies were prohibited and these instruments were confiscated from the blacks. When they had no permission, Africans who had *cabildos* in those large houses with a grand interior patio put a few benches in the front room, and people sat there to sing in choruses accompanied by clave sticks and a 'tres' guitar, a Spanish-derived music. Since there would be forty or fifty people singing loudly, those in the street couldn't hear the sounds of the drums in the patio. Those in the front room performed a refined type of party, while those out back performed the rites. In this way they could continue their rites, resulting in the popular saying: 'in the back room there's a rumba party', which means that there's a hidden ceremony."[217]

The architecture itself was a factor that made a ceremony like this possible in the middle of a fortified city. The inner courtyards of a cabildo house provided privacy, while the domestic spaces of the urban wealthy secluded the space from street activities. A traveler to Havana in the 1840s marveled at "the substantial manner in which even the most unimportant building is constructed; every one seems made to last forever. The walls of a single story house are seldom less than two feet in thickness; and to witness the erection of those of the larger ones, the masonry might readily be mistaken for that of some embryo fortification, destined to be cannon-proof . . . while the stout folding-doors, guarding the only entrance to the whole building, would not be unfit to protect that of a fortress."[218] These fortified domestic spaces with interior courtyards allowed inhabitants a certain disconnection from outside activity, distancing the noise of the streets.[219]

Continuing his narrative, Andrés reported, "The 'Efórisún' lodge received a long title ending with 'Usagaré'.[220] Efórisún was the capital of Efó territory in Calabar.[221] The treaty recited mentions the name and title given to this first lodge of Efó territory, as well as the names of the Africans who served as witnesses. Also mentioned are the godparents, who represented the prince of Ápapa Efó land." The last term of Efórisún's title, *Usagaré*, identifies this lodge with Usaghade, a community in southwestern Cameroon.[222] Both Ékpè and Abakuá know Usaghade as the source region for their club.[223] Nigerian musicologist Samuel Ekpe Akpabot confirmed the legend of Ékpè's sources in Usaghade, "Tradition has it that Ékpè originally came from a place called Usangade [sic] where the Efot ethnic group live . . . it was they who let the . . . people of Uruan into the secrets of the cult."[224]

El Chino Mokóngo unraveled the meaning of Usagaré: "In Cuba, according to the stories of the old men, the first Efó lodge was called Efórisún Efó. Efórisún Lilí is a lagoon in Africa.[225] The treaty of Efórisún Lilí belongs to the "treaty of the three brothers" from Usagaré territory in Africa, when the three brothers Efórisún, Usagaré, and Bakokó received the original fundamentos of Efó."[226] Abelardo added, "The treaty of Eforisún Lilí was in Africa, when they made the first consecration in Usagaré, on the hill of Ibondá. All the men from Usagaré gathered and invited the princes from Isún to see the great consecration of Efó territory. This treaty was recited during the foundation of Efori Isún here in Cuba." These interpretations, as well as Cross River pronunciation, identify the Cuban Efórisún as *Efut Isu* in Èfìk, meaning "the shrine of Efut."[227]

Andrés continued, "After Ápapa Efó founded Efórisún, they said these words to express their satisfaction: Abasí erominyán Ékue úyo makurí Abasí Ékue butón." According to El Chino Mokóngo, "This phrase of salutation to Ékue means 'While adoring God, the Ékue gives Voice.'"[228] In other words, the mystical Voice of the leopard sounded, confirming the transfer of Cross River autonomous organizations into Cuba.

Andrés went on, "Then they said, 'Asarorí Ékue Efó sése mokumbán.'[229] That means 'A great feast in Efó territory.'" El Chino Mokóngo explained, "This phrase comes after greeting the Ékue. It means 'the Voice was strong because of the sacred medicines.'"[230]

The Second Lodge from Efó Territory (Baróko of Efóri Nkomó)

Andrés told me, "There was an agreement to create another lodge called Efóri Enkomón; Efóri are the herbs used in sorcery, and Enkomón means 'drum.'"[231] In Calabar,

Efóri Enkomón is readily understood as "Efut Èkòmò," the drum from Efut.[232] El Chino Mokóngo reported the title as: "Efori Enkomón komo íreme taipo Efóri Ikondó,[233] the Íreme who guarded the fundamento during the consecration of Efó."[234] The full name of an Abakuá lodge often reveals their family lineage, with the original ancestor listed last. In this case, the term *Efóri Ikondó* is easily recognized by Calabar Ékpè as Efut Ekondo, the name of Efut communities in Calabar and in Cameroon.[235]

Andrés continued, "They finished the founding ceremonies of the Eforisún lodge at night, and could not continue. In the morning of the next day [January 6], in order to create another lodge, they performed the baróko 'Ekóko Nyángan Séne.'" The reason they could not continue was cosmological. Rites of Abakuá, like Ékpè, must be performed at certain times of night or day, as indicated by an Èfìk Ékpè chant from Calabar: "Eyen Edidem abanékpe okon eyo /A prince is initiated into Ékpè at night."[236] Cuban scholars have confirmed the night rituals of Abakuá; for instance, Lydia Cabrera wrote, "At midnight when the ceremony begins, the officiates join the procession."[237]

Ekóko Nyángan Séne

According to Andrés,

> Ekóko Nyángan Séne was the baróko performed in Cuba by the Africans of Ápapa Efó who gathered to "begin the daybreak." At 12 midnight they left the Fambá room in procession with the Eribó drum. Moruá [the chanter] praised the Eribó: Eribó maka maka, Eribó maka téréré.[238] This is a praise song to the plumed Eribó drum, representing the mother [Sikán] and the four kings [who founded the religion, each from a different tribe]. It means: "the plumed drum is everlasting."[239]
>
> They began to chant inside the Fambá room, then all the tribes exited in procession and encircled the patio. When returning to the Fambá room, Moruá chanted: Eribó maka maka, Eribó maka tere asánga baróko.[240] This means: "The Eribó is moving, and will return to its place of origin, the Fambá." Next day in the morning, the Efóri Enkomón lodge was established.[241]

El Chino Mokóngo responded,

> Yes, it is possible to create two juegos in two days, one after the other. One starts at six a.m. until six p.m. At night, this work cannot be done because according to the African ritual these works were born with the daybreak. At six a.m. with the rising sun, the procession Nyangan séne is made to greet the sun, after which the ceremony begins.

In Cuba the Abakuá always performed their plantes [ceremonies] at night, as they were done in Africa. One would begin at night by worshipping the stars, and would finish in the morning by worshipping the sun. At six a.m. the procession Nyangan Séne would greet the sun, because we ask the permission of the stars for our rites. Most of the ceremonies are held at night, but the birth of a potency must be done by day, with the authorization of the sun."[242]

Abelardo agreed, "The koko nyangan séne was made while the sun was rising: Asére ebión endayo atrofó mokayirén. Greetings to the power that illuminates the four cardinal points."[243] Abelardo indicates that reverence to the four directions—a principle in ceremonial drum activities around the world—is basic to Abakuá practice.[244]

In Uruan settlements on the Cross River, Ékpè leaders also perform rituals according to the movements of the sun.[245] For example, because a ruler "sits" upon Ékpè, it is believed that when he dies its power escapes into the bush and must be recaptured at night, the domain of the nocturnal leopard. An Uruan chief described the process: "About twelve midnight . . . there is the traditional hunting and shooting of Ékpè. The Ékpè is captured, taken to and caged at the Efe [temple] by about five a.m. From the time after the caging of Ékpè till the evening of that day . . . several traditional dances and plays are staged."[246]

Andrés continued his narrative, "After the first baróko of Efó territory, the Africans gave the [maritime] barrio of Belén the title of Engóro Éké ánbeleké, meaning 'Belén was recognized as the beachhead for Efó territory in Cuba.'[247] With the creation of one lodge from Efí territory and two from Efó, the people were content. The Africans taught the creoles, Ékue jura katínde akanarán enkrúkoro, Bongó itá. This means: 'The same there or here, Bongó Itá means the Voice is one.'"[248]

The concept expressed through Bongó Itá in Cuba is pervasive in Cross River Ékpè practice (as described earlier in "The Voice" section).[249] The meaning is that all settlements with Ékpè are equal and abide by the same laws, and the Voice of Ékpè signals their autonomy. The Cuban term akanarán, Abakuá for "mother," may derive from akani nwan, an Ìbìbìò term for "old woman."[250] In other words, as initiates, "all are sons of the same mother." Furthermore, akani aran is an Èfìk idiomatic expression meaning "original power or source," often used as a praise greeting.[251]

The success of Abakuá made it a club of prestige, but only those who met specific requirements could join. Andrés continued,

Because many men aspired to become dignitaries, other juegos were born.[252] In the early development of Abakuá there was a rigorous process for acceptance into a lodge; one had to be approved of by the Africans. The ndisimes [aspirants] were presented by the members to the Africans, who would act as judges and guides in the process of giving faith to the new initiates, but only after these demonstrated their respect for the Abakuá sacrament.

The African dignitaries began to confide in the creoles and delegated leadership responsibilities to them. Bit by bit they surrendered their secrets so that the creoles could act independently. There were many Africans who didn't reveal the content of their language—in my opinion this was a mistake—and knowledge was lost.

Orú Territory

According to oral tradition, after founding the Èfìk Obutong lodge in 1836 and the Efórisún lodge in 1840, a third ethnic lineage was established later in the decade. El Chino Mokóngo recounted, "In the colonial days, Orú Ápapa was a cabildo in the barrio de Jesús María.[253] Named the Cabildo of Orú, it was known as Ápapa Orú, and from there they named the potency Orú Ápapa."

Andrés Flores continued, "When the Abakuá was being established, a potency called Orú Ápapa was 'born.' When asked about its origin, the members of this collective said that their title was 'Orú Ápapa akondomína mefé Sése Bibí kóndo asikeleke nambele kabia ekuénte mesóro Bongó Orú Ápapa.'[254] Because of the well-known difficulties in colonial times, some lodges were created in *encerronas* [hidden gatherings]." After discussing this title with scholars and Ékpè leaders in Cross River communities, we concluded that the Cuban Orú is likely Uruan, while Bibí is clearly Ìbìbìò.[255] Uruan is a community in Ìbìbìò territory, with a historic tradition of Ékpè.

In nineteenth-century Cuba, with the founding of Efík Obutong, Efórisún, and then Orú Ápapa, the three major Abakuá ritual ethnic lineages were established. These lineages have been maintained continuously to the present. Andrés confirmed that the lodge "Orú Ápapa sponsored almost all the lodges of Orú territory and they still function today." From the 1840s onward, the triumphant narrative describing the recreation of Ékpè in Cuba takes various branches intermeshing with the wider society, including other communities of African descendants, the discovery of Abakuá meetings by police and their subsequent persecution within the penal system, and the collective participation of Abakuá in both local and international anticolonial movements.

Conclusion

When Cross River peoples in Havana formed cabildo groups from the mid-1700s onward, Ékpè members were likely among them. Tensions between those born in Africa and their Cuban offspring were a factor in the hesitancy of Ékpè to teach their culture to creoles and then organize them into lodges. Scholars generally agree that by 1836, the first Abakuá lodge, composed of black creoles, was established by African sponsors. With the sponsorship of Cross River experts, the three major ethnic lineages of Abakuá—Efí, Efó, and Orú—were established by the 1840s. In the Cross River basin, Ékpè functioned as a multi-ethnic practice that enabled mercantile interaction and safe travel between autonomous settlements with distinct ethnic identities but speaking Èfik as a lingua franca. Following this model, Cuban Abakuá members cultivated a practice of autonomous lodges with clearly defined "ethnic" lineages. At the base of this system were well-defined codes of ritual authority passed from African-born Ékpè teachers to creole offspring. Cuban Abakuá was established based upon a Cross River mythology wherein the Efut, the original possessors of a "perfected" Ékpè system, shared it with the Èfiks. In Cuba, a representative group of Efó (Efut) sponsored the first Cuban lodge, designated as Efí (Èfik). This ethnically designated process remains active in Cuba, wherein Efó lodges may sponsor Efí lodges, but not vice versa. In the creative process of regrouping and adaptation in the Caribbean, Cross River people followed clearly defined procedures based upon homeland concepts.

2. The Fortified City

■ ■ ■

In Cuba there was not one black society, but diverse coexisting societies.

—MANUEL MORENO-FRAGINALS[1]

In the 1660s a buccaneer who sailed past San Cristóbal de La Habana with Sir Henry Morgan described the city's defenses and international reach. He paid special attention because their plan was to sack the city: "This City is defended by three Castles, very great and strong, two of which lie toward the Port, and the other is seated on a Hill that commands the Town. It is esteemed to contain about 10,000 Families. The Merchants of this Place trade in New-Spain [Mexico], Campechy [Yucatan], Honduras, and Florida. All Ships that come from the Parts before-mentioned, as also from Caraccas, Carthagena, and Costa Rica, are necessitated to take their Provision in at Havanna to make their Voyage for Spain; this being the necessary and strait Course they must steer for the South of Europe, and other Parts."[2]

Havana's prominent role in trans-Atlantic history was determined by geography. Its deep, bottlenecked harbor, lying at the outer rim of the Spanish American empire and along the Gulf Stream flowing toward Europe, made Havana Spanish America's largest port, thus the setting where peoples of the world would encounter one another.[3] For three centuries of Spanish expeditions into Latin America, Havana was used as a point of return to the Iberian Peninsula. Its vibrant musical culture and characteristic hospitality was shaped early on to accommodate the hundreds of sailors who waited, sometimes for months at a time, for the end of hurricane season.

In 1624 the Spanish crown decreed Havana "The Key to the Gulf"; it was also known as "Key to the New World."[4] Expeditions sailed through Havana to and from the viceregal seats of Peru (in Lima), New Granada (in Bogotá), La Plata (in Buenos Aires), and Vera Cruz (in New Spain).[5] Shipments arrived from Asia along the Macao–Manila–Acapulco route through Vera Cruz.[6] Being the focal point of the route to the Indies, Havana became a militarized zone as well as the economic and political center of

FIGURE 9. Havana's official seal, the Key to the Caribbean, on el Gran Teatro, Havana. King Philip II of Spain granted Havana its official title as a city in the 1590s, with this coat of arms. The three castle fortresses represent the Fuerza, Moro, and Punta that guard the bay, and the key represents Havana's role in unlocking the Americas for Spain (Scarpaci 2002: 18). Photo by I. Miller.

Cuba.[7] By the 1850s, an American annexationist described Havana's as "undoubtedly one of the safest, best defended, and most capacious harbors in the world."[8]

African migrants arriving from the sixteenth century onward helped build the limestone fortresses that defended colonial Havana from invading armies and buccaneers.[9] At the entrance to Havana's bay the Castillo del Morro sits above the village of Casablanca, near the cavern where Abakuá was born. To construct this fortress, while responding to the growing numbers of escaped Africans, in 1610 the Havana Cabildo (city council) ordered two decrees announced throughout the city. First, all fugitives reporting within fifteen days would be absolved of punishment; that those remaining fugitives, male and female, would have their noses cut off; those who resist will be killed. Second, "all the neighbors and residents of this city that have fugitive slaves must report them in the following three days before the scribe of the City Council. Be advised that those slaves missing three days from now are condemned to serve without salary for three years in the construction of the Castillo del Morro."[10]

Brutal chain-gang labor would be the pattern for hundreds of years. Historian Manuel Moreno-Fraginals described the process: "The black and mulatto slaves in Havana's urban area were principally employed in military and civil construction and in the shipyards. Fortresses like La Fuerza, La Punta, El Morro, Cojimar, Bacuranao, the extensive wall that surrounded the city, the fortified tower of San Lázaro and, in the eighteenth century, the enormous La Cabaña fortress and the castles of El Príncipe and Atarés, required an extraordinary volume of labor.... The study of these constructions demonstrates that in many years there were more slaves working on military projects than on the plantations."[11]

Captured Africans were brought to the Spanish Caribbean from the early six-teenth to the mid-eighteenth century under the asiento system, whereby the Spanish crown sold rights to specific European powers and individuals to ship Africans to Cuba and other colonies (Plate 12).[12] Parallel to this system of "legal" slaving existed a largely undocumented forced migration of captured Africans organized by merchants who did not pay for the rights to do so.[13] The British occupation of Havana in 1763 virtually ended the asiento system, marking the beginning of an unrestricted (known as "free") slave trade that escalated the influx. From 1763 to 1792 nearly 70,000 enslaved Africans arrived in Cuba.[14] With the collapse of sugar production in Haiti due to the revolution (1791–1804), Cuban planters seized the opportunity to build the world's most lucrative sugar industry. From 1790 to 1820 the estimated total of Africans arriving in Cuba was 300,000.[15]

The opulence of Havana elites went hand in hand with the repression that protected them. In 1825 the captain generals were decreed "almost unlimited powers" that remained in operation through the 1850s.[16] The most infamous of these, Captain General Miguel Tacón, ruled Cuba by martial law from 1834 to 1838. The opera house he built in his own name was estimated, "with the exception of the Grand Theatre at Milan, to be the largest and handsomest of the world."[17] Convict labor built the Teatro Tacón, and taxing the (illegal) entry of slaves to the island paid for it.[18] Tacón also had the Havana Prison constructed, about which a contemporary traveler wrote, "It is said, its erection did not add to the expenses of the city; that it was built by the labor of the convicts . . . I passed a long shed near the prison, under which about a hundred convicts were busily employed in breaking stone. They were under a guard of soldiers, and seemed very attentive to their work, perhaps from the dread of a heavy whip, which an overseer held in his hand."[19]

Whereas the elites profited from slavery, the enslaved resisted by organizing community networks using models of West African institutions, like Ékpè lodges, or like the Yorùbá ilé (house) system (see the discussion of the Aponte Conspiracy of 1812 later in this chapter). In this process, if demography and the presence of knowledgeable culture bearers were important, so too were the oppressive conditions that convinced African Ékpè that the future of their communities depended upon their sponsoring lodges of creole Abakuá. It was precisely during Tacón's tenure that Africans and black creoles established Abakuá as a force of liberation and an alternative to authoritarian models of society.

Abakuá was organized within a very complex urban milieu, where the interactions among various distinct communities created a rich environment hidden from colonial authorities. The communities involved were black artisans, African nation-groups, militia members, the black curros (Ladino migrants from Seville), urban fugitives, and the various resistance movements—whether they succeeded or not—that all fertilized the soil in which Abakuá grew.

INSIDE OF THE TACON THEATRE.

FIGURE 10. Teatro Tacón from Hazard's *Cuba with Pen and Pencil* (1871).

Africans and the City

Colonial Havana was encircled by a fortified wall built from the 1630s to 1797.[20] Inside the walls were institutions and people dear to the Spanish Crown, including "the residence of the Captain General of the Island, maximum representative of the Crown; the Cathedral, the military quarters, the [many] churches . . . the convents of Belen, San Francisco . . . the great residences of the Havana bourgeoisie and the tenements where the workers lived."[21]

The servants and slaves of the dominant class who lived within the walled city became self-organized, even renaming their barrios. Instead of the official Catholic names of Belén, San Francisco, Santo Angel, and Santo Cristo, they chose "La Pluma [the Feather], La Lejía [the Lye], Campeche [Yucatan], Cangrejo [Crab], Los Doce Pares de Francia [Twelve Pairs from France]."[22] Many of the Africans and their descendants who built the city's structures and fortressed walls remained living within them. By renaming the city and its barrios, they indicated a parallel social system operating underneath the official one. The early black creoles may have used Spanish names, but as Africans arrived by the thousands in the early 1800s, the city was also given names in West African tongues.[23] They renamed the city, and they renamed the creoles participating in their communities, especially those initiated into ritualized systems. This cultural process culminated in what may be the most profound achievement in the history of the colony: the establishment of African-derived institutions within the very walls of the fortress.

The incubators of these institutions were in many cases the community-organized African cabildos, some of them located within the walled city.[24] Others resided in the barrios just outside the walled fortress, most famously the "celebrated and turbulent barrio of Jesús María, with its zone of the Manglar [Mangrove], where the feared 'negros curros' lived and the part known as the Basurero [Garbage], when from time to time, the numerous gangs of blacks and mulattos—distinguished with the names of the Arabs, the Mayorquines [Majorcans], the Vizcaínos [Biscayan], etc.—settled their differences. . . . Outside the city walls, the cabildos were more numerous and the sound of drumming was heard on Sunday afternoons, accompanying the chants and dances of the Congos, Carabalís, Lucumís, and others."[25]

Once the walls were built, the cannons boomed nightly at nine o'clock (as they still do) to signal the closing of the city gates. This was when African descendants could meet in the extramural barrios on their own terms. In this manner, from within a police state in Spain's "Antillean Pearl," Abakuá emerged to organize and educate communities for self-defense.

Black Artisans

The importance of Abakuá to Cuban history is reflected in the many different communities that shared its networks, including the "nation-blacks" (African cabildos), the various groups of freed blacks that included the black curros and the Battalions of Loyal Black and Mulattos. At first appearance, these groups seemed to be at opposite poles of social aspiration, but members of each became prominent Abakuá initiates. Officially, these groups were considered marginal, yet without them Havana would not exist.[26] Their activities contradicted received notions of "marginal" peoples vis-à-vis the dominant group. The process of assimilation into a host culture, for example, is often believed to occur most effectively when new arrivants live in close contact with those who set the norms. For those enslaved, this would amount to "the imitation of the master." As historian E. K. Brathwaite explained, "this imitation went on, naturally, most easily among those in closest and most intimate contact with Europeans, among, that is, domestic slaves, female slaves with white lovers, slaves in contact with missionaries or traders or sailors, skilled slaves anxious to deploy their skills, and above all, among urban slaves in contact with the 'wider' life."[27]

Imitation of the powerful is axiomatic in any society. But for Africans who already had a strong sense of self and identity, who may have already spoken several homeland languages, interacting with members of the Spanish elite would have been just another milieu within which they learned to operate. In Havana, artisans, soldiers, and dockworkers maintained or assumed specific African identities through membership in the Abakuá, Lukumí, Kongo, and other traditions. In many cases the intimacy between the dominant class and their African-descended workers produced not assimilation but tolerance.[28] Historian Gerardo Castellanos García reported that in the nineteenth century "many ñáñigos [Abakuá] were servants and sons of very dear slaves, who lived in the homes of influential, wealthy, and intellectual whites." This situation produced a tolerance to the extent that if these Abakuá were accused of an offence, they were defended as godchildren by their patrons, who were often lawyers or functionaries.[29] The relationship between a godfather and godchild in the Church of colonial Cuba was a profound one that contributed to a tacit relationship in Havana between the dominant class and their servants. This phenomenon was engendered by Havana's large Spanish settler population, in sharp contrast to the tendency in the Anglophone Caribbean for absentee owners.[30]

The symbiosis between both groups was enabled by an architecture within which masters and slaves coexisted. Havana's elites typically lived in a three-storied home: the first floor being a warehouse for agricultural products, the second housed the slaves and administrative offices, while the master family resided on the top floor.[31] The enslaved learned the ways of their legal owners, but as an intellectual in Havana observed in 1837, the exchange went both ways: "The slaves have influenced not only the customs, the wealth, and the intellectual powers of the whites, . . . since you know they have introduced an infinity of inhuman and barbarous terms and phrases in the speech habits of our societies of both sexes that call themselves cultured and refined. The same influence is observed in our dances, and in our music. Who does not see in the movements of our boys and girls as they dance a contradance or waltz, an imitation of the gestures of the blacks in their cabildos? Who doesn't know that in the bass tones of the dance music of the island are the echo of the drum of the *Tangos*? All is African."[32]

This vibrant milieu was merely one prism in the kaleidoscope of Havana's colonial society. Slavery crushed many, but the contradictions inherent in the system created spaces that Africans exploited fully. Compared with Cuba's rural plantations and with other colonies, Africans in colonial Havana existed within a relatively ample social space. Historian Moreno-Fraginals claimed that the self-determination and economic capabilities of Havana's African-derived population "differentiates the social history of slavery in Cuba from that of other non-Spanish islands in the Caribbean."[33] An important element was the high percentage of freed blacks, and so-called "jornal slaves," who had liberty to move throughout the city, as long as they paid a fixed sum to their legal owners.[34]

Another key element was the *coartación* (gradual self-purchase) system, whereby human property could buy themselves.[35] Moreno-Fraginals observed that in the long run, the system of coartación "gave rise to a social sector of free black and mulatto artisans, who in the eighteenth and early nineteenth century dominated almost all of the urban occupations, including the most exclusive such as music, silversmithing, engraving, painting and woodcarving."[36]

The situation was starkly contrasted in the rural sugar zones, where colonists created: "a plantation society where blacks were slaves for life, where existed a bestial imbalance in the percentage of sexes (80% men and 20% women, when it wasn't 100% men) as well as no communication with the outside world. To this plantation society . . . would never arrive the legal mechanisms to acquire liberty, nor the alternative of apprenticeship for trades, nor the possibility of going to the tribunals to denounce unjust treatment."[37]

In eighteenth-century Havana, there were many documented cases where enslaved men and women gained free status by challenging their owners in court.[38] Although these rights existed on the books, all the jurors were white male property-owners, making Moreno-Fraginals wonder what mechanisms blacks used to give value to their rights. Self-organization was key: "Ample documentation proves that these Havana blacks developed a deep communal sense in defense of their interests and created secret social cells that were profoundly feared by the whites."[39] Like many other historians, Moreno-Fraginals identified the Abakuá as an exemplary defense system for black communities. Its Cross River precedents, mutual aid functions, and strict ethical codes maintained a coherence that has been sustained into the twenty-first century.

Fugitive Communities in the Americas

Throughout the Americas, a common form of rebellion against slavery was to escape and then set up independent communities in hidden places.[40] Among prominent examples, the quilombo (fugitive community) of Palmares in northeastern Brazil existed for nearly a century before destruction by "the largest military force ever mounted in the Americas by the Portuguese and Brazilians."[41] The Spanish called fugitives *cimarrones* (thus *maroons* in English). Maroon towns in the Esmeraldas province of Ecuador and in sections of the Blue Mountains and the Cockpit Country of Jamaica existed for equally long periods.[42] In New Orleans, the Mardi Gras or Black Indians have been described as "contemporary urban maroons" whose roots are found in the communities of fugitives located in the estuaries surrounding the city, areas that allowed access to the city's marketplace while affording protection from authorities.[43] In the Haitian revolution of the late eighteenth century, maroon groups were important participants.

In colonial Havana as elsewhere, freed blacks commonly aided fugitives in collective actions against the government. Twentieth-century historians identified fugitive communities in Cuba as forms of resistance that culminated in the Mambí rebel army for national independence in 1868. The cimarrones set the model for American independence movements, according to one Cuban writer: "In the palenque [fugitive communities] . . . emerged the spirit of social solidarity, the rebels appeared as collectives, and with them came organization, discipline, and hierarchy. . . . 236 years before the Congress at Philadelphia prohibited the slave trade, our apalencados [fugitives] went forth throughout the mountains of the island with their desire for liberty."[44] The ability to romanticize fugitive solidarity at the foundation of American societies may reflect the scarcity of documentation about this phenomenon, yet the social consequences pervade collective memory and popular culture (musical examples are discussed in chapter 7).

In some cases, ethnic solidarity was a basis for underground networks, as demonstrated among Africans in Cuba who harbored fugitive members of their same homeland nation.[45] Similar cases existed in Brazil, where nineteenth-century "sources insist that the many candomblés of Bahia served as hideouts for fugitive slaves."[46] In Havana, Bahia, and other urban zones, spiritually based ethnic communities functioned in some ways similar to the Underground Railroad in the United States. Instead of moving North to freedom, Africans here created community networks for mutual defense. Using the Ékpè model of a multi-ethnic, regional system of independent lodges, Abakuá was particularly well suited for adaptation in a cosmopolitan heterogeneous environment where secrecy was required.

Freemasonry and Abakuá

Cuba's first independence movement was organized in 1810 in Havana by Joaquín Infante, who wrote a constitution for an independent Cuba, and Roman de la Luz. Twelve other participants were described as military officers, intellectuals, and men of color, both free and enslaved.[47] Before activating their plot, all were captured and imprisoned in Spain. Infante and Roman de la Luz were members of Cuba's first Freemason lodge, chartered by the Grand Lodge of Pennsylvania.[48]

Freemasonry was a vehicle for Enlightenment ideals like "the liberty of man" in both Europe and the Americas. In the period of the North American Revolution, leaders such as George Washington, the Marquis de Lafayette, Voltaire, Benjamin Franklin, and Andrew Jackson were members.[49] Parallel to its role in other American colonies, many nineteenth-century Cuban rebel leaders were Freemasons, including Carlos Manuel de Céspedes, who initiated the first war in 1868; José Martí, known as the apostle of Cuban independence; and Antonio Maceo, Cuba's greatest military hero, who fought in all three wars.[50]

Masonic conspirators in Cuba interacted closely with African descendants seeking liberation, a trend that grew in the Wars of Independence (1868–1898). Because all groups were underground, there is little hard evidence about them. However, it is clear that by the mid-nineteenth century, social and cultural ties developed among both groups and many Abakuá leaders became Freemasons.[51] By the 1890s these relationships were embodied in the figure of Felipe Espínola, a Freemason, a leader in the Mambí army, a foreman on the wharves, as well as an Abakuá title-holder in two Matanzas lodges (more on Espínola in chapter 6).[52] The parallel functions of both institutions inspired Alejo Carpentier to praise Abakuá as "a true popular masonry."[53]

Urban Palenques

Throughout Spanish America, communities of fugitives were called *palenques* and their members *cimarrones.*[54] One historian described nineteenth-century Havana as an "immense urban palenque," where some Africans eluded their would-be owners for many years by using community networks to hide and disguise themselves "in the barrios of the walled city, or in the hamlets outside the walls, converting themselves into urban cimarrones."[55] Urban fugitives had counterparts in rural areas, where Carabalí were also present, for example the famous fugitive known as Miguel Carabalí "the Black Tiger" of Camagüey (in central Cuba).[56]

Havana slave owners who sought fugitives in the first half of the nineteenth century placed hundreds of descriptive ads in newspapers that distinguished between male and female, African born and creole, skilled and unskilled, literate and multilingual, and those with African-styled facial cicatrisation.[57] Some fugitives were *jornaleros* (wage earners) who already lived apart from their owners and simply left. Many succeeded in eluding recapture for years by assuming new names, creating false papers, joining militias of *pardos y morenos* (mulattos and blacks), and living in the homes of their freed African compatriots.[58]

Interaction between enslaved and freed Africans in Havana stimulated the enslaved to flee to urban zones outside the city walls where free blacks lived.[59] In

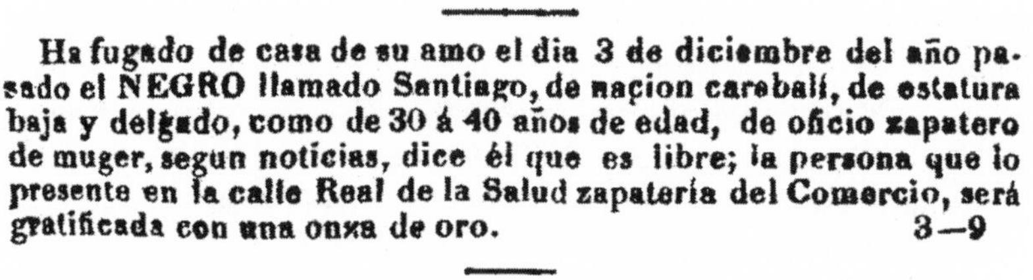

Ha fugado de casa de su amo el dia 3 de diciembre del año pasado el NEGRO llamado Santiago, de nacion carabalí, de estatura baja y delgado, como de 30 á 40 años de edad, de oficio zapatero de muger, segun noticias, dice él que es libre; la persona que lo presente en la calle Real de la Salud zapatería del Comercio, será gratificada con una onza de oro.   3—9

FIGURE 11. Advertisement in search of a fugitive from the Carabalí nation. From the Havana newspaper *Diario de la marina*, February 9, 1845. "A fugitive from the house of his master since December 3 of last year, the Black called Santiago, of the Carabalí nation . . ." Archives of the Library of Congress.

response, the colonial government built a depot in Havana where those captured could be reclaimed by legal owners. In 1831, the depot recorded that more than 10 percent of the enslaved population was arrested for escape.[60] Many Carabalí were among the fugitives, as evidenced in the ethnic terms used to describe them, including "the Brican nation" ('Bríkamo' is a term for the Abakuá language); the "carabilí macuá nation"; "Carabalí viví"; "carabalí ososo"; "the carabalí suamo nation"; and finally two "carabalí ibibí" born in Africa, whose homeland names were Usó and Umúa.[61] Ụsọ̀ is a personal name meaning "dexterous hands" in Ìbìbìò, precisely the ethnic background given to this fugitive in Cuba. Umúa is a name given to a child born in the market.[62]

Outside the walled city, the barrio of Jesús María was a destination for fugitives. This barrio of blacks contained the "celebrated and feared Mangrove refuge of the so-called black curros," who were free descendants of Africans born in Spain.[63] Deported to Havana in the late 1700s, the black curros were underworld characters feared by authorities. They lived in the backwaters of the Havana port called Manglar (mangrove), until this barrio was finally burnt down by authorities. As will be discussed later in this chapter, there is evidence that "the Africans from Calabar were associated with the so-called black curros of the Manglar and the foundation of the Abakuá secret society."[64] The relationship between African-derived initiation societies and fugitive communities in the Americas made both objects of fear in official dispatches, contributing to prejudices against mutual aid societies like the Abakuá that have persisted in the present.[65]

Cofradías: Black Catholic Brotherhoods

Africans in Havana were able to regroup through two distinct institutions: the Catholic *cofradías* (brotherhoods) organized by the Spaniards and the *cabildos de nación* (nation-groups) organized by Africans themselves. Both groups were sometimes referred to using the Spanish term *cabildo*, because it means both a municipal institution (a town council) and an ecclesiastical institution (a brotherhood). Sometimes the African cabildos sought the protection of the Church and were authorized by it, and sometimes the cofradías were subversively used to perpetuate African traditions. However, whereas the cofradía was a continuation of a medieval Spanish institution, the cabildos de nación were an American phenomenon created by Africans.

In 1573 the Havana town council ordered that all free blacks participate in the procession of Corpus Christi.[66] This was an emerging strand in the Latin-American tradition of cofradías begun in medieval Seville, where the Catholic Church organized a portion of the sub-Saharan Africans as they had the gypsies and North Africans before them.[67] The first documented black brotherhood in Seville was founded by the archbishop between 1393 and 1401.[68] A contemporary chronicler noted that the dances and celebrations of enslaved Africans had a king acting as chief and judge among them.[69]

In Spain, the brotherhoods acted as mutual aid societies organized under the name of a particular saint.[70] Church authorities organized immigrants into brotherhoods to Christianize them, while Africans used this vehicle for their own purposes.[71] From the fourteenth to eighteenth centuries, the original black brotherhood of Seville became the model for ethnic brotherhoods in neighboring Andalusian cities like Cádiz and Jerez, as well as Valencia.[72] This model was used throughout Spanish America and Brazil from the sixteenth century until national independence, when in many cases they continued using other names.[73]

Canoe Houses in West Africa

The self-organization of Africans in Cuba and Brazil into nation-groups had precedents along coastal West Africa, especially in the Niger Delta, Bonny, and Calabar, where trade with European merchants led to the reorganization of communities through competitive Canoe Houses. Both "a co-operative trading unit and a local government institution" that could include some 300 to several thousand people, Canoe Houses existed in Old Calabar by the late 1600s.[74] The heterogeneous Canoe Houses incorporated wives, slaves, and other outsiders into federated units, where social movement was possible for energetic and talented people.[75] In nineteenth-century Old Calabar, traders attached to Èfìk houses, even if enslaved, sometimes rose to prominence: "A head slave of the Duke family became a great trader, creditor to King Archibong II and a prominent member of the Ékpè society. He had over 3000 slaves himself and could purchase an imported storey house, allowed only to holders of the highest Ékpè grades."[76] Famous in this regard was King Jaja, who as a child was enslaved in the Ìgbo hinterland and brought to Bonny, where he eventually became a merchant. In 1870 he founded the trading state of Opobo. In the process, fourteen of the eighteen Canoe Houses existing in Bonny declared their allegiance and moved to join him.[77]

There are myriad ways of forming federated associations that are not uniquely determined by descent (actual kinship) but that nevertheless present the idiom of descent (ethnicity or fictive kinship). In any case, the process of establishing Canoe Houses was outside "the patterns of lineage of house expansion observed in other Ijo or hinterland communities."[78] Yet in some cases there was a fictive kinship element, since all members called the House head "father," and the senior wives were called "mother."[79] There is not necessarily a correlation between the models of the Canoe Houses of West Africa and the nation-groups of Cuba and Brazil, but the existence of Canoe Houses demonstrates a precedent for creative regrouping that Africans in the Americas would have used.

Carabalí Cabildos in Havana

Africans in Cuba created cabildos de nación by collectively reestablishing fundamental aspects of their homeland practices, in the process laying the foundation for the existing African-derived religions and their sacred music traditions. The cabildos played a foundational role in Cuban society by receiving African migrants in a communal, urban context.[80] Historians report that of all the American colonies, "Cuba received the greatest mix of African peoples," most of them entering through Havana.[81] In this situation, one would expect the loss of an African identity through mixture. Instead, the cabildo structure enabled Africans to regroup in order to teach homeland languages and customs to their offspring.

As Cuba transitioned from a "settler society with slaves" to a "slave society" in the second half of the eighteenth century, the ruling class attempted to use the cabildos for their own interests. In 1755 Bishop Morell in Havana "officialized the cabildos created spontaneously by the Africans since the sixteenth century," in order to evangelize their members, assigning to each a priest, as well as the image of a saint or the Virgin.[82] Morell documented twenty-one cabildos then existing in Havana, five of them Carabalís.[83] As did the black brotherhood in Seville, nineteenth-century African cabildos de nación had selected kings who were the "political link that legally united [the cabildo] to white society . . . the king was accredited before the Captain General as ambassador of . . . the respective African nation."[84]

Cabildos were important centers for the conservation of African languages and cultural practices. Through them, Cross River peoples in Cuba established several collective traditions, including, "the Bríkamos, who had cabildos in Havana and Matanzas, . . . the Isuámas in Trinidad and Santiago de Cuba; the Olugos in Santiago de Cuba; and the nyányigo or Abakuá society, prevailing in Havana, Regla, Guanabacoa, Cárdenas and Matanzas."[85] The Carabalí cabildos of eighteenth-century Havana included Ékpè members who sponsored the Abakuá society among the creoles.

Many cabildos selected their captains and matrons from among the free and propertied blacks in Havana society. Several captains were also officers in the black and mulatto battalions or were foremen on the wharves.[86] For example, in 1831 the captain of the Carabalí Ososo cabildo was a first sergeant in Havana's battalion of Pardos Leales (Loyal Mulattos). A funerary director, he had $17,000 in savings.[87] The profile of this free propertied creole who worked in the military and led a Carabalí *cabildo* gives insight into the multiple spheres of Abakuá presence at the time. These relationships were not articulated directly, but when reading between the lines—a requisite skill for grasping the dynamics Cuban society—the various strands make a tight net.

Even in the present generation, Abakuá maintain close ties with certain funeral homes, some of whose owners were Abakuá, enabling a lodge to perform rites legally within the society but also within the protective space of their own community (a reoccurring strategy in Abakuá history). Indigenous West African customs included the burial of esteemed leaders within the earth deep beneath their family compounds, rather than in a cemetery apart from the town.[88] Abakuá funerary rites were therefore gradually adjusted to conform to the laws of the Catholic colony while maintaining their own philosophies and expressive qualities. In spite of nineteenth-century legislation to stop it, contemporary Abakuá funerary rites include masked dance and a portion of activity in the home of the deceased.[89]

By the eighteenth century, as the cabildos were incorporated by parochial churches, the majority had their own meetinghouses. For example, the cabildo Carabalí Isuama owned a house in 1783 in Havana[90]; the cabildo of the Carabalí Okeya nation owned a house valued at $4000 in 1831; the cabildo of the Carabalí Ososo nation bought a house in 1832.[91]

Several Carabalí cabildos in Havana had been organized long before their existence was officially documented. In 1772 there were requests to "reauthorize the Carabalí Ungua cabildo," and "to authorize the fourth Carabalí cabildo of Nuestra Señora del Carmen."[92] A cabildo of the Carabalí Isuama Isieke nation was founded in 1793.[93] The cabildos Carabalí Iziegue and Carabalí Ugrí of Havana appeared in legal archives in 1812 and 1825, respectively. In 1812 the cabildo Carabalí Iziegue "facilitated the liberation of fifty African slaves" who were to join the cabildo.[94] Before they did, a government official dissolved the cabildo for fear they would liberate more Africans.[95] These findings document the mutual aid tendencies of the cabildos, as well as ethnic terms important in Abakuá history. An Abakuá member in the mid-twentieth century recalled the solidarity among Carabalí: "The Abakuá groups have funds for misfortunes: sickness, accidents and burials, as did the cabildos of any nation in the past; although for the help of their brothers, nobody was like the Carabalí."[96]

Several cabildos involved in the foundation of the Abakuá society were known as Apapá.[97] One cabildo of the Carabalí Apapá nation, founded in 1714, owned a house in Havana.[98] Two Carabalí cabildos documented in 1799 had the names Apapá and Apapá Chiquito (Apapá the Second).[99] One of them bought a house in Havana in 1810, where its members gathered in 1833, appearing again in documents in 1843.[100] In Calabar, the term Apapá is interpreted as "apá apá," meaning "the first, the original."[101] Interpretations in Havana support this. El Chino Mokóngo told me, "Ápapa means 'birth.' One may say Ápapa Efí, Ápapa Efó, or Ápapa Orú," a reference to the birth of the three Abakuá lineages.[102]

Two years after Ápapa Efó founded the Eforisún lodge inside the city's walls in 1840 (as described in chapter 1), cabildo activities were banned from within the city. Many members relocated to the extramural barrio of Jesús María, where the Abakuá have been active since.[103]

Pardo y Moreno Battalions

The battalions of free blacks (*morenos*) and mulattos (*pardos*) have a long history in Cuba, but they were expanded enormously after the British occupation in 1762.[104] In 1763 in Havana a pardo infantry battalion and a moreno battalion of light infantry were organized with 800 men each.[105] By 1770 more than 3000 colored militiamen, among them about 130 officers, existed among the total army of 11,667.[106] Black battalion members were the only African descendants in the colony sanctioned to carry arms, a privilege institutionalized in 1779.[107]

The port of Havana had the largest labor force in the city, where from 1763 onward ships were loaded and unloaded by teams of freed blacks who had served in the black battalions of Havana.[108] Meanwhile, the storing of goods on board ships was work reserved for a group of about 100 white men. Contact between these groups was relevant to the later entry of whites into the Abakuá society, in the 1860s.[109]

Many black militia members on the Havana harbor were Carabalí, and several were foremen who acquired capital and property.[110] The testimonies and wills of Carabalí nation members from the 1820s to 1845 document the cohesion of their community in terms of "military-labor and national identity." For example, José María Fuertes, a "carabalí suama" dock foreman and first sergeant of the battalion, died in 1833, leaving property that included six houses, and fourteen slaves.[111] There were intimate, if underground, ties between the Abakuá society, the leadership of the Carabalí cabildos, the colored militias, the dock foremen, and property ownership by blacks.[112]

Black Curros, Cabildos, and Militiamen

The black curros were free men and women of African descent with immediate origins in Seville and Madrid, Spain.[113] After arrival in Havana in the late 1700s, curros often served as strongmen to the colonial bourgeoisie. By the early 1800s they were legendary for their colorful dress, gold earrings, slang, and aggressive behavior.[114] The black curros inhabited the barrio of Jesús María, a center for African cabildos and future Abakuá activity. Archival evidence shows that they participated in the formation of Abakuá.[115]

A system of Abakuá's magnitude in Cuban society would have emerged from community networks impenetrable to authorities. As described in eighteenth-century chronicles, certain marginal barrios of Havana and Matanzas, "became bounded enclosures where the white repressive forces did not dare enter." Police reports from the late 1700s state that, "in some years, more than 80 of 100 crimes went unpunished because the authorities could not locate their authors."[116]

In 1824 in the barrio of Jesús María, authorities intervened in a feud between two groups of black curros. The resulting investigation revealed that the members of two barrios disagreed about the capacity of a black creole to dance with an African-style mask. Authorities assumed that Oró Papá was a group of black curros. They were alarmed that a costume used in their dances was found in the home of a Carabalí nation member, and that the director of the Oró Papá dances was also a soldier in the First Company of Havana's Battalion of Pardos Leales (Loyal Mulattos).[117] The interwoven community links between the black battalions, black curros, black creoles, and African cabildos were just the kinds of networks necessary to produce the Abakuá. Based upon the police report, Pedro Deschamps-Chappeaux concluded, "Until this moment, there had been no evidence for the existence of Abakuá in 1824 and even less of the dances of the black curros . . . we must conclude that there is nothing more similar to a nyányigo [Abakuá] than a curro of the Manglar."[118]

Black curros of this era, like the creoles, were assuming West African identities and organizing groups called "Mandingas, Isicuatos, Isieques, and Dearrumbambá . . . their fandangos and dances were . . . in the 'nation' style."[119] Isieke is a place name in the Niger Delta; there was a cabildo Carabalí Iziegue in Havana at this time.[120] Other groups of enslaved creoles were reported to have filed their teeth, "following carabalí custom, without doubt for the fame of those Africans from Calabar as being *cheches*, brave and rebellious. These [creoles] were associated with the so-called black curros of the Manglar and the foundation of the Abakuá secret society."[121]

That the Carabalí sponsors of Abakuá interacted with the black curros is further evidenced in a coded verse from 1825, in décima form, about the Oró Apapá group.[122] Written in both Èfìk and Spanish, this may be the first popular song to mix these idioms. Beginning with the name of the groups' dance director (also a Havana Battalion member), it praises Cross River tradition:

> Antonio Basabe has said
> without any precaution
> that Orú Apapa is already in session.
> Obon Iya canyon dirán [The Sacred Fish appeared]
> And without any fuss
> He says: "O Sisi Yamba-O!" [Praise to the Iyámba grade]
> The initiate comes to dance.[123]

Abakuá leaders understand Orú Apapa as a cabildo. This song confirms the presence of Ékpè and possibly Abakuá members within Carabalí cabildos by 1825 in Havana, as Andrés Flores had reported.

Another anonymous song attributed to nineteenth-century black curros uses vernacular Spanish and Abakuá. Called "Décimas" after its poetic form, it expresses a shared cultural practice wherein black curros and Cross River Ékpè fused to create a poetic-braggadaccio characteristically Habanero, male, and working class.[124] Two of five stanzas are heavily informed by Abakuá language. Each stanza seems to be a distinct voice. It begins: "Sámbila of Habana arrived/ I am the black curro."[125] After two boastful stanzas in black Spanish, the battle continues with a verse representing Efó territory (or an Efó lineage):

> You are as stupid as my horse
> when it's ill
> You surrender to my flag
> If not I part you in two
> We will see, fool
> Naeriero amoropó [I greet your head] . . .
> Inuá aborobuto ékue [I speak Èfìk to greet Ékpe]
> Momí asarorí abanékue [I am a blessed initiate]
> Abaíreme ékuefó [who comes from Efó]. . . .[126]

The speaker of the next stanza represents Efí territory:

> I am abanékue Efí [I am an initiate of Efí]
> since 1881,
> I fear nobody,
> I swear this to Abasí.
> I have seen the Anamanguí [funerary masquerade]
> inuándo [dancing] with the Nyanyako [Abakuá],
> and upon seeing me, he said [figurative for "gestured"]: amako [look]
> kuri kufón [come to the temple], because Ékue
> needs an abanékue [figurative for "to guard him"].[127]

These stanzas contain Abakuá terms understood by Ékpè masters in Calabar today (as detailed in the appendix of chants). For example, in Calabar Nyanyako is understood as Nyanyaku, an early Èfìk Ékpè masquerade assigned the responsibility to execute a judgment after its delivery by a council.[128] The mixture of Cross River terms with Spanish reflects the process of Abakuá's foundation with the participation of Ladino black creoles.

These findings detail the interactions of various groups participating in Abakuá's foundation. Deschamps-Chappeaux argued that this was evidence for Abakuá's foundation in 1824. More likely, the Oró Papá nation was a cabildo that sponsored the Orú Apapá lodge in the 1840s.[129] Abakuá leaders regard antiquity as a factor in the legitimacy of a lodge. If Oró Papá was indeed the first Abakuá group in Cuba, it would be highly unusual that that there would be no memory of it, because most founding rituals were performed collectively.

In summary, documentation from Havana in the eighteenth and nineteenth centuries indicates that various communities of Africans, freed blacks in the Crown's militia, as well as underworld curros were interacting and reorganizing using Cross River models. Their interactions were part of the zeitgeist in which resistance movements became ever more prominent.

Aponte's Conspiracy of 1812

Without the African descendants who resisted slavery and Spanish domination, Cuba would have had an entirely different history. Fernando Ortiz wrote, "It is sufficient to mention as historic heroes the black Aponte and the mulatto Maceo. Without the liberation of the slaves and cooperation of the blacks, the Cuban people, of which they form an integral part, would not have been able to achieve independence."[130]

José Antonio Aponte, a carpenter, was a retired first corporal of the black militia. In 1812 he led what has been described as, "the largest and best organized conspiracy which, in colonial Cuba, had as an objective the liberation of slaves," through the overthrow of the colonial regime.[131] The conspiracy was international in scope, including an officer from Santo Domingo and strategic intelligence from black militia who sailed throughout the Caribbean, and it was believed to have inspired revolts in New Orleans, Santo Domingo, and Brazil at the time.[132]

A Yorùbá descendant, Aponte was Oni-Shangó, a son of Shangó, the divinity of thunder, as well as leader of the Lukumí cabildo Shangó-Tedun.[133] He was believed to have been a hereditary member of the Yorùbá-derived Ògbóni secret society, recreated in Havana after the arrival of thousands of enslaved Yorùbá speakers.[134] Using his skills and status, and inspired by a constellation of contemporary ideas and leaders such as Toussaint-Louverture and George Washington, Aponte built a multi-ethnic movement that used a protocol of secret oaths to pass along information.[135] Their procedure was so effective that even after their movement had inspired revolts in urban centers across the island in 1812, colonial authorities remained unaware of their links with a larger conspiracy.[136] A Cuban historian concluded that these oaths were derived from the Abakuá tradition, because "a conventional sign used as a signature by the Abakuá" was discovered by authorities among the papers of a colleague of Aponte.[137] Few details are known about this process, but clearly African-derived initiation systems derived from Cross River Ékpè and Yorùbá Ògbóni were functioning for collective action.[138]

Lukumí Revolt of 1835

In another example of how African descendants self-organized using African models, an armed uprising of some fifty Lukumís took place in 1835 outside the walled city in the barrio del Horcón.[139] This is the first known urban rebellion in the history of Havana. One of their leaders was a free black Lukumí priest, known as Taita (Father), who had a following within the community. As a symbol of their faith and the purity of their intentions, the rebels wore white clothes and hats, while Taita carried an *ìrùkẹ̀* horsetail fly-whisk in his hand, a symbol of leadership.[140] They planned to enter the city, inspire the slaves to join them, and smash the colonial government. The governor general sent the cavalry to crush the movement. "The principal leaders of the rebellion ... were executed and their heads exposed on the Puente de Chávez by command of the Military Commission."[141] If anything, this event demonstrates the dire consequences for Cuban communities that resisted openly, therefore the need for Abakuá strategies of developing ever more impenetrable codes of communication.

The 1839 Abakuá Raid

In 1839, three years after Èfìk Obutong was established in Regla, colonial authorities invaded an Abakuá meeting in the barrio of Jesús María. They discovered papers belonging to a dockworker named Margarito Blanco, a title-holder in a Carabalí cabildo. The title, written as 'Ocongo', was Mokóngo, a leading Abakuá title that derives from southwestern Cameroon Ékpè tradition.[142] Authorities were alarmed that the papers included a summons to Mokóngos of other Abakuá groups to create a new cabildo, Orú Apapá.[143]

Former participants in the Aponte conspiracy were implicated in this meeting. One of them, a black sublieutenant named Pilar Borrego, the founder and director of the cabildo de Nuestra Señora de Belén, had been exiled in 1812 for his political ideas.[144] Also arrested was León Monzón, captain of the Loyal Blacks of Havana, with more than thirty-five years of military service and honored with the coat of arms (*escudo*) of fidelity to the king. Among his papers was found a pamphlet containing the phrase, "No hay patria, sin libertad" (There is no country without liberty). A list of associates belonging to an entity called Empresa de Comercio (Business Enterprise) contained the names of 110 members, who were called "brothers."[145] Four associates of Monzón, also officers in the black militia, were arrested.[146] Also detained were seven members of Abakuá groups, as well as other Carabalí descendants. One held the title of Ocongo of Ososo[147]; another held the Abakuá title of Empegó (the scribe) of Bacondo of Obani.[148] Another was Ocongó of Efó, a cabildo.[149] Papers found in the house of one slave proclaimed the laws of an association entitled Nueva Constantino-pla, Habitantes de la Luna, Hijos del Sol y Academia Nuestra Señora de los Dolores (New Constantinople, Inhabitants of the Moon, Sons of the Sun and Academy of Our Lady of the Dolores).[150] It appears that alongside the Abakuá existed other secret societies based on European models, like the Freemasons, that professed ideals of the Enlightenment.

Participants were found to belong to three distinct groups: those from the Far Orient (who claimed to belong to the Catholic Church), the military, and Abakuá members, led by Margarito Blanco, who were also wood, quarry, and dock workers. Authorities were alarmed that black creoles practiced Cross River culture: they "dem-onstrated a certain pride in calling themselves Apapá chiquitos [Apapá the second], for being sons of Apapá Carabalíes."[151] Margarito Blanco's aim was to create a group called Arupapá (or Orú Apapá).[152] Blanco's cabildo was called Ultán or Papaultán, perhaps from "Old Town," the British name for the Obutong settlement in Calabar.[153]

In 1840 the majority implicated in this Abakuá meeting were sentenced to per-petual banishment to the Iberian Peninsula.[154] As a result, little is known about the later foundation of the Orú Apapá lodge of Abakuá. Known popularly as Uria Ápapa, its official name is Orú Ápapa, a title interpreted as the "owners of Orú territory." Various contemporary Obónes of this lodge told me that the exact date of their foun-dation is unknown; they believe it to be between 1847 and 1848 in Guanabacoa.[155] Des-champs-Chappeaux concluded that: "The name of the group or cabildo Oró Papá is of carabalí origin and its foundation in the year 1824, with all the characteristics that we have outlined, alters in our judgment, the date that we have for the foundation of the Abakuá."[156]

Deschamps-Chappeaux's findings offer provocative insight into the period, but do not necessarily overturn the narrative that Èfìk Obutong was the first creole lodge in the 1830s, as accepted by Abakuá masters. Even if the generally accepted date of 1836 is not necessarily accurate, the chronology for the foundation of early lodges is fairly clear. Also, if there were already an Oru Ápapa lodge in 1824, why would there have been a meeting in 1839 calling for the formation of Oru Ápapa? The answer to these mysteries may have been carried to the grave by those who witnessed them.

Expansion and Repression

The formation of Abakuá lodges was part of a larger trend of expressing an emerging Cuban identity. Early forms of nationalist thought in journalism and literature appear in the 1820s—some published by exiles in New York—while Cuban literary discourse was established in the 1830s with the founding of the Cuban Academy of Literature by José Antonio Saco, Domingo Delmonte, and others.[157]

Havana and Matanzas comprised the most cosmopolitan region of nineteenth-century Latin America, with communication and transportation systems more modern than those of Spain. In 1819 steamship service was inaugurated between Havana and Matanzas. In the 1830s the railroads were built in Havana, and by 1851 the telegraph linked Havana with Cárdenas and later Matanzas.[158] Built to augment agricultural productivity, these systems were also used by African descendants to network within their own cultural systems. Abakuá lodges, for example, were diffused specifically in zones with the most modern transportation of the era. Havana and Matanzas were connected by railway in the 1850s, and Abakuá was established in Matanzas by 1862.[159] By 1858 a train ran from Havana to Guanabacoa, an important center for Abakuá activity.[160] By 1870 passenger trains ran regularly between Havana and the outlying village of Marianao, which became a center for Abakuá activities.[161]

In addition, the Carabalí in Havana and Matanzas successfully regrouped in the port regions. Deschamps-Chappeaux confirmed that "the initial and majority participation by the Africans of Carabalí origin, as much among the *jornaleros* [day workers] as among the foremen, allowed them to make the wharves a zone under their dominion."[162] The extent to which they dominated the wharves is still an open question, but by all accounts, their presence was considerable and multi-layered.

Among the benefits of having a presence on the docks was communication with sailors who brought news about events throughout the Atlantic world, a privilege that only increased in 1818 when Cuba's ports were opened to unrestricted world trade.[163] Black sailors arriving from throughout the Atlantic region, including New York City, Calabar, and Britain, reported on current events,[164] including news of antislavery activity in Brazil, Jamaica, Haiti, and the southern United States.[165] In Havana and Matanzas, the Carabalí and Abakuá were a conduit for these communications.

The contradictions inherent in the frenetic international economic activities of the ports and the colonists' desire to keep workers and slaves there ignorant was consistently resolved through censorship of the press and martial law. In the wake of the conspiracies of Infante and Roman de la Luz, Aponte, and the multiple rebellions by the enslaved, the Spanish Crown resorted to martial law. The repression sought to contain the effects of British antislavery agents in Havana in the 1830s and 1840s, who were thought to have inspired a series of revolts in the early 1840s that became known as the Conspiracy of La Escalera (the Ladder), after a ladder-like device that suspected conspirators were tied to for torture and execution by Spanish and Cuban authorities.[166] Several leading foremen of the Havana docks were executed by authorities as a result of La Escalera, thus eliminating the few propertied blacks and mulattos of the era.[167] Among them, José Agustín Ceballos died in a Cuban prison in 1844, known as "the year of the lash."[168] Among the accused that year was an Abakuá title-holder from Efó territory.[169] The repression of La Escalera extended into the early 1850s as many

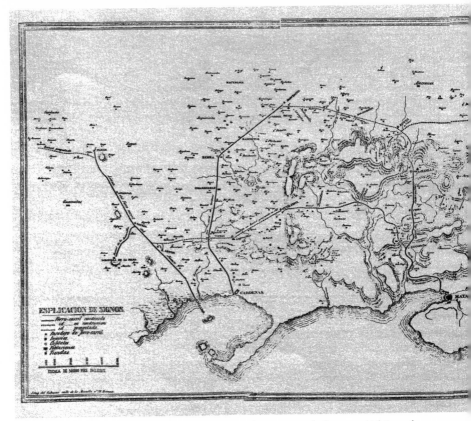

FIGURE 12. Map of Cuba showing the ports of Havana and Matanzas at the bottom, which is north (a view from Florida). Drawn by Manuel J. de Cabrera, 1846 (from Marrero 1972–1987, vol. 11).

wasted away in prisons and others were sent into exile.[170] Even within this desperate context, Abakuá forged ahead to create new lodges.

Conclusion

Colonial Havana was a fortified city built largely by African labor and partially financed by taxing the entry of Africans brought to sustain the burgeoning sugar industry. Africans in urban centers often regrouped based upon homeland identities to create cabildos (nation-groups) and sometimes were recognized by authorities as Catholic brotherhoods, or cofradías. After the British occupation of Havana in 1763, Spain regained control and

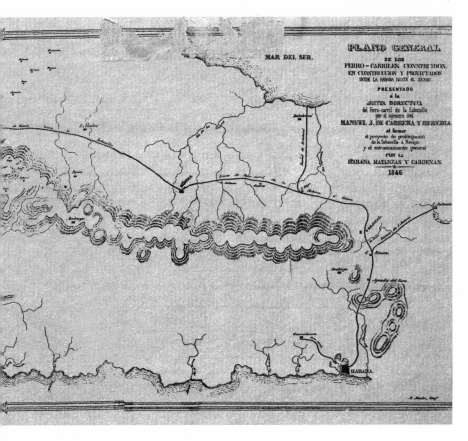

former trade restrictions were gradually opened, the black and mulatto battalions were expanded to help defend the colony, and Freemasonry was established (with its Enlightenment ideals). With the success of the Haitian revolution in the early 1800s, Cuba effectively transitioned from a "society with slaves" to a "slave society." The plantation system dominated the economy, being sustained by the thousands of Africans pouring into the city from the regions of Senegal to Mozambique and all points between. Expelled from Spain, groups of Ladino black curros settled into the marginal barrio of Jesús María, soon to be an Abakuá center. All these African-descended migrants participated in renaming the city using homeland terms and created communities based on homeland systems.

The interactions of many communities, including African nation-groups, free black artisans, the black and mulatto militias, urban fugitives, and black curros, created underground networks through which Abakuá emerged. Members of Carabalí cabildos and Abakuá lodges worked along the wharves, where they maintained international communication through black sailors. To escape detection, Abakuá developed intricate codes of communication, based upon Ékpè codes called nsìbìdì. As anticolonial movements were organized from the early 1800s onward, secret oaths in the manner of Freemasonry and Abakuá were operative. The first plan to overthrow Spain (including Freemasons and African descendants) was detected and crushed in 1810. Two years later, Aponte's conspiracy against colonial rule and slavery (with possible Abakuá and Ékpè participation) was also crushed. The captain general of the island received omniscient powers in 1825, the same year police discovered black curros and militia members participating in proto-Abakuá or Ékpè groups. Once begun, martial law continued until the 1850s. Abakuá was established in the 1830s, the same period an organized Lukumí revolt attempted to overthrow Havana. Responding to the agitation, the colonists violently suppressed the population in 1844, known as "the year of the lash." This resulted in the absence of significant anticolonial activities until 1868, with the first war of independence. In spite of myriad obstacles, Abakuá groups were created and functioned as antislavery cells that helped maintain a sense of morality and history among their communities.

3. Planting Abakuá in Cuba, 1830s to 1860s

■ ■ ■

The king is dead, long live the king!
—ÉKPÈ AND ABAKUÁ SAYING[1]

Cross River Ékpè lodges governed each autonomous community. As villages grew into urban areas, such as the nineteenth-century city-state of Old Calabar, former towns became neighborhoods, yet maintained their own lodge. To the north, in Arochuku, each ward had an Ékpè lodge that "was an effective integrative factor in the heterogeneous community."[2]

Ékpè concepts of autonomy were sustained in Cuban Abakuá lodges, self-described as "'small states' governed by four grand chiefs."[3] The full expression of independence was not possible, yet Abakuá councils disciplined the membership in their jurisdictions. The function of Abakuá as a basis for moral laws is conveyed in the Cuban phrase, "God is in heaven and the Abakuá are on earth."[4] The phrase has clear precedents from Calabar, where missionaries sought to end Ékpè's rule, replacing it with Christian law, to which Ékpè leaders responded, "God [is] in the sky, but Ékpè [is] on the land" (Plate 15b).[5]

This confidence displayed by Ékpè in the face of adversity was carried into Cuban Abakuá. The emergence of Abakuá coincided with the expansion of Havana into *barrios* outside the walls. Lodges became identified with particular barrios, becoming a social club of prestige for men; an informal school for historians, musicians, and dancers; a vehicle for organizing labor; as well as a place to hold funerals. As Abakuá activities shaped neighborhood life, each barrio developed a distinct character linked to its resident lodge(s). The most public aspect of barrio identity was expressed in carnival groups, where Abakuá leadership was prominent (as discussed in chapter 7).

Examining the foundation of Abakuá lodges within their barrios can give a deeper picture of how marginal people organized themselves as the city expanded geographically. With the establishment of Abakuá's three ethnic lineages (Efí, Efó, and Orú) by the 1840s, its leaders sponsored new lodges.[6] Ten years after the founding of the Èfìk Obutong lodge, "there were some forty lodges, to the point where these were greater in number than all the other nation-groups put together."[7] Because Africans arrived in Cuba until the late 1860s, Carabalí arrivals in Havana and Matanzas would have encountered a familiar community structure.[8]

In what follows, I have listed Abakuá lodges chronologically according to their "birth," with reference to their barrio of origin. The titles of many Cuban lodges were created using Cross River terms for towns, regions, ceremonial objects, or ritual events; wherever possible, I offer interpretations of them.

EFÓRI ENKOMÓN, 1840

The Efóri Enkomón lodge (in Èfìk, Efut Èkòmò) was born under the Arco de Belén (Arch of Bethlehem), the walled city, in 1840.[9] If the baróko (founding ceremony) was performed within the city, regular meetings would have been held outside its walls in Jesús María. El Chino Mokóngo recounted that, "All the early lodges—except Efí Buton—were born in the barrio Jesús María. Here, outside the walled city of Old Havana, lived many freed blacks in the zone called El Manglar [Mangrove]. Nowadays it is named Jesús María."

EKLÉ NTÁTI MACHECHERÉ, 1840

Ntáti Machécheré are Bibí from Orú territory. Founded on February 24, 1840, in the barrio of Los Sitios, outside the city walls, its full name is Eklé Ntáti Machecheré.[10] Its title was "Ntáti Machécheré baróko munyón kai," meaning "the first owners of the plumes."[11] This title refers to the plumes brought by the Orú people who participated in the foundation of Ékpè.[12]

Cuban legend tells of several Ékpè pilgrims who went to Orú territory to perform a baróko (ceremony).[13] They spoke with a prince named Bibí Okondo (or Ibíbio Kóndo), who agreed.[14] The pilgrims brought only plumes (munyón) and a banner (standard) as their representation.[15] In Cuba, the plumed staffs, called *munyón*, represent Cross River ancestors who helped found Abakuá.[16] In the Calabar region, the Mmònyó is a plumed staff "symbolizing supreme spiritual authority" that is used in funerary processions of Ékpè leaders.[17] Both the Cuban munyón and the Cross River Mmònyó are associated with the title Iyámba (Plate 13).[18]

BETONGÓ NARÓKO EFÓ, 1843

Betongó Naróko Efó was founded in Jesús María in 1843 by a lodge of Africans named Nglón Afabábetó.[19] Its title is Betongó Naróko Síro Nánguro Apá.[20] Cuban narratives

FIGURE 13. Betongó Naróko Efó
lodge seal (from Rodríguez 1881: 21).
This image of the medicine horn is
related to the title Nasakó, named after
the diviner who according to Cuban
treaties organized the society in Africa.
Compare with Plate 11 of the emblem
on front door of the Efut Assembly in
Calabar. Compare with Figure 14, a
photograph of this seal on the temple of
the contemporary lodge. Reproduced
by Leandro Soto, 2006.

refer to Betongó Naróko as a king of the tribe Betongó Naróko of Efó territory, who
participated in the ceremonies that perfected Ékpè in Usagaré, when the energy of the
fish Tánsi was directed to create the Voice of Ékpè (Plate 14).[21]

Other Cuban narratives refer to Betongó's interactions with Calabar during the
slave trade, wherein Betongó was ultimately defeated, losing control of commerce.[22]
These narratives demonstrate how Cuban tratados (mythic histories) document aspects
of the expansion of the Èfìk Ékpè empire.[23] An Ékpè leader told me, "Etonko Naroko is
an Efut community from Usaghade; they have Ékpè. They migrated to Oron, then to
Calabar."[24]

EFÍ ABAKUÁ, 1845

Andrés reported that, "The potency Efí Abakuá was born in 1845. After Efík Ebúton
disintegrated, Efí Abakuá became the youngest son of the Ubáne region [Efí terri-
tory].[25] It is asked, 'Ekuéri tené emba une néwe Ubáne?' [Who is the youngest son
of Ubáne region?][26] 'Efí Abakuá kende maribá.' Its title is Efí Abakuá Kénde Maribá,
Maribá Kendé, Kúna Maribá. Maribá means 'sea,' because they were fishermen

FIGURE 14. Betongó Naróko lodge seal, Los Pocitos,
Havana. The arrows pointing downward symbolize
life and birth. Photo by I. Miller.

in Calabar."[27] In Balondo (Efut), *mariba* is "water."[28] In the language of the Qua (Ejagham) M̀gbè, *mariba* identifies the water source of the Voice. The phrase states that the power of Abakuá comes from the water.[29] Cabrera documented this meaning: "Èfìk Abakuá kende Maribá: to receive the Fundamento and the title of Èfìk Abakuá, the Èfìk gathered at the wharf of the sacred river to worship and give offerings to the sea."[30]

According to a sign painted on its temple, Efí Abakuá was born on December 5, 1845, a date confirmed by Fernando Ortiz (Plate 15). A title-holder of this lodge told me it was founded in Regla, sponsored by the lodge Ékue Barondó Enyenisón, its grandparents being Efík Ebúton—neither lodge exists today. The name Ékue Barondó Enyenisón translates easily into Cross River languages: Ékpè Balondo Enyenisong. Balondo are Efut people; *Enyenisong* means "son of the soil" in Èfìk, and idiomatically "owner of the land." Therefore, "Efut Ékpè is supreme."[31]

ENYÓN BAKOKÓ EFÓ, 1845

In Cuba, "Nglón Afabábetó founded Enyón Bakokíro, which in turn founded Enyón Bakokó Efó in 1845.[32] Its title was Enyón Bakokó Awana Mokóko Awana Bekúra Mendó, after Wana Bekúra, a king of Efó in Africa." El Chino Mokóngo told me, "Bakokó is a territory of Usagaré, of Wana bekura mendó," whose representatives were consecrated in the first ceremony in Usagaré.[33] In southwestern Cameroon, Bakoko is a Balondo-speaking group; migrants from there established a Bakoko settlement in Calabar.[34]

The Cross River region of Enyong may be a source for the Cuban term *enyón*. The Enyong Creek empties into the Cross River at Itu, the place of a large slave market in the nineteenth century; Enyong is identified with the nearby Uruan settlements, whose founders claim Usaghade origins (linking them with Bakoko).[35] In southwestern Cameroon, ancient migrants from Enyong are claimed as founders for two settlements in the Usaghade community.[36]

In Cuba, Bakokó Efó was also called Bakokó írióngo meaning "the source of the Voice."[37] In Èfìk, *idiongo* means "a sign, a symbol," meaning in this context, " 'the heart of Ékpè,' because even those permitted to see it will not know its value unless they are taught."[38]

From the barrio of Belén, members of Enyón Bakokó transformed Cuban society forever by disregarding ethnicity and race as factors for membership. From the 1860s onward, leaders of Bakokó sponsored seven lodges with white members who could pass the rigorous tests of morality and strength of character. In effect, they universalized the Abakuá, so that worthy men of any background could be eligible. This achievement has been extolled in many Abakuá chants recorded in the twentieth century (and discussed in chapter 4).[39]

EFÍ ABARAKÓ SISI, 1846/1863

The lodge Efí Abarakó Sisi (or Efí Abarakó Eta) was founded in Regla, some say in 1863.[40] A title-holder in this lineage, however, reported its foundation date as 1846, explaining that when the police confiscated the fundamento in 1863, its members fabricated new ritual objects (Plates 16 and 17).

According to Andrés, "Efí Abarakó Sisi was founded with the tratado [mythic history] of the hill Abarakó in Africa. Abarakó was where the Efó and Efí gathered to share Ékpè."[41] *Sisi* means "first," as a second Abarakó potency was created later. In Qua (Ejagham), Eta is a royal name associated with a founder of a place.[42] El Chino Mokóngo told me, "The phrase 'Entereré enyúgue abarakó' is chanted; it speaks of the fees paid by the Efí tribes of Abarakó to participate in the consecration, to belong to the Abakuá."[43]

In Calabar, Abarakó was interpreted as Mbarakom, a ward of Creek Town held to be foundational to modern Èfìk Ékpè history.[44] This interpretation appears to be supported by Cuban data, because "Mbarankonó abarakó" is an Abakuá phrase.[45] In Èfìk history, Mbarakom is known as a place where important transmissions of Ékpè culture occurred, through ceremonies in which Efut shared aspects of Ékpè.[46] This is precisely the legend of Abarakó in Cuba. Creek Town is a place of many springs; known in Èfìk as Obioko, it is remembered in Cuba as "Ubioko: a spring of water in Èfìk Ubioko."[47] The Cuban phrase "Ubioko Èfìk Ekue anyangasi" is interpreted as "a river in which Ékpè was regenerated."[48]

Another interpretation of Abarakó offered in Calabar was: "Barakong is a traditional meeting place, usually attached to the house of a high chief with Ékpè rank.[49] A meeting there may be taken as meeting in a high place, or place of the most high."[50]

EFÍ MBEMORÓ, 1846

Efí Mbemoró was founded in 1846 in the barrio El Vedado.[51] In Spanish *vedado* means "prohibited," because during the colonial period this outer region of Havana was a reserve forest for the Crown. It happens that the lodge's title, Efí Mbemoró, Awaranyóngo Ekómbre, awanasita moréré, refers to the forest as a source for Ékpè. Mbemoró is interpreted as "highway" (i.e., a river) or "embarking point" (i.e., a beach head). Andrés told me, "Awaranyóngo means 'forest'; Ekómbre means 'offering'; awanasita means 'to give'; moréré means 'food' [an offering]." Thus, this potency represents the highway/embarking point of Efí territory where food was given as an offering.[52] Abelardo Empegó said, "The road of Ubáne Mbemoró crossed through the jungle.[53] Because there was no other way, those passing had to pay fees." The founders of Efí Mbemoró may have chosen this forested zone for ritual purposes, the same way that the founders of Efí Obutong had chosen Regla a decade earlier, as the appropriate environmental setting to perform their rites. The Efí Mbemoró lodge has been celebrated in Cuban commercial recordings from the first half of the twentieth century onward.[54]

In Calabar, Mbemong is an Èfìk settlement on the Great Kwa River, the route for travel from Calabar to Oban.[55] The name Mbemong means "by the river"; therefore any riverbank settlement would be known popularly as *mbemong*, followed by the name of the original settler. For example, *Mbemong Orok* is pronounced similarly to *Mbemoró* of Cuba.

ÉKUÉRI TONGÓ ÁPAPA UMÓNI, 1848

In 1848 in Havana, a lodge called Ékuéri Tongó Ápapa Umóni was founded by a group of Calabarí named Ékuéri Tongó.[56] This lodge originally belonged to the barrios of Los Barracones and San Leopoldo, outside the city wall.[57] Its title, Ékuéri Tongó Ápapa Umóni Ékue úyo unkeno okóbio Umóni, has various interpretations. On one hand, Abakuá leaders told me that, "Umón represents a spring dividing the beach in Calabar"; they are "representatives of a spring in Efí." On the other hand, "Ekueri Tongó" is praised as "the greatest part of Efí territory."[58]

The source of Havana's Ékuéri Tongó is clearly *Ekoretonko*, an indigenous name for the Cohbam House of Creek Town and Calabar.[59] Its title reflects trade relations on the Cross River; during the nineteenth century, traders from the Cross River island of Umon arriving to Creek Town or Calabar would land at an Ekoretonko beachhead.[60] By the early 1800s, Èfìk merchants were trading up the Cross River to Umon, beyond which they could not travel.[61] This Cuban phrase, then, identifies the extent of the reach of the traders from Ekoretongo in Calabar.[62] Approximately fifty miles upriver from Calabar, the Umon market was frequented from the late 1700s by Èfìks from downriver, by Arochukwu to the northwest, and by traders from upriver.[63] A visitor to Calabar in 1805 was told that "the richest and most powerful king in the neighbourhood of Calabar" was in Umon.[64]

In Cuba, Abakuá elders identified "Ékuéri Tongó" and "Umon" as distinct entities.[65] The lodge name, Ékuéri Tongó Ápapa Umóni, suggests that Ékpè members of both Ekoretonko and Umon joined forces in Havana. This kind of regrouping is consistent with the formation of other African-derived institutions in the Americas, wherein diverse groups of people sharing a common language would gather to create an umbrella organization.

Abakuá titles begin with the lodge name and usually end with the name of their sponsor (or even grandfather lodge); as one reads right to left, one goes chronologically backward in the lineage. The phrase "Ekueri Tongó Ápapa Umóni Ékue úyo unkeno okobio Umóni" could be interpreted as "our brothers from Umon gave the Voice of Ékpè to Ékuéri Tongó."

Further identifications of Cross River places are contained in a treaty of this Havana lodge, recited as, "Ekoi Efí Meréme Boki bomia Asemene nyóngo Ekuenyón Ékuéri Tongó Ápapa Umoni Ékue úyo unkeno Efí Meremí Unbiara." Abakuá leaders told me that in Africa, "Efí Meremí Unbiara was an Èfìk king, in whose territory was a spring" and "Ékuéri Tongó Ápapa Umon Kende Mefí, Kende Mefó, was the name of a spring in Calabar." Responding to several terms in this Cuban phrase, a leading elder from Umon told me, "Ekoi, Boki, and Umon are interrelated since early Umon people migrated from Ekoi (Ejagham) through Boki and into Umon, in other words from Cameroon to the Cross River.[66] Ekoretonko and other Èfìk communities were related to Umon through trade."[67] In Cuba, Boki were remembered as Carabalí.[68] This nineteenth-century Havana treaty demonstrates how some Abakuá narratives reflect trade relationships and migration in the Cross River region.

Ekueritongo is linked to the Abakuá origin myth through another Cuban phrase: "Usagaré Eforisun bakokó Ekueritongo."[69] In its deepest sense, the phrase names the three Efó (Efut) groups that participated in the foundation of Abakuá in Usagaré.[70] But the role of *Ekueritongo* is not obvious, since it belongs to an Èfìk lineage in both Cuba and in Calabar. Ékpè leaders in Uruan and Calabar, however, reported that *Ekoretonko* is an Efut term historically linked to Usaghade.[71] These claims are controversial in both Calabar and Cuba, but they are consistent with narratives in both places of the Efut (Balondo) and Ekoi (Ejagham) sources of Ékpè in the Usaghade region.[72]

URIABÓN EFÍ, 1840S

The origins of Uriabón Efí are related to the founding of Abakuá in Cuba.[73] Its title is Uriabón Ereniyó Brandi Masóngo Makrí Ubáne Ekue Efí Mbemoró.[74] This lodge was founded in the barrio of Colón, outside the walled city.[75]

In both Cuba and in Calabar, variants of *uria* and *iria* are interpreted as "to eat."[76] In an Ékpè context, *ùdíábon* means "food for kings," derived from *ùdíá* and *obong*.[77] Thus, *ùdíábon Ékpè* would be "food for Ékpè title-holders"; Abakuá have the same interpretation. The sharing of food is a fundamental aspect of both Ékpè and Abakuá gatherings.[78]

A related interpretation identifies "udi Obong" as an Èfìk phrase for the process of burying a deceased Ékpè leader and installing another person to carry his Ékpè title.[79] An Uruan Ékpè leader surmised, "When they went to Cuba, there must have been an important chief who was the custodian of Ékpè fidelity in Cuba. When that first leader died, they buried him, and the lodge was named to immortalize him. In Uruan, when a ruler dies, he is not buried where anyone can see, he is buried inside the Ékpè shrine, so that *udiobong* can also represent the burial place of a king. During these rites, we have such festivities with many people cooking food, so the name *ùdíábong* could be used to represent the sort of festivities they performed."[80]

In Cross River Ékpè, when a title-holder died his body was ritually cleansed, marked with nsìbìdì writing, and then interred. Before his death was publicly announced, he was buried while the Voice of Ékpè sounded.[81] The belief was that with the death of a chief, the spirit of Ékpè would escape, returning to the bush. Therefore, Ékpè members would seek to recapture it at night, unsuccessfully. Having no other recourse, Ékpè leaders would request an elder woman from a ruling family to evoke the aid of the ancestors in recapturing the spirit of Ékpè to the town.[82] This rite alludes to the importance of powerful women in the mechanics of Ékpè and to the male/female balance expressed in the female Ndèm and male Ékpè organizations. In the Cross River region, Ékpè abandons the lodge at the death of a chief, only to be recaptured through elaborate funerary rites, during which a new chief is installed to "sit upon" Ékpè. This concept was continued in Cuba, where the phrase "Uriabón Efí" symbolizes the continuation of the spirit of Ékpè, despite the death of important African-born leaders. Cuban Abakuá say, "Man dies, but the Abakuá does not," as well as "The king has died, the king is installed."[83] In Calabar, the comparable phrase is "The Obong is dead, long live the Obong."[84]

Herskovits identified an elaborate funeral as "the true climax of life" in many West African societies, because the rites were viewed as an essential mechanism to earn the support of the ancestors.[85] In the Americas, this approach toward funerals was continued by many African-descended communities, as in the example of Uriabón in the Cross River tradition.

IRIANABÓN BRANDÍ MASÓNGO, 1853

Irianabón Brandí Masóngo was sponsored by Uriabón Efí in the barrio of Jesús María, in 1853s.[86] Its title is Irianabón Brandi Masóngo Makrí Ubáne Ekue Efí Mbemoró. Irianabón was a prince, and this potency is considered "owner of the beach of the prince Irianabón." Brandí Masóngo is the "medicine" of Efí territory, the basil leaf used to sprinkle water upon the participants at a ceremony to purify them. In both Calabar and Uruan, *udianabong* means "successor to the Obong," that is, the person next in line to become king.[87] This is a fitting title for the offspring of *udiobong* (or Uriabón), their sponsors in Cuba.

EROBÉ EFÓ, 1853

Erobé Efó was founded in 1853 by Efóri Entoki, a lodge sponsored by Eforisún.[88] Eforisún and Efóri Entoki have disappeared, while Erobé Efó remains active. Its title, Erobé Efó ateme nkányo asawaka bongó, is a reference to the "myth of the woman who discovered the Voice."[89] The temple of Erobé Efó is in Guanabacoa, a hill town on the outskirts of Havana.

EKEREWÁ MOMÍ, 1863

The lodge Ekerewá Momí was founded by Efí Akana Bióngo in the barrio of Jesús María in 1863.[90] In Cuba, Ekerewá Momí is interpreted as, "I am a great man from Efí."[91] Ekerewá is clearly derived from Ekeng Ewa, a family name from Henshaw Town, Calabar.[92] In Èfìk, Ekerewá Momí means, "Ekerewá is here!"[93]

As told by El Chino Mokóngo, the title of this lodge is Unkerewá Momí, Síro Amako Asíro, Síro Akanabión.[94] It is asked: "Siro amako siro, siro akanabión bengue?" "Who is the mother of Akanabión?"[95] The answer is, "Siro nagurupá akanabión bengué!"[96] "Sikán gave birth to Akanabión!"

This title resonated with Èfìk speakers, because *akaní obio* means "old town," a common reference for a place one migrated from.[97] After the founding of Duke (New Town), for example, Obutong became known as Akani Obio (Old Town).[98] Another interpretation was linked to the spiritual dimension of Ékpè: "Akanabión is probably Akan Obiong, that is, he or she who has power to prevent, block, etc. Idiongo means 'sign'; idiong means 'sacrifice.'"[99] Another Abakuá term in this title, *nsiro* (family), is pronounced similarly to Nsidung, the indigenous name for Henshaw town.[100] In Calabar, "Nsidung akani obio" is a common phrase used to refer to earlier Nsidung locations.[101]

In Havana, the Ekerewá lodge is famous for the banner they carry during processions. Andrés related that, "When the *berómo* [procession] of the Ekerewá lodge leaves the Fambá temple, they carry the *suku bakarióngo*, the standard of power that represents the sacrificial leopard skin, although a goat skin is now used. This is the only lodge in Cuba to practice this tradition."[102] This Abakuá standard reminded Cross River Ékpè leaders of their Ukara cloth with leopard symbols, as well as the wild cat skins, that they use in processions from the Ékpè bush to the lodge at the installment of a new leader (Plate 7b).

USAGARÉ MUTÁNGA EFÓ, 1863

Mutánga Efó was founded by Usagaré Munankebé Efó in the barrio of Los Sitios, outside the city walls, on December 13, 1863.[103] Its title is Usagaré Mutánga Efó Akaribó Abasí. Mutánga is a hill in Usagaré territory, and Akaribó means "sacred drum." This phrase means "The fundamento that was presented to Abasí [God] at the top of Mutánga hill" (Plate 15b).[104]

Usagaré is clearly Usaghade, the place where Ékpè/M̀gbè was perfected, according to both Cuban and Cross River legend. Mutanga is singular of Batanga, a Balondo clan of southwestern Cameroon, as well as the name one of the founders of Abakuá.[105] Mutanga may be related to Mutaka, an ancient name in southwestern Cameroon.[106]

FIGURE 15. View of Efori Buma lodge from the patio, looking through the temple to the street. Photo by I. Miller.

EFÓRI BÚMA, 1865

Efóri Búma was founded by Efóri Ntoki of Havana in 1865.[107] Its title is Efóri Búma Bongó Basaróko. In Cuba *búma* means "thunder bolt"; in Èfìk and Ìbìbìò the term is *obuma*.[108] Efóri Búma would then be Efut Obuma, meaning "the thunderous Voice of Efut."

AMIABÓN, 1867

Amiabón was founded by Irianabón Brandi Masóngo in the barrio of Jesús María in 1867.[109] Their title is Amiabón Brandí Masóngo Makrí ubáne Ekue Efí Mbemoró.[110] In Èfìk, *ami* means "I am" and *amiobon* means "I am a king."

In the nineteenth century, Amiabón had another title: Amiabón Inéyo Ikomáwa Enyógoro Máwa.[111] This means "money is of the Devil." This was interpreted provocatively as, "Nyógoro mawá: a rich Èfìk king who sold many slaves to the traders of ebony."[112] Roche noted, "Ikomanawan—He who sells another person."[113] The message of this title, then, could be "in spite of Èfìk merchants selling their brothers, I remain a king in exile." The identification of Èfìk slavers is borne out by shipping records from Calabar from the eighteenth and nineteenth centuries.[114] Boastful Èfìk phrases from the nineteenth century reflect attitudes regarding their hinterland neighbors: "Èfìk can inflict any injury it pleases on the country around; Èfìk feeds on all the neighbouring tribes, and therefore has supremacy."[115] Cross River merchants were famous for their participation in the trans-Atlantic slave trade.[116] The interpretation of these Abakuá phrases indicates the codification of this historical memory in Abakuá practice.

SANGÍRIMOTO EFÓ, 1869

Usagaré Moton Bríkamo Sangírimoto was founded by Usagaré Munankebé in Jesús María in 1869.[117] Cabrera wrote, "In Sangrimoto, a place in Usagaré, where the first consecration was performed."[118]

How Abakuá Came to Matanzas

As they had done earlier in Havana, Carabalí leaders renamed their new sphere of influence. While establishing the first Matanzas lodge, they named this region Ítiá

Fondogá.[119] This phrase and its use can be interpreted through Èfìk Ékpè. The Cuban *Fondogá* may be derived from Ifondo, a village ruled by Atakpa (Duke Town), but ancestrally part of Obutong.[120] *Ítiá fondó* can be interpreted in Èfìk as *itiat ifondo*, or "Place of Ifondo." A rural farmland belonging to Atakpa, Ifondo has no Ékpè shrine, so its members go to Atakpa to "play Ékpè."[121]

Èfìk society is built upon the House system, where autonomous Houses in Calabar have rural possessions or principalities. The ruling houses, such as Atakpa (Duke Town) or Obutong (Old Town), each have their own dependencies or farm villages.[122] This system is expressed in the process of Ékpè administration. The Ékpè shrine of Atakpa, for example, controls the villages that belong to Atakpa. Therefore, Ékpè members from these villages belong to the Ékpè lodge of Atakpa.[123]

In Cuba there is no House system, but in the 1860s Matanzas was effectively a rural zone, as Havana's population was nearly ten times it size.[124] The Havana lodges that initiated neophytes from Matanzas were from Èfìk lineages. It makes sense that their leaders would have made the comparison between urban Obutong (or Atakpa) and rural Ifondo by using the phrase "Itiá Fondongá." Even in contemporary Abakuá practice, a similar relationship exists between the urban and rural areas of Matanzas Province: Abakuá members who live in rural villages (where no lodges exist) belong to lodges in Matanzas city.[125]

In the early 1860s, Abakuá lodges were founded in the port city of Matanzas and sponsored by lodges in Havana. The first Matanzas lodge, Uriabón Efí, was named after the already existing Havana lodge, indicating that the networks between the two cities used a common mythological base. Andrés told me, "In the past century Pedro 'Fresquesita' was Obonékue of the juego [lodge] Irianabón Brandí Masóngo in Havana. He was called Fresquesita because he knew a lot, and asked very difficult questions in the *redondas* [round gatherings]. To avoid a prison sentence, he escaped to Matanzas, where he acquired many friends with the passing of time. He encouraged them and in 1862, together with his *ekóbios* [brothers] of the juego Irianabón, the first juego was created in Matanzas, called Uriabón Kuna Maribá."[126] El Chino Mokóngo responded,

It is certain that a man from Havana went to Matanzas and created the first juego, because in the past a man who committed a crime left for another town to avoid the police. In this way, some left for Matanzas to take refuge, because the police then were not organized as nowadays.

The first juego in Matanzas was sponsored by Uriabón of Havana. The Uriabóns of Havana made Uriabón of Matanzas. I know this because it's documented in our manuscripts. In my opinion they were men of the same tribe in Africa who were distributed to different places in Cuba; when they met and recognized each other, those from Havana reported that they had a potency called Uriabón in memory of that territory, and they agreed to establish a potency in Matanzas.[127]

The Carabalí, reported as the largest African community in urban Matanzas, had created nine cabildos by the 1850s.[128] According to Cuban scholar Israel Moliner-Casteñeda, "the principal Carabalí cabildo in the city," founded before 1816 and called the Cabildo Carabalí Bríkamo Niño Jesús, "organized the first potency or group of Matanzas nyányigos on 24 December of 1862."[129] Havana Abakuá traveling to Matanzas organized the first potency there with the support of a Carabalí cabildo. In the process, they maintained another important function of Ékpè in West Africa, that of protecting members who traveled throughout zones that shared this culture. In West Africa, "the common possession of Ékpè lodges by different communities was politically important rather as a means by which individual rights could be transferred from one community to another, so that a person passing between communities was given some protection."[130] Continuing this practice in Cuba, Abakuá who traveled between Havana and Matanzas could demonstrate membership to receive protection away from their home.

URIABÓN EFÍ, 1862

According to Andrés, "The first juego of Matanzas was Uriabón Kuna maribá (Plate 18).[131] Uriabón was a prince of Ubáne territory; Kuna maribá is the sea. The potency's title is Uriabón Efí Makrí Ubáne Brandi Masóngo."[132]

During the plantes (gatherings) of Uriabón of Matanzas in the late twentieth century, members would display a map of mythic Calabar painted on canvas. Placed next to the altar inside the temple, scores of names on this map indicated the major Cuban potencies of the Efó, Efí, and Orú lineages, including Bakokó, Ekerewá, and Isún.[133] The map was not based upon the work of contemporary cartographers, but upon the interpretation of oral traditions inherited from Cross River ancestors. This visual representation of Abakuá sources illustrates how African-derived communities in Cuba use their ceremonial practices to document their history as a people.

EFÍ ABARAKÓ, 1862

Efí Abarakó of Matanzas was founded by Biabánga in 1862.[134] Its title, Efí Abarakó Nankábia Itiá Berómo Kánko Maribá, can be interpreted as "Efí Abarakó represents the first procession to the sea," a reference to ceremonies performed in the water.[135]

After the first potencies were born in Matanzas, in the 1870s and 1880s many Abakuá from Havana fled there as a result of police persecution. Cabrera wrote, "In the period of the persecution by [colonial authorities] Rodríguez Batista and of Trujillo Monagas, the obonekues [initiates] took refuge in Matanzas, and Biabanga began to establish new Potencies there."[136]

BETONGÓ NARÓKO, 1875

Betongó Naróko Ítiá Fondogá was founded in Matanzas in 1875 by either Biabánga Efó Piti Naróko or Uriabón. Despite conflicting versions, all agree that the first Matanzas lodges were established with the support of Havana lodges, and using the same titles, demonstrating that the foundation of the Èfìk Obutong lodge in Havana had ramifications for all subsequent Abakuá lodges.

BAKOKÓ EFÓ, 1877

Bakokó Efó was founded in Matanzas by Betongó Naróko on January 1, 1877.[137] Its title is Bakokó Efó Irondá Naróko. Andrés told me, "Abayí, the first Iyámba of Bakokó Efó Irondá, was a Basaibéke," an Abakuá master.

The Suáma and Bríkamo Languages

In nineteenth-century Matanzas, Abakuá spoke a language called Suáma, a variant of Ìgbo.[138] Never central to Abakuá practice and today only a memory, Suáma was displaced by Bríkamo Carabalí, Abakuá's standard ritual language.[139]

Andrés Flores explained why: "The founders of Uriabón obeyed the African treaty that explains how groups from Suáma territory were incorporated into the Abakuá. At the hour of performing rituals, the Suáma, as well as the Efí, would follow the traditions of the Efó, because the society has its rules. When the Abakuá of Matanzas spoke Suáma, those in Havana ignored the contents of their language. But during rites, the Efó, the Efí, and the Suáma would speak the same language.[140] On occasions the explanation of this history has brought disagreement and hatred. Notwithstanding this, when men of the two provinces gather, they conduct themselves as they should in order to avoid confrontations." El Chino Mokóngo agreed, "Suáma, Efí, and Efó are different, but all our rites follow the consecration made by the Efó. In our consecrations, Suáma cannot be spoken. Whether the lodge is from Efí or Efó, the language must be Bríkamo. According to the stories of the birth of Abakuá, the consecration was made by Efó. There is a language that says: 'Manyón bríkamo manyón usagaré.'[141] This means that Bríkamo is more important than Suáma, since it was used in Usagaré."

The term *Bríkamo* in Cuba is a reference to Usagaré, the place where Ékpè was perfected. Cuban explanations about the formation of the Abakuá language, like most whys regarding Abakuá practice, are based upon African treaties. In the scenario described, Cross River communities that shared Ékpè with others taught an initiation language as part of the culture. This process is reflected in Cross River Ékpè practice. During the early period of the trans-Atlantic slave trade, Èfìk traders of Old Calabar participated in the creation of a modern form of Ékpè, by including important elements from Usaghade (and other Cameroon sources) as well as the phrases to describe them. Èfìks taught this form of Ékpè throughout their trading empire.

From an Ìbìbìò region up the Cross River, musicologist Samuel Akpabot reported a mythic history quite similar to those of Cuba: "Tradition has it that Ékpè originally came from a place called Usangade [sic] where the Efot ethnic group live in the [peninsula near] Calabar; it was they who let the Ìbìbìò people of Uruan into the secrets of the cult."[142] Evidence for this history includes the use of non-Ìbìbìò language in Ìbìbìò Ékpè ceremony. Akpabot wrote, "Members of the Ékpè society greet one another with these code words: Cantor: Uyo bari bari nya nkpe . . . they are not Ìbìbìò words and their origin is not easily traceable. They are more like nonsense words with a special meaning to Ékpè society members."[143]

The terms are likely Ejagham or Balondo, two languages common in southwestern Cameroon, of which Usaghade forms a part.[144] From this region, Prince Mosongo agreed that Ékpè sources are "traced from Usak-Edet (Balondo land) in Cameroon. This is reinforced by the fact that most Ékpè songs are in Balondo language."[145] If Ékpè songs in Cameroon are in Balondo, in cosmopolitan Calabar they include terms from Èfìk as well as Ejagham and Efut (Balondo).[146] This issue requires further research by linguists. It is significant that West African and Caribbean interpretations of the process reinforce each other.

Conclusion

Cross River Ékpè organized Cuban creoles into ethnic-based lodges in the 1830s. Within a decade, scores of new lodges were sponsored as Abakuá expanded throughout Havana. By 1862, Havana lodges sponsored lodges in Matanzas. In both cities, Abakuá activities related to labor organization, the expressive arts, and life-cycle rites shaped the character of many barrios. In this chapter, I documented most of the lodges created from 1840 to 1877 and offered preliminary interpretations of their names and titles through Cross River languages. Abakuá leaders report that a standard Abakuá language, called Brícamo, was used by all lodges, while other Cross River languages such as Isuama (Suáma) disappeared. The reasons why are explained through African treaties that describe how the Efó of Usagaré, in the process of sharing Ékpè centuries ago with the Efi and Orú, taught them a ritual language. A similar scenario is reflected in Cross River Ékpè mythology and practice. Most of the Cuban lodges discussed in this chapter exist to the present, and they continue to function as schools for the continuation of Cross River philosophies.

4. From Creole to Carabalí

∎ ∎ ∎

Who conquered who?

—CONTEMPORARY ABAKUÁ LEADER REFERRING TO THE EXPANSION
OF AFRICAN-DERIVED SYSTEMS IN COLONIAL CUBA[1]

Something unprecedented and momentous transpired in Havana in the 1850s, when Bakokó Efó sponsored a lodge of white men. The effects reverberated throughout the Abakuá, as well as the larger society. Many twentieth-century Abakuá leaders believed that the intended and lasting result was the salvation of their brotherhood from extinction by its persecutors.[2] Several lodges were created in the 1840s and 1850s, yet in the same period, authorities unleashed waves of repression, culminating in "the year of the lash" in 1844 (as discussed in chapter 2). These pressures, combined with an "intense commercial depression" that ruined many Cubans, encouraged creole workers to seek a safety net in the Abakuá and other mutual aid societies whose activities were foundational to the Cuban worker's movement.[3] Abakuá members worked as professional "firemen, cigar workers, bricklayers, carpenters, cooks, tailors, bakers, carriage drivers, shoemakers, stevedores, etc."[4]

But economic safety was not the only consideration, since the lodge of whites included the sons of Spanish elites.[5] Their participation was an expression of creole consciousness, part of a wider movement pushing for separation from Spain.[6] Connections between Abakuá practice and political consciousness have rarely been made in the Cuban literature, perhaps being inconceivable to the dominant class.[7] This was confirmed in the 1920s by Havana police chief Roche, "According to the documents we have acquired, the nyányigos, when first created, were a cult that respected all other societies and it was believed that 'they had no politics.'"[8] To the contrary, Abakuá was useful as a political technology that defended the interests of members, making it a prestigious club within the barrios, defended at all costs by each generation of initiates.

By opening their ranks to incorporate representatives of the racial and ethnic makeup of the city long before any colonial institution, and half a century before the nation was born, Abakuá leaders made their club a model for the integration of Cuban institutions.[9] By transcending class, race, and ethnic boundaries, this act was met with resistance by orthodox Abakuá on the one hand and by colonial authorities on the other. Because Abakuá was a rare space in the colony where African descendants held leadership positions, there was considerable resistance to recognizing initiated Spaniards and their descendants as leaders of an autonomous lodge. In this process of expansion and adaptation to Cuban realities, Abakuá was moving ever further from a pretext of maintaining its African-derived ethnic-based groupings. There were no real precedents from Èfik Ékpè, even though some individual European merchants in nineteenth-century Calabar were initiated in order to give them more leverage in business dealings (as discussed in chapter 5).[10] But there is no evidence that these guests learned the inner teachings of the system.[11] The white Abakuá lodge was radically different, since its leaders were instructed in all aspects of running a lodge. In Cuba, Abakuá leaders shifted the emphasis to preserving the moral and spiritual foundations of Ékpè. They did this by selecting men of any heritage with the requisite moral conditions, as expressed in the Abakuá maxim of eligibility: "one must be a good friend, a good father, a good brother, a good husband and a good son."[12]

The initial resistance by many Abakuá to the white lodge was overcome in time, as the white brothers learned the culture and earned the respect of their brothers. As a result, in contemporary Cuba, one can see above the doors of some lodges the symbol of two hands clasping, one black and the other white. The rejection of skin-based hierarchies by the brotherhood became an important psychological tool for combating racism, for Abakuá themselves and for the larger society.

Abakuá's practice of integration contributed to an urban environment that allowed intellectuals to envision a society that transcended race. Decades later, independence leader José Martí (1853–1895), who was born in Old Havana, wrote passages such as, "The man of color has a right to be treated according to his qualities as a man"[13] and "A man is more than white, black or mulatto. A Cuban is more than mulatto, black, or white."[14] Following the visions of an integrated society expressed by Martí, and General Antonio Maceo before him, at the end of the nineteenth-century Cuban nationalists articulated their cause as one of "joint political action by armed black, mulatto, and white men fighting in a war against the colonizer."[15]

The Reformation of Petit

Nearly every phase of Abakuá's expansion was engineered by Abakuá leadership with a specific goal in mind. Evidence shows that each new social group allowed to enter Abakuá—from the first black creoles in 1836 to the first white creoles in the 1860s, to

the first Chinese creoles soon afterward—did so based upon decisions made by Abakuá leadership to strengthen the society.

In the late 1850s, a leader of the Bakokó Efó lodge began the process of organizing
a new lodge that would include the sons of society's elites. Andrés Petit held the title
of Isué of Bakokó. He was a free mulatto with strong ties to the Catholic Church, as
well as a leader of Kimbisa, a Cuban-Kongo practice he helped establish in Havana.[16]
El Chino Mokóngo narrated a legend of Petit's learning process, "Andrés Petit founded
the Kimbisa Rule in Havana after he had gone to Monte Oscuro [Dark Mountain] in
the mountains near Las Tunas, where many Africans used to live. Nobody could enter
that place, and he went there to learn Kimbisa."

Upon his return, Petit's vision of religious coexistence without racial distinctions
led him to fuse elements from all these practices. Petit consecrated the objects for a
new Abakuá lodge in 1857; after six years of selecting and organizing its first members,
he initiated them in 1863.[17] According to legend, with initiation fees paid by the whites,
Petit bought the freedom of many slaves. In the process, he and his colleagues transformed Cuban society, to the extent that this movement has been called "the Reform
of Petit," likened to the Protestant and Judaic reform movements begun in Germany.[18]
As a result, Petit has been called a "forger of the Cuban nation."[19]

El Chino Mokóngo recounted,

> White men were introduced in the Abakuá through the mediation of Andrés
> Valdés Petit Cristo de los Dolores, who was Isué of Bakokó in the nineteenth
> century.[20] Andrés Petit was an intelligent man, he was Franciscan in the Chris-
> tian church and had powers in the Mayombe religion.[21] As a missionary of St.
> Francisco de Asís, he came into contact with important personalities. When he
> established the first juego of white people, their members were powerful people;
> they were slave owners and the Abakuá were slaves. If he initiated as Abakuá a
> marquis who owned forty slaves, at least ten of them were Abakuá, and as they
> were now "brothers" of the marquis, their lives improved.[22] With the money he
> received to create the potency, he bought freedom for many slaves of different
> juegos. The Abakuá in Cuba must venerate Andrés Petit; he imposed rules of
> fraternity among men in the religion.
>
> When Andrés Petit consecrated those marquises and counts, owners of
> slaves, he made them brothers of their own slaves through the religion.[23] In his
> era, he sought equality between black and white through the religion. Petit was
> criticized in his time, but today it is understood that he made a great brother-
> hood, he magnified the Abakuá religion.

A century after its foundation, Cuban society "demonstrated a remarkable pluralism with significant participation in the economy by the non-European element," including free Africans and American Indians.[24] Having a significant free population for some

250 years, Cuban society was complex and diverse. As the plantation economy emerged in the 1800s and Cuba became a full blown slave society, social categories became more rigid, the distinction between free and not free more prominent, and "manual labor became identified with non-whites."[25] Responding to the worsening social conditions, the Abakuá movement to integrate creoles of any heritage was based upon preexisting networks of multiracial communities. Even within the new rigidity, ancient customs of intimacy bound elite whites to their black servants, for example, through the institution of "godfathering" in the church.[26] The resulting ties, as reflected in the words of an Abakuá elder, were documented by Cabrera in the 1950s: "The Efor and Èfik Ápapas in Cuba were slaves; some freed, but all were aristocrats. That is, slaves of rich and influential owners . . . and they relied on the protection of their owners.[27] Due to my age, I can tell you that the nyányigos of those times were backed by their owners, as much in Regla and Guanabacoa—where the Abakuá was born—as in Havana, . . . and that this greatly favored nyanyiguismo. As time went on, when the Abakuá had grown and the Creoles were initiated, the whites also wanted to be initiated. The white sons of Spaniards, and Spaniards. Yes sir! . . . the Spaniards really like our thing."[28]

Some of the white Abakuá neophytes were from wealthy families, and Petit knew that their influence would help defend the brotherhood from Spanish authorities. By all accounts, the Abakuá reform continued the assimilation of non-Africans into their core belief system. Initiates had to learn passages in the "Carabalí" language, learn the performance of dance and ritual actions, and make oaths to defend the brotherhood until death.

Abakuá practice offers a radically different model for how Africans grappled with transmitting ethnicity to their offspring than those on the North American mainland.[29] As Cuban creoles of all backgrounds were allowed to enter the society, they formed identities based on ritual kinship with West Africa. Abakuá was the first multiracial Cuban institution. By joining it, Cubans became simultaneously "more Cuban" as well as "Carabalí." In the twentieth century, many Abakuá of European descent shared leadership roles in the society. North American scholar Harold Courlander, after attending an Abakuá ceremony in Guanabacoa in 1941, recounted his experience: "Something bothered me a little, and I sensed it only vaguely. It later came to me with a shock that many of the spectators and *ocobíos* were white. White men singing Carabali songs. When I closed my eyes there was no way of distinguishing who was white and who black. The white *ocobíos* were as completely 'African' as the Negroes. Their singing gestures and postures, too, were African. I have a great admiration and respect for those white 'brothers' who have somehow leaped the great gap between the *guahiro* [Spanish-descended peasant] or Castilian attitude of mind and that of the direct and legitimate heirs of Africa."[30]

In the United States and many other parts of the Americas, African ethnicity was replaced by race as a prime marker of identity. Abakuá innovation created an alternative, wherein creoles of all backgrounds assumed a Calabarí ethnic identity through ritual kinship. The primary literature identifies the first white Abakuá as members of wealthy families of Regla, so their motives were not economic. Whites joined Abakuá as an anticolonial force they were sympathetic to, because in becoming Abakuá they gained access to Havana communities in profound ways related to creole solidarity and aesthetic preferences.

Okóbio Mukarará Efó, 1863

According to Cuellar-Vizcaino, a black intellectual from Havana's Club Atenas, "the initiation of white nyányigos had two objectives: liberty for slaves and liberty for Cuba."[31] Andrés Flores recounted: "This religion descended from Africans, but since whites also wanted to belong, thanks to the intuition of Andrés Petit, his lodge Bakókó Efó created the first juego of whites.[32] Named Okóbio Mukarará Efó, it was created in the Arco de Belén in 1863."[33] Okóbio Mukarará Efó means "white brothers of Efó." In Cuba, *okobio* is interpreted as "brother"; in Èfìk, as "it belongs to us" (figuratively, brother).[34] In Balondo (Efut), *mukara* is "white person."[35]

Some scholars argue that whites joined the Abakuá for protection in the struggle for Cuban independence. Cuellar-Vizcaino, who gathered information from Abakuá members, wrote:

> organizations of white nyányigos emerged, precisely in order to have
> secret support to conspire against Spain. . . . Young white patriots, residents
> of the barrios of Montserrate, Colón, Punta and San Leopoldo, gathered to
> study how to conspire without danger of being denounced, thinking prefer-
> ably in a secret organization that would function like the nyányigos, with
> extreme bravery and exemplary sanctions. They called upon the patriot
> and nyányigo Andrés Petit, Isué of the juego Bakokó, as an advisor; he told
> them: "'What for we blacks is a religion, could be the secret society you need,
> and we could give you the principal rules in order that you organize inde-
> pendently." This is how Okobio Mukarará, the first juego of white nyányigos,
> emerged.[36]

José Gómez, a leading title-holder of a lodge in the white lineage, wrote: "the hon-orable Andrés Petit, Isué of Wanamokóko Efor [Bakokó], consecrated the first group of whites, that included several young wealthy students, without religious agendas except the protection of the first principle of the religion: that men cannot be infor-mants, and they conspired against the criminal and enslaving Spanish regime. They completed their historic role: some died fighting in the trenches and others became members of the Republic of Cuba, some being Chiefs of the Matanzas District Attorney."[37] Supporting this perspective, Cabrera reported, "Petit consecrated the first juego of whites because of patriotic fervor, because the founders of this juego were young men from good families, students, who had been accused of conspiring against Spain."[38] For good reasons, then, colonial authorities regarded this movement as menacing. They understood that this process required the recognition of black leaders and African-centered philosophies by white initiates.[39]

White Lineages

Arcadio, a famous Ocha and Palo Monte diviner from Guanabacoa, said, "Here, the most legitimate white man has something of the blacks"[40] According to Andrés Flores, "Andrés Petit sold the secret of the Abakuá to the juego Mukarará Efó, and when the other juegos of the era began to censor him, in his defense he told them that he had charged the whites thirty ounces of gold and that with this money he would liberate some slaves who had been already initiated.[41] This defense was accepted by some juegos, although the great majority still did not agree, and there were conflicts. Many Africans said that this religion was African and in their country there were no whites,

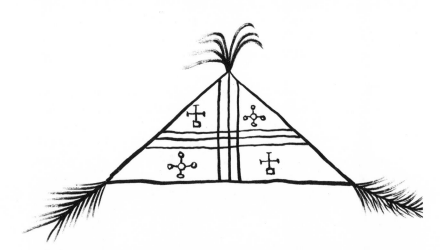

FIGURE 16. Acanarán Efor lodge seal (from Rodríguez 1881: 20). The triangle is a universal symbol of stability; its use in Abakuá designs was interpreted as representing the "Hill of Ibondá" in Usagaré, where Ékpè was perfected (Cabrera 1975: 185, 187). The triangle could also be a reference to the parallel institution of Freemasonry, of which many nineteenth-century Abakuá were members. In this context, the equality of the sides is a political representation of "liberty, equality, and fraternity." Reproduced by Leandro Soto, 2006.

PLATE 1. Andrés Flores, El barrio de Belén, 1995. Photo by Jon Kaplan. Used with permission.

PLATE 2. Abelardo Empegó, El barrio de la Victoria, Havana, 2001. Photo by David Garten, cubaphoto.com. Used with permission.

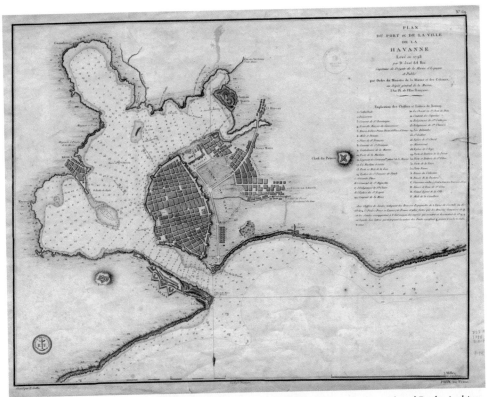

PLATE 3. Map of Old Havana (1789) indicating El Horcon, Jesús María, Old City, the Arsenal, and Regla. Archives of la Biblioteca Nacional José Martí. Used with permission.

PLATE 4. Painting of Carabalí cabildo, Three Kings' Day, nineteenth-century Havana. "Fiesta de ñáñigos" by M. Puente, 1878. From left to right, an Íreme with leaves in hand greeting a woman, and the Enkríkamo title-holder guiding his movements. Behind him a man plays a drum of the biankoméko orchestra, another plays the ekón bell with a stick, a man carries a staff symbolic of his grade, and men play the marugas (reed shakers) and the bonkó enchemiyá drum. Behind them men chant in the chorus. In the background another Íreme dances, dressed in black. Other very important objects, like the Sese Eribó mother drum, are hidden from the public to avoid capture by the police. Used with permission of El Museo de Bellas Artes, Havana.

PLATE 5. In Ékpè practice, Ukara cloths are worn exclusively by title-holders and are hung in the lodges to authorize the Voice. This Ukara cloth hangs at the front of the M̀gbè *butame* of Abijang-Ibunda, Etung L.G.A., Cross River State, 2005. Photo by I. Miller.

PLATE 6. Painting of mythic Calabar in the home of an Abakuá member in Miami, based upon the original published in Roche y Monteagudo (1925: 99). The figure at the base of the tree has the form of a manatee. The temple door on the left has the signature of Efí, based on a cross, and that on the right has the signature of Efó, based on a circle. In each, arrows point downward to signify initiation and birth. The figure in leopard skin represents the Iyámba. The river curving into the brilliant sun is a *gandó*, a symbolic design based on those ritually drawn during the foundation of Èfïk Obutong in Cuba. The river represents the community of ancestors who authorized the lodge, the sun's rays are a metaphor for contact with the divine. Photo by I. Miller, 1994.

PLATE 7. Painting of a leopard emblem in the home of an Abakuá member in Miami, based upon the original published in Roche y Monteagudo (1925: 99). The leopard mauls a man with his front paw, indicating the political power of Ékpè and Abakuá, while the background depicts the origin story in Usagaré. This painting has the signature (gandó) of the river into the sun, representing the communication with the ancestors. This is of a genre with the Èfìk Obutong *firma* (figure 7) in which the serpent leads to the skull at high noon. Photo by I. Miller, 1994.

PLATE 7B. Ékpè/M̀gbè members carry and protect the Ekpe hut, covered with Ukara cloth (with leopard symbols) and a Serval (Leptailurus serval) skin, during the traditional funerary rites of the Ikot Ansa Qua Clan (Ekonib), Calabar Municipality. This practice was reproduced in Havana, Cuba, where the Ekerewá Momí lodge was distinguished for the standard of power they carried in processions to represent the sacrificial leopard skin. Photo by I. Miller, April 2008.

PLATE 8. Painting in the home of a Moñongo Efó lodge member in Regla depicts the inside of a fambá shrine with an Eribo drum on the altar, while a masked dancer performs. Photo by I. Miller, 1990s.

PLATE 9. Mural from the Orú Bibí lodge patio wall in Guanabacoa (1990s), inspired by the original published in Roche y Monteagudo (1925). In the center is a title-holder with the Eribó drum with plumed rods; the white dove above signifies the Holy Spirit. Photo by I. Miller, 1990s.

PLATE 10. Two coconuts with plumes and an Abakuá drum. Home of an Abakuá leader, barrio de la Marina, Matanzas (1990s). This is a spiritual work that speaks to the ancestors in an Abakuá context. The plumed staffs represent Abakuá leadership. Photo by I. Miller.

PLATE 11. Emblem on front door of the Efut Assembly, Anantigha, Calabar, carved in 1995. Depicts a dugout canoe with an Ékpè masker at front. The cap on the paddler identifies an Ékpè title-holder. Medicine horns contain protective herbs. In Havana, the seal for the Betongó Naróko lodge is based upon the medicine horn (see Figures 13, 14). Photo by I. Miller, 2004.

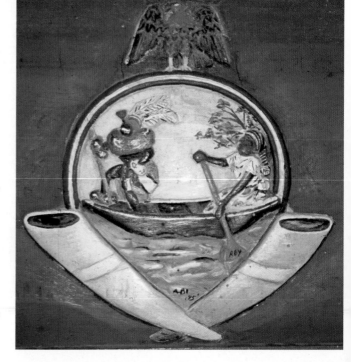

PLATE 12. The Wall of Havana, 1762. Detail of a lithograph depicting the British "Expedition against the Havannah in the year 1762." Used with permission of the Archivo Nacional de Cuba.

PLATE 13. Ékpè/Mgbè traditional funerary rites of the Ikot Ansa Qua Clan (Ekonib), Calabar Municipality. A title-holder carries the Mmọnyọ́ staff with plumes, and holds a red feather in his mouth, which signals a state of meditation. The Mmọnyọ́ staff, a symbol of supreme spiritual authority in the Calabar region, is usually carried by the Iyamba title-holder. Cuban Abakuá identified this staff as similar to that used by the Iyámba title-holder in some Cuban lineages, with a plumed stick (*munyón*) at the top. Photo by I. Miller, April 2008.

PLATE 14. Certificate from the Betongó Naróko Efó lodge, recognizing Gerardo Pazos del Cristo (El Chino Mokóngo). Note the 1843 foundation date of the lodge, the emblematic palm tree, Íreme masquerader, ritual signatures, and the titles of Iyámba and Mokóngo.

PLATE 15. Entrance to the Efí Abakuá lodge, Guanabacoa. Note foundation date of 1845, as well as emblematic ceiba tree and Íreme masquerader on the sign above the door. Photo by I. Miller, 1990s.

PLATE 15B. View from the patio of the Usagaré Mutánga Efó temple, Los Pocitos, Marianao. Above the doors to the inner sanctum reads: "Dios en el cielo y Mutanga en la tierra" (God in the sky and Mutanga on the land). ME means Mutanga Efó. At left, an Enkríkamo title-holder with drum leads the íreme at right. Photo by I. Miller, 1990s.

PLATE 16. Detail of the portal of Efí Abarakó Sisi (Abarakó Eta) temple grounds in Regla. Sculpted in iron are the signature of Mokóngo (at center), and of the lodge seal (at right). Photo by I. Miller, 1990s.

PLATE 17. The entrance to Efí Abarakó Sisi in Regla, with a sacred forest (Ekón Abasí). Photo by I. Miller, 2005.

PLATE 18. Framed image hanging in the front room of the Uriabon Efí temple in Matanzas. Ivor Miller archives, 1990s.

PLATE 19. Portrait of Andrés Petit, nineteenth-century Abakuá leader. Archives of El Chino Mokóngo, a member of a lineage founded by Petit. Photo by I. Miller, 1998.

PLATE 20. "La fuerza del mambí" (Power of the Mambí), 2001, by Jorge Delgado, Havana. This painting represents an ancestral spirit emerging as a Mambí warrior through the *prenda* or *fundamento* of Sarabanda, Palo Monte divinity of war. With a waist chain representing the seven powers, the spirit rides a leopard into battle. At left the Tata Nkisi, wrapped in leopard skin and with a serpent tail, summons the power from the *fundamento*. Photo by Daniel Swadener. Used with permission.

PLATE 21. Abakuá mask with seven points on the head, seven being the magic number of Abakuá (there were seven tribes of Efó, seven of Efí, and seven of Orú). Made by Jesús Cruz, mask-maker in Matanzas. Photo by I. Miller, 1990s.

PLATE 22. Ekerewá Ikanfioró Nankúko lodge patio entrance, with an 1873 date. Photo by I. Miller, 1990s.

PLATE 22B. View from the patio of the Munyánga Efó lodge temple, in the barrio "La cuevita" (Reparto Nuñez), San Miguel de Padrón. This is the former lodge temple. From left reads "1871 Ecue Munanga Efo 1977", with the lodge seal below. Two doorways are standard in West African Ékpè lodges. Photo by I. Miller, 1990s.

PLATE 23. Orú Abakuá temple façade with a triangular pediment of Greek classical architecture commonly used on Masonic temples. Embellished with sculpture in high relief are seven staffs (representing the seven tribes of Orú), three chain links (Efó, Efí and Orú), and a symbolic eye (International Order of Odd Fellows). The small window at left is based upon the Star of David. Above the pediment sits "El santisimo," the Holy Sacrament of Catholic tradition. By publicly displaying these symbols, this lodge proclaims the recognition and respect of Abakuá leaders for ecumenical practices. Photo by I. Miller, 1990s.

PLATE 24. Cannon in the patio of a former Èkpè lodge called Èfé Èkpè Iboku (Adak Uko Ward), Creek Town, Nigeria. The new lodge, created in 1964, also has a cannon at its front patio. The canon represents authority, being gifted by British merchants to their Creek Town partners during the regime of King Eyo Honesty, among other Èfik rulers. Photo by I. Miller, 2004.

PLATE 25. Part of the Nyóró funerary rites for an Ékpè/M̀gbè title-holder in Calabar. Isim Ékpè performers hold bows and arrows, as well as a red feather in their mouths; some have plumed rods on their heads. Behind them protrude isim (tails) representing the leopard with peacock feathers. The Isim represent the male principle in regeneration, they symbolize here the continuation of the culture at the death of its leaders, as new leaders are initiated as part of the funerary process. The bow and arrow motif is expressed in many nineteenth-century Abakuá firmas with feathers and arrows (see Figures 7, 14, 51–54, 56). Photographed in Ikot Ansa, Calabar Municipality during the traditional rites of H.R.H. Ntoe Pius Ansa Okon Effiom II. Photo by I. Miller, April 2008.

PLATE 26. Eribó drum with plumed rods and the body covered in leopard skin cloth. Made by Felipe García-Villamil, a Matanzas Abakuá member, in the Bronx, New York, 1990s. Photo by I. Miller.

PLATE 27. Ceremony in progress at the Orú Bibí lodge, Guanabacoa. Photo taken outside the temple grounds, with an observant crowd. On the patio, members participate in *la valla*, where music and dance are performed, while esoteric ceremonies proceed inside the *fambá* (temple). Photo by I. Miller, 1990s.

FIGURE 17. Abakuá Efó lodge firma (from
Rodríguez 1881: 20). Reproduced
by Leandro Soto, 2006.

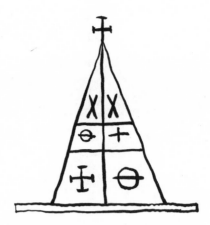

that they had been sacrificed and mistreated by the whites and therefore could not
accept them as brothers in the religion."

Conflicts stemming from the creation of the Mukarará lodge forced both Bakokó
and Mukarará to wait more than a decade before sponsoring others.[42] The many
versions detailing the emergence of this lineage reflect the complexities of documenting the past of a hermetic and persecuted institution. Whatever else happened, Abakuá leadership followed the African-based treaties in the process, with the result that

FIGURE 18. Ekório Efó the First lodge
seal (from Rodríguez 1881: 20). Reproduced by Leandro Soto, 2006.

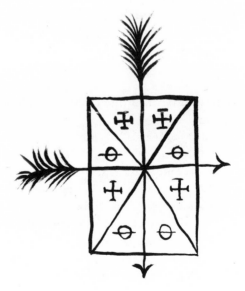

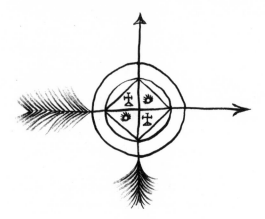

FIGURE 19. Ekório Efó the Second lodge firma (from Rodríguez 1881: 20). Reproduced by Leandro Soto, 2006.

the fundamentos of the white lodges were created equal to any other, as expressed in the maxim, Bongó Itá meaning "one voice" (as discussed in chapter 1). According to the treaties, the Mukarará lodge received the title Akanarán Efó, meaning "mother of Efó."[43] In Èfìk, *akanawán* means "old woman," a term of reverence that can be used to mean "original power or source."[44]

This lineage expanded to have a major influence. El Chino Mokóngo listed the lodges created by the 1880s, which in turn sponsored many others in the twentieth century, "Under the guidance of Andrés Petit, Enyon Bakokó founded seven juegos of whites, in this order: Okobio Mukarará Akanarán Efó, Ekório Efó Ita, Ekório Efó Taibá, Ekório Efó Third, Ebión Efó, Enseniyén Efó, and Abakuá Efó."[45] Abakuá musicians in the twentieth century recorded aspects of this history in chants that extol their ancestors who saved their brotherhood by "universalizing" it into a model for integration.[46]

Transforming the Eribo Drum on the Inside

According to El Chino Mokóngo,

> A war emerged between the white potencies and those black ones that did not accept whites as part of the religion, and this is why Andrés Petit made the Eribó of the juegos of whites different from the others.[47]
>
> To protect the whites he consecrated as Abakuá, Andrés Petit first initiated them into Kimbisa [Palo Monte, a Cuban-Kongo practice]. And he made the Eribó chalice-shaped to put *efori*, the medicines of Kimbisa, inside the drum. During this process they chanted, Obonékue morúmba entiéro sése anamó kim-

bán, "The séseribó is charged with kimbisa" [medicines]. After doing this, Petit told them: "Sese anamó kimbán," which means that "this Seseribó is charged with kimbisa."[48] Petit charged the Seseribós of his godson juegos with medicines to defend them.[49]

All Cuban juegos having a chalice-shaped Eribó belong to the lineage of Bakokó, whose Isué was Andrés Petit. This Eribó either carries an ebony cross, or a cross is placed in a cup on the altar where it is kept. In my juego we use this type of Eribó because our lineage is that of the whites. The others have *kankómo*, as those used in Africa. [In Èfìk, called èkòmò].

Petit's cultural activism integrated several strands of Cuban Abakuá, Kongo, and Catholic practice in the process of initiating the whites. But the individual strands were not confused; even today, practitioners know that the Catholic symbols (like the chalice shape) are external, that the Kimbisa was a Kongo medicine inserted into the Eribó, and that the rest is Carabalí.

The Eribó (or Seseribó) is a fundamento instrument representing the founding mother of Abakuá in Africa.[50] This legendary founder, known as Sikán, is regarded as a divine representative of Mother Nature. Through initiation by the Eribó, all men are reborn as sons of the same divine Mother, making all equals; it was therefore the correct instrument for Petit to use to integrate the society. Because this drum is seen publicly but not played, its hollow cavity was an ideal place to insert magical medicines.

Anthropologists tend to divide religion and magic by defining the former as "a matter of belief" and the later as "as set of techniques."[51] David Graeber asserted, "magic is a public performance meant to sway people . . . not a mistaken technique for swaying things."[52] If Petit "charged" the Eribó drums of the white lodges he created with Kimbisa medicines, he also let those lodges opposing his actions know about it. History has proven Petit's actions to be both effective and visionary. His Regla de Kimbisa is now practiced throughout Cuba and many parts of the Americas, Abakuá groups have become integrated, and Petit's memory is cherished by the vast majority of contemporary practitioners.[53]

The Golden Chalice: Adorning the Eribó Drum

The Mukarará (white brothers) expressed their adoration for Abakuá by adorning their ritual objects with silver and gold, in the manner of their own cultural base, the Catholic Church. This became a point of tension between the newly formed white lodges and some of their darker brethren. Andrés explained, "Since the white potencies had more economic power, they transformed the attributes of their juegos by adorning them with gold and silver, disrespecting the African tradition that the attributes were originally made of wood and shells. The juegos Abakuá Efó, Enyegueyé Efó, and Ekório Efó Táiba [all of the Bakokó and Mukarará lineage] had their staffs wrapped with gold and silver and proclaimed themselves as better than the others.[54] They thought that they were the best and forgot the phrase 'Bongó Itá.' Silver and gold have created tragedies the world over—especially when people want to mix money with religion—why then would they cover their attributes with this mineral?"

El Chino Mokóngo responded, "The men Andrés Petit consecrated in Mukarará Efó were wealthy; they adorned their Abakuá attributes according to their economic power, which means that they were different from those of the Africans. Attributes can be better or worse according to economic power, but this has no connection with the functioning of religion."[55]

Andrés pointed out that the conspicuous exhibition of wealth added to the already tense situation of early white initiates in the Abakuá. The exhibition of precious metals would only have added to the suspicion of black Abakuá that whites might attempt to create a hierarchy of wealth and race within the brotherhood.[56] Abakuá leaders were determined that all would be equal before the divine Mother, the Sése Eribó.

On the one hand, there was nothing in the liturgy to prohibit the use of precious metals. On the other, there was no liturgical reason to use them. Being that Abakuá objects are made from wood, skin, fiber, iron, and herbs and that persecution by authorities ensured that the most important aspects of the brotherhood were embodied by its leaders, and not imbued in its objects, the use of precious metals was merely an aberration. The whites, mimicking the Catholic Church tradition, adorned the chalice with silver and gold as a sign of devotion. As Andrés Petit had already made the Eribó of the whites in the form of a chalice, the association was logical.

The perspective of Andrés represents that of African descendants trying to maintain their cultural inheritance, who would be leery of those attempting to transform their traditions. A similar perspective was given by an Abakuá elder from Matanzas, while recounting his nineteenth-century visit to the temple of Erobé Efó in Havana.[57] Upon arrival he was told, "'Here we are old Carabalí Bríkamo. The same protocol is not used in all regions, because we are not all the same, and not everyone can enter our Potency [likely a reference to the white Abakuá].[58] Their Ekue was covered with the head and the whole skin of the goat, with the testicles upon it, and the three legs were adorned with Guinea shells. It was a big Ekue. On the leg corresponding to Iyamba was a dry fish and on that of Mokongo, a doll completely covered by shells and a gourd on her head. Their sacks—the íremes' costumes—had patches of authentic leopard skin."[59]

This description of an orthodox "Cross River-styled" altar is striking in contrast with those of the Mukarará lineage and its Catholic influences. Being autonomous, each lodge has its own traditions—there are many ways of doing things within the brotherhood. As the Ékpè of Calabar tell it, "We share the stream; we do not share pots." All variants of Ékpè and Abakuá share common sources, each developing their practices and philosophies in their own way.

One of the engines for creating variation is aesthetic competition, a powerful motor in the process of innovation. In his description of Ékpè practice in the Calabar region, Talbot noted a "great rivalry between the different towns as to which can produce the most gorgeous robes for 'images' [masquerades] and members. The financial state of a place can be told by a glance at one of the 'plays,' as the local resources are strained to the utmost in the hope of outdoing neighbouring towns."[60] In Cuba as in Calabar, inherited practice is embellished through the flamboyant expression of chant, dance, and masquerade, in order to "gain reputation and recruits."[61] In the 1990s, the Havana lodge Orú Abakuá was known for the well executed dances and music on their temple patio, as many of its members were performers in the Conjunto Folklórico Nacional de Cuba (National Folklore Ensemble).[62]

Three Kings' Day Processions and the Abakuá's Use of Catholic Symbols

Abakuá emerged in a Catholic society that condemned other religions. To protect the brotherhood, Andrés Petit incorporated visual symbols of the Church into Abakuá, as a way of presenting a point of agreement, despite their obvious differences and agendas. Because he used a Catholic celebration to orchestrate this maneuver, a review of a typical Three Kings' Day procession of African cabildos in nineteenth-century Havana gives an idea of the context: "At noon all proceed to the Plaza de Armas to greet the Captain General . . . As the cabildos arrived, they entered the patio of the Palace to offer their best chants and dances. The cabildo king, accompanied by his flag runner and treasurer, climbed the stairs to receive from the hands of the Captain General the half-ounce of gold with which the representative of his Catholic Majesty awarded his faithful and loved subjects.(!) They gave thanks and retired to give room for the chiefs of the other cabildos. From the balconies of the Palace were tossed cigars, cigarettes, and coins that the blacks avariciously gathered."[63]

Abelardo Empegó remarked that, "In Abakuá, the Three Kings' Day was called 'Obón paraisún,' paying tribute to the kings of the capital [obón means "king"; isún, "capital"]." In other words, Abakuá terms were used to describe Spanish colonial phenomena, just as they had been used to rename the city.

Andrés Flores continues with the legend of Petit:

One January 6, Three Kings' Day, the Bakokó Efó lodge, led by Andrés Petit, set out in a berómo [procession] formed by slaves and those curros [free blacks] who were Abakuá.[64] The procession included men from the juego Mukarará as well as many others. As they passed the Church of Jesús María, the parish priest came out and all Abakuá knelt.[65] Petit had organized this encounter with the priest beforehand. Then the priest took out the crucifix, blessed them all and gave them the crucifix. At this moment Andrés Petit said the word "Abasí," and since then, this has been the name with which the crucifix is baptized in Abakuá.[66] The crucifix was placed in front of the procession that passed along the streets of Jesús María, through the wharves of the barrio of Belén, to the Palace of the captain general of the island of Cuba, where the cardinal of Havana was waiting. When he saw the crucifix he said, "Where God is, Religion exists" [or "Wherever God is, there is religion"]. And since then the Abakuá have carried a crucifix in their processions and ceremonies.

Throughout the Cross River region, Àbàsì is a widespread term for the Supreme Being.[67] Like other Cuban adaptations of Ékpè not based upon an African treaty, the use of the crucifix and the consecration of a title-holder who carries it are controversial and not uniform. Cabrera wrote, "Abasí—Jesus of Nazareth—created by the abanekues, i.e., by the creoles, 'Havana nyányigos.'"[68] While some contemporary potencies include a title called Abasí, most do not.[69]

Until 1884, on Three Kings' Day, the captain general and other officials would receive African cabildos as they arrived to the official residence one by one, each with their king and queen as representatives.[70] As described in the late nineteenth century, Abakuá used the opportunity to organize publicly in the margins of the city:

From the first light of dawn, one heard the monotonous rhythm of those great drums throughout the city . . . The servants left the houses early in the morning; and the enslaved workers arrived from the nearby rural estates; some, by crowding into the rear wagons of the train; others, piled into the carts that transport the enormous casks of sugar, and not a few on foot. All ran to incorporate themselves into their respective *cabildos*, each generally having as a chief, the eldest of the tribe or nation to which they belong . . .

At twelve noon the entertainment arrived to its apogee. In the [intramural] streets of Mercaderes, Obispo and O'Reilly was an uninterrupted procession of *diablitos* [masquerade dancers]. All headed toward the Plaza of Arms. Soon after the crowds overwhelmed the place; with great difficulty one could move along the sides of the Government Palace. . . . in turn, the cabildos entered the patio of the Palace. . . .

In the furthest barrios and least crowded streets, the nányigos, covered in hoods of coarse cloth, did as they pleased . . . It was something to see with what ferocious enthusiasm the masses of the lowest class of the population—without a

distinction of age, sex or race—followed that ridiculous wooden plumed symbol
[the Eribó] brandished by each one of those savage groups.[71]

This description of Abakuá marching in the furthest reaches of the walled city coincides with the legend of the procession through Jesús María to the Governor's Palace.
The writer confirms the Eribó as a powerful symbol for urban men, women, and children of all colors.

The Three Kings' Day processions in Cuba are best understood in the context of
the global mission of the Catholic Empire. In medieval Andalusia, African cofradías
(brotherhoods) performed in public on saints' days. Because the mythic African king
(Balthazar) was celebrated on Epiphany or Three Kings' Day, January 6 became the
day when African cabildos throughout the Spanish empire would greet the authorities and swear their loyalty.[72] In Güines, Cuba, in the 1840s an eye-witness wrote that
each cabildo, "having elected its king and queen, paraded the streets with a flag, having
its name, and the words *viva Isabella*, with the arms of Spain, painted on it."[73] In Rio
de Janeiro, Brazil, a "brotherhood of King Balthasar" was created by Africans in the
1740s; Brazil's black brotherhoods of the rosary held important events on January 6.[74]
A description of African "nation" dances in Montevideo on Three Kings' Day in 1827
indicates a parallel tradition.[75]

In the Three Kings' Day events, we find that myth encountered myth. Ortiz
advised that the ahistorical myth of Balthazar was calculated to foster the Catholic
global mission, "The black king only begins to appear in history in fifteenth-century
images, when black Africans were reintroduced in large numbers as slaves into Christian societies, as a consequence of the discoveries and outrages of European Christians
against black Africans . . . With the three 'races' of the 'magi kings' they meant to symbolize those of the entire world: the white, yellow and African."[76]

In Cuban urban centers, January 6 became a day for African nation-groups to
perform publicly, while receiving the traditional aguinaldo (Christmas gratuity) from
the governor general and the public. Being one of the few social spaces allotted to
Africans, they intelligently worked with it.[77] In the example of Andrés Petit, he used
the Church's own method of incorporating powerful symbols to its benefit. In this case
the Church was incorporated to defend the Abakuá: "Seeking mutual understanding
between the priests and the Abakuá, Andrés Petit named the crucifix 'Abasí'. He did
this to demonstrate that the defamations of our religion were not true, because we
respect any religion in order that ours be respected too." Nowadays each juego has the
crucifix among its attributes to represent the son of God.

El Chino Mokóngo clarified, "The Abasí, the crucifix, is used by all juegos, but the
plaza Abasí is not. In the past, the Mokóngos, Iyámbas, Isunékues, or Isués [the leading Abakuá grades] had a relative or close friend, and in order to give them a title they

said, 'You are Abasí.' The god of Abakuá is the fundamento. How can God be sworn in? This is a title that does nothing. Nowadays that title is not made because they have understood that Abasí is the fundamento. In my juego there is no title of Abasí. The crucifix in the religion signifies the sacrifice which one needs to make, because Jesus Christ sacrificed himself for his religion. This is what Andrés Petit made the brothers understand when he introduced the crucifix."

These actions reflect another conscious decision of Abakuá leaders to integrate or delete elements of Catholicism according to their own needs at specific historic moments. This example illustrates the intentional fusion of distinct practices by innovators within a community-based tradition, who are often criticized by the traditionalists.[78] This point was necessary because Church purists have consistently characterized non-Christian practices as "syncretic," therefore false. The various traditions emerging from this activity evidence why traditions like Abakuá, Santería (Ocha), and Palo Mayombe cannot be contained within a ritual recipe book, because their ceremonies are never stagnant reproductions, but ritual theater and artistic enterprises that develop according to the mastery of those present.

The Significance of White Abakuá

The tensions created when Petit orchestrated the creation of white lodges were resolved over time, when various Abakuá lodges made pacts, by "crossing staffs" and working together. In the streets, white and black Abakuá greeted each other with respect. From this situation the following phrase emerged, "La amistad a un lado y el nyányigo por separado" (Friendship is one thing, and Abakuá is another).[79]

In the early twentieth century, police official Roche understood the significance of the white Abakuá for social integration. After noting the initial turbulence caused by the entry of whites into the Abakuá, Roche noted, "in 1875, on the San Joaquín Hill in Regla, the group *Abacua Efor* was baptized, with which the African society . . . humane, fraternal, charitable, and even moral—being of blacks, passed to become a true conglomerate of whites . . . whites who spoke *nyányigo*."[80]

In 1920, a self-described "Anglo-Saxon" travel writer visiting Havana ruminated upon Abakuá influence. His racism did not blind him from grasping Petit's achievement in creating a potency of white members, in which "Spanish nobles and professional men were assisting in the rites."[81] In his own experience in Richmond, Virginia, the dominant mythology of "natural laws" (racial hierarchies) formed men who "wanted black black and white white, with no transition, no blurring of the edges; this was their dream."[82] Yet in the actions of Petit, he saw an alternative, "a different humanity from any which had yet appeared outside rare individuals . . . but that vision seemed, to me, as fantastic as the sentence in Carabalíe Bricamó that gave it expression,

Enkrukoro enyenison komun bairán abasí otete ayeri bongo—We of this world are all together. The truth was, honestly at heart, that I couldn't commit myself to all, or even a quarter, of what this would have demanded. Impersonally I was able to see that, as an idea, it was superb ... but it was useless to pretend that I could begin to carry it out."[83]

The Virginian may not have understood that Cuban elites also believed in "natural laws," and that the Abakuá integration was an expression of working-class men who countered this Western ideal, not unlike the actions of John Brown and other nineteenth-century white abolitionists who put their lives on the line to struggle with blacks against the U.S. slavery regime.

Chinese Creole Abakuá

Some 142,000 male Cantonese laborers migrated to Cuba between 1847 and 1875.[84] Due to international blockades on the trans-Atlantic slave trade in this period, Chinese migration replaced the diminishing availability of Africans. Planters encouraged this labor source, fearing that another revolution like that of Haiti could occur if more Africans were brought Cuba. Although on paper the Chinese were "contracted laborers," in practice they lived and died in Cuba like slaves.[85]

As did Africans and Europeans, Chinese migrants in Cuba established secret societies based on homeland institutions.[86] These were recreated in Havana as mutual aid societies to help members find work and housing, as well as to defend them from persecution. Chinese societies were for Chinese only. Noting the Abakuá model of inclusive membership, Pérez de la Riva observed, "for the Chinese this would have been simply inconceivable."[87] As a consequence, the Chinese-derived societies did not last, and many Chinese Cubans joined Abakuá groups later in the century. For example, the lodges Efí Etété and Ubáne Sése Kóndo of Matanzas were particularly famous for their members of Chinese descent.[88] The Cuban census of 1899 found that Chinese "were most numerous in Matanzas, where they formed 2.1 percent of the population."[89] Chinatowns were created in nineteenth-century Havana, Matanzas, and Cárdenas, the same urban zones where Abakuá was established.[90] Like their initiation-brothers, Chinese Cubans joined the independence movement as Mambí warriors.

Conclusion

In an unprecedented strategy, Abakuá leaders established a lodge of whites in Havana in the 1860s. Second only in importance to the founding of Èfìk Obutong in the 1830s among black creoles, it marked a watershed moment in Abakuá's expansion. As a consequence, Abakuá lodges soon included members of African, European, and Asian descent, making them a foundational institution on the island, in the sense that they reflected the racial and ethnic makeup of the society half a century before the nation-state was inaugurated. The integration of Abakuá became an example that others followed, as intellectuals in the movement for independence envisioned a nation that was unhindered by racism.

In terms of social theory, Abakuá's integration was significant because the process demonstrates how its leadership collectively guided the course of their cultural innovations. The entrance of white men from the dominant class was a strategy to defend the brotherhood against persecution by colonial authorities. In a related example, the Catholic crucifix was used by the newly formed white lineage as a visual symbol, meant to communicate with leaders of the Catholic Church as to the assimilation of Abakuá to Catholic norms. But the further example of how Andrés Petit reshaped the Eribó drum after the Holy Chalice, in order to contain protective medicine, demonstrates the use of exterior symbols from the dominant culture merely to continue African-derived systems of interacting in a communal network.

In the United States and many other parts of the Americas, African ethnicity was replaced by race as a prime marker of identity. Abakuá created an alternative by teaching initiated creoles of all heritages the language, rites, music, and dances of their lineage, thereby assimilating them into a Calabarí ethnic identity through ritual kinship.

5. Dispersal

ABAKUÁ EXILED TO FLORIDA AND SPANISH AFRICA

■ ■ ■

Ebongó meta eee, wasangandó maribá.
The fundamento crossed the sea.
—CHANT OF AN ABAKUÁ IN A SPANISH AFRICAN PENAL COLONY

Spanish authorities faced a problem in Cuba when the creole descendants of Africans joined the nation-groups of their parents to learn African-centered identities. In 1868, as the first War of Independence began, an official memo prohibited the enrollment of creoles in the African cabildos, stating that "to the contrary these should be inclined with prudence and tact to complete extinction, following the death of the blacks born in Africa."[1] By prohibiting creoles to join the cabildos of their parents, authorities hoped to encourage their assimilation into Spanish-based identities. Instead, some joined the Abakuá, fueling the growth of its lineages in the 1870s.[2] Meanwhile, momentous events within the Spanish-American empire led to the arrest and deportation of creoles participating in the independence struggle; among them were many Abakuá leaders.

Although Abakuá leaders traveling throughout the Atlantic world maintained their identity as Abakuá, they did not found lodges outside of Cuba. This chapter examines the reasons why, and in the process underscores the exceptional characteristics of this communal practice and its maintenance by orthodox leadership.

The Eight Medical Students

On November 27, 1871, a group of medical students from the University of Havana was accused of profaning the tomb of a Spanish journalist whose inflammatory writings argued for the extermination of the Cuban population.[3] A militia of Spanish Volunteers pushed for their execution. In order to appease them, after a third trial a raffle was held among the accused forty-five students, and eight were selected for execution.

Andrés told me, "In 1871, when the eight medical students were shot in the Royal Prison at the Punta fort on Prado Avenue, the juego Okóbio Mukarará was celebrating a plante.[4] Their leaders learned about the problem and set out to rescue the corpses of the students before they were defiled. They were not successful, but their attempt marked the outstanding presence of Abakuá in that critical moment. The police retaliated against those Abakuá who protested the colonial government's murder of the medical students, and assassinated them.[5] In order to avoid problems with the government their names were not released, but among the Abakuá it is known that they were members of the juego Okóbio Mukarará Efó." In a similar version, El Chino Mokóngo told me, "When the eight students were shot, the juego Efóri Awána Mokóko, godson of the juego of Andrés Petit, was performing a plante in Belén, and when they heard the news a group set out to rescue the students. They clashed with the authorities and there were several dead from Awána Mokóko."

In the 1850s, Spain had set up a Voluntary Corps in Cuba to supplement its army.[6] The reactionary Voluntary Corps became powerful enough to remove the liberal-minded Captain General Domingo Dulce in 1869 in their attempts to suppress the independence movement.[7] Tension between the *peninsulares* (those born in Spain) and creoles ran so deep that in the 1850s a visitor wrote, "There is no doubt that Creoles and Spaniards live here as dogs and cats locked up in the same cage."[8] The situation came to a head during the first War of Independence in 1869, when a group of "Volunteers opened fire on the Louvre Cafe, a point of gathering for [white] youths supporting the independence cause."[9] The café was a meeting place for a group of well-bred white youths known as the Tacos (Dandies) of the Louvre, among whom were "journalists, literary types, musicians, painters, conspirators and participants in the War of '68."[10] The Volunteer's attack took place after Spain enacted laws demanding the execution, without judicial proceedings, of insurgency leaders and anyone collaborating with them, as well as any males fifteen years or old caught outside of their plantation or place of residence without justification.[11]

These events are part of the standard history of Cuban independence. Less known is the Abakuá participation at key moments. Several of the Tacos of the Louvre were members of the Okobio Mukarará lineage.[12] *Taco*, like *curro*, meant "well-dressed men with elegant mannerisms," a model for the Tacos being the black curros, who by then had nearly disappeared as a social group, but whose cultural imprint was still felt in Havana (and some say still is).[13]

During the Wars of Independence, persons conspiring against the monarchy were subject to exile in Spanish penal colonies in North and West Africa, and Abakuá were among them.[14] A witness, Balmaseda wrote that on January 24, 1869, General Dulce ordered the Spanish "Volunteers throughout the city, armed and in groups, since they feared an insurrection of the men of color in the barrios of the Manglar and Jesús María, who had given heroic proof of their love for the cause of liberty."[15] Those caught were exiled to Fernando Po (today Bioko), an island in the Bight of Biafra. A magistrate on Fernando Po wrote, "in 1869, when General Don Domingo Dulce, in the midst of a Cuban insurrection, ordered the deportation of some rebels to the island of Fernando Poo, many of them, blacks and mulattos, carried the rites of this [Abakuá] sect there from the distant Pearl of the Antilles [Cuba]."[16] Abakuá were part of the resistance during the Wars of Independence. Some fought actively, while others resisted culturally by establishing new lodges. Meanwhile, exiled members carried their ideas and practices to foreign lands.

Colonials felt threatened by the expansion of the Abakuá mutual aid society during the economic crisis of the late 1850s. As a living example of racial integration, Abakuá demonstrated the hollowness of Spanish claims that the War of Independence was "another Haiti" (a race war). Many scholars have identified the participation of Abakuá in anticolonial efforts. For instance, "More civil guards or Spanish soldiers died in the streets of Havana than in the rural areas, since they were under the shadow of the skilled knives of the Abakuá."[17] The day after the executions of the students in 1871, the chief of the firing squad sent a letter to his brother describing the resistance, "Some black men shot their guns at a group of artillery volunteers, killing their lieutenant and injuring another individual."[18] Abakuá narratives present these as valiant attacks by earlier members responding to the executions of the students.[19] Pablo Gutierrez-Nuñez, an Abakuá title-holder born in 1906, told me:

> The students were falsely accused by Spanish Volunteers of profaning the tomb of Castañón. The nation was shocked by this process, and the Volunteers were fanatically involved in it, pressing for the shooting of the students. They were escorted from the police station, chained and handcuffed to one another, by a large group of Volunteers shouting: "Shoot! Shoot! Long live Spain! Down with Cuba libre!" As they came along the street, a group of slaves, all of them with knives in their hands, gathered at a court named Peña Pobre. As the students were arriving to this corner, the black men rushed at the Volunteers and began to stab them fiercely. The Volunteers gave way, but the students could not escape because they were chained. This was a historical deed of the black slaves who were finally killed by the authorities. They were twenty or thirty. It is said that most of them were Abakuá.[20]

Another Abakuá title-holder recounted that those defending the students were members of the black lodge Ibiabánga, who were able to kill many Volunteers but were then overcome and pushed into the sea on the Malecón.[21] In spite of their variations, all anecdotes confirm Abakuá participation in the struggle for nationhood.

The significance of this event has diminished little with time. In the aftermath of this conflict, José Martí, known as the Apostle of Cuban Independence, wrote a "poetic ode to the student demonstrators shot on the streets of Havana on November 27, 1871, [that] . . . had an electrifying effect on Spanish public opinion."[22] A century later, a Cuban historian remembered the students as "the first martyrs of the student body in the cause for Cuban Independence."[23]

The Wars of Independence and Abakuá Exiles

As the first War of Independence raged on hundreds of miles from Havana in Oriente, rebel troops broke through the Spanish barricades in 1875, moving through the island's center toward Havana.[24] La Trocha, as the Spanish barricades were called, represented Spain's ability to keep the rebel armies contained to one side of the island. Their trespassing symbolized Spain's loss of control. The same year, authorities made Abakuá illegal when they learned of the formation of white Abakuá groups.[25] According to Roche y Monteagudo, "On 12 March 1875, by superior decree, nyányigo groups were declared illicit associations."[26] Governmental officials feared that Abakuá "identified themselves with the Mambís," the independence army of which African descendants were a majority (as discussed in chapter 6).[27]

Police captured some Abakuá members by tricking them into self-identification through spontaneous reverence of an imitation Sése Eribó drum that undercover agents carried through the streets. The Sése Eribó drum is used only during ceremony; it is a symbol of peace that represents Abakuá's most elevated values. The manipulation

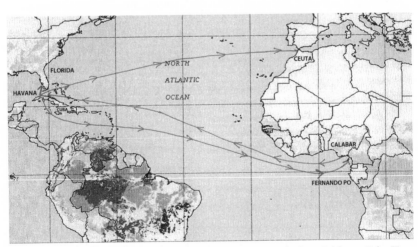

FIGURE 20. Map indicating original movement of Cross River peoples from Calabar to Cuba. Then after 1875 the movement of Abakuá members from Cuba to Florida, to Ceuta in North Africa, and to the island of Fernando Po in the Bight of Benin.

of this symbol by colonists demonstrated a deep cynicism that could have only ended in tragedy. Ortiz wrote, "Before this ardent proof of the faith in Abakuá, the police arrested the ingenuous and devoted believers and in this way discovered ... those who later were confined in Fernando Póo, Ceuta or the Chafarinas Islands and other Spanish penal colonies."[28] In the Ceuta prison in North Africa, Spanish penal official Salillas noted that Abakuá were treated as criminals, "Finally, the nyányigo was conceived of as a dangerous being, shown clearly by the mass deportations during the last period of our dominion, that accumulated a large number of nyányigos in Ceuta, in Cádiz, and in the Castle of Figueras."[29]

Cuellar-Vizcaino wrote, "When we review the colonial press and read 'shipment of Nyányigos for Ceuta or Chafarinas,' these nyányigos were mostly patriots, regardless of whether they were black or white, since the whites joined nyanyiguismo, or better said, organizations of white nyányigos emerged, precisely in order to have secret support to conspire against Spain."[30] As the arrests continued, the police records became a repository for the activities of Africans in Cuba. For example, "In 1876 the police detained 167 individuals involved in the creation of a juego in ... the old barrio of Belén."[31]

Spanish Penal Colonies

CEUTA

At the entrance to the Mediterranean Sea, Ceuta—across the Straits of Gibraltar from Spain—is one of the two "pillars of Hercules." By the 1840s Ceuta had become a penal colony for Cuban insurgents.[32] In the 1850s, the leader of a defeated *palenque* (fugitive community) in Camagüey was deported to Ceuta.[33] In 1880, some 350 blacks arrested in Santiago de Cuba were shipped to Havana to await transportation to Ceuta.[34] Into the 1890s, hundreds of Cubans of all classes and colors were deported there, including the prominent African-descended intellectual Juan Gualberto Gómez, as well as the Generals José Maceo and Guillermo Moncada.[35]

Abakuá was certainly practiced in Ceuta. In 1889 a Spanish penal authority visiting the fortress of Ceuta witnessed prisoners performing Abakuá drumming and dance:

We heard the sounds of an uproar and of drums, and the prisoner in whose cell we were in that instant lost his gloomy aspect and sat up with joy, exclaiming: 'The ñáñigos!' The prisoner was black. I understood in that instant he felt more than ever the yearning for liberty ...

Soon afterward we went to the esplanade, nearly meeting a procession of strange figures, some dressed in fantastic masquerades, playing primitive drums, chanting, gesticulating, and dancing. It was an authentic ñáñigo exhibition, as

LOS ÑAÑIGOS EN CEUTA

Lámina 4.ª

Aberiñan y Murna-Erivó.

FIGURE 21. "Los Ñáñigos en Ceuta; Aberiñan y Murua-Erivó." Cuban Íreme masker with skull image at the back of head and Moruá caller (kneeling). Photograph taken in the Ceutas penal colony of North Africa, 1889 (from Salillas 1901).

authentic as those seen on the streets of Havana, with actors from that country who had brought with them their customs and rites. . . . This was not a reference plagued with adulterations. It was a living thing.[36]

Penal authority Salillas organized a series of staged photographs of prisoners in ceremonial Abakuá regalia. These, taken in what seems to be a private home, have been regarded by some as evidence for the creation of an Abakuá lodge in Ceuta. Certainly there were many knowledgeable initiates there.[37] Salillas claimed that in addition to Cubans, Africans born and initiated in West Africa were among the prisoners in Ceuta.[38]

Historian Ruth Pike demonstrated that inmates of Spanish colonial prisons in North Africa, at least in the 1700s, enjoyed the relative freedom to practice artisan trades in the nearby towns.[39] In the 1890s, Salillas described a similar atmosphere, where prisoners created drums, costumes, and enacted ceremonies. Cuban scholars Ortiz and Cabrera refer to his publication as evidence for Abakuá ceremonies, whereas Sosa concluded that Abakuá "formed new potencies" in Spanish prisons far from Cuba.[40]

Even with the relative freedom described by Pike, there is little evidence that an Abakuá lodge was recreated in Ceuta. After examining the photographs from Salillas' essay, an Abakuá title-holder commented that, "In Ceuta a folklore troupe was made, perhaps because they were told they would never be able to leave."[41] In Figure 21, the skull symbol indicates a funerary mask, while the colorful squares of the suit indicate an initiatory function. One mask cannot perform both functions. In other words, this photograph was not evidence of ceremonial action.

Nevertheless, Cabrera seemed on target by saying, "They also 'planted' in the penal colony of Ceuta—in 1888—where the nyányigos were deported in great num-

FIGURE 22. "Los Ñáñigos en Ceuta; Mecongo y Mesongo." Two men with Abakuá staffs; that with the crescent moon represents the title of Abasónga in Èfìk territory; that with the cross represents either Iyámba or Mosóngo. The signs on their bodies are those used during a baróko (a consecration of a title-holder). Their act of crossing staffs is an Abakuá sign for unity. Photograph taken in the Ceutas penal colony of North Africa, 1889 (from Salillas 1901).

LOS ÑÁÑIGOS EN CEUTA

Lámina 1.ª

Mecongo y Mesongo.

bers."[42] After viewing the photographs titled "Los Ñáñigos en Ceuta", Abakuá leaders in Havana recounted oral narratives wherein members of two lodges performed a ceremony in Ceuta requiring the presence of the Voice.[43] This photograph depicting two men crossing staffs was regarded by these contemporary leaders as possibly documenting an initiation ceremony in Ceuta. The staff with the half moon is that of the title of Abasóngo (from an Efí lineage), while that with the cross is that of the title Iyámba or Mosóngo.[44] The chalk markings on their legs and arms are that of a baróko (ceremony) that may have been performed in Ceuta. For this purpose, an object could have been created to represent the original fundamento in Cuba. There is an important distinction, however, between the creation of a temporary ritual object to represent an already existing one and the creation of a new lodge in a foreign land.

One outcome of Cuban presence in Ceuta was that rebels from across the island could confer. Because there were practitioners of Carabalí systems from both Havana and Santiago de Cuba in Ceuta, it is possible that they learned from each other, then returned to their respective Cuban regions to enrich the local tradition. Carabalí cabildos existed in Santiago de Cuba from at least the early nineteenth century. The seven Baracoa brothers, free black creoles and Mambí warriors, were among the directors and founders of the cabildo Carabalí Isuama, which has been celebrated in popular song.[45] Fernando Baracoa, deported to Ceuta for his participation in the independence struggle, returned to Cuba.[46] It is possible that his interactions with Abakuá from Havana resulted in a cross-fertilization of ideas that influenced popular music (see next section for details).

Isla de Cuba: Ñáñigos conducidos á la cárcel de la Habana. (De un croquis sacado por nuestro corresponsal señor Gimenez, en el lugar de la ocurrencia).

FIGURE 23. "Island of Cuba: Ñáñigos led to the Havana jail. (From a sketch drawn on-site by our correspondent, Mr. Jiménez)." Published in Guerrero (1896: 617).

CHAFARINAS

The island of Chafarinas, located off the Mediterranean coast of Morocco, became a Spanish penal colony in 1847.[47] En route to Chafarinas in 1896, political prisoner Bacardí Moreau reported 200 fellow prisoners on board, detained "under the pretext of being nyányigos."[48] Among those deported to Chafarinas during the last War of Independence, Matanzas Abakuá members Carlos Estorino "Larguito" and "Niñito" Calle eventually returned home.[49]

El Chino Mokóngo told me, "In Havana, Abakuá leader Felipe 'Cara de gallo' [rooster face] was captured by the Spaniards and sent to prison in Chafarinas.[50] He chanted this march in 'the days of Spain':

Ebongó meta eee	The fundamento
Wasangandó maribá	Crossed the sea.[51]
Ebongó meta eee.	The fundamento

Felipe chanted this march while crossing the sea to prison; it means that he carried his faith. He came back from Chafarinas and died in Cuba.[52] In a certain moment of the baróko, this chant is still used in Cuba, to tell people about the faith of this man, and to stimulate the current title-holders to have a similar faith."

It is instructive to contrast this Abakuá chant of steadfast faith with another nineteenth-century song about desolation and death in Chafarinas and Fernando Po.[53] The Abakuá chant demonstrates the role of Abakuá spirituality in helping its members survive tragedy, whereas the song in the Habanera genre is completely bleak. The confidence expressed by this chant and others speaks volumes about how the Abakuá system functions to sustain Cuban communities.

Deported to Africa, Cubans from across the island interacted. The exchange of ideas between an Abakuá leader from Havana like Felipe Villavicencio (Cara de gallo) and a Carabalí cabildo leader from Santiago like Baracoa would have influenced the practice of Carabalí-derived aesthetics upon their return. This might explain the relationship between two very different instruments, one used exclusively in western Cuba the other developed in eastern Cuba, that have similar names and can produce similar sounds. In the west, an Abakuá fundamento called Bongó Ékue is revealed only to specific titled elders. In the east, the double-headed bongó drum used in popular music is held to be of Kongo derivation in the Cuban literature.[54] The received tradition is that the bongó and its name arrived in Havana with *son* music from Oriente Province by the early 1900s.[55] Fernando Ortiz thought that the secular bongó was named after the Bongó Ékue.[56] The meeting of Carabalí Cubans in Ceuta or Chafarinas may be relevant to this homonym. In early son recordings, the secular bongó was often manipulated to recreate both the roar of Abakuá's Voice as well as the speech of the bonkó enchemiyá drum also used in Abakuá ceremony (see chapter 7 for examples).[57]

FERNANDO PO, "AFRICAN CUBA"

Some forty miles south from the entrance to the Calabar river, the island of Fernando Po was another meeting place for nineteenth-century Abakuá and Ékpè.[58] By the mid-nineteenth century under Spanish jurisdiction, it was an island of slaving, plantations, and penal colonies with distinct populations, not all of them "assimilated."[59] The British used its capitol as a base to suppress the trans-Atlantic slave trade from 1827 to 1843.[60] In 1849, the British Consul for the Bight of Biafra was established on Fernando Po.[61] Having continuous contact with both Calabar and Cuba, this post had the distinction of receiving exiled Abakuá as well as Èfìk merchants who were Ékpè. By 1828, Ékpè merchant Great Duke Ephraim of Atakpa was contracted to supply British officers In Fernando Po with their daily beef. In 1861, King Eyo III of Creek Town made a diplomatic visit to the Spanish governor of Fernando Po.[62] After the Henshaw Town/Duke Town War of 1874, Èfìk trader Joseph Henshaw traveled to Fernando Po, "to relate to the British Consul his town's displeasure with the terms of settlement of the conflict."[63] In addition, some members of the Eyamba family (of Atakpa) migrated to Fernando Po in the nineteenth century from Calabar.[64]

Among the population of workers in Fernando Po who came from southeastern Nigeria and southwestern Cameroon, many were undoubtedly knowledgeable about Ékpè.[65] In contemporary Calabar, the memory of those who left for Fernando Po to find work on plantations in the nineteenth century remains strong. In the 1980s, a group of Ékpè musicians recorded this popular phrase:

Ete unyeneke ubok utom   you say you are unemployed
anana ubok utom di ika Panyá   if you are jobless let's go to Panyá.[66]

Panyá is a rendering of the name España (Spain) into some local English varieties of Nigeria and Cameroon. Here it refers to Fernando Po (Bioko) as part of the Spanish Guinea colony.[67] We have seen that Abakuá document their history and geography through chants; this example shows that in Calabar, geographic locations important to Ékpè history have been documented in song. As we shall see, some form of Ékpè and Abakuá was recreated in colonial Fernando Po.

Hundreds of Cubans were deported to Fernando Po between 1850 and 1897, many never to return.[68] In 1872 a Cuban political prisoner wrote, "An epidemic swept throughout the island. The dead are burnt in great bonfires."[69] Free to roam the island, many prisoners stayed in the port town of St. Isabel. As one wrote, "There were no iron bars, only sky, sea and desolation."[70] In their attempts to colonize the island, Spain used black Cubans and "emancipated" Africans as workers.[71] Such was the Cuban presence that cigars made from tobacco grown on Fernando Po plantations won the Amsterdam Prize in 1878. After his expeditions to Fernando Po in 1884–1886, Dr. Ossorio referred to it as "African Cuba."[72]

In 1895–1896, during the final War of Cuban Independence, nearly 600 men considered nyányigos were deported to Fernando Po.[73] Abakuá's cultural imprint in Fernando Po was not documented until the 1940s, when a Spanish colonial authority described the early-twentieth-century processions during Christmas and New Year celebrations.[74] What Moreno-Moreno called "comparsa" or "tumba" (carnival troupe) seems to be a variant of the cabildo nation-group processions of nineteenth-century Cuba:

> But the stridency reaches a climax on Christmas Eve. Then . . . the comparsa processions through the streets and the din of their various instruments reaches its maximum intensity. . . .
>
> Each of these "tumbas" or dance groups is proud of their presentation; but none has the prestige, the richness and tradition of that of the "yangüé" . . .
>
> The "yangüé" sect, also called "ekuó" (devil), this last term having a meaning different than we give it, being closer to "spirit," since with it one alludes to the visible representation of the spirit of the ancestors, to whom homage is given

on these days. The "yangüé" is not autochthonous; its place of origin is English Calabar [from where] . . . were carried [to Cuba] the slaves, their customs . . . the so-called "yan-kué", a term that there became "nyányigo," with which the institution we now write has been and is known there.[75]

Moreno-Moreno's *yangüé* is the Abakuá term *nyámpe*, itself likely derived from Nyámkpè, the name of a high grade of Ékpè Èfìk.[76] In southwestern Cameroon, Nyánkpè is the name of the Ékpè society itself.[77]

In Ékpè Èfìk tradition, the Nyámkpè ídèm masquerade appeared in the town as "an arm of government, with the authority to discipline and police."[78] Even today in Calabar, Nyámkpè is performed only among the Ékpè membership; all others leave for fear of fines or corporal punishment.[79] In 1805 in Calabar, Peter Nicholls reported, "This was grand yampia day, when no person who had not purchased yampia dare be seen out of their houses."[80] The fact that Nyámkpè was public in Fernando Po may be a sign of the deterioration of Ékpè there, if it ever did exist. Judge Moreno-Moreno continued, "Being that 'nyányigo' and 'yangüé' have the same origin, it is not surprising that similarities exist between them. Both, in effect, are secret societies, and in both, their dances participate in the same exalted and liturgical character. But in Cuba the ancestral fanaticism of the race, united with abundant libations of alcohol, exacerbates the hatred of whites, and has occasionally produced aggressions against them; in Fernando Poo, to the contrary, due to the pure influences of the primitive sect, furnished by the neighboring Calabar, it has conserved more of its exclusive character as an association geared to revering the memory of the ancestors and with a marked religiosity."[81]

Given the presence of white Abakuá members in Cuba, Moreno-Moreno's reference to "hatred of whites" seems to be a euphemism expressing frustration for the anticolonial attitude of Abakuá. Unable to control their subjects, Spanish authorities resorted to interpreting their rebellion as "racial hatred." Abakuá of any color would therefore become "black" in their descriptions. Moreno-Moreno continued:

> The Isabelenian "yangüé" has experienced a great evolution. There was a time when, to join this sect, the neophyte was subjected to tests of bravery, the act of wearing the multicolored and fantastic clothes of the ceremonies being reserved for them; women were prohibited, and those who divulged the secret were punished in diverse ways. At the same time, the prestige of the sect among the indigenous population was such that, while traversing the streets in masquerade, traffic would stop, and the other comparsas would greet them with great respect.
>
> For a long time, entry remained limited to a prerogative of the powerful and most distinguished indigenous of Santa Isabel, and today one could say that even these do not belong today, having degenerated to the extreme of giving the

generic denomination of "yangüés" to any of the several comparsas that fill the air with the stridency of their music.[82]

This description of interactions between masquerades and the indigenous population indicates that if this tradition had Cuban elements, these were incorporated with those of Calabar to create a local variant.[83] According to the author's description, the processions had either lost their authority and become merely entertainment, or Yangüe had transformed from a type of nation-group procession into a generic name for local carnival troupes. Either way, this is no evidence that Abakuá lodges were established on Fernando Po. This renewed contact of Abakuá members with people of the Biafran region, however, presents the possibility that Abakuá could have learned first-hand about the Ékpè society and language, then reinfused Cuban practice with this information upon their return.

Migration to Key West

With the first Cuban War of Independence in 1868, many Cuban cigar workers migrated to Florida, forming large exile communities.[84] Their contributions to the independence efforts were memorialized when a Havana barrio was named Cayo Hueso after the Florida Key where many lived.[85]

The earliest known reference to Abakuá in the United States comes from Raimundo Cabrera, the father of the great Cuban folklorist Lydia Cabrera. In 1892 he described the arrival of his passenger ship from Havana to Key West, "Just as the boat came close to the shore, one saw the multitude that filled the wharf and heard the special whistles that came from it, to which were answered others of the same modulation from the passengers who occupied the prow. I realized the meaning of these whistles! They are tobacco rollers from Havana who recognized and greeted one another. This greeting of *nyányigo* origin was imported to the yankee city."[86]

Abakuá greetings normally consist of coded handshakes and phrases, but on special occasions whistles were used for communication.[87] One Cuban remembered his grandfather's explanation that African-born Abakuá "spoke through their flute with the íreme, as he did with his neighbors in the hills with a [conch] shell. Shells, flutes, and drums spoke language."[88] This Abakuá practice is comparable to those in West African regions with tonal languages, where instruments of all kinds (drums, flutes, and iron) are commonly used to convey messages. In southeastern Nigeria, for example, Robert Armstrong observed an "elaborate secret language" expressed on "drums, flutes, and horns."[89]

Since the late nineteenth century, Abakuá presence in Florida has been largely undocumented. Most studies of Cuban migration to Florida were structured using

Anglophone concepts of race.[90] Although important for other reasons, they are not adequate to describe the multiracial Abakuá. With the foundation of Ybor City, the cigar-making company town just outside Tampa in 1886, many Havana cigar workers (among them Abakuá) migrated there, making it the largest Cuban settlement in the United States.[91]

From a lineage of white Abakuá descended from Andrés Petit's lodge Bakokó Efó, El Chino Mokóngo was a third-generation Abakuá in Havana. He told me about his family members who migrated to Key West and Tampa in the late nineteenth century:

> My grandfather Juan Pazos [1864–1951] was born in the barrio of Jesús María, the son of a Spaniard. He was obonékue of the juego Itá Baróko Efó [The First Baróko of Efó].
>
> Many Cuban tobacco rollers went to Tampa, Florida, and stayed there, including my grandfather's brother, who was a member of the juego Ekoria Efó.[92] They left during the persecution of the Abakuá by the Spaniards and later by the Cuban government. Many left in schooners to Florida, because those captured were sent to Fernando Po, Ceuta, and Chafarinas. I knew several elder men of color sent there who told me their stories. They were very tough prisons, and many Abakuá who were deported there died. My grandfather's brother lived in Tampa, and he never told me that they "planted" in Florida. No Abakuá elder ever told me that they "planted" there.[93]

El Chino Mokóngo, like many other Abakuá leaders, reported that even though Abakuá title-holders lived in Florida, they conducted no ceremonies, because this would have required establishing a lodge there with the sponsorship of a Cuban lodge. A series of publications, however, have erroneously claimed Abakuá ceremonies were held in Florida. For example, Cuban scholar Enrique Sosa argued for the "certainty of the existence of nyányigos" (i.e., Abakuá lodges) in Key West in the late nineteenth century among exiled tobacco workers.[94] Sosa uncritically cited earlier publications and was in turn cited by later scholars, forming a chain of errors.[95] Sosa's primary source was Stetson Kennedy, a Works Progress Administration writer who in 1940 documented Abakuá influence in Florida's past. Kennedy wrote, "A Nanigo group was organized in Key West, and enjoyed its greatest popularity between 1880 and 1890. They gave street dances from time to time, and dance-parties on New Year's. As it had no rival, the Nanigo group in Key West was rightly considered to be a harmless fraternal organization. . . . In 1923 the last Nanigo street dance to be held in Key West was performed 'for fun' by Cuban young people, attired in make-shift costumes."[96]

Not knowing the Cuban context, Kennedy did not realize that he was describing a carnival group. El Chino Mokóngo responded to Kennedy's depiction, "It is not

FIGURE 24. "El Ñáñigo," 1870s, by Victor Patricio Landaluze (1881).

possible even that they left in 'berómo' a procession, without 'planting' [evoking the Voice]. It is possible that *comparsas* paraded around with representations of Abakuá with similar costumes and rhythms, but this is not an Abakuá ceremony."[97] An Abakuá ritual procession must be authorized by the Voice, and that existed only in Cuba. Nevertheless, Kennedy cited a WPA survey with "fragmentary mention of Nanigo in Tampa: 'Nanigo rites were recently enacted in West Tampa. To the accompaniment of a *bongó*, a *diablo* appeared in a dress suit of black and white, adorned with feather. A savage-looking knife dangled from one side of his belt, while on the other side hung a live rooster, fastened by the legs. His lively contortions followed the primitive rhythms of the *bongó*.'"[98] This description is actually humorous to those in the culture. The idea of a black and white Íreme, with rooster hanging from the belt, is obviously patterned after the famous Landaluze lithograph from Havana in the 1870s. Landaluze's imprint is clear, since in ritual practice a rooster is not hung from the waist, but held in the hand (see Figure 24).

I spoke with Kennedy, who admitted his ignorance of Spanish at the time of research and that he had no proof of Abakuá's existence in Key West.[99] Instead, he gathered recollections among exiled Cubans about the society as it existed in Cuba. The following from an official Florida guide is clearly based upon Kennedy's work, "When the cigar workers migrated from Cuba to Key West and later to Tampa, societies of 'notorious Nanigoes,' as they were branded by Latin opposition papers, were organized in these two cities. The Nanigo in Key West eventually became a social society that staged a Christmas street dance. . . . The last of the street dances was held in 1923."[100] Part of Kennedy's evidence for Abakuá in Key West was the painted wood sculpture "Manungo's Diablito Dancers" by Mario Sanchez, depicting his memories of the "nyányigo street dance" in 1919. In it, one sees a street jam session with a bongo player, a trumpet player, and full body masquerades in the style of those from Loisa Aldea, Puerto Rico, not those of Cuban Íremes.[101]

Louis A. Pérez Jr., author of several histories of Cubans in the United States, reported to me, "I have not come across any Abakuá references in Tampa during the late nineteenth and early twentieth centuries."[102] Anthropologist Susan Greenbaum, author of *More Than Black: Afro-Cubans in Tampa*, a study involving the mutual aid and Cuban independence group the Club Martí-Maceo in Tampa, reported that during her fifteen years of research, "Nanigos were the subject of hushed and infrequent references. There could have been an active Abakuá underground here, but I never heard of it."[103]

Unauthorized Immigration: An Abakuá Fundamento in the United States

In 1994, at the request of Andrés Flores, I visited in Miami his friend Luis "el Pelón," an Ifá diviner as well as Abakuá title-holder. Regarding Abakuá activities in Miami, Luis told me, "Here in Miami there are *ceiba* [kapok] and palm trees, but since the most important thing—the fundamento—is in Cuba, no Abakuá group can be consecrated here. I have met with all the Abakuá who live here and we have had celebrations, but not consecrations, with my set of *biankomó* [drum ensemble for music]."[104]

Unlike the fundamentos of other Cuban religions, those of Abakuá are thought to have never left the island. In 1998, however, the birth of the first Abakuá lodge in the United States was announced by its founders in Miami, who sent letters to various Abakuá title-holders in Cuba pronouncing their existence.[105] They called their lodge Efík Ebúton after the first Abakuá lodge in Cuba. Abakuá leaders I spoke with in Cuba regarding this matter unanimously considered it a profanation: The birth of an Abakuá group without a sponsor is not valid.

El Chino Mokóngo, who was also a *babaláwo* (Lukumí Ifá diviner) reflected, "It is not possible that a juego was created in Miami, because no Cuban there has the authority to perform the required transmissions. Whoever would create a juego in Miami would have to come to Cuba and carry a fundamento from there. It is not the same with the Yorùbá religion. Because I, Gerardo Pazos, Mokóngo of Kamaroró, do not know of anyone in Miami or anywhere in the United States with sufficient knowledge to create a tierra [land]."

According to Cuban lore, Abakuá was created by knowledgeable Cross River Ékpè leaders who had the authority to establish lodges in Cuba. Because Ékpè leaders could not return home, they moved forward and created. But Abakuá outside of Cuba can return, and according to the society's rules they must be authorized by Cuban lodges to establish a new lodge, wherever it is. El Chino Mokóngo continued, "Those Abakuá who have migrated to the United States do not have the knowledge to create a potency there, because this process is very profound. In addition, when a potency is created, one must pay the *derecho* fee of one rooster to all the existing potencies in order to be recognized by them. If a juego is born in Havana, it must pay this fee to the other juegos in Havana. If it is born in Matanzas, then to the others in Matanzas. The juego they tried to create in Miami had no sponsor. It cannot exist."

IFÁ IN CUBAN MIAMI

To appreciate the containment of Abakuá to a section of western Cuba, in spite of the global travels of its members and even the desire of some to establish lodges abroad, it is instructive to note a parallel movement in the Yorùbá-derived Cuban practice of Ifá. Like Abakuá, Ifá is thought to have been established in Cuba in the first half of the nineteenth century.[106] Before the 1959 Revolution, the estimated 200 babaláwos in Cuba all knew each other.[107] By the 1990s, leading Cuban babaláwos gave me estimates of 10,000 to describe their numbers, and neophytes were arriving from throughout the Americas, Europe, and elsewhere to receive Ifá consecrations and travel home with them.

In 1978 highly specialized Ifá ceremonies performed in Miami intended to reproduce there the foundation of Ifá in Cuba some 150 years earlier.[108] The ceremonies were led by Yẹmí Elébùìbọn, the Àwíṣẹ of Ọṣogbo, a leading Nigerian babaláwo, who traveled to Miami for the occasion.[109] Two of the participating Cuban babaláwos were also Abakuá leaders, Luis Fernández Pelón and José-Miguel Gómez, both of whom are cited in this study.[110] The point is that Ifá consecrations can be led by one babaláwo, while Abakuá consecrations involve scores of men acting in concert, in addition to the required tributes paid to the existing lodges in Cuba.

White Men Can't "Hear"

All the issues of protocol regarding the dissemination of Ékpè and Abakuá throughout the Atlantic world are applicable to another facet of Ékpè history: those nineteenth-century British merchants and early European colonists who bought Ékpè titles in Calabar and southwestern Cameroon. Contrary to the evidence, one scholar speculated that Europeans brought Ékpè to England before the Èfìk Obutong lodge was established in Cuba.

In the 1820s, presumably received from the Duke Town lodge, a "Captain Burrell of the ship *Haywood*, of Liverpool, held the rank of Yampai, which is of considerable importance, and found it exceedingly to his advantage, as it enabled him to recover all debts due to him by the natives."[111] Using this example, Palmié stated that, "*ekpe* reached Liverpool before it ever reached Cuba."[112] If Ékpè could reach Liverpool through Burrell by his being an initiate, then Ékpè had reached there long before, through the sons of Èfìk elites who were educated in England from the 1700s onward, who would have been knowledgeable members.[113] In Burrell's case, there is no indication that he knew details about the cultural practice. The grade he received, Yampai, an Anglicization of Nyámkpè, was indeed important.[114] Each Ékpè grade, however, has several tiers and Burrell would have occupied an entry-level tier.[115] Even so, in order to harness ones' grade, one needs a great deal of cultural information to communicate with other members. Did Burrell know any Nsìbìdì (the gestural language of Ékpè)? Did he know how to chant Ékpè? There's no evidence.

In another case, a document from Duke Town in 1874 showed that a Liverpool agent named Hartye purchased six Ékpè titles. This document was clear that, "Mr. Hartye's initiation did not qualify him to be a chief officer of Ékpè. He was only to enjoy the rights, claims and immunities of the Ékpè grades into which he had been initiated."[116] Every indication is that merchants of the time joined Ékpè to enhance their business dealing in Calabar, but were not taught, nor authorized, to become leaders in its cultural manifestations.[117] In his diary in 1841, an English captain with palm oil interests, "recorded the purchase of two 'Egbo' [Ékpè] grades, which facilitated the collection of outstanding debts before he set sail."[118] There are many similar examples, but Talbot sums it up by describing, in reference to trade in the nineteenth century, how creditors seeking to recover debts brought cases before an Ékpè council in the debtor's town: "If the claim was thought justified, the Club drum would be beaten through the streets, and the defaulter ordered to pay. He was also bound to provide a 'dash' for the Egbo [Ékpè] society."[119]

These internal mechanics of Ékpè have been maintained to the present. In 2001 during meetings with members of the Èfìk National Association in the United States, I was told of current attempts by Èfìk Ékpè to establish a lodge in the Western Hemisphere. Due to the complex protocol, it had not yet happened. If not among Èfìks themselves, then how could an individual Brit bring Ékpè across the water? According to a contemporary Cross River historian, who is an Ékpè member, "the art of mboko sound which Europeans referred to as 'blowing Ékpè' are kept secret and only known to very disciplined Ékpè members of certain titles."[120] The truth of this statement is reflected by its parallels in Cuban Abakuá practice. Like so many dynamics in the Ékpè –Abakuá continuum, the ideas of one region are reflected in the narratives and practice of the other. From Cuba, an Abakuá phrase seems to confirm what the West African literature reports about the nineteenth-century British merchants: "Èfìk Butón mukarará mango: in Èfìkland the mukarará—the whites—did not hear Ékpè."[121] In Nigerian parlance, to say one "cannot hear" a thing means he "cannot understand" it.

Confusion over the Term *Ñáñigo* (*Nyányigo*)

Because colonial authorities associated *Nyányigos* with crime and other antisocial behavior, Abakuá members reject this term. Throughout the literature, the term

FIGURE 25. A Kongo cabildo during a burial rite in Matanzas, 1899 or 1900. Caption reads, "Strange burial rites of the secret negro society known as ñañigos." However, the Yuka drums, clothing, cabildo flag, and hats indicate that this is a Kongo cabildo, whose members were Mambí soldiers. The sword is a symbol of power and authority. The elder female sitting at right of the drums is the cabildo queen; sewn into her dark sash is the phrase, ". . . Presidenta de la Sociedad Africana." Ivor Miller archives.

nyányigo has been used to refer to Abakuá, but also indiscriminately in reference to members other African-derived traditions, and even more generally to working-class black males. In nineteenth-century Cuban literature, issues related to race and culture were collapsed, so that terms such as *black, African, Abakuá, Lukumí,* and *witchcraft* were confused and interchangeable. Instead of being recognized as representatives of distinct traditions, in the literature a diviner of Palo Monte traditions might be called a *nyányigo* or an Abakuá called a *santero*.[122]

American war correspondent Grover Flint, who moved with the Mambí army across Cuba for four months in 1896, observed that the "Pro-Spanish guerrilleros often referred to Afro-Cuban insurgents as nyányigos, an indication that they perceived them as criminals empowered with secret African magic."[123] In the 1890s, Flint wrote, "Nányigo: a term of reproach. . . . originally applied to negroes addicted to mysterious voodoo practices."[124] In one scene, Flint described a Spanish captain accosting and then murdering a Cuban peasant: "'Thou art a Mambi.' . . . Calling him a traitor, a shameless one and a nanyigo, they dragged him from his house."[125] This term as used here is merely derogatory (not ethnically specific), because to outsiders all African-derived practices were confused.[126] Ortiz concurred, "Many absurdities and falsehoods have been published concerning nyányiguismo, even by Cuban writers of certain reputation, and generally, in Cuba, they are confused with very distinct religious cults and practices of sorcery."[127]

Twentieth-century writers continued using the term *nyányigo* to signify "working-class black culture." A famous example being the verse "Ñáñigo al cielo" (Nyányigo to heaven) by Puerto Rican poet Luis Palés Matos (1898–1959). There is no Abakuá society in Puerto Rico; the poet used this Cuban term to convey the idea of "an ordinary black man in heaven."[128]

The sources of the term *nyányigo* are obscure, and its usage has transformed in time.[129] Upon hearing this Cuban term, new possibilities were presented by Èkpè leaders in Calabar. One Èkpè elder and mask-maker identified *nyanyá* as the term for the raffia chest piece representing the lion's mane on Èkpè masquerades.[130] Another Èkpè master reported that Nyanyaku was an early Èfìk mask that was integrated into modern Èkpè.[131] These Cross River terms resemble those in Cuba; they also have similar meanings as used by members. In Cuba, *nyanya* and variants of this term mean "Íreme, or masquerader."[132]

Abakuá used the term *Nyányigo* in the nineteenth century. An 1882 document signed by leaders of the first white lodge is titled, "Instructions and regulations for the society of white nyányigos."[133] In the same period, Trujillo wrote that *nyányigo* was "the name adopted by the black creoles after they were constituted in a society, because its true name in Carabalí is *nyanguitua*."[134] The veracity of this usage is confirmed by contemporary Abakuá, who privately continue to refer to their rites as *nyangaíto*.[135]

Because nyányigos were declared illicit in 1875, Abakuá leadership came to reject this term publicly because of its pejorative implications in the wider society.[136] To my knowledge, the term *Abakuá* was rarely, if ever, used in the early literature on the brotherhood, becoming popularized only with the 1958 publication of Lydia Cabrera's *La Sociedad Secreta Abakuá*. Abakuá themselves, however, are documented as using the term as early as 1928 in public. According to Ortiz, "Around 1928, in a theater of the city of Guanabacoa, a drama was presented, entitled *Apapá Efí o por culpa de un Abakuá* [Apapá Efí or because of an Abakuá]. It was a brief episode or scenic interlude, composed and represented by real nyányigos."[137] Based on this evidence, we can infer that sometime between the 1880s and the 1920s, Abakuá discontinued the public use of the term *nyányigo* and its variants.

Abakuá Collective Practice

From the 1870s to the present, Cuban Abakuá members exiting Cuba have regrouped in foreign lands. Some reports suggest that Abakuá created lodges in the Cuban Diaspora, including Florida and the Spanish penal colonies in northwestern Africa, as well as Fernando Po. To the contrary, I found little evidence for this. The collective and hierarchical nature of Cross River Èkpè was firmly reproduced in Cuban Abakuá. Based on their protocols, a lodge cannot be established outside the Havana-Matanzas jurisdiction without the consent of every existing lodge, a complicated and expensive procedure. Èkpè Èfik express their collective behavior with the phrase "inuá tiet" (one voice). The transfer of Èkpè to Cuba was achieved through the collective action of authorized title-holders and their supporters. Even today, Abakuá is the only African-derived institution in Cuba to maintain a collective identity and decision-making process affecting the entire membership. Èkpè transmission to Cuba linked the new variant, Abakuá, to specific port zones of northwestern Cuba, in spite of attempts to create groups in other cities.[138]

The collective process involved in the creation of the first Abakuá group is repeated throughout the Cuban literature.[139] In 1882, police authority Trujillo wrote about the procedure of his day, "The contemporary nyányigos create their lodges in the following manner: Twenty-five men gather and name godfather from one of the already consti-tuted lodges in any neighborhood. The sponsors accept, and impose a contribution of more than 200 pesos to the godchildren, used to pay the work of the sponsors . . . To be recognized by the other lodges, it is also necessary to pay a contribution delivered to the chief of each, consisting of a rooster. Some days before the initiation, invitations are sent to the chiefs of all lodges."[140] The payment of fees, the support of a sponsoring lodge, and the presence of representatives from other lodges are basic to the investi-ture of Abakuá authority. Trujillo also described something of the hierarchy within the lodges, "In order to create a lodge, it is necessary . . . to complete the twenty-five titles that constitute the Potency by forming a permanent board of directors, each one with a particular name that designates the charge they fulfill in the council. . . . To say that a lodge needs these twenty-five title-holders to be founded does not mean that once constituted, all those brothers who want to, without limit, can join, but that, those not among the twenty-five title-holders have the simple title of Abanicués [abanékpe], the lodge being governed by the four chiefs who direct the ceremonies."[141] Protocol, there-fore, requires a number of specific title-holders and a sponsoring lodge to create a new entity.

Oral tradition in both Cuba and the Cross River region indicate that a settlement known as Usagaré or Usaghade (now officially called Isangele), in the estuary region near the present Cameroon-Nigeria border, was an important center for the perfection of Èkpè.[142] From there, title-holders shared the Voice with the lodges of other settle-ments.[143] In the Cross River, "Going by Ekpe principle, the rites of purchase of Ekpe by a community is performed firstly at the Itiat Ekpe [Ekpe stone] of the seller before subsequent planting of a new Itiat Ekpe at the domain of the purchaser."[144] A similar process is used in Cuba, when a new lodge is birthed from the lodge of the sponsors. In an epic form, contemporary Abakuá detail the process in ancient Usagaré, through the performance of chants and ritual actions.

These insights into Abakuá/Ékpè practice indicate why Cuban scholar Sosa was on shaky ground when arguing for "the creation of a 'tierra' in prison by fourteen imprisoned Obonékues in 1874," or "that in 1888 was founded in the Spanish prison of Ceuta, at the north of the African continent, an 'Abakuá tierra' by Cuban nányigos."[145] As important as they are for the society, obonékues (abanékpe, first-level initiates) are without authority to direct ceremonies.

Conclusion

From the first War of Independence against Spain onward, colonial authorities made Abakuá illegal. As such and misunderstood by outsiders, Abakuá members became scapegoats, accused of committing heinous acts. Captured Abakuá members were exiled to penal colonies throughout Spain's African empire, in Ceuta, Chafarinas, and Fernando Po. Others escaped to Florida, where large communities of Havana tobacco workers flourished in the late nineteenth century. Abakuá leaders who traveled throughout the Atlantic world regrouped and maintained their identity as Abakuá, but they did not found lodges outside of Cuba. Following the model of Cross River Ekpe, Abakuá have a well-defined protocol for the creation of new lodges, in which ritual authority is passed from a sponsor to a new group. Unlike the fundamentos of other Cuban traditions, those of Abakuá have not left the Havana-Matanzas region, despite some documented attempts. Nineteenth-century Abakuá were known as *nyányigos*, after the Èfìk Ekpe term *Nyanyaku*, but since outsiders used it depreciatively as an umbrella term for all forms of black culture, including antisocial behavior, Abakuá now reject the term.

6. Disintegration of the Spanish Empire

...

Liberty is won with the edge of the machete; it is not asked for.
—ANTONIO MACEO[1]

By 1882, when some eighty-three Abakuá lodges existed in Havana,[2] Cuba's governor general planned to destroy the African cabildos because of their links to the Abakuá: "The African cabildos . . . must not continue, and must not be allowed to perpetuate themselves; on the contrary, civilization and the well-being of all Cubans advise that they be stopped with the last African. . . . These cabildos of Africans have given birth here to some black associations to which there already belong some whites of the lowest class who themselves are called the societies Juegos de Nyányigos. They must be prohibited as illegal societies."[3]

Hoping to encourage the population's loyalty to "mother Spain," colonial authorities thought that destroying the cabildos would erase the historical memory of Africa.[4] To increase the probability, nearly 100,000 Spaniards migrated to Cuba between 1882 and 1892, in an official effort to visually whiten as well as culturally influence its population.[5] With the end of slavery imminent, in 1884 a ban was placed upon new cabildos de nación and existing ones were permanently eliminated from processions on January 6, Three Kings' Day.[6] Emancipation became official in Cuba in 1886, and by the following year no worker was legally enslaved.

The existing cabildos had to annually renew their licenses and identify their groups with a Catholic saint and its local church.[7] The former Cabildo Carabalí Acocuá became a mutual aid society known as "San Diego de Alcalá," and the Cabildo de Congos Reales (Royal Kongos) became a mutual aid society dedicated to "el Santo Cristo del Buen Viaje" (the same patron evoked by Andrés Petit for the Kimbisa practice with which he defended his Abakuá godchildren).[8] The majority of African cabildos were unable to survive this process. When a cabildo was terminated, "its wealth became property of the Church."[9] Ortiz wrote, "In contradiction to their announcements, governmental agencies made war on the cabildos . . . the authorities of the time believed that the cabildos and the secret nyányigo societies had dangerous relations among themselves, and that their organizations were identical in their aims, if not their forms, and all were given the same treatment."[10]

The demise of the cabildos had grave consequences because, like Abakuá, their mutual aid services protected members against poverty and illness.[11] Initiated in 1897, one member articulated how Abakuá continued the mutual aid practices of the cabildos, "If one has a peso in one's pocket and one's initiation brother has nothing, the duty is to share with him and be content. Give, even if one isn't happy about it! What the conscience demands is not always what one wants. The lodges have funds for bad times; sickness, accidents, and funerals, as was the custom before in the cabildos of any nation."[12]

Despite these benefits, many cabildos were coerced to reject Abakuá publicly. For example, the Cabildo Arará Magino, legalized in 1890, required members to be "*honorable* and have never been a member of the *extinguished* association of nyányigos."[13] Such pronouncements concealed links that were maintained through family and community, among the cabildos de nación, the Abakuá, and the newer societies for instruction and recreation (formed from 1878 onward).[14] These groups were commonly thought to represent distinct populations with conflicting aims: the cabildos of Africans, who sought to perpetuate homeland customs; the Abakuá creoles, who universalized their practice to include Cubans of all heritages in an underground mutual aid system; and the societies for instruction led by integrationist black creole elites, who rejected an African cultural identity, seeking instead participation in the institutions of dominant society through formal education.

Many Cuban families in fact had relatives in each of these groups. A prominent example was that of Brindis de Salas, whose family included Calabarí Africans, Abakuá members, and elite performers of European classical music. Havana-born violinist Claudio José Domingo Brindis de Salas (1852–1911) appears to have been the grandson of a Carabalí woman.[15] Music historian Alejo Carpentier described Brindis as, "the most extraordinary of the black musicians of the nineteenth century . . . a singular person whose case is without precedents in the musical history of the continent."[16] Trained in the Conservatory of Paris, he came to be extolled by the media of his day as "the black Paganini" or "King of the Octaves."[17] He spoke six or seven languages, played concerts with a Stradivarius, and taught violin to the German monarchy. Considered the first black musician to triumph in modern Europe, he married into an aristocratic German family, was honored as a Caballero of the French Legion of Honor, and received the titles of Caballero de Brindis and Barón de Salas from the emperor of Germany.[18] His nephew was an Abakuá leader in the late nineteenth and early twentieth centuries. Andrés Flores told me, "Román Brindis de Salas was the Ekuenyón in the juego Bakókó Efó.[19] He gained the affection of the men in his potency because he was upright and was always seeking to learn about the religion from the Africans. He learned all the issues of the religion and he carried them out to the letter." Román Brindis endured imprisonment in Ceuta during the Wars of Independence and returned to Cuba.[20] If the experiences and aspirations of many Cuban families ran this spectrum, these dynamics were rarely expressed in public.

To the contrary, in the political sphere some prominent black Cuban intellectuals encouraged cultural assimilation to European models, while portraying the Abakuá as "centers of immorality," of "malign ignorance," in the words of black journalist and politician Martín Morúa-Delgado.[21] Morúa-Delgado followed Cuba's governor general in stating that the Abakuá and other African-centered networks should be forgotten as vestiges of slavery.[22] Other black Cuban elites, perhaps with a larger view of the problems facing African descendants, worked with all groups. Juan Gualberto Gómez, described as "an illustrated vanguard member, in the European sense,"[23] created a directorate to link all black organizations whose aim was to unite all the societies of color to advocate for civil rights.[24] The social links between diverse organizations created by African-descended peoples is evidenced in a figure like Lino D'Ou, himself a member of the Directorio, a Freemason, an Abakuá, as well as a Mambí warrior.[25] (D'Ou is discussed later in this chapter).

By 1890, while a diminished number of cabildos continued a specific African ethnic identity, the Abakuá was officially nonexistent. Ironically, and prophetically, by being illegal and therefore outside the reach of the law, Abakuá has persisted to the present, whereas the cabildos and later societies have not.[26] Because of its many positive functions, Abakuá was maintained by its membership "contra viento y marea" (against winds and tides).

Delivering Fake Drums

Continuing their war on the cabildos and Abakuá, police raided Abakuá temples in the 1880s. Contemporary police reports document their confiscation of ritual objects, as well as the surrender of sacred drums to police by some Abakuá leaders. This is an unresolved issue in Cuban society, because some of these objects are still displayed in museums.[27] In some cases, fake copies of fundamentos were delivered. Regarding this problem, El Chino Mokóngo said, "In the nineteenth century the police confiscated many Abakuá fundamentos. It is also true that the plazas handed jew [unconsecrated] pieces to deceive the police while hiding their true fundamento. The fundamento is the life and soul of the Abakuá—it is hard to believe that they would deliver it to the police without fighting.[28] That is why, today in 1998 the religion exists and the government still attempts to know the secrets of the religion, but they do not."

Police thought that by capturing the ritual objects of their enemies, they would conquer them. If important objects were destroyed, others were created to replace them, and the cultural practice continued. In Cuba, several lodges documented as being destroyed in the 1880s still exist in the twenty-first century. Some of the public deliveries of Abakuá objects seem to have been part of a tacit understanding between authorities and Abakuá, where the latter would feign their demise, while hiding their activities from public view. It is significant that the majority of lodges documented as delivering their fundamentos to the police were from the white lineage of Okobio Mukarará, that is, the sector of the Abakuá community the police could most easily communicate with.[29] Police reports listed the white lodges Ekório Efó the First, Second, and Third, as well as Ebión Efó as among those whose leaders delivered their fundamentos to police in 1889.[30] The Ekório Efó lodges no longer exist, but Ebión Efó does.[31] Most Abakuá doubt the veracity of those ritual objects delivered, yet even if they were captured, others could be fabricated to replace them.[32] The same year, the title-holders of Enyegueyé Primero of Guanabacoa were reported to have delivered their fundamentos to the Town Hall of Guanabacoa.[33] A local historian, Gerardo Castellanos García, wrote that the mayor called the leadership of the Enyegueyé lodge to his office, where they promised to renounce their membership, "to which end they delivered a collection of drums, staffs, costumes, various ritual objects, along with a masquerade costume."[34] Neither Enyegueyé Efó the First nor Enyegueyé the Second survived this period.

Another lodge documented as being destroyed by police was Bakokó, its members sent to Spanish penal colonies.[35] This is unlikely because today the lodge Bakókó Efó, popularly known as Awana Mokokó, functions in Havana.[36] Leaders of Erón Entá were also documented as delivering fundamentos to municipal authorities. Castellanos García wrote, "Chiefs of the group Erón Entá . . . presented themselves at the Town Hall. . . . delivering objects that they used in their lodge."[37] Erón Entá, however, exists in the present.[38] In 1889 the leadership of Erumé Efó was reported to have delivered their fundamentos to the police; the black title-holders of Iyámba and Mokóngo of this lodge "presented themselves announcing the dissolution of their juego, and delivering other pertinences [ritual objects]."[39] Likewise, Erumé Efó continues to exist. In addition, a black member of the lodge "Enclentá" (Eklé Ntáti Machecheré) reportedly delivered "a luxurious diablito costume that, according to the Guard, was 'checkerformed of scarlet cloth in different colors.'"[40] The humor in this passage is that delivering an old masquerade costume would in no way effect the functioning of a lodge, since another one could be easily made. Eklé Ntáti Machécheré exists today.

Among the strong evidence that the eradication of Abakuá was an intentional farce, both Fernando Ortiz and Lydia Cabrera reported that Don Carlos Rodríguez Batista, civil governor of Havana Province in the last years of the colony, was a member of Mukarará Efó: "It is tradition among the nyányigos that Rodríguez Batista, son of Regla and raised among its population (situated in the Bay of Havana and birth place of Cuban nyányiguism) [was initiated] . . . The initiation of the governor Rodríguez

Batista into nyányiguism appears certain; as such he would know its organizations, rites, attributes, customs, and the name of his friends and coreligionists. This more than anything explains his spectacular success [in 'eliminating' Abakuá], and with such a pacific and insincere method, that had no effective transcendence."[41] In spite of reports of the demise of Abakuá during Batista's tenure, Ortiz observed that afterward, "the supposedly disintegrated 'juegos' functioned as before." In other words, some of the "confiscated" objects donated by Batista to the Museo de Ultramar in Madrid, the same objects that inspired Ortiz's early career (as discussed in the Introduction), were fakes.

Rafael Roche's book, *La policía y sus misterios en Cuba* (1908), is held to be a classic of the Cuban underworld, infamous for criminalizing the Abakuá. Nevertheless, many Abakuá leaders have identified valuable information in his book for their own historical research. El Chino Mokóngo and several other Abakuá leaders, while noting Roche's hostility, agreed that some of the tratados he documented were accurate and useful. Lydia Cabrera, who criticized Roche's work as, "completely incorrect and barren of information,"[42] also documented an Abakuá as saying, "The one who discredited nyanyiguismo was the chief of the police, Roche, who was a nyányigo."[43] This leads to the realization that Roche's book, in three editions, may also have served as an official cover for his own participation in the society. Such an irony is not unusual in Cuban society, where survival sometimes requires camouflage.[44]

Summing up the difficulty of being Abakuá in the colonial period, Abelardo Empegó told me,

> We have never been recognized as a religious group. For many years we were not allowed to perform plantes [ceremonies] and we had to do it in hidden places, in a *solar* [tenement], with people watching at the corners for the possible arrival of the police. Many fundamentos were confiscated; it is known that in the university there is a set of drums and staffs from an Abakuá potency confiscated during the Spanish government. Until now no one knows the name of the juego that owned those attributes. I cannot talk about this because it is a black story and there were many deaths. I will carry that story to my grave.[45] Since the colonial times the Abakuá was a phantasm. Children were told, "Watch out! The nyányigo is coming; he will take you away if you don't behave well." And they made people believe that the Abakuá was a horrible thing, that it was backwardness.

In order to survive, members disguised their practice through metaphor, as Cabrera described, "In the years truly difficult for the Abakuá, when evading the vigilance of the authorities determined to persecute every vestige of African 'barbarism,' it was essential 'plantar,' 'play' (celebrate the rites and ceremonies of the society) in a reduced space of a room of some tenement or rented house in Havana, and even to fill the betraying cowbells of the 'diablitos' [masked dancers] with paper, so they wouldn't sound and alert the police; they represented the ceiba [kapok] and palm trees with chalk signs, and the river Oddán [Ndian] ... was reduced to a washbasin or a tray filled with water."[46] By reducing their visibility and noise level, by using chalk signs (known as *nsibidi* in the Cross River region) to represent key environmental elements like rivers and trees, urban Abakuá camouflaged their activities in order to continue transmitting their cultural values.

End of Spanish Rule

MACEO'S WAR

Among the founding families of the Cuban nation, the Maceos reign supreme. Regarded as the "Mother of the Cuban Nation," Mariana Grajales Cuello bore nine children by Marcos Maceo.[47] Her entire family fought in the Cuban Wars of Independence, where her husband and eight sons perished.[48] Her son Antonio Maceo (1845–1896) has been called "one of the truly great figures in the history of the Hispanic-American wars of independence."[49] In 1878 General Maceo organized a rejection of Spain's peace offer, in what became known as the Protest of Baraguá, declaring his commitment to continue the struggle until independence with emancipation were achieved.[50] His biographer wrote, "When virtually all the political leaders of the republic-in-arms, and most of the military commanders as well, were ready to agree to peace in the Treaty of Zanjón, Maceo alone refused to surrender. Rejecting the minor political concessions the Spaniards were willing to make, he openly defied the Spanish general, Martínez Campos."[51]

Maceo's protest encouraged the war efforts to continue. Nearly twenty years later, Maceo became the hero of the Invasion of the West (October 1895 to January 1896), when his troops marched across the island from east to west, breaking through the Spanish *trochas* (barricades) meant to contain them. Maceo is an enduring symbol of Cuban patriotism. Even into the second half of the twentieth century, the Cuban masses commonly referred to the last War of Independence as "Maceo's War."[52]

MACHETES, MAMBÍS, AND PALENQUES

Cuba's Wars of Independence were fought by a ragtag group of rebels using machetes against a numerically far superior army with modern arms.[53] The rural population supported the rebel troops by supplying them with information on the movement of Spanish troops.[54] Spain tried to demoralize the rebels and their supporters by presenting the conflict as a "race war." The Cuban insurgents were called "Mambí," using a Cuban-Kongo term with connotations of "evil." Ortiz thought that this term was popularized by enslaved Kongo who translated the hatred of their legal owners toward the rebels.[55]

Kongo scholar Dr. Fu-Kiau Bunseki interpreted *mambị* as the KiKongo term *ambi* meaning "bad, evil, rotten, gross corrupt, offensive"; "*mâmbu mambi*, bad words/news; *n'kisi miambi*, bad medicines."[56] Another related meaning of *mambị* in Cuba is "cimarrón (maroon), a fugitive from slavery."[57] In Cuban Kongo ritual practice, however, *mambi-mambi* refers to a consecrated medium between the ancestors and the living, while *mambị* is a variant of Zambí, a reference to the Supreme Being.[58] These allusions to the spiritual dimensions of African presence in the rebel army are sustained by other anecdotal evidence, to follow. With all these connotations, rebels described themselves with the term *Mambí*, which became a badge of honor.[59] Far into the twentieth century, Cuban musicians and intellectuals continued to interpret the term as such.[60]

There was poetic justice in calling the rebel army Mambí, since African descendants were in the majority. For hundreds of years, fugitives from slavery had created camps in rural areas, known as palenques. Founded in the early 1500s by Taino and Arawak Indians, palenques later incorporated Africans and by the nineteenth century included fugitive whites.[61] Networks of Cuban palenques conducted illicit trade with the islands of Jamaica, Santo Domingo, and Haiti through European merchants. Never successfully destroyed, these networks became a major support system for the Mambí rebels.[62] With the first war for Cuban liberation in 1868, "cimarrones were incorporated to the forces commanded by general Antonio Maceo."[63] From 1869 onward, Maceo used some palenques as bases to heal and shelter his troops.[64] He used their preexisting trade networks to receive medicines, food, and weaponry from the aforementioned islands.[65] Maceo repeatedly defeated Spanish troops while attacking sugar plantations. As he liberated the enslaved, he explained that the purpose of the war was to end slavery. Consequently, large numbers of freed blacks joined the rebel troops.[66]

PALO MONTE

West-Central Africans in Cuba organized many palenques, and the Matiabos were among them.[67] With a reputation as warriors, the Matiabos were more appropriately called Tata Ngangas, specialists in the herbal arts who work with powerful fundamentos in Palo Monte traditions.[68] Because an estimated 70 percent of the Mambí army were Africans and their descendants, many of them would have been devotees of Palo Monte.[69] In a rare documented example, based upon the memoirs of Maceo's doctor, one historian concluded, "The rank and file believed so strongly in traditional remedies that they were reluctant to see commanders resort to modern medicine. When Antonio Maceo fell seriously ill during the preparation of the western invasion, he sent for the chief of the Sanitary Division. His escort and soldiers, however, insisted that only a healer's manipulation could save him."[70]

If Antonio Maceo and other generals were not practitioners of African-derived healing systems, their surrounding community insisted on their protection by them.[71] And if the generals were practitioners, their authority would only have increased in the eyes of their troops. Given the African sources of the rebel army of the time, this was to be expected. Throughout sub-Saharan Africa, preparations for war included evoking the ancestors and divinities to aid in the struggle.[72]

In contemporary Cuba, at least two black generals, Antonio Maceo and Quintín Bandera (1833–1906), are commemorated as devotees of Palo Monte.[73] Invocations at Palo Monte ceremonies name deceased members of the house lineage, and then the names of important initiates in Cuban history. In contemporary Havana, one can hear recited "Antonio Maceo Ngo La Habana" (literally, leopard of Havana), the ritual title of the general, whose portrait is placed upon some Palo Monte altars.[74] As for General Bandera, his Kongo *prenda/nkisi* (shrine) was called Briyumba Zámbe Ndio Ngo La Habana, interpreted as "the divine power of the leopard came to Havana."[75] Bandera was the Tata Nkisi, or head custodian, of this nkisi, and General Antonio Maceo was the *bakonfula*, or assistant.[76] This nkisi was carried from Oriente to Matanzas in a saddlebag to protect the warriors during the Invasion of the West; it was used to evoke the power of Sarabanda, the Kongo divinity of war.[77]

This legend is referred to in many forms of popular culture.[78] In the 1950s an Abakuá-led percussion ensemble recorded a march where the chorus repeats "Ngo" as the lead singer improvised about arriving to Havana. Those who know the codes understand the references to Maceo's Invasion of the West.[79] More recently, this theme was represented in a painting grounded in Cuban Kongo philosophy (Plate 20), where the spirit of a Mambí warrior rides a leopard into battle.[80]

That the nkisi of insurgent generals was linked to Sarabanda would be obvious to Palo Monte practitioners, because the only weapon available to the majority of Mambí warriors, the machete, is both a tool, as well as a symbol of Sarabanda/Ògún, the respective Kongo and Lukumí divinities of war.[81] The shrine of the leaders of those bearing machetes would necessarily be linked to the power of iron. In 1896 a North American journalist witnessed Maceo's column attack a Spanish regiment. He wrote, "I shall never forget that night. It was a fitting tribute to the god of the machete."[82] Legends of this type may be omitted from official history texts, but those familiar with marginal areas of Havana know that they continue to be transmitted orally through ritual lineages; the Kongo title of General Bandera is recited each time a particular nkisi is activated in ceremony.[83]

THE ABAKUÁ AND MACEO

According to Andrés Flores, there is a famous anecdote among the Abakuá concerning Antonio Maceo that is little known by others:

> General Antonio Maceo visited Havana and was hosted in the Hotel Inglaterra. He was going to a meeting and his life needed protection; the patriots of Havana addressed him because they wanted to assign him bodyguards. But Maceo firmly

refused, saying that it was not necessary. The patriots, having no alternative but to withdraw, contacted the Abakuá world and told them about the need to protect Maceo until the meeting, and to bring him back discreetly so that he would not notice their protection. On the day of the meeting, when Maceo left the hotel, he did not notice the two blacks standing on the corner, nor did he observe three other blacks walking along the sidewalk in front of him. Four more blacks walked along the other block, and so on, up to the meeting place. Maceo was not aware of his protection by the Abakuá.

In fact, Maceo visited Havana in 1890, arriving from exile after receiving a guarantee of safe conduct by the Captain General Salamanca.[84] While staying at the Hotel Inglaterra, he met with Spanish as well as rebel leaders several times.[85] An account of Maceo's protection in Havana was published in a memoir by a member of the "youth of the Acera del Louvre" (discussed in chapter 5), a social group who met in cafés next to the Hotel Inglaterra, and among whom were many Abakuá. Gustavo Robreño wrote that during Maceo's visit, his group "constituted the Honor Guard of the great warrior staying in the Hotel Inglaterra."[86] Among the messages of these anecdotes, that Maceo would need protection in spite of the safe conduct pass from the colonial authorities, has a solid basis. A decade earlier, Cuban rebels leaders, including two of Maceo's brothers, surrendered on the condition of their safe passage from the island. On the open seas, however, they were captured by a Spanish warship and imprisoned in Africa.[87] Antonio Maceo's brother Rafael died in an African prison, and Spanish agents attempted to assassinate Antonio Maceo three times.[88]

During the process of research, I learned several versions of the Maceo anecdote from Abakuá leaders. El Chino Mokóngo told me, "The Abakuá fought for Cuba during the Independence Wars. There is a well-known story about a secret meeting Maceo attended in Havana where he was protected by the Abakuá. I do not know the potencies they belonged to." It may be tempting to suggest that these narratives are a recent invention, related to a contemporary desire to link Abakuá with patriotism. But in the 1950s, Lydia Cabrera had learned that "nyányigos served the independence movement, as in the high and intellectual spheres served the masons."[89] Antonio Maceo, like many Cuban rebel leaders, was a Freemason. The narratives describing the collusion of Abakuá, Kongo warriors, and Freemasons in the rebel army seem to have been consistent throughout the twentieth century, although rarely documented by scholars.

Luckily, Abakuá leaders guided me to those with special knowledge about the historical activities of their lodge. Salinas brought me to the home of an Abakuá titleholder who was born in 1906 in the barrio of Belén.[90] Salinas introduced the topic, "There is an anecdote about Maceo's visit to Havana. He was being sought by Spaniards, and a group of Abakuá from the barrio of Belén hid him. The next morning they escorted him to the train station and he left for Oriente. Speak about this." Pablo Gutierrez-Nuñez responded:

That was during the war of '95. The late Guevara, a handsome mulatto, was the best tailor in Havana; he worked in a famous shop owned by a Spaniard. His family was respected, notwithstanding that he was Abakuá, from my juego Kanfioro Nankúko.

In those times, we had wealthy men in my juego. We had a Spaniard surnamed Canales who owned a large barbershop; another white man was the manager of the piers located in San Pedro; we also had a black man named Enca-dilao Acuesta, known as "the mason"; another was a council member for many years, Juan Borre. These wealthy men were not title-holders, but they were loyal to their oaths and always helped and supported any lodge activities.

Salinas persisted, "Tell him how Maceo left from here." Pablo replied,

General Antonio Maceo was coming from Tampa to go to the eastern provinces, and he was told to meet Guevara. Maceo arrived to Guevara's home and handed him a letter from José Martí, an acquaintance of Guevara. Maceo explained that he needed to be informed about the police movements to avoid arrest at the station. He said that he wanted to leave on the first Central train in the morn-ing. Guevara told him, "Don't worry, General, I am in charge." He met with four Obonékues of his juego and told them, "I need you to go at night to the Villanueva station and observe the movements of the police there and inform me." Then, he told the owner of the shop where he worked. "I come to bother you because I need a ticket for the Central train leaving at 6 a.m. tomorrow." The owner's secretary got the ticket immediately. The next morning Guevara breakfasted with Maceo, and they walked to the Villanueva station that was located where the Capitol building is today, only seven or eight blocks from here. The train arrived at 5:30 and they traveled with Maceo to Matanzas, where they got off, leaving Maceo to continue traveling to the Oriente Province. That was Guevara, my brother in religion.[91]

I documented several variations on the theme of the Abakuá protecting Maceo in Havana, and they are generally consistent with written documentation of Maceo's visit to this city. Contemporary Abakuá continue to recite these stories, reflecting a desire that the activities of their nineteenth-century ancestors be recognized as integral to the official narratives of the birth of the Cuban nation.

ABAKUÁ IN THE LIBERATION ARMY

The Abakuá presence in the Mambí army is another understudied facet of Abakuá history. During research I learned of several figures, although there were undoubtedly many more.

Lieutenant of the Mambí cavalry of Matanzas, Felipe Espínola was a foreman on the Matanzas docks, a Freemason, and the Mbákara of Efí Embemoró Second, founded in 1890. When the Odán Efí lodge was founded in 1893, Espínola received the title of Isué there.[92] Together with Federico Gil, Espínola directed a *clave* choir ensemble named "Los Amalianos" (more on this form in chapter 7). He was taken prisoner and shot on August 24, 1896. After Espínola's execution, Pedro Isasi, a Mambí soldier, replaced him as Isué of this lodge. Above the altar inside the house/temple of Odán Efí, I saw hung a gilded Freemason square, indicating rarely documented relationships between Abakuá and Freemasons.[93] This evidence supports the conclusion of one writer regarding Abakuá, "Cuban nationalists joined the cult, finding the secretiveness of its meetings well-adapted to planning revolutionary activities against the Spanish authorities."[94]

While visiting Matanzas in the late 1990s, I saw the public monument in Espínola's memory that was erected in 1922. El Chino Mokóngo reported, "Concerning Felipe Espínola of the Liberation Army, up to the 1940s an homage was held in Matanzas." Other Abakuá told me this homage is still performed, "Every January 6, when the Abakuá celebrate the anniversary of their foundation in Cuba, many lodges hold plantes. In Matanzas, the Abakuá set out in procession from the temple of Uriabón (on Salamanca and América Streets) to the statue of Espínola, placing flowers around his statue.[95] During this homage a representative speaks about his revolutionary character in that era and his performance as Isué of Odán Efí. Even if only one lodge celebrates a plante, Abakuá of the entire region will be present."

Another Mambí, a Cuban creole of Chinese-Filipino descent named Quirino Valdés was initiated into the Akaranán Efó lodge. In 1875 he cofounded Abakuá Efó, becoming a title-holder there.[96] Valdés fought in the Mambí army during the last War of Independence (1895–1898), later becoming "the secretary general of laborers of the Regla warehouses, and founder of the Labor Federation of the Bay."[97]

Lino D'ou, a lieutenant colonel of the Mambí army, was also a writer, a member of the national House of Representatives (1909–1912),[98] a Freemason, as well as a member of the Abakuá lodge Bakokó Efó.[99] In 1935, D'ou's lecture on Abakuá history was broadcast by radio from Havana; it was meant to explain "the origin, meaning, and ends of Abakuá in Africa and in Cuba," as well as "advocate for the respect and consideration of an African institution whose morality and altruism have nothing to learn from Masonry, for example, nor from any religion."[100]

Cuba's national poet, Nicolás Guillén, knew Lino D'ou to be an Abakuá member.[101] His famous verse "La canción del bongó" (The Song of the Bongó) was dedicated to D'ou in 1931. Scholars often interpret it as expressing Cuba's imagined "binary" heritage, where a fusion of African and Spanish cultures resulted in the national culture. In addition to this reading, Abakuá insiders receive a deeper interpretation that resonates with the dedication to D'ou. The poem begins by describing the authoritative voice of the bongó: "Esta es la canción del bongó: Aquí el que más fino sea, responde, si llamo yo" (This is the song of the bongó: He who is most refined here, responds, if I call.)[102] In Abakuá practice, the bongó would be the Bongó Ékue, the Abakuá epicentrum. In both Ékpè and Abakuá practice, when the Voice sounds, title-holders must respond to affirm their presence.[103]

Guillén identified the presence of Spanish aristocratic titles and African ethnicity within the same family, "y hay títulos de Castilla con parientes en Bondó" (and those with Castilian titles have relatives in Bondó.) Bondó is a reference to Efí Ibondá, an Abakuá lodge. Referring to this poem, Benítez-Rojo wrote, "Guillén's poetry speaks of black men and women who . . . proclaim their laborious cultural victory."[104] This example shows again how Cuban artists have used codes while referring to Abakuá's symbolic role in the nation's history, so that the deeper meanings are perceived only by those in the know.

CLOSE OF THE CENTURY

With the close of the nineteenth century, Spain finally lost her "Pearl of the Caribbean."[105] Until the end, colonial authorities saw the Abakuá as a target, as Spanish authority Domingo Blanco wrote in 1900, "While I was in Cuba, Governor Don José Porrúa and Chief of public order Don Manuel de La Barrera organized a campaign of persecution against the nyányigos that was applauded by all honorable people."[106] In spite of their intentions, the persecutions were not successful. According to a Cuban historian, "Neither in Havana nor in Regla were the order of the colonial authorities of 1875, nor the later and continual persecutions, nor the repeated police raids of the municipal governments, nor the deportations to Ceuta and Fernando Poo, sufficient to liquidate 'nyanyiguism' [Abakuá]."[107]

In response to their persecution, African-derived communities seem to have resisted with similar intensity, a dynamic that continued into the twentieth century. The tension between authorities and Abakuá has never been resolved, in part because the memory of struggles to maintain Abakuá has been passed on through the generations and because twentieth-century authorities have continued attempts to assimilate them, with varying degrees of intensity.

Conclusions

During the Wars of Independence, colonial authorities sought to erase the memory of Africa and foster loyalty to Spain by prohibiting African descendants to participate in African cabildo groups. Both Abakuá and the African cabildos became illegal. In 1886, with the legal end of slavery, the Three Kings' Day processions were terminated and the cabildos linked to Catholic churches that received their properties. Nevertheless, underground ties between the remaining cabildos, the Abakuá, and the newly created societies for instruction were maintained through community networks. In highly publicized police raids in Havana, Abakuá objects were confiscated and placed in museums. Several title-holders agreed to stop their activities, but instead delivered fake objects to police. Some lodges may have been terminated in the process, while many others continued. Reports that even leading police officials were members of lodges show the interwoven nature of Havana society, and how tacit agreements between authorities and Abakuá have protected the brotherhood.

General Antonio Maceo is the personification of Cuban patriotism as well as the African-derived presence in the rebel army. Called Mambí after a West-Central African term, the insurgent army was composed of 70 percent African descendants. Maceo helped defeat the Spanish by using networks of palenques (fugitive communities) and by liberating the enslaved on plantations, who then joined the ranks. The Kongo-derived practices of many Mambí warriors is recognized among specialists, but not reflected in the official histories. Lesser-known is that General Quintín Bandera and Maceo were also practitioners and their ritual names and fundamento are still evoked in contemporary Cuba and its Diaspora. In Havana, Abakuá recount narratives of how their ancestors protected Maceo during his visit to Havana in 1890 to rekindle war efforts. Several Abakuá leaders were Mambí warriors, whose legacies are commemorated in collective ceremony, and even in verse by Cuba's national poet, Nicolas Guillén. The close of the nineteenth century ended Spanish domination on the island, but not the persecution of Abakuá. In response, African-derived communities have resisted with equal fervor.

7. Havana Is the Key

ABAKUÁ IN CUBAN MUSIC

■ ■ ■

Cuba contributed more than it received.

—ALEJO CARPENTIER[1]

Music is integral to all facets of Abakuá practice, whose very origins are linked to the reverberations of the Divine Voice in Cross River estuaries.[2] Abakuá ceremonies reenact African foundations through sequences of chants and corresponding actions that articulate the significance of ritual objects and symbols, dances, and moral codes. Narratives of Abakuá's foundation in Cuba, as summarized in chapter 1, are expressed in chants recited in contemporary ceremonies.[3] The chants themselves, even if performed a capella, are structured upon time-line patterns usually articulated through hand drumming on skin. Drum skins, once living membranes, are considered transmitters of ancestral forces whose vibrations serve to purify initiates, defending them against negative forces.[4]

Music is fundamental to African-derived communal practice, but nineteenth-century Havana resounded with music from around the world, whose practices were cross-fertilized in exhilarating ways, fusing the sounds of diametrically opposed groups. For example the European airs of the *country dance/contredanse/contradanza* of the British, French, and Spanish aristocracy were transformed in Cuba through the *cinquillo*, an African-derived time-line pattern.[5] Even during an official act to begin the destruction of the walls of the city in 1863, contradanzas were composed and performed, one called "The Demolition" (*El derrumbe*).[6] That is, despite the desire of elites to erase their dependence upon African workers, even their representative musical forms were permeated with African rhythms.

These and many other examples demonstrate how popular music can be a key to the social history of Cuba. After a lifetime of study, Fernando Ortiz concluded, "Every social upheaval of Cuba has its repercussions in the music, in which it sounds and resounds, into which it escapes and is barely heard. To study Afrocuban music is to investigate the entire ethnography and social history of Cuba as well as the position of blacks and whites within it. The historical formation and trajectory of the Cuban people are expressed in their music."[7]

This chapter discusses several facets of Cuban music relevant to Abakuá presence in Cuban history. I gathered these fragments over several years and then reviewed them with Abakuá leaders and musicians, who helped me transcribe and understand their intended meanings. Only through an awareness of the kaleidoscopic nature of metaphors in various genres of the music, whether purely sonic or verbal, can one begin to grasp the significance of this art for its creators.

Contradanza, Danza, and Danzón

During the Invasion of the West in 1895, several columns of the Mambí army traversed Cuba to counteract Spanish pretences of controlling the island. When Maceo's column passed through the Spanish trocha (barricade) at Camagüey, their military band celebrated with music. Days before, a composition dedicated to Maceo called "The Invading Hymn" was created by a Cuban general.[8] Nearly a century later, the victories of Maceo and other rebel leaders were evoked by professional musicians with the classic rumba phrase "se quema la trocha" (the barricade is burning), which became the basis for a national dance hit.[9]

A cornet player and composer in the army of Antonio Maceo, Enrique Peña (1881–1922) was an Abakuá member.[10] His 1921 composition "El ñáñigo" (on the accompanying CD, track 1) pays homage to the role of Abakuá in the Wars of Independence. "El ñáñigo" is a danza that begins with the tune of a military call to arms (*llamada a combate*), then segues into a dance tune.[11] The implication is that Abakuá were rebel warriors who moved with elegance and strength. This danza is distinctive for its use of a lively 6/8 meter in the second part, standard for Abakuá ceremonial music, as well as a melody from an Abakuá chant.[12]

The black and mulatto battalions of Havana (as described in chapter 2) included Abakuá members and wharf leaders. Graduates of their military bands organized orchestras that performed modified contradanzas for local parties.[13] From this milieu in the mid-1800s, some composed contradanzas with Abakuá titles, such as "Los ñáñigos" and "La fambá,"[14] with fambá being the inner sanctum of an Abakuá temple. In Calabar, "Efamba [is] a secret display of Ékpè artifacts" in a temple.[15] In other words, the epicenter of activities for the entire society, the *fambá* is a place of intense energy where collective bonds are reaffirmed. Such contradanza titles are among the first signs of Abakuá emerging as a national symbol.[16]

In the mid-nineteenth century in Matanzas city, the *danzón* emerged from the contradanza. Early danzones used Abakuá, Kongo, and Lukumí musical ideas. The most popular danzón, "Las alturas de Simpson," first performed in 1879, was composed

FIGURE 26. "Andante ñañigo," a section of a suite composed by Miguel Failde in the second half of the nineteenth century. From the Archives of the Museo de la Música, Havana.

by Miguel Failde (1852–1922), who was likely an Abakuá member.[17] One of Failde's suites had a section called "andante ñáñigo"[18]; Failde's dexterous use of this material implies his contact with practitioners of its systems. Other composers titled their danzones using Abakuá phrases like "Chévere Macumchevere," "Íreme maco Íreme," and "Íreme."[19] The phrase "Chévere Makóngo Machevere" extols the mythic bravery of Mokóngo, a leading Abakuá title. Íreme is the masquerade dancer that symbolizes the participation of important ancestors in ceremonies (Ídèm in Èfìk Ékpè). In nearly every genre of Cuban popular music from the nineteenth-century danzón to the twenty-first-century *tímba*, one finds the presence of Abakuá musicians and obvious signs of their influence. Fundamental elements and genres of the music were taught to me by Abakuá musicians. The process required learning about the interwoven nature of Havana, its music, and the role of Abakuá codes therein. Since the cultural life of Africans in the early colony was not documented in detail, the student must glean from the existing fragments, as well as compare notes with their continental source regions.

The Shipyards and the Claves

To fill its coffers with silver and gold, the Spanish Crown needed an American shipyard. In Havana, the shipbuilding industry begun in the late 1500s lasted for three centuries.[20] By 1735 the shipyard was next to the barrio of Jesús María, soon to become a center for the black curros and Abakuá activities.[21] (See Plate 3, the 1789 map of Old Havana that identifies the arsenal [dockyard] next to Jesús María.)

Havana's prodigious shipyard was a key to Spain's empire, but it produced more than floating vessels.[22] The musical practices of its workers, the galley slaves, and black laborers contributed to Cuban popular music by refining the use of the two hardwood sticks known as claves. These sticks and the rhythms they express are among Cuba's enduring contributions to popular music. Claves have been used subsequently by musicians across the world. The official historian of the city of Havana, Emilio Roig de Leuchsenring, wrote, "The 'claves,' percussion instruments frequently used in our popular music, are nothing but the hardwood 'pegs,' hand secured by carpenters on the shore to strengthen the joints, planks, and frames of the ships. The black population of Havana, who resided in great numbers at the time in *El Manglar* [The Mangrove], an extramural barrio near the shipyards, conceived of using them to accompany their songs and dances. In this way resulted that . . . the clave is genuinely from Havana."[23] Since the twentieth century nearly ubiquitous throughout Cuban music, the claves may have emerged from Havana's harbor in the 1600s. Fernando Ortiz identified the source of its name, "the Cuban *clave* instrument [was] born in Havana in the centuries in which this city was known as 'the key to the Indies,' or the 'key,' as we could say playing with words, of the entire colonial and maritime structure of Spain."[24]

The Africans, Spaniards, Asians, and American Indians who built Havana's fortresses—as free laborers, slaves, or galley convicts—also worked in its shipyards.[25] The round hardwood pegs, known as *clavijas*, they used to join the planks in ships were reconfigured to mark rhythms.[26] Called claves (or "keys"), these sticks are commonly used to mark the time-line patterns in Cuban popular music, which are "necessary to organize polyrhythmic music."[27] Ortiz viewed the claves as quintessentially *mestizo*, thus a Cuban instrument, "The clave of Cuban music was born in Havana, through the mixed marriage of the rhythm-making sticks of the black slaves of Africa with the castanets of the galley slaves of Andalucia. Born mulatto, incarnate without doubt in the 'clave' pegs of the shipyards, where the blacks and whites joined their desires, their labors, and their sorrow, and because of the lack of their accustomed instruments in the prison."[28] If the materials were Cuban, the ideas were trans-Atlantic; the African precedents for time-line patterns are obvious and ubiquitous in West and West-Central Africa.

Time-Line Patterns

A historian of African music, Gerhard Kubik reported the widespread use in West and Central Africa of what Cubans call "clave rhythms."[29] Used to structure the music, these time-line patterns are found in African regions whose peoples migrated to Cuba, namely the west coast (Yorùbá, Akan, Fon), Calabar, and the Kongo. One of these patterns is a five-stroke version, found in Nigeria, southeastern Cameroon, Angola, and Brazil. The time-line patterns are the "metric back bone of these musics." Because of their ubiquitous use, Kubik argues that they were stable elements existing much earlier than the seventeenth century. For this reason, "The presence or absence of one of the African time-line patterns in Afro-American music can be considered diagnostic for historical connections with specific African cultures."[30] Regarding the one time-line pattern from the Nigeria/Cameroon borderland, Kubik wrote that, "with the slave trade this pattern was exported to various places in the Caribbean, notably Cuba, and to Brazil, where it survives in the Candomblé religious ceremonies."[31] Summarizing their utility for historical research, Kubik argued that, "The most important fact about the asymmetric time-line patterns is that their mathematical structures are cultural invariables, that is, their mathematics cannot be changed by cultural determinants. They are immune to all social, cultural, or environmental influences. One can change a time-line pattern's instrumentation, accentuation, speed, starting point, and the mnemonic syllables used to teach it, but not its mathematical structure. Any attempt to change that dissolves the pattern. For this reason time-line patterns are formidable diagnostic markers for detecting historical connections between certain New World African Diaspora musical styles and those of distinctive language zones on the African continent."[32]

Kubik identified the "asymmetric time-line patterns" as "a distinctive Kwa and Benue-Congo phenomenon."[33] Because the cultural base of the Cross River peoples, as well as their creole Abakuá descendants who worked in the shipyards, came from this part of Africa, it was no accident that they used the clave pegs to make these rhythms.

If the clave sticks and their rhythms emerged in the seventeenth century, they remained local to Havana until the nineteenth century.[34] The clave sticks were integral to the music of the dockworkers, the rumba, in both Havana and Matanzas. After the colonial era, when clave sticks began to be used in *troubadour* and son music, their use became nearly ubiquitous on the island. Through commercial recordings in the early twentieth century, claves became an international phenomenon.[35]

The Cabildos and the Rumba

The cabildos de nación, as cultural centers for the performance of African-based expressions in colonial Cuba, are the embarking point for the study of ethnic music and dance. Because there are no recordings of the music of these groups, travelers' descriptions are important sources of information. In the 1840s a traveler in urban Matanzas described the cabildos: "in numerous places on the hill back of the town, and in the [barrio of] Pueblo Nuevo, will be seen flags raised on high staffs. These point out the spots where [Africans] congregate and indulge in their national dances, for the different tribes introduced here from Africa retain all their custom and habits."[36]

Wurdeman's 1844 description of a cabildo dance is consistent with the *yuka* dance, a recreational genre performed in some Kongo cabildos, using three drums, hand clapping, with a male and female pair dancing competitively: "To the music of two or three rude drums, formed by stretching an untanned cow-hide over the extremity of a hollow trunk of a tree, the crowd of men and women, gaudily dressed, keep time with their hands. Presently a woman advances, and commencing a slow dance, made up of a shuffling of the feet and various contortions of the body, thus challenges a rival from among the men. One of these, bolder than the rest, after awhile steps out, and the two then strive which shall first tire the other; the woman performing many feats which the man attempts to rival, often excelling them, amid the shouts of the rest."[37] The yuka dance is regarded by music scholars as the major source for the rumba, a nonethnic form. In 1850 on a large sugar plantation in rural Matanzas, Fredrika Bremer described a multi-ethnic Sunday dance sanctioned by the owner that was also consistent with the yuka dance:

> In the shade of [a] tree were assembled between forty and fifty negroes, men and women all in clean attire, the men mostly in shirts of blouses, the women in long, plain dresses. I here saw representatives of the various African nations— Congoes, Mandingoes, Luccomées, Caraballis, and others . . . The dance always requires a man and a woman, and always represents a series of courtship and coquetry; during which the lover expresses his feelings, partly by tremor in all his joints . . . as he turns round and round his fair one, like the planet around its sun, and partly by wonderful leaps and evolutions, often enfolding the lady with both his arms, but without touching her . . . One negro, a Caraballis, threw one arm tenderly round the neck of this little lady during the dance, while with the other he placed a small silver coin in her mouth.
>
> . . . it is the custom that if any one of the bystanders can thrust a stick or a hat between two dancers, they are parted, and he can take the man's place. In this manner a woman will sometimes have to dance with three or four partners without leaving her place. Women, also, may exclude each other from the dance, generally by throwing a handkerchief between the dancers, when they take the place of the other who retires . . . The dancing of the women always expresses a kind of bashfulness, mingled with a desire to charm, while with downcasts eyes, she turns herself round upon one spot . . . and with a neckerchief or colored handkerchief in her hand, sometimes one in each hand, she half drives away from her the advancing lover and half entices him to her. . . . The spectators stood in a ring around the dancers, one or two couples accompanying the dance with

singing, which consisted of the lively but monotonous repetition of a few words which were given out by one person in the circle, who seemed to be a sort of *improvisatore*, and who had been chosen as leader of the song. . . . The music consisted, besides the singing, of drums. Three drummers stood beside the tree-trunk beating with their hands, their fists, their thumbs, and drumsticks upon skin stretched over hollowed tree-stems. They made as much noise as possible, but always keeping time and tune most correctly.[38]

All the elements here—three drums, couples moving with playful eroticism, exchanging partners, gesturing with cloth, responding vocally in chorus—are elements of contemporary rumba.

The yuka dance became the basis for the *yambú*, an early variant of rumba dance established by the 1870s.[39] The yuka dance performed during cabildo gatherings in Matanzas and Havana was within reach of the Carabalí cabildos and the nascent Abakuá, all of whom contributed to the rumba. Among "the most notable rumba players of Matanzas" were members of the Carabalí cabildo that organized the first Matanzas Abakuá lodge.[40] As the rumba developed over the next century, many of its leading artists would be Abakuá members. The yuka dance and its derivative the rumba yambú, both considered to be aspects of Bantu-Kongo traditions, were also being played by Carabalí and Abakuá, with the rumba emerging as a creole form where musicians of any nation could participate.[41]

Rumba and Abakuá

According to a Cuban television program, "The rumba complex was the typical expression of the humblest workers, particularly the stevedores. These expressions could not have developed without a social base to promote it. This base was the society known as Abakuá."[42] Abakuá's deepest ties with popular music are found in the rumba, played by community-based percussive ensembles that seem to have emerged simultaneously in Matanzas and Havana. Given the railroad and shipping lines that connected these contiguous port cities, as well as their shared Abakuá practice, this is what one would expect. Cuban musicologists have identified the rumba as emerging from a Bantu-Kongo cultural base. The earliest variant, yambú, was created by 1850; other variants, rumba-guaguancó and rumba-columbia, emerged later in the century.[43] The son of a Kongo man told Lydia Cabrera in the 1950s, "the rumba Guaguankó was born from the Tahona, created by we the creoles of the last century"; "Wawankó. Born from the Tahona. 'When I was born, in the last century the Tahona was no longer played . . . The Guaguankó strengthened my legs."[44] Fundamental elements of the rumba emerged from Kongo traditions, but they also incorporated North African and Andaluzian vocal and gestural styles, brought by Spaniards who lived and worked alongside Africans. The result was an inter-African fusion to which Carabalí and creole Abakuá contributed.

This history is referred to within the rumba tradition itself. In a famous example, the Muñequitos of Matanzas, many of whose members are Abakuá, recorded a *guaguancó* extolling the poetic power of the rumba. Its chorus, "Carabalí—Congo Reales," names two African cabildos that developed the form.[45] Matanzas scholar Israel Moliner affirmed, "the contributions of [Abakuá] music have not been slight on the formation and later development of the urban styles of the rumba or the guaguancó, in Havana as in Matanzas."[46] One specific strand of Abakuá music evident in the guaguancó is that "the rhythm of the *abí-apá* drum (the 'one hit' Abakuá drum) influenced the basic movements of the tumbador of the rumba."[47]

Coros de clave

After the 1884 ban on the Three Kings' Day cabildo processions, public drumming was prohibited for several decades. During this period, African descendants in Havana and Matanzas responded by creating ensembles known as *coros de clave* (rhythm choruses), which used clave sticks, but apparently no drums.[48]

The first coro de clave of Matanzas included Carabalí-descended rumba players who participated in a Kongo cabildo, confirming the bonds between these groups.[49] Organized by barrio, the coros de clave performed songs accompanied by a time-line pattern and partner dancing.[50] Because many leaders of these choruses were Abakuá members, they fused Abakuá elements to the new rumba variations.[51] In 1894 in Matanzas, Abakuá title-holder Felipe Espínola became founder and director of the chorus Los Marinos.[52] The Abakuá, like the drum, was prohibited, so its members used the clave chorus format to disguise their activities. In Havana members of the lodge Ekoria Efó Taibá created the clave chorus called El Clavel (the Carnation) in 1884.[53] A police chief noted the presence of Abakuá in Havana coro de clave performances in the early twentieth century: "In the afternoon of January 1, 1908, a numerous and compact *clave* [coro de clave] traversed the streets of Alambique and Florida, in the center of which, covered by the those present, appeared an individual with a ñáñigo masquerade and all its attributes. . . . In the evening of February 23 of the same year, while celebrating a *clave* [coro de clave] on the Road of Belascoaín and Jesús Peregrino, a skirmish was sustained by [the lodges] Betongó and Munyánga, resulting in three wounded."[54] This observation, used to portray the criminality of Abakuá, confirms the early interaction of Abakuá in rumba ensembles. According to a Cuban television program about the history of the rumba, "There is no evidence of an institution of popular artistry that has not been promoted and directed by Abakuá members, or related to them."[55]

Andrés Flores talked about Abakuá in the development of the coro de claves, as well as in the rumba:

> From 1900 to '12 the coros de clave became popular throughout the barrios of Havana.[56] Most were integrated by Abakuá from the lodges Irianabón, Uriabón, and Efóri Enkomón. The chorus from the barrio of Colón was called Tercio de Colón [Group from Colón] and its composer was called Nicanor Asencio— father of the famous rumba composer Tío Tom [Uncle Tom] and a member of Irianabón.[57] The chorus of Jesús María was called Los Lugareños [the Villagers] and that of Carragüao, Paso Franco.[58] The composer for Paso Franco was called Severino Durán, an Abakuá member.[59] The chorus of the barrio Pueblo Nuevo was called Los Roncos [the Singers][60]; its composer was Ignacio Piñeiro, a member of Efóri Enkomón.[61] Ignacio Piñeiro was one of the most respected and loved men in the barrio of Pueblo Nuevo. He had a very high pitch and it was terrific when he began to sing with the chorus Los Roncos of the barrio of Pueblo Nuevo.[62] He also composed and arranged Abakuá chants for the clave choruses, for rumba groups, and for son septets.

With this passage, Andrés mentioned some of the greatest names in Havana rumba history. Tío Tom's compositions are classics of the genre, while Ignacio Piñeiro went on to compose hundreds of rumba-infused son compositions.[63] Through interviews with Ignacio Piñeiro in the 1960s, Rogelio Martínez-Furé learned that the coros de clave performed protest songs against the social conditions in which the masses lived; they were made illegal by the government in 1913, thus ending this tradition.[64] Because the music of these local groups was not recorded, too little is known about them.

Havana's Carnival Comparsas

EL ALACRÁN (THE SCORPION)

Carnival comparsa (carnival troupe) performances, parading with music and dance, have occurred for centuries in Cuban society.[65] There were two carnival traditions in colonial Cuba: that of the African cabildos street processions on January 6 and the pre-Lenten carnival of the white elites in February.[66] The 1884 banning of the January Three Kings' Day cabildo processions terminated the parade of African nation dances. Black comparsa troupes participated marginally in the pre-Lenten carnival, but over time the presence of white elites receded, and carnival became defined by the performance of troupes representing the marginal barrios.[67] For example, the troupe El Alacrán (The Scorpion), commonly thought to have been founded in 1908 as a white troupe using blackface to represent African-descendants, were in fact merely imitating an already existing black comparsa.[68] The theme of this troupe is based upon an African-derived story recounting how a Kongo healer was able to cure the bite of a scorpion where all others failed.[69]

Although not originally Carabalí, many Havana comparsa traditions acquired a pronounced Abakuá profile.[70] Abakuá leaders played key roles in the early-twentieth-century comparsas. This is to be expected, because many barrios had their own Abakuá lodge, itself defined as a tierra (territory) that was significant to the identity of many barrio residents. A Cuban television program recognized that "Abakuá lodges were converted, over time, into true potencies that controlled specific territories or specific neighborhoods."[71] Organized by barrio, the carnival comparsas were huge collective ensembles with people of all ages who performed for the glory of their barrio in citywide competitions. Dr. Mercedes Herrera, whose father was an Abakuá title-holder and a comparsa director, explained why the comparsa directors would be Abakuá members:

> It is like that because these people are respected in the barrio, they are not weak, because to organize a comparsa one must have a strong hand. They must be people who everyone respects in order to avoid problems in the comparsa. Otherwise there would be a debacle. The comparsa is from the "hood" and directed by people who are responsible and respectful. The comparsa directors were united as brothers, like Pedro Lagrimita (a member of Ibondá Efó) of La Jardinera [The Gardeners], Miguel Chappottín (a title-holder of Ikanfioró) of Los Dandys of Belén [The Dandies of Bethlehem], Arturo (a member of Usagaré Sangírimoto) of Las Bolleras [The Lolypops], Santos Ramírez of El Alacrán [The Scorpion], Nolasco (a member of Usagaré Sangírimoto) of the Marahá de la India [Maharaja of India]. These men were known in Havana, and those who joined their comparsas knew that they had to maintain their composure therein. Because when my father said, "Go away," that person did not return. Almost all the directors were Abakuá.[72]

In the ethos of the participants, the carnival comparsas seemed to take on the role of a nation-group during nineteenth-century Three Kings' Day, each ensemble working together to win the prize. After performing annually in the early Republic, the comparsas were banned until 1937, when many became reorganized.

Santos Ramírez (1903–1975), who held the title of Iyámba in the Sangírimoto Efó lodge, reorganized the comparsa El Alacrán.[73] Ramírez wrote the theme song of El Alacrán, "Tumbando caña," in the conga genre (on the accompanying CD, track 2).

In its day, it had the most overtly political message of any comparsa song.[74] The 1938 performance of this comparsa had a white overseer who whipped a lash as all sang:[75]

Oye colega no te asustes cuando veas	Listen colleague, don't be surprised when you see
el alacrán tumbando caña	The scorpion cutting cane
costumbre de mi país	A custom of my country
me hermano	my brother
Sí, sí, tumbando caña.	yes, yes, cutting cane.[76]

By depicting a land where even the crustaceans are sent to cut cane, the Alacrán performance alluded to the continued use of forced labor to produce Cuba's sugar, well into the twentieth century.[77] In this comparsa males danced from side to side (like crabs, who do not move forward), with machetes in their hands.[78] Santos Ramírez was a leader and a composer of popular music. In 1926 he cofounded a son group whose musical theme was the composition "Errante o Ecue" (Wandering or Ékue), a clear reference to Ékue, the epicenter of the Abakuá society.[79] Santos Ramírez used Abakuá terms to name his compositions, including "Chévere," and "Con su guaraguara [wárawára]," the latter being an Abakuá code for solidarity (more on this ahead).[80]

Abakuá leaders organized comparsas and composed music. Rhythmic influence from the Abakuá is found even in comparsa music, known as conga. In the rhythm of the comparsa Las Bolleras of the barrio of Los Sitios, the bí-apá (the one-hit Abakuá drum) influenced the playing of the *salidor* drum of the conga.[81] These example demonstrate how in the twentieth century some Carabalí cabildo traditions were continued through comparsa ensembles.

"EL CERRO TIENE LA LLAVE"

In the 1930s Ramírez moved to the barrio of the Cerro, bringing his lodge and comparsa with him, where they still exist. According to legend, some rumba players, referring to the cultural power of both the comparsa and the lodge, coined the phrase "El Cerro tiene la llave" (El Cerro has the key). The "key" metaphor had been present in the rumba since at least the early 1900s, deriving from the original idea that Havana was "Key to the New World."[82] An Abakuá leader interpreted the phrase using the words of the apostle of Cuban independence, "José Martí said, 'Be cultured to be free.' Cultural manifestations are keys to unchain the enslaved soul. For example, the cabildo processions each January 6 during the colonial days are an example we still turn to each time a comparsa goes to the streets."[83]

In the 1940s Arsenio Rodríguez recorded "El Cerro tiene la llave," composed by an Abakuá rumba player.[84] This phrase refers to Santos Ramírez's moving his lodge from Jesús María (Amalia) to El Cerro, which is reflected in a related phrase still sung in popular music referring to the Abakuá *bonkó* drum: "El Cerro tiene la llave, mira!, porque Amalia se la dió, bonkó!" (El Cerro has the key, look!, because Amalia gave it to them, Bonkó!).[85] The lyrics of "El Cerro tiene la llave" (on the accompanying CD, track 3) use a constellation of metaphors alluding to some core meanings of Abakuá in twentieth-century Cuba:

La bola se va extendiendo[86]	The ball soars outward
Cañonazo de 'hit'	Shot like a cannon
Con un grupito en el Cerro	With a group in the Cerro
Que ellos saben compartir	Who knows how to enjoy
Sin alavbanza ninguno	Without ostentation
Y le cantan un rumbón	They sing a rumba
Calientico y suavecito	Hot and smooth
El Cerro tiene la llave	The Cerro has the key
Wárárá la rumba	Play the rumba
Wárárá la llave.	Play the key.

The metaphors here relate to the group concept shared by successful sports teams, rumba players, and Abakuá lodges. The coded lyrics refer sequentially to a baseball game in the El Cerro stadium, to the rumba phrase "El Cerro has the key," and then to Abakuá mythology with the term *wárárá*.[87] *Wára* is derived from the Abakuá term *Awárandária*, a reference to the society's mystic origins in West Africa. El Chino Mokóngo told me, "Awárandária Kúsundária are two brother Íremes; they are guardians of the Abakuá fundamento in the land of Usagaré."[88] *Wára*, then, refers to a guardian of the culture. Andrés Flores told me, "Awárandária and Kúsundária were two watchmen in a forest. They were wise men and every time they met, they began to debate in order to know who had more knowledge." In a rumba context, *wárárá* means "to play"; it is a code referring to a group of men who live in peace, who get along well, enjoying debates about the richness of their cultural history, because they have mystic bonds as Abakuá members.[89] The last phrase of the song, "wárárá la llave" means "play Abakuá," because this was the key Ramírez brought to El Cerro. The song's message is that through collective efforts, team players will always come out winning. Cuban lodges are likened to teams, where members work together for the success and prominence of their group.

Abakuá Lineages in Music

The migration experience from Africa destroyed bloodlines and dynasties. Cuban national poet Nicolas Guillén expressed the idea that all Cubans are of mixed heritage in his poem "Balada de los dos abuelos" (Ballad of the Two Grandfathers). Nevertheless, generational continuity has been maintained in many Abakuá lodges, as male members of a family commonly belong to the same lodge or lineage. Examples abound in popular music, including the carnival comparsas already examined. After Santos Ramírez died, his son Domingo replaced him as Iyámba and Santos Jr. took another title in the same lodge; their brother known as "El Moro" was a title-holder of Isún Efó.[90]

Another leading comparsa, Los Dandys de Belén, was founded in 1937 and directed by Miguel Chappottín, a title-holder of Ikanfioró, a lodge whose very foundations are linked to the Chappottín family.[91] Miguel Chappottín's son, Miguel Jr., who sang rumba with Yoruba Andabo until his retirement, is a member of Ikanfioró.[92]

In the 1960s, a rhythm called Mozambique was the rage in Havana.[93] It was created by "Pello el Afrokán" (1933–2000), a member of Efó Kondó.[94] Pello's grandfather founded the lodge in 1922; his father, Roberto Izquierdo, was a title-holder in the lodge, and worked as a captain of the wharves.[95] Pello's brother Gilberto was also a title-holder of this lodge, while his brother Roberto, a member of Orú Ápapa played bongó in Ignacio Piñeiro's Septeto Nacional.[96] The family lineage of Pello el Afrokán is one among many indicating Abakuá's deep roots in Cuban society. Of the spectrum of African ethnic traditions that arrived to this island, Abakuá is among the few to have expanded to incorporate members of distinct ethnic lineages.[97]

Following the Mozambique craze, Los Van Van, founded in 1968, became Cuba's most popular dance band for decades. "El Yulo," a founding member as a *tumbador* player, was a title-holder of Isun Efó, the lodge where his father was also a title-holder.[98] Another member of Los Van Van, percussionist and singer Armando Cuervo, is a member of the Munandibá Efó lodge. Cuervo went on to play with Cuba's premier jazz ensemble, Irakere. His father, Octavio Cuervo, was a member of the Amiabón lodge and a professional singer.[99]

Guaguanco Maritimo Portuario was founded in 1961 by dockworkers in Havana; in 1986 they became known as Yoruba Andabo. Among its founders was Juan Campos-Cárdenas "Chang," a title-holder in the Muñánga Efó lodge.[100] His stepfather, Abakuá member Mario Carballo, played bongó drums in both the Septeto Nacional de Ignacio Piñeiro and the Sexteto Habanero.[101] Chang's son, "Siki," who performed as a dancer with Yoruba Andabo, is a member of Muñánga Efó.[102]

In the 1990s, the Charanga Habanera stormed Havana with its high-powered tímba music. One of their trumpet players, Leonel Polledo, is a member of Erón Entá. His father was a title-holder of Usagaré Mutánga Efó.[103]

These few examples—merely the entrance to a labyrinth—indicate the ubiquitous presence of Abakuá family lineages within Cuban popular music. This phenomenon indicates that since the nineteenth century, Abakuá has been a school for artistic production in Cuban society, one that is maintained within communities, independently from other institutions.

The Barrios and the Abakuá

Havana is a city of distinct barrios. Coded in terms derived from the colonial period, Abakuá themes underlie many twentieth-century recordings considered classics. In the 1940s and 1950s, musical genius Arsenio Rodríguez extolled Havana's barrios in his recordings, among them "El Cerro tiene la llave," "Los Sitios Asere," and "Juventud Amaliana." All refer to Abakuá themes.[104] Amaliana is a nineteenth-century code name for the barrio of Jesús María, a center for Abakuá activities.[105]

"YAMBÚ OF THE BARRIOS"

In the 1950s Abakuá title-holder Alberto Zayas and his Afro-Cuban Group recorded some of the first authentic rumba recordings in Cuban history.[106] Called "El Yambú de los barrios" (on the accompanying CD, track 4), the title implies that Zaya's Yambú is the people's music, because in Cuban parlance el barrio is where the people's culture is maintained.[107] The lyrics name several of the historic barrios, with special mention of their rumba singers. Unarticulated, yet implicit, is that many Abakuá lodges were founded and still exist in these barrios, where they continue to sustain social networks.

Diana: Bele beli / beli bele–oye lo!	Attention: I will sing, listen!
Hay quien habla de la rumba	Some speak against the rumba
Sin motivo y sin razón	Without motive or reason.[108]
Aye, lindo Yambú	Oh, pretty Yambú.
En Amalia tengo amigos	I have friends in Amalia [Jesús María]
Y en los Sitios también	And in Los Sitios as well
Por eso siempre consigo lo que quiero	This is why I also find what I
allá en Belén	need in Belén.
El Colón con su va y ven	El Colón with its to and fro.
Allí soy muy distinguido	I am welcomed there by its inhabitants
También soy muy conocido en el	I am also well known in the
barrio de Atarés	barrio of Atarés.
Aye, lindo yambú	Oh, pretty Yambú.
Si me remonto en mi campo	If I go to my countryside
Al Vedado llegaré	I will arrive in Vedado
Allí también gozaré	There I will also enjoy
Oyendo a los cantadores	Listening to the singers

Que hechan por su boca flores	Who throw flowers through their mouths
Como bien claro se ve.	As one can easily see.
Aye, lindo Yambú	Oh, pretty Yambú.
Desde El Pilar te diré	From El Pilar I tell you
Hasta Carragüao de la clave	Until Carragüao "of the key,"
Que El Cerro tiene la llave	That El Cerro has the key
De los buenos cantadores	Of the good singers
En Cayo Hueso, señores	In Cayo Hueso, gentlemen,
Me quieran a mi también	They love me also
Pueblo Nuevo te diré	Pueblo Nuevo I tell you
Era donde yo nací	Is my birthplace
Por eso te digo a ti	This is why I say
Yo nunca te olvidaré	I will never forget you.
Aye, lindo yambú	Oh, pretty Yambú.
Yambu que me muero	Yambú [is so sweet it's] killing me.
Yambú para Amalia ee!	Yambú for Amalia!
A todos los barrios quiero!	I love all the barrios!

Without mentioning Abakuá directly, the description of distinct barrios and their rumba players are obvious allusions to the Abakuá, for those who know the codes. The rumba of this era corresponded profoundly to the history of the city. The first stanza proclaims the prejudice of those who condemn the rumba—and by extension the population it represents. The second stanza was interpreted by an Abakuá and rumba master from Havana as, "My Abakuá brothers live in Amalia, Los Sitios, and Belén (the port zone), that's why I can walk there with tranquility, even while outsiders speak about them with fear."[109] The barrio of Atarés is named after the fortress of Atarés; this song, therefore, "compares the power of the fortress for defense, with the power of the culture to defend its members. Abakuá can enter this zone, because the brotherhood is their defense."

"OUR BARRIO"

In the 1960s in New York City, Cuban musicians "Patato" and "Totico" recorded a rumba that illustrates the ties between the comparsa and the Havana barrios.[110] The lyrics of "Nuestro barrio" (on the accompanying CD, track 5) begin with:

Jesús María, Belén, Los Sitios Asére	Jesús María, Belén, Los Sitios Asére
son tres corazones en uno	Are three hearts in one

que unido estarán para siempre	That will always be united
en un lazo de amistad	In the bonds of friendship
que nos une con sinceridad	That unites us with sincerity
Oye, tiene mi barrio Los Sitios caramba	Listen, my barrio Los Sitios
un ambiente colectivo	has a hell of a collective feeling

As the story goes, in the early twentieth century three comparsa troupes—The Dandys of Belén, The Gardeners of Jesús María, and Las Bolleras of Los Sitios—spontaneously encountered one another at an intersection in Los Sitios.[111] While the lyrics speak of unity, the context was one of great tension, because the comparsas, representing their barrio territories and Abakuá lodges, were in the heat of competitive performance. An inspired poet resolved the situation by improvising the lyrics of this song, calming the situation.[112] Following protocols of respect in all African-derived systems, the eldest comparsa left first, then the next in age, and finally the Gardeners.[113]

This rumba is a favorite among musicians for alluding to the meaning of comparsas for many Havana residents. The leaders of traditional comparsas consider their ensembles as the continuation of the nation-group processions of Three Kings' Day. An Abakuá leader told me that the traditional comparsas are still considered "the military band of a 'nation,' and the institution where the youth of a barrio go to encounter their identity and develop their talents as musicians, dancers, and singers, meanwhile developing a love for their barrio that can transcend the love for the city and even country."[114] By this reckoning, then, the performances of the traditional comparsas are a form of historical narrative, where the residents of a barrio proclaim their presence as a community that continues to uphold the banner of its African-centered identities.[115]

Abakuá Document Social History in Their Compositions

Lacking recording devices, important aspects of Abakuá history in their chanted forms were not recorded during the nineteenth century, but the ideas and themes of that era persisted in popular music that was recorded. Thus, the commercial recordings in which Abakuá composers documented aspects of their history are primary sources of information for a discussion of Abakuá perspectives on nineteenth-century Cuba.

"LOS CANTARES DEL ABACUÁ"

Ignacio Piñeiro (1888–1969) was known as "the poet of the son" for his some 400 compositions.[116] His "Los cantares del abacuá" (The Abakuá Chanters) describes a perpetual colonial theme: an Abakuá gathering disrupted by a police raid. Recorded by María Teresa Vera in the early 1920s, this may be the first commercial recording in the

Americas in a non-European language.[117] The song (on the accompanying CD, track 6) is in a troubadour (*vieja trova*) style with guitar accompaniment and two voices, but the 6/8 meter expressed on the clave sticks is called the "clave ñáñiga" by Cuban musicologists.[118]

En cuanto suena el Bonkó	When the Bonkó drum sounds
todo el mundo se emociona	everybody is moved
el maso feliz entona	the participants happily chant
junto con Sése Eribó	together with the Sése Eribó drum
los cantares del Abakuá.[119]	the Abakuá chanters.
Nangandó mariba[120]	They went to the river to consecratey en eso
llegó enkabúyo[121]	but the police arrived
y el Íreme Mboko con el bonkó	and the Íreme masker escaped
se desprendió.	with the bonkó drum
huye!	huye![122]
pero el Iyámba caliente	but the Iyámba, furious
le gritaba a su monína	shouted to his brother,
"el Bongó se desafina si no cantamos"	"the Bongó will lose power if we do not sing."[123]
"Asére asére asére mana	"Praise the birth of the Abakuá
kankúbia komo índia abakuá	through the drum.
Asére asére asére mana	Praise the birth of the Abakuá
kankúbia komo índia abakuá"	through the drum."[124]
huye!	huye!
manyóngo empábio	The spiritual work[125]
no se puede continuar	cannot continue
Mbákara esta bravito	Mbákara [a title-holder] is upset
por que le falta el diablito	because he is missing the Íreme dancer
que compite a verdad[126]	who truly competes
metale!	Go ahead!
por eso no están de acuerdo	because of this they don't agree
Mosóngo, el sese Yuanza no quiere cantar	Mosóngo, the Sése Yuánsa will not chant[127]
metale!	Go ahead!
ay yumba abanékue yumba	Initiations bring unity.
yúmba abanékue yumba	Initiations bring unity.[128]

Piñeiro mentioned enough title-holders (Mbákara, Iyámba, Mosóngo), ritual objects (the Sése Eribó and Bonkó drums), and ritual actions (Nangandó maribá, manyóngo empabio) to describe an initiation ceremony. The tendency in Piñeiro's compositions to describe local customs makes them part of a *costumbrista* genre used in various ways throughout Latin America, but in Cuba specifically to express anticolonial sentiment.[129] During the colonial period, most Cuban costumbrista works describe and define the creole as distinct from the peninsular Spaniard.[130] Piñeiro's composition, however, reveals the limits of nationalism in the abstract by depicting the Abakuá as distinct in language and aims from other Cubans, while being the targets of state aggression in the early republic. In other words, he describes Abakuá as a "nation within a nation."

"CRIOLLA CARABALÍ"

The composition "Criolla Carabalí" deals with Abakuá's foundation among the creole black population of Havana and the entry of white members in the nineteenth century. Whereas Piñeiro's "Los cantares del abacuá" of 1920 may have been the first commercial recording to use Abakuá phrases, the Sexteto Habanero recording of "Criolla Carabalí" of 1928 appears to be the first using exclusively Abakuá language.[131] "Criolla Carabali" (on the accompanying CD, track 7) contains ceremonial Abakuá rhythms and phrases.[132]

Iya yo	The sacred Fish appeared
Wana nyóngo entómbre	Power in the river and forest[134]
Efí Méremo Bijuraka - o Mokóngo	An Èfik king authorized by the Efó[135]
indiminua sanga Abakuá	Abakuá began to function
[affirmed through the sound of glissade on bongó]	
Aaa Eee, Aaaa Eee	Aaa Eee, Aaaa Eee
Efí Abarakó eyeneka Mokóngo	The Efí Abarakó lodge are our brothers.
Machébere.	Mokóngo is valiant.[136]
[affirmed through the sound of glissade on bongó]	
Anawe Eriero Bonkó	Why do we praise the drum?
Subusu nkaníma awana Bakokó	Because with it the Bakokó Efó lodge[137]
Abakuá Efó, nkrúkoro abanékue	Created Abakuá Efó, making us
Iyámba-O	brothers
Banbankó banbankó suko bakarióngo.	We carry our banner with pride.[138]
Yayo Eee Yayo ma-ee	
ákua bero akanawán Morua awa boribó	A reference to the birth of Abakuá
Yayo Eee yayo ma-ee.	in Africa.[139]

The lead vocal in this recording, Abakuá member Gerardo Martínez, extols a drum used for initiation:

Heyey bario bakongó!	Attention, I greet the fundamento![140]
Sése Eribo eróko mbóko baróko nansáo[141]	The Sése Eribo drum initiates title-holders
Abairémo Efí, abairémo Efó, bongó Ita	making all people, the Efí and the Efó, as one.
Sése akanarán	The Sése drum is our mother [is from Orú]
biankomo komo iremo	The music drums [biankomo, are from Efí]
munyangué Efó akari bongó	The Bongó came from Efó
Abasí ama Abasí manyobino.	Abasí [God] loves all.

The chorus then praises the founding of Enyegueyé Efó, in the lineage of white Abakuá (as discussed in chapter 4 and the appendix of potencies), repeating "Ekóbio Enyegueyé monína son ekóbios" (The members of Enyegueyé are our brothers). In referring to the ritual kinship of the Orú, Efí, and Efó people of the Cross River basin and then to a lodge of white Abakuá, these lyrics reaffirm that in Cuba all Abakuá members are "one people" and that race is not a obstacle to initiation.[142]

This composition became a model for later recordings, for example, those by Chano Pozo (1947), Victor Herrera (1962), and Patato y Totico (1967). All have some of the same lyrics and melodies as the Sexteto Habanero original, as well as a similar musical feeling.[143] When I shared this recording with Ékpè elders in Calabar, they responded with great enthusiasm, claiming that this Sexteto Habanero performance was strongly influenced by Cross River Ékpè aesthetics.[144]

"PROTESTA CARABALÍ"

Recalling the theme of the danza "El ñáñigo" from the 1920s, the composition "Protesta Carabalí" links Abakuá to anticolonial struggles.[145] The arrangement by "Román" Díaz (on the accompanying CD, track 8) was conceived of as a conversation among three parties who joined forces to fight in the Wars of Independence. They meet around a Cuban-Kongo fundamento, making their pact a sacred one. The first voice represents a Kongo leader, a Tata Nkisi, the second voice that of a Spanish creole, the third voice that of a Carabalí Abakuá.[146] The three representatives are "cruzando bastones" (crossing staffs) to join in common cause.[147] Each belongs to an initiation society, Freemasonry in the case of the Spanish creole.[148] The rhythmic structure is rumba-guaguancó, the ethnically mixed Cuban creole form used to express *cubanía* (Cuban-ness).

The structure of the composition represents the majority participation of West-Central African peoples in the Mambí army,[149] which is indicated by the first voice performing a *mambo* (chant) in the Kongo tradition, like the chorus throughout.[150]

Yo mambé!–Dió	I am consecrated; God bless you![151]
Salam Alekum	Peace unto you
[respuesta] Alekum Salam	[response] Peace unto you[152]
Yo jura nganga arriba ntoto	I am consecrated on the earth[153]
Yo soy bacheche arriba ntoto	I am fully consecrated[154]
Yo soy bacheche arriba Nganga[155]	By the Nganga fundamento.
Kwiri yo!	Listen up!
Kinani kuenda munanzo Kongo?	Who knocks at the door of my Kongo temple?[156]

The second voice extols Carlos Manuel de Céspedes, a native of Bayamo whose family owned a sugar plantation, La Demajagua, in this region near Yara. On October 10, 1868, commander Céspedes freed his thirty slaves from plantation labor, enrolling them in his small army, and thus commencing the first Cuban War of Independence (1868–1878). Céspedes' famous statement in favor of abolition is known as the Grito de Yara (Shout of Yara). The next year, a follower of Céspedes composed a martial song, "La Bayamesa," that developed into the Cuban national anthem.[157]

Heye! nació en Bayamo en el 1816	He was born in Bayamo in 1816
y a '42 a terminar su carrera de abogado	and in '42 after finishing his law career
cruzó a España	he left for Spain
participó en una conspiración	to participate in a conspiracy
por la cual fue desterrado de España	for which he was banished from Spain.
un hombre de grandes conocimientos y un trata afable	A man of great knowledge with an afable character,
el cuadillo Bayamés	the Bayamés leader.
cuando Martínez Campos y otros generales españoles	In the time of Martínez Campos and other Spanish generals
la Demajagua sonó	the battle of Demajagua began.
Carlos Manuel de Céspedes sus esclavos liberó	Carlos Manuel de Céspedes freed his slaves
les dijo 'vamos a luchar'	He told them, "Let's fight"
ese hecho constituya una gran epopeya para los tiempos modernos	The event has great significance for modern times
el grito dado por el caudillo Bayamés	The shout of the Bayamés leader
ese hecho ¿cómo se llamó?	This event, what was it called?
Ese hecho se llamó El grito de Yara.	This event was called the Shout of Yara.

The first voice responds,

Si Malembe malembe	Calling the *nfumbi* (ancestors) to solve a problem.[158]
Chichiri bakó	Bone will hit bone. [Malembe will come out fighting.]

The third voice, a Carabalí Abakuá member evokes the Voice of Abakuá, as well as specific Cross River warrior traditions as memorialized in Cuba:

Heyey baribá bakongó	Attention, I greet the fundamento![159]
Etie momi achocho ucho kambo	I belong to an ancient potency.[160]
Efí Efí Gueremo	A warrior king from Efí
Ikuar ikuá	A knife.[161]
Arafantogoyó	Strangulation.[162]
Uriabon ereniyó	A founding Èfik potency
Barondí kama.	The river Barondí kama.

Three ethnic voices and three secret societies (Kongo Palo Mayombe, Cuban Freemasonry, and Carabalí Abakuá) use phrases from their language to evoke common cause in a war of liberation. Their conversation articulates—albeit in coded forms that only initiates will comprehend—how African-derived traditions were harnessed in the Cuban colony for defense. This example is part of a tradition in Cuban popular music, where coded discursive performance, once recorded commercially, becomes a fixed part of the historical record.

Conclusion

Being integral to all facets of Abakuá practice, music is a vehicle for the expression of Abakuá's cultural history. The lodges function as informal schools for teaching Abakuá aesthetics, and many Abakuá musicians have become professionals, contributing to the formation of popular music genres in Havana and Matanzas, including the nineteenth-century contradanzas, danza, danzónes, and rumba, as well as the twentieth-century son and carnival congas.

The clave sticks and the African-derived time-line patterns they express are keys that structure most genres of Cuban popular music. They emerged as early as the 1600s in Havana's shipyards, where Carabalí Abakuá worked and where rumba ensembles were formed. The cabildos de nación were important centers where African ethnic traditions fused to create creole genres like rumba. Earlier scholars identified the rumba as derived primarily from Kongo traditions; overwhelming evidence points to Carabalí and Abakuá influence from mid-nineteenth century onward.

Abakuá have influenced nearly every genre of Cuban popular music, particularly that commercially recorded. They have been leading musicians of genres like the coros de clave, as well as the carnival comparsa traditions that are an extension of the colonial Three Kings' Day cabildo de nación processions. In their compositions and recordings, Abakuá musicians have documented aspects of their history, including their patriotism during the Wars of Independence, as well as their contributions to the formation of Havana, the nation's capitol. The activities of Abakuá lodges have shaped many Havana barrios to the point where each lodge is identified with its barrio. Commercial recordings describing Havana's barrios include coded allusions to their lodges. In other examples using Abakuá phrases, conversations about Abakuá history are camouflaged in codes that only members will understand.

When twenty-first-century Ékpè members in Calabar heard the recordings discussed in this chapter, they responded with recognition of its language and rhythmic structures. Abakuá terms identify Cross River settlements and their Ékpè practices, indicating the orthodox fashion in which its narratives have been maintained. Although the migration experience from Africa destroyed bloodlines and dynasties, many Abakuá lodges have cultivated generational continuity, as male members of a family commonly belong to the same lodge or lineage. This continuity is sustained within many Cuban musical families who are also Abakuá, a phenomenon that continues into the present.

8. Conclusions

■ ■ ■

Through Abakuá, African migrants in colonial Cuba reorganized their homeland government and passed it onto their offspring in the form of a mutual aid society. West Africans collectively refashioned an institution in the Americas, resulting in the liberation of many from slavery and strengthening the struggle for independence from a European colonial power, thus shaping the emerging nation-state in lasting ways.

In West Africa in the eighteenth and nineteenth centuries, the Èkpè leopard society of the Cross River basin was a multi-ethnic sodality that served as the local government, enabling mercantile interaction and safe travel between autonomous settlements. Cross River mythology describes the Efut of Usaghade as the source of a perfected Èkpè system, who later shared it with Èfiks and eventually with other groups including the southeastern Ìgbo. Following this pattern in Cuba, a representative group of Efó (Efut) sponsored the first Cuban lodge, designating it as Efí (Èfik). In the creative process of adaptation to the Caribbean context, Cross River peoples followed clearly defined procedures from West Africa.

From the 1600s onward, West African coastal societies were reorganized in the process of trade with European merchants, such as the Èfik Canoe House system that incorporated wives, servants, and other outsiders into federated units in the Cross River capital of Calabar, as Onwuka Dike's 1956 study demonstrated. Such precedents suggest that Cross River migrants in Cuba's urban centers, who were known as Carabalí, used models from home as they regrouped in cabildo nation-groups from the mid-eighteenth century onward. When Èkpè members within Carabalí cabildos established the first Cuban lodge for their offspring in the 1830s, they named it Èfik Obutong after a settlement in Calabar with direct links to the Usaghade cultural source. Many more Cuban lodges were named after Cross River settlements, each lodge belonging to a specific ethnic lineage, Efí, Efó, or Orú, which correspond to the Cross River Èfik, Efut, and Uruan peoples. The entire Cuban system was called Abakuá, probably after the Àbàkpà (Qua Ejagham) settlement in Calabar.

This heretofore unknown story was pieced together using oral narratives from Cuba, which were fixed in writing in the nineteenth century in the Abakuá ritual language, with interpretations into Spanish. Unpublished and intentionally maintained by Abakuá masters in a piecemeal form, some of these narratives were exceptionally made available to me for the purpose of documenting historical aspects of Abakuá's foundation. These narratives were juxtaposed with (and in large part confirmed) by others in police records, colonial legal documents, and ethnographies by earlier Cuban scholars. Later fieldwork in West Africa among Ékpè leaders provided details regarding the Cross River sources of Abakuá materials, as well as the importance of comparative trans-Atlantic research to assess the legacies of Africans in the Americas. Such research was possible only through cooperative engagement with the Cuban descendants of Cross River peoples, including the contemporary Abakuá leadership, and their West African counterparts. Key data required to grasp the profundity of African cultural heritage in the Americas are maintained within communities who have shielded this information from outsiders. Collaboration with insiders requires nurturing meaningful relationships with leaders of African-derived communities, who may share aspects of their knowledge with scholars if they feel that their values are appreciated and that their communities would benefit from this interaction.

Colonial Havana was a fortified city built largely by African laborers, who also participated in renaming the city using homeland terms. Cross River peoples named Havana Núnkwe, understood in Èfik as "a place not seen before." During the foundation of Abakuá, the port town of Regla was renamed Itiá Ororó Kánde, understood in Èfik as Itiat òyóyò Nkàndà, "foundation of the great Nkàndà," the name of a leading Ékpè grade. Using Cross River language, symbols, and philosophies, West Africans created an institution that existed parallel to the Spanish regime and was largely undetected by it.

Abakuá expanded its urban networks through the interactions of many communities, including African nation-groups, free black artisans, the black and mulatto militias, urban fugitives, and African descendants from Spain. Abakuá secret codes of communication, based upon Ékpè codes called nsìbìdì, were useful in nineteenth-century anticolonial movements, where secret oaths in the manner of Freemasonry and Abakuá were operative.

In a society where humans were bought and sold as merchandise, Abakuá groups functioned as antislavery cells that maintained a sense of morality and history among their communities. Although members paid dues, one could not buy membership. Instead, candidates for initiation underwent a long period of probation to verify their moral character among family and community members. The ability of Abakuá to maintain silence about their activities is alluded to in the phrase "Friendship is one thing, and the Abakuá another."

Havana was among the most cosmopolitan regions of nineteenth-century Latin America, with transportation systems more modern than those of Spain. Built to link the sugar plantations with the ports, Africans used the railroads for their own agendas, for example, when Abakuá from Havana traveled to the nearby city of Matanzas to sponsor new lodges there in the 1860s.

Abakuá continually expanded its networks by adjusting its restrictions on membership. First emerging as a club exclusive to those born in Africa, it later incorporated the offspring of Africans into separate lodges in the 1830s. In the 1860s, Abakuá became universalized, that is, it was opened to incorporate members from any background, when a lodge of white men was established in Havana. From this moment onward, lodges would include the descendants of Africans, Europeans, American Indians, and Asians, making Abakuá a foundational institution in Cuba, in the sense of reflecting the racial and ethnic makeup of the island long before any colonial institution did. The incorporation of white men from the dominant class was a strategy of defense against persecution by colonial authorities. The success of Abakuá's integration became a model that others followed, most famously nationalists such as José Martí, the 'apostle of Cuban independence', who in the 1880s envisioned a nation unhindered by racism. During the same era, Abakuá themes became symbolic of the Cuban nation, as represented in publications and staged plays of the period.

Fernando Ortiz once remarked that innovations like the universalization of Abakuá made what were once "things of blacks" into "things of Cuba," by which he meant "available to all Cubans," because Abakuá had been in fact a Cuban institution since the 1830s. Because nations do not exist in the abstract, however, it may be more accurate to say that Abakuá's inclusiveness extended Carabalí cultural influence into the lives of any eligible Cuban, assimilating them into a core belief system that made them Carabalí-Cubans. Initiates had to learn passages in Carabalí language, learn the performance of dance and ritual actions, and make oaths to defend the brotherhood until death. This phenomenon was paralleled in other African-derived communities of the era that incorporated members of any heritage to make them, for example, Lukumí-Cuban or Kongo-Cuban. To become Abakuá during a period of great tension between the privileged Spanish peninsulares and the marginalized Cuban creoles was to side with the creoles, becoming simultaneously "more Cuban" as well as "Carabalí." This trend was quite different from that of the United States, where African ethnicity was gradually replaced by race as a prime marker of identity, as Michael Gomez's 1998 study has shown.

Abakuá's success was met head-on by colonial authorities who banned the institution and exiled captured Abakuá members to penal colonies throughout Spain's African territories, while others escaped to Florida. Abakuá leaders who traveled throughout the Atlantic world maintained their identity as Abakuá, but contrary to some erroneous reports they did not found lodges outside of Cuba. This was not possible because Abakuá have well-defined protocols for the creation of new lodges based upon the model of Cross River Ékpè in which ritual authority is passed from a sponsor to a new group. Unlike the fundamentos (core ritual objects) of other Cuban religions of African derivation, those of Abakuá have not left the Havana-Matanzas region, despite some documented attempts.

In the 1880s Spain officially ended slavery in an attempt to diffuse the independence movement, a process that also targeted African cabildos and Abakuá for annihilation, with the aim of assimilating Cubans. By the time Spanish domination had been eclipsed on the island in 1898, the Abakuá not only remained but proceeded to expand in new lodges. Oral narratives from the final War of Independence detail the key roles of African descendants in this struggle, including the Abakuá's protection of rebel generals such as Antonio Maceo, who was the personification of Cuban patriotism.

Abakuá activities in both Havana and Matanzas guided the development of labor organizations, the expressive arts, and life-cycle rites that shaped the character of many barrios. Lodge activities include teaching of Abakuá aesthetics, and many Abakuá musicians have become professionals who contributed to the formation of nearly every genre of Cuban popular music. The compositions of Abakuá musicians have documented aspects of their cultural history in codes that only members will understand. Although the migration experience from Africa severed lineages, many Abakuá lodges have cultivated generational continuity, where male members of an extended family commonly belong to the same lodge or lineage, a phenomenon that continues to date.

This study is the result of my decades' long struggle to understand the cultural continuities between West Africa and the Caribbean. When I presented twenty-first-century Ékpè members in Calabar with recordings of Abakuá music and when they actually met Abakuá members in a cultural festival, their response was a detailed recognition of its language and rhythmic structures. That Abakuá terms could be understood by contemporary Nigerian Ékpè members indicates an unusually orthodox practice of cultural transmission that has been sustained to the present. Future volumes will describe the continuing activities of Abakuá, whose estimated 150 lodges presently contain more than 20,000 members.

Epilogue

CUBANS IN CALABAR: ÉKPÈ HAS ONE VOICE

∎ ∎ ∎

Ibuana idim; nyin ibuanake abang.
We share the stream; we do not share pots.
—ÉKPÈ SAYING

On a late afternoon in December 2004, as the sun lowered over the grounds of the Cultural Center of Calabar, Nigeria, a crowd of some 2000 people opened a wide circle for the performance of Ídèm (masquerades) in the International Ékpè Festival, organized by leaders of the Ékpè society, the traditional government of the region.[1] This event was the Nyóró (Ídèm display and competition), and for the first time two Cuban musicians who are Abakuá members, Román Díaz and Vicente Sánchez, were there to participate in the homeland of their ancestral practice.

After plantain leaves were placed over the high table and libations poured on the ground with incantations, a signal that Ékpè was in session, several Ídèm masquerades formed a line. One by one they were summoned to perform by an Ékpè specialist, the first using a rattle while chanting, another communicating only with a hand-held drum.[2] Starting from the far side of the fifty-meter circle, the specialist guided the masker—who responded with coded gestures while holding a branch of Oboti leaves in one hand and a staff in the other, spinning, stomping, shaking, sounding a bell at his waist, hopping, and running—to the high table in a display of strength and elegance.

During their short stay, the Cubans had already recognized a host of similarities with their Havana Abakuá practices, including specific drums, visual and gestured symbols, phrases, and ways of using them. For example, in Calabar an Ékpè Nyóró is a display of masquerades commonly held during the funerary rites of an important elder, a competition for the aesthetic pleasure of the participants.[3] In Cuban Abakuá, *nyoró* refers to the funerary rites of an Abakuá member, in which Íreme maskers play a fundamental role.[4] Even the term *Íreme* is derived from *Ídèm* of the Cross River (as discussed in chapter 1).

When the Cubans were invited to perform, they requested the Ékpè drum ensemble to play as they normally would. Having the same instruments played in essentially the same ways as in Cuba, the ability of both groups to communicate was matter of fact. Sánchez began to improvise with a Cuban Abakuá talking drum brought for the occasion, and Díaz, while marking time on a Cuban hand-held drum nearly identical to those used by the Ékpè ensemble, stepped into the circle to exclaim, "Heyéy heyéy aaaah!" (Attention, I will speak!).[5] Moving slowly, chanting with all his might, Díaz repeated the phrase once and then again. Being a standard opening in both Cuba and in Calabar, the entire crowd caught on and responded in chorus: "Heyéy heyéy aaaah!" Because there had been no rehearsal, Díaz calmly waited for the ensemble to find their groove, then continued, "Iyá eeee, Obon Tánsi Iyá kondondó!" (The Fish, Lord Tánsi the great Fish!). After repeating this phrase several times, the entire crowd responded by echoing, "Iyá kondondó!" (Track 10 of the accompanying CD has a recording of this chant.[6])

In Cuba, this chant refers to the founding of the society in West Africa, when a sacred fish was discovered in the water. In the Èfìk language of Calabar, *iyak* means "fish."[7] So too in both Èfìk and Abakuá, *Obon* means "king" or "ruler." In the neighboring Ejagham language, *Tánsi* can be interpreted as "lord fish." Did the spectators understand this? Or were they responding to the rhythmic structure, the way of performing in call and response? Inspired by the response, Díaz put down his drum and began to dance, using steps as would a masked dancer, while the spectators exclaimed with delight.

After other performances, the Cubans were asked to conclude the event. Without hesitation, Díaz entered the circle to chant, "Heyéy baribá benkamá!" (Attention, I will speak!), and the crowd responded "Wey!," a standard opening in both Cuba and Calabar. Díaz chanted, "Nangandó maribá" (We are going to the water),[8] "Ékue uyo" (The Voice of Ékpè is sounding).[9] Díaz continued to chant the history of Ékpè as recounted in Cuba, wherein the fish Tánsi announced its presence in the river with a roar; it was captured and used to create the Ékpè society, where its voice still sounds today. He emphasized this by chanting, "Dibó dibó dibó" (The Voice, the Voice).[10] The crowd responded on cue, "Yey yey yey!"

Díaz performed with total conviction. Because we were in Calabar, on a piece of land surrounded by three rivers, and in the presence of representatives from three ethnic groups known in Cuba as the "owners" of Ékpè, Díaz seemed to be announcing the existence of Abakuá to the ancestors of this land, to the forces of nature in Calabar: the rivers, the stars, the four directions, the drum skins, as well as the Ékpè title-holders present. After these and other historical passages, Díaz turned his attention to the matter at hand, the nyóró competition, chanting, "Awananyóngo eeeeh!" (The forest!) "Ékue wananyóngo" (Ékpè is in the forest.)

This was a summons to the masquerade dancer, who seemed to miraculously appear just then.[11] The Íreme costume he wore had been brought from Cuba for this occasion. In both Cuba and Calabar, the Íreme/Ídèm masks represent ancestral figures, as well as leopard spirits who live in the forest. The performer was a Calabar Ékpè initiate, who had spontaneously put on the Cuban mask. Díaz proceeded to guide the Íreme/Ídèm to the high table: "Etié, tié, tié, tié, tié!" (Come!).[12]

Unlike the Ékpè specialists who either rattled and chanted or intoned a message through the drum, Díaz held a drum symbolically while chanting.[13] Thinking to help, a local Ékpè man came to shake his rattles to bring out the masker, but the elders waved him away, wanting to see what the Cuban would do. Díaz continued chanting, holding the drum—in both Cuba and Calabar a symbol of authority—out to the masker, who responded, shuffling and gesturing with herbs, moving to the high table, shaking the Cuban *nkaniká* (bells) at his waist.[14] Once there, Díaz called out several titles used in Cuba for Èfìk leaders: "Efí méremo" (an Èfìk king) and "O-Iyámba" (Iyámba, a lodge leader in both Cuba and Calabar).

To bring in the audience, Díaz chanted a classic Cuban phrase that signals unity: "Yumba abanékue yumba!" (Through initiation there is unity).[15] The crowd repeated this as the percussion ensemble picked up the march and the masker danced. To conclude, Díaz commanded the attention of all:

Heyey baribá benkamá!	Attention! I will speak!
Emomí enkányo su Abasí	I am a servant of God.[16]
Abasí menguáme enkrúkoro![17]	May God bless all gathered here.

While many terms here have correspondence in Èfìk, all present understood Abasí as the Supreme Being. As the crowd responded with shouts of surprise, some with laughter, and much applause, the event came to a close.

In 2004 in Calabar, the Cuban Abakuá were received by various lodges and entered the Efe Ékpè (temple) of Obutong and Eyo Ema (Ekoretonko), both of which had representative lodges in nineteenth-century Cuba. Ekoretonko (Ékuéritongó) still exists in Havana, and both Cuban visitors were members of that lodge. After introductions and the evocation of Ékpè by Calabar leaders, both groups exchanged signs and phrases that left each confident in their affinity. The fact that obvious differences also exist did not diffuse the awareness of a bond, because Ékpè itself has many variants. The diversity of Ékpè practices are understood throughout the Cross River, so the recognition of a Cuban variant was not difficult for Ékpè leaders. It is said that "Ékpè is one," but it's not the same in each place, and these differences are respected. The Iyámba of Obutong recited, "Nyámkpè: ami ke ufọk ete mi, afo ke ufọk ete fo; ami ye afo inyanga nso?" (Nyámkpè song: I am in my father's house, you are in your father's house; what are we struggling about?).

One of the defining factors that led Ékpè and Abakuá leaders to recognize their deep ties is the Voice of Ékpè, the resonant sound that emits from the *butame* (temple) to confirm the presence of Ékpè. To articulate this idea, the same Iyámba of Obutong recited, "Ibuana idim; nyin ibuanake abang" (We share the stream; we do not share pots) interpreting thusly: "Everyone goes to the stream, but they each do what they like with their water. Ékpè be like spring. When you go to the main spring, you take the water, then you go to your house. And the way you treat it, we don't have argument or discrimination.[18] But all one, we know, is Ékpè. As that time when you people come from Cuba, you come in the full stream of Ékpè. You enter the Ékpè hall, you stay as a big man, we have to receive you and enjoy you. Even if we don't do everything the same way. But so many things almost are the same thing. It's the same thing. When we come to Cuba you will receive us, we chop there, you just look at the tradition there, and we are happy. 'Inua tié': 'one voice'. Ékpè has one voice."[19]

APPENDIX I

Cuban Lodges Founded from 1871 to 1917

■ ■ ■

The lodges of Cuban creoles founded from the 1830s to the 1860s are discussed in chapter 3, with some preliminary interpretations of their Cross River sources. This appendix continues the process by documenting lodges founded 1871 to 1917. The Cuban process of creating lodges was discontinued during the final War of Independence, due to the extreme hardships of the period. Only after the Republic of Cuba was established in 1902 did the process continue. Being outside the scope of this study, the twentieth century deserves detailed treatment elsewhere, but several twentieth-century lodges whose practices and treaties are relevant to the comparative method of this trans-Atlantic study are included here.

USAGARÉ IBONDÁ EFÓ, 1871

Usagaré Ibondá Efó was founded by Usagaré Munankebé on December 24, 1871, in the Havana barrio of Jesús María.[1] Ibondá Efó is known as "the hill of the consecration of Usagaré," a place in West Africa where Abakuá was first founded. The lodge's title is Asoíro Ibondá Efó Tété Kairán Akuáro Bénya Akuaro Benyan Moto Unbríkamo Manyongo Usagaré, akuaro binyán. This means "The sound emitted by the mother of fish above the hillock of Ibondá, when she was sacrificed to authorize the embarking point of Usagaré."[2]

Cabrera wrote, "Asoiro Ibondá . . . place in Ibondá where the first magic operation was made that produced the Voice—the sound of Ekue"; "Ibondá Usagaré Manyón Bríkamo: in Usagaré, Nasakó made the first witchcraft and on its hillocks called the Spirits and founded the Abakuá religion."[3] Ibonda is an Efut clan of western Calabar whose ancestors migrated from the Dibonda village, near the Ndian River of southwestern Cameroon.[4] During my visit there, Ṁgbè elders confirmed that their ancestors settled the Efut Ibonda community of Calabar.[5] Elders from the Usaghade community of Cameroon told me that, because part of Usaghade is Efut, the phrase "Usaghadé Efó" is used in their town, just as in the name of this Cuban lodge.[6]

BARONDÓ EFÍ, 1871

Andrés Flores told me, "Barondó Efí was born on December 26, 1871, in the barrio of Jesús María. Its title is Efí Barondó, Barondina Atabó. It was sponsored by Barondí Nataó Ubáne Efí (Ékue Barondó Nankúko) an African juego that witnessed the consecration of Èfík Ebúton in 1836.[7] Barondó, like Biabánga, belongs to two territories, Efí and Efó."[8]

In West Africa in the 1880s, explorer H. H. Johnston wrote, "Barondo (who inhabit the coast and advance in little isolated settlements into the Calabar district), are the first tribes speaking purely Bantu languages which are to be met with in journeying from Old Calabar toward the Cameroons."[9]

According to linguist Bruce Connell, "The Efut claim affinity with the Balondo, a people living in southwestern Cameroon, east of Usaghade. Efut is the Èfìk term for the Balondo-speaking people."[10] There is a Balundu village in the Usaghade community of southwestern Cameroon, where Ékpè was perfected.[11] The Cuban lodge named Barondó Efí, then, likely refers to the Efut settlements of Èfìk-speaking Calabar.[12] This would explain the received knowledge in Cuba that Barondó "belongs to two territories."

IBIABÁNGA MUNYÓN PITI NARÓKO, 1871

Ibiabánga Munyón was founded in 1871 by Piti Naróko Efí in the barrio of Jesús María.[13] Its title is Úbiabánga Munyón Piti Naróko Mbemoró. *Úbia* means "voice"; *Bánga* means "big".[14] Ibiabánga belongs to Efó.[15] In one of its meanings, Ibiabánga is a border region symbolizing the union of Efí and Efó.[16] In southwestern Cameroon, Babiabanga is a village name of the Batanga clan.[17]

In Cuba, Úbiabánga is known as a hill in Efó, whose leader ruled the seven tribes of Efí and the seven tribes of Efó who lived there.[18] This myth is used to explain why this Cuban lodge has a scepter with seven feathered plumes, representing the seven tribes (Plate 21). The theme of seven is pervasive in both Abakuá and Ékpè history. In Calabar in the 1920s, Talbot wrote that during a funerary rite of an Èfìk Ékpè leader, "the chiefs of the 'seven tribes of Calabar' were invited to be present."[19] Uruan people of the Cross River basin have a seven-clan structure "depicted during the coronation or transition of the Edidem Atakpor, the Nsomm [paramount ruler] of Uruan by the presence of the seven traditional bow-men, seven spear-men, seven sword-men, and seven royal staff-men, each representing his Essien Uruan or traditional clan."[20]

The Abakuá feathered scepter is clearly derived from another used by Cross River Ékpè during the funerary rites of important chiefs. This scepter with a plumed end is called Mmònyó in Èfìk (and munyón in Cuba).[21] According to the history as received by Cross River Ékpè leaders, when Èfìks migrated hundreds of years ago from Uruan to found Obioko, they brought symbols of royal authority, including the Mmònyó, as part of the installation regalia for their Edidem (paramount ruler).[22] An ancestor named Ibanga is a historical figure who brought part of this regalia.[23] The Cuban lodge Ibiabánga Munyón, then, may be interpreted as Itiat Ibanga Mmònyó, "the foundation stone of Ibanga who brought Mmònyó" to Obioko.[24] Ibanga is known as one of two original ancestors of the Èfìk people of the Calabar region.[25] He is also credited with bringing the Ntìnyá (the royal crown) from Uruan to Obioko, which was used to authorize the crowning of Èfìk Edidem (paramount rulers).[26] The Ntìnyá from Uruan is memorialized in the Abakuá phrase "Ntìnyá Obón Bibí," (the crown of the Bibí).[27] Uruan peoples speak Ìbìbìò and have been historically identified with this group.[28] The grandsons of Ibanga were legendary founders of Atakpa (Duke Town), Calabar's most powerful mercantile port in the nineteenth century, and therefore of its Ékpè shrine, the symbol of their independence.[29]

MUNYÁNGA EFÓ, 1871

Munyánga Efó was founded on January 6, 1871, in the barrio of Pueblo Nuevo.[30] Its title is Munyánga Efó Akari Bongó Abasí, Bongó Aterenyón Nankúku, Aterenyón Kamá, Okobio Efóri Enkomón. This means "Munyánga was born from the fundamento of Aterenyón, itself born from Efóri Enkomón, the oldest extant lodge in Cuba" (Plate 22b).[31]

During its foundation, Efóri Enkomón and Aterenyón Nankúko gave the following title to Munyánga Efó: Munyánga Efó, Munyánga mbóto, Pití biróko, Akarawáso ndibó Aterenyón Nankúko Bongó amana mbóri okámbo, Bongó Efóri Nkomón. This title mentions the fathers, grandfathers, and other family of Munyánga Efó. The phrase "Bongó amana mbóri okámbo" means, "the goat skin of the ancient fundamento."[32]

Andrés told me, "The bravery of a white man called 'El Guajiro' is well known. He was the first Iyámba of Munyánga Efó and preferred to lose everything in order to save its fundamento. He was the cook of a marquis, and hid the fundamentos of his juego in the marquis' home in order to save them.[33] Later on, El Guajiro died at the hands of Spanish guards in Oquendo Street, where, because he was Abakuá, they laid a trap for him."[34]

NCHEMIYÁ IBONKÓ, 1871

In 1871 Nchemiyá Ibonkó was sponsored by Ntáti Machecheré in Los Sitios, Havana. Ntáti Machecheré are considered "Bibí from Orú territory," and Nchemiyá Ibonkó are considered Efí.[35] Abakuá mythology explains why a group from Bibí (Ìbìbìò) would found a group from Efí (Èfík), based upon the sharing of Ékpè between both groups in West Africa. This mythology may be based upon the historical migration of Èfík communities from Uruan (likely the Cuban Orú), considered part of Ìbìbìò territory, to settlements in Calabar centuries ago.

The name of this Cuban lodge derives from the Bonkó Nchemiyá drum, considered by Cubans as the original sacred drum of Efí territory.[36] In Calabar, Ebonkó is a prominent title associated with Ékpè's spiritual facets and the Voice (úyò Ékpè).[37]

EKEREWÁ IKANFIORÓ NANKÚKO, 1873

Andrés told me, "Ikanfioró was founded by Efí Akana Bióngo in 1873 in the barrio of Belén.[38] It is also known as Ekerewá Ikanfioró Nankúko, after the name of its African territory."[39] In Abakuá, *Ikan* means "fire," and Ikanfioró refers to an active volcano in Africa.[40] All these terms are interpreted into Èfík.

In Calabar, Ekeng Ewa is an Èfík family name from Henshaw Town, today a section of Calabar city.[41] Ikang is one of the three houses of Obutong, their name means "fire."[42] Ikanfioró may be derived from historical figures in Obutong history, like Ikang Efí Oyo, Ikang Efíon Uyo, or Ikang Efío Eyo.[43] In nearby southwestern Cameroon there is an active volcano, Mt. Cameroon. Cabrera wrote, "Nankuko: great warrior."[44] In Èfík and Ìbìbìò, *uko* means "courage, bravery."[45] There is a community in Creek Town called Adak-uko (place of the brave).[46]

The terms comprising the name of this Cuban lodge, as understood by Èfík speakers, indicate that Calabarí peoples from various towns in Old Calabar regrouped in Cuba to form a community. But, in fact, Calabar was always mixed. The Iyámba of Obutong explained, "When we hear a mixed name like Ekenewa Ikan, usually it means that Ekenewa, from Henshaw Town, married from the Ikang family of Obutong, and they had a child. Because of intermarriage, Henshaw and Obutong are related through many people. We say, 'Nturukpom enyene mba iba' [an eagle has two wings], that is, a person has two wings [two parents], anywhere he goes, he will wave them. Eken Ewa of Henshaw Town cannot talk bad of Obutong when he marries from here, or vice versa. By extension, Uruan is a part of Èfík, since the first place that Èfík settled was Uruan, before we moved to Arochukwu. Then, some of our people went there. Only a foolish person will speak against them, but a clever man will laugh, saying, 'All is my people.'"[47]

Makarará in this Cuban lodge's title is interpreted as "albino," based upon a legend where albinos lived on a volcanic mountain. In Cameroon, legends of the Bakweri people who live at the foot of the volcanic Mt. Cameroon report that albinos were used as sacrificial victims to appease the spirit of the mountain when it erupted.[48] Makarará may also be a variant of *mukarará*, a Balondo term for "white man." Another possibility is "Okarárá, a place in the Oban district, close to Efut territory, home to renowned black magicians; there is no real road to the place, one can get lost in the forest."[49] In Calabar Ékpè practice, elders would call out "Okarárá!," meaning that one has gone far and can strike fear into others.[50] "During Ékpè Èfìk chanting, if one says 'Okarará' (a reference to this town of magicians), the music will switch to that of the Nyámkpè grade, and those not authorized to see Nyámkpè must leave."[51]

A treaty of this lodge speaks of a mythological struggle among various groups for possession of the *bakarióngo* standard in Ekerewá territory, where there was a large volcano.[52] The elevated regions of the Cross River region seem to be of volcanic origin, from the Oban Hills, to Mt. Cameroon, to the peak of Fernando Po (now Bioko).[53] In addition, the Cuban treaty of Ekerewá Ikanfioró may memorialize conflicts between the Èfìk settlements of Henshaw Town, Obutong, and Duke Town, begun in 1871 and ending with Henshaw Town's defeat in 1875.[54]

Andrés Flores narrated that after the battle for the standard, "The Bakarióngo remained in Ekerewá territory, and that is why the Ekerewá received the title Suko Bakarióngo. This is a legend told by Africans." Abelardo Empegó added, "The Ekerewá composed a march that is chanted: 'Banbankó suku bakarióngo, tero makotero.' They chanted this march as they carried the bakariongo." (Some Calabar perspectives on this discussion are documented in chapter 3, "Ekerewá Momí").

ERUMÉ EFÓ, 1874

Erumé Efó was founded by Erobé Efó on August 8, 1874, in Guanabacoa. According to Cabrera, "Erume: the Voice of Ekue."[55]

ENSENIYÉN EFÓ, 1876

Enseniyén Efó was founded in 1876 in the barrio del Pilar.[56] El Chino Mokóngo told me, "Their title is Eseniyén Efó Ita kono bongó taibá."[57] Various Obónes of this lodge place the date between 1876 and 1881 and named Ekório Efó Taiba as the founders. Others say that Bakokó, the founder of Ekório Efó, was the sponsor. In either case, the founders were from the Bakokó lineage.[58]

In Cuba, *Enseniyén* means "the sky." Several interpretations were offered through Cross River languages: Nsañinyañ is a place name within Ekoi, "on the east bank of the Cross river."[59] "One meaning of *nsañ* is 'red earth' (presumably laterite); *inyañ* is 'river.'"[60] *Enseniyen*, an Èfìk verb, means "to probe, inquire."[61] *Enyene nyin* means "belongs to us." Thus, the phrase "Isong enyene nyin" means "the land belongs to us."[62] "En'-yọñ, n. 1. The heavens; the firmament; the lift; the sky."[63] This translation resonates directly with Abakuá usage. It is also convincing because the lodge Enyón Bakokó (sky of Bakokó) was the sponsor. In Ékpè practice, *Nseniyen* is chanted as a boast that the speaker is a title-holder and has also initiated his offspring.[64]

ORÚ ABAKUÁ ENDÚRE, 1877

Orú Abakuá Akondomína Mefé, founded by Orú Ápapa in 1877 in Guanabacoa, is popularly known as Orú Abakuá Endúre.[65] The "Carabalí Induri" cabildo existed in Havana as early as 1802.[66] *Nduri* is an Èfìk term.[67] In Ékpè practice, *Nduri* literally means "tug of war," the act to arrest Ékpè on the run but tracked down to an Ékpè bush, pulled, and caged. It is a dramatized saying, "The King is dead. Long live the King." An Ékpè title-holder in Calabar offered that in Cuba, "Orú Abakuá Nduri may be a specialist institution dedicated to higher teachings, such as linkages in creation, reincarnation, resurrection, and immortality of soul."[68]

Andrés Flores told me, "The lodge title is Okobio Endúre akondomína mefé Sése erini bondá enyuáo, Sése Eribó akanarán."[69] According to El Chino Mokóngo, Akondomína mefé is interpreted as the "depths" or "mist" of the forest where the baróko was performed. The title mentions the Sése Eribó drum because it originates in Orú territory (Plate 23).

EKÓRIO EFÓ I, 1874/1878

Ekório Efó was founded in the barrio of Colón in 1874 or 1878.[70] Its title was Ekório Efó Brándi Masóngo. *Ekório* means "reunion." A second lodge, Ekório Efó Taiba, was founded in 1880.

ENYEGUEYÉ EFÓ, 1881

Enyegueyé Efó was founded by Ekório Efó in 1881, according to a document internal to this lineage.[71] Enyegueyé Efó founded Enyegueyé Second; both were from Guanabacoa.[72] From the Mukarará (white) lineage, the role of Enyegueyé in Abakuá integration is celebrated in popular music.[73]

In the Cross River, Eningheye is an Ejagham settlement between Calabar and Oban that was key to Cross River trade routes.[74] They are called Eningheye in Èfik and Aningeje in Ejagham.[75] So too in Cuba, Enyegueyé has a variant pronunciation, evidenced in a distinction made between the Enyegueyé lodges of the nineteenth century and the Inyiguiyí lodge from the early twentieth century.[76] The Cuban use of these related terms may reflect the variant pronunciations in Èfik and Ejagham.

EFÍ ANARÚKIE, 1881

Efí Anarúkie was born in 1881 in Matanzas. Its title is Efí Anarúkie Bongó Ubáne.

EBIÓN EFÓ, 1882

El Chino Mokóngo reported, "Ebión Efó was founded by Okobio Mukarará in the barrio of San Lázaro, and Andrés Petit acted as witness."[77] The first Iyámba of Ebión Efó was Carlos Indarte, who was also the Isué of Mukarará; he came from a wealthy white family.[78] Ebión's title is Ebión Efor, Ekori Entenisún, Efí méreme Natákua, Fambá Nitánga Kufón Nafokó, Bongó Okobio Mukarará.[79] Ebión is the sun; Cabrera wrote, "Ebión Efor: 'God and the rays of the sun.' Name of a Potency, literally, Sun-Efor."[80] Efí méreme is understood in Cuba as an Iyámba title-holder from Efí. Natákua is clearly Atakpa (Duke Town).[81]

ERÓN NTÁ, 1888

Erón Ntá was founded by Eklé Entati Machecheré in 1888 in Guanabacoa.[82] One version of its title is Eron Entati Ibióno Ana Muteke Ana Mendó. *Erón* means "ram" in both Èfik and Abakuá.[83] El Chino Mokóngo said, "They are from Orú. Erón Ntá means 'land of the ram.'"[84] The third term, *Ibióno*, means "music with swing," or in its deepest sense, the Voice of Ékpè.[85]

The case of Erón Ntá exemplifies how Abakuá interpret inherited phrases and the difficulties therein without information from African source regions. The phrase composed of *erón* (ram) and *ibióno* (music) does not make good sense, because according to mythology the ram skin did not function well as a drumhead.[86] Therefore, El Chino Mokóngo suggested that *ibióno* should be *bibí*, "It must be Erón Ntá Bibí, because in 2001 this lodge sponsored Bibí Okóndo Orú, a new lodge in Regla.[87] It seems like *Ibióno* is a mistake." This interpretation was documented in the 1950s, Cabrera wrote, "Erón Ntá Bibí: Potency of Guanabacoa."[88]

FIGURE 27. Cuban Abakuá instruments, including a marímbula (lamellophone). Photo on the left by Pierre Verger, 1957, Havana; drawing on the right from Talbot (1969/1926: vol. 3, 813); "Rattle used by the Semi-Bautu on the Cross River."

EFÍ MBEMORÓ SECOND, 1890

In Matanzas, Efí Abarakó founded Efí Mbemoró First in 1875, which founded Efí Mbemoró Second in 1890. Its title is Efí Mbemoró bongó ubane achacha úcho kambo. The phrase "Achacha úcho kambo" means "old," in other words, that the fundamento was born from an old (therefore powerful) fundamento.[89] As detailed in chapter 3, Mbemong is an Èfìk phrase for "by the river"; Cross River fishing ports are commonly called by this name.[90]

ODÁN EFÍ NANKÚKO, 1893

Odán Efí Nankúko was founded in 1893 by Efí Mbemoró Second of Matanzas.[91] El Chino Mokóngo told me, "Its title is Odán Efí nankúko awana ríbe benkamá. It means 'When the Fish spoke, he passed along the Efí river, but the men of Efó caught it.'" *Odán* means "river"; *benkamá* means "spoke."

In Cross River languages, *nkama* means "to declare."[92] In Abakuá tradition, Odán is the river where the Divine Voice was heard, its secret was discovered.[93] Thompson identified the Cuban Odán as the Ndian, a river flowing through the heart of the Usaghade peninsula in southwestern Cameroon.[94]

EFÍ EFÍ GUÉREMO, 1893

In Matanzas, Efí Efí Guéremo was sponsored by Uriabón Efí in 1893.[95] Its title, "Efí Efí Guéremo Bakondondó Abakuá," means Efí Guéremo founded Abakuá in Efí territory.[96]

Abakuá generally interpret Efí Guéremo as a variation of Efí Méremo, whom they consider the first Iyámba of the Èfìks.[97] Abakuá phrases identify Efí Méremo as "king" of Atakpa, the economic center of Calabar in the nineteenth century.[98] Calabar narratives do recount the first Èfìk Iyámba as a historical figure from the 1700s.[99] A few generations later, the title was held by the Atakpa lodge, which later sponsored a lodge named Iyámba.[100]

The Cuban Efí Méremo could derive from the personal name of an Èfìk Iyámba. One Ékpè leader suggested an historical figure from the early 1700s: " 'Efimémemo' sounds like 'Efiem Ekpo,' Ibanga's grandchild, who was the king after Eyo Ema."[101] Another suggestion was "Efiom Edem, who was Eyamba, the leader of Ékpè, as well as a leader of Duke Town in the late eighteenth to early nineteenth

centuries."[102] By 1805 Efiom Edem (Duke Ephraim), was "by far the greatest trader" on the Cross River.[103] Efiom Edem "was in 1814 the supreme interpreter [of Ékpè laws] as Iyámba Ékpè Èfik Iboku. As each of the seven Ékpè Èfik lodges of the seven Old Calabar clans had its own Iyámba, he even tried to introduce the office of 'Grand King Egbe' or 'Iyámba Mme Iyámba Ékpè Èfik Iboku' (Iyámba of Iyámbas of Ékpè Èfik Iboku)."[104] "By 1828 Duke Ephraim was *Obong, Eyamba*, sole comey [port dues] recipient, and virtual monopolist of the external trade.... He was the most influential man in Èfik history."[105] If this interpretation is correct, it is a rare reference in Abakuá to a known historical figure.

EFÍ KONDÓ ÍREME, 1903

In Matanzas, Efí Kondó Íreme was founded in the barrio of the Marina.[106] Its title, Efí Kondó Íreme, Efí Méreme Akanawán, means, "An Efí Íreme clad in a pretty suit, like a king." Efí Kondó was an Íreme of Efí territory; *Akanawán* is "a suit."[107] In Èfik, *Akanawan* is "old woman."[108] The Cuban use of this term makes sense, because in Calabar the Èfik Ebonko Ídèm masquerade represents a feminine aspect of the Ékpè system.

The treaty of Efí Kondó Íreme recounts a cultural exchange between Efó (Efut) and Efí (Èfik) in Africa, wherein the Efó exchanged their music for the hand drums and cloth suits of the Èfiks, in a place called Efí Kondó.[109] El Chino Mokóngo told me, "The Efó exchanged their own music for the íremes of Efí, for the suit worn by the people of Efí Kondó. This music was the marímbula of Efó. The Abakuá marímbula is a square box with seven keys made of cane (sometimes metal is used). A small replica is placed on the altar as a tribute in memory of Efó territory."[110] In other words, the presence of the marímbula, of the four-piece drum ensemble, and of the flashy masquerades, are explained in terms of historical exchanges in Africa between the Efó and the Efí. Cross River Ékpè representatives understand such exchanges as standard elements in the development of their system. The keyed instrument, as well as the drums used by Cuban Abakuá, are ubiquitous in eastern Nigeria and southwestern Cameroon. A traveler's report from the 1830s in Duke Town (Atakpa) described the same "bamboo cane" keyed instrument as did El Chino.[111]

Calabar Ékpè continue to use a costume that represents the time before cloth was used. Called "Ékòng Ikọng Ukom," literally "masquerade of plantain leaves," it is considered by some, "the most senior in Ékpè, and in public all others pay their respects."[112] There are places in greater Calabar where all other masquerades (Ékpè and otherwise) disappear the moment it appears. This Ídèm is made of dried plantain leaves, and only princes may wear them, and so they are called Ídèm eyen obong (son of king)."[113] In Cuba, Abakuá narratives tell that in Èfìk territory, "The first íreme of Ubáne was made with the leaves of trees like palms."[114]

EFÍ KUNÁKWA, 1908

In Matanzas, Efí Kunákwa was sponsored by Efí Kondó in 1908.[115] Its title is Efí Kunákwa Enyuáo Kuna unamberetó, Efí Kóndó, Ubáne Mbemoró. This means, "The forest in Efí territory where the íremes gathered and the costumes were manufactured." Efí Kunákwa is a forest in Efí territory; *enyuáo* means "to consecrate."[116] Cross River Ékpè leaders understood Kunákua as Ekong Anaku, an Ejagham village near Oban; it is in a deeply forested region and has M̀gbè.[117] In the early twentieth century, Efí Kunákwa godfathered the following three lodges whose names and symbols are relevant to lower Cross River history and culture.

EFÍ ETÉTE, 1913

In 1913 the Efí Etéte lodge was founded by Efí Kunákwa of Matanzas. Its title, Efí Etéte wananyóngo ekómbre unsendé keáfáróká, is interpreted as "A fortress of warriors that represented the staff and greeted with gunfire."[118] Efí Etéte is the staff of Efí (authority), *wananyóngo* means "the forest," and *ekómbre* is the "gunfire" of Efí territory.

In Calabar, Ntete is an Èfìk name meaning "great-grandfather," while Etete means "grandfather," that is, persons whose authority would be represented by their staff (or walking stick), as is common in this region.[119]

During the rites of both Cuban-Kongo and Abakuá, small amounts of gunpowder are lit, their explosion meant to "activate" the spirits being summoned.[120] This Abakuá lodge in Matanzas, however, went so far as to use a small cannon, its blast signaling the activation of the fundamento. I was able to see the Matanzas rite as an extension of maritime history by walking through the Calabar beachhead settlements of Creek Town (Obioko) and Duke Town (Atakpa), where antique cannons still lay along the roads and in the historic compounds of former merchant families.[121]

The Cuban term *ekómbre* (gunfire) is interpreted in Èfìk and Ìbìbìò as *otombe* (cannon).[122] In Matanzas, the Efí Etéte lodge is famous for commencing ceremonies with the blast of a small cannon. This practice emerged in the maritime gun salutes to settlements along the coast of West Africa, as described repeatedly by Barbot during a slaving voyage in 1699: "saluting the [Mina] castle with seven guns"; "we saluted the Black king of Great Bandy, with seven guns"; and "I came before the town of Calabar, and fired three guns, to salute the king."[123] In 1765 an English seaman who participated in slave raiding expeditions with an Èfìk chief described their equipment, "The canoes . . . had two three pounder cannons, one fixed in the bows and the other in the stern."[124] In the 1780s, "The Èfìk fortified the beach with cannon and also fired cannon at funeral obsequies or to salute the arrival of European ships."[125] English explorer Mr. Nicholls "arrived at Old Calabar (Duke Town)" in 1805, where he, "went on shore after saluting the town with eleven guns, the town returning five guns, and two other ships in the harbour five guns each, at the same time hoisting their ensigns and pendants."[126] In the 1850s, King Eyo's canoe trips from Creek Town (Ekuritunko/Obioko) to Duke Town (Atakpa) were "accompanied by a train of large canoes, from one of which a gun is fired to announce his approach."[127]

According to a title-holder in the Efe Ékpè Iboku, where a cannon still sits in the lodge's patio, "the cannon was used by King Eyo Honesty (Eyo Nsa I). It came from the supercargoes in

FIGURE 28. Cannon in the prow of King Eyo Honesty's canoe, nineteenth century (from Waddell 1863).

the 1700s and was used to make wars and bombard territories in the area. It is presently a symbol of authority for the community. It is only used for a very big occasion, like the installation of the Obong, or during the arrival of the Obong to Creek Town, at which point we would place it in the appropriate position and blow it seven times to announce the arrival of the Obong. Then the talking drums will herald the arrival of the king. Then, the Ékpè will now take over the entire ceremony, that is, Mbókò will sound. The cannon is used only for very important activities that concern kingship."[128]

The contribution by European merchants of arms and gunpowder to the Calabar region, memorialized in the ceremonial cannon of the Cuban lodge Efí Etéte, have come to symbolize both spiritual as well as military power. In may not be a coincidence that past members of Efí Etéte belonged to the Tactical Army of Matanzas, including a sergeant of the National Cuban Army that Ortiz interviewed.[129] In contemporary Cuba, when something is well done, Abakuá are prone to say, "plantó como Efí Etété" (it was done like Efí Etété), in reference to the superb spectacle of their cannon announcing the presence of the Voice.

SIERÓN NAMPÓTO, 1915

Sierón Nampóto was founded by Efí Kunákwa of Matanzas on December 12, 1915.[130] Its title is Sierón Nampóto, Mányené mpoto Ékuéri Tongó mácheberé. El Chino Mokóngo said, "This title means 'The place where the stone was extracted from the river in the territory of Ékuéri Tongó.' *Sierón* means 'a stone' and *mpóto* 'extract.'"[131] Other interpretations claim that Sierón is a territory.[132]

In Calabar, Sierón is understood as Nsidung, the indigenous name for Henshaw Town.[133] Ámbótò is a Qua settlement north of Calabar in Akampka L.G.A.[134] As discussed in chapter 3, Ékuéri Tongó is *ekoretonko*, an indigenous name for a ward in Creek Town and Calabar. *Mácheberé*, meaning "valiant," "wonderful," has been popularized throughout Latin America and then around the world through Cuban popular music as "chébere."

The importance of a sacred stone in Abakuá is certainly reflected in Ékpè practice. Religious traditions worldwide use stones to represent the strength of their foundation, among other things; so too in Ékpè and Abakuá. Regarding the phenomenon in Nigeria, Talbot reported among Cross River peoples, "stone worship reaches its greatest intensity."[135] To be recognized as autonomous, the Ékpè temple of every Cross River settlement must have its own itiat stone.[136] "A popular saying in Ékpè is 'Esio Ékpè Ke Itiat,' meaning Ékpè is born from a rock."[137] In Cuban lore, the stone was essential during the creation of Abakuá in Africa.[138] Because Abakuá lodges were illegal throughout the nineteenth century, they could not own land or construct temples openly.[139] Instead of planting a stone in the ground, Ékpè fashion, in Cuba a stone was placed on all altars "in memory of the origins of the Abakuá."[140]

EFÍ IRONDÓ, 1917

Efí Kondó founded Efí Irondó in 1917 in Matanzas.[141] Efí Irondó's title is Irondó Efí Ita Békó Bambi Nobane Bonkó Enchemiyá. "Irondó: a mine in Èfìk territory."[142] Idundu (pronounced Irundo) is a village near Calabar; they have their own Efe Ékpè.[143] Idundo is a family name in the Oron village of Usaghade, southwestern Cameroon.[144]

APPENDIX 2

Comparing Ékpè and Abakuá Masks and Their Symbols

■ ■ ■

In the nineteenth-century Cuban literature, Abakuá masks were often called *diablitos* (little devils). The association of masked dances and the Devil was made in medieval Spain, where saints' days processions were mobile performances representing virtue and sin to the public. Catholic clergy and their symbols represented good, while masked dancers represented sin (the bad life). As Africans arrived in Seville from the fourteenth century onward, they were incorporated into the processions of the Catholic brotherhoods to represent sin, the term *diablito* used to refer to them.[1] As a result, masquerade performances are referred to as *diablito* throughout the Iberian Peninsula and Latin America and indeed throughout the Christian world.[2] Through comparative research with Cross River sources, following the foundational work of Ortiz, Cabrera, and Thompson, I here present new evidence that indicates paths for future research, which would further describe the details of the Ékpè–Abakuá continuum in their own terms.

The performance of masked dancers is emblematic of both Ékpè and Abakuá. One can better understand the historical relationships of both groups by comparing their masking practices. Because both have diverse types of masquerades that represent specific functions and grades, the masks reflect the structure of these institutions. Since the early nineteenth century, Calabar Ékpè have had nine grades, many of them represented by a specific mask. Each grade has at least three tiers—the highest being Obong and then Isung (Deputy)—resulting in some twenty-seven Ékpè titles.[3] Two leading Abakuá titles are Obón Iyámba and Isun Ékue, among the some twenty-five Cuban titles, many of them represented by masquerades. In other words, lodges in both regions have a similar number of chieftaincy positions, with corresponding names in many cases.[4]

Cross River material culture was not brought directly to Cuba during the colonial era, but recreated there with the available materials. Because there is so far no evidence of reciprocal communication between Calabar and Cuba after arrival, and because visible signs of Abakuá were hidden in Cuba to avoid persecution, any similarities between West African and Cuban costume designs and their uses would be remarkable. For example, the blue and white Ukara cloth is used in Calabar exclusively by Ékpè as a banner for their temples and as a loincloth around the legs (cf. Plates 5, 13, Figure 29). Calabar Ékpè charge fines to members who wear Western-style pants during ceremony, but contemporary Ékpè members who do not have a loincloth handy when Ékpè is evoked can tie a handkerchief at the waist to represent the cloth. In Cuba there were no loincloths because these would have been visible markers of membership. Instead, Abakuá leaders often rolled up their pant legs and sometimes wore a sash cloth around the waist (cf. Figure 22), a very specific modification that resonates with Cross River usage. As discussed in chapter 1, Cubans use variants of the symbols found on the Ékpè Ukara cloth, but draw them with chalk, for the same purpose of authorizing ritual action. In other words, many symbols and their concepts are shared between

FIGURE 29. Nkàndà mask in initiation in Ùsé Uruan, an Uruan village, 1950s. The ancestors of the Uruan people were migrants from Efut of Cameroon. The five-drums initiation is an early Efut practice that depicts the full temple initiation assembly. This Nkàndà Ékpè ceremony uses five drums, a bell, and a mask. The man third from left sits on a drum to play the skin with his heel. The man second from right holds a large metal idiophonic bell (nkong) in one hand, between his legs is a symbolic drum. The man next to the Nkàndà mask has just been initiated, as the marks on his body indicate. Archives of Chief Bassey. Used with permission.

Ékpè and Abakuá, but the vehicles through which they are expressed vary according to the environment.

During Three Kings' Day processions in the nineteenth century, some drums and masquerades were performed publicly (cf. Plate 4), but more intimate fundamento objects were revealed only in hidden, private contexts. In 1879, "any Abakuá mask or sign not permitted by authorities was prohibited" from the Three Kings' Day processions, and known members were exiled to penal colonies.[5] The need to reduce visible signs in Cuba helps explain why the art of chanting was developed there into an epic form.[6]

Despite the adverse situation, there is abundant evidence that multiple forms of Cross River masking were recreated and maintained in Cuba. This fact was not controversial in Calabar, where the Ídèm masquerades are considered a form of writing; they are stable forms with specific meanings that should not be altered spontaneously.[7] Regarding the nineteenth-century painting of an Abakuá procession on Three Kings' Day in Havana, specifically the mask to the far left (Plate 4), Calabar Ékpè identified the very specific "design of the hat, the point of its top piece, and the general arrangement of its costume," as representative of the Ékpè Oku Akama grade.[8] The identification of Abakuá masks as belonging to specific grades of Ékpè is a significant finding that indicates directions for future research. Several other examples follow.

NKÀNDÀ

The Landaluze lithograph from the 1870s (Figure 30, left) is the most widely known symbol of Abakuá in the colonial period and beyond.[9] Ortiz compared this to a photograph of an Ejagham Ṁgbè (Ékpè) ídèm from the early twentieth century by Talbot (Figure 30, right), because of the obvious similarities in the cloth pattern and overall design. My research has found this comparison valid, with significant new details.[10] But other scholars have been critical of the assumption of a direct relationship with these masks, primarily because the Cuban representation appeared some three decades before the first photograph from West Africa.[11] But this is merely a problem of documentation, which occurred in Cuba first and later in Africa following the presence of colonial regimes. Ékpè title-holders in Calabar recognized several details in the Landaluze image that, buttressed by further evidence from Abakuá texts, has led to a new hypothesis of Abakuá's foundation in Cuba.

Calabar Ékpè identified the Landaluze Íreme as their own Ídèm Nkàndà, according to the cloth designs and the shape of the head projection. A comparison of Landaluze's drawing with an Nkàndà mask in Uruan from 1962 (Figure 31) shows obvious relationships. In Calabar, Ékpè masks are used as teaching tools, and the projection of an Ídèm's headpiece indicates the spiritual degree of a grade.[12] The enlightened state indicated by the vertical projection of Nkàndà's headpiece is shared in the Cuban Íreme. The checked cloth pattern is specifically that of Nkàndà, representing the claws of the leopard.[13] This pattern was described in 1825 on a Carabalí masquerade in Havana, where the "Oró Papá" group used a silk costume for celebrations, "like that of the costume of Pierrot [the harlequin], a checked cloth with a yellow base."[14] The checked-cloth masquerades of Three Kings' Day processions in nineteenth-century Havana were often described as "Harlequin."[15] These Cuban references resonate with others from the Calabar of Ékpè masquerades wearing a "harlequin costume" in the 1840s.[16] As already mentioned, in Calabar the checkered pattern, nsìbìdì for the leopard's spots, is used today on the Ukara cloth used by Ékpè, specifically the Nkàndà grade.

In both Calabar and Cuba, each part of a masquerade ensemble has a function and a name. Masquerade ensembles in both regions have a thin disk attached to the back of the masks' head. In Cuba this is called itá musón meaning "hat of the ancients."[17] In Calabar, itàm uson means "hat for the aged."[18]

In both Calabar and Cuba, many masks are made from sisal hemp and raffia. The same 1825 reference from Havana described another Carabalí masquerade made of sisal hemp with, "a large wide shirt" and trousers, "both with hemp fringes at the ankles and wrists."[19] This feature remains standard in many Ékpè and Abakuá masquerade designs, where the hemp or raffia fringes represent the sacred forest, the source of Ékpè. In Cuba, Nyanya is a general term for Íreme, while its raffia chest fringe is called nyángaduro.[20] In Calabar the raffia chest piece is called nyanya.[21]

At their waists, both Ékpè and Abakuá masks wear a bell called nkaniká (see Figures 30, right; 32, right).[22] The earliest Cuban description from 1825 indicated that "on the waist [the masquerades] carried a small bell."[23] It is significant that a single bell was used, in the manner of Èfik Ékpè Ídèm masks. In Calabar many masquerades look like those of Ékpè to the untrained eye; it is their use of a small bell on the waist that distinguishes them as Ékpè masks.[24] The Cuban Nkàndà drawn by Landaluze has many bells around the waist, which appears to have been the custom from that point onward. A description of a Three Kings' Day procession claims that the dancers were "shaking the many bells they carried bound to their waists."[25] To the present, Abakuá masks use multiple bells around the waist to the front of the dancer. In Calabar, Ékpè masks generally use one bell at the back but in rare cases also wear multiple bells as in Cuba.[26]

Ékpè in Calabar offered culturally grounded interpretations of the Abakuá language and material culture. In the case of Landaluze's drawing, their identification of it as an Nkàndà mask

FIGURE 30. (Left) Cuban Íreme (Landaluze lithograph), 1870s, displays a checkered pattern representing a leopard pelt and the upward projection of the headpiece, symbolizing spiritual achievement. (Right) An Ejagham Ídèm, West Africa, 1910s (Talbot 1926: 786). Both share striking similarities in the checkered pattern, the cloth and bell at waist, the raffia at the wrists, ankles, and chest. Despite their similarities, these masks have very different functions, as indicated by the projections of their headpieces. Verticality is synonymous with spirituality. Calabar Ékpè identified the Cuban mask as the Nkàndà grade and the Ejagham mask as the Nyámkpè grade.

supported the interpretation of an Abakuá phrase regarding the foundation of the first lodge in the 1830s. The place of Abakuá's birth, the town of Regla, is known as "Itia Ororo Kánde." In Èfìk, this was interpreted as "Itiat oyóyò Nkàndà," meaning "the birthplace of Nkàndà in Cuba" (details are discussed in the appendix of chants). This interpretation follows those made earlier by Thompson, who identified early-nineteenth-century Abakuá signatures as inspired by symbols from the Ékpè Nkàndà grade.[27] More evidence is the pronounced use of arrows and feathers in the signatures of nineteenth-century Cuba (Figures 16, 18, 19); Calabar Ékpè use bows and arrows during the Isim performance to represent male energies in a cosmic dance of regeneration (see caption for Plate 25).[28] The identification of Nkàndà in Cuba is of great significance to West African Ékpè, because this grade represents the attainment of elevated spiritual awareness in their system.

EBONGÓ

A wide variety of Cuban masquerades have been documented, starting with those of the Carabalí cabildo Ápapa Efí, the sponsors of the first Cuban lodge in 1836, who "were accustomed to parade in the streets on King's Day . . . with Abakuá masquerades; with the only difference that they were made of skins, as used in Africa . . . Also, the hood that covered the head was round at its extremity, and not pointed as that of today."[29] Íremes made of animal skins continue to be part of the Abakuá tradition, even if rarely used.[30] The rounded hood is still a part of Ékpè practice for the Ídèm Ikwo, the messengers who wear a knitted suit with a small tuft of raffia on the head.[31] As described earlier, Ékpè leaders consider their masquerades a form of nsìbìdì writing that communicates in codes through dance and that its elements that have not been altered significantly since the early nine-

teenth century.[32] Thompson extended this idea to the Ékpè–Abakuá continuum, "the whole panoply of Ǹgbe/Abakuá messengers, with their costumes, characteristically trimmed with fiber at the wrists and ankles, could be accurately characterized as *nsìbìdì* or *anaforuana* in material form."[33] Given the multiple forms of Ékpè and Abakuá masquerades that seem to have existed for centuries, the variations documented in Cuba are not necessary new inventions changing in time, but different facets of a rich tradition as displayed publicly by culture-bearers at their own discretion.

As a general rule, Cross River Ékpè masking seems to have more variations than the Cuban practice, and the same follows for drumming patterns. For example, there are five major Ékpè rhythms in contemporary Calabar that correspond to specific grades, while Cuban Abakuá use the same rhythm in two tempos, faster and slower, which represent the Efí and Efó styles.[34] After hearing Cuban Abakuá music, several Ékpè leaders in West Africa responded that it reproduced the rhythm of their Ebongó grade, an Ékpè processional.[35]

The Ebongó mask has a vertical headpiece similar to that of Nkàndà, signaling a state of spiritual transcendence (Figure 33).[36] But instead of the checked pattern of Nkàndà, Ebongó has sequined cloth with brilliant colors and its movements are "feminine," since Ebongó represents the universal mother who makes initiates reborn as *eyeneka*, children of the same mother, a term used both in Calabar and Cuba.[37] The Ebongo mask of Calabar (Figure 32, right) is clearly the model for the most common form of Abakuá Íreme, who join the fiestas or initiation ceremonies wearing brilliant colors (Figure 32, left).[38]

AKUARAMÍNA

The Cuban mask with plumed rods rising from the head is a rarely seen variant of Cross River masking styles (Figure 6, right). The mask has seven plumed rods attached to a calabash crown with signatures of authorization and crocodile teeth. Abakuá narratives about the first mythological mask

FIGURE 31. Nkàndà mask with upward projection of headpiece, demonstrating parallel functions with the mask depicted by Landaluze in nineteenth-century Havana. Initiation rite in Ùsé Uruan, an Uruan village, 1962 (the woman was invited to join the team for the photograph; Chief Engineer B. E. Bassey to right of Nkàndà). Archives of Chief Bassey. Used with permission.

describe its crocodile symbols; in Calabar, the crocodile represents the divinity of the water, known as Ndèm (Èfìk) or Nimm (Ejagham), as detailed in chapter 1. Referred to as Akuaramína (spirit), this Cuban mask is directly related to the Eribó drum (Plate 26) that represents the mother of Abakuá.[39] This mask uses a constellation of symbols that resonate those of Cross River initiation societies, both male and female, that allude to the regenerative powers of a divine mother.

Cross River Ékpè use plumed rods *basonko* during the installation of a paramount ruler or in the funeral proceedings for an Ékpè title-holder (Plate 13; Figure 6, left).[40] In addition, their use in Cross River masks can represent women's power as life-givers (Figure 8; as discussed in chapter 1). In both Cuba and Calabar, white is the color of Ndèm and the ancestors. The white plumes on the Cuban headpiece correspond to the white plumed crown worn by Ndèm priestesses during rites, whose assistants carry a gourd marked with nsìbìdì.[41] In both Calabar and Cuba, the calabash gourd represents the role of a woman in the perfection of Ékpè, as well as the womb where initiates are reborn.

Abakuá may be the only example of Ékpè's recreation in the Americas, but evidence for Cross River aesthetics in Jamaica was documented in the same decade as Abakuá's foundation, in a famous lithograph by Isaac Mendes Belisario (1837–1838). The telltale signs are the four plumed rods rising vertically from the headpiece of the mask.[42]

NYANYAKU

Nyanyaku was an early Èfìk masquerade that was integrated into modern Ékpè as a grade centuries ago, according to some Calabar Ékpè leaders.[43] This grade and its representative mask are likely sources for *nyányigo*, the nineteenth-century Cuban term for an Abakuá member (as discussed in chapter 5).

FIGURE 32. (Left) Jesús Cruz, Abakuá masquerade maker, Matanzas. Photo by I. Miller. (Right) Ebongó masquerade, Oron, near Calabar (Ward 1911).

Thanks to the thoughtful reflection of Calabar Ékpè leaders, we now have many new interpretations of Abakuá materials through Cross River languages. The following are the names of several Abakuá titles whose representative masquerades perform vital functions.

ÉRIBÁNGANDÓ

Íreme Éribángandó leads the procession in Abakuá ceremonies to "open the way."[44] Abakuá interpret the term as comprised of *Eri*, an alternate name for Tánsi the sacred Fish, and *gandó*, meaning "path." In the myth of Ékpè's perfection, Éribángandó appeared to help the Fish along the path, that is, when Sikán caught the Fish in her calabash, this Íreme protected her from the crocodile and serpent that tried to stop her from bringing it to her village.[45]

In Calabar, Éribángandó was interpreted as "eri ban kando," a rhetorical statement or a challenge, said by an initiate to anyone attempting to excel him. A boast, "one cannot excel an initiation done with 'Eri ban kando.'"[46] In a Cuban context, this would mean that the role of Éribángandó in the ceremony guarantees the best initiation.

ABASÓNGO

Íreme Abasóngo represents the first Èfìk initiate in the Abakuá origin myth. That is, when the Èfìks received the Voice from the Efó, Abasóngo was the first initiate from Efí. During the foundation

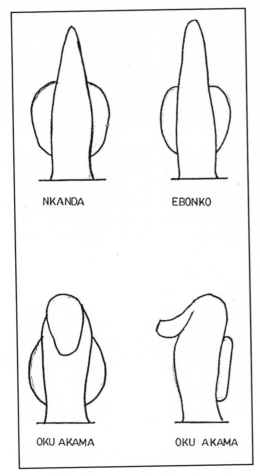

NKANDA

EBONKO

OKU AKAMA

OKU AKAMA

FIGURE 33. Figures of Ékpè masquerade heads from Bassey (2001: 77). The symbols of the Nkàndà, Ebonko, and Oku Akama shapes are discussed in the appendix of masks.

of lodges from Efí lineages in Cuba, Abasóngo is the first title to be consecrated. The staff of Abasóngo represents the autonomy of the lodge.[47]

In Cross River Ékpè, a basonko is a plumed stick used for important occasions, like the funeral or initiation of a title-holder. The fact that the basonko has a deep significance in Ékpè Èfìk practice, not accorded to the Ékpè/Ìgbè of other groups like Ejagham, Efut, or Uruan, resonates strongly with the Cuban practice of Abasóngo in Efí lineages.

ABERISÚN

In Abakuá, the title of Aberisún is represented by a masquerade who participates in the sacrifice of a goat during the initiation of a title-holder. In Èfìk, this term was interpreted as Eberédé Usun, meaning "opener of the door or way," following the idea that sacrifice opens the way. Also, Eberi Usun is "one who shuts the door or way."[48]

ENKANÍMA

Íreme Enkaníma is a Cuban masquerade who represents the forest and carries all sacrificial offerings to the bush.[49] In Èfìk, *ékàn ímá* means "greater than love." This praise name describes an attribute. If you take all the sacrifice to the bush, in fact, the bush is blessed. If you continuously take sacrifice to a particular bush, that bush is blessed, and this is in fact "greater than love."[50]

APPENDIX 3

Abakuá Chants and Their Interpretations in Cross River Languages

■ ■ ■

Hundreds or possibly thousands of Abakuá phrases are expressed by intellectuals of this informal school to narrate the history of their ancestors' activities in Africa and later in Cuba. During ceremonies, the phrases are performed competitively as masters challenge each other to go further into the subject at hand. This appendix contains selected phrases referred to in the chapters (presented according to their order of appearance) to offer preliminary interpretations into Cross River languages. First presented is a transcribed Abakuá phrase, followed by an English translation of the Spanish phrases and terms used by Abakuá leaders to interpret them. After this, translations into Èfìk or another Cross River language are presented, as identified by Engineer Bassey Efiong Bassey, Etubom Bassey Ekpo Bassey, Chief P. O. E. Bassey, Orok Edem, Chief Eso Archibong Eso, and Callixtus Ita, linguist Prof. Eno Urua, all native speakers, or Bruce Connell, an authority on the languages of the Cross River region, and from published sources, mainly Rev. Hugh Goldie's 1862 *Dictionary of the Efìk Language*, the standard work. Because these multilayered interpretations are difficult to read, I used a graphical device to identify terms in the text that correspond to West African terms. For example: anything in Goldie or another published source is placed in square brackets [ ], and anything identified by my colleagues is placed in angle brackets < >. Where both kinds of sources identity an item, then both kinds of brackets are used. Immediately under the Cuban interpretation, each bracketed expression is translated with a citation. My own comments on the interpretation, if any, follow this.

A comparison of Cuban with Cross River terms demonstrates that the oral history materials of enslaved Africans in Cuba, passed on for 200 years, may in some cases be more accurate than the errors documented by European visitors, especially regarding place names. For example, the Cuban *Natakua* is clearly *Atakpa* or Duke Town. After his voyage to Old Calabar in the 1840s, Esquire W. F. Daniell (1848) reported that the "chief commercial towns . . . are three in number: Attarpah [Atakpa], or River Town, the metropolis; Abbutong [Obutong], or Old Town; and Occorotunko [Ekoretonko], or Creek Town." All three are memorialized in Cuban Abakuá. This simple example demonstrates the necessity for emic perspectives, rather than the documents created by Europeans to comprehend this topic. By and large considered the marker of objectivity and accuracy by academic historians, the documents created by Europeans have been among the obstacles necessarily bypassed by the author to gain insight into the inner mechanics of the Abakuá language.

As an esoteric language used exclusively for ceremonial purposes among initiated men, Abakuá is likely a mixture of various "initiation dialects" (called "argots" by some scholars) of the Cross River region. This possibility must be seriously considered because many West and West-Central African guilds have initiation languages unknown to noninitiates, such as the *ẹnà* (initiation language) of the *bàtá* and *dùndún* drummers guild (called Àyàn) of the Ọ̀yọ́ Yorùbá.[1] Among the Ìgbo, members of the Àyáka society learn "secret or fancy words."² The titled elders in the Ìgbo kingdom of Nri used a "secret language" called *ólú* to communicate among themselves to maintain "ritual/economic monopoly."³ The language of the Yevegbe initiation society in an Ewe-speaking region of Ghana has "complex linguistic structures that make it difficult to be understood or spoken by an Ewe speaker who does not have any training in Yevegbe."⁴ In West-Central Africa, initiates of the Kongo Kimpasi society "were taught a new language, like Kikongo, but with subtle changes in grammar and vocabulary which made it sound strange and not always intelligible."⁵ A Kongo prince reported that, "My brother had been taken away by my uncle to be initiated into the offices of *nganga* and was taught a different and particular language, which no one but the *ngangas* were allowed ever to learn."⁶ Similarly, we would not expect facile translations of Abakuá terms directly from Cross River languages, but perhaps from their "initiation dialects."⁷

From Chapter 1

1. Éntre enyúge ororó amána semé unkayo Núnkue [néwe] amanisón erieron?
At what part of Cuba did the first Carabalís land?
In Abakuá, Néwe is an interrogative.

[Néwe] "E-we', v. . . . Which? Which one?" in Èfïk (Goldie 1964/1862: 96).

2. <Núnkue> <Amanisón> Bióráma
Those in Havana were consecrated in the African way.
Núnkue, Havana; Amanisón, a person prepared to be initiated in the African way; Bióráma, a title, "from there."⁸ This phrase refers to the Africans who were not members of Ékpè, but who were initiated in Havana.

<Núnkue>, 'nung nkwe,' I have also not seen; this could refer to a place (Havana) not seen before by the speakers (Engineer Bassey, pers. comm.; Prof. Eno Urua, pers. comm.).

<amanisong> "àmànìsòng, the rulers of a place; native, original, local" (Engineer Bassey, pers. comm.).

3. Anasakó enkrúkoro enchemiyá [mbóko] Nékre Ákamaró.
Mbóko, the Voice (Cabrera 1988a: 113); the roar of the Fish Tánse (Cabrera 1975: 183); the Voice from the River (Cabrera 1975: 21, 25); the Íreme who helps bring the Voice (Cabrera 1975: 240, 242–243).

[mbóko] Mboko is used from the Cross River region to West-Central Africa to mean Voice, with mystic and legal implications. For Ki-Kongo, see Fehderau (1992: 139), Swartenbroeckx (1973: 322); for Cameroon, see Matute (1988: 37); for Calabar, see Bassey (2001/1998: 109).

4. <Okobio> <[Enyenisón]>, <awana <bekura> mendo>/ <[Núnk]ue <[Itia] [Ororo] [Kánde]> <[Efí Kebutón]>/ Oo <[Ékue]>
Our African brothers, from the sacred place [i.e., Usagaré]/ came to Havana, and in Regla founded Efík Ebúton / we salute Ékpè.

<Okobio> it belongs to us, in Èfïk (Engineer Bassey, pers. comm.).

[Enyenisón] "Eyenisón: Africa"; "Nyisón nyenisón: African" (Cabrera 1988a: 223, 420). "Ẹ-yẹn'-i-sọñ. *n.* 1. Child of the soil; a native. 2. A free man. Ata ẹyẹn isọñ, Free by both parents" (Goldie 1964/1862: 97; *Story of the Old Calabar* 1986: 75).[9]

<Enyenisón> "enyenison, son of the soil, meaning 'We are owners of the land' " (Edem, pers. comm.).

<bekura> "Bekura is a village east of Usaghade, adjacent to or part of Ekondo Titi. This is Londo (Balondo) country" (Connell, pers. comm.).

<awana bekura mendo> Awana ekure mendo, the fight is over, take it. Awana, to fight (wana); ekure, is over; mendo, take it (Engineer Bassey, pers. comm.).

Cuban narratives describe a conflict between Èfìk and Usagaré settlements before Ékpè was eventually shared. This interpretation is consistent with some narratives from southwestern Cameroon.[10] The phrase *awana bekura mendó* as used in this chant posits a chain of transmission from the sources of Ékpè in Usagaré to the foundation of Obutong in Cuba. There is a village of Bekura in southwestern Cameroon, near Ekondo Titi and Usaghade that has Ékpè.[11] The history of this settlement is unknown to me, but it is common that new settlements are named after earlier ones. According to Cuban legend, Awana bekura mendó was an Efó region near Usagaré where the Voice sounded for the first time.[12] The phrase is written in Cuba variously as *wanabekura* or *awana bekura*; in the transcription of spoken phrases into words, Cross River terms may be joined or resegmented (cf. Miller 2005).[13]

<Núnkue Itia ororo kánde Èfìk Ebúton> "You cannot push that stone farther than the Èfìk Obutong. Itiat, stone; oro, that. Ukan . . . kande, more than, overpower, overwhelm. This standard Èfìk boast means: 'We are stronger than anyone else' " (Edem, pers. comm.). Details of this interpretation are discussed in Miller (2005).

[Núnk] "Nuk . . . to push; to push aside or away" (Goldie 1964/1862: 234).
[itia] "I'-ti-at, *n.* 1. A stone" (Goldie 1964/1862: 139).
[itia] ítíát, a stone, in Ìbìbìò (Urua et al. 2004: 61).
[ororo] "O'-rụ, *dem. pro.* That" (Goldie 1964/1862: 256).
[kánde] "U'-kan, *n.* . . . Superiority; mastery" (Goldie 1964/1862: 312).

<Itiá ororó kánde> Itie/itiat Nkàndà, Place of Nkàndà. "Itiat Ékpè is buried at the entrance to each Ékpè house. Itie is the position of authority in Ékpè cosmology" (Edem, pers. comm.; Miller 2005: 46).

<[Itia Ororo Kánde]> Itiat òyóyò Nkàndà, the foundation of Nkàndà in Cuba.[14]
Itiat, stone (symbolizes foundation); Ororo, oyóyò, beautiful, the greatest; kánde <Nkàndà, an Ékpè grade (Engineer Bassey, pers. comm.; cf. Aye 1991: 59, 105, 116).

[Kánde] In Ìbìbìò, Nkàndà is "a large bird with long colorful feathers, it lives near the river; a play connected with Ékpè society, by the old men of the society, many drums are used" (Urua et al. 2004: 99).

[Kánde] Ekande is a Bakweri village southwestern Cameroon (Matute 1988: 11).

As supporting evidence to *kánde* as Nkàndà, Ékpè Èfìk leaders identified the Cuban masquerade depicted by Landaluze in the 1870s (see Figure 24) as their own Nkàndà masquerade (see the appendix of masks). Another parallel between Cuban and Calabar practice supports the influence of Nkàndà in Havana. Cross River Ékpè music ensembles generally have three drums and an ekón bell, while Abakuá ensembles have four drums and a bell. In both systems, additional drums are used on special occasions, often as symbols of authority.[15] In particular, the Nkàndà grade uses a four-drum ensemble.[16] Given the available evidence, it is possible that Nkàndà's use of four drums was the inherited model of Cuba.

5.1. <Ékue [asanga] abiá [epó]> nípó
Ékue came to the land of the whites.[17]
In Abakuá, *asánga* means movement, walking (cf. Cabrera 1958: 55).

[asanga] "ásáñà . . . walking" in Ìbìbìò (Essien 1990: 147). "I'-sañ, *n*. . . . A walk; a journey; a trip . . . A voyage" (Goldie 1964/1862: 135). "To move, in whatever manner . . . asaña" (Goldie 1964/1862: 264).

[epó] "Ékpó, *n*. ghost . . . spirit" (Aye 1991: 32).

<Ékue asanga abiá epó> "If one interprets 'abia' as 'obio,' town in Èfik, one could get 'Ékpè that walks around in the land of the ghosts.' 'Walking' is used in a boastful context" (Connell, pers. comm.; Edem, pers. comm.). In one Ìbìbìò village, "The 'Obio Ekpo' is the village of souls beneath the earth where the souls of the departed stay and wait for reincarnation."[18]

5.2. Endafia awereké [Abasí] <[obon]> Efí
We give thanks to God (Abasí) and to the Èfik rulers (Obones).

[Abasí] Àbàsì is the Supreme Being throughout the Cross River region (Amoah 1992: 84; Connell 1997: 26; Goldie 1964/1862: 2;).

[Obón] Obong; "A chief; one having authority. 2. A principal ruler; a king" (Goldie 1964/1862: 3).

5.3. <Afotán konomí Ékue> Enyemiyá
I came from Enyemiyá land.

<Afotán konomí Ékue Enyemiyá> "Àfò ètín ònò mí àbáná Ékpè; Àfò, you; ètín, inform; ònò, give; mí, me; àbáná, about; Ékpè" (Engineer Bassey, pers. comm.).

5.4. Jura [Natakuá]
I was consecrated in the land of Natakuá.
Cubans understand Natakuá as the center of the Èfik Ékpè, as in the phrase: "Èfik atákua irión Èfik atákua irión mokabia sisi"[19]; "Atákua is an Èfik place with profound Ékpè."[20]

[Natakuá] Atakpa; "A-tak'-pa, Duke Town, the largest town in Calabar" (Goldie 1964/1862: 355).[21]

6. [ndem] efí ndem efó.
The spirit of Efí and Efó.

"The Èfik believe that Ékpè originates from Ndem . . . the elemental spirit of water" (Engineer Bassey 2001/1998: 41). Goldie (1964/1862: 200) wrote, "N'-dem E'-fik, *n*. The great idem of Calabar—the tutelary deity of the country. The priest of keeper of this object of superstitious reverence enjoys the title of Äböng [Obong] Efik."

7. <Anáwe kamanba Èfìk Ebúton?>
Tell me who is the mother of Èfìk Ebúton?

<Anáwe kamanba Èfìk Ebúton?> Ànéwò Ákámàn Èfìk Òbútòng, "'Who gave birth to Èfìk Òbútòng?' A question, a challenge" (Engineer Bassey, pers. comm.).

8. [Efórisún]
Efórisún is the capital of Efó.
This Cuban lodge was created in 1840.

[Eforisun] Efut Isu, face of Efut, in Èfìk meaning the shrine of Efut. Or, Ìsún Éfút, harbinger/fore-runner of Efut (Engineer Bassey, pers. comm.).

[Isún] "I'-sụ . . . The face; the countenance"; "I-sụ A-bas-i, n. The little round mound, as an altar . . . before which prayer was wont to be made to Abasi" (Goldie 1964/1862: 137–138).

9. <[Efóri Nkomón]>
The Drum from Efó.
Efóri has two meanings in Cuba: a title from Efó during the perfection of Ékpè in Usagaré; herbs used for *wemban* or medicinal arts.

[Efóri Nkomón] Efut Èkòmò, the drum from Efut, in Èfìk.[22]
[nkomón] "e-kọm-ọ, n. A short drum; the Egbo [Ékpè] drum" (Aye 1991: 30; Goldie 1964/1862: 73).

<nkomón> " 'ikomo' probably is a Londo (Efut) word, whereas Èfìk has ekomo. -komo is a wide-spread root for 'drum,' found in many Bantu languages" (Connell, pers. comm.; cf. Nebengu 1990: 81, 101).

<Efóri Nkomón> Èfòrì, peel; e-kọm-ọ, drum. "In Èfìk, efori ekomo means unveil or cleanse the drum for use. Efori in this context would be Ékpè usage, since in daily speech, one would not 'peel' a drum, but it makes sense in Ékpè usage" (Engineer Bassey, pers. comm.).

10. [Obonékue] <efión> [enkíko]>, obonékue efión [bonkó].
Initiates were cleansed; rooster blood was given to the bonkó drum.
In Abakuá, *obonékue*, initiate; *efión*, blood; *enkíko*, rooster.

[Obonékue] Àbànékpè, an Ékpè initiate. The term abanékue has been used in Cuba to mean initiate, from the nineteenth century onward (Cf. Cabrera 1975: 22; Castellanos García 1948: 588; *Causa* 1884: 43; Courlander 1944: 469; Guirao 1938: 14; Ortiz 1981/1951: 496; Roche y Monteagudo 1925/1908: 123; Trujillo y Monagas 1882: 369).

<efion> Fiọn, to wound (Èfìk). Giving the phrase: the cock was wounded (blood was spilt) for the candidate (Engineer Bassey, pers. comm.).

[enkíko] "E'-kikọ, v. Ekikọ-unen, n. The cock; the male of the domestic fowl" in Èfìk (Goldie 1964/1862: 72). In Ìbìbìò, nkíko is rooster. In Cuba, the term nkiko-une (meaning rooster) was recorded on *Ibiono* (2001), track 5 (at 4:06 minutes).

<efión enkíko> "The rooster is used for sacrifice in Ékpè Èfìk practice. They use it only when an adept dies in his house, to demonstrate the descent of spirit into matter. When the cock moves, a bell rings, then you know things are happening, creation is about to take place. They cleanse the entire house with the cock, then the cock is killed in the end" (Engineer Bassey, pers. comm.).

<bonkó> Ebonko is a leading Ékpè grade associated with a particular drum.

11. [Íreme] [iya] iya [isún] Anarukíe erukábia abesumbí.
An Íreme masquerade with a crocodile head.

[Íreme] In Èfìk usage, ídèm Èfí, an Èfìk masquerade, is nearly identical to Íreme (Etubom B. E. Bassey, pers. comm.; Ortiz 1952a: 111).[23] Even within the Cross River region, as Essien (1990: 13) wrote about Ìbìbìò, "the free variation involving [d] and [r] very often occurs."

[Iya] "I'-yak, n. A fish; the general name" (Goldie 1964/1862: 142). Also in Èfìk, "I'-yä, n. A public offering of food made at certain times by the people of Äkäbä, Efiat, and other places, to the objects of worship" (Goldie 1964/1862, addenda: 9).

[Isún] "I'-sụ . . . The face; the countenance" in Èfìk (see 7 above).

12. Sése [Ekoi] efórí [Ibondá].
Sacred Power of Ibondá.
This phrase refers to a spiritual power from the Ekoi people/region. In Cuba, "The Ekoi were the owners of Ékpè. . . . Ekoi beromo: the Great Power of Sese" (Cabrera 1988a: 163).

[Ekoi] Ekoi is an Èfìk term for the Ejagham and other peoples in their region (Ardener et al. 1960: 230; Jones 1984: 191; Talbot 1912a: 153).
In Calabar, Ekoi was historically used as a term for the Ejagham people. Ejagham historian Dr. Sandy Onor responded to this Cuban phrase with, "Àkàtà òtò Ekoi." Àkàtà is a secret society, and this phrase means Àkàtà originated from Ekoi; it is said in non-Ekoi regions where Àkàtà is danced. In other words, he recognized a parallel use of terms in Cuba and Calabar to speak of cultural sources in the Cross River.

[Ibondá] Ibondá is a settlement in southwestern Cameroon as well as in Calabar (see discussion in the appendix of potencies).

13. <Eribó> maka maka, Eribó maka tere <asángo> <baróko>.
The plumed drum is everlasting.
Maka maka, feather; ateréré, everlasting, infinite; asángo, to move; baróko, foundational ceremony. Chanted while the Eribó drum is being carried in procession.

<Eribó> Edibo is a mythic founder of Ékpè in Uruan settlements. Uruan Ékpè leaders interpreted the Cuban Eribó drum as a monument to their eponymous ancestor (Obong Nyong, pers. comm.; Iberedem Essien, pers. comm.). Edibo is Dibó, a reference to the spirituality of the Ékpè institution used throughout the Cross River region (Engineer Bassey, pers. comm.; Etubom Bassey, pers. comm.).

<asángo> asang, to move in Èfik (see discussion in 5.1 above).

<baróko> Mboroko (or Boroko) is a masquerade in Calabar that appears only at the death of an Iyámba or a highly ranked Ékpè chief. Boroko is connected with grief (Engineer Bassey, pers. comm.). As discussed in chapter 3, after the death of a titled-holder, an initiation is held to fill the vacant position. Among the Qua (Ejagham), during the coronation of the Ntoe (Clan Head), the Mboroko comes out first thing in the morning to announce the commencement of a big ceremony. It is a high-ranking part of the Ṁgbè tied to Mbọ́kọ̀ (Ndidem Oqua III, pers. comm.; cf. Ekpo 2005: 74).

14. Asére <[ebión] [endayo]> atrofó mokayirén.
Greetings to the sun and the four directions.
Ebión endáyo, sunrays (El Chino Mokóngo, pers. comm.; cf. Cabrera 1958: 187, 1975: 22).

[ebión] Eyo, sunshine in Cross River usage (cf. Goldie 1964/1862: 606; Talbot 1912a: 53).

<ebión endayo> "Throughout Lower Cross, 'eyo' (or a cognate form) is usually 'sunshine' (i.e., the rays or light of the sun). Endayo may be related to terms for sun/sunshine in some of the Bantu languages of that area (Bantu A15), or indeed ultimately related to Lower Cross 'eyo' " (Bruce Connell, pers. comm.).

15. <Ékue jura katínde [akanarán] enkrúkoro, Bongó itá>
The same there or here, the Voice is one.
Bongó Itá, the Voice is one. Akanarán, mother; nkrúkoro, united (i.e., we have the same mother). What Abakuá metaphorically call mother represents the female ancestor Sikán, who was associated with the spirits of the water (Ndem). In Cuban mythology, a masked dancer named Akanawán appeared in a ceremony; it was the spirit of the founding woman, Sikán, and her chant was "Ndeme Èfik yereká okobio" (Cabrera 1975: 298).

<Ékue jura katínde> Ékpè jura ketinde, I want to tell you (Engineer Bassey, pers. comm.).

<akanarán> akani nwan, old woman in Èfik. Ákánàràn <Ákánì Áràn, literally means old oil—a repository of knowledge. Furthermore, *akani aran* is an Èfik idiomatic expression meaning original power or source, often used as a praise greeting. In greetings, this would be akin to "You're the man!" (Engineer Bassey, pers. comm.).

[akanarán] Akaninwan: "A-kan'-ni, *a.* 1. Old; aged; ancient"; "ñwan, a woman" (Goldie 1964/1862: 7, 80). It makes sense that what Abakuá metaphorically call mother would be an ancestor.

<akanarán> Akanawán (old mother) is a personal name given by the Ndèm water spirit to her devotees (Akanawán, pers. comm.; cf. Udo-Ema 1940: 321).

<enkrúkoro> ekrue koro; <Bongó itá> Ekomo Ékpè ita, three Ékpè drums. "Together, these phrases mean: all that is Ékpè issues out from the Ékpè fundamento (mboko), the creator of all that is Ékpè. It may also mean: Three (ita) original Ékpè lodges [as in the Cuban origin myth]. I see this as a statement or a question: In the end, what is Ékpè? The drum. The drum is a vehicle for creating things. A statement: 'Originally there were three of them, but in fact, there is one.' " (Engineer Bassey, pers. comm.).

From Chapter 2

16. The first stanza of "Décimas"

16.1. naeriero [amoropó]
I greet your head.
In Abakuá, "Molopo, head. The same as in Duala" (Martín 1946: 20); "Koropó . . . head" (Cabrera 1988a: 318); "Akorofó or akoropó: head" (Cabrera 1988a: 39); "moropo (head)" (Cabrera 1969: 164).

[moropó] In Èfìk, "Skull, *n.* Mkpọkpọrọ" (Goldie 1964/1862: 598).

16.2. [inuá] [aborobuto] ékue
I speak Èfìk to greet Ékpe.
In Abakuá Ínuá, aburubútu ínua means we're going to speak a lot of language. "Inuá borobutón borobutón inuá ke afonkemio: many speak what they know; others know what they speak" (Cabrera 1988a: 238).

[inuá] In Èfìk, ìnùa means mouth and can mean boastful, as in "eneminua, *n.* a flatterer. . . . Owo inua inua, a boaster" (Aye 1991: 56).

[aborobuto] In Calabar, Eburutu is interpreted as Èfìk, thus the Èfìk language. In Cuba this came to mean speak, since the language was Èfìk based. "E-bur-u-tu, *n.* Said to be a man who lived in former times, to whom Calabar and Akáyöng are said to belong. Hence the phrase Èfìk Eburutu" (Goldie 1964/1862: 58).

16.3. <momí> asarorí [abanekue].
I am a blessed initiate.
"Emomi, I" (Cabrera 1988a: 398); *asarorí*, positive; *abanekue*, initiate.

<momí> In Èfìk, *mmọ mi*, is here (Chief Eso Archibong Eso, Iyámba of Obutong, pers. comm.).

<momí> In Èfìk, *ami ke*, *idem mi*, I, myself (Engineer Bassey, pers. comm.).

[abanekue] Àbànékpè, an Ékpè initiate (see discussion in 7).

16.4. abaireme <ekuefó>
An Íreme from Efó.

<ekuefó> Ékpè Efut; the Efut Ékpè.

17. The second stanza of "Décimas"

17.1. I have seen the <Anamanguí>
A funerary masquerade.

<Anamanguí> Anam ama nkwé; Anam ma nkwé; Nam ma nkwé. These are idiomatic expressions in Èfìk for a performer who does not remember his actions. That is, he cannot talk about what he did in the *fambá*. This in effect means that whatever you do during the funeral rites as Anamanguí, when

you leave there, you don't remember. If anyone asks you what happened, he's just wasting his time (Engineer Bassey, pers. comm.).

17.2. inuándo with the <Nyanyako>
Dancing with the masquerade.
Inuándo literally means speaking, but figuratively is dancing, because masquerades speak through gestures.

<Nyanyako> Nyanyaku', an early Èfìk Ékpè masquerade.

[inuá] ìnùa, mouth in Èfìk (see 16.2 for discussion).

17.3. <kuri> [kufón]
Come to the temple.

<kuri> kuri, is it? (Engineer Bassey, pers. comm.).

[kufón] Kufok means "in the house" in Èfìk, derived from *ke ufok*. House is ufok in the Èfìk, Ìbìbìò, and Oron languages (Akpanim 1998: 26; Waddell 1863: 675).

From Chapter 7

18. <[Mbákara]>
An Abakuá title.

<Mbákara> Mbàkàrà is an Ékpè title. In Ékpè practice, this grade signifies a transition from one state of being to another (Engineer Bassey, pers. comm.; Etubom Asuquo Etim, pers. comm.).

[Mbákara] "Mbàkárá, *n.* a white man; a European; white men generally. Things or animals that were first introduced to the coast on the early days of European contact with Africa . . . Unen mbakara, the white man's hen" (Aye 1991: 71).

<Mbákara> The Ékpè title Mbàkàrà and the Èfìk term Mbàkárá—meaning those who govern, that is, white men—are distinct terms (Engineer Bassey, pers. comm.). In Èfìk, Mbàkárá is derived from kárá, rule, which is quite possibly a semantic extension of kárá, encircle (Connell, pers. comm.). Ékpè leaders claim that in Ékpè the title Mbàkàrà had been in use long before European contact with Old Calabar. The Ékpè title Mbákárá is used in Calabar, but not in Oron, nor in Ejagham M̀gbè, implying that this title may be an Èfìk contribution (Connell 2004: 235). In Cuban Abakuá, both terms are used maintaining Cross River meanings. For example, Ngomo Makará is "white chalk" (Cabrera 1975: 377).

From the Epilogue

19. [Iyá] eeee, [Obon] [<[Tánsi]> Iya <[kondondó!]>
The Fish, Lord Tánsi the great Fish!

In Cuba, Iyá is the sacred Fish, the Fundament, the Mother; Tánsi or Ékue is the divine fish; Kondó: greatness.[24]

[Iyá] Iyak, fish. See Èfìk interpretations in 11.

[Obon] See discussion in 5.2.

<Tánsi> Ta-nsí, lord fish, from Tata, lord, Nsí, fish, in Ejagham. Tata nsí would mean big fish or lordly fish (P. O. E. Bassey, pers. comm.).

[Tánsi] Tansí, a "combination of the Efut word for 'lord' or 'father,' *Ta*, with the standard Ejagham for 'fish' (*nsi*)" (Thompson 1983: 242). Tone markers are important here, since Nsìí means earth, whereas Nsí means fish in Ejagham (P. O. E. Bassey, pers. comm.).

<kondondó> "Ordinarily Ekondo means domain, earth, etc., but Ekondo Ekondo is the universe. In Èfìk, *ekundu* is a row boat, distinct from canoe, known as *ubom*" (Engineer Bassey, pers. comm.).

[kondondó] "É'-kụn-dụ, *n*. The inhabitants of the earth collectively; the nations" (Goldie 1964/1862: 77). The term *èkòndò* is world in Ìbìbìò (Urua et al. 2004: 44). The implication is that the universal or mystic Fish represents a universal principal of regeneration.

20. <Heyey bariba <ben[kamá]>! . . . Wa!> (response)
Attention, I will speak! . . . We are ready! (response).[25]

<Heyey baribá benkamá . . . Wa!> Yei ekama bariba (Wa!)—all acclaim.
This sentence is a good example of nsìbìdì: It cannot be understood literally, but from the translation given, one can begin to understand what the original sentence would be (Engineer Bassey, pers. comm.). One hypothesis is that in colonial Cuba, where many Cross River language speakers were present but not all participated in Ékpè, initiates would have sought to disguise their language from the non-Ékpè people, thus transforming terms to disguise it. This is a form of nsìbìdì practice. Cross River Ékpè and M̀gbè have an initiation dialect, derived from local languages by switching their codes to be unintelligible to a noninitiate (cf. Miller 2000b; Ruel 1969: 231, 245).

<Heyey baribá benkamá—Wa!> "'Oye bari . . . ooo . . .' Assuming one enters a crowd of Ékpè people and wants to call everybody's attention or call to order before business or a speech could begin. 'Wa!' here confirms this kind of identification because after the salutation or call to order all present would answer, 'Uwa . . .'" (Edem, pers. comm.).

<benkamá> "Likely 'be nkama': be, tell a story in Londo (Efut) and other Bantu/Bantoid languages in the area (cf. Ìbìbìò: bo, speak, tell), while *n-kama* is I declare" (Connell, pers. comm.).

<kamá> "*ekama*, to call people to attention, to begin, to declare" in Èfìk (Edem, pers. comm.).

[kamá] "*kámá* . . . share in the play by displaying your knowledge of its secrets as an initiate or member" (Aye 1991: 61).

21. [Nangandó] [maribá]
We are going to the water (i.e., the place where initiates are consecrated).

Nangandó derives from ngandó, an Abakuá term meaning outline (signature), representing a path. The Abakuá phrase *ngandó mokómbre* (outline of a reptile) refers to a legend where the original *gandó* was a mark left by a reptile on the bank of a river in Usagaré (Usaghade) in what is today Cameroon (Andrés Flores, pers. comm.).

[Nangandó] Ngando or Yangando, crocodile in the Balondo language of southwestern Cameroon (Mosongo 1995: 29); ngàndo is crocodile in the Mòkpè (Bakweri) language of southwestern Cameroon (Connell 1997: 14). Ngando was also a personal name meaning Caiman/Alligator in coastal southwestern Cameroon (Ardener 1996: 138; Austen and Derrick 1999: 40). Ngandu, crocodile in the Luchazi language of Angola-Zambia, is represented in the Tussona-Luchazi ideograph vocabulary (Kubik 1987: 42–43, 188); -gando/-gandu are noun roots in many so-called Bantu languages (Johnston 1922, vol. 2: 277).

[maribá] In Balondo land of southwestern Cameroon, *mariba* or *maliba* is water, and the name of a specific stream (Mosongo 1995: 29; Nebengu 1990: 36, 42). Madiba is water in Duala (Ardener 1996: 19, 37–38). See also Hair et al. (1992, vol. 2: 678). Talbot (1912a: 43) documented an Ejagham ceremony of Oban called Mariba, "performed in the depths of the forest and with the greatest secrecy." In Ejagham and Qua Ṁgbè, mariba identifies the water source of the Voice.

22. Ékue <[úyo]>
The Voice of Ékpè.
"Ekue Uyo," the Divine Voice (Cabrera 1958: 64). "Èfíke Butón Ekue Uyo," the Voice of Èfìk Obutong (Cabrera 1988a: 146).

<úyo> úyò Ékpè, the Voice of Ékpè is one, in the Ékpè practice of Uruan settlements (Obong Nyong, pers. comm.).

[úyo] Úyò is "voice, order, edict" in Èfìk and Ìbìbìò (Goldie 1964/1862: 335–336; Urua et al. 2004: 111).

23. <[Dibó]> dibó dibó.
The voice, the voice.
A chant to evoke the Voice.

<Dibo> dí bo, come and get, in Èfìk and Ìbìbìò (Prof. Urua, pers. comm.).

[Dibo] "Ndiva means deep water to the Bakweris [of southwestern Cameroon] and other sister ethnic groups of Bantu origin," and is used in the context of their water spirit worship (Matute 1988: 40).

[Dibo] "Bap dibó!" is an Ékpè phrase uttered in reference to the grade of Nyamkpe (Hart 1964: 59, para. 167; Sosa-Rodríguez 1984: 97).

24. Awana[nyóngo] eeeeeh!/ Ékue wana[nyóngo]
The forest!/ Ékpè is in the forest.
"Manyongo: forest" (Cabrera 1988a: 331).

[nyóngo] Nyòngò is witchcraft in the Mòkpè (Bakweri) language of southwestern Cameroon (Connell 1997: 70, 122; Matute 1988: 30). Nyongo is a Bantu term, not known in Èfìk or other Lower

Cross languages (Connell, pers. comm.). In Bakweri, near Mt. Cameroon, there is a "special kind of witchcraft also known among the Duala but of Bakossi origin. This witchcraft is called 'nyongo'" (Ardener et al. 1960: 339).

25. <Efí méremo> <[O-Iyámba]>!
An Èfìk king.
Iyámba is a lodge leader in both Cuba and Calabar. "Efimeremé . . . This Èfìk king received the first sacred drum skin from the Efor"; "Efiméremo Natakua: King 'of the Akanarán Èfìk'" (Cabrera 1988a: 150–151).

<Efiméremo> "Efiméremo sounds like Efiem Ekpo, Ibanga's grandchild, who was the king after Eyo Ema" (historical figures from the early 1700s; Chief Eyo, pers. comm.).

<Efiméremo> "Efiom Edem, who was Eyamba, the leader of Ékpè, as well as a leader of Duke Town in the late eighteenth to early nineteenth centuries" (Connell, pers. comm.; see also Hart 1964: 69, para. 188, 153; Miller 2005: 38–39). If this interpretation is correct, it is a rare reference in Abakuá to a known historical figure (see appendix of potencies for details of this discussion). These Cuban interpretations documented by Cabrera (above) support that of Connell, because Natakua would be Atakpa, Duke Town in Calabar. Akanaran could be interpreted as "A-kan'-e̩-ren, n. An elder; an old man" (Goldie 1964/1862: 7), that is, an authority.

[Iyámba] Iyámba. The leader of the "Nmgbe society in Oban and in many communities in the Cross River State is the Iyamba. The word Iyamba is a diminutive of the Ejagham word *Ayamba*, meaning one who opens the way. . . . Iyamba means small ayamba, or leader of a small community—the select community of . . . Nmgbe" (P. O. E. Bassey 2004: 15). Ayamba refers to the first-born twin (P. O. E. Bassey, pers. comm.).

<Iyámba> Eyamba, name of the ruling Èfìk House of Atakpa. This is not an Èfìk term, and evidence suggests that Eyamba is an Ejagham word. In the Calabar rural areas a nocturnal masquerade called Àkàtà, or ekpri Àkàtà, comes out to gossip and will chant this song: Ekpri àkàtà ótò Ekoi/ Eyamba-ba oto Ikom edi! (Ekpri Akata hails from Ekoi/ Eyamba came here from Ikom). Ikom is an Ejagham (Ekoi) settlement (Etubom B. E. Bassey, pers. comm.). Other sources point to the Efut origin of the term Eyamba (Cf. Hart 1964: 67, para. 185). The historical relationship between Efut (Balondo) and Ejagham has not been studied in depth. My aim here was to confirm that the Cuban identification of a first Èfìk Iyamba coincides with narratives from Calabar.

26. <Abasí menguáme enkrukoro!>
May God bless all present.[26]

<Abasí menguáme enkrukoro!> "menguáme > guáme > kpeme, Èfìk 'watch' (over). Enkrúkoro, kpúkpùrù, Èfìk 'all'; thus: Àbàsì me ekpeme kpúkpùrù, God watches over all. (In Èfìk 'all' would be qualified by 'thing' or 'person')" (Connell, pers. comm.; Miller 2005: 46).

<Abasí menguáme> Àbàsì men kama means "God take control" in Èfìk (Etubom B. E. Bassey, pers. comm.).

From the Appendix of Potencies

27. \<ibióno\>
Music

\<ibióno\> "Íbiono means good intonation in the music. In the deepest sense, the term *ibiono* may be rhythm [or voice] that comes from the sea." As used in the lodge title Erón Entá Ibióno Sése Kóndo Maribá, it means that "the Voice comes from the sea" (Abelardo Empegó, pers. comm.).

\<ibióno\> Ibiono is an Èfìk term meaning a barrier, that is, meant only for the initiated (Engineer Bassey, pers. comm.). In Calabar, as this Èfìk chant tells, the language and signs are not understood unless one is trained:

Ètè ìtíé ntè àmì	You compare yourself with me
Dí ìkà ké èfé	Let us go to Ékpè shrine
Òmódiòngó nsìbìdì Ékpè	Do you understand nsìbìdì Ékpè?
Dí sèm ìsé kàbádé nò nyìn	Come and listen and interpret for us.

[ibióno] In Èfìk and Ìbìbìò, úbíongó means a barrier; the verb 'bị̀ọ̀ñọ́' means "become obstructed . . . in the way" (Uruan et al. 2004: 31).

\<ibióno\> Another possible source is the Ìbìbìò town called Ìbiònó (located in the present Akwa Ibom State). Ìbiònó apparently did not receive Ékpè until the 1920s, but it is possible that Ìbiònó people taken to Cuba inserted this place name within Abakuá practice (Etubom B. E. Bassey, pers. comm.; Engineer Bassey, pers. comm.).

GLOSSARY

■ ■ ■

Abakuá: A male initiation society in Cuba, based on a West African ethnolinguistic identity and its emblematic masked dance performance. Abakuá lodges exist in the port cities of Havana, Matanzas, and Cárdenas in western Cuba. The source for this term may be *Àbàkpà*, an Èfìk term for the Qua Ejagham of Calabar, West Africa.

Àbànékpè: In Calabar and nineteenth-century Cuba, an Ékpè term for first level initiate. Cuban Abakuá use the variant terms *abanékue* and *obonékue*.

Àbàsì: Supreme Being in several Cross River basin languages, as well as in Cuban Abakuá (as *Abasí* in Cuba).

Akanarán: In Abakuá, mother; a term of reference for a powerful fundamento. In Èfìk, *akani nwan* means "old woman," a term of reverence related to the Ndèm priesthood.

Ápapa: In Abakuá, birth. Early Havana Carabalí cabildos had names such as Ápapa Efí, Ápapa Efó, or Ápapa Orú. In Èfìk, the phrase *apá apá* means "the first, the original."

Atakpa: The center of trade activity in nineteenth-century Calabar, also known as Duke Town. In Cuba, *Natákua* is memorialized as a prominent source for Èfìk Ékpè.

Atakpo: The principal deity of the Uruan people. They called themselves "Uruan Inyang Atakpo," meaning that the identities of Uruan people and the Atakpo divinity of the river are intertwined. In Cuban Abakuá, *Natacho* is evoked as an ancient divinity in the Calabar region that predates Ékpè.

Baróko: In Cuba, a high-level ceremony. In Calabar, *mboroko* is a masquerade that appears only at the death of a highly ranked Ékpè chief.

Barondo (Balondo): An Èfìk name for the Efut people of Cameroon. The Cuban lodge Barondó Efí memorializes the Efut settlements of Èfìk -speaking Calabar.

Barrio: In Spanish, neighborhood.

Basaibéke: Wise man; a person learned in Abakuá. This Cuban term may derive from "Abasi (or Basi) Eke, a person from the region of Calabar, the Bakasi Peninsula, and Usaghade. Abasi Eke or Basieke is a popular personal name associated with success" (Engineer Bassey 2006, pers. comm.).

Bríkamo: The Abakuá language; a funerary tradition maintained by the Calle family of Matanzas city. In colonial Cuba there was a Carabalí Bríkamo cabildo. One Èfìk interpretation was *mbré kámá*, meaning "share in the play by displaying your knowledge of its secrets as an initiate or member." *Brika mmọ* means "this one is good" or "authentic" in the Ñkòmè language spoken by the people of urban Ikom.

Briyumba: See *Palo Monte.*

Butame: In Cuba, the inner sanctum of the Abakuá temple from where the Voice emerges. In Cross River Ejagham, the Ékpè (Ṁgbè) temple is called the *butame*, whereas *mutámé* means "the mystic sound of Ṁgbè."

Cabildo: In colonial Cuba, a self-organized nation-group comprised of Africans from related ethnicities, a common language group, or a common port of embarkation from Africa.

Carabalí (Calabarí): A Caribbean term of reference for Africans from Calabar or the entire Cross River region and its hinterlands, possibly including the Kalabarí of the Niger Delta.

Chébere: In Cuba, a popular exclamation, derived from Mácheberé, a title of Mokóngo meaning "valiant," "wonderful." Through Cuban popular music, the term was popularized throughout Latin America and now the world.

Cimarrón: A fugitive from slavery; *maroon* in English.

Coartación: During slavery in Cuba, a legal category wherein the enslaved could gradually purchase his/her own freedom with down payments. A person who had begun this process was known as *coartado*.

Cofradía: A lay fraternity linked to the Catholic Church. Based upon Iberian precedents, in Cuba cofradías were commonly composed of free blacks who practiced a trade.

Comparsa: An ambulant carnival troupe in Cuba.

Cuban Wars of Independence: A series of three wars that resulted in the legal emancipation of the enslaved and the end of Spanish colonial rule in Cuba. The first from 1868 to 1878, known as the Ten Years' War; the second from 1879 to 1880, known as the Small War; the final from 1895 to 1898, known as the War of Independence. The last war is commonly referred to in North America as the Spanish-American War.

Ebongó (Ebonko): In Èfik Ékpè, a grade related to the deeper spiritual functions of the society. In Cuba, *ebongó* is a name for the fundamento, that is, the Voice of the Leopard.

Èfik: An ethnolinguistic identity predominant in the Cross River State capital of Calabar, Nigeria. Known as Efí among Cuban Abakuá.

Efí Méremo: In Cuba, known as the first Iyámba of the Èfiks. This title likely derives from the name of an Iyámba of Atakpa (Duke Town) in the late eighteenth to early nineteenth centuries.

Efut: An ethnolinguistic identity predominant in the Cross River State capital of Calabar, Nigeria. Known Balondo (or Balundu) in southwestern Cameroon and as Efó among Cuban Abakuá.

Ekóbio: In Abakuá, ritual brother. Also called *okobio*, a term understood in Èfik as "it belongs to us."

Ekoi: An Èfik term for the Ejagham-speaking people. In Cuban Abakuá, Ekoi indicates "power," because they participated in the foundation of the society in Africa.

Èkòmò: In Èfik, a drum used for music. In Abakuá, known as *kankómo* or *nkomo*.

Ékpè: In Èfik, leopard. In Ejagham, *Mgbè/Ǹgbè* means "leopard." In Usaghade, *Obè* means "leopard." Each of these Cross River language communities uses their term for leopard to refer to their traditional government. In Cuba, the term became *Ékue*.

Ékpènyòng: In Èfik and Ìbìbìò, a reference to Ndèm, the water divinity. It was an Ékpè title in Oron. In Cuba, Ekuenyón is an important Abakuá title.

Ékue: Abakuá fundamento; the epicenter of Abakuá activity; derives from *Ékpè*, the Èfik term for leopard. Its sound, likened to the roar of a leopard, is alluded to as the Divine Voice. Ékue has various names, depending on the context, including Bongó.

Eribó: A fundamento drum, also known as Sése or Sése Eribó; one of several representations of the Mother, or female founder of the Abakuá. The Eribó is believed by Cubans to come from Orú, likely the Cross River community of Uruan, Nigeria, where Ékpè leaders claim Edibo as an ancestor who founded their Ékpè. Ékpè of Calabar interpret Edibo as Dibó, a reference to the spirituality of Ékpè.

Eyeneka (Èyéneka): In Èfik, a child of the same mother. Ékpè and Abakuá use the term to mean "brother," since through initiation members are reborn through the same spiritual womb.

Fambá: Abakuá temple; derived from the Ékpè term *efambá*.

Firma: Signature, a drawn symbol used in rites (see also *gandó, nsíbidi*).

Fundamento: Fundament; a consecrated object imbued with spiritual energies. Abakuá practice requires several fundamentos working in concert, including the Sese Eribó, the *bonkó nchemiyá*, the *ekón* bell, and the masquerades.

Gandó: In Cuba, a type of firma. The gandó represents a camino (path), thus the related terms Nangandó, meaning "procession," and the title Eribangandó, a masquerade who protected the founding woman on her path from a crocodile.

Ìbìbìò: An ethnolinguistic identity in southeastern Nigeria. Known as *Bibí* among Cuban Abakuá.

Ibiono: In Abakuá, music with swing. In the Cross River region, Ìbìònó is an Ìbìbìò town, while in Èfìk, *úbíongò* is "a barrier," that is, meant only for the initiated.

Ídém: In Calabar, body.

Ídèm: In Calabar, masquerade (see *Íreme*).

Íreme: A masquerade ensemble used in Cuban Abakuá rites. Íreme is derived from the Èfìk term *ídèm*.

Irióngo: In Abakuá, a place deep within the temple. In Èfìk, *idiongo* means "a sign, a symbol," in this context "the heart of Ékpè," a reference to the temple's inner sanctum.

Isué: An Abakuá grade whose function is essential to the consecration of initiates. In Calabar, there is a title called Isu Ékpè.

Itiá: In Cuba, land, usually referring to an African territory that the Cuban lodge is named after. In Cross River Ékpè, *itiat* is the foundation stone every lodge must have to signal its autonomy.

Iyá: In Abakuá, fish. In Èfìk and in Calabar, *iyak* means "fish."

Iyámba: A paramount title of both Abakuá and Ékpè. The term is derived from the Ejagham language.

Jew: Not consecrated. In African-derived traditions of Cuba, the term *Jew* means "not baptized."

Juego: Abakuá lodge (see *tierra, potencia*). A multi-faceted metaphor, *juego* can also mean "game," "play." Cross River Ékpè also describe their activities as "playing" Ékpè, implying aesthetic mastery and physical discipline.

Kankómo: An Abakuá drum used for music, also called *nkomo*. In Èfìk, *èkòmò* means "drum."

Kimbisa: See *Palo Monte*.

Mambí: A member of the Cuban liberation army of the late nineteenth century. A Kongo-derived term, in a ritual context refers to a traditional healer.

Matiabo: In colonial Cuba, a term for Tata Nganga, a specialist in the herbal arts who works with powerful fundamentos in Palo Monte traditions. Matiabo seems to be derived from Angola, where *ma-diabu*, derived from the Portuguese *diabo* (devil), was used pejoratively by Catholics.

Mayombe: See *Palo Monte*.

Mbákara (Mbàkàrà): A title in both Abakuá and Ékpè. In Ékpè practice, this grade signifies a transition from one state of being to another. Ékpè leaders report that the title Mbàkàrà had been in use in Ékpè long before European contact with Old Calabar. The Ékpè title Mbàkàrà and the Èfìk term Mbàkárá, meaning "those who govern" (popularly used to mean "white man") are not the same.

Mbókò: A grade in both Ékpè and Abakuá whose name refers to the sound of the Divine Voice.

Mbóri: In Cuba, goat. In West Africa, *mboi* means "goat" in Qua (Ejagham) and in related languages in southwestern Cameroon.

Mimba: In Abakuá, cane liquor. In Cross River languages, *mimbo* is palm wine.

Mokóngo: An Abakuá title-holder, a lodge leader. In southwestern Cameroon, Mukongo is also a title of Ṁgbè.

Mokúba: The drink prepared by Cuban Abakuá for initiations. In Nigeria, *bokuba* is the ritual drink of Uruan Ékpè.

Moruá: In Cuba, the chanter. The Abakuá title Moruá Yuánsa has the function of chanting in ceremony. In contemporary Calabar, Murua (announcer, communicator) is an assistant to an Ékpè Obong, a leader.

Mosóngo: An Abakuá title. In Ejagham Ṁgbè, Musungu is a title, the equivalent of Iyámba among the Èfìks.

Mukarará: In Abakuá, white man. The first lodge of white Abakuá was called Mukarará Efó. In Balondo (Efut), *mukara* means "white man."

Muñón (Munyón): A plumed rod. In Calabar, *Mmọ̀nyọ́* is a long scepter, at the end of which is placed a plumed rod. In Cuba, *munyón* represent ancestors who participated in foundational rites in Africa. In both Calabar and Cuba, the Mmọ̀nyọ́/munyón are associated with the title Iyámba.

Ñáñigo (Nyányigo): A Cuban term used popularly in reference to an Abakuá member, as *ñáñiguismo* was used to refer to Abakuá activities from the nineteenth century onward. Considered pejorative by contemporary Abakuá. The source for this term may be *Nyanyaku*, held to be an early form of Èfìk Ékpè.

Nasakó: An Abakuá grade who functions as a diviner and herbalist. Abakuá know the original Nasakó as a Kongo ancestor who orchestrated the foundational ceremonies among the Efó (Efut) in Usagaré.

Ndèm: A water divinity throughout the Cross River region, with variant names in each settlement. In Abakuá, *ndèm* is a reference to the spiritual base of the practice.

Ndisimes: In Cuba, those aspiring to become initiated. In Calabar the term means "ignorant," those who are not initiated.

Néwe: An Abakuá interrogative term meaning "which," "what." In Èfìk, *ewe* is "which, which one?"

Ngangulero: A practitioner of Kongo-derived Palo Monte. Derived from the KiKongo term *nganga* or Tata Nganga, referring to one who works with a fundamento of this tradition (called a *prenda* or a *nkisi*).

Nkàndà: Among the supreme symbols of Ékpè, Nkàndà is a grade whose masquerade ensemble was reproduced in colonial Cuba. Èfìk Ékpè have interpreted the Cuban term *kánde*, a reference to the birth of Abakuá in Cuba, as Nkàndà.

Nsìbìdì: A coded form of communication in the Cross River region used among Ékpè members, which includes the use of coded gestures, drum signals, and drawn and material symbols. Cuban Abakuá use similar techniques; the visual symbols are commonly known as *firmas* (signatures) or *gandó*.

Nyámkpè: An Èfìk Ékpè grade. In parts of southwestern Cameroon, Nyánkpè is the name of the society among Ejagham. The term was used in the penal colony of Fernando Po in connected with Ékpè/Abakuá practice. In Cuban Abakuá, the term *nyámpe* is a funerary rite, related to the executive functions of West African Ékpè.

Nyóngo empábio: In Cuba, the herbal arts used by the title Nasakó to activate Abakuá ceremony. Also known as *manyóngo empábio* or *nyóngo*. In southwestern Cameroon, *nyongo* was a form of traditional medicine.

Nyóró: In Calabar, an Èfìk term for a masquerade dance, usually performed at the funeral of an important Ékpè leader. In Cuba, *nyoró* (or Spanish *llanto*) is an Abakuá funerary rite, where a masquerade dancer has an essential function.

Obón (Obong): In Cuba (Calabar), refers to the highest category of an Ékpè title, such as Obong-Iyámba. In twentieth-century Calabar, Obong also became the title of a "paramount ruler."

Obonékue: See *àbànékpè*.

Obutong: An early Èfìk settlement in Calabar. The African founders of Cuban Abakuá named the first creole lodge Efìk Obutong after this settlement.

Ocha: Yorùbá-derived Lukumí religion, widely known as Santería.

Palenque: A community of fugitives; in Brazil, *quilombo*.

Palo Monte: Kongo-derived religion in Cuba. Palo Monte has several branches: Palo Mayombe is considered the oldest, followed by Briyumba. Kimbisa is a third branch founded by Andrés Petit in the nineteenth century.

Plantar: Spanish, to plant. In Cuba, to perform a ceremony, an Abakuá gathering. Cross River Ékpè interpret their term "to plant" (to evoke Ékpè) in Èfìk as *ntuak nda wuk.*

Plaza: In Cuba, a title or grade of an Abakuá lodge. Each lodge may have up to twenty-five distinct titles. In Calabar, the term used is "title-holder."

Potency/Potencia: An Abakuá lodge (see *juego, tierra*).

Sikán: The Divine Mother of Abakuá, known as an Efó princess who "discovered the secret" at the bank of a river in Usagaré. In Cameroon, some Efut (Balondo) groups name Sirkan as the woman in their Ékpè origin story.

Tánsi: In Cuba, the Lord Fish of the Abakuá origin myth. *Ta-nsí* is "lord-fish" in Ejagham, derived from *Tata,* "lord," *Nsí,* "fish."

Tierra: Land; an Abakuá lodge (see *juego, potency*). The concept of tierra refers to the group and its mythic origins in a specific land or territory in Africa. For example, the tierra Èfìk Obutong was recreated in Cuba to represent the Obutong settlement of Calabar.

Tratado: Treaty; mythic history; a charter; a pact or alliance treaty containing key information about an African-derived spiritual tradition in Cuba. Among the Abakuá, some founding treaties are shared by all lodges, while each lineage has its own treaty, as do many lodges.

Uruan: An Ìbìbìò and Èfìk-speaking community north of Calabar on the Cross River; likely the source for the Orú lineage of Cuban Abakuá.

Usagaré: Sacred homeland of Abakuá; place where Ékpè/Abakuá were perfected, according to Cuban and Cross River myths. In southwestern Cameroon, the community of Usaghade, as it is known locally, is officially called Isangele.

Úyó: In Abakuá, the Voice. In Calabar, *úyò* is voice (see *Voice*).

Valla, la: In Spanish, literally the cock-fighting pit; a metaphor for the competitive nature of Abakuá chanting, dancing, and percussion during gatherings.

Voice: In both Calabar and Cuba, Voice (*úyò, úyó*) is a code name for the regenerative forces of a universal Mother who protects lodge members; the Voice is a resonant sound that emits from the inner sanctum, often described as a leopard's roar.

NOTES

■ ■ ■

A Note on the Typography and Word Usage

1. According to linguist Bruce Connell (2007, pers. comm.), "What is sometimes mistakenly called a 'mid' tone is really what we call a 'downstepped high.' The difference is one of distribution; downstepped high can only occur after another high tone, whereas a 'mid' would be able to occur freely, that is, after a low tone as well as a high tone, as in the case of Yorùbá."

Introduction

1. Corrected by Engineer Bassey from that documented by Hugh Goldie from 1846 to 1861 in Calabar and reproduced in Aye (1991: 145), Burton (1969/1865: 365), and Goldie (1960: 17): "Obume mbume okup usem." Thanks to Professor O. Essien for providing the tone markers.

2. Abakuá members commonly refer to their system as a "religion," but the fact that they exclude women and children and only initiate men by invitation after a process of inquiry into their behavior, indicates not a religion, which are inclusive, but a club of prestige. Scholars have often referred to it as a "secret society," a "sodality," an "initiation club," or a "mutual aid" society for males whose practice includes reverential homage to the spirits of their ancestors. Cf. Martínez-Fure (1979: 158)

3. Cf. Cabrera (1975: 28).

4. On Èfìk as a regional lingua franca, cf. Jeffreys (1935: 49); Ward (1911: 47).

5. Àbàkpà is an Èfìk term for the Qua (Ejagham) settlement in Calabar (Baikie 1966/1856: 351; Goldie 1964/1862: 239; Jeffreys 1935: 24; Nair 1972: 294). In the early 1800s, Old Calabar was referred to as "the kingdom of Qua" by a Liverpool merchant who traveled there (Robertson 1819: 312). The term Àbàkpà has other meanings in the upper Cross River region (cf. Dike and Ekejiuba 1990: 48–49).

6. An autonomous community, also defined as a clan or pricipality, would necessarily have its own Èkpè lodge. Outlying villages administered by a larger settlement would not have had an Èkpè lodge, but its leaders would belong to the lodge of their principality (Etubom B. E. Bassey, pers. comm.; Ekpo 2005: 35, 83). For a modern legal definition of an autonomous community, see Uwazie (1994: 94).

7. Several prominent scholars of Cross River basin cultures have been initiated into Ékpè/Mgbè: Keith Nicklin in Usaghade (Isangele), Cameroon; Asuquo Anwana in his hometown of Oron, Nigeria; and Engineer Bassey in both Uruan and Calabar. Malcolm Ruel (1969: 210) was initiated into a traditional association of southwestern Cameroon.

8. In Calabar, Engineer Bassey (2001/1998: 57–58) used the sun and planets as metaphors for Ékpè teachings. In Havana, a lodge named Ebión Efó, interpreted as "the sun of Efó," is a metaphor for the radiance of Abakuá's inner teachings (see appendix of potencies for more on this lodge).

9. Cf. Brandon (1993: 133)

10. "The Greeks of the post-Homeric period, the 'classical' Greeks and their successors, that is, those Greeks who were literate and have left articulate records of their beliefs, considered that one of the episodes in the early history of their own race was the Trojan War.... it was a piece of history, not a piece of legend or myth; and the main characters and the essential course of events were matters of general agreement" (Lattimore 1961/1951: 12).

11. As Cross River Ejagham peoples established new settlements, "the first ceremony of all is the choosing of the new site" for the Ékpè shrine. The shrine built, an offshoot of a certain tree from the old settlement is planted in front of it (Talbot 1912a: 262, 266–267).

12. In Èfìk and Ìbìbìò, "Ndìsímé, n. folly; foolishness; stupidity" (Aye 1991: 89; Goldie 1964/1862: 605; Urua et al. 2004: 87). Young Ìbìbìò girls waiting to be initiated into the female Nyama Society went "by the name of *ndisime*" (Jeffreys 1956: 15). In Cuba, "Endisimó, a jew" (Roche y Monteagudo 1925/1908: 140). El Chino Mókongo defined: "Indisimí, jew; one who has been presented and is to be consecrated" in Abakuá. Being an historically Catholic-dominated society, Cubans use the term *jew* to mean "not consecrated" (Ortiz 1939: 88).

13. Cf. Gomez (1998: 94–95).

14. Brathwaite (1985/1974: 43) made this observation in the Anglophone Caribbean: "Because of its history, however, Afro-Caribbean culture has remained largely invisible within the region, and the representatives of this culture, though in a majority throughout most of the area, are treated (and *behave*) like a minority."

15. The Divine Voice "became the source of certainty" (Thompson 1983: 243).

16. Northrup (1978: 3–5, 108–109); *Story of the Old Calabar* (1986: 115–116). Regarding Calabar, Hart (1964: 130, para. 289) wrote: "The Èfìk state at the beginning of kingship was a conglomeration of tiny republics.... What linked them together—loosely—was the Ekpe Society." Cf. Hart (1964: 45, para. 129; 51, para. 144; 52, para. 148, 149). Regarding coastal southwestern Cameroon, Anderson (1933: 21, para. 62) reported: "Each village had its own Ekpe house which was the scene of all trials."

17. Ékpè is the Èfìk term, Ǹgbè (or Ṁgbè) is Ejagham, and Obè is the term in Isangele (Usaghade; cf. Anderson 1933: 16, para. 48; Mosongo 1995: 40; Nicklin 1991). "Among the Èfìk, Ìbìbìò, Oron and Cross River Ìgbo, Ékpè means Leopard" (Anwana 2002: 6).

18. Membership in Ékpè was a requirement for leadership: "A non-member was a person of no consequence whatever in the town" (Talbot 1969/1926: vol. 3, 786). "As late as 120 years ago Ékpè was the acknowledged symbol of manhood and statehood.... Without it neither the man nor the community was accepted to possess defendable rights. Both could be plundered, enslaved or simply done away with almost at will by those in possession of fraternity rights and privileges" (Engineer Bassey 2001/1998: 33). In the twenty-first century, Ékpè lodges still exist throughout the region. In urban areas like Calabar and Uyo, their judicial and executive powers have largely been replaced by the modern state. But in rural communities, Ékpè still performs judicial and executive functions (Dr. Anwana 2005, pers. comm.; Ebot 1978: 128–129).

19. Waddell (1863: 314). British writers visiting the region referred to Ékpè as Egbo, confusing the Ekpo society of many Ìbìbìò communities with the Ékpè of other communities (Talbot 1969/1926: vol. 3, 780). Such confusion, like that between Kalabari of the Niger Delta and Old Calabar of the Cross River region, has been termed "errorism" by Victor Manfredi (2004).

20. These indications come from contemporary oral history, as well as colonial reports, themselves largely based upon oral history. "Trade between Cross River merchants and European ship captains

increased in the 1630s and 1640s" (Behrendt and Graham 2003: 56). Anthropologist Edwin Ardener (1968, 1996: 19, 21, 26) used the records of seventeenth-century European merchants to demonstrate the existence of trading settlements in the coastal Rio del Rey area (southeast of Calabar) by the 1600s, a narrative documented by Anderson (1933, paras 11–20) from local tradition. This is the region of Usaghade (Isangele), known as Usagaré in Cuba, the legendary source of a "perfected" Ékpè. Given the foregoing, it is probable that early trade in the Isangele region effected the stature of their Ékpè. This supposition is supported by the finding that Ékpè emerged later in Calabar than in Cameroon (Latham 1973: 36).

21. Cf. Ijoma (1998: 22–23); Jones (1988a: 115); Manfredi (2004: 239). "The Aro, and their neighbours the Ututu and Ihe, have the Ekkpe Club in all its seven grades and its full ceremonial derived from Calabar" (Talbot 1969/1926: vol. 3, 782). "At the end of the eighteenth century some 7000 slaves a year for the Atlantic trade were exported from Old Calabar and Cameroons" (Chilver 1962: 237). By the mid-1800s, there were "well defined slave-trading routes" from the Grassfields of Cameroon into Calabar (Chilver and Kaberry 1967: 149).

22. Nigerian historian O. E. Uya (1986: 30) wrote, "it is now generally accepted that secret societies as a vital instrument of social control . . . and the Nsìbìdì script found in Ìgbo land, were all borrowed through Ìgbo contact with the Cross River peoples." The secret men's association of the southern Ìgbo-speaking people, Ọkọnkọ, is also known there as Ékpè (Forde and Jones 1950: 20; Green 1958; Hargreaves 1987: 112–113; Talbot 1969/1926: vol. 3, 781). On the islands of Trinidad and Carriacou, the Ọkọnkọ was documented as "Hokonko" in the nineteenth century (Warner-Lewis 1991: 182). In Maroon communities of Jamaica, Okonko is remembered as a founding general (Bilby 2006: 82).

23. Cf. Anwana (2002: 84); Engineer Bassey (2001/1998: 23); Talbot (1969/1926: vol. 3, 787).

24. Cf. Dr. A. O. Anwana (2002). The expansion of the Èfìk trade networks went hand in hand with the development of eclectic forms of Ékpè. During the settlement of Creek Town, some forms of Ékpè were brought from Uruan. "The destruction of Tom Shott's Point in 1821 by Duke Ehpraim marked the culmination of 200 years of Èfìk expansion and aggrandizement" (Behrendt and Graham 2003: 56; cf. Crow 1830: 270–271; Latham 1973: 50); it also marked the reception by Èfìks of the important Ékpè grade of Nkàndà from Tom Shott's (cf. Oku 1989: 15–16, 65–66).

25. Ékpè masking aesthetics are found at the further reaches of Old Calabar trade networks. For example, in the region of Buea, Cameroon, Ardener (1996: 266) noted the resemblance of a "Nigerian Ékpè dancer" to the "Moseke" figure in the Bakweri elephant dance. In Bamum, Cameroon, a photograph of masqueraders from the early 1900s depicts an Ékpè-inspired costume (Geary 1988: 116–117, fig. 75). The cultural cross-fertilization of the Cross River and Cameroon Grassfields regions was pronounced (Brain 1981: 357). Until 1900, "The Cross River . . . remained the highway of cultural interchange between the various people of the region" (Erim 1990: 185). The Grassfields regions is described as an "ecumene," one of whose distinguishing characteristics was a masked regulatory society (Chilver and Kaberry 1967: 128, 148; Kopytoff 1981: 372)

26. Africans became victims of the trans-Atlantic slave trade in various ways, as prisoners of war, as debtors, as banishment for antisocial behavior, and through treason. For examples from the Cross River region, see Talbot (1969/1926: vol. 3, 664); Waddell (1863: 429).

27. Baikie (1966/1856: 313) documented a sighting of more than twenty enslaved people in Cuba who had passed through "A'ro" to "Old Kalabár." Ékpè members or not, they would have recognized the codes of this system. In "Arochukwu," for example, the Ékpè society "promoted the assimilation of aliens into the Aro cultural system" (Dike and Ekejiuba 1990: 77). Ékpè cultural and political themes were understood at various levels by all inhabitants of the region.

28. From the 1650s onward, the term Kalabari—as used in slave records in the Americas—may have meant either a person from New Calabar, where the Portuguese and Dutch traded, or from

Old Calabar, where the Dutch and English traded (cf. Jones 1963: 34; Northrup 2000: 9). The first known European slaving vessel in the Cross River region was "The Portuguese slaver *Candelaria*, which disembarked 114 enslaved Africans from 'Calabar' in Veracruz on 25 June 1625" (Behrendt and Graham 2003: 41). "'Calabar' was a generic term for all captives from Biafra," the key ports of which were Bonny and Calabar (Nwokeji 2000: 634). In reference to the inhabitants of Old Calabar as well as the Niger Delta Kalabari, the term Kalabari was used in Freetown, Sierra Leone, after 1807, when the British government sent "recaptive" Africans into the region (cf. Fyfe 1960: 110, 113, 2005, pers. comm.). Evidence suggests that the term *Calabarí* for the inhabitants of Calabar was created as a result of trans-Atlantic trade from the seventeenth to nineteenth centuries.

29. Hall (1992a: 299); Landers (1999: 48–49); Wood (1974: 339). "Calabars" were documented in early seventeenth-century Bahia, Brazil (Sweet 2003: 23; see also Verger 1976: 595). A Calabar High School was built by the West Inidan Pioneers of the Presbyterian Church of Scotland Mission, who had worked in Calabar (Oku 1989: xi).

30. Miller (2000b, 2005); Trujillo y Monagas (1882: 364).

31. Jean-Marie Teno, a filmmaker from Cameroon, in *Afrique, je te plumerai* (Africa, I Will Fleece You), 1992.

32. Andrés Flores (pers. comm.); Cabrera (1992/1954: 286).

33. Martínez-Furé (1968: 64).

34. Orozco and Bolivar-Aróstegui (1998: 226).

35. The towering exceptions are several foundational works by Lydia Cabrera, namely *El Monte* (1992/1954); *La sociedad secretá Abakuá* (1958); *Anaforuana* (1975); and *La lengua sagrada de los ñáñigos* (1988a).

36. Nicklin (1984: 25).

37. Esen (1982: 4). According to Jeffreys (1935: 53), "a number of words in Goldie's dictionary are wrongly interpreted."

38. Herskovits explained the rationale for this method with the term "non-literate folk." In Cuba, however, many historical narratives are documented in manuscripts, then memorized and recited.

39. Herskovits (1967: vol. 2, 321).

40. Ellis and Barwick (1987: 41).

41. Ellis (1983: 136, 141, 143); Ellis and Barwick (1987: 43).

42. Gladwin (1970: 129, 131); Lewis (1994: 9).

43. Lydia Cabrera (1958: 62) referred to this phenomenon by naming one chapter of her classic work on Abakuá, "Geography through Memory" (*geografía a traves del recuerdo*). One Cuban chant maps out a journey from one Cross River settlement to another: "India Obane Mbemoró Odán sanga maribá mbairán kurí aroropa Usagaré: 'one leaves Oban, arriving to Mbemong, to the Ndian river, in a boat, and arrives to Usaghade by sea'" (Cabrera 1988a: 236). Other examples are found in Abakuá signatures representing journeys from one settlement to another in West Africa: "from the territory of Wana Bekura to Ibondá" (Cabrera 1975: 189). See also Cabrera (1975: 248, 254). The relationship between these Cuban terms and their interpretations in Cross River place names is discussed in later chapters. All are identified on Figure 4.

44. Ortiz may have been following the ideas of Talbot here, but for different reasons. In the fashion of many Africanists of his day, Talbot (1912a: 40) concluded that: "there seems to be a close resemblance between [Ékpè] secrets and the Eleusinian and ancient Egyptian mysteries." In Cuba, where the reigning ideology held that Abakuá was a product of slavery, therefore incapable of embodying a moral philosophy, Ortiz (1950a: 26) defended Abakuá practice by comparing its structures to those of ancient Greek drama.

45. Cf. Di Leo (2005: 54, n. 38); Fernández-Ferrer (1998: 20, notes); Ortiz (1939: 86); Roche y Monteagudo (1925/1908: 63). The provenance of these objects is discussed in chapter 6.

46. Ortiz (1955a: 252–253). Robert Farris Thompson (1998) relocated several of these items and wrote about their significance.

47. Rodríguez-Solveira (1975: 10).

48. Ortiz (1986: 5). Ortiz described Abakuá as, "one of the most curious and original phenomena of the African transculturations in all the Americas."

49. Ortiz (1943: 2–3). This passage was reproduced from an earlier book, published in 1906.

50. Ortiz (1924a: 376) wrote, "I have in the making a sociological book hundreds of pages long about *The Black Ñáñigos*, an in-depth study of this curious ethnographic phenomenon and destroying many prejudices about it." Ortiz (1929: 23) later wrote, "the secret society called ñáñiguismo, formed by blacks from Calabar in Cuba, and whose study, already very advanced by me, will comprise at least a thick volume." Ortiz (1929: 24) wrote that "nánigos rites" "will deserve greater development in my next book, *The Black Ñáñigos*."

51. Courtesy of Jane Gregory Rubin.

52. At his death, Ortiz left materials in preparation for the publication of some twenty books, at least one of these was a study of the Abakuá (Rodríguez-Solveira 1975: 16).

53. Muri Joseph Bassey's actual words were: "If you were not to be an Ékpè title-holder, I would not allow you to appear as he is appearing now." Muri Joseph Bassey Anating-Edem VI is the Clan Head of Efut Ekondo Clan, Calabar South.

54. Adediran (2004, pers. comm.). The Museum Curator, Mr. Nath Mayo Adediran, and his staff graciously supported by research in Calabar during all my trips there. For example, in 1714 "King Ambo" of Creek Town was one of two merchants who delivered 360 enslaved Africans to the London ship *Florida*. Creek Town's position as the dominant settlement was eclipsed by Obutong in the 1750s and by Atakpa (Duke Town) in the 1770s (Behrendt and Graham 2003: 43–44, 50).

55. This visit to Calabar was supported by a grant from the West African Research Association.

56. At the table were Dr. Okon E. Uya, chair of the History Department at the University of Calabar; Dr. Ekpo Eyo, the former director of the National Museums of Nigeria; Dr. Jill Salmons, senior researcher into Cross River traditional arts; Mr. Larry Esin, the managing director of tourism for Cross River State; "Etubom" Bassey Ekpo Bassey, the Iyámba (leader) who presides over Efe Ékpè Eyo Ema, the Calabar lodge responsible for the coronation of the Obong, or traditional ruler of the Èfìk people; "Etubom" Ekpo Eyo, president of the Museum Society. Èfìk society is organized into Houses, groups based on an extended family lineage including ancestors and descendants, as well as incorporated exogenous members (wives, servants, etc). Etubom is a title meaning "Head of House." Goldie (1964/1862: 93) wrote: "Ë-te'-u-büm, *v*. Ètubüm, *n*. 1. Captain of ship; headman of canoe. 2. The chief or principal in any undertaking."

57. Efut Ekondo was founded by Efut (Balondo) migrants who came in waves from Cameroon in the nineteenth century and earlier. The head of an Efut (Balondo) village is called *Muri* (Nebengu 1990: 63). In 1805 a British explorer traveling through Calabar referred to "Cameroon Town," near Duke Town and Henshaw Town, an early reference to Efut Ekondo (Hallett 1964: 201). In Cuba, the Efó (the Efut of Calabar) are considered the founders of Ékpè.

58. Chief Ekong Edim Imona was advisor to the contemporary Ndidem. Chief Imona passed away in 2006.

59. Among them Robert Farris Thompson, Keith Nicklin, Jill Salmons, and Amanda Carlson.

60. I am grateful to the late Chief (Honorable) P. O. E. Bassey, who held the Ṁgbè grade of Ntoe Okpoho in Big Qua Town, who arranged for my visit to the lodge.

61. *Yoruba Andabo: Del Yoruba al Son* (1997) "Enyenisón Enkama 2" (D. R.). 9.49 minutes. Arrangement and lead voice, Ogduardo "Román" Díaz Anaya. Magic Music/Universal. CD FMD 75141, La isla de la música, vol. 6.

62. I am grateful to Dr. Anwana of the History Department of the University of Calabar, Mr. Etim Ika of Efut Ifako (son of Muri Edet), and Etubom Bassey Ekpo Bassey for accompanying me to various lodges in the Cross River region. All are knowledgeable Ékpè members.

63. For their support of my research in southwestern Cameroon, I am grateful to Dr. Roland Ndip, Dr. Fongot A. V. Kinni, Dr. Agbor A. Enoh Richard (all faculty of the University of Buea), Chief Nyuja Ndengi George of Bekura Barombi village, Edmundo Nofuru (my first contact and guide), and Chief Esoh Itoh Stephen, Paramount Ruler of the Balondos, of Ekondo Titi, Ndian Division.

64. This passport consisted of a statement in English of my investiture, attached to it was stapled a leaf from the Oboti tree (*Newbouldia laevis*), used by Ékpè as a symbol of their authority, the tree being found next to Ékpè lodges throughout the region (Keay et al. 1964: vol. 2, 428–430). The Iyámba of Obutong told me: "All lodges [Èfìk, Efut, Qua, etc.] use the Oboti tree, that is like the general flag among us, like a national flag" (Archibong Eso 2005, pers. comm.). This leaf was understood by Ékpè members I presented it to from Umuahia in Abia State, Nigeria, to Ekondo Titi in Cameroon. In Oron, Udo-Ema (1938: 314) wrote, "an initiated member [of Ékpè] in one locality will be recognised as such in any other locality, provided that he uses the correct watchword, or wears an emblem signifying his rank and section." In the Usaghade (Isangele) region, Anderson (1933: 10, para. 28) documented a legend whereby a local dispute was settled when one representative "returned wearing a leaf round his neck which indicated that he wished to have a discussion with the Isangelis." Likely an Oboti leaf, this act would have made the matter surpass individual interests and pertain to the regional membership.

65. Engineer Bassey (2001/1998: 39–40) wrote that: "Nsìbìdì are secret writings that employ symbolism, hieroglyphs, secret signs, sounds, colours and dance forms for secret communications and rituals. They are not limited to Ékpè. . . . Nsìbìdì Ékpè is a natural ingredient of Ékpè culture. Its use prevents unwanted intrusion of non initiates and the profane into Ékpè secrets." See also Kalu (1980/1978: 82–83).

66. Thanks to Professor Okon E. Essien, Department of Linguistics, University of Calabar, for identifying the tone markers for the Èfìk Ékpè chants.

67. Recorded in Calabar in 1981 on the LP *Nka Asian Mkparawa Eburutu: Cultural Group Calabar*. Director, Etubom Asuquo Etim. Thanks to Mr. Demmy Bassey (2004, pers. comm.), an Ékpè member and former highlife musician, who transcribed and translated the lyrics on this recording; his work was then reviewed by formally educated Ékpè leaders (Etubom B. E. Bassey 2004).

68. The term *anaforuana* was used by Cabrera (1975) to name her monumental study of Abakuá signs. Not common in contemporary Abakuá parlance, the term seems to have fallen from use (Soto Rodríguez 2006, pers. comm.). In 1962, the phrase "Ékue anaforuána" was performed by Abakuá title-holder Victor Herrera in the recording "Enkame" (at 1:45 minutes, *Musica afrocubana*. 1993). See glossary and appendix of chants for a discussion of *gandó*.

69. I am grateful to North American artist Ben Jones, who also supported this application.

70. In New York City, Juan Boza (d. 1991), an artist and *santero* born in Camagüey and formally educated in Havana, Cuba, was my principal teacher (cf. Miller 1995b).

71. Miller (1994, 1995a, 1995b).

72. I learned about this use of language during the process of my initiation in the Efe Ékpè Eyo Ema, where after a group consensus, an exception was made so that the Obong Ékpè could use English in order to communicate with me (Etubom B. E. Bassey 2004, pers. comm.).

73. An exception to this is Tato Quiñones (a member of the Muñánga Efó lodge), who wrote several original works on Abakuá history and who graciously shared some of his insights with me in the 1990s.

74. My Ph.D dissertation (1995b) treats the Yorùbá-derived Santería religion (Ocha and Ifá) during Castro's regime. Yorùbá studies are more developed in part because West African Yorùbá have created a standard language and a body of literature about their history and culture.

75. In Cuba, one of Cabrera's main teachers was called *Saibeke*, an Abakuá term meaning "wise-elder" (Cabrera 1994: 57–58). See *Basaibeke* in the glossary for an interpretation into Èfik.

76. Only years later in Calabar did I appreciate the full significance of the staff and cap. In West Africa, these are privileges worn only by Chiefs or title-holders of local traditions such as Ékpè. Some Abakuá continue this tradition, including Pedro-Alberto Suarez-Gonzáles "Pedrito el yuma," one of the leading ceremonial directors of contemporary Abakuá, who holds the title of Moruá Eribó Engomo of the lodge Betongó Naróko Efó.

77. This anecdote was told to me by Andrés' childhood friend and schoolmate, Abelardo Rodríguez Fornaris, a title-holder of the Munyánga Efó lodge of Havana, with whom I worked for two years (2000–2002) reviewing the testimony of Andrés.

78. Abímbólá (1973: 43).

79. Bourdieu (1994: 119) used the phrase "rites of institution" instead of rites of passage, because the process "transforms the person consecrated: first because it transforms the representations others have of him and above all the behaviour they adopt toward him . . . and second, because it simultaneously transforms the representation that the invested person has of himself."

80. I am grateful to Idania Díaz (1993–1996) and to José-Antonio Fernández (1997–2002) for their help in transcribing interview materials in Cuban Spanish.

81. In Abakuá ceremonies, chanters gather in "la valla" to publicly display their knowledge of treaties. In African-derived religions of Cuba, lead chanters use ritual language to identify themselves, the ethnic sources of their rites, as well as the nature of the ceremony at hand. The dancers and drummers have conversations with gesture and rhythm. All of this occurs from the doorway of the temple outward. Fernando Ortiz's study *Los bailes y el teatro de los negros en el folklore de Cuba* (The Dances and Theater of Blacks in Cuban Folklore; 1981/1951) was possible only because Abakuá, Palo Monte, and Santería rites, while having components for initiates only, also include the performance of music and dance for the public.

82. Luis Salinas (b. 1920s, d. 1995) held the title of the Ekueñón in the lodge Abarakó Sisi. I recorded a videotape of Andrés and Salinas in October 1994 as they demonstrated how the Abakuá language was used to recite history.

83. Okobio asarorí Moní bonkó Endibó Efó.

84. The versions of Andrés and Ortiz were not identical, suggesting that Andrés did not read Ortiz but learned from a similar school of thought.

85. Ortiz (1954: 20).

86. Martínez-Furé (2001: 195) referred to this process in the Regla de Ocha (Santería) as the invention of "modern *patakines*" (origin myths), based on a "dialectical movement from orality to written text to orality."

87. Abelardo was a member of the lodge Munyánga Efó, the same lodge that Andrés Flores aspired to join as a youth.

88. Abelardo died on 31 October 2005, just a week after I visited him in Havana. Juan Campos Cárdenas "Chan," the Isué of Muñánga Efó, confirmed that Abelardo received his title 27 January 1963, but later stopped attending reunions of his lodge.

89. In *The Many-Headed Hydra*, Linebaugh and Rediker (2000: 327, 329–330) contested the criminalization of workers by bourgeois historians: "Marx . . . argued that the colonial system . . . converted 'the worker into a crippled monstrosity'"; "Thus our first step has been to remember the proletarian body. We have had to translate it out of the idiom of monstrosity." I found that the best way to effectively re-envision Abakuá outside the frame of the colonial literature was to travel to its source region in West Africa. Dr. Wáñdé Abímbólá (1996, pers. comm.) urged me to travel to Calabar before publishing about this theme; his advice has proven pivotal.

90. Ortiz (1991d/1954: 123) wrote, "Abakuá, in the past century, was shrouded in a sinister atmosphere of criminality, more legendary than truthful."

91. The name Sikán has variants in the Cross River region: "Sikán must be from Nsikan, an Ìbìbìò name, not used by the Èfìk. The full name is Nsikanabasi (Nse ikan Abasi), 'nothing is greater than God'. This name is literally a question: 'what surpasses god?'" (Connell 2004, pers. comm.; cf. Essien 1986: 60). Some Efut (Balondo) groups of Cameroon name "Sirkan" as the woman in their Ékpè origin story (Engineer Bassey 2007, pers. comm.).

92. In the same year, 1882, *Los Ñáñigos. Su historia . . .* was published by an anonymous author. This 24-page pamphlet has, word for word, the same information appearing in Trujillo y Monagas' book.

93. Trujillo y Monagas (1882: 368).

94. Trujillo y Monagas (1882: 368); *Los ñáñigos* (1882: 13). For the sake of the reader in English, I have altered the spelling to be phonetic, from "ñampe" to "nyámpe," from "gelley" to "heyéy." Andrés explained to me that this is a poorly transcribed funeral chant that includes the phrase "heyéy bario" out of context, since this would be used only in the context of a feast. This entire phrase is interpreted in Abakuá, and much of it can be interpreted in Èfìk. For example, in Cuba *Nyámpe eyeneká* means "a brother has died." In Èfìk *eyeneka* is "a full brother" (Goldie 1964: 97). *Nyampke* is a grade in both Èfìk Ékpè and Ejagham Ǹgbe (Ruel 1969: 226); *nyámkpe* is interpreted as death in Cuba (see n. 76 in chapter 5).

95. I heard this phrase repeatedly used by the M̃gbè leadership of Oban, an Ejagham village northeast of Calabar, in 2004. Oban (or Ubáne) is regarded as an important territory for Cuban Abakuá.

96. Andrés and I worked from the 3rd ed. (1925).

97. Roche y Monteagudo accurately documented the existence of Abakuá lodges in Guanabacoa, such as Enyegueyé Efó I and II, and Nandibá Efó, none of which exist today.

98. Roche y Monteagudo (1925/1908: 10–11).

99. The statement that no organized business transactions occur in Abakuá gatherings holds true for other Cuban traditions, like Ochá, Ifá, and Palo Monte, with the exceptions that fees are paid for certain rites and that money circulates through the purchase of food and drink shared by the community. So too in the Cross River Ékpè, where ceremonies do not include business transactions, but instead the bonds created through ritual activity are used when appropriate in business activities elsewhere.

100. Arístides Sotonavarro (1980: 277). Those who know Cuban society intimately understand that in this period, publications rarely expressed ideas and opinions outside those of officialdom.

101. Fernando Ortiz came to the study of African influence through his training in criminology. About his first book he wrote: "My book *Los negros brujos* [The Black Sorcerers] was published in 1906 . . . It is true that I, as shortly before had the Dr. Nina Rodrigues in Brazil, came to ethnographic studies from the field of criminal anthropology, where I had my most fervent interests" (Ortiz 1939: 85; cited in Ortiz 1995: 8). Fernando Ortiz was able to reinvent himself as a scholar, particularly from 1937 onward, discarding the criminological ideology in his later works.

102. "The living sources of information that have made this work possible, and that we have found principally in Matanzas" (Cabrera 1958: 22).

103. Cabrera (1950: 45, 1992/1954: 285).

104. Cabrera (1950: 45).

105. Cabrera (1958: 119).

106. Lovejoy and Richardson (1999: 348).

107. These accounts were typically self-serving reports by British colonists or missionaries to justify their "civilizing" presences. For example, British Consul Thomas Hutchinson (1861: 335) repeated hearsay about the terrorists of his day: "every eighth day a man goes about the town during Egbo [Ékpè] meeting, dressed in disguise to simulate a spirit, and he has leave to flog every slave, man, woman, or child, whom he meets to his heart's content, in order to keep the system *in terrorem* over the heads of the serf population."

108. While in Calabar, I met an Ékpè member from Umon whose mother paid for his membership, so that he could enter the town while Ékpè was in session. This was a common practice. A Calabar folktale offers a local perspective, describing the appearance of Ékpè during a village celebration: "'Nyamkpe,' the cult masquerade, came unannounced. The big brass bell around its waist was ringing 'umam! umam! umam!' . . . Everyone knew the cult of the wealthy had come out to perform in public. Mothers ran out to drag their kids indoors. The uninitiated villagers returning from the farms couldn't come into the village. The same was true of others coming back from the streams. Such unfortunate returnees hid in the bush for fear. 'Nyamkpe' drum was an automatic curfew in Bokondo." (Ñkaña 1984/1933: 31–32).

109. Following their analysis by Hobsbawm (1959: 30), early forms of Mafia are difficult to classify, being somewhat fluid organizations existing somewhere between social banditry and social movements: "Whether the tinge of social protest by the poor determines their general colour, as in Calabria, or that of the ambitions of the local middles classes, as in Sicily, or pure crime, as in the American Mafia, depends on circumstances" (Hobsbawm 1959: 30). "Public discussion has been confused, partly by all manner of journalistic romancing, partly by the simple failure to recognize that 'what appeared to the Piedmontese or the Lomard as 'Sicilian delinquency' was in reality the law of a different society . . . a semi-feudal society'" (Hobsbawm 1959: 32).

110. Hobsbawm's (1959: 36) description of the situation in Sicily seems appropriate here: "No doubt Sicilian peasants have throughout history lived under the double régime of a remote and generally foreign central government and a local régime of slave or feudal lords . . . they were never, and could never be, in the habit of regarding the central government as a real State, but merely as a special form of brigand, whose soldiers, tax-gatherers, policemen and courts fell upon them from time to time." To paraphrase Thomas Hobbes (1991/1651: 31), 'One man calls cruelty what another calls justice'. French essayist Michel de Montaigne (1533–1592) wrote: "Each man calls barbarism whatever is not his own practice; for indeed it seems we have no other test of truth and reason than the example and pattern of the opinions and customs of the country we live in" (Montaigne 1958: 152).

111. By comparison, could one use the example of the Catholic Inquisitions as the defining moment for Christian history and values? Pleading the case of Ékpè in the context of contemporary Christian Calabar, Engineer Bassey (2001/1998: 130–131) argued that despite its misuse by some ancestors, Ékpè has enduring values linked to the identity of Cross River peoples: "The illusion of quick rewards led many, including Ékpè initiates, to abandon pious activities and the path to invest in oppression, parochialism and evil desire . . . This should not be the end of Ékpè if man invests to redeem what is redeemable, and in the process help himself to remember his past."

112. This point was made by Talbot (1912a: 37). After observing that Ejagham adopted many Èfik customs and laws, he reported that "those to the North [of Oban] still keep their old Egbo [Ékpè] practically unchanged."

113. Palmié (2006: 109). In Èfik mercantile towns of the nineteenth century, money was indeed a key for receiving Ékpè titles (cf. Bassey 2001/1998: 56), but this appears not to have been the case in other areas. Membership in Ékpè remains key to the identity of being an Èfik, Efut, or Qua male from Calabar, and some Ejagham communities have schools for children to learn the customs. Ethnicity, however defined, remains important to participating in Ékpè culture. Offiong (1989: 73) reported that in the 1970s, a non-Èfik governor of Cross River State did not receive an honorary title because of his ethnicity. Regarding Oban, P. O. E. Bassey (1999: 7) wrote: "The method of choosing Oban kings has been well established and consistent from time immemorial. . . . He must be of pure Oban blood, that is: free born with no trace of slave blood among his ancestry." In the case of Europeans who were initiated to establish mercantile relationships, Commissioner Hart (1964: para. 168) concluded that: "There is no evidence to show that a non-Èfik ever became a title-holder in Ékpè. This distinction was reserved for Èfiks alone." In Oban, the first chieftaincy title conferred upon an outsider was in the late twentieth century, to "an American professor honored for his service to the community" (P. O. E. Bassey 1999: 69). But 'ethnicity' was always a fluid category. The common ideology in Calabar that slaves could not receive Ékpè titles (cf. Noah 1980: 68, 70), for example, is contradicted by the famous case of Eyo Nsa. Nsa was a slave in the late 1700s whose heroism led Èfik royalty to make him a "son of the soil" (enyenisong); he received a wife from a royal lineage as well as an Ékpè title; Nsa's son became King Eyo Honesty II, an important trader and Ékpè leader credited with bringing the Okpoho grade into Èfik Ékpè practice (Chief E. E. Eyo 2005, pers. comm.; Hart 1964: para. 67, 207, 282, 287, 289; Oku 1989: 114, 140, 176–178, 193).

114. The process was similar throughout southeastern Nigeria; for an example from Ìgbo title-socieites, see Uwazie (1994: 95).

115. Calabar musician Ékpè Ita recorded this phrase on the track "San Ikese Ekpabrukim" (1975). Transcription and interpretation by Demmy Bassey and Etubom B. E. Bassey, Calabar (2004). This phrase is a standard, recorded on other records by the same musician. In Cuba, this tradition has been continued. Cabrera (1975: 9) documented the anecdote of an African-born Ékpè member who oversaw the initiation of his Cuban grandchild. Some lodges have a tradition of inheriting titles within a family lineage.

116. Ward (1911: 37). Engineer Bassey (2001/1998: 161) noted, "Until recently, tradition required a father to initiated his loved ones into Ékpè." By "until recently," Bassey refers to the attack of West African indigenous practices by Christians. Ward (1911: 83) reflected this stance by referring to Ékpè and other indigenous institutions as "hindrances lying athwart the path of advancement of the kingdom of Jesus Christ . . . evil habits have so rooted themselves into native life that they are strongly supported by the influences of prestige and fashion."

117. Anderson (1933: 17, para. 52).

118. Two letters from 1842, signed "King Eyamba V" and "King Eyo Honesty," were addressed to the commander of a war ship, requesting instructional aid to increase agricultural production, as well as missionaries to teach reading (Goldie 1894: 9–10; Waddell 1863: 663–664). In 1846, the Church of Scotland Mission in Calabar began.

119. Waddell (1863: 503). This opinion was echoed decades later by British High Commissioner Sir Claude MacDonald, who described Ékpè as "a sort of superstitious fetish worship kept by the kings, chiefs and free-born of Old Calabar by means of which they keep the lower classes in subjugation." (Sir Claude MacDonald to Marquis of Salisbury, 1889; enclosure in File No. CP 1716, Calprof, National Archives Enugu; cited in Nwaka 1978: 190).

120. Talbot (1969/1926: vol. I, 199).

121. Nair (1972: 98–102); Noah (1980: 55–57). The conflict was documented by the Rev. Hope Waddell. While conversing with King Eyo of Creek Town in 1849, wrote Waddell, Eyo "drew my attention

to an affair in which Mr. Edgerley had acted somewhat rashly at Old Town—he had gone he said into the palaver house and broke the Egbo drum; a very serious offence in this country and which would cause a bad feeling against the Mission. 'It was a thing I could not do myself' said Eyo, 'No Calabar man could do it on pain of death.'" (Waddell 1846–1855, vol. 7, entry for 4 December 1849, 49).

122. By 1856 the Mission House of Duke Town in Calabar declared itself politically independent from Ékpè and local authorities. Ékpè leaders "blew Ékpè" (sounded the Voice) to sanction locals from attending the mission house. The British consul negotiated, and sanctions were lifted, with "a naval force ready to enforce the decree." With this conflict, "instead of improving Ékpè from within, the missionaries were now breaking it from without by creating the nucleus of a new order" (Nair 1972: 103–104).

123. Tamuno (1966: 102) contrasted the effectiveness of traditional legal systems in Nigeria with the disorder resulting from colonial law. I heard like perspectives expressed in the Cross River region regarding the contemporary chaos and explanations for its persistence. Messenger (1971: 217) reported that in the mid-twentieth century a theme in Ìbìbìò theater performance was "Bribery in the Native Courts ... Reflected here is the widely held opinion that in precolonial times the courts were largely incorruptible." In a 1941 petition to colonial authorities, Ìbìbìò leaders wrote, "Prior to the arrival of the British, the Idiong [society] was our most powerful means of lessening and checking crime and its drastic measures against offenders did cause crimes ... to be a scarcity" (file no. 18816, CSE, National Archives Enugu, 'Idiong Society, Abak District: Petition to Resident Calabar', 15 April 1941; cited in Nwaka 1978: 189).

124. This famous adage in Calabar means that no one stood above Ékpè law (Chief Ekong Edim Imona 2004, pers. comm.).

125. The 1856 the British consult affirmed "the right of sanctuary of the mission house" in Duke Town, Calabar (Nair 1972: 104). Colonists proscribed "secret" societies that enforced customary law. "Thus by direct and indirect administrative action, the taproot of traditional society, respect for elders and religion, before the intrusion of alien religions and political systems, had been cut" (Tamuno 1966: 115–116). In the 1960s, an American anthropologist reported that the increase of immorality and crime in southeastern Nigeria was directly related to the acceptance of the Christian concept of forgiveness. According to Messenger (1967: 183, 185), "Protestantism ... and Roman Catholicism, by introducing the sacrament of confession, have fostered, however unintentionally, the widespread belief among young people that the Christian God forgives all sins. ... The acceptance by youth of the concept of a forgiving deity has greatly reduced the efficacy of supernatural sanctions and has actually fostered immorality."

126. Noah (1980: 59); Waddell (1863: 310). Talbot (1969/1926: vol. 3, 604) reported that although Old Calabar had three or four authonomous communities, "The Obbong of Èfìk, of Duke Town, was usually acknowledged as the head-chief."

127. Talbot (1969/1926: vol. 1, 199). This reference indicates that European initiates into Ékpè did not have the power to evoke Ékpè at their will.

128. Noah (1980: 72). Talbot (1969/1926: vol. 3, 618) wrote that throughout southern Nigeria, "the executive and judicial powers ... were always combined in the chief ruler, or rulers, of the people. ... In those places where the administration was carried on by a secret society, such as ... Ekpe and Idiong among the Semi-Bantu, the judicial power was also kept in its hands. ... Considerable intelligence is displayed by the average judge, and ... it is probable that the right decision is given with as much certainty as in a European Court."

129. Anwana (2002: 187), citing Calprof 4/1, vol. 1 NAE (National Archives, Enugu).

130. For example, Ékpè was evoked to legitimize a protest against the recent International Court of Justice award of the formerly Nigerian Bakassi Peninsula to Cameroon. In 2004, when Bakassi's

Paramount Ruler Etim Okon Edet and many residents protested, a BBC report included a photograph of an Ékpè masquerade, with the caption "Even traditional dancers have taken part in protests over the world court ruling, which was based on a 1913 colonial agreement" (BBC 21 June 2004).

131. Weber (1968: 506; cited in Peel 1990: 350).

132. In Calabar, council-made decisions were fundamental to Ékpè practice. Hope Waddell (1863: 504) observed during an Ékpè council in 1852, that even the voice of the powerful "King Eyo" of Creek Town "was no more than that of any other." A British commander requested earlier that King Eyo change a local custom, but "Eyo could do nothing without calling his council together." (Waddell 1863: 406). Èfïk merchant Antera Duke, who kept a diary in the 1780s, described a similar scenario with the leaders of his day (cf. Asuquo 1978: 42, 51). Throughout southern Nigeria and southwestern Cameroon, including the Grassfields, councils made political decisions (Erim 1990: 171; Hart 1964: para. 173, 181, 387; Koloss 1985: 100; Messenger 1959: 67; Talbot 1969/1926: vol. 3, 565; Ukpong 1982: 162).

133. The literal interpretation of codes contained in these lyrics would require an essay. This recording affirms that essential values of African-derived traditions have been maintained through coded forms that remain misunderstood outside their hermetic communities. Los Muñequitos de Matanzas recorded "La plegaria" (The Prayer) sometime between 1956 and 1963. This composition was briefly referenced by Yoruba Andabo on *Del Yoruba al Son* (1997), track 6 (at 3:12 minutes).

134. Part of the process includes divination in the Lukumí system and, among Abakuá, a critical analysis of one's character and behavior.

135. Goldenberg (1984: 130, 131).

136. Goldenberg (1984: 134).

137. Goldenberg (1984: 158).

138. Goldenberg (1984: 167).

139. Cabrera (1992/1954: 8).

140. Among Abakuá, even if a passage is obscure, or if sages have conflicting interpretations, the terms are maintained for their sacred value as the inheritance of the society's African founders. Price and Price (1991: 26) observed a similar phenomenon among Saramaka narratives in Suriname.

141. Cf. Adams (1823: 144–145); Àyándélé (1966: 3–4, citing the Waddell journal entries for 16 and 17 April and 2 May 1846); Goldie (1894: 9); Latham (1990: 72–73); Lovejoy and Richardson (2001); Robertson (1819: 313); *Story of the Old Calabar* (1986: 80); Waddell (1846–1855, journal entry for 17 April 1846, 31–32).

142. Andrés and I communicated until his death in September 2001. Even though our work was essentially finished in 1999, I visited him whenever I was in town. Arriving in Havana in October 2001, I learned from his neighbors about his death six weeks earlier, peacefully at home, and his burial in the cemetery of Colón.

143. Carney (2001: 142).

144. Sweet (2003: 6–7, 9).

145. Sweet (2003: 136).

146. "An understanding of New World Negro culture will reciprocally deepen our comprehension of the relevant African cultures themselves, give unity to a broader field of research, and open the door for an interchange that cannot but be fruitful for Africanists and Afroamericanists alike" (Herskovits 1948: 1).

147. Cf. Cohen (1999); Mann and Bay (2001).

148. I am grateful to all the members of Efe Ékpè Eyo Ema (Ekoretonko) of Calabar and Creek Town for their support in myriad ways during my visits to Calabar. Their invitation to make me a

member of their lodge, motivated by their recognition of the strength of the Cuban Abakuá materials I presented in Calabar, was the highest form of support for my research. Thanks in particular to Etubom B. E. Bassey, Iyámba, and to Chief Effiom Ekpenyong Eyo, Mboko-mboko.

149. *Efe Ékpè* means "Ékpè temple" in Calabar (cf. Engineer Bassey 2001/1998: 83; Simmons 1956: 23). Cuban Abakuá refer to the innermost sanctum of their temple as "Fe-Ékue"; also "Fó-Ekue" (Cabrera 1958: 268, 273, 1975: 20, 221).

150. The title Mbákara was mentioned in the first commercial recording of Abakuá music, from the 1920s, by Ignacio Piñeiro, "Los cantares del abacuá" (see description in chapter 7).

151. P. O. E. Bassey (2004: 15).

152. Talbot (1912a: 43) wrote: "The head priest of the whole Egbo [Ékpè] Society is called Iyamba, the old Ekoi equivalent for which was Musungu." Chief Imona (1996: 2), who wrote a history of Qua (Ejagham) Town in Calabar, is Head of Mosongo Iseri Royal family Idundu Qua Clan and the village Head of Asamanka. Mosongo is an Efut name (Ekpo 2005: 72).

153. Deschamps-Chappeaux (1987: 75).

154. In this preliminary study, all interpretations offered are *probable*, based upon the information available to the author, and do not rule out other possibilities. For example, 'Ekwe' means leopard in the Ododop (Korop) language of the Cross River region, as reported by Talbot (1912a: 430). In another region, Ekwe is a large wooden drum in "the Oreyi group of drums" among the Ìgbos of Nigeria's Eastern Central State (Akpabot 1971: 37, 1975–1976: 36). Both examples resonate with Cuban usage.

155. Essien (1986: 9, 2005: 344).

156. The Abakuá terms *asére* (greetings), *ekóbio* (ritual brother), and *monína* (ritual brother) are used as standard greetings among urban Cuban males. In Abakuá chants, *asére* is a greeting, but in the larger society its new meaning is that of "friend." So too *Ekóbio* and *monína* have also become used to mean "friend" outside of Abakuá ritual practice. Jorge Ibarra (1985: 267–268) affirmed the importance of vocabulary in the creation of national identity.

157. In essence, "Mokóngo machébere" means that "Mokóngo is great, he is powerful, his sign authorizes the meetings and gives validity to the rites. Without his consent there is no gathering" (Cabrera 1975: 17). Cabrera documented three versions: "Mocongo Macheveré, when he parades in the procession" (1950: 38); "Chabiáka the Mokóngo of Èfik territory, the valiant man, gallant" (chébere) (Cabrera 1958: 168); "Mokongo Machébere: title of Mokongo. The valiant, the warrior" (Cabrera 1988a: 348). Cabrera (1958: 10) wrote that the title "Mokóngo Ma' chebere" gave origin to the Cuban popular phrase "chébere, for pretty, good, elegant, gracious." This title was documented in an Abakuá chant in Cabrera (1975: 17).

158. Anthropologist Dr. Kinni (2005, pers. comm.) of the University of Buea in Cameroon reported, "The Mukongo is the assistant of the Ékpè." Among Balondo (Efut) settlements of Cameroon, "Mukongo" is the executive officer of the "secret society" (Nebengu 1990: 69, 106). Mokongo is a ceremonial figure in Kundu settlements of southwestern Cameroon (Valentin 1980: 14). Mokongo is also a name used in southwestern Cameroon, such as in the Bakweri village Soppo Mokongo (Matute 1988: 11), and as I saw on sign boards in Buea in 2004.

1. Arrival

1. As told to me by Andrés Flores. Cabrera documented several versions of this phrase (1974: 270, 1988a: 127, 128).

2. Bartolomé de las Casas (1474–1566), Bishop of Chiapas, was often accused of giving the Spanish monarchy the idea of shipping enslaved Africans to the Americas, in his 1517 letter recommending the use of Africans to substitute indigenous Americans. In fact, they had already arrived by the time (since 1502 in Hispañola; Palmer 1976: 8, 9, 167).

3. The Crown's policy of importing exclusively Ladinos, or Spanish-speaking, Christianized blacks from Spain to the Antilles was abandoned as early as 1510 (Franco 1961: 98–99, 1973: 9; Klein 1989/1967: 66; Landers 1993: 141).

4. "In 1513 the Crown established the *asiento* system whereby licensed contractors sent an estimated 75,000–90,000 enslaved Africans to Spanish America by 1600" (Klein 1989/1967: 67; Landers 1999: 11). Four Africans were carried to Cuba in 1513 (Donnan 1930: vol. 1, 15, n. 67).

5. English trans-Atlantic slaving commenced with the clandestine smuggling of Africans into the Caribbean by Admiral Sir John Hawkins, whose first voyage left in 1562 (Donnan 1930: vol. 1, 8, 10, 44–45).

6. In the Cross River region many people were captured in battles or enslaved for debt (Warnier 1985: 138–139). Others were accused of adultery, witchcraft (i.e., antisocial behavior), or were undesirable, as in the case of twins (cf. Lieber 1971: 36, 53). Also, powerful ritual specialists were sometimes enslaved as threatening to the status quo (Chief Eso Archibong 2005, pers. comm.), as Herskovits (1990/1941: 105–109) found in Dahomey.

7. The Congo Real cabildos in Cuba were thought to have been composed of peoples from Mbanza Kongo, the Kingdom of Kongo (Martínez-Furé 2006, pers. comm.).

8. The titles of "king" and "prince" as used by Andrés are a form of code-switching, or translations of West African terms for leadership, but do not necessarily refer to hereditary rulers of a monarchy. A similar usage was common in Old Calabar (Jones 1956: 126). Andrés named these men as: "Enyón Bakokó, Enyón Bakokíro, Efí Enyumáné Búton Koibá, Efí Abakuá, Ápapa Efí Ákamaró, Efí Unwetón, Nglón Chambéyo, Nglón Afabábetó, and Usagaré Mesón." Cabrera (1988a: 61, 62, 150, 514) documented several variants.

9. Many were from Efí, but the following were from Efó (Efut in Nigeria): Bakokó, Bakokíro, Nglón Chambéyo and Afabábetó, as well as Usagaré (cf. Cabrera 1975: 288).

10. Ebúton derives from Obutong, a Calabar settlement; Enyóng is a Cross River settlement; Bakokó settlements are found in Calabar and Cameroon; Abakuá <Àbàkpà (the Qua of Calabar); Usagaré < Usaghade, a community in the Nigeria/Cameroon estuary borderland.

11. "Brícamo," a person from the Calabar region (Pichardo 1985/1875: 103); Bríkamo (Ortiz 1924a: 103). "Hablo bríkamo" (I speak bríkamo) (Cabrera 1988a: 361, 129); "In the *Papel Periódico de la Habana* of 16 August 1792, a slave of the *carabalí bricma* nation is referred to. I suppose this is the same as Brícamo" (Ortiz 1975a/1916: 44).

12. Èfìk was a regional trade language, and many Cross River peoples were bilingual, so that speakers of the languages mentioned by Andrés, Bibí (Ìbìbìò) and Suáma (Ìsú-Amá Ìgbo), which are not mutually intelligible, could communicate. In southwestern Cameroon, Mòkpè (Bakweri) is one of several very closely related languages in a small area known as Northwest Bantu (Connell 2006, pers. comm.).

13. King Peppel of Bonny, who reigned from 1792 to 1830 (Dike 1956: 68), sailed the Atlantic as a youth. Captain William F. Owen of the Royal Navy wrote, "At the Bonny King Pepple is the principal man or merchant . . . This man was a boy in one of Mr. Thomas Tobin's Ships of the Liverpool Slave trade, and in remembrance of his kindness gives his ships the preference, if not the monopoly in the palm oil trade of that river." Public Record Office, London. Admiralty 1/2259–2276, Captain's letters 1808–1839. ADM I.2273, Owen, n. 91, 14 July 1828. Reference number: TNA050017550.

14. Clinton (1961: 182–188); Oku (1990: 34–35); Talbot (1969/1926: vol. 1, 191); Waddell (1863: 310). Oku reported that Eyo II was born soon after his father's marriage in the 1760s.

15. "Otu Mbo and Afiong Mbo, children of the Obutong Chief, Mbo Otu who had died in the massacre of 1767, had been educated in England" (Asuquo 1978: 53; Oku 1990: 39). In 1804, Mr. Archibald Dalzel, author of *The History of Dahomy* (1793), remarked "there is rarely a period that there are not at Liverpool, Callabar Negroes sent there expressly to learn English" (Hallett 1964: 195).

16. In the early 1800s, African and African-American sailors were important transmitters of information in subversive trans-Atlantic networks (Linebaugh and Rediker 2000: 312; Scott 1991; Verger 1976: 286). In Cuba, Aponte's conspiracy of 1812 involved black militia sailors from throughout the Caribbean (Franco 1974). In 1812 some "22 percent of all the free blacks in New England were seafarers." The percentage of free men among black seamen was seven times that of the national average (Dye 1991: 222–224). Born in Old Calabar in 1773, John Jea became a trans-Atlantic maritime cook and preacher. His autobiographical, antislavery narrative was published in England in the early 1800s (Hodges 1993: 18–34).

17. This identification, made by Ortiz (1955a: 254), was confirmed by Nigerian Ékpè in 2001 (Miller 2005).

18. Duke Town was also known as New Town (cf. Simmons 1956: 67–68).

19. The Obutong massacre of 1767 was one of several battles between Calabar settlements for domination of the trade with European merchants. Many of the vanquished became victims of the trans-Atlantic slave trade (Clarkson 1968/1808: 305–310; Miller 2005: 29–31; Oku 1989: 144–145; Simmons 1956: 67–68; Williams 1897: 535–538).

20. About the conflicts, see Hallett (1964: 204); Lovejoy and Richardson (1999: 346); Northrup (1978: 37); Waddell (1863: 251, 310). Of course, the vast majority of the enslaved came from the hinterlands.

21. Williams (1897: 544). Lovejoy and Richardson (1999: 341–42, 351, 353) identified Ephraim Robin John and "Grandy King George" as the same person. The sons of Ephraim Robin John did not arrive in Cuba, but were sold in Dominica, escaped, were re-enslaved in Virginia, and then traveled to Bristol, where they became enmeshed in a legal battle over their status and eventually returned to Calabar (Paley 2002; Sparks 2002).

22. In 1762 the *Nancy* disembarked 423 at Barbados and Havana; in 1763 the *Indian Queen* disembarked 496 at Kingston and Havana; in 1785 the *Quixote* disembarked 290 at Trinidad and Havana; in 1804 the *Mary Ellen* disembarked 375 in Havana. In all cases, the port of primary disembarkation was Havana (Eltis et al. 2000). The voyages are numbered 75899 (*Nancy*), 17552 (*Indian Queen*), 83268 (*Quixote*), 82646 (*Mary Ellen*).

23. In the mid-eighteenth century, there were five Calabarí cabildos de nación (nation-groups) in Havana (as discussed in chapter 2).

24. "In 1860 Cuba produced nearly one-third of the world's sugar" (*Encyclopædia Britannica Online*, Cuba entry, 2006).

25. *Accounts and Papers* (1849: 67 ff, 140); Aimes (1907: 171, 207); Eltis and Richardson (1997a: 8, 1997b: 20); Franco (1961: 107–108); Hutchinson (1970/1858: 112–113); Jameson (1821: 31–33); Marrero (1972–1987: vol. 9, 108); Moreno-Fraginals (1986: 11, 143); Moros y Morellón and de los Ríos (1844: 30); Sundiata (1996: 52); Thomas (1998/1971: 83, 136–137, 156). Trans-Atlantic slavery ended in Old Calabar and Bonny in 1842 (Alagoa 1999/1980: 254; Goldie 1964/1862: 356; Lovejoy and Richardson 1999: 337; Thomas 1997: 699).

26. Núnkwe is a term for "Havana" (Cabrera 1988a: 419). See appendix of chants for interpretations into Cross River languages.

27. Hale (1998: 206).

28. So far, there is no evidence in Cuba of the Kalabari language of the Niger delta, but the nineteenth-century Havana cabildo "Carabalí Iziegue" is named after a place in the Niger delta (see chapter 2 for details).

29. Lohse (2002: 78) gave parallel examples from the Mina and Arará groups.

30. In Spanish, *cabildo* means a "town assembly hall." In urban Cuba, many African cabildos also had an assembly room or meetinghouse (cf. Bremer 1853: vol. 2, 379 *ff.*; Hazard 1989/1871: 196). Africans organizd many cabildos in Cuba; in some cases these were sanctioned by Spanish authorities (Montejo-Arrechea 2004: 24, 41). The Cabildo Carabalí brícamo San José of Havana was extralegal in 1871, that is, not recognized by authorities. The foundation date for cabildos in legal documents was often the date of authorization for preexisting organizations; for instance, the Arará Magino cabildo was "founded or legalized" in 1890 (Martínez-Furé 1979: 155–156; Ortiz 1984b: 25–26). The cabildos de nación were an American invention, not to be confused with the Spanish tradition of cofradías (brotherhoods), ethnic-based groups of free blacks attached to a church. The African cabildos were similarly structured and existed parallel to the cofradías (Martínez-Furé 2006, pers. comm.).

31. Andrés interpreted Anayúgue as a variation of Ananúnkue, "Havana" (cf. Cabrera 1988a: 56). Besun kányo, good; *anawe* (or 'néwe), interrogative; *kório abakuá*, Abakuá collective.

32. Cf. Trujillo y Monagas (1882: 364). In 1805, the cabildo Carabalí Osso raised 240 *pesos* during Christmastime (Childs 2006b: 229–230).

33. Cf. Jameson (1821: 21).

34. In 1839 colonial authorities invaded an Abakuá meeting in Havana; the Executive Military Commission found that one purpose of the society was "to emancipate any of their membership who were enslaved" (Deschamps-Chappeaux 1964: 107–108). Many African cabildos purchased the freedom of their enslaved members (Childs 2006b: 210–211, 218–219, 227; Franco 1961: 129; Howard 1998: 4). For parallel examples from eighteenth-century Brazil, see Mulvey (1982: 39, 40, 49–52).

35. Cf. Cabrera (1988a: 324). In Èfìk, *súng súng* means "gently," and when expressed as *ting súng súng* can mean "speak in low tones (Etubom B. E. Bassey, pers. comm, 2008; cf. Aye 1991: 126).

36. Brathwaite (1985/1974: 45, 28).

37. Cf. Thompson (1983: 244–268).

38. In other words, West African Ékpè members reorganized themselves into lodges in Havana, but they did not consecrate anyone else until creating the lodge Efík Ebúton in 1836.

39. Cabrera (1958: 47). *Creole* as I use it means "born in Cuba," following Brathwaite (1985/1974: 10). For more on the tension between African and Cuban forms of Abakuá, see Cabrera (1972: 81, 2004: 72) and De Briñas (1898).

40. Ékpè leaders in Cuba waited for decades before authorizing a lodge of other Africans or creoles (cf. Ortiz 1955a: 310).

41. This tendency in Abakuá was paralleled by other African groups. In 1836, a black cofradía in Matanzas invited mulattos into their group (likely their creole offspring), without authorization (Montejo-Arrechea 2004: 25).

42. According to the constitution of some African cabildos, those born in Africa had full membership, while creoles had no representation (Childs 2006b: 210–11). Abakuá's foundation with separate lodges for creoles was a partial resolution of this problem.

43. Cf. Trujillo y Monagas (1882: 364).

44. The use of Abakuá narratives to express continuity with West African sources makes them conceptually distinct from those documented among the Saramaka by Richard Price (1983), which seem to mark a new beginning in Suriname.

45. Jones (1963: 190).

46. Suarez (2006); also Soto Rodríguez (2006, pers. comm.). "Fundament . . . sacred object charactersitic of Afrocuban cults, in which have been imbued supernatural forces" (Alfaro Eschevarria 1981: 185; see also Cabrera 1975: 15).

47. This phrase literally expresses the sharing of ritual authority from Efó to Efí to establish the Ebúton (Obutong) lodge in Cuba. Cf. Cabrera (1988a: 146).

48. Cuban mythology reports that a founding African ceremony was performed in a cave named Boko Bebá (see chapter 3, footnote 19 for the lodge Betongó Naróko Efó). There are many caves in the limestone hills along Havana's harbor. Caves were also refuges in Cuba for fugitives (Franco 1973: 93, 94).

49. In Cross River Ékpè, *itiat* is the foundation stone; in Cuba, *itiá* means "land," usually an African territory represented by an Abakuá lodge (cf. Cabrera 1988a: 258).

50. Engineer Bassey (2001/1998: 109). In the lower Cross River, *Mbọ́kọ̀* refers to the epicenter of Ékpè/Mgbè practice.

51. Enkrúkoro Enchemiyá, to work collectively to transmit Mbóko, the Voice (cf. Cabrera 1988a: 113).

52. This passage indicated that the concept of fundamento includes knowledgeable elders who lead the tradition; the lodge activities are authorized by their words and actions.

53. Cabrera (1988a: 145) documented a phrase that confirmed the preexistence of fundamentos among African Ékpè in Havana.

54. In a process of cultural diffusion, the impact of even one master can influence a large population. Cf. Cohen (2002: 27); Kubik (1999: 97–98).

55. The creation of this Efí lodge therefore required the authorization of leaders from Efó, because Cuban mythology reports that in West Africa the founders of the society were from Efó. Cf. Cabrera (1958: 50, 1988a: 146, 201, 1992/1954: 196, 277, 279). Seeming to corroborate this Cuban tradition, an official Qua [Ejagham] publication reported, "All through history no Èfìk Obong or Egbo [Ékpè] shed has ever given an order which is binding on the Quas" (QCCA 2003: 29). That the Ejagham and Efut (Balondo) are related historically is not controversial among local historians and settlement leaders (Ika 2005, pers. comm.; Ntui Erim Onongha 2005, pers. comm.; Onon 2004, pers. comm.).

56. According to Andrés Flores, "Efík Ebúton, Representation of Africa in Cuba; Efí Méremo, king of Èfìk (an Iyámba of Èfìk); Wafatá, name of the first baróko in Núnkue (Havana). The title of the juego was 'Efík Ebúton Efí Méremo, Akanarán Núnkue.' Akanarán Núnkue is 'mother of the Abakuá in Cuba.'" Another title of this lodge was Èfìk Ebúton Ápapa Efí Akamaroró, after the prince Ápapa Efí Ákamaró who sponsored Efík Ebúton (Andrés Flores, pers. comm.; Abelardo Empegó, pers. comm.).

57. Cf. Cabrera (1988a: 71).

58. "This is the name of the first consecration in Cuba: Embara, hand; Núnkue, Havana; Ororó, center; Amuramo, name of the baróko. This means: 'We give our hand to those present and we salute the land'" (Andrés Flores, pers. comm.). "Mbara: hand" (Cabrera 1988a: 334). In Ìbìbìò, mbàrá are fingernails (Urua et al. 2004: 75).

59. Amanisón, a person prepared to be initiated in the African way; *bióráma*, a title, meaning "from Africa" (Andrés Flores, pers. comm.). This phrase refers to those born in African who were initiated in Havana.

60. Guaguancó Matancero (Los Muñequitos de Matanzas) recorded "Ritmo abakuá," in praise of the Abakuá's foundation in Havana (the phrase transcribed above is at 1:35 minutes into the recording). In later recordings, Los Muñequitos recorded the variant phrases, "Erendió Efík Ebutong, krúkoro ekóbio enyéne abakuá," (at 1:34 minutes, "Wenva," 1995), and "Erendió Èfìk Obutong nandibá mosongo" (The authorization of Èfìk Obutong came from the river), that is, Abakuá was

authorized African leaders ("Lo que dice el Abacuá," 1983). Erendió is interpreted as "to believe, to revere, honor, greet" (Ángel Guerrero 2007, pers. comm.).

61. Cf. Cabrera (1975: 29, 1988a: 319).

62. As early as the 1920s, Ignacio Piñeiro composed "En la alta sociedad," with the chorus: "Sanga prokama nandiba ekóbio" (the procession of brothers moves to the river), as recorded in 1956 by María Teresa Vera (1994). See chapter 7 for details on Piñeiro.

63. "Ekoria, birth; Otán, first; 'the birth of the first baróko in Havana'" (El Chino Mokóngo). *Ekoea* (or *Ekorri*) is forest in Qua, possibly the source for *Ekória*, birth in Abakuá, since Abakuá itself comes from (or is born in) the forest (Ndidem Oqua III, pers. comm, 2008; cf Ekpo 2005: 33).

64. Cf. Cabrera (1975: 21, 1988a: 387). This phrase was recorded by Abakuá masters on *Ibiono* (2001), track 1 (at 2:07 minutes).

65. Cf. Ortiz (1950a: 27).

66. In southwestern Cameroon, "Ndiva means deep water to the Bakweris and other sister ethnic groups of Bantu origin," and is used in the context of their water spirit worship (Matute 1988: 40). In Ékpè chanting, "Bap dibó!" is a reference to the Nyámkpè grade (Hart 1964: 59, para. 167; Sosa-Rodríguez 1984: 97).

67. Cf. Ortiz (1981: 75). This phrase was performed by Román Díaz on the composition "Enyenisón Enkama 2," by Yoruba Andabo (1997), at 30 seconds (track 9 of the accompanying CD has a recording of this chant). A variant phrase was recorded by Abakuá masters on *Ibiono* (2001), track 6 (at 7:06 minutes): "Erendió itiá ororó kánde kóndo mína mofé."

68. Miller (2005).

69. Cf. Johnston (1888a: 436).

70. From the archives of El Chino Mokóngo, as inherited from Jesús Capaz "Chuchu." A version was recorded by Los Muñequitos de Matanzas (1983) in "Abakuá #3." Cf. Martín (1946: 28); Cabrera (1975: 375).

71. Alagoa (1971: 567–568).

72. The name Asibong Ekondo is associated with the foundation of Ékpè in Obutong and evoked by contemporary Ékpè in Calabar. Cf. Aye (2000: 71–72); Hart (1964: paras 176, 177, 180, 182, 184, 185, 398); Nair (1972: 5, 286). It is relevant that: "Obutong and Ekondo are Efut villages in the Cameroons" (Engineer Bassey 2007, pers. comm.). Talbot (1969/1926: vol. 1, 185) placed the foundation of Obutong by Creek Town (Obioko) settlers around 1650.

73. The names vary, but the story of the woman at the center of Ékpè's origins are "the same in Èfìk, Usaghade and Efut" (Engineer Bassey 2007, pers. comm.).

74. Precolonial trade between Calabar and "Rio del Rey" (Usaghade) is reflected in a Cross River folk tale (Dayrell 1969/1910: 135), and oral narratives from Usaghade (Anderson 1933: 8, para. 20).

75. "É'-kün-dü, n. The inhabitants of the earth collectively; the nations" (Goldie 1964/1862: 77); "èkòndò" is world in Ìbìbìò (Urua et al. 2004: 44).

76. Chief Eso Archibong Eso (2005, pers. comm.). Thanks to Eso Asibong, the chief's son, for help in interpretation.

77. Cf. Ukpong (1982: 168, 170). Rites with water are a human "universal," with many variants throughout West Africa (Herskovits 1990/1941: 233).

78. Cf. Cabrera (1988a: 147, 161, 514); Roche y Monteagudo (1925/1908: 93).

79. Cf. Cabrera (2000: 132–133, 1975: 7, 9).

80. Lovejoy (1989: 383); Castañeda (1995: 141, 144).

81. 'Ńdèm' [HL] (Essien 1986: 91). Among the Ejagham of Cameroon, "Ndèm" was a "Female Association" (Ebot 1978: 130, 132). Calabar Ékpè told me that, "Ékpè and Ndèm are one."

82. Cf. Talbot (1969/1926: vol. 2, 344).

83. Cf. Hackett (1989: 181–182); Röschenthaler (1998); Talbot 1969/1926: vol. 3, 780; Thompson (1974: 210); Valentin (1980: 36, 37, 46).

84. Ms. Okpo Akanawán (2005, pers. comm.) of Creek Town is an Ndèm priestess as well as an Ékpè member. Cf. Hart (1964: 53, para. 150).

85. Cf. Goldie (1901/1890: 43); Hart (1964: para. 124).

86. "The Èfik believe that Ékpè originates from Ndèm . . . the elemental spirit of water." (Engineer Bassey 2001/1998: 41). Cf. Goldie (1894: 4, 1964/1862: 200); Nair (1972: 56); Talbot (1926: vol. 2, 347); Waddell (1863: 314).

87. Ñkaña (1984/1933: 80). Ndèm Èfik, the goddess of the Èfiks, mammy water or mermaid. Ete mi, my father; Ndèm Èfik ete mi, The goddess of my father, i.e., The goddess which the Èfiks my parents, worship. (Thanks to Calixtus Ita of Calabar, 2007). Cf. Goldie (1960: 3).

88. Thanks to Ángel Guerrero (2005, pers. comm.). Cf. Cabrera (1988a: 387, 1975: 203). The chant "Ndèm Efí, ndèm Efó" was performed by Abakuá title-holders on "Apapa Efí," track 3 of *Ibiono* (2001). A variation, "Ndèm ndèm Efí yeneká, unkóbio," is ubiquitous in recordings, including Mongo Santamaría's "Afro Blue" (at 1:43 minutes) *Live at Jazz Alley* (1990); in "Encame de Abakuá (Efó-Efí)" (1987; at 2:50 minutes) by the Conjunto de percusión de Danza Nacional de Cuba; in "Ya Yo E" (at 1:45 minutes) by Patato y Totico (1967); in "Acere" (at 5:35 minutes) by Grupo Afro-Cubano de Alberto Zayas (1950s); in "Marcha Abakuá" (at 2:25 minutes) by the Coro Folklórico Cubano (2001). The variant, "Ndèm Efí Ubane" was recorded in 1940 (at 2:10 minutes; Courlander *Cult Music of Cuba* 1949).

89. Cf. Cabrera (1988a: 501); Engineer Bassey (2001/1998: 41).

90. As in Ékpè, during Abakuá rites a portion of the offerings are sent to the river (cf. Cabrera 1975: 49).

91. This chant was performed by Abakuá title-holders on "Orú Afiana," track 6 of *Ibiono* (2001), at 7.12 minutes. Abakuá lodge titles begin with their name, and end with the ultimate source or sponsor; in this case, the source of Èfik Obutong was ultimately Ndèm.

92. Hart (1964: para. 7, para. 30).

93. Cf. Oku (1989: 114). Before 1902, the title of the paramount ruler for the Èfiks was Edidem, but it officially became Obong thereafter (Hart 1964: 213–214; Nair 1972: 211). Edidem means the representative of the Ndèm deities (Etubom B. E. Bassey 2005, pers. comm.). Its use in an Ékpè context indicates the intimate ties between Ndèm and Ékpè. In Ìbìbìò, *àsábọ* is python (Urua et al. 2004: 23; cf. Akak 1982: 297; Aye 1991: 27; Ekong 1983: 134; D. Essien 1993: 16, 64; Hackett 1989: 181; Hart 1964: 74, para. 199).

94. Cf. Asuquo (1978: 46–47; entry for 24 March 1787 in Antera Duke's diary); Hart (1964: para. 183, 200); *Story of the Old Calabar* (1986: 78). In Cuba, the title Nasakó represents the legendary southwestern Cameroon diviner, a priest of Ndèm who organized the Ékpè society (as discussed in n. 128 in this chapter).

95. Iberedem Essien (2008, pers. comm.); Obong Nyong (2005, pers. comm.).

96. Ndèm is known as Atakpo in Uruan and Oron, Anansa in Obutong, Nimm in Ejagham, for examples (cf. Aye 1967: 28; Engineer Bassey 2001/1998: 42; Essien 1986: 91; Lieber 1971: 39, 65; *Story of the Old Calabar* 1986: 75, 78; Talbot 1969/1926: vol. 4, 221; Waddell 1863: 549, 551).

97. A linguist wrote the term variously as "Àtâkpò" and "Átâkpò" (Essien 1986: 13, 91; cf. D. Essien 1993: 3, 8, 13; Hackett 1989: 180; Ñkaña 1984/1933: 20, 2000/1933: 12). The Èfiks refer to this divinity as Atakpo Ndèm Uruan (Etubom B. E. Bassey 2008, pers. comm.).

98. Cf. Essien (1993: 82). Thanks to Chief E. Eyo of Adakukó (2005, pers. comm.), and Obong Nyong of Uruan (2005, pers. comm.).

99. Ndèm and Atacho are evoked in Cuban practice as historical deities (Cabrera 1958: 93, 1975: 15, 22, 25, 26, 380, 1988a: 310, 384, 449). So too in Ékpè, it is protocol to evoke Ndèm (Offiong 1989: 57). One can hear the chant "untacho natacho nabere tacho" performed by Abakuá title-holders on track 5 (6:30 minutes left to track) of *Ibiono* (2001).

100. MacGaffey (1977: 173) gave a parallel example from West-Central Africa.

101. Roche y Monteagudo (1925/1908: 101).

102. Dayrell (1969/1910: 145–152); Nicklin and Salmons (1988: 142).

103. Koloss (1985: 64); Nicklin (1991: 15); Talbot (1915: 105); Uya (1984: 23).

104. Talbot (1912a: 2, 1912b: 34; cf. Ekpo 2005: 58).

105. Nicklin and Salmons (1988: 142). These hairstyles were called *Offiom Inyang*, literally "crocodile" (cf. Goldie 1964/1862: 105, 134; Urua et al. 2004: 14).

106. Talbot (1912a: 24).

107. Talbot (1912a: 24). In 2004 and 2005, I saw the crocodile depicted on the pillars of many Ékpè lodges in Calabar, including that of Obutong (Efe Ékpè Asibong Ekondo) and Cohbam Town (Efe Ékpè Eyo Ema).

108. Footage from Oban 22 July 2004 (Mini DV #4, at 9 minutes, Ivor Miller Archives) documents a crocodile skin hanging prominently in the Efe Ékpè of Oban; it was the only animal skin displayed in the lodge.

109. This tratado was documented an inherited manuscript in Havana (Anonymous).

110. Cf. Cabrera (1958: 66).

111. Pierre Verger's photograph of the Íreme "Akuaramina," as identified by Cabrera, shows its crocodile teeth. This image was published in Cabrera (1958: 5); Thompson (1983: 238). David Brown (2003a, plate 18) photographed the same mask in 1992 as exhibited in the Casa de Africa in Havana.

112. "Korópo, head; *mekondó* (mokondó), masquerade ensemble; *unpón* (ponpon), head of the Íreme; *awaremí*, Íreme; Erómbe, a Kongo man; Ubáne, Oban; *néwe*, a question; *ákua*, to kill; *eromísón*, a dove" (Andrés Flores, pers. comm.) This phrase refers to the sacrifice made during the consecration the first Íreme.

113. Cabrera (1988a: 243) documented a variant.

114. "Isun, face; Anarukíe, a place. The mask was 'the face of Anarukíe' or 'the representation of Anarukíe'" (El Chino Mokóngo, pers. comm.).

115. The Amiabón lodge was founded in 1867 in Havana (see chapter 3 for details).

116. Mario Vinajera, an Abakuá title-holder and artist, made this particular masquerade. El Chino Mokóngo learned this anecdote from Juan Sotolongo, who held the title of Moruá Eribó of the Amiabón lodge in Havana.

117. Cabrera (1992/1954: 278). In the Cross River region, "an earthen pot—always a female symbol" (Talbot 1912a: 52).

118. Talbot (1912a: 45). Cf. Jones (1988a: 110); Talbot (1912a: 52–53); Thompson (1974: 210–212).

119. Nicklin and Salmons (1988: 142); Talbot (1912a: 24). Messenger (1971: 211) reported a variant from the Annang people near Calabar.

120. Goldie (1964/1862: 14).

121. Cabrera (1992/1954: 278). Cf. Cabrera (1975: 76, 82, 98, 1988a: cover image).

122. Cabrera (1988b: 19).

123. Thanks to Abakuá title-holder Sr. Pedro Suarez (2006, pers. comm.) of the lodge Betongo Naroko for identifying this image documented in Rodríguez (1881: 17), as a firma of the Èfìk Obutong lodge. Other variant firmas are documented in Cabrera (1975: 345–347).

124. Cabrera (1975: 90, 230).

125. Cabrera (1975: 68, 1988a: 169, 331, 1992/1954: 282). The term *Nyóngo* is a variant of *nyóngo-empabio*, as heard in the Abakuá chant, "Nyongo beko maná" recorded by Afrocuba of Matanzas, "Abakuá" (1998). For the sake of readers in English, I have transformed the Spanish "ñ" to the English equivalent "ny," even in published sources; e.g., in this passage "manyóngo" was written by Cabrera as "mañóngo."

126. Ardener et al. (1960: 339); Connell (1997: 70, 122); Matute (1988: 30). See also Ardener (1996: x); Nyamnjoh (2006: 183). Francis Nyamnjoh (2005: 243) described the contemporary usage of the term.

127. Cf Cabrera (1975: 224–228). There is obvious resonance here with the Rod of Asclepius and the caduceus, two symbols for healing in ancient Greece, used by contemporary western medical associations. Nineteenth-century Africans in Cuba may have made this association, but since their concepts and practices of healing were not borrowed, there was no real reason for them to do so.

128. Nasakó was a priest of "Obón Tacho," the Ndèm water spirit (Cabrera 1975: 449). Cf. Cabrera (1988a: 143, 1988b: 19). Cross River Ìbìbìò narratives also refer to powerful diviners from Cameroon (Talbot 1915: 101–106).

129. Cabrera (1988a: 133) referred to the parallel practice of Nasakó and Tata Nkisi in Cuba, inferring an African precedent.

130. Cabrera (1979: 59, 1984: 97, 1988b: 19, 1992/1954: 296, 479).

131. Much has been written in Cuba to identify parallels between the Kongo and Carabalí/Abakuá systems (cf. Cabrera 1977: 3–4, 1986: 69; Ortiz 1952c: 311; Pérez-Fernández 1986: 25, 27); as well as the Lukumí, Kongo, and Abakuá symbols (cf. Cabrera 1979: 128, 1988b: 17, 18).

132. Joseph (1974: 347–348); Talbot (1912a: 2, 1967/1932: 321–322, 1969/1926: vol. 3, 733).

133. Nowak (1991: 1301–1302); Grzimek (1972: 523).

134. Cabrera (1988b: 123).

135. Hutchinson (1970/1858: 145); Simmons (1956: 77, n. 91).

136. Ward (1911: 38).

137. Hallett (1964: 203–204, 205).

138. Hallett (1964: 209).

139. Cabrera (1988a: 319).

140. Nicklin (1991: 10). Bateka is a Balondo (Efut) village, a group known as Efó in Cuba. Cubans consider Efó the founders of Ékpè.

141. Cabrera (1975: 211, 1988a: 101, 131, 206, 269). Ejagham M̀gbè call their temple the *butame* (Ntui Erim Onongha 2005, pers. comm.). In Ejagham, *mutámé* means "the mystic sound of M̀gbè"; *ke butame* means "let us dance to the sound" (P. O. E. Bassey 2004, pers. comm.). In Kundu settlements of southwestern Cameroon, the sound that emerges from the shrine is *Butame* (Valentin 1980: 12–13, 15).

142. Fine and Ladich (2003).

143. Marine-life specialist Dr. Paul Skelton (2004, pers. comm.) noted, "There are a few [West African] freshwater fish species that are well known to emit sounds, especially when caught and taken from the water, cf. Pellegrin (1929); Sauvage (1879)." Cf. Mamonekene and Teugels (1993: 39–42); Reid (1989: 69); Teugels et al. (1992: 78–79, 82).

144. Hutchinson (1970/1858: 139–140) wondered about "the remarkable echoes in the Old Kalabar river. Is the refraction of sound due to the density of the atmosphere [?] . . . a booming sound of ordnance comes over the swamp from Creektown—it rolls and rolls away down the river, and over the country by Henshaw Town. The gradual diminution of echo at every reverberation at once attracts my listening faculties. [etc.] . . . the voice of the children . . . may be heard re-echoing over the dense bush which abounds in the neighborhood of Duketown."

145. Cf. Achebe (1984/1959: ch. 6, 46).

146. Goldie (1901/1890: 43).

147. Talbot (1912a: 30).

148. In Calabar-South I saw a cloth-draped silk-cotton tree along the river that was used as a shrine to Ndèm. Talbot (1912b: 38); Ward (1911: 51).

149. The Efe Ékpè Efut Ifako, Efut Ifako Clan, Odukpani LGA. Thanks to Prince Etim Ika (2005).

150. Cabrera (1988a: 504–505).

151. For parallel examples from the Cross River, see Jeffreys (1956: 18); Johnston (1888c: 745); Talbot (1923: 113); Ukpong (1982: 177, 181).

152. This tree stands a block away from the temple of the Muñongo Efó lodge.

153. Abakuá consider the royal palm as representative of the birth of Abakuá in Africa. Cuban Lukumí identified the royal palm as belonging to the divinity Changó, because during storms this tall tree acts as a lightning rod. Cf. Cabrera (1988b); Jameson (1821: 2–3). For Cross River examples, see Ebot (1978: 143); Lieber (1971: 40); Talbot (1923: 18).

154. In Cuba (Cabrera 1975: 33); in Èfìk (Aye 1991: 139).

155. Goldie (1964/1862: xlvii); Talbot (1912a: 429). Goat is *mboli* in the Mòkpè (Bakweri) language of southwestern Cameroon (Connell 1997: 26).

156. These phrases, "Chekendéke longorí semó eeeeee/Chekendéke longorí mayé" (one must have heart to go to war) and "ákua mbóri aborokín nyángé" (kill the goat), were recorded on the track "Canto Abakuá," sometime from the 1950s to 1970s (*La Música del pueblo de Cuba* 1972).

157. This phrase was recorded on *Ibiono* (2001), track 6 (at 5:14 minutes). Silvestre Mendez performed it on "Ñáñigo," at 2:15 minutes (*Bembé Araguá* 1957).

158. For examples from Cameroon, see Ebot (1978: 50–51); Huet (1996: 145); Ruel (1969: 49–51, 53); from the Onitsha Ìgbo, see Baikie (1966/1856: 295); Henderson (1972: 276–277); from Òyó Yorùbá and Benin, see Bem-Amos (1983: 52); Talbot (1969/1926: vol. 3, 733); Verger (1957: 374, 395); from Danhomè [Dahomey] kingdom see Blier (1995: 400, 406); from the Kuba Kingdom see Anderson and Kreamer (1989: 73); Cornet (1982, plates 240, 303, 305, 318); Vansina (1964: 102–103); among the Bakongo see Weeks (1969/1914: 189); in the Cross River, see Talbot (1910: 649); Uya (1984: 73).

159. Camerounian anthropologist Fongot Kinni (2004, pers. comm.) told me, "In my region, the Grasslands of the Bamenda and the Bamileke region, our Chiefs/Kings or Fons are called 'children of the leopard', 'Muo-Ngue' (Muo-Ngi-nyam, Muo-Ngue-nyam). No person can become king who is not born on a leopard skin. It's a symbol of agility, of dexterity, and productivity; it is believed that as a son of Ngui-nyam you can escape danger mystically or naturally."

160. Vansina (1990: 104).

161. This occurred in Calabar into the 1940s (Chief Effiom Ekpenyong Eyo 2005, pers. comm.).

162. Goldie (1901/1890: 43). See also Hutchinson (1970/1858: 146); Johnston (1888c: 756). Early photographs line the walls of the palace of the Obong of the Èfìks in Calabar that depict earlier Obongs receiving leopard tributes. I thank the Obong of the Èfìks for inviting me into his palace to observe them (in 2004).

163. A Cuban phrase used to convey this myth is "Ekuenyón ákua yebengó akurí akanawán eribó," meaning "Ekueñón went to the bush and killed a leopard to wrap the Eribó" (Rodríguez-Fornaris, Abelardo Empegó, pers. comm.). In addition to the term *Ékue*, Abakuá also refer to the leopard as *yébengó* (Cabrera 1988a: 527; Ortiz 1954: 3), apparently from *ngo*, the term for leopard in southwestern Cameroon and many West-Central African languages (Connell 1997: 35). Linguist Bruce Connell (2006, pers. comm.) wrote: "'ngo' is cognate with mkpe, ekpe, etc."

164. Connell (2004: 235); Iyanam (1998: 47); Uya (1984: 44).

165. Engineer Bassey (2008, pers. comm.); Ebot (1978: 138); Essien (1986: 14); Hackett (1989: 180); Lieber (1971: 52); Simmons (1956: 67); Waddell (1863: 397).

166. Oku (1990: 28); Talbot (1912a: 137).

167. According to a plaque in the permanent exhibit of the National Museum, Calabar, "The leopard was a sacred animal under the protection of the Ékpè society. Any killed animal was taken to the Efe Ékpè [Ékpè shrine] where some parts of its body were removed and preserved as sacred objects, the skin was given to the Obong Ékpè and the rest of the body thrown, by special messengers, into the sea" (August 2004).

168. The term *Uyo*, "the Voice of Ékue," derives from *úyò* "voice; order edict" in Ìbìbìò (Essien 1986: 10; Ortiz 1955a: 233; Urua et al. 2004: 111). "'úyò Ékpè' is all that is Ékpè. If we went a bit further we may say, 'all that there are, is energy.'" (Engineer Bassey 2007, pers. comm.).

169. Cf. Kubik (1971: 5–6, 1987: 51).

170. Cf. Engineer Bassey (2001/1998: 109); Talbot (1912b: 35).

171. Cf. Röschenthaler (1998: 41); Valentin (1980: 27).

172. In West Africa: Forde (1964: 158, 277), Ruel (1969: 220); in Cuba: Courlander (1944: 468), Trujillo y Monagas (1882: 366).

173. Ortiz (1955a: 236).

174. Engineer Bassey (2001/1998: 93); Johnston (1922: vol. 2: 254); Ortiz (1954: vol. 4, 434).

175. Cf. Cabrera (1975: 21). The variant phrase: "sánga Abakuá, ebongó itá" was recorded by Abakuá masters on *Ibiono* (2001), track 5 (at 7:14 minutes).

176. Cabrera (1975: 388). The interpretation is wholly mine. In another version, "In Efike Butón, here in Cuba, as happened in Africa, the Secret sounded" (Cabrera 1975: 63).

177. Eyom, sound; Mbókò, a vehicle; na, from; mmutami, inner sanctum; eri, is; jit, one (Ntui Erim Ononomgha 2005, pers. comm.).

178. Ika (2005, pers. comm.).

179. Thanks to Ernesto Soto Rodríguez "El Sambo" (Itia Mukandá), Pedro-Alberto Suarez Gonzáles "Pedrito el yuma" (Moruá Eribó Engomo de Betongó Naróko Efó), and many others in their community (October 2005).

180. Cabrera (1992/1954: 213); Goldie (1964/1862: 174). See references to Íreme Mboko in the song "Los cantares del abacuá," in chapter 7.

181. Cabrera (1988a: 113, 115). The phrase "bonkó eroko mboko efori sisi-yamba," evoking the bonkó drum and "the Voice," *mboko*, was recorded on *Ibiono* (2001), on track 3, at 7:02 minutes. Another phrase, "Sése Eribo eróko mbóko baróko nansáo," evoking the Eribó drum and "the Voice," *mboko*, was recorded on Sexteto Habanero's recording of "Criolla Carabalí" (1928), as discussed in chapter 7.

182. Fehderau (1992: 139); Swartenbroeckx (1973: vol. 2, 322).

183. Valentin (1980: 24).

184. The cabildo of San Antonio in Quiebra Hacha, western Cuba, maintains a hidden instrument called Kinfuíti that produces a "roar" (Cabrera 1958: 66). I visited this cabildo in 2000 to participate in its annual ceremonias. For their reception and generousity in teaching me their history and customs, I thank the cabildo leaders, including Rigoberto Laza-Laza, Mario Pedro, Cesáreo Cuesta López, Jesús Pedro Medina, Lázara Ester Robaina López, and Reinaldo Acosta Rodríguez.

185. Matute (1988: 37).

186. Talbot (1912a: 46–48).

187. Ruel (1962: 101, 1969: 30) provided a parallel example from Cross River Banyang communities.

188. Uruan is likely the source for the Cuban Orú lineage (discussed later in this chapter). Cubans regard the Eribó drum as from Orú territory that was incorporated into Ékpè during foundational ceremonies in Usagaré. Contemporary Uruan Ékpè claim that their ancestors migrated to their

present sites from the Usaghade (Usagaré) region with the Edibo drum in the distant past (Iberedem Essien 2008, pers. comm.; Obong Nyong 2005, pers. comm.).

189. Iberedem Essien (2008, pers. comm.); Obong Nyong (2005, pers. comm.). Cuban legends also relate the Eribó drum to the leopard, by recounting that in Africa the title-holder Ekuenyón hunted a leopard to bring its skin to cover the Eribó.

190. I recorded this phrase in Uruan as performed by Obong Nyong, while officiating a ceremony to consecrate me within Uruan Ékpè traditions, to help me continue my research. Present at witnesses were Cardinal Offiong of Uruan, Etubom B. E. Bassey, Iyámba of Ekoretonko, and Prince Etim Ika of Efut Ifako, Creek Town (February 2005).

191. Cuban references to Eribó confirm its relationship to Cross River rulers, for example, the phrase "Obón Eribó," meaning "Eribó the Obón" (ruler); cf. Cabrera (1975: 24). Another phrase, "Eribó Tacho," confirms the relationship between Eribó and the Uruan settlements, where Tacho (or Atakpor) is the local divinity (Cabrera 1975: 26).

192. The Eribó is known in Cuba as Sése Eribó, or Sése. An Abakuá phrase, "sése Akanarán," means "the sése (Eribó) is my mother" (Miller 2004b).

193. Ortiz (1954: vol. 4, 43).

194. This phrase and the significance of the plumes are further explained in the notes for the lodge Eklé Entáti Macheceré, chapter 3, and in the appendix of chants.

195. Ardener et al. (1960: 230); Jones (1984: 191); Talbot (1912a: 153). The term *Ekoi* (or *Koi*) is made in reference to the foundation of Abakuá, particularly the Eribó drum and its plumed rods (cf. Cabrera 1975: 25, 26). Ibondá is discussed in the appendix of potencies.

196. Ñkaña (1984/1933: 64–66).

197. Cf. Onyile (2000).

198. See the discussion of the *munyón* plumed rods in chapter 3 regarding the Cuban lodge Eklé Entáti Macheceré, 1840, and in the appendix of potencies regarding the lodge Ibiabánga Munyón, 1871.

199. Cross River folktales with parallel themes were documented by Dayrell (1913: 19, 26–27, 99, 1969/1910: 107–114, 126–132).

200. In Cuba, "plantain" is *aberenyón*; in Èfìk *mbri-enyöng* (Goldie 1964/1862: 567). In Cuba, *mimba* is "cane liquor" (Cabrera 1975: 21); in Cross River languages, *mimbo* is "palm wine" (Connell 1997: 105; Goldie 1901/1890: 205; Hallett 1964: 201; Latham 1990: 75; Mzeka 1980: 88; Waddell 1863: 248, 379).

201. Roche y Monteagudo (1925/1908: 93). I have spelled Roche's transcriptions phonetically in the English translation. Originally it was "Anague camanba Efique buton . . . Cambito."

202. Roche y Monteagudo (1925/1908: 93).

203. Cabrera (1975: 342, 387, 1988a: 145); Palmié (2006: 108).

204. Cf. Brandon (2004); Cabrera (1988a: 145, 307, 1992/1954: 403–404).

205. In Uruan Ékpè, the ritual drink is called *bokuba* (Engineer Bassey 2004, pers. comm.).

206. El Chino Mokóngo (pers. comm.); Ortiz (1955a: 255–256).

207. Cf. Cabrera (1988a: 143).

208. Engineer Bassey (2001/1998: 34).

209. Cabrera (1975: 13).

210. Engineer Bassey (2001/1998: 50).

211. Talbot (1969/1926: vol. 3, 869).

212. Abakuá has its own laws and administers justice within its own ranks. Each lodge may form a tribunal to judge the trespasses of a member (cf. Cabrera 1975: 276). Abakuá's separatist relationship to the national administration parallels that of other groups, at one point or another in their his-

tory, such as the Nation of Islam in the United States, the Amish communities of Pennsylvania, the Accompong Maroons of Jamaica (cf. Bilby 2006: 44–45).

213. Hart (1964: 58, para 165).

214. Jameson (1821: 71).

215. Wurdeman (1844: 83–84).

216. In the colonial period on Three Kings' Day, Abakuá meetings were so prevalent that a firma was created for this occasion (cf. Cabrera 1975: 456).

217. Dr. María-Terésa Lináres Savio (1997, pers. comm.).

218. Wurdeman (1844: 44–45); see also Scarpaci et al. (2002: 29).

219. The courtyard housing typical of colonial Havana was and is ubiquitous and generic throughout southern Spain and the Magreb (Berber and Muslim) and is also a common feature of West African compounds, Muslim or not. An ancient form, it was used during the Roman Empire (Labelle Prussin 2005, pers. comm.).

220. In Calabar, this title was interpreted as "the Efut shrine from Usaghade." Andrés Flores said, "The title is Efórisún Lilí Enkrúkoro Mambre Asuku Anabénabia Anababurecha Awana mukundun Wanglón Nglón Chambéyo Eforisún Usagaré. Enkrúkoro, reunion. This title consists of the names of Africans who witnessed the creation of this group, for example, Nglón Chambéyo."

221. Cf. Cabrera (1958: 72, 1988a: 159).

222. Officially known as Isangele, this community is commonly referred to by Cross River inhabitants as "Usak-Edet" and by some locals as "Usak-Ade" (Mosongo 1995: ii), both with a very light *k*. Linguist Bruce Connell (2007, pers. comm.) uses "Usaghade," because locals do not pronounce *k*, but a very light *g*. This coincides with Cuban usage. Other West African variants of Usaghade are Usahadit, Usarade, and Usakere. The region is also called Bakasi or Backasey (Nicklin 1991: 8). As a result of Portuguese contact in the early 1500s, the region "has historically been referred to as Rio del Rey" (Connell 2001: 53).

223. Engineer Bassey (2001/1998: 21) wrote, "Èfìk agree that the Efut introduced Ékpè to them and Usak Edet is the actual source." In Oron, Rev. Ward (1911: 37) learned similarly that Ékpè "was brought into the country from the Cameroons."

224. Akpabot (1975: 30).

225. Cf. Cabrera (1958: 72).

226. Cf. Cabrera (1992/1954: 285). This treaty is also known as Bongó Yukáwa (also referred to in n. 21 of chapter 3, n. 147 of chapter 7).

227. Goldie (1964/1862: 137–138). Ékpè leaders in Calabar identified the term Eforisún as *Efut Isun*, meaning the "face" or shrine of Efut (see details in appendix of chants). The equation of Efóri with Efut was confirmed in Cuba (Cabrera 1992/1954: 285).

228. Cf. Cabrera (1988a: 18). El Chino interpreted it as, "Erominyán, adoring; Abasí, God; úyo, voice; butón, voice." Butón, from Obutong, is interpreted as "voice" as in "the first Voice," according to Cuban narratives, since the first Voice or fundamento of the creoles was received through the Èfìk Obutong lodge. Some Cross River narratives also identify Obutong as an early source of Ékpè for the Èfìks (Engineer Bassey 2004, pers. comm.).

229. Andrés interpreted, "Asarorí, when the fundamento is 'fragayando' (sounding) powerfully." Cf. Cabrera (1988a: 71).

230. El Chino interpreted: "sése, sacred; Mokumbán, mokúba, the ritual drink of Abakuá."

231. Cf. Cabrera (1958: 38, 1988a: 406). In Abakuá, *efóri* has two meanings: "herbs," as well as an Efut tribe named Efori. The birth of Efóri Nkomón lodge is celebrated in a composition by Ignacio Piñeiro, "Iyamba Beró," recorded in the 1920s (Miller 2000b).

232. See discussion in the appendix of chants.

233. Cf. Cabrera (1988a: 158).

234. El Chino Mokóngo interpreted, "taipo, first; ikondó, food, sacrifice." Andrés Flores said, "Its title was Ékue nyanya komo Íreme táipó. This title says the names of the Íremes that appeared during the treaty of Bongó Yukawa in Africa, Efó territory."

235. Cf. Thompson (1983: 300, n. 33). The permanent exhibit in the Calabar Museum reports one of several migratory waves of "Efut Ekondo and Efut Abua people . . . in 1833 from Cameroon," (as seen by the author in 2004).

236. Literally, "a representative of Ndèm becomes an Ékpè initiate at night" (Etubom B. E. Bassey 2005, pers. comm.). This phrase is a further indication of the intimate ties between Ndèm and Ékpè. Commonly heard in Èfìk Ékpè ceremonies, this chant was recorded by Ékpè Ita on "Ifot Ufok Etemi," *"Ase"–Traditional*, vol. 2 (1976).

237. Cabrera (1992/1954: 216). See also Cabrera (1975: 13); Ortiz (1950a: 27).

238. This chant was recorded in Guanabacoa, outside Havana, by Harold Courlander on *Cult Music of Cuba*, track 4, (1949). Arsenio Rodríguez recorded it in "Canto Abakuá" (1963).

239. The term *maka maka*, means "feather"; *ateréré*, "everlasting, infinite."

240. Cf. Cabrera (1988a: 207).

241. Because the Efórisún lodge did not last, Efóri Enkomón became the source of sponsorship for the lineage of Efó territory, and it is today the eldest lodge in Cuba. Cf. Cabrera (1988a: 158).

242. Cf. Cabrera (1969: 168–169).

243. Cf. Cabrera (1992/1954: 217).

244. A Cross River example is found in Nicklin (1995: 372). Other examples from around the world are in Mickey Hart's *Planet Drum* (1991).

245. For example, in Qua (Ejagham) practice, "the preparation of the Ṃgbè Lodge or shrine must commence early before sunrise to benefit from the blessings of Obasi which come with the Eho (the rising sun)" (Ekpo 2005: 57).

246. Written by Chief Akan (1992) of Uruan in the program notes to a funerary ceremony.

247. Abelardo Empegó responded, "Yes. 'Engóro mambé nángereté,' the Africans said this when they founded Efóri Enkomón in Belén.

248. Cf. Cabrera (1988a: 193).

249. Contemporary Èfìk Ékpè say; "inua tiet, one voice," as the equivalent of the Cuban "bongó ita." It means "Ékpè is one" wherever it is found, and that members "speak with one voice" once their decision upon a matter has been established (Chief Archibong Eso, Iyámba of Obutong 2005, pers. comm.).

250. *Akan nwan* is Ìbìbìò; *Akani awan* is Èfìk (Engineer Bassey 2008, pers. comm.); Goldie (1964/1862: 7, 80).

251. Engineer Bassey (2004, pers. comm.).

252. Cf. *Los Ñáñigos* (1882: 7). Abakuá title-holders are sworn in for life. Therefore, the *abanékues*, the first-level initiates who aspire to be title-holders, must either wait for the death of a title-holder in their own lodge or create a new lodge to receive titles.

253. El Chino specified that the Orú cabildo was located "on San Nicolás Street between Vives and Esperanza Streets." See discussion of the lodge Orú Abakuá Enduré in the appendix of potencies for more on this lineage.

254. Cf. Cabrera (1988a: 460, 517). The phrase "Okobio Orú Ápapa Akondomina Mofe" was recorded by Abakuá masters on *Ibiono* (2001), track 6 (at 3:26 minutes). "Orú Ápapa Akondomína Mofe" is a chorus (at 6:33 minutes) on the same track. Silvestre Mendez performed it on "Ñáñigo,"

(*Bembé Araguá* 1957, at 2:10 minutes). See appendix of potencies for an interpretation of the phrase "akondomína mefé."

255. In a preliminary interpretation of Abakuá terms through Cross River languages I wrote, "Orú is likely Oron, a Cross River ethnic group" (Miller 2005: 34). After meeting with scholars and Ékpè leaders from Oron, Uruan, and Calabar, we have reasoned that Uruan is the more likely source. Oron was not an important slave port (while Uruan was). Uruan has a strong tradition of Ékpè historically tied to that of the Èfïks of Calabar. Early Cuban variations of the term Orú include Urua, as in "uru ápapa," "Oruá Apapa," or "Uruá Abacuá" (cf. *Los Ñáñigos* 1882: 16; Rodríguez 1881: 14, 22); later versions include "Urua ápapa", "Uruápaoa", "Uruana: name of a Carabalí settlement" (Cabrera 1988a: 517, 247). Cuban narratives also relate Orú to "Uyo Bibene" (Cabrera 1988a: 460), Uyo being a town adjacent to many Uruan settlements in the Ìbìbìò-speaking region.

2. The Fortified City

1. Moreno-Fraginals (1996: 92).

2. Exquemelin (1741/1678: 130).

3. Kuethe (1991: 13). See also Mante (1772: 398).

4. Arrate (1949/1830: 8). See also Russell (1929: 303).

5. Cf. Rout (1976: xiii). By 1543 Havana was ordained the port of gathering for ships in the first regulations for the return voyage of the *flotas* (Spanish fleet) back to Cadiz (Marrero 1972–1987: vol. 2, 148).

6. Kuethe (1991: 14). In the 1690s "el dottor Gio Francesco Gemelli Careri took this route when sailing from the Philippines to Acapulco to Havana (cf. Gemelli Careri 1699–1700: vols. 5, 6).

7. Early Havana was "a castle in a dominant position" (Franco 1972: 4). Havana was the political and economic center of Cuba for the Spanish Crown from 1553 to 1898 (cf. Carpentier 1989/1946: 36).

8. Ely (1853: 119).

9. Cf. Linebaugh and Rediker (2000: 46–47, 49).

10. *Memorias* (1842: 445–447). See also Pérez-Beato (1893b: 131).

11. Moreno-Fraginals (1996: 86). See also Scarpaci et al. (2002: 14).

12. Asiento: "A contract . . . between the king of Spain and other powers, for furnishing the Spanish dominions in America with negro slaves (J.). *spec.* That made between Great Britain and Spain at the peace of Utrecht in 1713." *Oxford English Dictionary*.

13. Palmer (1981: 85).

14. The period beginning in 1763 was characterized by an end of commercial monopolies and a general opening up of Cuba to commercial, educational, and agricultural development (Cantón-Navarro 1998: 33). The number of 70,000 African arrivals per Bergad et al. (1995: 25). In 1789 the Spanish Crown declared free trade in trans-Atlantic slavery. The document is in the Archivo General de Indias, Seville, fondo Indiferente General, file 2823 (Childs 2006b: 240, n. 29). Meanwhile, from the 1760s to 1790s, during the height of the trans-Atlantic slave trade to Old Calabar, Èfïk merchants exported some 3000 to 5000 people annually (Behrendt and Graham 2003: 51–52).

15. Childs (2006b: 215); Martínez-Vergne (1989: 186).

16. Ely (1853: 120); Foner (1962: 104); Kimball (1850: 54–56); Knight (1970: 102); Martínez-Vergne (1989: 187).

17. Hazard (1989/1871: 186). By the "world," Hazard meant the West.

18. Franco (1961: 107); Hazard (1989/1871: 135); Jameson (1821: 107); Madden (1839); Marrero (1972–1987: vol. 14, 245).

19. Wurdeman (1844: 59–60).

20. De la Torre (1857: 102); Jameson (1821: 87); Roig de Leuchsenring (1963: 134); Scarpaci et al. (2002: 27).

21. Deschamps-Chappeaux (1972b: 19).

22. Deschamps-Chappeaux (1972b: 19). Cf. Cabrera (1975: 496).

23. Abakuá names for Havana and Regla are described in chapter 1; the Abakuá name for Matanzas is discussed in chapter 3.

24. Deschamps-Chappeaux (1972b: 19).

25. Deschamps-Chappeaux (1972b: 20).

26. Cf. Mintz (1984: 298).

27. Brathwaite (1971: 299).

28. Many Cuban narratives recounted by members of African-derived systems tell how some elite whites in the colonial period helped protect leading practitioners. For example, babaláwo Mayito Angarica (1993, pers. comm.) told me about the wealthy white patrons of Adeshina, a nineteenth-century Ifá diviner in Regla who helped found Cuban Ifá practice.

29. Cf. Blanco (1900: 147); Castellanos García (1948: 589).

30. On English-dominated Caribbean islands, property owners with large holdings tended to live in England, whereas Cuban property owners lived there, usually residing in Havana. Jameson (1821: 8, 45) cited as exemplary the twenty-nine Havana residents with Spanish titles of nobility who had never actually been to Spain.

31. Scarpaci et al. (2002: 312).

32. Carta de Félix M. Tanco a Domingo del Monte, 1837 (*Domingo del Monte* 2002: 107–108). Félix Manuel Tanco was a Colombian whose parents were Cuban.

33. Moreno-Fraginals (1996: 86).

34. Moreno-Fraginals (1996: 87).

35. Castañeda (1995: 147); Jameson (1821: 41–42).

36. Moreno-Fraginals (1996: 90).

37. Moreno-Fraginals (1996: 92).

38. Moreno-Fraginals (1996: 90) located 102 such cases in the eighteenth century.

39. Moreno-Fraginals (1996: 90–91).

40. Cf. Price (1996).

41. "In Central Africa, the *ki-lombo* referred to a merit-based, male warrior society that not only cut across lineage boundaries, but actually erased lineage ties based on natal descent" (Sweet 2003: 50).

42. Knight et al. (1989: 769). See also Bilby (2006).

43. Smith (1994: 13). Cf. Hall (1992b: 78); Johnson (1992: 38).

44. Entralgo (1953: 18–19).

45. "Ethnic" solidarity was maintained among the descendants of Africans well into the twentieth century. Cf. Calderón et al. (2000: 64–65).

46. Reis (2001b: 130).

47. Morales-Padrón (1972: 353). Cf. Foner (1962: 89–90).

48. Ponte-Domínguez (1944: 8); Torres-Cuevas (2005: 68). Cf. *Diccionario Enciclopédico de la Masonería* (1883: 228); Kimball (1850: 52); Torres-Cuevas (2005: 63, 66–67).

49. Fox (1997, 2001: 15, 21, 64).

50. General Máximo Gómez, General Adolfo del Castillo, General Quintín Bandera, and many other Cuban rebels were also Freemasons (Padrón-Valdés 1991: 151). I learned about the masonry activities of these figures from the library at the Grand Lodge of Havana, in 1993, where I spoke with archivists and consulted publications, including *Diccionario Enciclopédico de la Masonería* (1883).

Masonic lodges were centers for the Cuban rebellion against Spain (Ponte-Domínguez 1944: 19, 27).

51. Deschamps-Chappeaux (1964: 108). One indication of these ties may be the coded handshake, used by Freemasons and Abakuá, but not by Cross River Ékpè, whose gestured communication does not involve body contact, as far as I know.

52. Another example is Francisco Rodríguez Lavín, an Abakuá title-holder and Freemason from the late nineteenth century. See footnote 34 in appendix of potencies, for the Munyánga lodge.

53. Carpentier (1989/1946: 266). Cf. Ortiz (1943: 2–3, 1981/1951: 465).

54. Arrom (1983) found that *cimarrón* likely derived from a Taino root term, as it came into common usage in the Spanish Caribbean before being globalized.

55. Deschamps-Chappeaux (1969b: 162, 147). A similar phenomenon was observed in eighteenth-century Virginia (cf. Mullin 1972: 117–121).

56. Cairo (2005: 222–223, citing Martínez-Furé 1976); Martínez-Furé (2006, pers. comm.).

57. Deschamps-Chappeaux (1983: 41–46) lists descriptions of facial cicatrize of fugitives according to ethnicity in Havana from 1800 to 1845.

58. Deschamps-Chappeaux (1969b: 155).

59. Deschamps-Chappeaux (1983: 5).

60. Deschamps-Chappeaux (1983: 24–25). Cf. Deschamps-Chappeaux (1983: 22); Franco (1973: 66).

61. The fugitives included: a "ladino [Spanish speaker] of the Brican nation" in 1815; a "black bozal [African born] from the nation carabilí macuá" in 1821; "the black female Pilar, *carabalí*" in 1831; a "Carabalí viví" in 1831; a "black carabalí ososo" in 1831; two "bozales" (African born) "from the nation carabalí suamo" in 1831 (Deschamps-Chappeaux 1969b: 149, 154, 158, 156).

62. Essien (1986: 89). *Usó*, meaning "dexterous hands," would be used for anyone who is an artist, a blacksmith, a tailor, etc. (Engineer Bassey 2006, pers. comm.).

63. Deschamps-Chappeaux (1983: 5–6).

64. Deschamps-Chappeaux (1983: 41).

65. Franco (1973: 21).

66. Carpentier (1989/1946: 60); María de la Torre (1986/1857: 162). See also Carpentier (1989/1946: 265–266).

67. Ortiz (1984: 38, n. 27); Rout (1976: 17).

68. Moreno (1997: 20).

69. Ortiz (1984b: 14).

70. Ortiz (1984b: 14).

71. Ortiz (1984b: 15, 37–38, n. 25). Cofradías and authorized cabildos were the only means through which urban blacks could meet without arousing fear among the master class (Levine 1990: 6; Moreno 1997: 62).

72. Moreno (1997: 19); Ortiz (1984b: 14, 37, n. 22).

73. The earliest dates I have found for African-based mutual aid societies are: Hispaniola, 1540s; Cartagena de Indias, 1573; Mexico, 1609; Peru, sixteenth century; Argentina, eighteenth century (cf. Howard 1999: 138, 141; Molina and López 2001: 337; Olivera-Chirimini 2001: 258; Ortiz 1984b: 37, n. 24; Thornton 1998a: 202–203). In Brazil, the brotherhoods date to the late sixteenth century (cf. Russell-Wood 1974: 575, 597–598). For brotherhoods in Bahia, Brazil, see Verger (1976: 462–465).

74. Aye (2000: 91); Dike (1956: 34); *Story of the Old Calabar* (1986: 78).

75. Cf. Anene (1966: 9–10); Behrendt and Graham (2003: 50); Dike (1956: 34–37); Jones (1956: 132–135, 1963: 159).

76. *Story of the Old Calabar* (1986: 131).

77. Anene (1966: 42–43); Jaja (1977: 13, 43); *Roots of King Jaja* (1997: 23, 32–33).

78. Jones (1963: 166).

79. Jones (1963: 163–164).

80. Deschamps-Chappeaux (1972b: 25).

81. Eltis et al. (1999: 30).

82. Marrero (1972–1987: vol. 8, 159–160). Cf. Thornton (1998: 301).

83. From the 1750s to 1820s, the number of cabildos grew to at least fifty (Childs 2006b: 215–216).

84. Ortiz (1984b: 13).

85. Moliner-Casteñeda (1988: 14); see also Pérez-Fernández (1986: 25, 27). A recording of Bríkamo music from Matanzas is found on the CD *Grupo AfroCuba: Raíces Africanas/African Roots* (1998).

86. See also Childs (2006b: 222–223).

87. Deschamps-Chappeaux (1971: 32–33).

88. The type of cemeteries created in Spanish colonies, with a separate ground walled and usually outside the city center, did not exist in West Africa. In the practice of Òyó Yorùbá, various Ìgbo-, Ejagham-, and Èfik-speaking groups in the Cross River region and in the Cameroon Grassfields, prominent deceased persons were buried within a family compound (cf. Baikie 1966/1856: 315; Balmaseda 1869: 195; Dayrell 1913: 25; Matute 1988: 7; Valentin 1980: 32; Waddell 1863: 336; Walker 1877: 123; Ward 1911: 45).

89. Cf. Deschamps-Chappeaux (1972a: 39–40). Abakuá funerary rites are a long process, aspects of which continue to be performed in private homes, as Rogelio Martínez-Furé (2006, pers. comm.) witnessed during the last rites of his father in 1993, who held the title of Mokóngo of a Matanzas lodge.

90. Deschamps-Chappeaux (1968b: 50) found reference to a lawsuit between the Cabildo Carabalí Isuama, founders of the Cabildo Carabalí de Oro, and the Cabildo Carabalí Isuama Abaya Ocuite Nuestra Señora de Regla for possession of a house in Havana owned by the Isuama Isieques.

91. "Okeya" was spelled "Oquella" in the original Cuban manuscript. The cabildo of the Carabalí Ososo nation bought their house with money lent by María de Jesús de Soto, a free black woman identified as a Carabalí Isuama. Many of the cabildo houses were originally within the walled city (Deschamps-Chappeaux 1971: 36–38). If Ososo in Havana is the same as the Ososo language identified on the Nigerian language map (cf. Crozier and Blench 1992), then Isauma and Ososo are both Ìgbo related. Ortiz (1975a: 50) mentioned a "cabildo carabalí ibó" in Havana, but without a date.

92. Landers (1999: 312, n. 7).

93. Isieke was spelled "Isieque" in the original Cuban manuscript (Deschamps-Chappeaux 1971: 38).

94. Landers (1999: 312, n. 7). This cabildo has the same name as a group of black curros, suggesting a relationship between them, as both existed in Havana at the same time.

95. Howard (1998: 41, 36, 49–50).

96. Cabrera (1950: 20).

97. The first lodge of Regla "was sponsored by the Apapá Carabalíes" (Rodríguez 1881: 5–6).

98. Deschamps-Chappeaux (1971: 37). A document from 1759 reported a "Carabalí apapa" nation in Havana (Marrero 1972–1987: vol. 6, 36).

99. Ortiz (1975a: 41, 1984b: 17). The term *chiquito* means "second" or "junior," as in "son of."

100. Howard (1998: 44, 36, n. 25). There exists an archive of the "cabildo de Apapa" from 1808 to 1830 in the Archivo Nacional de Cuba, Havana, fondo Escribanía Antonio Daumy, file 583, no. 5, fols. 82-v (Childs 2006b: 242, n. 67).

101. Engineer Bassey (2004, pers. comm.).

102. Cf. Cabrera (1958: 50, 1992/1954: 277).

103. The *cabildos de nación* were repeatedly expelled from the walled city (first in 1792, then again in 1842), implying that they did not leave willingly or easily (Ortiz 1975a).

104. Klein (1966: 18–19).

105. Kuethe (1986: 38).

106. Historian Klein (1966: 20–21) estimated that at this time, "one out of every five free colored males was a member of the militia."

107. Kuethe (1986: 49, 75, 176); Navarro (1929: 103–104).

108. Deschamps-Chappeaux (1971: 89–90). Black Battalions were established throughout the Spanish Americas: in New Orleans after 1769 (Sublette 2004: 106); in 1801 in Uruguay (Olivera-Chirimini 2001: 258; Rama 1967: 21) and in Haiti (Trouillot 1982: 355).

109. Deschamps-Chappeaux (1974: 17). Cf. Jameson (1821: 15).

110. Deschamps-Chappeaux (1971: 94–95, 1974: 19). For more examples, see Deschamps-Chappeaux (1971: 91, 1974: 18). The Carabalí "enjoyed the reputation of being … avaricious, thrifty and wealthy" (Cabrera 1950: 16).

111. Deschamps-Chappeaux (1971: 95–96). For the issue of African-descendants who owned slaves, see Berlin (1998: 9); Cabrera (1979: 111–113); Deschamps-Chappeaux (1971: 51–53).

112. Deschamps-Chappeaux (1971: 93–94).

113. The term *curro* derives from *currataco*, used to describe an underworld social group of eighteenth-century Madrid with a peculiar dress and behavior.

114. Deschamps-Chappeaux (1972a: 37).

115. The first scholar to treat this topic, Fernando Oritz, thought that the Abakuá and the curros were two distinct groups (Ortiz 1927, 1986: 5–8). Later, Deschamps-Chappeaux (1972a: 41) presented evidence for multiple links between both groups.

116. Moreno-Fraginals (1996: 91).

117. Deschamps-Chappeaux (1972a: 38, 40). Authorities thought that Oró Papá was a group of black curros, but Abakuá understand Orú Apapá as a Carabalí cabildo, as mentioned by El Chino Mokóngo in chapter 1.

118. Deschamps-Chappeaux (1972a: 40–41).

119. Deschamps-Chappeaux (1972a: 35–36).

120. Anoka (1979: n.p.) identified four places named "Isieke" in the Nigeria Local Government Areas of Bende, Ideato, Isuikwauto/Okigwe, and Oru.

121. Deschamps-Chappeaux (1983: 41). Ortiz (1929: 22) documented a creole grandson of a Carabalí who had his teeth filed, according to "Carabalí Bibí" usage. Compare with Talbot (1923: 215).

122. Deschamps-Chappeaux (1983: 41).

123. Antonio Basabe was a soldier and director of dances in the Oró Papá cabildo, known to have black curro members. Basabe was a participant in the 1825 feud discussed earlier in this chapter. "Ha dicho Antonio Basabe/ sin nada de precautela/ que ya el bombo está en la escuela. Después aparecen las palabras de origen carabalí: Oban lla canyon dirán/ Y sin nada de aparato/ Y dice o sisi dia mato/ Critiano salga a bailar. Posiblemente esta décima, donde se dice que el bombo es oruapapá, sea la primera manifestación popular, en que con cierta armonía, se mezclan palabras del castellano y del carabalí." (Deschamps-Chappeaux 1972a: 39). The term *el bombo* (bass drum) in the original text was a code for *oruapapá*, as Deschamps-Chappeaux (1972a: 39) learned from Abakuá sources. It's obvious that "bass drum" is an indirect reference to the Voice of Ékpè. Many terms here are clearly Abakuá, others are illegible, likely due to a poor transcription by an authority ignorant of Abakuá language. At any rate, the general message of the décima is understood. "Oban lla [ya]" is closest to "Obon Iya," a reference to Lord Fish (in Èfìk), the sacred Fish Tánse. The phrase "canyon dirán" is likely a diminished form of "sankantión manantión dirán," a phrase of reverence before an Abakuá shrine (cf. Cabrera 1988a: 477). "O sisi dia mato" was interpreted as "O sisi Yambá-O," a variation of "Efóri Sisi Iyamba-O," title of the grade Iyámba (Cabrera 1975: 21, 25, 26, 28, 29, 31, 181, 199, 1988a: 160, 268, 488–489).

124. Guirao (1938: 14). Décima is a poetic form used in various Cuban and Puerto Rican genres, originating in seventeenth-century Spain. The décima consists of ten-line verses in rhymed octosyllables.

125. "Yegó Sámbila habanero:/ yo soy e negrito curro."

126. "Nesio eres cual mi bayo/ cuando le sale epereja;/ te rindes a mi bandera/ o si no te parto el guayo./ bamos a ber, sosipayo,/ naeriero amoropó/ aproseme y a copó,/ inuá aborobuto écue,/ momí asarorí abanecue/ abaireme ecuefó." For interpretations into Èfìk, see appendix of chants.

127. "Yo soy abanecue Efí/ desde el año ochentaiuno,/ y no le temo a ninguno,/ lo juro por Abasí./ Yo he bisto el anamanguí/ inuando con el ñañaco,/ y al berme me dijo: amaco/ curi cufón, porque écue/ nesesita un abanecue/ que condocá dia afomaco" (Guirao 1938: 14–16). Translating black Cuban speech, as well as Abakuá, is not a linear process. Thanks to Abakuá leader Ángel Guerrero (2004, pers. comm.) for help interpreting the obscure and antiquated "street" usage terms in this poem.

128. Engineer Bassey (2006, pers. comm.).

129. As discussed later in this chapter, Deschamps-Chappeaux (1964) described a meeting in 1839 held to organize a new "cabildo" named Orú Apapá, implying that it did not exist before then.

130. Ortiz (1955b: 8).

131. Marrero (1972–1987: vol. 9, 34).

132. Franco (1974: 154, 184).

133. Based on archival research as well as historical memory maintained in Havana, historian Franco wrote that, "the elders, who arrived from Nigeria, transmitted to the creole José Antonio Aponte the powers that only a great man could have in Africa" (Franco 1974: 148–149).

134. The precolonial Ògbóni initiation society was a religious brotherhood/sisterhood with political dimensions that gathered powerful men and women in each Yorùbá town under the protection of secrecy to venerate the earth in its aspect of the universal mother (cf. Abímbólá 1977: 39; Abraham 1958: 484; Drewal et al. 1989: 136, 242 f.n.; Talbot 1969/1926: vol. 3, 762; Thompson 1983: 74).

135. This movement included "Mandingas, Ararás, Congos, Carabalíes, Macuá, Bibis and others . . . as well as groups of blacks and mulatto migrants from Haiti, Santo Domingo, Jamaica, Panama, Cartagena de Indias, and the United States" (Franco 1974: 150).

136. Franco (1974: 177).

137. Franco (1974: 179). "Under a secret oath—whose reach and gravity only the Abakuá knew—the brigadier Narciso [of Santo Domingo] agreed with Aponte to lead the rebels once they had weapons in their power" (Franco 1974: 154).

138. Franco (1974: 154). Ortiz (1955a: 310) thought that "the secret Ogboni society of Nigeria . . . undoubtedly had some early relation with the founders of the ñáñigo [Abakuá] society of Cuba." In Cuba, Ògbóni seems to have not survived into the twentieth century.

139. Deschamps-Chappeaux (1972b: 20).

140. Deschamps-Chappeaux (1968b: 51, 1987: 76, 1990: 102).

141. Franco (1972: 8). Franco cited the Legajo 11, no. 1, Comisión Militar, Archivo Nacional de Cuba.

142. As discussed in n. 158 of the Introduction.

143. Margarito Blanco, of the Cabildo Ultán or Papaultan; his papers included a summons to "the 'Ocongos' of Obane, Ososo, and Efó, to create a new Cabildo . . . Arupapá or Oru Apapá." (Deschamps-Chappeaux 1964: 98, 101, 105–106).

144. Deschamps-Chappeaux (1964: 98–99).

145. Deschamps-Chappeaux (1964: 101–102).

146. Deschamps-Chappeaux (1964: 102).

147. Ósoso was a Carabalí group that figured in the foundation of Abakuá (Andrés Flores, pers. comm.). Cf. Cabrera (1958: 71); Deschamps-Chappeaux (1969a: 72).

148. As discussed in chapter 3, the Cross River settlement of Oban became known in Cuba as Obani or Ubáne.

149. Perhaps the reference to the "Ocongó of Efó," held to be a cabildo, really was an Efó Abakuá lodge. If so, this would push the accepted date of 1840 for the first Efó lodge back a year.

150. Deschamps-Chappeaux (1964: 103).

151. Deschamps-Chappeaux (1964: 105).

152. Deschamps-Chappeaux (1964: 105).

153. Brown (2003a: 255).

154. Deschamps-Chappeaux (1964: 109).

155. The "juego Oruá Apapá" appears in the book *Los Ñáñigos* (1882: 16).

156. Deschamps-Chappeaux (1972a: 40).

157. Benítez-Rojo (1986: 20–23). Cf. Benítez-Rojo (1996b: 440, 446); Bueno (1985: xiii).

158. Alfonso Ballol et al. (1987: 13); Hazard (1989/1871: 318); Pérez (1999: 18, 85); Scarpaci et al. (2002: 36). In all cases, these technologies arrived in Cuba through the United States soon after becoming available on the mainland.

159. Pezuela (1863: vol. 2, 336); Zanetti Lecuona and García Alvarez (1987: 52–53). In 1839, the Real Junta de Fomento (a Spanish colonial institution in Cuba), published the Reglamento para el camino de Hierro de la Habana a Güines (Regulations for the railroad from Havana to Güines), which stated that African descendants could ride in second and third class cars (thanks to Mercedes Herrera Sorzano, Febrero 2006). See also Hazard (1989/1871: 217), O'Kelly (1874: 42–45).

160. *Directorio* (1859: pt. 3, 22–24; pt. 5, 7–11).

161. Hazard (1989/1871: 260); Imbernó (1891: 84). After the streetcar system was installed in Havana in 1900, Abakuá temples were constructed near its path on the outskirts of Havana, in Los Pocitos.

162. Deschamps-Chappeaux (1971: 93).

163. Kuethe (1986: 173, 1991: 33). See also Andueza (1841: 43–44); Jameson (1821: 131, 134).

164. In the late 1700s, slave ships hired African "deck slaves," who were in constant communication with the crew, as well as human cargo (Svalesen 2000: 35–36, 110, 114). As a result of the battle of 1767, known as the "Massacre of Old Calabar," two Èfìk brothers were carried across the Atlantic as slaves, but in 1773 in Virginia they met two of their "countrymen, crewmen on the British ship *Greyhound*" (Clarkson 1789: 8–9, 1968/1808: 305–310; Eltis, et al. 2000, voyage no. 17807 [*Greyhound*] Paley 2002: 168; Richardson 1991–1996: vol. 4, 31). That the vessel had both crew and captives from the Cross River region and that these crew enabled their "countrymen" to sail to Bristol gives rare insight into underdocumented networks of communication between African sailors, crew, and port workers.

165. Deschamps-Chappeaux (1964: 99, 1971: 21–22, 1987: 75–76, 1990: 104). See also Bolster (1997: 172, 199); Burrows and Wallace (1999: 350); Linebaugh and Rediker (2000: 223–224, 299); Scott (1991: 46–48, 51); Stuckey (1994: 30); Turnbull (1969/1840: 70); Verger (1976: 285–309).

166. Paquette (1988); Sarracino (1989). The South Carolina physician John Wurdeman (1844: 354–357) traveled to Cuba in 1844 and described the "system of terror" unleashed by the colonists.

167. Balsameda (1869: 148–151) gave an account of the destruction.

168. Deschamps-Chappeaux (1974: 26). See also Helg (1995: 149); Thomas (1998/1971: 205).

169. Deschamps-Chappeaux (1964: 108).

170. Lapique (1979: 26). The removal from Cuba of free blacks who resisted Spanish rule was sought as early as 1845 (Unzueta y Yuste 1947: 397–399), leading to mass exiles in African penal colonies of the 1860s to 1890s, as discussed in chapter 5.

3. Planting Abakuá in Cuba, 1830s to 1860s

1. Cuban Abakuá render this as "Rey muerto, rey puesto." In Calabar, it is "the Obong is dead, long live the Obong."

2. Dike and Ekejiuba (1990: 77–78). Also in Yakö villages of the middle Cross River region (Forde 1964: 167, 172).

3. Cabrera (1992/1954: 201).

4. Ortiz (1954: 40); Cabrera (1988a: 386). This phrase was recorded in Abakuá as, "Abasí mofe/kiñóngo Abakuá Abasí obón Efi." Performed by Román Díaz on "Enyenisón Kamá 2," Yoruba Andabo (1997), at 4:55 minutes.

5. For the missionary context, see Waddell (1863: 445). Thanks to the Iyámba of Obutong (Archibong 2005, pers. comm.). Cf. Thompson (1974: 185). Cross River Ékpè express the phrase as: Àbàsì ké ènyóng; nyámkpè ké ísòng (Àbàsì édì ìbà). God is in the heavens; Nyámkpè is on earth (there are two Gods; Etubom B. E. Bassey 2004, pers. comm.). During my visit among the Ejagham of Abijang, an Ǹgbè ensemble chanted a phrase they interpreted as, "There are two gods: god above and god below" (Ntui Erim Onongha 2005, pers. comm.).

6. While this statement is true, the situation was complicated when parallel ethnic lineages were established independently by Carabalí immigrants. For example, although Èfìk Obutong may have been the first Èfìk lodge in Cuba among creoles, it was not necessarily the source of all subsequent Èfìk lodges. For example, the Ekuéri Tonkó lodge (discussed later in this chapter) was founded in Havana in the 1840s by a group of Èfìks, but not necessarily from the Èfìk Obutong lineage. This process and the chronology of lodges within lineages is a subject of debate among Abakuá intellectuals. This chapter offers the most commonly agreed upon chronologies, as I have learned them.

7. Trujillo y Monagas (1882: 365).

8. How many Carabalí entered Cuba is not clear. Trans-Atlantic slaving purportedly ended in Calabar in 1841, but continued clandestinely in a diminished form. Estimates from British commissioners in Havana were cited in Murray (1980: 244).

9. Andrés Flores told me that Efóri Enkomón moved to the barrio of Pueblo Nuevo in the decade of 1870. When this potency celebrated its centennial in 1940, they were given the following title for being the eldest in Efó territory: Efóri Enkómo Íremeta Íremepó mana mbóri okámbo. (Efóri, witchcraft [divine herbs]; Enkómo, drum; Íremeta Íremepó, the Íremes [masquerades] that appeared; manambóri okámbo, old consecrated skin.) Cf. Cabrera (1988a: 155).

10. This date was told to me by an Obón (leader) of this lodge. There is confusion in Havana between the names Ntáti and Eklé (or Nklé/Ekre) Ntá. Some say they are two related lodges, that in the "times of Spain, the lodge Ntáti Machécheré" sponsored "Eklé Nta," whose title is Ekre Ntá Anabí Ekoi Ntáti Machécheré. After consultation with many Abakuá leaders, we have resolved that they are the same lodge, because Ntá and Ntáti are variants of the same term.

11. Ntáti, or Ntá, first; Machecheré, munyón, or plumes. Cf. Ortiz (1954: 54). In Ìbìbìò, nta (pl. of ata) can mean "practitioner, specialist, expert" (Urua et al. 2004: 94). The title phrase "Ntáti Machecheré baróko muyón kai" was recorded by Abakuá masters on Ibiono (2001), track 6 (at 57 seconds).

12. "Ekré Ntá was a tribe of Bibí territory whose members placed the munyon [plumes] on the Sése [Eribo] drum" (Andrés Flores, pers. comm.). El Chino Mokóngo responded, "Enklé Entáti are from Orú (Bibí) territory. They brought the feather plumes to Munyánga territory for consecration in the first baróko of Usagaré." He then explained several steps in this process, "Sese embugaraso was the land in Africa where the plumes were made. After Ntáti Macheceré, they carried them to Munyánga territory and put them on the Eribó. Later they took them to consecrate the Eribó in Usagaré, on

Ibondá hill, during the first baróko in Africa. This phrase is related to the Nklé Ntá lodge of Guanabacoa. It is said, 'Sése embugarasó asokano nklé ntá abiga ekoi?' What did they do in Nklé Ntá? Ntáti Macheceré made the plumes. 'Sése Ekoi efórí Ibondá.' They took it to Ibondá hill and placed it on the Eribó during the consecration."

13. Cf. Cabrera (1975: 254). Cuban narratives locate Orú, "in the center, dividing the Efó and Efí territories." The likely West African source for Orú is Uruan, a community of settlements with Ékpè, located in the Ìbìbìò region, where Èfìk lived before migration to Calabar. Uruan leaders claim to be historically Efut from Usaghade.

14. Cf. Cabrera (1988a: 111). The phrase "Bibiokóndo Oru" was recorded by Abakuá masters on *Ibiono* (2001), track 6 (at 26 seconds).

15. The banner would have been the Ukara cloth, used throughout the Cross River to authorize the Voice.

16. Cf. Cabrera (1958: 93); Ortiz (1954: 43).

17. Aye (1991: 85); Engineer Bassey (2001/1998: 97); Goldie (1964/1862: 194).

18. In the Ejagham village of Abijang, I learned that "Monyo is the staff of Iyamba" (Ntui Erim Onongha 2005, pers. comm.). In Cuba, munyóns are used on the staff of Iyámba (Soto Rodríguez 2006, pers. comm.)

19. The lodge Nglón Afabábetó no longer exists (Andrés Flores, pers. comm.). Betongó Naróko Efó moved later from Jesús María to the barrio of Cayo Hueso. It is known as "the great China," because it had hundreds of members (cf. Franco 1975b: 213). Cuban treaties inform that in Usagaré, the lodge Betongó Naróko was created in a cave named Boko Bebá. In Cuba, the ceremony to recreate Betongó Naróko Efó was named Baróko Boko Bebá, after the original cave. In the context of a chant for "Betongó Naróko Efó," the phrase "baróko Boko bebá" was recorded by Abakuá masters on *Ibiono* (2001), track 1 (at 6:28 and 7:30 minutes). Cf. Cabrera (1992/1954: 284).

20. Cf. Cabrera (1988a: 109, 487, 375).

21. The phrase "Tánse Naróko nandiwára," from the treaty Bongó Yukáwa, refers to the sacred Fish. Cabrera (1992/1954: 282) described the process in Spanish.

22. The Calabar communities mentioned in the tratados of Betongó are Ekerewá, Ikanfioró, and Mbemoró. Each group has a lodge in Cuba and a clearly recognizable source in Calabar. For details, see the entries for Ekerewá (1863), Ikanfioró (1873), and Mbemoró (1846) in this chapter and the appendix of potencies.

23. Cabrera (1988a: 364) documented a version of this legend, specifically as related to conflicts between Èfìk and Efut communities over the slave trade from southwester Cameroon. In this version, Ekerewá and Èfìk Mbemoró went to war against Betongó and won, therefore taking control over the slave commerce of Betongó. These three communities have been identified as Henshaw Town in Calabar (Ekenewá), Mbemong (on the Akwa Yaffe River near Cameroon), and Betongó, a part of Usaghade, implying that this Cuban narrative reflects aspects of the expanding Èfìk Ékpè empire. Supporting narratives from Cuba imply that Ekerewá took control of Betongo's land, "Ekerewá: a land that belongs to those of Betongó" (Cabrera 1988a: 162), or that geographically, Betongó in Usaghade is indeed near Mbemong, a settlement between there and Calabar, "Betongó Naroko … a territory of Betongó bordering that of Èfìk Mbemoró" (Cabrera 1988a: 109).

24. Adam Eyamba (2005, pers. comm.). Chief Oku of Efe Ékpè Esien Ékpè recognized Etonkó Naroko as an Efut settlement in Usaghade (2005, pers. comm.).

25. "Ebúton" was reported as existing in 1882 (Trujillo y Monagas 1882: 370). Ortiz (1954: 14) reported the burial of Èfìk Obtuong's fundamentos in Havana. Andrés Flores reported that members of the lodge Nchemiya Ibonkó, founded in 1871, were present. The burial must have been after this date.

26. Andrés Flores said, "This means, 'The eldest Potency that functions in Efí.'" Cf. Cabrera (1988a: 191).

27. Cf. Cabrera (1975: 299, 1988a: 332).

28. Chief Hayford Solomon Edet (2007, pers. comm.); Mosongo (1995: 29). In addition, in Balondo (Efut), *mariba* is water. See appendix of chants for more discussion.

29. El Chino Mokóngo interpreted as, "Èfik Abakuá, the beach; kénde, embarking point of Efí, where the river met the sea."

30. Cabrera (1988a: 142). My translation abbreviates the original baroque Spanish.

31. Could also be interpreted as, "Balondo is the originator of Ékpè" (Engineer Bassey 2006, pers. comm.).

32. Nglón Afabábetó founded the potencies Betongó Naróko, Usagaré Embosi, and Enyón Bakokíro, in this order. López-Valdés (1985: 166) placed the Bakokó lodge in the barrio of Belén.

33. Cf. Cabrera (1958: 118, 1988a: 489). Abakuá identify Bakokó as an Efó (Efut/Balondo) group.

34. Bakoko settlements exist from south Cameroon to Calabar (cf. Anderson 1933: 19–20, para. 58; Ardener et al. 1960: 322; Austen and Derrick 1999: 8–9, 19–20; Greenfell 1882: 648; Mosongo 1995: 233; Nicol 1929: 12; Nofuru 2002: 10; QCCA 2003: 18).

35. An early Uruan settlement in Enyong was referred to as "Akani Obio Eniong" after Uruan people left it behind (Hart 1964: 33, para. 97).

36. Anderson (1933, paras 11–20); Connell (2001a: 54).

37. Cf. Cabrera (1975: 126, 1988a: 120, 247). The phrase "Bakokó irióngo" is heard on *Ibiono* (2001), track 1 (at 1:37 minutes).

38. Engineer Bassey (2006, pers. comm.). For Èfik Ékpè, the term *idiongo* means "the more you look, the less you see," a reference to the temple's inner room where the source of the Voice is kept, a place literally called *etak èfé*, meaning "the bottom of the house" (Chief Archibong Eso 2005, pers. comm.).

39. The phrase "awana Bakokó," a reference to this lodge, was recorded in the classic "Criolla Cara-balí" by Sexteto Habanero (1995). See description in chapter 7.

40. Their birthdate is 6 September 1863.

41. Cf. Cabrera (1988a: 17).

42. For example, Eta Nyak and Eta Ntisong both were founders of Big Qua and Akim Qua clans (Chief Hayford Solomon Edet 2007, pers. comm.).

43. "Enyúgue, a fee; *enteré*, to give" (El Chino Mokóngo, pers. comm.). The phrase "entereré enyúgue abarakó" was recorded by Abakuá masters on *Ibiono* (2001), track 5 (at 4:30 minutes). Another example from Sexteto Habanero (1995) is discussed in chapter 7.

44. Goldie (1894: 26). Thanks to Chief Ekpenyong Eyo (2005, pers. comm.); Etubom B. E. Bassey (2005, pers. comm.); Engineer Bassey (2006, pers. comm.).

45. Cf. Cabrera (1975: 28). Abakuá interpret *Mbarankonó* as a "tribe" and *Abarakó* as "the hill they lived upon' (Ángel Guerrero 2007, pers. comm.).

46. Mbarakom was an Èfik term of reference to people from the Mamfe area of Cameroon (cf. Jones 1970: xiii; 1988b: vol. 3, 503). Cubans know Abarakó as a place in Cameroon.

47. Cabrera (1988a: 503). "Ubioko Sese Efí" was the name of an Abakuá lodge in a Cuban novel (Cofiño 1977: 54, 81–82).

48. Cabrera (1988a: 503). This phrase indicated that Ékpè was brought to Ubioko from elsewhere and recreated.

49. *Barakong* is believed to be an Èfik interpretation of "balcony," because this is the place where meetings take place (Engineer Bassey 2006, pers. comm.). Cf. Lieber (1971: 31).

50. Engineer Bassey (2006, pers. comm.).

51. Andrés Flores (pers. comm.). Mbemoró is mentioned in *Los ñáñigos* (1882: 17); see also Cabrera (1988a: 149). Its contemporary temple is in the Parraga division, Havana. The Mokóngo of Efí Mbemoró, Orlando Caballero (2005, pers. comm.), told me that his lodge's leadership understands 1851 to be the foundation date. This date is painted on the lodge's temple.

52. Andrés Flores told me, "Mbemoró was a highway of Efí territory, in which one had to pay a fee in order to pass. As it was so powerful, the town of Efí Nuróbia Bongó Ubáne did not have to pay."

53. The phrase "Ubáne Mbemoró" is one of many claiming Ubáne as an Èfìk territory. The Cuban Ubáne (or Obane) is likely Oban, an Ejagham settlement with Ékpè (cf. P. O. E. Bassey 1999: 81; Jones 1988b: vol. 3, 504, 541–542; Talbot 1912a: 41–42, 1969/1926: vol. 3, 786). After studying the forest around Oban, British forester D. R. Rosevear (1979) observed that it was mostly secondary growth and theorized that in the 1800s the area was extensively farmed, but that the Atlantic slave trade had depopulated the region.

54. The recording "Efí Embemoró" (Afro-Ñáñigo) by Cheo Marquetti (1939) celebrates the foundation of this lodge with the chorus phrase, "Amanambá amanambé, ekoria Abakuá Mbemoró" (our hands clasp as we greet our brothers in Mbemoró). Cristóbal Díaz-Ayala (2002, pers. comm.) reported that this composition was by Ignacio Piñeiro and was recorded by his Septeto Nacional as early as 1933.

55. Mbemong is in Akpabuyo, south of Calabar. The first road from Calabar to the Kwa River was built in the 1980s; before then canoes were the only means of transport (Aye 1994: 97–102). This Mbemong was founded in the 1880s, but many earlier settlements share the name (Aye 2000: 190).

56. The phrase "Bonkó Ekuerí tonko" was recorded on "Enyenisón Enkama 2," by Yoruba Andabo (1997), at 7:18 minutes; chanted by Román Díaz (a member of this lodge).

57. The barrios of Los Barracones and San Leopoldo extend from Belascoain Street to Galiano Street and from Reina Street to Zanja Street (Andrés Flores, pers. comm.). Today this area is known as Centro Habana. The nineteenth-century barrio del Barracón was named after the prisons where newly arrived Africans were held before sale (cf. Jameson 1821: 77).

58. In 2005, I was invited by the leaders of Ekuéri Tongó to their new temple in the barrio of La Korea, San Miguel de Pádron, to share information about Cross River Ékpè.

59. Contemporary Ékpè chiefs of "Ekoretonko" spell their name thusly (cf. Jones 1956: 119). There have been many variations in the literature, e.g., "Ikoritungko" (Waddell 1863: 309); "Okuritunko (Creek Town)" (Walker 1871–1872: 136); "Ikot Itunko" (Jeffreys 1935: 31; Northrup 1978: 37–38).

60. Leading members of the Cobham House (anglicized from the Èfìk name Akabom) abandoned Creek Town to found Cobham Town next to Atakpa in two waves, the first in the mid-1700s, the second in 1830 (Engineer Bassey 2004, pers. comm.; cf. Hart 1964: 28, para. 73; Oku 1989: 114, 176–178; 193). The two Ekoretonkos are distinguished as Upper and Lower Cobham Town, that in Calabar proper is also known as "Ekpri [small] Ikorotonko or Cobham Town" (Hart 1964: 3, para. 7; 156, para. 327; Goldie 1964/1862: 75).

61. Erim (1990: 172). King Eyo Honesty II of Creek Town maintained relations with Umon by strategically marrying the daughter of Umon's wealthiest man (Northrup 1978: 99).

62. *Story of the Old Calabar* (1986: 128).

63. Umon is 70 miles (110 km) from the ocean. Thanks to Chief Aniyom, a surveyor from Umon, who helped make the *National Atlas of the Federal Republic of Nigeria* (Lagos: Cartographic Unit of Federal Surveys, 1978). The diary of Èfìk trader Antera Duke from 1785 to 1787 records Umon (referred to as "Boostam") as the place of a slave market (Forde 1956: 39).

64. Umon was referred to in this report as "Eerick Boastwain" (Hallett 1964: 203; Northrup 1978: 101).

65. Thanks to Román Díaz (2004, pers. comm.); cf. Cabrera (1988a: 507).

66. Chief Aniyom (2005, pers. comm.). Boki communities had a form of Ékpè (cf. Talbot 1969/1926: vol. 3, 787). "so-called 'Ekoi' groups like the Boki are clearly distinguishable from one another" (Andah 1990: 29).

67. "Umon merchants settled on Mission Hill in Atakpa in the nineteenth century, very close to Ekoretonko" (Chief Aniyom Eyamba 2005, pers. comm.).

68. Cf. Cabrera (1988a: 113).

69. Roche y Monteagudo (1925/1908: 95). See also Ortiz (1955a: 224).

70. Most Cuban Abakuá origin narratives refer to participation of three Efó groups in Usagaré. There are in fact three distinct communities in Usaghade (Amoto, Bateka, and Oron), each with the own Ékpè lodge. For the theme of three, see Cabrera (1958: 118, 1975: 183, 1992/1954: 285).

71. Engineer Bassey (2004, pers. comm.); Simmons (1956: 72, n. 45). The original meaning seems to be lost (cf. Hart 1964: 37, para. 113). The likely translation is: Ikot Itunko, "they are called (or people of, followers of) Itunko." Itonko is a pet name. This is pronounced as "ekoretonko." (Etubom B. E. Bassey 2004, pers. comm.; Engineer Bassey 2005, pers. comm.). Supporting evidence is found in the use of the term *Etongo* in Havana by a lodge from an Efó lineage, Betongó Naróko Efó.

72. The main evidence lies in the Efut sources of the term *Ekoretonko*, the rest is historical myth. During the founding of Creek Town in the early 1600s (Behrendt and Graham 2003: 43; Latham 1973: 9–10), the Ekoretonko shrine of Obioko (Creek Town), known as Èfé Asabo, was derived from the Èfé Atakpor (Atakpor shrine) of Uruan (Essien 1993: 82). It arrived with Eyo Ema during Èfìk migration from Uruan (Hart 1964: 40) and continues to be fundamental to the coronation of the paramount ruler of the Èfìks.

73. Abakuá narratives report that a group of Africans named Uriabón Efi participated in the founding of Èfìk Obutong in Havana; a lodge was later created in their honor. Cf. Cabrera (1958: 142, 1988a: 515, 516, 246).

74. Andrés reported that Uriabón Ereniyó means "the eyes of Efi territory." Cf. Cabrera (1958: 68, 178). This phrase was recorded by Abakuá masters on *Ibiono* (2001), track 5 (at 0:15 minutes).

75. Uriabón has no temple. In the 1990s they performed plantes in the temple of their godchildren, Irianabón Brandí Masóngo in Pogolotti.

76. Cf. Cabrera (1988a: 515).

77. Engineer Bassey (2006, pers. comm.) told me, "Uriabón or Uriabong means 'food for kings or noble men'; Uria mbon Èfìk, 'Èfìk cuisine'; Uria mbong Èfìk, 'cuisine for Èfìk kings or noble men.' It is doubtful if these words refer to towns or settlements (as Cabrera documented). After all, Efe Ékpè is a gathering of initiates. In contemporary churches where Èfìk is spoken, *ùdíáobon* or *iria obon* are terms for 'the Lord's supper.'" Cf. Goldie (1964/1862: 304); Jeffreys (1935: 50).

78. The Èfìk saying "Ékpè edi udia" (Ékpè is food) refers to the functions of Ékpè as financial insurance for members (*Story of the Old Calabar* 1986: 75). In the 1780s in Calabar, a feast called Udia ikot Ékpè (Bush Ékpè Chop) was held in the process of commemorating a deceased Èfìk leader and selecting a candidate to fill his post (Asuquo 1978: 46; entry for 30 April 1787 in Antera Duke's diary). Several Abakuá ritual signatures authorize the sharing of food in ceremonies (Cabrera (1975: 143–146).

79. "Udi, grave; Obong, ruler" (Urua et al. 2004: 105; cf. Goldie 1964/1862: 303). In Atakpa, Chief Eyamba (2005, pers. comm.) described the process, "Udióbon is part of Ékpè because when an Obong died, a certain amount of days after the burial, Ékpè members go to his grave to play and call on the man who died, to take back his position. If the man was an Iyámba, then the next person to be Iyámba will start from there. If he is Nyámkpè, Ebonkó, or any of these top positions, then the next person will take over from that time."

80. Iberedem Essien (2005, pers. comm.); Obong Bassey A. Nyong (2005).

81. Simmons (1956: 22–25) refers to the elaborate burial practices of Èfïk Ékpè.

82. Cf. Talbot (1969/1926: vol. 3, 513–515, 524–525) cites examples from Èfïk and Ejagham settlements.

83. Andrés Flores (pers. comm.); Soto Rodríguez (2005, pers. comm.). Cf. Cabrera (1988a: 267).

84. Hart (1964: 178, para. 373).

85. Herskovits (1990/1941: 63).

86. According to a plaque on the ledge's temple, Irianabón was born on 16 December 1853. Irianabón was born in Jesús María, but later moved to the barrio of Colón. López-Valdés (1985: 167–168) wrote, "Urianabón . . . of the barrio of Colón," but it should be "Irianabón." Three distinct lodges are often confused: they are Úria, Íria, and Ámia. Uriabón Eréniyó founded Irianabón Brandi Masóngo and later, Irianabón founded Amiabón Enéyo. Irianabón, commonly called Idianabón, has a temple in the barrio of Pogolotti, Marianao.

87. Chief Eyo (2005); Chief Eyamba (2005). Among Èfïk, an udianobong is not necessarily *the* successor to the throne, since there are several potential successors (Engineer Bassey 2006, pers. comm.). Cf. Goldie (1964/1862: 304).

88. According to the date written on its temple, Erobe Efó was founded in 1853.

89. Cf. Cabrera (1975: 27, 1988a: 210, 398, 478, 124).

90. The lodge Efí Akana Bióngo no longer exists. On the Ekerewá's lodge's pantheon in the cemetery of Colón is written in iron, "Great Abakuá Lodge Ekeregua Momi, 1863 to 1965." Cf. López-Valdés (1985: 166).

91. Cf. Cabrera (1988a: 353, 1992/1954: 281). A march for the Ekerewá lodge with a related phrase was recorded by Harold Courlander in the 1940s, "Akunanbére emomí, anewe bonkó Ekerewá" (*Cult Music of Cuba* 1949).

92. Archibong Eso (2005, pers. comm.); Chief Henshaw (2005). Cf. Asuquo (1978: 46; entry for 31 August 1787 in Antera Duke's diary); Jones (1963: 192–193). Henshaw itself derives from Ansa, an Èfïk name (cf. Hart 1964: 128; Nair 1972: 174).

93. In Èfïk, *mmọmi* means "is here." If one asks, "Where is Ekenewa?" The response would be "Ekenewa mmọmi!" (Ekenewa is here!) (Archibong Eso, pers. comm.). In Calabar: "Ekerewa Momi, Ekerewa is here (because I am present). One asks: Ekere Ewa? Are you Ewa? The response: Nkèrè Ewa! I am Ewa! (I have authority). The statement indicates that Ekerewa was an important person, or group, assumed or earned. Ekere Ewa, we are Ewa. Ewa Ekeng is a name for the Nsidung ward of Calabar" (Engineer Bassey 2006, pers. comm.).

94. The phrase "Síro Akanabión" was recorded by Abakuá masters on *Ibiono* (2001), track 3 (at 1:33 minutes) in relation to Ekerewa territory in Africa.

95. "Síro, family; Amako, to look; bengué, the woman, or Sikán" (El Chino Mokóngo, pers. comm.).

96. "Nagurupá, give birth" (El Chino Mokóngo, pers. comm.).

97. Examples from Eniong, Uruan, Oron, and Calabar are documented (cf. Essien 1993: 18; Hart 1964: para. 65, 82, 87, 97; Lieber 1971: 64; Nair 1972: 291, 294).

98. Archibong Eso (2005, pers. comm.).

99. Engineer Bassey (2006, pers. comm.).

100. Nsidung means "what people are these", derived from *nso*, "what," and *idung*, "people." The term implies "not peaceful," "confusion," "trouble," or "what a heroic people!" (Noah 1980: 63).

101. The first Akani obio Nsidung was located on the Calabar River between the nineteenth-century locations of Atakpa and Obutong (cf. Oku 1989: 13).

102. Cf. Cabrera (1958: 70, 1975: 282–283, 336, 1992/1954: 283); Ortiz (1950a: 139). "Bakarióngo" is chanted on "Criolla Carabalí," recorded in 1928 (see chapter 7 for details). This phrase was recorded by Abakuá masters on *Ibiono* (2001), track 3 (at 6:05 minutes): "Efí Ekerewá/ suku bakarióngo/ Efí Ekerewá/ bakarióngo Efí/ Efí Ekerewá/ Ekerewá Momí."

103. The lodge Usagaré Munankebé Efó no longer exists.

104. The temple of Usagaré Mutánga is in Los Pocitos, Marianao. The dates 1868–1955 are sculpted in marble in its collective crypt in the Colón cemetery of Havana.

105. Cf. Austen and Derrick (1999: 14); Grimes (2000); Nicklin (1991: 11); Nofuru (2002: 22); Reid (1989: 17, fig. 1); Zöller (1885). For Batanga in the Cuban myth, cf. Cabrera 1958: 94.

106. In Calabar, Mutaka is remembered as an Efut man from Usaghade who played a prominent role in modernizing Ékpè Èfìk in the 1700s. The role of Mutaka is common knowledge among Ékpè leaders in Calabar, since the name is recited during libations to evoke Ékpè (Engineer Bassey 2001/1998: 21, 51, 99; Hart 1964: para. 185).

107. The Efóri Ntoki lodge was sponsored by Eforisún. The Efori Búma temple is in the barrio of Los Pocitos, Marianao. According to information sculpted in iron on its door, the "Efori Buma" lodge was born in 1865.

108. In Cuba, cf. Cabrera (1988a: 130, 19). In the Cross River, cf. Goldie (1964/1862: 247); Marwick (1897: 258–259); Talbot (1969/1926: vol. 2, 16); Urua et al. (2004: 10).

109. The founding ceremony for Amiabón was held in a home on Revillagigedo Street, corner of Esperanza, in the barrio of Jesús María.

110. The sponsors were Irianabón, therefore Amiabón is "grandchild" of Uriabón. Cf. Cabrera (1988a: 49).

111. Cf. Cabrera (1958: 72–73).

112. Cabrera (1988a: 420). See also Cabrera (1988a: 197).

113. Roche y Monteagudo (1925/1908: 144).

114. For example, shipping documents from the 1720s show that heads of Èfìk lineages from Creek Town (Obioko), Obutong (Old Town), and Atakpa (Duke Town) received the largest share of the fees for trading in enslaved people (Behrendt and Graham 2003: 45–46, 48–49). The diary of Antera Duke of Old Calabar, documenting the years 1785–1788, has many references to the sale of enslaved locals to European traders (cf. Hair 1990).

115. Anene (1970: 61, cites Calprof 8/2, Macdonald's observations, 26 October 1895; repeated in Erim 1990: 169). Cf. Uya (1990: 200).

116. Cf. Sparks (2003).

117. El Chino Mokóngo interpreted this lodge's name: "The authority to perform blood sacrifice was given in Usagaré territory. Moto, authorization; *bríkamo*, language/region; *sangírimoto*, blood." Cf. Cabrera (1988a: 124, 361, 453, 462).

118. Cabrera (1950: 45).

119. "Ítia Fóndogá means 'Matanzas'" (El Chino Mokóngo, pers. comm.); "Ítiá fondogá, 'a land beyond the city' [Matanzas]. It was when the first juego was created in Matanzas" (Abelardo Empegó, pers. comm.)

120. Goldie (1964/1862: 358, 75).

121. Archibong Eso (2005, pers. comm.); Chief Nsan (2005). Fondo is also a village name in southwestern Cameroon (Nofuru 2002: 27).

122. The same holds true for the Nsidung (Henshaw) and Ekoretonko (Cobham) Houses.

123. Chief Nsan (2005). The vast majority of villages in Akpabuyo belong to houses in the city-state of Calabar.

124. Cf. Levine (1990: 14).

125. Cuban intellectual Martínez-Furé (2006, pers. comm.) traveled to Jovellanos and other rural Matanzas towns in 2006 to present his recent book *Briznas de la memoria*. While there, he confirmed the presence of local Abakuá who belong to lodges in urban Matanzas.

126. Cabrera (1988a: 416) documented a similar story for Uriabón.

127. Given the confusion between the three lodges of the same lineage: Uriabón, Irianabón, and Amiabón (as discussed earlier in this chapter), the discrepancy between Irianabón and Uriabón is not unusual.

128. Cf. "Documentos" (1924: 281–283); Moliner-Casteñeda (1992: 26).

129. Moliner-Casteñeda (1988: 14). This cabildo was maintained by members of the Calle family into the 1950s (Martínez-Furé 1979: 174–176).

130. Ruel (1969: 254–255). See also Anderson (1933: 17, para. 52).

131. The temple of Uriabón Efí is on Salamanca and América Streets in the barrio Simpson, Matanzas. This lodge was founded in 1862, according to the date painted inside its temple.

132. One version holds that the sponsors were Irianabón Brandi Masóngo of Havana, another that they were Biabánga of Matanzas (now defunct), founded by Ntáti Machechere of Havana. In the latter scenario, after their founding by Biabánga, Uriabón of Matanzas made Wanariansa (unification) with Irianabón of La Habana, adding Brandi Masóngo to its title as a consequence. Both versions were documented by Moliner-Casteñeda (1988: 14, 1990: 31, 1998/1990: 399). The Biabánga version was documented by Cabrera (1988a: 37), and affirmed by Abakuá leader Francisco Zamora "Mininí" of Matanzas, who helped me verify the history of Matanzas potencies by speaking to leaders of each group. In other words, after receiving information from Havana oral traditions, I cross-checked with Matanzas Abakuá leaders and learned other versions that compliment and enrich the first. Comparative research by Abakuá leaders will no doubt clarify this history.

133. Thanks to Ángel Guerrero (2004, pers. comm.), an Abakuá title-holder who witnessed this map from 1982 onward.

134. Biabánga was a Matanzas lodge. Another lodge named Biabánga was founded in Havana in the 1870s, as discussed in the appendix of potencies.

135. Berómo, procession; *maribá*, sea. Ntati Macheceré of Havana sponsored Biabánga in Matanzas. Biabanga then founded both Uriabón Efí and Efí Abarakó in 1862. In 1875, Abarakó founded Efí Mbemoró First. Cf. Cabrera (1988a: 416). Thanks to Francisco Zamora Chirino "Mininí."

136. Cabrera (1977: 1).

137. Cabrera (1988a: 95) documented "Bakokó Efor" of Matanzas as founded in 1863. Abakuá from Matanzas responded to me that Cabrera mistook this date, because Betongó, which was born in 1875, founded Bakokó in 1877.

138. Ortiz (1954: 19). Suáma derives from Ìsú-Amá, an ethnic term for an Ìgbo subgroup. Ìsú is a clan of the Ìgbo people, *Amá* means "of the road," that is, "Ìsú Diaspora" (Afigbo 1981: 12–13; Manfredi 1998, pers. comm.). See also Crowther (1860); Ottenberg and Knudsen (1985: 42).

139. Cabrera (1958: 69, 1988a: 129). Bríkamo may be a transformation of *mbré kámá*. This Èfik term (literally play and carry) means "share in the play by displaying your knowledge of its secrets as an initiate or member" (Aye 1991: 75, 61; also Goldie 1964/1862: 174, 145). *Brika mmọ* means "this one is good" or "authentic" in the Nkòmè language spoken by people of Uruan Ikom (Chief Agbor Esija, 2008 pers. comm.; Edang Bassey, 2008 pers. comm.).

140. Abelardo Empegó agreed, "All the treaties are in Bríkamo. Mario Vinajeras of Matanzas spoke Suáma and Bríkamo. It is possible that in the past in Matanzas they spoke Suáma, but during Abakuá rites the consecrations were in Bríkamo." Mario Vinajera (d. 1970s) was the second Iyámba of the Efí Irondó lodge (see discussion in appendix of potencies).

141. Mañón, embarking point; Brikamo, a territory; Usagaré, a land. In Matanzas city, the Calle family, who are the descendants of Calabarí, conserve the Brikamo tradition. Abakuá leaders believe that the term indicates sources in Usagaré.

142. The original quote was "in the island of Calabar." Because Calabar is not an island, I corrected the phrase (Akpabot 1975: 30). The multiple villages of the Uruan community within the present boundaries of Akwa Ibom State are Ìbìbìò and Èfìk speaking. They claim distinct historical origins and identity from both groups (Essien 1993; Nyong 2005, pers. comm.).

143. Akpabot (1975: 32). Akpabot gave an unusual transcription; the common usage is "Oje bari Nyámpkè!" after the Ékpè grade Nyámpkè. Research indicates the Ejagham origins of these terms (Anwana 2002).

144. Cf. Ruel (1969: 231), who found that in the Ǹgbè practice of the Banyang of the upper Cross River region in Cameroon, "Many songs are in Ejagham; others are in Balundu."

145. Mosongo (1995: 80). Even among Qua (Ejagham) communities, "Some of the Ṁgbe songs are sung in the Efut language by sophisticated members of the society" (Ekpo 2005: 72).

146. Connell (2004); Manfredi (2004); Miller (2005).

4. From Creole to Carabalí

1. Anonymous (2004, pers. comm.).

2. Cabrera (1958: 53).

3. For workers' movement, cf. Montejo-Arrechea (2004: 31–35). Regarding the economic depression of the late 1850s, cf. Franco (1975a: 26).

4. According to the earliest documentation, police records of those arrested accused of being "ñáñigos" from 1876 to 1902 (Sosa-Rodríguez 1982: 307–308).

5. Carpentier (1989/1946: 266).

6. Tension between Spaniards and creoles was well documented in contemporary first-hand accounts (cf. Ely 1853: 104; Wurdeman 1844: 198).

7. Trouillot (1995: 93, 95) made this point regarding the reaction of slave-owning countries to the Haitian revolution.

8. Roche y Monteagudo (1925/1908: 117).

9. Miller (2000b: 171). Other attempts at legal integration were opposed by authorities (cf. Montejo-Arrechea 2004: 62).

10. Cf. Dike (1956: 161–162); Northrup (1978: 109).

11. Cf. Hart (1964: para. 168); P. O. E. Bassey (1999: 69).

12. Cf. Cabrera (1958: 244, 1992/1954: 199). A parallel process was described for Ékpè aspirants in Calabar (Engineer Bassey 2001/1998: 11).

13. José Martí, 1889, in a letter to Serafín Bello (Martí 1977: 308). José Martí was the son of Spaniards, who in 1892 founded the Cuban Revolutionary Party in New York. Martí's ideas on race were radical in the Cuba of his day (James 1998: 246), but the mulatto General Antonio Maceo had expressed them in the 1870s (Ferrer 1999: 133).

14. José Martí, 1883, "Mi Raza," *Patria* (New York), 16 April (Martí 1977: 313).

15. Ferrer (1999: 4). See also Ferrer (1999: 127, 138).

16. Petit founded *La Regla Kimbisa del Santo Cristo del Buen Viaje* (cf. Cabrera 1977; see also Bolívar and González 1998: 50). "The Church of Santo Cristo del Buen Viaje, founded in Cuba in 1640 by Franciscans (*Habana: Guía* 1928: 261), had very powerful interests in sugar production"

(Moreno-Fraginals 1986/1978: 125). Petit's use of Catholic, Kimbisa, and Abakuá elements was a nineteenth-century form of liberation theology.

17. Sosa-Rodríguez (1982: 141). "In 1857 the first lodge of whites was organized, and in 1863 they were baptized, their godparents being the lodge Bakókó Efor no. 1 and Efí Ebuton" (*Causa* 1884: 89). See also Brown (2003a: 244); Cabrera (1977: 1); Roche y Monteagudo (1908: 14); Trujillo y Monagas (1882: 369). Cabrera (1958: 56) wrote that the first white men were initiated in 1857 in Akanarán Efor, and in 1863 the Obónes (title-holders) were sworn in. This cannot be, since the first initiates of any lodge are the Obónes.

18. Ortiz (1954: 70–71).

19. Mosquera (1996: 256). See also Moliner-Casteñeda (1988: 14–15).

20. Andrés Facundo Cristo de los Dolores Petit (Cabrera 1958: 25). According to an investigation based on the Church's files, Petit was born 27 November 1829 and died 20 May 1878 in Guanabacoa (Muzio 1996: 11).

21. Mayombe, like Kimbisa, is a Cuban-Kongo spiritual practice. Cabrera (1977: 3) wrote that Petit "lived with the Franciscans in their convent in Guanabacoa and collected alms for them" (habitaba con los franciscanos en el convento de estos en Guanabacoa y recogía limosna para ellos.)

22. In the 1840s, most of the nobility of Cuba were "twenty-nine marquises and thirty counts," more than half "created since 1816; Ferdinand 7th, alone, made eleven marquises and fifteen counts from 1816 to 1833. Most of them had acquired their wealth by sugar plantations, and are jocosely called 'sugar noblemen'" (Wurdeman 1844: 197). Cf. Ely (1853: 105); Jameson (1821: 8); Philalethes (1856: 20).

23. Cf. Cabrera (1992/1954: 197).

24. Knight (1988: 12, 16).

25. Knight (1988: 19).

26. Cf. Knight (1970: 61); Jameson (1821: 40–41).

27. Cf. Cabrera (1958: 60); Deschamps-Chappeaux (1964: 97); Rodríguez (1881: 5).

28. Cabrera (1958: 50).

29. In his study of the formation of an African-American communities from 1770 to 1830, Gomez (1998: 11) found that, "The creation of the African American collective involved a movement in emphasis away from ethnicity and toward race as the primary criterion of inclusion." See also Gomez (1998: 2–3, 15). While there was certainly a deep racial consciousness in Cuba, the historical record is replete with examples of multi-ethnic organizations among African descendants, such as the Aponte conspiracy of 1812 (cf. Franco 1974).

30. Courlander (1944: 465).

31. Téllez (1960: 2).

32. Okóbio Mukarará was sponsored by Bakókó Efó (*Causa* 1884: 89); Trujillo y Monagas (1882: 369).

33. Cabrera (1988a: 454); Trujillo y Monagas (1882: 369).

34. Engineer Bassey (2004, pers. comm.).

35. Chief Esoh Itoh, Paramount Ruler of the Balondo People of Cameroon (2004, pers. comm.).

36. Cuellar-Vizcaino (1956b) created a list of the founding lodge members: "Ocobio Mucarará was founded by Carlos Valdés, Antonio Romay Infante, Cirilo Mirabal, Adolfo García, Celestino Per-domo, el niño Miguel Parrado, who later became colonel; Vicente Prado, a Spaniard; Félix y Celes-tino Iglesias and, among others, a descendent of the Marquee of Indarte."

37. José-Miguel Gómez (2003), the Mokóngo of Ebión Efó from 1926 to 2003.

38. Cabrera (1977: 1).

39. Cf. Brown (2003a: 137); Fernández-Carrillo (1881: 143).

40. Luis and Cuervo Hewitt (1987: 12).

41. Cf. Ortiz (1954/69); Roche y Monteagudo (1925/1908: 117); Trujillo y Monagas (1882: 369).

42. Trujillo y Monagas (1882: 370).

43. An Abakuá leader from the lineage of Mukarará wrote, "Carlos Indarte, the Marquis of Indarte, loved the Abakuá, and being Isué of Ocobio Mukarará created seven groups of whites, for which motive the title of Ocobio Mukarará was changed to Akanarán of Efor (Mother of Efor)" (José-Miguel Gómez 2003). Cf. Cabrera (1988a: 454); Ortiz (1954: 82). Also from this lineage, El Chino Mokóngo ripostes, "It was not like that. Akanarán Efó means Mother of Efó because the religion was born according to the narratives of Efó. Akanaran Efó founded three juegos: Enyegueye First, Enyegueye Second, and Nandiba Efó. [These three lodges were from Guanabacoa; none exist today]. The name Akanarán means mother (or first) of the lineage, not godfather of all the juegos in the lineage." This lodge was also had the title Akanarán Efó Muñón Ekobio Mukarará (Quiñones 1994: 38; cf. *Causa* 1884: 88, 91).

44. Chief Archibong Eso, Iyámba of Obutong (2005, pers. comm.); Engineer Bassey (2004, pers. comm.). In Cuba, Ortiz (1954: 82) wrote, "In the Èfìk language, Akanarán Efo means the 'ancient and superior men of Efó.'"

45. El Chino Mokóngo continued, "Many think that Mukarará made Abakuá Efó, but Mukarará was only a witness to what Bakokó was doing." Many title-holders from Matanzas and Havana with whom I spoke told me that Mukarará founded Abakuá Efó. A document written before 1884 by a member of the "Ecoria Efó Taiba" lodge stated that "Ecoria Efó Ita" godfathered Abakuá Efó in 1875 (*Causa* 1884: 91). Because Ekório Efó Ita was founded in 1874 or 1878 and the author of that document is unknown, I follow the oral history. It is certain that the four lodges are from the same lineage. El Chino Mokóngo described Petit as director of the ceremonies of Abakuá Efó and many other lodges, and that Mukarará, as godsons, acted as witnesses, not godfathers.

46. "Criolla Carabalí," recorded by Sexteto Habanero in 1928, contains references to the Bakokó and Enyegueyé lodges in the context of their efforts to unify Cubans of all skin colors through Abakuá. The phrases "awana Bakokó," "Abairémo Efí, abairémo Efó, bongó Ita," and "Ekóbio Enyegueyé monína son ekóbios" are chanted to evoke this historical period and its consequences. See description in chapter 7.

47. Ortiz (1954: 69) described this conflict as a merely local struggle for turf and muscle. Ortiz may not be mistaken, but this is only part of the story. The process of receiving the highest Abakuá titles and corresponding ritual objects is equated by Abakuá leadership with the highest spiritual ideas and profound responsibilities.

48. Cf. Ortiz (1954: 74).

49. Cf. Alfaro Echevarria (1981: 184).

50. The idea that consecrated objects represent founding ancestors is expressed throughout sub-Saharan Africa, such as Àyàn in Yorùbáland (Euba 1988: 7; Láoyè 1959: 10), *minkisi* in central West-Central Africa (Laman 1962: 67).

51. Graeber (2001: 239). "Magic, then, is about realizing one's intentions . . . by acting upon the world. . . . about humans actively shaping the world, conscious of what they are doing as they do so" (Graeber 2001: 240).

52. "magical statements . . . are poetic or rhetorical, expressive rather then instrumental" (Graeber 2001: 241, 242). Graeber (2001: 240) asserted that the "usual Marxist critique [of fetishism] would not apply" to magic practices, because those who perform them are aware they are swaying people, not objects.

53. La Regla de Kimbisa is widely practiced in Maracay, Venezuela, where I met several Tata Nkisi who practiced this form, and knew Andrés Petit as its founder (July 2007, thanks to Santos López).

54. Cf. Cabrera (1958: 54, 61).

55. Abelardo Empegó agreed with El Chino, "One can adorn the Eribó and the staffs according to the economy of the *juego*; as long as one follows the model of earlier fundamentos, precious metal can be used. The staffs and the Eribó may be made of brass, silver, and gold. But the drums for the music—the *nkomos* and the *bonkó enchemiyá*—must be uniform, only wood and skin."

56. This conflict echoes tensions in the thirteenth to fourteenth centuries between the Franciscan Order and the Pope, regarding the Doctrine of the absolute poverty of Christ (cf. Eco 1983: 66).

57. According to the date written on its temple, Erobe Efó was founded in 1853.

58. Trujillo y Monagas (1882: 369) reported a case wherein white Abakuá attempted to enter the *fambá* lodge of Efí Embemoró. Resistance to their entry resulted in the death of one man and wounding of four others.

59. Cabrera (1969: 160).

60. Talbot (1912a: 44–45).

61. Aesthetic rivalry, a human universal, has specific qualities in African and African-American communities, in the performance of music and dance. Brown (2003a: 83) described how "the challenge of marked aesthetic competition" was used by Abakuá lodges to "gain reputation and recruits."

62. The reputation of the Orú Abakuá Endúre lodge has been established for decades. On 26 December 1999, I witnessed the initiation of an Iyámba, an Mbákara, two Íremes, and another plaza into this lodge. Luis Chacón is a member of this lodge and a master rumba player.

63. Roig de Leuchsenring (1925: 30).

64. Cf. Cabrera (1958: 276).

65. The Church of Jesús María still stands on Diaria Street, between Águila and Revillagigedo, in the barrio of Jesús María.

66. Cf. Cabrera (1958: 55–56, 1975: 23).

67. Used throughout the Cross River region, *Abasi* is "God" in Ìbìbìò, Èfìk, Oron, and Eket (cf. Amoah 1992: 84; Goldie 1964/1862: 2). Connell (1997: 26) reported *Òvàsè* as "God" in Mòkpè (Bakweri) in southwestern Cameroon, as cognate with Èfìk Abasi.

68. Cabrera (1992/1954: 204). Cf. Cabrera (1958: 238, 1988a: 18).

69. El Chino Mokóngo observed, "Not all the juegos make Abasí, because who is going to baptize Christ? In Cuba, Andrés Petit, as a religious person, introduced Christ to represent the religion; this is the motive for the existence of Abasí, but the plaza is not made."

70. Ortiz (1960: 28, 1984b: 22).

71. Meza (1891; cited in Franco 1959: 72–75).

72. Balthazar was patron saint for blacks of the Río Plata region, including Argentina, Uruguay, and Paraguay, since the 1770s (cf. Andrews 1980: 138–139; Molina and López 2001: 336–337; Olivera-Chirimini 2001: 262; Ortiz Oderigo 1974: 37–40; Rodríguez 2001: 321).

73. Wurdeman (1844: 83).

74. Kiddy (2002: 164, 178–180).

75. On 6 January 1827, French scientist Alcides d'Orbigny (1802–1857) witnessed and described "nation" dances of Africans in the Plaza del Mercado in Montevideo.

76. Ortiz (1960: 21–22) prefaced this statement with, "There is no evidence of the number nor names of these mythological Three Magi. The Gospel of St. Mathew, the only one to refer to these Magi, conveys nothing. In the so-called Christian countries there is great confusion about this. In some, the black king is Melchior; in others, Balthazas or Caspar. Furthermore, the black king is a purely folkloric invention, without historical basis." Cf. Griffith (1997: 26); Watts (1985: 77); *New Catholic Encyclopedia*, 2nd ed., vol. 9 (Detroit, 2003), 34–35; *The Book of Saints: A Comprehensive Biographical Dictionary*, 7th ed. (New York, 2002), 365.

77. In Havana "in 1796 there was a *Cabildo de Congos Reales* [Royal Kongos] dedicated to the Magi King Saint Melchior" (Carpentier 1989/1946: 266).

78. Anthropologist George Brandon (1993: 175) observed that, "The statement that syncretists do not know that they are practicing two religions or have confused the two [or three] . . . is [not] necessarily true for those who are actually creating and carrying out the process. . . . In the transitions between periods, borrowing does not go unnoticed because not everyone agrees with introducing new materials into the religious tradition. Furthermore there is always a more or less prolonged period in which the old forms and the new coexist."

79. Cabrera (1975: 498); Trujillo y Monagas (1882: 370).

80. Roche y Monteagudo (1925/1908: 118).

81. Hergesheimer (1920: 225).

82. Hergesheimer (1920: 238).

83. Hergesheimer (1920: 226) wrote, "Eruco en llenison comunbairán abasí otete alleri pongó." Because he rendered this common phrase with many errors, I have written it clearly. An Abakuá title-holder interpreted this as, "We in Cuba are brothers of the Africans through the transmission of the bongó" (Nostros aqui de Cuba, somos hermanos de la gente de Africa a través de la trasmisión del bongo).

84. Helly (1993: 20).

85. García-Chavez (1930: 313, 537); Scarpaci et al. (2002: 26).

86. Pérez de la Riva (2000: 243).

87. Pérez de la Riva (2000: 243–244).

88. Franco (1975b: 213). Efí Etété, founded in 1913, sponsored Ubáne Sése Kóndo in 1932 in Matanzas; they have since moved to Cárdenas (Andrés Flores and El Chino Mokóngo, pers. comm.).

89. U.S. War Department (1900: 96–97). Cf. Hazard (1989/1871: 273–274).

90. Pérez de la Riva (2000: 250). Hazard (1989/1871: 267) referred to Chinese laborers in the sugar warehouses of the wharves of Regla.

5. Dispersal: Abakuá Exiled to Florida and Spanish Africa

1. Deschamps-Chappeaux (1968b: 50; see also Montejo-Arrechea 2004: 44, 109–110).

2. Deschamps-Chappeaux (1968b: 50; see also Montejo-Arrechea 2004: 109–110).

3. In 1870 Spanish journalist Don Gonzalo Castañón published a series of essays in Cuba titled "Reconstrucción, repoblación," expressing his desire for the extermination of Cubans, in order that Spanish migrants would completely repopulate the island. He died soon afterward in a duel with a Cuban (Le Roy y Gálvez 1971: 57).

4. The names of the participating lodges vary in the documentation, but are often from the same lineage (cf. Cuellar-Vizcaino 1971: 19; Hernández-Serrano 2001: 10; Téllez 1960: 2).

5. A monument commemorating the murder of the eight students of medicine stands at the base of Prado Avenue, across from the Punta fortress.

6. Cf. Knight (1970: 163); Martínez-Vergne (1989: 190); Miguel (1990: 13).

7. Knight (1970: 151; see also Franco 1975a: 51–52). Balmaseda (1869: 10) reported the presence of 9000 armed Volunteers in Havana in this era.

8. Philalethes (1856: 22). Cf. Foner (1962: vol. 1, 52–53); Knight (1970: 89); O'Kelly (1874: 94); Pérez de la Riva (1963: 25).

9. Cantón-Navarro (1998: 48); Franco (1975a: 51–52); Leal (1982: 64–65); Moreno-Fraginals (1996: 237); Robreño (1925: 251).

10. The "Acera del Louvre" (sidewalk of the Louvre), at the heart of nineteenth-century Havana, was a center for social elites and underworld figures, including many white Abakuá members (cf. Blanco-Aguilar 1992: 7–8). See also Ferrer (1999: 146).

11. Cantón-Navarro (1998: 49).

12. In his book on the Acera del Louvre, based largely on personal memories, Gustav Robreño (1925: 26–27) identified two groups of Tacos, one aristocratic, another working class and linked to the Abakuá as: "ebiones or enyegueyés or akaniranes or batangas" (all are Havana lodges), he also mentioned the lodges Macaró and Ekório Efor.

13. Deschamps-Chappeaux (1972a: 41, 42). See also Lapique (1995: 158).

14. Balmaseda (1869: 9–10, 19–20) documented the deportation of 250 Cuban political prisoners to Fernando Po in 1869. They came from all sectors of society: peasants, students, lawyers, and merchants; among them were several Freemasons. See also Cantón-Navarro (1998: 49); García del Pino (1969); Ponte-Domínguez (1944: 21); Stewart (1999: 95); Villaverde (1992/1882: 442).

15. Balmaseda (1869: 40).

16. Moreno-Moreno (1948: 411–412).

17. Cuellar-Vizcaíno (1956b).

18. Le Roy (1971: 389) documented the "letter that Ramón López de Ayala, chief of the firing squad, sent to his brother Adelardo, the day following the executions." In spite of this document, Le Roy (1971: 140, 389 f.n.) dismissed the idea that Abakuá, black or white, participated as a group in the resistance to this event. At the time of that publication the idea of Abakuá participation in Cuban liberation was not encouraged in Cuba.

19. For example, Ricardo Abreu "Papín" (1999, pers. comm.), elder brother in the world-famous rumba group Los Papines as well as an Abakuá title-holder, told me, "The Abakuá in the nineteenth century came to the defense of the medical students, this is why our religion has always been respected."

20. Gutierrez-Nuñez was the Mbákara of Ikanfioro Nankúko of Havana. Thanks to Abakuá title-holder Luis Salinas, Ekuenyon of Abarako Nankábia, for arranging this interview.

21. Soto Rodríguez (2006, pers. comm.). Soto Rodríguez referred to an essay in the *Juventude Rebelde* newspaper that narrated this story in the 1990s, on the anniversary of the execution of the medical students. The Ibiabánga lodge was in the process of its formation at the time of the students' execution.

22. Foner (1977: 113). Martí published this work in Madrid on 27 November 1872.

23. Le Roy y Gálvez (1973: 8).

24. Franco (1975a: 85). Cf. Martínez-Vergne (1989: 190).

25. Colonial authorities across the Americas criminalized black-white cooperation. For an example in 1873 in Salvador, see Bahia (cf. Reis 2001b: 121); for an example in 1741 in New York City see Linebaugh and Rediker (2000: 206–207).

26. Roche y Monteagudo (1908: 39). Cf. Castellanos García (1948: 591); Deschamps-Chappeaux (1968b: 51). The campaigns to exile Abakuá and other conspirators continued into the 1890s (cf. Deschamps-Chappeaux 1968a: 44).

27. Castellanos García (1948: 591).

28. Ortiz (1954: 51; cf. Salillas 1901: 339). Other Spanish penal colonies included those in Cádiz and the Castle of Figueras in Catalonia, where several Abakuá died (Helg 1995: 271, n. 150).

29. Salillas (1901: 339).

30. Cuellar-Vizcaino (1956b).

31. Deschamps-Chappeaux (1968a: 44).

32. Pike (1983: 111); Stewart (1989: 59). In 1844 a military commission condemned ten Africans in Matanzas, who were accused of conspiracy "against the whites," "to the Ceuta prison for ten years." (*Sentencia pronunciada* 1844: 4.a).

33. Franco (1973: 101–102).

34. Foner (1977: 102).

35. Helg (1995: 82). Juan Gualberto Gómez (1854–1933) was born to enslaved parents on a Matanzas sugar mill. Having freed status, he was educated in Havana and in Paris, where he became a journalist. In 1887 the constitution for the Directorio Central de las Sociedades de la Raza de Color was created through his initiative. The aim of this umbrella organization was to unite all existing black and mulatto societies to advocate for civil rights. Deported to Ceuta in 1880, Gualberto Gómez returned to Cuba in 1890. From 1892 to 1895, he worked with José Martí to coordinate the activities of the Directorio (in Cuba) and the Partido Revolucionario Cubana (in exile) to begin the final War of Independence (Montejo-Arrechea 2004: 81, 116–119).

36. Salillas (1901: 337, 341–342).

37. Cabrera (1958: 23).

38. Salillas (1901: 343).

39. Pike (1983: 115, 121, 151).

40. Cf. Ortiz (1906: 131); Cabrera refers to Salillas' essay as evidence for "planting," engaging in a ceremony (1958: 11, 58–59, 1988a: 10). Sosa-Rodríguez (1982: 325) wrote, "Many ñáñigos, under the accusation [of being antislavery and revolutionary separatists] were sent to Spanish prisons far from Cuba, where they achieved the formation of new lodges."

41. Ángel Guerrero (2004, pers. comm.).

42. Cabrera (1958: 58).

43. Elders of the Kanfioró lodge taught younger members that in Ceutas, members of the Kanfioró lodge "cruzaron bastones" (crossed staffs) with those of Orú Abakuá Endúre. The crossing of staffs is a ritual pact between lodges that requires a fundamento. For this purpose, an improvised fundamento would have been fabricated.

44. Cross River Ékpè use a plumed stick called *basonko*. During the installation of a king, *basonko* will be inserted into a regal scepter to signify Ékpè. The basonko is used in funeral proceedings in Calabar to indicate that the deceased was an Ékpè title-holder (Ika 2005, pers. comm.). In Ékpè Èfìk practice, the basonko has a deep significance not accorded to the Ékpè/Mgbè of other groups like Ejagham, Efut, or Uruan. The Èfìk relationship with basonko is likely reflected in the Cuban title Abasóngo, known as "owner of the staff" (cf. Cabrera 1975: 302). In Cuba, this title exists only in lodges of Efí lineages. See discussion in n. 21 to the Ibiabánga Munyón lodge, appendix of potencies.

45. This cabildo was reorganized in 1894, based upon earlier models, as a cabildo comparsa that functioned as a "recreation and mutual aid society" (Pérez-Rodríguez et al. 1982: 12, 35). The cabildo Carabalí Isuama in Santiago de Cuba was the inspiration for the composition "Carabalí" by Félix Caignet. A celebration of the integration of African culture into Cuban society, "Carabalí" was performed by Rita Montaner in Paris in the late 1920s (Caignet 1993; Moore 1997: 174). In 1928 both Rita Montaner (Spottswood 1990: 2123–2124) and Ronda Lirica Oriental (Caignet 1993) recorded the song.

46. Pérez-Rodríguez et al. (1982: 9–13, 55).

47. Ceuta had heretofore been a prison fortress, not a colony.

48. Bacardí Moreau (1973: 21) was a member of the Bacardí rum producing family.

49. Carlos Estorino "Larguito" was Obonékue of Embemoró 1 and Isué of Úkano Bekonsí; "Niñito" Calle was from the Calle family, inheritors of the Bríkamo religious tradition of Matanzas ("Minini" 2000, pers. comm.).

50. Felipe Villavicencio (d. 1917) was Íreme Eribangandó of Orú Ápapa (Castellanos García 1948: 594). See also Ortiz (1955a: 217).

51. Cf Cabrera (1988a: 344).

52. Castellanos García (1948: 594).

53. María-Terésa Lináres Savio (1974: 58) documented a song in the Habanera genre composed during the nineteenth century in reference to exile in Africa: "En una triste y oscura bartolina/ Lo vi encerrado y me saludó./ Me llevan, dijo, con rumbo a Chafarinas/ O a las desiertas playas de Fernando Póo./ . . .Y si sucumbo del África en las playas,/ tan solo en ella,/ tan solo en ella pensaré al morir." (In a sad and dark cell/ I saw him confined, and he greeted me/ They will take me, he said, to Chafarinas/ Or the deserted beaches of Fernando Po./ . . . If I succumb to the African beaches/ so alone there/ So alone there, I will think of dying.)

54. In fact, two-toned or double-headed drums were found throughout West and West-Central Africa. In the Cross River region, "Among the Ekoi are some drums with a double head, each covered with a skin, made out of a small tree trunk where it forks, in the shape of the letter Y" (Talbot 1969/1926: vol. 3, 811).

55. Cf. Miller (2000b).

56. Ortiz (1955a: 242).

57. This understudied theme promises to illustrate the function of sonic symbolism within the music of the entire region. On the one hand, the Carabalí nation-groups of Oriente undoubtedly influenced the regions' popular music, namely the Changüí, a source for the early son. In the 1970s, Changüí musicians played *bongos* using a *glissade* (sliding a finger across the drum skin) to produce the "roar" famous in early son recordings, and identified this sound as related to African-based religious practice (*Orígenes desde el Changüí* 1986). Changüí musicians also use a ceramic jug as a bass wind instrument and a *marimba*, both of which are used in the Cross River region. Lapidus (2005, 2007) has demonstrated the influence of Haitian music in Changüí. In Haitian Vodún, the glissade, "known as 'siye' (see-yay), is most associated with the bass drum of two rhythms: 'Kongo Frank' and 'Kongo Piyet,' and is considered the sound that 'brings down the *loa* (spirits)'" (Thanks to Steve Deats of Troupe Makandal 2007, pers. comm.). In Cuba, founding *son bongosero* Agustin Gutierrez, an Abakuá member, reproduced the "roar" on early son recordings in the 1920s. The Abakuá and Carabalí interaction in colonial Chafarinas suggests that the "roar" of the bongo had multiple meanings, related to the spiritual practice of Haitians and Carabalí in Oriente, as well as Abakuá in Occidente (cf. Miller 2000b; Ortiz 1955a: 422–424).

58. Goldie (1901/1890: 79). Named after a fifteenth-century Portuguese navigator, Spain claimed the island from 1778. Talbot (1969/1926: vol. 1, 41) wrote: "1777. The Portuguese handed over Fernando Po to the Spaniards in exchange for an island and strip of coast in Brazil. The latter desired it as base for slave-trading, but abandoned the island in 1782 owing to the hostility of the natives and unhealthiness of the climate."

59. Cf. Baikie (1966/1856: 345); Talbot (1969/1926: vol. 1, 59); Unzueta y Yuste (1947: 205). Spain used Fernando Po as a base to protect slaving ships, because by 1844 five percent were lost to accidents and 25 percent were captured by British antislaving forces (Moros y Morellón and de los Ríos 1844: 30–34).

60. Cf. Balmaseda (1869: 131); Owen (1833: 339); Sundiata (1996: 6); Talbot (1969/1926: vol. 1, 44–47, 49); Unzueta y Yuste (1947: 206–207); Waddell (1863: 240).

61. Jones (1956: 125).

62. An eye witness, Muñoz y Gaviria (n.d.: 207–209) described the 1861 visit of King Eyo III to Fernando Po in the steam ship *King Calabar*, with an armed retinue, one carrying his umbrella, while

the king held his Ékpè staff. See also Talbot (1969/1926: vol. 1, 207–208); Unzueta y Yuste (1947: 196, 317).

63. Latham (1973: 127); Nair (1972: 177); Uya (1984: 64). Joseph Henshaw was known in Efik as Effanga Ekang Ansa (Oku 1989: 203; Talbot 1969/1926: vol. 1, 210). In another example, Fyfe (1960: 110) reported that Calabar native Peter Nicholls, who traded palm-oil in Creek Town, "went to Fernando Po and complained vainly to the acting-Consul" in 1855 regarding a seizure of his property by a Liverpool Captain (cf. Dike 1956: 119).

64. Engineer Bassey (2005, pers. comm.). "An adult male from Eyamba House—likely a title-holder—migrated to Fernando Po in the nineteenth century due to a problem in Calabar. He was a brother of Chief Eyamba's great-grandfather. There was no communication with Calabar after he left" (Chief Eyamba 2005, pers. comm.).

65. Cf. Baikie (1966/1856: 307, 346); Balsameda (1869: 17); Goldie (1894: 28–29); Sundiata (1996: 57). The capital, Santa Isabel, formerly called Clarence by the English, is presently called Malabo.

66. Recorded in Calabar in 1981 on the LP *Nka Asian Mkparawa Eburutu*. Thanks to Mr. Demmy Bassey (2004, pers. comm.); Etubom B. E. Bassey (2004, pers. comm.).

67. The name Panyá for Fernando Po is also used in southwestern Cameroon (Nebengu 1990: 77). A Cuban exile in Fernando Po documented the term as "Apanaá" in the later nineteenth century (Valdés-Infante 1898:68).

68. Because of the high death rate, it was said in 1862 in the Spanish courts that "deportation to Fernando Póo should be considered a death penalty" (Unzueta y Yuste 1947: 206–209, 224, 283; cf. Balsameda: 1869: 12–13). Among the Spanish political prisoners in the early 1860s were socialists from Andalusia who died of yellow fever (Unzueta y Yuste 1947: 284, 286). The first Cuban political prisoners arrived in 1866, whereas indentured laborers came in 1862 (Unzueta y Yuste 1947: 319).

69. León (1976: 8). Cf. Balsameda (1869: 161–162); Unzueta y Yuste (1947: 231).

70. León (1976: 7). Cf. Balsameda (1869: 130); Unzueta y Yuste (1947: 229).

71. Black Cubans were selected for colonization because the Europeans died quickly of fever, and the indigenous inhabitants refused to work. In 1862 the Spanish government decreed that if enough volunteers did not appear, that "all convenient methods of persuasion to incline them to volunteer for the voyage should be adopted" (Unzueta y Yuste 1947: 401–402). That year, 200 African descendents from Havana arrived as laborers indentured for seven years (Unzueta y Yuste 1947: 209–211, 225, 284). During the decade, at least 563 people arrived from Havana to Fernando Po, either as *emancipados* (liberated from the illegal slave traffic) or black creoles intended for agricultural and artisan labor (Franco 1980: 359–360; Sarracino 1988: 144–145; Sundiata 1996: 53; Unzueta y Yuste 1947: 402–403). In 1860 a government census listed 150 emancipados from Havana living in Fernando Po's capital. Balmaseda described them as Congos "rescued" from slave ships in Cuba, then converted into indentured workers, and later deported to Fernando Po as workers in 1862 (Balmaseda 1869: 130, 138, 147–149; Unzueta y Yuste 1947: 285–286, 397–398).

72. Ossorio (1886: 350); Unzueta y Yuste (1947: 285, 320).

73. Cf. Helg (1995: 83, 107); Roche y Monteagudo (1908: 53); Unzueta y Yuste (1947: 288, 323); Valdés-Infante (1898: 84–88). Many prisoners on Fernando Po were later deported to other penal colonies of Spain; those who survived were returned to Cuba in 1898. According to Roche y Monteagudo (1908: 52–53), part of the evidence against them were their tattoos, a bogus claim, since tattoos were common among maritime workers and other groups of workers in the city.

74. Ortiz (1954: 426–427).

75. Moreno-Moreno (1948: 411).

76. In Cuba, the term *nyangé* means "to kill, to sacrifice," as in the phrase, "embori nyangue tansíro" (the sacrificial goat represents the fish; Chino Mokóngo, pers. comm.). Cf. Cabrera (1975: 377, 1988a:

426). Formerly, the Èkpè Nyámpkè grade was used for enforcing a judgment, arresting offenders, the same function as a court bailiff (Engineer Bassey 2006, pers. comm.).

77. Cf. Anderson (1933: 16, para. 48); Nebengu (1990: 34); Valentin (1980: 15, 37, 42). Regarding an Ejagham region, Ebot (1978: 126, 128) wrote: "Nyankpe . . . is said to have come from the Èfìks"; "If the village council makes a law, for example, it is announced by the Nyankpe drum and called a Nyankpe law."

78. Ebutom Essien Efiok (2003, pers. comm.).

79. The Iyámba of Obutong told me, "What we hide is Idem Nyámkpè, Okpoho, Oku-Akama, Nkándá; we don't play them openly" (Archibong Eso 2004). I saw this in practice on several occasions.

80. Fyfe (1960); Hallett (1964: 203). In his entry of 8 February, Nicholls wrote that "grand yampia day . . . commences with the appearance of Egbo, who is grander upon that day than any other, making a noise very like a bear" (Hallett 1964: 203).

81. Moreno-Moreno (1948: 411–412).

82. Moreno-Moreno (1948: 412).

83. A Cuban deportee on Fernando Po in 1897 mentioned the weekly dances of the indigenous people, with no reference to Abakuá (Valdés-Infante 1898: 67). The lack of reference by a Cuban witness living in the period to the activities described by a Spanish authority forty years later either indicates ignorance of the phenomenon or brings Moreno-Moreno's descriptions into question.

84. "Key West had become the world's largest cigar manufacturing center by 1870; and many Cuban patriots who fled to Key West prior to the Spanish-American War were employed in the factories." Federal Writers' Project (1940: 198). This source is likely edited from the writing of Stetson Kennedy.

85. Louis Pérez (2006, pers. comm.); Orovio (2005: 85). The name Key West is an English gloss upon the earlier Spanish name, Cayo Hueso. The Cuban communities of Cayo Hueso in Florida actively countered the Spanish regime (Foner 1977: 120; Le Roy y Gálvez 1971: 58; Montejo-Arrechea 2004: 104).

86. Raimundo Cabrera (1892: 3–4).

87. Cabrera (1988a: 109); Ortiz (1955a: 300, 301, 309).

88. Cabrera (1988a: 232).

89. Armstrong (1954: 361). Armstrong's example was from southern Idoma (Benue State, north of Cross Rivers). In Calabar, Jeffreys (1935: 89) observed, "natives could converse by whistling. Such an impromptu command as, 'Bring me a fowl's feather to clean my pipe,' was whistled, and correctly acted upon by the recipient." In Oshogbo, Nigeria, Gerhard Kubik (1962) recorded a blacksmith speaking by tapping on his anvil (Kubik, 6 June 2000, pers. comm., New York City).

90. "Black Cubans made up about 21 percent of the Cuban population in Florida in the 1870s" (James 1998: 232).

91. In 1900 an estimated "791 Afro-Cubans and their children had settled in Tampa" (James 1998: 234–237).

92. The lodges Ita Baróko Efó and Ekoria Efó no longer exist. Many references indicate the presence of Abakuá among the cigar workers (cf. Rivero-Muñiz 1961: 167).

93. Kennedy (1940: 154–155) reported, "Nanigo came to Florida for various reasons. There were naturally some Nanigos among the Cubans who immigrated first to Key West and later to Tampa, seeking employment in the cigar factories and other industries. Others were revolutionary patriots seeking refuge from the tyranny of Spain."

94. "Lo que extraemos de su lectura [de Kennedy y Wells] nos lleva a la certeza de la existencia de ñáñigos [en Key West]" (Sosa-Rodríguez 2001: 165).

95. Sosa-Rodríguez (2001: 166–167) referred to an essay by José Martí (1893), yet in it, Martí (1992/1893: 324) described an order of Africans where members rejected use of a drum, wanting

instead to create a school (cf. Ishemo 2002: 256; Muzio 2001: 71–72; Sosa-Rodríguez 2001: 167). This could not have been an Abakuá lodge, because they require specific drums. Sosa-Rodríguez was cited by Ishemo (2002: 268), who described José Martí's "visit to a ñáñigo *famba* (a sacred room in the temple)" in Key West. The "secret society of Africans" as described by Martí required that the holder of the "third grade" be able to read. Abakuá lodges have no such requirement, nor are their grades numbered.

96. Kennedy (1940). Cf. Wells (1982: 48).

97. The phenomenon of processions in the 1880s in Key West, patterned upon those of the Día de Reyes in Havana, is no evidence that Abakuá lodges were recreated in Florida. My skepticism is supported by extensive conversations with Abakuá title-holders in Matanzas and Havana, all of whom confirmed their oral traditions have no reference to Abakuá activities in Florida.

98. Kennedy (1940: 155).

99. I spoke by phone with Kennedy in April 2002, who referred to his lack of fluency in Spanish at the time (cf. Kennedy 1939: 21). In a letter to the author, Kennedy (2002a) wrote, "I do not know much about *naniguismo* beyond what I have read in Dr. Fernando Ortiz's *Los Negros Brujos* . . . and my own article." In his next letter, Kennedy (2002b) wrote, "I do not now recall the contents of my *nanigo* article, or whether it even implied that there might have been nanigo organizations in Florida. I suspect that it would be difficult to prove either that there had been, or had not been."

100. Federal Writers' Project (1940: 133).

101. Cf. Proby (1981). The masquerades depicted by Mario Sanchez are called Vejigantes or diablitos in Loiza Aldea (R. F. Thompson 2007, pers. comm.). Proby (1981: 19–20) cited Sanchez as stating, "They didn't remember their magic rites for the populace to witness as did their kinsmen in Cuba. It was just for fun." Sanchez carved this piece in the 1930s.

102. Louis A. Pérez, Jr., 2004 letter to the author.

103. Greenbaum (2003).

104. *Biankómo*, an Abakuá term for music-making drums, is derived from *èkòmò*, an Èfìk term from drum. Luis "el Pelón" died in 1997 in Miami; his body was transported to Havana to receive Abakuá ceremonies and burial.

105. The ceremony was held in Miami on 6 January, believed to be the birthdate of Cuba's first creole lodge. Mr. Ángel Freyre "El chibiri," president of the Abakuá Bureau (la Organización para la Unidad Abakuá) in Havana, showed me his copy of the letter sent from Miami.

106. Cf. Brown (2003b: 64–65); Ortiz (1954: 315–316) reported on the founding of Yorùbá-derived Batá drums in Havana in the 1830s.

107. Cf. Bascom (1952: 171).

108. The ceremony performed in Miami was the creation of the first Olofis, a ritual vessel possessed only by high-ranking *babaláwo*. A 1978 Miami newspaper article reporting on the event stated that the first Olofis were made in Havana by Yorùbá babaláwos more than "200 years" before.

109. Thanks to Mr. Nath Mayo Adediran, curator of the National Museum, Calabar, for the correct title and spelling (2005, pers. comm.).

110. From a Miami newspaper article published in 1978, in the archives of Luis Fernández Pelón. For a detailed report on this process, see Brown (2003b: 93–95). In Miami, I saw and videotaped a photograph of Luis Fernández and two other Cubans in Òṣogbo, Nigeria, in 1978, taken there during their initiation as babaláwos. I also saw a photograph of Yẹmí Elẹbù̀ibọn dedicated "To my godson José-Miguel Gómez" (Caballero 2005, pers. comm.).

111. Holman (1972/1827: 392).

112. Palmié (2006: 109–110) went on to argue that Ékpè "extended its reach all the way onward to Berlin," through Alfred Mansfeld, an early twentieth-century German colonial authority who was

initiated (see Mansfeld 1908). This fanciful reading is out of sync with the documentation from Cross River history.

113. As referred to in the Introduction.

114. Cf. Hart (1964: 59, para. 166).

115. Following tradition, in the early 1960s the Efe Ékpè Èfìk Iboku lodge of Calabar had three men representing three tiers of the Nyámkpè grade: "Obong Nyamkpe Ekpe," "Isung Nyamkpe Ekpe," and "Murua Nyamkpe Ekpe" (Hart 1964: 55, para. 157). In Calabar, most Ékpè grades have four levels.

116. According to an 1874 agreement between "Emperor Eyamba VIII, King, chiefs and members of Egbo of Old Calabar" and "Harry Hartye Esquire of Matilda, an Agent to Messrs Thomas Harrison of Liverpool," Hartye "bought and paid for" six Ékpè titles (including Nyámkpè; Hart 1964: 59, para. 167–168).

117. Referring to the case of Mr. Hartye, Dr. Anwana commented, "the membership of Ékpè by foreigners in the eyes of Africans did not confer political rights and privileges (an exclusive preserve of the African members), but was seen as a means to facilitate and enhance their economic interests" (Anwana 2002: 140). Cf. Hart (1964: 59, para. 166); Walker (1877: 121).

118. Northrup (1978: 109). See also Adams (1823: 245); Ward (1911: 38).

119. Talbot (1912a: 45–46).

120. Anwana (2002: 215).

121. Cabrera (1988a: 145).

122. Cf. Cabrera (1992/1954: 198); Carpentier (1989/1946: 214).

123. Helg (1995: 81). See also Téllez (1960: 2).

124. Flint (1898: 94).

125. Flint (1898: 99).

126. Cf. Helg (1995: 107, 113).

127. Ortiz (1991d/1954: 124).

128. Luis Carbonell (2000, pers. comm.). Palés Matos' verses were performed to music by Cuban vanguard composer Amadeo Roldán in 1929, as "Danza Negra" (Gómez 1977: 68–69). The poet would have learned the Cuban term from members of the Afrocubanismo movement of this era (Palés Matos 2000: v–vi, 35–41). For more on Afrocubanismo, see Moore (1997: 2–3).

129. Earlier attempts to interpret the term appear in Martín (1930: 176, 175); Ortiz (1924a: 376, 1954: 3, 1993b/1950: 42).

130. Etim "Bambam" (2004, pers. comm.); Engineer Bassey (2001/1998: 71, fig. 13; 76, fig. 14; 107, fig. 20; 174). In Èfìk, "Nya-nyang-a, n. 1. Guinea grass; any kind of strong grass" (Goldie 1964/1862: 240).

131. The Nyanyaku grade is specifically Èfìk, not forming a part of the Efut, Qua, or Uruan practice of Ékpè (Engineer Bassey 2006, pers. comm.). Cf. Akak (1982: 288); Hart (1964: 30, para. 81; 34, para. 101; 63, para. 176). See the appendix of masks for details.

132. Cf. Pichardo (1985/1875: 228); Roche y Monteagudo (1914: 21); Rodríguez (1881: 4–5); Salillas (1901: 357). See also Cabrera (1988a: 257).

133. Deschamps-Chappeaux (1968a: 45); Sociedad de los ñáñigos blancos (1893).

134. ñanguitua (Trujillo y Monagas 1882: 364); ñangaíto (Roche y Monteagudo 1908: 14); Ñangaípó (Roche y Monteagudo 1925/1908: 95); Ñaitúa (Cabrera 1988a: 423, 1992/1954: 205); Ñangaítua (Cabrera 1988a: 424).

135. The Abakuá phrase "bongó nyaituá, kurumína nyaituá" refers to the spirit of Sikán in the bongó: "'Bongó ñaituá akurumína ñaituá' was chanted in Usagaré to say that the spirit of Sikán was reincarnated in the bongó" (Anonymous).

136. Cf. Courlander (1949: 2); Cuellar-Vizcaino (1956b).

137. Ortiz (1981/1951: 446).

138. Deschamps-Chappeaux (1968a: 44–45). Attempts to establish Abakuá in Cienfuegos in the nineteenth century were unsuccessful, in spite of the Carabalí influence there (Soto Rodríguez 2006, pers. comm.).

139. Rodríguez (1881: 5–6) referred to the payment of fees to create Cuba's first lodge, a process consistent with Cross River and later Cuban practice.

140. Trujillo y Monagas (1882: 365).

141. Trujillo y Monagas (1882: 369).

142. Nicklin (1991: 10).

143. Cf. Nicklin (1991: 12–13).

144. Engineer Bassey (2006, pers. comm.).

145. Sosa-Rodríguez (1984: 24). Sosa's source is likely Trujillo y Monagas (1882: 367–368), who referred to fourteen Abakuá members jailed in Havana in 1879 who "formed a lodge inside the prison, selecting for it various imprisoned men." Palmié (2006: 110) accepted this narrative, then built a hypothesis upon it.

6. Disintegration of the Spanish Empire

1. Antonio Maceo, 14 July 1896, in a letter to Francisco Pérez Carbó (Foner 1977: 239).

2. Trujillo y Monagas (1882: 372).

3. Howard (1998: 155–156, citing "Correspondencia de [Ramón] Blanco por el Ministerio de Ultramar," 24 May 1882, in Archivo Histórico Nacional de Madrid, Sección de Ultramar, leg. 4787, exp. S-1). Ramón Blanco was governor of Cuba from 1879 to 1881, then again in 1897 (Thomas 1998: 1523–1524).

4. Cf. Scott (1985: 266–267).

5. Efforts to whiten the population began in the early 1790s (Jameson 1821: 100–101; Lamounier 1995: 186) and continued into the 1900s (Scarpaci et al. 2002: 53). Censuses of the late 1880s declared whites a majority on the island (Ferrer 1999: 96).

6. Deschamps-Chappeaux (1968b: 51); Montejo-Arrechea (2004: 49–50); Ortiz (1984b: 22).

7. Ortiz (1984b: 21; see also Montejo-Arrechea 2004: 45; Ortiz et al. 1945–1946: 139).

8. Also, the Cabildo Carabalí Isuamao Isiegue de Oro became known as the Cabildo de Oro, Carabalí, Isuama Isueque de la Pura y Limpia Concepción, Nuestra Señora del Rosario, San Benedicto y San Cristóbal (Ortiz 1984b: 22–24). By the same law of 1887, the Cabildo Carabalí Olugo of Santiago de Cuba became La Sociedad Nuestra Señora de Carmen (Millet and Brea 1989: 8–9). Ortiz (1984b: 23–24) cited a registry from the provincial government of Havana of 1909 listing several extant cabildos or "mutual aid societies," including "Sociedad de Socorros Mutuos del antiguo Cabildo de la Nación Carabalí" and "La Sociedad de Socorros Mutuos del Cabildo Carabalí Ungrí." "The Nation and Cabildo Carabalí Brícamo San José" was mentioned in a Cuban court case of 1911 (Ortiz 1984b: 26).

9. Ortiz (1984b: 27, 22).

10. Ortiz (1984b: 28). For more on persecution in the 1880s, see Ortiz (1954: 79–80).

11. Ortiz (1984b: 28).

12. Cabrera (1992/1954: 199–200).

13. Oritz (1984b: 25; italics in original).

14. Martínez-Furé (1979: 175) noted that many of the cabildos, officially called societies after Spanish rule, continued the functions of the cabildos and were popularly called cabildos by their members.

Montejo-Arrechea (2004: 59) concluded that many of the societies of instruction and recreation formed in the 1880s "were converted to true centers for the promotion of culture, and in many cases of mutual aid. Some were merely new masked forms of what they had always been: a place for the preservation of ancestral culture."

15. Cabrera (1979: 112). His father, Claudio Brindis de Salas (1800–1872), was second lieutenant in Havana's battalion of Morenos Leales and a professional musician whose orchestra was popular with the creole nobility. The son of a free black in Havana who was first sergeant of the Real Cuerpo de Artillería, Claudio Brindis de Salas was a slave owner by 1838. He was exiled from Cuba along with many other free blacks in 1844, "the year of the lash," but eventually returned (Deschamps-Chappeaux 1971: 106–109).

16. Carpentier (1989/1946: 134).

17. Carpentier (1989/1946: 136) referred to him as the "Cuban Paganini."

18. Bianchi Ross (2005: 164–168); Deschamps-Chappeaux (1971: 109); Orovio (1992: 70–71).

19. Andrés reported that Román was a cousin of the violinist. Contemporary Abakuá leaders in Havana investigated this claim and reported that Román Brindis held the title of Empegó or Ekueñón in this lodge and he was the nephew of the violinist (Soto Rodríguez 2006, pers. comm.; Placencia-Romero 2006, pers. comm.). Another family member, Pablo Justamante Brindis de Salas, held the title of Isué of Mbemoró in the twentieth century; he died in the 1980s (Caballero 2005, pers. comm.).

20. Cabrera (1958: 23).

21. A central character in Morúa-Delgado's novel *La familia Unzúazu* (1891) was once a loyal mulatto slave; but after joining the Abakuá, he became a fugitive from slavery, a negative figure in the norms of the slave society (Cairo 2005: 104–108; Sosa-Rodríguez 1982: 325).

22. Howard (1999: 135). See also Ortiz (1984b: 28).

23. Montejo-Arrechea (2004: 37).

24. Through Gualberto's initiative, the Havana-based Directorio Central de las Sociedades de la Raza de Color created a constitution in 1887.

25. Montejo-Arrechea (2004: 73–75), after analyzing the registers of several of these societies, observed that their members were also Freemasons (like Juan Gualberto Gómez and General Antonio Maceo) and some were Abakuá.

26. Deschamps-Chappeaux (1968b: 51); Scott (1985: 268–269).

27. In one example among many museums where Abakuá objects are displayed in Cuba, the Abakuá sala of the Museum of Guanabacoa displayed a representation of the Ékue fundamento, as I saw in February 2006. The museum director told me that the Abakuá were pleased about this. But when I asked Abakuá leaders, their response was acidic (Soto Rodríguez 2006, pers. comm.).

28. Several Abakuá leaders told me that their elders taught that the Abakuá delivery of ritual objects was a trick; it was inconceivable that Abakuá leaders would deliver their sacred drums to police (Anonymous 2004, pers. comm.).

29. Similarly, information published about Abakuá in this period derived from the Mukarará lineage (cf. *Causa criminal* 1884; Pérez-Beato 1892, 1893a).

30. Roche y Monteagudo (1908: 43, 1925: 56–59); Trujillo y Monagas (1882: 370).

31. Cabrera (1958: 55) confirmed that the lodge Ekório Efó no longer functioned by the 1950s.

32. Supposing that some of the fundamentos delivered to police were authentic, one narrative holds that the lodge Ebión Efó was reconstructed by the lodge Ekório Efó Taibá, giving them the title Ebión Efó Ékue Entenisún. The ceremony was directed by Manuel Fernández, Moruá Eribó of Ekório Efó Itá. Both lodges were sponsored by Andrés Petit (El Chino Mokóngo, pers. comm.).

33. Maujarz, *Actas*, Casa Consistorial de Guanabacoa, 1889, cited in Pascual (1997: 20).

34. Castellanos García (1948: 593).

35. Ortiz (1954: 70).

36. During research, I learned several versions that Bakokó and Awana Mokóko, while intimately related, are two different lodges (cf. Cabrera 1988a: 521). Contemporary title-holders in this lodge reported to me, however, that they are one and the same lodge.

37. Castellanos García (1948: 593) also wrote, "They offered to renounce their posts and dedicate themselves to work." This description indicates a tacit agreement between authorities and Abakuá for public relations: the Abakuá renounce their errors, they will be good, and go to work. Since Abakuá have always prided themselves in being workers, this is a non sequitur.

38. The Erón Entá lodge created a pantheon in the Old Cemetery of Guanabacoa for its members (cf. Castellanos García 1948: 594).

39. Castellanos García (1948: 593).

40. Castellanos García (1948: 593).

41. Cabrera (1992/1954: 199); Ortiz (1954: 81–82).

42. Cabrera (1958: 59 n.). Here Cabrera was citing Salillas' (1901) phrase to condemn Trujillo y Monagas' 1882 work.

43. Cabrera (1992/1954: 199).

44. After the 1958 Revolution, for example, Cuban Communist Party members could not openly profess their religious practice until the 1990s. Noting this dichotomy, Vélez (2000: 177) wrote, "the 'official' position, [was] not shared by everyone and at times not held privately by those who advocated it publicly. Since the 1980s there has been a major change in the official position of the government with respect to the Afro-Cuban religions."

45. This is a rare acknowledgement; in spite of reports that police captured several Abakuá fundamentos (Brown 2003a: 134–135; Roche y Monteagudo 1908: 43–49, 1925/1908: 56–59). This matter is generally taboo among Abakuá leaders, thus the persistent popular belief that "the police never captured the Ekué sacred drums" (Ishemo 2002: 269 citing Muzio 2001: 67–68).

46. Cabrera (1992/1954: 205). The Ndian River is discussed in the appendix of potencies.

47. Rodríguez-Sarabia (1957). In the way that Antonio Maceo's role in Cuba's independence has been likened to that of Toussaint L'Ouverture in Haiti, Mariana Grajales' role in Cuba is likened to that of Nanny of Jamaica, a founding female warrior (Stubbs 1995: 297). See also Foner (1977: 155); Martí (1992/1893); Sociedad cubana de estudios (1950: vol. 1, 428).

48. Cf. Foner (1977: 295).

49. By "Hispanic-American" wars are meant those of the Philippines, Puerto Rico and Cuba, ending in 1898. Among Maceo's many other epithets are: "the greatest man of color in Cuban history" and "one of the great guerrilla fighters of all time" (Fernández-Mascaró 1950: 9, 10; Foner 1977: 16, 24, 252).

50. Ferrer (1999: 71). This event was celebrated in the mid-twentieth century in a bolero by El Conjunto Chappottín y sus estrellas, "La Protesta de Baraguá," composed by Luis "Lili" Martínez Grinan (LP Puchito 594, 1960s).

51. Foner (1977: 254).

52. In the 1960s, Cuban folklorist Rogelio Martínez-Furé interviewed elder descendants of Africans throughout the island. He found that the texts of anonymous popular songs from the Wars of Independence onward mentioned Maceo's name with greater frequency than that of Martí. Maceo was known by the Cuban population, whereas Martí, who lived in exile for many years, became known on the island through his collected writings after his death. See also Ferrer (1999: 68); Foner (1977: 257). "Both in Cuba and abroad, Maceo appears to have been better known in his time than even Martí. . . . the [New York] Times' special correspondent in Havana, observed: 'Maceo, one of the

Cuban idols in the war of independence, was a back man. All Cubans of whatever color, look upon him as one of the noblest of their countrymen'" (Foner 1977: 260).

53. "By the end of 1897, there were 240,000 [Spanish] regulars and 60,000 irregulars on the island." For the Cubans, "For the greater part of the war, the effective combatant force amounted to about 30,000" (Foner 1977: 172). "Adding paramilitary troops—Spanish volunteers, and Cuban guerrillas—to the regular forces, Spain unleashed some 600,000 soldiers against the Cuban troops (*mambises*) on an island with 1.5 million inhabitants" (Scarpaci et al. 2002: 52; Mario Coyula, 19 June 2005, pers. comm.). For the Cubans, "the only standard weapon that was available in abundance was the machete." A contemporary wrote, "There has been more hand-to-hand fighting in Cuba than in any war of modern times" (Foner 1977: 173–174).

54. Foner (1977: 180).

55. Ortiz (1924a: 315).

56. Dr. Fu-Kiau Bunseki, letter to the author (27 June 2000): "maṁbị; evil (things)" (cf. Fehderau 1992: 127).

57. The term *mambí* was used for cimarrón in Cuba, Santo Domingo, and Brazil (cf. Bachiller y Morales 1883: 318). Another interpretation offered by Bachiller was that *mambí* means "twice a man," derived from *man* in English and *bis*, "twice."

58. Cabrera (1984: 32); Santa-Cruz (1988: 34). Contemporary Cuban Abakuá, Kongo, and Ocha practitioners have confirmed this interpretation (Román Díaz 2006, pers. comm.).

59. For example, a group of Cuban insurgents published a newspaper in the nineteenth century with the title Mambí (Bachiller y Morales 1883: 318).

60. In 1957 Arsenio Rodríguez composed and recorded "Adorenla como a Martí," a song praising the Mambís and imploring patriots to fight for democracy and liberty in Cuba in the manner of Bandera, Maceo, Martí, and other independence leaders (Thanks to Eugene Godfried 2007, pers. comm.).

61. The white fugitives indicate the presence of "white serfs," whose migration from poor Catholic countries such as Ireland and Italy was encouraged in an effort to "whiten" the Cuban population (Franco 1973: 78–79, 104–106).

62. Benítez-Rojo (1996: 254); Franco (1973: 82, 114–116).

63. Deschamps-Chappeaux (1987: 78).

64. Maceo's use of the palenques made him unusual among rebel generals. Some insurgent leaders persecuted these fugitive communities, believing that the cultural forms maintained on the palenques were incompatible with civilization (cf. Ferrer 1999: 35–37).

65. Foner (1977: 27); Franco (1975a: 53).

66. Franco (1975a: 53–54; see also Foner 1977: 28–29).

67. Ferrer (1999: 35–37); Miller (2004b: 207); Ortiz (1956b: 317–320, 130).

68. Ortiz (1955b: 9, 121).

69. Cf. Ortiz (1956b). No scholar doubts that blacks were a majority of the Mambí forces, growing proportionally from 1868 to 1898; the percentage is usually estimated at 70 percent (cf. Ferrer 1999: 48; Foner 1977: 172, 191, 243). Some scholars report estimates of 80 to 85 percent (Fermoselle 1974: 26; Thomas 1998: 323). See also Duque (1923: 144); Kunz (1909: 12); Pérez (1983: 106).

70. Helg (1995: 64; citing Fernández-Mascaró 1950: 16–17). The folk treatment was indeed given in this case, because the doctor was told that if he did not allow it and Maceo died, the locals would hang him for malpractice.

71. The knowledge of herbal arts and the healing powers of Antonio Maceo's mother were proverbial. Using them, Mariana Grajales saved Antonio's life several times (Stubbs 1995: 312).

72. In the early twentieth century, Dayrell (1913: 22) documented an example from the upper Cross River region of Ikom. Of course, military techniques brought by Africans would have also been a factor, but I am unaware of references to this theme in Cuba (cf. Thornton 1999).

73. "Quintín Bandera, the son of free black parents, joined the rebellion of 1868 as a private, and was among the last to surrender, as a general, in 1878." Bandera joined Maceo at the Protest of Baraguá in 1878 to reject the peace offer of Spanish General Martínez Campos. By August 1897, "Bandera was perhaps the most powerful and popular of the revolution's nonwhite leaders. . . . Rebel sympathizers recited poems and sang songs about him, and Spanish soldiers confessed that he was one of the few leaders they truly feared (the other two were Antonio Maceo and Máximo Gómez)" (Ferrer 1999: 57, 66, 173). "El terror de los españoles en la Habana era Quintín Bandera" (Camejo 1910: 54, notes).

74. *Ngo* means "leopard" in many West-Central African languages, such as Kikongo (Fuentes Guerra and Schwegler 2005: 65). "*Ngo* is cognate with *mkpe*, *ekpe*, etc. (Proto-Bantu *n-gu*)" (Connell 2006, pers. comm.). *Njo* is "leopard" in languages of southwestern Cameroon, such as Mòkpè (Bakweri; Connell 1997: 35). In the early twentieth century, the hereditary leader of the coastal Duala interpreted his title as "le Seigneur de pays des sujets de Njo" (the King of the nation of subjects of the Leopard; Joseph 1974: 347–348).

75. Briyumba, territory, or a *prenda* from the region of Kongo Luango; [N]zámbe, God; Ngó, leopard. "Ngó: leopardo o tigre" (Cabrera 1984: 92, 1988a: 393).

76. Bakonfula, interpreted as "the one who lights the gunpowder," likely derives from Portuguese *polvora*, transformed to *fula*. Small amounts of powder are lit to activate the spirits (C. Daniel Dawson 2004, pers. comm.).

77. Among the many forms of Nkisi is a portable one, an amulet called Makuto (cf. Cabrera 1984: 21, 137).

78. Oral narratives by contemporary Cubans refer to the *prenda* of Bandera and Maceo as an active presence. One version holds that the prenda Ngo La Habana was buried beneath a ceiba in the Quinta de los Molinos in Havana, where General Máximo Gómez resided in 1899 at the conclusion of the war (Ruíz 1986: 36). This ceiba is highly regarded by practitioners of many African-derived systems in Havana. The "ceiba with fundamento as shrine" is a common narrative in Cuba (cf. Miller 2000c). Another version holds that Bandera's Palo Monte prenda is maintained by a Cuban-Kongo lineage in Miami, as told to me by a Cuban *santero* and *ngangulero* in Little Havana in 1994. This legend is contested by ngangueleros living on the island, who insist the prenda is still in Regla, across the bay from Havana. The dynamics of this issue indicate an axiom of Cuban society: "For the palero to have an old *nganga*, from the colonial days, is a priceless trophy. It represents the greatest prestige for him, and assures clientele" (Barnet 1995: 129). Cuban intellectuals noted that because the Spanish army was defeated by Mambí troops led by black generals who were believed to have been supported by Kongo spirits, these traditions became popular throughout all sectors of the society and practiced by political leaders during the Republic (Antonio Benítez-Rojo 2002, pers. comm.; cf. Cabrera 1979: 120).

79. "Ngo, ngo, ngo. Cuando yo vengo a la Habana," in the song "Angoa," *Afro-Frenetic*, Grupo Afro-Cubano de Alberto Zayas (1950s). This march seems to be in the conga genre (thanks to John Amira for this recording). While *Angoa* is a variation of *Ngo* (cf. Cabrera 1984: 153), it is also the title of a danzón composition by Felix Reina in the 1940s (Orejuela 2003). The record producer seems to have confused the two terms. The "inspirations" of the lead singer, while describing arrival in Havana, are not meant to be coherent; they are a nonsensical diversion, a camouflage for the hidden message of this composition. Members of Zayas' group were highly knowledgeable practitioners of Abakuá, Lukumí, and Kongo traditions.

80. Artist Jorge Delgado was initiated into the Kongo-derived practices of his family. He was inspired by well-known legends of Palo Monte practice among the Mambí warriors that include Maceo and Bandera. In another example, a Tata Nkisi from Havana referred to the legend of Ngo in the Wars of Independence through the chorus "Ngo saludando Batalla" meaning "the leopard greets the battle" ("Ngo Batalla"on *Lemba Kongo Muna Kongo* 2002). The lead chanter, "Muerto Vivo" (2004, pers. comm.), learned detailed legends of the fundamento Ngo La Habana and its use to protect the Mambí troops by Antonio Maceo and Quintín Bandera from his grandfather, Quintín Nicolas, who was a Mambí warrior.

81. Cabrera (1992/1954: 134–136) documented various perspectives of the meaning and history of Zarabanda, some saying it is a creole innovation in Havana, others that it is an ancient Kongo divinity. Thompson (1983: 110) reported that the term derives from "Ki-Kongo: 'nsala-banda', a charm-making kind of cloth." Linguists Fuentes Guerra and Schwegler (2005: 234–235) reported that in KiKongo, "Zarabanda < Sarabanda . . . Literally 'work something sacred.' . . . Kik. sála 'work' + Kik. Bánda 'something sacred.'"

82. Journalist Syme-Hastings (1896: 4) accompanied Maceo's column outside Havana. Syme-Hastings continued his description of the attack in a burning cane field, "The roar of the flames, the crackling of the cane, the screams and curses of the wounded, the harsh frightened cries of the royalists, the wild, discordant yells of the maddened 'Cubes,' 'Cuba libre,' 'viva Maceo,' the sharp clash of steel, all blended into a song to the god of the machete." The battle of Las Begoñas took place on 1 September 1896 (Centro de Estudios Militares 2003: vol. 2, 44).

83. The chant "Briyumba Zámbe Ndio, Briyumba Ngo La Habana" evokes the power of Bandera's nkisi. Information regarding Bandera, Maceo, and the Kongo nkisi came from several Tata Nkisi (leading practitioners), including Sr. Ricardo Montabán Vega, a Palo Monte initiate since age seven. When I spoke with him in 1998, he had been a Tata Nkisi (ritual leader) for twenty-seven years. An image of Antonio Maceo was placed upon his Palo altar in San Miguel de Padrón, Havana.

84. Maceo visited Havana from January to July 1890, arriving by sea from Jamaica via Haiti. Maceo had not set foot in Cuba since 1878, and this was likely his first time in Havana.

85. Foner (1977: 135–141).

86. Robreño (1925: 89).

87. Centro de Estudios Militares (2001: vol. 1, 230–232); Foner (1977: 102–103). Remembering this betrayal, Antonio Maceo wrote an open letter to members of the liberation army on 2 May 1896 (Maceo 1998/1952: vol. 2, 194; Miró 1945: vol. 2, 274).

88. Cf. Foner (1977: 158).

89. Cabrera (1958: 60).

90. Salinas held the title of Ekuenyón of Abarakó; Pablo Gutierrez-Nuñez held that of Mbákara of Ikanfioró Nankúko.

91. After Maceo's visit to Havana in 1890, he departed for Santiago de Cuba in July (Foner 1977: 142).

92. Mbákara and Isué are both leading Abakuá titles.

93. Blanco-Aguilar (2000: 15). I photographed this altar and Freemason square in the Odán Efí lodge in the 1990s.

94. Kennedy (1940: 154).

95. The statue of Espínola stands in the Parque de los Pinos, on the corner of Abayí and Pedro Betancourt Streets on the main road to Varadero. A plaque beneath it reads, "The lieutenant Felipe Espínola y Travieso was a humble stevedore in the ports of this city: moved in his soul for the ideal of Cuban independence, he became a hero and was immortalized through martyrdom. Matanzas, proud of its son, erects this monument in memory of his patriotic virtues."

96. Brown (2003a: 24); Cosme-Baños (1998: 51). Valdés held the title of Abasónga in Abakuá Efó (Brown 2003a: 245, n. 21).

97. Cosme-Baños (1998: 51).

98. Cf. De la Fuente (2001: 38).

99. Victor Vicente Martí Labarrer, Isunékue of Awana Mokoko (Bakokó Efó), told me that according to the manuscript books of his lodge, Lino D'ou was Obonékue of Bakokó Efó and was also a Freemason (2001, pers. comm., La Habana). Conversations with Lino D'ou were fundamental to Franco (1974: 186) during research about Aponte's conspiracy of 1812 and the Abakuá participation within it (see also Cabrera-Peña 2007: 35; Helg 1995: 150).

100. Urrutia (1935: 17–20).

101. Sosa-Rodríguez (1982: 324–325).

102. This phrase was referenced in a popular song about Cuban identity, specifically in the context of the palenque, while the chorus chants "Bruca Maniguá," a reference to Arsenio Rodríguez's song about a Carabalí who escapes his enslaved condition ("Somos Cubanos" by Los Van Van, at 3:42 minutes). This album, *Llegó . . . Van Van* (1999) is famous for its references to Abakuá history, in the track "Appapas del Calabar." *Brucu* means "African born and recently arrived in Cuba" (Pichardo 1985/1875: 104); *Manigua* means "forested hills"; the phrase refers to an African born captive in Cuba who escaped to the palenques (rural emcampments).

103. Cf. Cabrera (1975: 39).

104. Benítez-Rojo (1996: 125).

105. For an insightful study on the complex dynamics that ended the war in 1898, see Tone (2006).

106. Blanco (1900: 147).

107. Castellanos García (1948: 598).

7. Havana Is the Key: Abakuá in Cuban Music

1. "Cuba aportó mas que recibió" (Giro 2006, pers. comm.). Leading Cuban musicologist Radamés Giro attributed this phrase to Carpentier (cf. Carpentier 1989/1946: 7–8).

2. Cf. Cabrera (1988a: 317) regarding the primordial Voice that founded the religion.

3. Excellent samples of ceremonial chants are recorded on *Ibiono* (2001). Each track evokes a particular terrirtory (Efó, Efí, or Orú), articulating the West African territories, as well as the contemporary Cuban lodges named after them.

4. Thompson (1998) referred to this function of skins in Cross River societies. Abakuá rites are defensive, that is, used to proctect the group from negative forces.

5. Cf. Acosta (2004: 46–47); Lapique (1995).

6. Lapique (1979: 39).

7. Ortiz (1993a/1950: 65).

8. The composer was General Enrique Loynaz del Castillo. Maceo's column breached this trocha in November 1895 (Miró 1942, vol. 1: 125–126; Foner 1977: 199).

9. For example, Carlos Embale (1975) "Y a Matanzas." The chorus includes the phrase, "Güiro bombero, se quema la trocha" (Alert the firemen, the barricade is burning). Cuban bandleader Adalberto Álvarez (1979) composed the dance tune "Se quema la trocha." In its deepest sense, the phrase announces warriors who elude military opponents who claim to be stronger. Metaphorically, it refers to the arsenal-like power of a percussion ensemble that defeats its competitors.

10. Cf. Díaz-Ayala (1994: 121–124); Juan "Juanillo" Febles (1996, pers. comm.). Febles (1914–2004) was a professional musician in Havana his entire life. As a son of babaláwo (Ifá diviner) Ramón

Febles and brother of Ramón Jr. (a member of the Abakuá lodge Efóri Búma), Juan Febles had information from oral traditions as both a musician and as a member of a prominent family within African-derived traditions of Havana.

11. Danza is a variant of the European contradanza.

12. Frank Oropesa (2006, pers. comm.), *bongosero* of the Septeto Nacional de Ignacio Piñeiro and an Abakuá title-holder, confirmed the melody of "El ñáñigo" as derived from Abakuá vocal styles. Some musicologists like to refer to this pattern as a 12/8 meter, being the length of one full clave cycle, but Cuban scholars tend to describe it as 6/8 (Lináres Savio 1998).

13. Cf. Acosta (2003: 39). For example, Claudio Brindis de Salas, father of the great violinist (discussed in chapter 6) was second lieutenant of the battalion of Morenos Leales (Loyal Blacks) of Havana, who gave dance lessons and played music for the creole elites of the early nineteenth century (cf. Deschamps-Chappeaux 1971: 105–107).

14. Lapique (1979: 40–42).

15. Engineer Bassey (2001/1998: 22). In Èfìk, "èfámbá, n. . . . Efamba Ekpe, Nkanda Ekpe house where all types of Ekpe grades are displayed" (Aye 1991: 27).

16. Another important example is a *zarzuela* (light opera) by Raimundo Cabrera from 1888 that used Abakuá images. In one scene, processions of *gallegos* (Spaniards from Galicia) and of *ñáñigos* (Abakuá) cross the stage to create the mood of Havana city (the Abakuá appear in scene 22 (R. Cabrera 1888; cf. Lane 2005: 233–234). This was among the first signs by Cuban intellectuals of the Abakuá emerging as an integral element of Cuban identity, and thus a national symbol. Cuban elites of Cabrera's day rarely distinguished between the ñáñigos and members of African-derived groups. However, Sr. Cabrerea (the father of Lydia Cabrera) was exceptionally informed, as his later writings demonste. Refererences to Abakuá had appeared in early Havana theater traditions, but they appear to be lost. In 1868 a group pf working-class artists created the Compañia de Bufos Habaneros, (a form of comic theater influenced by U.S. minstrel shows), whose reperatory represented the customs of the time, including "rumbas of Manglar, ñáñigos in their fambá" (Leal 1982: 20). Jorge Ibarra (1985: 214–215) referred to the Teatro Bufo's use of references to poular culture, including *ñáñigo* language, as a culture of resistance that transformed "folk culture" into "a rhythm, a style, a sound and a language distinct from that of Spain."

17. Lapique (2006, pers. comm.); Moore (1997: 24). "Las alturas de Simpson" (the Heights of Simpson) refers to a Matanzas barrio that sits upon a hill. Abakuá lodges existed in Matanzas by 1862, and Failde lived in a barrio with Abakuá traditions. More fieldwork is needed to confirm his membership. Failde was indeed a full initiate of Santería, whose *orichá* (divinity) was Oyá (goddess of wind and transformation; Martínez-Furé 1999, pers. comm.). Dr. Martínez-Furé learned about Failde from his grandmother, who was his neighbor and also an initiate.

18. Another section of this suite is called "andante congo mundele" (thanks to Zoila Lapique).

19. Orquesta Antonio María Romeu (n.d.); Urfé (1992). Composer and flautist Octavio "Tata" Alfonso blended elements of Abakuá liturgy into his danzones (Urfé 1977: 234–35). See also Rodríguez-Domínguez (1967: 103).

20. Jameson (1821: 112); Marrero (1956: 308, 1972–1987: vol. 8, 1, vol. 12, 177); Scarpaci et al (2002: 22).

21. Inglis (1985: 49–50); Kuethe (1991: 15–16, 23). When Britain ended their 1763 occupation of Havana, they utterly destroyed the shipyards on their way out, thinking to maintain their domination of the seas (Marrero 1972–1987: vol. 12, 174–177).

22. Kuethe (1991: 17); McNeill (1985: 173–174).

23. Roig de Leuchsenring (1963: 121).

24. Ortiz (1952a: vol. 1, 234). Rumba musicians in Havana continue using this metaphor. In the 1950s Abakuá member Alberto Zayas recorded "Si El Cerro tiene la llave, la Habana tiene la clave" (If

El Cerro has the key, Havana has the clave), a reference to the barrio El Cerro (discussed later in this chapter). Grupo Afro-Cubano de Alberto Zayas (2001, "Que me critiquen").

25. Centro de investigación (1997: 70); Lapointe (1997: 120–125); Marrero (1972–1987: vol. 9, 140, 198; vol. 12, 168; vol. 14, 245). Forced labor in the shipyards was yet another Spanish continuity in the Americas (cf. Pike 1983: 26).

26. Ortiz (1952a: vol. 1, 218–221) observed that each of the paired pegs are shaped differently, one considered male, the other female. The ship pegs were therefore a raw material that was refashioned based upon inherited musical ideas.

27. Sublette (2004: 168, 170–171).

28. Ortiz (1952a: vol. 1, 237).

29. Kubik (1979: 13–14) called them "time-line patterns," "percussive guiding patterns," or "one-note patterns."

30. Kubik (1979: 18–19).

31. Kubik (1999: 53). Its structure is (x.x.xx.x.x.x).

32. Kubik (1999: 56).

33. "Asymmetric time-line patterns are not universally distributed in sub-Saharan Africa. Actually, they are a distinctive Kwa and Benue-Congo phenomenon, and even there they are not known among all speakers of this language family" (Kubik 1999: 60).

34. Cf. Centro de investigación (1997: 71). From the mid-nineteenth century, the same period when Abakuá was transmitted to Matanzas, the claves were diffused to Matanzas and Cárdenas, nearby port cities (Centro de investigación 1997: 71). Cognizant of the tensions in the colonial society, it would be difficult not to conclude that racism was a predominant factor in keeping the claves outside of the colonial music.

35. Cf. Centro de investigación (1997: 71); Sublette (2004: 342–343).

36. Wurdeman (1844: 112–113).

37. Wurdeman (1844: 113).

38. Bremer (1853: vol. 2, 325–328).

39. Moliner-Casteñeda and Gutierrez-Rodríguez (1987: 42). Diosdado Ramos, a member of Los Muñequitos de Matanzas, noted, "slow down the *baile yuka* a little and you have the *yambú*" (Sublette 2004: 259).

40. Moliner-Casteñeda (1988: 14). See also Martínez-Furé (1979: 157, 174); Martínez-Rodríguez (1995: 142).

41. See Acosta (2004: 55–56) for an overview of the literature regarding the historical creation of the rumba through the synthesis of various African-derived forms. In Cuba, the musical forms of the cabildos de nación underwent an inter-African process of symbiosis, resulting in later forms like the rumba. Martínez-Furé (1979: 161) identified "Yorùbá-Carabalí syncretism from the nineteenth century" in Matanzas; Sweet (2003) described a similar process in Brazil.

42. "La Rumba: de donde viene la rumba" (1978).

43. Cf. Urfé (1977: 230–31, 1982: 153).

44. Cabrera (1984: 150).

45. "La viola," by Florencio "Catalino" Calle (Los Muñequitos de Matanzas 1977). Calle was Iyámba of the Matanzas lodge Efí Akanirán. Hear also "Yumurí (Yamorí)" by Los Muñequitos de Matanzas (1950s) and "Caumbia" (Mongo Santamaria 1953).

46. Moliner-Casteñeda (1988: 17).

47. Campos-Cárdenas "Chang" (2006, pers. comm.); Román Díaz (2005, pers. comm.). The tumbador is a low-tone conga drum that holds a basic pattern (cf. Howard 1967: 238).

48. Cf. Blanco-Aguilar (1992: 7–8, 116).

49. Blanco-Aguilar (2000: 15).

50. Urfé (1977: 231). See also Sublette (2004: 263).

51. Cf. Díaz-Ayala (1993/1981: 87).

52. Espínola was the Mbákara of Efí Mbemoró Second and the first Isué of the Odán Efí lodge (cf. Blanco-Aguilar 2000: 15). See discussion of Espínola in chapter 6.

53. Deschamps-Chappeaux (1968a: 45).

54. Roche y Monteagudo (1908: 55).

55. "La Rumba: de donde viene la rumba" (1978).

56. Also called "Coros de clave y guaguancó," these groups utilized 6/8 rhythms and sang many Abakuá chants (Lináres Savio 1998).

57. Nicanor Asencio was Obonékue of the lodge Irianabón.

58. Cf. Blanco-Aguilar (2000: 16, 117); Castillo (198?: 3).

59. Severino Durán was *obonékue* of Efóri Búman or Sangírimóto. He died in the 1950s.

60. Cf. Ortiz (1981/1951: 411).

61. Abelardo Empegó said, "Ignacio Piñeiro was from Jesús María, but he moved to Pueblo Nuevo." According to the register book of the lodge Efori Nkomón, Ignacio Piñeiro was consecrated into this lodge in 1917. As reported by Wilmaracio Orbeal, Abasí of Efori Nkomón (f. 2005). (Frank Oropesa 2005, pers. comm.).

62. No recordings of this group are known. In the 1950s Ignacio Piñeiro organized a recording of "Consuélate como yo" (Console yourself as I do) by Tío Tom (cf. Carlos Embale 1994), in order to reconstruct the choral style of Los Roncos.

63. Cf. Sublette (2004: 365–366).

64. Martínez-Furé (1999, pers. comm.).

65. Carnival celebrations were documented in Havana in 1585 (cf. Rojas 1947: 303).

66. In the February carnivals, both whites and blacks participated in distinct performance modes. For example, blacks paraded on foot, while elite whites often celebrated with masked balls inside a private home or paraded publically in carriages (cf. Gallenga 1873: 70–71). An Italian traveler described a group of extravagantly dressed blacks and mulattos in the carnival celebrations in Havana on 9 February 1698 (Gemelli Careri 1699–1700: vol. 6, 305). In Matanzas city in 1870, Hazard (1989/1871: 297–305) described a carnival scene and the different performance modes of each social group. He did not mention the month, but this was likely the February carnival. See also Orovio (2005: 10–11).

67. Cf. Ortiz et al. (1945–1946: 139).

68. Cf. Blanco-Aguilar (1992: 117); Moore (1997: 66–69); Orovio (2005: 9); Roig de Leuchsenring (1945–1946: 151).

69. An indication that the comparsa theme of a sacrificial snake or a scorpion is derived from African sources is that "in Cuba, there are no serpents, vipers, nor other harmful ophidians that kill" (Ortiz 1937c: 41).

70. As discussed in chapter 5, the cabildo Carabalí Isuama of Santiago de Cuba was reorganized in 1894 as a cabildo comparsa (Pérez-Rodríguez et al. 1982: 12, 35).

71. "La Rumba: de donde viene la rumba" (1978).

72. Dr. Mercedes Herrera (2000, pers. comm.) is daughter of the late Victor Herrera, Iyámba of Isún Efó and founder of the comparsa Los Marqueses de Atarés (The Marquees).

73. Iyámba is a leader of an Abakuá lodge. Ramírez's complete name was Santos-Eligio Ramírez-Arango (Radamés Giro 2005, pers. comm.). El Alacrán was founded in 1908 in Jesús María, directed by Gerónimo Ramírez, a black man who was principal dancer. The majority of members were white Abakuá, members of the Ekerewá lodge, who performed in blackface. In 1937, Santos Ramirez "El

Niño" (son of Gerónimo) restructured El Alacrán in El Cerro (*El Alacrán* 1999; Orovio 2005: 12–13, 31–34).

74. Ortiz (1981/1951: 572–573) refers to other popular songs of protest from the 1880s to the early 1900s.

75. Antonio Benítez-Rojo, an eyewitness (2000, pers. comm.). See also Roig de Leuchsenring (1945–1946: 170).

76. In 1941 in Havana, Chano Pozo recorded "Tumbando caña" (conga), attributed to Santos Ramírez and Julio Leonard (Martré and Méndez 1997: 39; Pujol 2001: 133). In 1955, Odilio Urfé recorded a historical recreation of the original written by Santos Ramírez (Urfé 1960s; see also *Festival in Havana* 2003; Moore 1997: 74). Carlos Embale (1992) recorded "Tumbando caña" (guaguancó).

77. This song was used subversively in the 1970s, when Fidel Castro mobilized the entire country to harvest 10 million tons of cane.

78. The down stroke of the machete came at the final beat of the conga rhythm, where the "conga kick" is usually placed.

79. Cf. Blanco-Aguilar (1992: 28). For more on Ramírez, see Blanco-Aguilar (1992: 42, 72–73, 94).

80. "Chévere" was recorded by Clave y Guaguancó (1996). "Con su guaragura" was recorded on *Carlos Embale–Septeto Nacional de Ignacio Piñeiro* (LP, Egrem PRD 067; Díaz-Ayala 2002, entry 1886), also on Carlos Embale (1992).

81. Román Díaz (2005, pers. comm.). Salidor is a second drum that carries a counter beat, over which the *quinto* drum improvises.

82. In the early 1900s, Ignacio Piñeiro's group Los Roncos sang the phrase, "El ronco tiene la llave" (The Ronco has the key; Andrés Flores 1990s, pers. comm.). Los Muñequitos de Matanzas (2003) recorded an homage to their group's founders; on the track "La llave" is sung, "lo único que yo digo es que mantengo la llave" (All I can say is that I maintain the key), meaning that the group's awesome musical skills are maintained by the present members of the ensemble.

83. Román Díaz (2005, pers. comm.).

84. "El Cerro tiene la llave" (guaracha) by Fernando Noa (Arsenio Rodríguez y su conjunto 1993). Fernando Noa "El cojo mojado," composer of "El Cerro tiene la llave," was abanékue of Orú Ápapa; he was famous in rumba gatherings of the 1950s ("Palillo" 2006, pers. comm.). Percusionist Candido Camero was a colleague of Chano Pozo and played in the Tropicana Nightclub. He migrated to the United States in 1946, where he played with Dizzy Gillespie, Billy Taylor, Tony Bennett, and Tito Puente. Raised in the barrio of El Cerro, Candido remembers learning the phrase "El Cerro tiene la llave" as a child in elementary school, that is, even young children in Havana know this phrase as part of their identity (Camero 2005, pers. comm.).

85. The phrase is sung as an inspiration to commence the quinto drum solo on Conjunto Rumbavana's 1985 version of "A Belén le toca ahora," written by Arsenio Rodríguez. This interpretation was confirmed by several Abakuá leaders, including Palillo (2006, pers. comm.), Moní Bonkó of Mutánga Efó and lifelong percussionist in Havana.

86. "La bola" refers to baseball, as there is a baseball stadium in El Cerro. Just as baseall is organized into juegos (teams), so too are these rumberos/Abakuá, who are just as popular in the barrio (Román Díaz 2000, pers. comm.).

87. The use of the term *wárárá* could be a reference to Ramírez's composition "Con su guaraguara" [wárawára]. The phrase "traigo la mano caliente andero, con su wárárá" was one of many stock phrases used since the nineteenth century by rumba players. In the mid-1950s it was recorded by Abelardo Barroso in "El guarjiro de Cunagua" to introduce the drum solo, another indication of its ties with African-based spirituality.

88. Cf. Cabrera (1988a: 89, 522).

89. Guara is a group of people who get along well. *Guara*, as used in the rumba, is derived from the Abakuá term *awarandaria*, from the phrase "warandaria kusundaria" (Anonymous 2000, pers. comm.).

90. Santos Ramírez Ugarte Jr. became Isunékue; "El Moro" was Moní Bonkó. Santos Jr. became the director of El Alacrán in the 1970s. By 2003, his son Santos Ramírez García became director (Bauza 2003).

91. Cf Díaz-Ayala (2002); Orovio (2005: 61); Pujol (2001: 106). Since its foundation, the Ikanfioró lodge has included members of the Chappottín family. Julio Chappottín was founding member of Ikanfioró. Of his three sons (Miguel, Julio, and Félix), Miguel Chappottín (d. 1991) was Moruá Yuánsa; Julio Chappottín Jr. was abanékue of Ikanfioró. Julio's great-great-grandson, Rogelio Chappottín "El Negro," is also a member of Ikanfioró. Félix Chappotín was one of the few members of the family not initiated, but his son "El Negro" Chappottín, who also played trumpet in the Conjunto Chappottín, was a member of Orú Ápapa (Soto Rodríguez 2006, pers. comm.; Miguel Chappottín Jr. 2006, pers. comm.). Paralleling their Abakuá lineage is the Chappottín musical heritage. Julio Chappottín Sr. was a musician (Miguel Chappottín Jr. 2006, pers. comm.). Julio Chappottín was a member of the son group Los Apaches, founded in 1915 in the barrio de Dragones, Habana (Blanco-Aguilar 1992: 19–20, 113; Díaz-Ayala 2002). In 1927, Félix and Miguel Chappottín created a son group called Sexteto Belén, named after the barrio (Blanco-Aguilar 1992: 41). In the 1940s, Félix became a member of the comparsa (Blanco-Aguilar 1992: 114). In 1951, when Arsenio Rodríguez left Cuba for the United States, Félix Chappottín organized el Conjunto Chappotín y sus Estrellas with members of Arsenio's old band (Blanco-Aguilar 1992: 88).

92. Miguel Chappottín Jr. was the second director of the rumba group Clave y Guaguancó, founded in 1945, after the demise of the first director. Information regarding the Chappottín family history is guarded jealously by its members. I was able to confirm what I learned only through extensive introductions by trusted members of their community and subsequent meetings with family members, to whom I am grateful.

93. The Mozambique is a rhythm in the conga genre and not a genre unto itself (Radamés Giro 2006, pers. comm.).

94. "Pello el Afrokán" (Pedro Izquierdo Padrón) was abanékue of the lodge Efó Kondó Éndibó Makaró Mofé. In the Yorùbá-derived Santería practice, he had Ochún "made" and was a babaláwo (Baba Eyobe).

95. Pello's father held the title of Nkóboro of the lodge Efó Kondó; Roberto Izquierdo is remembered as a dextrous quinto player in Jesús María (Martré and Méndez 1997: 40). His grandfather Damaso Morales "El mocho" Izquierdo was abanékue of Asoíro Ibondá, as well as the first Mokóngo of Efó Kondó (founded in 1922; Soto Rodríguez 2006, pers. comm.).

96. Pello's brother Roberto Izquierdo Padrón (d. 1995) was *obonékue* of Orú Ápapa and a babaláwo (Ojekú Opeleka Okana). Gilberto Izquierdo Padrón was Aberiñán of Efó Kondó and a babaláwo (Obara Ogbe; Soto Rodríguez 2006, pers. comm.). Pello's cousin, Mongo Santamaría, became a leading percussionist in the United States in the jazz circuit, where he made many important recordings with Abakuá conent.

97. For example, the Makua, a Bantu group from Mozambique, were present in nineteenth-century Cuba; Domingo Macuá was a famous cimarrón in western Cuba (Cairo 2005: 222, based upon Martínez-Furé 1976). Pello chose the name Mozambique for his rhythm because he knew his grandmother was Makua (Martínez-Furé 2002, pers. comm.; Miller 2005). But Makua-derived traditions, to my knowledge, have not been perpetuated in Cuba.

98. "El Yulo" (Raúl Cárdenas Jr.) was Moní Bonkó of Isún Efó. Later in his career he played with NG La Banda. His father, Raúl Cárdenas (d. 2006), was the Abasí of Isún Efó (Cuervo 2006, pers. comm.; Marino-García 2006, pers. comm.).

99. Armando Cuervo is obonékue of the Munandibá Efó lodge. He played with Los Van Van from 1972 to 1978 and with Irakere from 1978 to 1981. His father, Octavio Cuervo, an obonékue of Amiabón, sang with the son group Estrellas del Vedado from the 1950s to the 1970s. Armando Cuervo's maternal grandfather, Adolfo Pedroso, was obonékue of Orú Ápapa his paternal grandfather, Ambroso Cuervo, was an Abakuá member and a troubador; his maternal uncle, Gilberto Pedrez-Valera was obonékue of Amiabón and a rumba player. Armando Cuervo's sister, Caridad Cuervo, was a great singer of *guarachas* in the Tropicana for decades. His son Daody Cuervo is a percussionist with NG La Banda. Another Abakuá member of Los Van Van was flutist Orlando Canto "El Viejo espigón," obonékue of Ita Amana Enyuao (Cuervo 2006, pers. comm.).

100. Among its other founders were Abakuá members Justo Marino-García (Moní Bonkó of Efóri Enkomón), Pedro Celestino Fariña (Obonékue of Barondí Kamá), and Jacinto Scull Castillo "Chori" (Enkóboro of Irianabón Brandí Masóngo). Yoruba Andabo became a professional group in 1986. Later members were Miguel Chappottín Jr. (Obonékue of Ikanfioró); Ogduardo "Román" Díaz (Moní Bonkó of Ekueri Tonko Ápapa Umoní), and Orlando Laje "Palito" (babaláwo and Ndisime of Ita Amana Eñuáo; Marino-García 2006, pers. comm.).

101. All members of Chang's family were masters of the rumba de solar. His mother, Ana Luisa Cárdenas-Vergada, who sang in the *coro de los Roncos*, was a founder of the comparsa La Mexicana (barrio de los Barracones) in the 1930s. Chang's uncle Santiago Vergada was a singer in the Orquesta Habana Swing in the 1940s. Santiago's brother Alfonso Orna Vergada, likely a founding member of Muñánga, was the second Isué of Muñanga (his nephew Chang is the third). Chang is Isué of Muñánga Efó. Mario Carballo was abanékue of Munandibá Efó. Chang's brother, percussionist Ricardo Carballo-Cárdenas, cofounded the Conjunto Folklórico Nacional. Chang's biological father, Juan Campos, worked in the wharves; he was an obonékue de Efóri Nkomón, but since he knew how to chant well, he was called "Juansito el Moruá." Chang's brother Umberto Campos is abanékue of Efóri Nkomón and a babaláwo (Oberoso Ntekle; Campos-Cárdenas 2006, pers. comm.).

102. "Siki" danced Eleguá and Abakuá Íreme for Yoruba Andabo. Of Chang's other sons, one is a title-holder in Munyánga.

103. Leonel Polledo is abanékue of Erón Entá; his father was Abasí of Mutánga Efó.

104. Other examples are "A los barrios de La Habana" (To the barrios of Havana), "La juventud de Cayo Hueso" (The Youth of Cayo Hueso [a barrio]), "Pueblo Nuevo" [a barrio], "El rumbon de Luyano" (The Rumba of Luyano [a barrio]), "A Belén le toca" (It's Belén's Turn [a barrio]), and "Como se goza en el barrio" (the people enjoy in the barrio; Arsenio Rodríguez 1992).

105. A group of black curros in Jesús María called themselves Amalia, and the term became synonymous with this barrio into the present, its inhabitants being "amalianos" (cf. Deschamps-Chappeaux 1972a: 37, 41).

106. Alberto Zayas Govín "El Melodioso," held the title of Isué in the lodge Erobé Efó.

107. Grupo Afro-Cubano de Alberto Zayas (2001).

108. This was interpreted by an Abakuá and rumba master from Havana as, "Some people (that is, from the dominant culture) speak badly of the rumba, but they are ignorant of it, not being rumba players nor poor people, but the rumba does no harm to anyone."

109. Román Díaz (2006, pers. comm.).

110. "Totico" (Eugenio Arrango), an abanékue of the lodge Enchemiyá of the barrio Los Sitios, learned the song while playing rumba in his youth (Totico 2005, pers. comm.). Both Totico and "Curba" chant on this recording (Palillo 2006, pers. comm.). "Chabalonga" confirmed that his

brother Luis Dreke-Alfonso "Curba" (abanékue of Isun Efó) sings inspirations in the *montuno* of this recording (he also chants the Abakuá enkame in "Ya yo e", as well as the chorus on "Rezo Abacua," other tracks on this LP; Chabalonga 2006, pers. comm.). Carlos "Patato" Valdéz, also raised in the barrio of Los Sitios, played tumbador in the Conjunto Casino in Havana in the 1950s (Palillo 2006, pers. comm.).

111. "Nuestro barrio," composed by Silvio A. Pino of Los Sitios (the composer of "Los Sitios Asere"), became a rumba standard expressing deep barrio sentiments in Havana, referring to an encounter at La Plazuleta in Los Sitios between the three comparsas from Belén, Jesús María, and Los Sitios (the same three barrios referred to in Zayas' earlier "El Yambú de los Barrios"). Both Totico and Chang of Yoruba Andabo confirmed that Silvio Pino is the author (Chang 2005, pers. comm.). Silvio Pino's son, of the same name, is abanékue of Mutangá Efó as well as a babaláwo (Palillo 2006, pers. comm.).

112. During the montuno jam at the end of "Nuestro Barrio," the lead voice sings "Oye que viva María/ viva Italia/ Los Sitios Asére!," a reference to the barrios of Jesús María and Los Sitios, as a group of black curros from the early nineteenth century called themselves "Italia." Cf. Blanco-Aguilar (1992: 116).

113. Like the story of the three rings in Boccaccio's *The Decamaron* used to diffuse tension regarding the authenciticy of Judaism, Chirstianity, or Islam, the solution was arrived at by finding mutual respect, in the Cuban case with the added acquiescence to age.

114. Román Díaz (2005, pers. comm.). An example of this love for a physical place, rather than for an abstract nation, was articulated by Abakuá leader José de Jesús "Chuchú" Capáz from the town of Regla, who after leaving Cuba for the United States in 1967 said, "I am more from Regla than from Cuba" (Yo soy más reglano que cubano; El Chino Mokónko, pers. comm.).

115. I refer to the traditional comparsas such as El Alacrán, Los Componedores, and La Jardinera that were organized as community-based popular movements in the early twentieth century, modeled directly from the former calbidos de nación processions, and often maintained within particular families, as distinct from the government organized, top-down comparsas of the post-1959 revolutionary period, which had a distinctly secular and less popular appeal, that continued only as long as the state support was forthcoming (cf. Orovio 2005).

116. Thanks to Lázaro Herrera (1999, pers. comm.). Mr. Herrera played trumpet in Piñeiro's Septeto Nacional for some fifty years.

117. Díaz-Ayala (2005, pers. comm.). "Los cantares del abacuá" was recorded by Columbia, circa 1920 (cf. Díaz-Ayala 1994: 271). Notes from rerelease place the recording in 1923 (Vera, *María Teresa Vera y Rafael Zequeira* 1998).

118. Lináres Savio (1998, pers. comm.).

119. *El maso* means "the participants." This first stanza seems to have inspired the composition "Irimo" by the Gran Combo of Puerto Rico (*En Las Vegas*, 1978, CD, Combo 1925). Thanks to Stella Estrada, whose novel is named after this recording (2007).

120. The phrase "Nangandó mariba" is translated as "a procession to the river."

121. *Enkabúyo*, the police. Enkabúyo is a title of the Íreme Nkóboro, guardian of the fundamento (Ángel Guerrero 2007, pers. comm.), in other words, a costumed police officer (cf. Cabrera 1975: 22). In the Cross River region, the traditional police were masked representatives of Ékpè. Following this practice, Carabalí in Cuba referred to the colonial police after their term for "guardian." Cuban Lukumí had their own term for police, *aché-lu*, from the Yorùbá *Àṣẹ-ìlú*, "those who administer the town" (cf. Abímbọlá and Miller 1997: 120–121).

122. *Húye* or *úye* is a play on the Abakuá term *úyo* (the mystic sound of the Ékue drum).

123. This phrase means that the Voice will lose force. The Bongó fundamento is a defense mechanism for Abakuá to keep negative forces at bay (cf. Cabrera 1975: 19).

124. This Abakuá phrase is chanted during initiations to evoke the birth of Abakuá. Mana, manantión, "praise" (cf. Cabrera 1988a: 330); Kankubia, bakankúbia, "altar" (Andrés Flores, pers. comm.; Cabrera 1988a: 309); Komo, èkòmò, "drum" in Èfìk; Índia, "birth" (cf. Cabrera 1988a: 236). Índia may be derived from Ndian, the river along the Usaghade where Ékpè was perfected, that is, born.

125. See *nyongo empabio* entry in glossary for details.

126. Íreme dancers compete with each other for style mastery.

127. Mosóngo is one title-holder, Sése Yuánsa (commonly Moruá Yuánsa) is another. They do not agree on how to proceed after the raid.

128. The phrase "yúmba abanekue yúmba" has various meanings, including "through the sacrifices of our ancestors, we are able to initiate neophytes," so that our culture will continue. This phrase refers to the foundation of Ékpè in Africa, and can be interpreted to mean "unity with the ancestors" or "initation brings us in contact with the ancestors" (cf. Cabrera 1988a: 16).

129. "The development of *costumbrismo* followed a different trajectory in Cuba than on the continent, reaching its peak later and becoming allied with anticolonial sentiment rather than with postcolonial, national consolidation" (Lane 2005: 25).

130. Cf. Lane (2005: 21).

131. With the exception of one Spanish term *son* (are) in the phrase "Ekóbio Enyegueyé monína son ekóbios."

132. Sexteto Habanero (1995). The author of "Criolla Carabali" was Felipe Neri Cabrera, the lead voice and maraca on this recording, according to the notes on *Sexteto y Septeto Habanero* (vol. 3, 1928, Tumbao TCD 303). Guillermo Castillo, listed as author on the Harlequin release, played guitar on this recording.

133. In Èfìk, *iyak* means "fish."

134. Cf. Cabrera (1988a: 522).

135. See discusión of Efí Méremo in the Efí Efí Guéremo lodge (appendix of potencies). As lodge leader, one of Mokóngo's titles is Mokóngo Bíjuráka Mbóri (Cabrera 1988a: 348; Andrés Flores, pers. comm.).

136. Cf. Cabrera (1988a: 348). In Èfìk, "Èyéneka, n. brother or sister by the same mother"; composed of "Èyén, child"; "Èkà, mother" (Aye 1991: 39, 28; Goldie 1964/1862: 97). Arsenio Rodríguez utters this phrase in his "Canto Abacuá." *Leyendas/Legends:Quindembo-Afro Magic*. Sony Tropical DIC 8134/4–46974. Recorded in 1963, despite the error of 1973 in the liner notes (Dave Garcia 2001, pers. comm.).

137. This stanza celebrates the process by which the Bakokó lodge founded the Mukarará (white) lineage, including the Abakuá Efó lodge. Cf. Cabrera (1988a: 491).

138. Cf. Cabrera (1988a: 94). See discussion in chapter 3.

139. This full phrase chanted for the first obonékues in Africa was, "ákua bero akanawán Morua tan boribó Iyámba, yayo ee, yayo ma," referring to the birth of Abakuá with the death of Sikán. Contemporary Abakuá leaders reject Cabrera's (1988a: 39) interpretation as a phrase to call out an Íreme (Soto Rodríguez 2006, pers. comm.).

140. Thanks to anonymous Abakuá leaders. See also Cabrera (1975: 21, 27).

141. This phrase, "Sése Eribo eróko mbóko baróko nansáo," posits a relationship between the Eribó drum and the Voice (*mboko*) during a foundational baróko ceremony, as discussed in n. 181 of chapter 1.

142. Instead, qualities like an appreciation of collective consciousness, the bravery to defend oneself, and spiritual and artistic accomplishment are extolled by Abakuá.

143. A version of "Criolla Carabalí" was recorded by the group Sierra Maestra in the 1990s. The recordings referred to are Chano Pozo's "Abasí, " recorded in 1947 in New York City (*Chano Pozo*

2001); "Encame," performed by Victor Herrera in 1962 (*Música afrocubana* 1993); and "Ya yo e" and "Rezo Abacua," recorded by Patato and Totico in 1967 in New York City (*Patato y Totico* 1967).

144. Several Ékpè leaders observed that "Criolla Carabalí" by Septeto Habanero uses the rhythm of their Ebongó grade, an Ékpè procesional (Etubom B. E. Bassey 2004, pers. comm.). See also Talbot (1969/1926: vol. 3, 782).

145. Early versions were recorded by the groups Rumboleros (in 1975) and Yoruba Andabo (in 1992).

146. A Kongo fundamento is known as Nganga, Nkisi, or Prenda. A Tata Nkisi is a ritual leader who works with the Matiabo spirits that Ortiz (1955b) documented as vital participants in the Wars of Independence (cf. Cabrera 1984: 142).

147. Cf. Cabrera (1975: 476). This composition depicts the creation of a Cuban tratado, a pact between representatives of distinct communities to unite in common cause. This Cuban treaty is modeled upon an Abakuá tratado called Bongó Yukáwa, "also known as 'The treaty of the three brothers.' This was the consecration the Efó made in Ibondá for the birth of the first baróko and the sharing of the fundamento" (El Chino Mokóngo, pers. comm.). See also Cabrera (1958: 119).

148. The Spanish creole represents Carlos Manuel de Céspedes, who was a Freemason.

149. Speakers of Bantu languages were widespread throughout the island. The three voices of this composition are sustained by Kongo mambos. This structure reflects the Kongo presence in the ranks of the Mambí army, to the extent that their opponent, Spanish General Martínez Campos, was given the Kongo name Nfumo Nbanza Bana, "Big Man" (cf. Cabrera 1979: 113, 1984: 88, 109). The act of naming makes one known, in this case, a known target.

150. Cf. Cabrera (1984: 41).

151. Cf. Cabrera (1979: 165); Martínez-Ruíz (2002: 113, 116). Thanks to Félix "Pupi" Insuá-Brandis (2005, pers. comm.) for interpretations of Cuban Kongo terms in this composition. Pupi is Tata Nkisi Malongo, that is, a ritual leader in Cuban Kongo practice.

152. This Arabic greeting was brought to Cuba by African Muslims in the 1800s (cf. Madden 1839). This phrase became incorporated into Cuban-Kongo parlance, perhaps superimposed over an earlier KiKongo (cf. Cabrera 1984: 143).

153. Cf. Cabrera (1984: 152).

154. The term *bacheche* means "good, complete, no problem."

155. Cf. Cabrera (1979: 126, 1984: 40).

156. A question asked of someone who knocks at the door of a Cuban Kongo temple, in effect evoking those particular ancestors. *Munanso*, "house" (Cabrera 1972: 141, 1984: 46, 2004: 135); *Kuenda*, "to arrive" (Cabrera 1984: 46, 161, 163).

157. León (1990: 111); Thomas (1998: 242–245).

158. *Malembe* is a greeting (Cabrera 1984: 23, 143); Malembe is the name of an nfumbi ancestor (cf. Cabrera 1979: 24, 1984: 69; Insuá-Brindis 2005, pers. comm.).

159. This standard opening was recorded in "Criolla Carabalí" (discussed earlier), as well as the Los Muñequitos de Matanzas (1999) recording "Ritmo Abacua" (cf. Cabrera 1988a: 271–286). This Abakuá term is also a reference to a West-Central African ethnic group. Abakuá traditions indicate that Nasakó, a Kongo diviner, was the founder of the society in Africa.

160. "Achocho ucho kambo" (the skin of an old drum), a phrase for an ancient lodge, its age being a sign of authority. The title of the Matanzas lodge Efí Mbemoró Second used the term, as detailed in the appendix of potencies. Cabrera (1958: 93) referred to "the ancient gods Karabalío Okámbo" of the Abakuá foundation myth.

161. Cf. Cabrera (1988a: 235).

162. Cf. Cabrera (1988a: 65).

Epilogue. Cubans in Calabar: Ékpè Has One Voice

1. Èfìk Ékpè leader Etubom B. E. Bassey officiated the event with Chief Ekon E. E. Imona, a Qua M̀gbè representative on behalf of the Ndidem of the Quas and Paramount Ruler of Calabar Municipality.

2. Abakuá also use rattles to guide the Íreme (cf. Cabrera 1975: 24).

3. Cf. "Èfìk Dances" (1957: 167–169). In Calabar, *nyóró* is an Èfìk term for a masquerade dance, whereas *unek* is a person dancing without a mask (Etubom B. E. Bassey 2004, pers. comm.). "Nyóró (Èfìk): A gathering of ídèm for a dance display" (Engineer Bassey 2005, pers. comm.).

4. Cf. Cabrera (1958: 258); Ortiz (1954: 41).

5. Sánchez played the Bonkó Enchemiyá drum, a long drum held with a strap around the shoulders, used to solo over the time-keeping drums and to communicate with the Íreme masked dancers. Díaz held one of the three time-keeping nkómo drums of the Abakuá.

6. This phrase forms the basis for a field recording performed by Victor Herrera in 1960 (found on the accompanying CD, track 10), titled "Marcha Abakuá" (*La Música del pueblo de Cuba* 1972).

7. In Èfìk, *iyak* has a muted *k*, therefore sounding very close to the Abakuá *iyá*.

8. Meaning "the place where initiates are consecrated." Both terms have relevant meanings in local languages. In Balondo, a language of neighboring Cameroon, *Yangando* or *Ngando* means "crocodile." Through use of metaphor, *ngandó* means "path" or "movement" in Abakuá. *Mariba* is water in Balondo (Mosongo 1995: 29).

9. The term *úyò* means "voice" in Calabar (cf. Cabrera 1958: 64). The phrase "Ekue úyo" was used in Cuban popular music in the 1920s, when Ignacio Piñeiro composed "En la alta sociedad," a song ending with a call-and-response chant led by the Moruá Yuánsa (the singing dignitary): "Ekue Uyo Ke Akanapon dibio dibio dibio kondo" (The voice of our sacred mother Ékue is roaring; Vera 1994). The phrase "Ekue uyo ukeno" is heard in the recording *Ibiono* (2001), track 2 (at 3:20 minutes). This phrase is also part of the title of Ékuéri Tongó in Havana (see chapter 3).

10. Dibo is also an Ékpè grade in Calabar.

11. The dancer was Edem Effiong Ékpéyóng, an *abanékpe* in the Osam M̀gbè Akim Qua.

12. Cf. Cabrera (1988a: 221). The phrase "tie tie tié" is what one says to an Íreme "be careful," "watch what you are doing," "go easy," synonymous with *tébere* (Ángel Guerrero 2007, pers. comm.). The phrase is also used when summoning the Voice to the *butame* (temple) in ceremony (cf. Cabrera 1975: 31). This phrase was performed by Silviestre Mendez (1957) on "Ñáñigo" (at 53 seconds).

13. Talking drums are used throughout West and West-Central Africa. For southeastern Nigeria cf. Talbot (1969/1926: vol. 3, 810).

14. In Èfìk, "Ñ-kan'-i-ka, *n.* 1. A bell . . . Nyeñe ñkanika, *Ring the bell, by shaking it*" (Goldie 1964/1862: 214). Lit. "shake bell" (Connell 2001, pers. comm.).

15. The term *abanékpe* means "initiate" in both Cuba and Calabar. *Yumba* is literally translated as "blood of the female founder." Through her blood, the society was founded and the first neophytes were consecrated.

16. Cabrera (1988a: 283–288) gave several examples of this phrase in a context, without interpretation. *Emomi* is "I"; *enkanyo* is "good" (cf. Cabrera 1988a: 398).

17. Cf. Cabrera (1988a: 20).

18. On another occasion, Iyámba Archibong Eso clarified, "They way you like to use it, that is not our business, but we will not allow you to spoil the spring. So we don't want anybody to spoil the Ékpè" (Archibong Eso 2004, pers. comm.).

19. Archibong Eso (2005, pers. comm.).

Appendix 1. Cuban Lodges Founded from 1871 to 1917

1. On 28 June 1998, I witnessed the consecration and investiture of the Moní Bonkó of Ibondá Efó in the temple of Ororó Mayambéke in the barrio Obrero.

2. *Asoíro*, sound; *Ibondá*, hillock of the consecration; *téte*, fish; *kairán*, mother of fish; *akuáro bénya*, kill; *moto*, authorization; *bríkamo*, a territory; *manyóngo*, "prenda" (ritual pot) of Nasakó (Andrés Flores, pers. comm.; cf. Cabrera 1975: 22, 25, 26).

3. Cabrera (1988a: 77, 234). See also Cabrera (1992/1954: 285).

4. Cf. Becroft and King (1844: 261); Cotton (1905: 303); Goldie (1964/1862: 358); Nair (1972: 3, 106); Nicklin and Salmons (1988: 129); Waddell (1863: 444). The Dibonda village of southwestern Cameroon is on the Moko River, near the Ndian River (cf. Nebengu 1990: 7; Reid 1989: 19, fig. 3). I confirmed this chronology with the paramount ruler of Ibonda in Calabar (H. H. Muri Ita Okokon Mesembe 11th, Muri and Clan head of Efut Ibonda, March 2005, pers. comm.).

5. I visited Dibonda-Balondo in the summer of 2004.

6. H. H. Etínyin Edet Effiong Edet Atre and Chief Edet Eneyo Assato, both of Usaghade (2005, pers. comm., Calabar). See also Connell (2001a: 54).

7. Cf. Cabrera (1988a: 100). The phrase "Ékue Barondó" was performed by Silvestre Méndez on "Ñáñigo," at 3:41 minutes (*Bembé Araguá* 1957). See other references to "Ékue Barondó" in chapter 3. The Efí Barondí Kamá lodge of Matanzas was mentioned in a recording by Los Muñequitos de Matanzas (1983), "Abakuá #3" (at 2:26 minutes). Cf. Cabrera (1975: 358).

8. Cf. Cabrera (1988a: 100)

9. H. H. Johnston (1888b: 634). See also Nofuru (2002: 1, 5, 13).

10. Connell (2004, pers. comm.); Nair (1972: 3). See also Anene (1970: 62).

11. The village of Bateka in Usaghade was reportedly founded by "Balundu" peoples (Anderson 1933: 18, para. 53).

12. Barondó was a prince of Efí territory (Andrés Flores, pers. comm.). Cf. Cabrera (1988a: 100). Cuban interpretations of *barondó* vary from that of a historical figure to a river or a region. These ideas do not necessarily contradict each other.

13. Ibiabánga Munyón's foundation date is commemorated as 26 December 1871. Piti Naróko Efí was a nineteenth-century Ékpè/Abakuá lodge that no longer exists. The lodge "Otiabanga Muñon" is mentioned in the text *Los Ñáñigos* (1882: 16). Several phrases evoking this Cuban lodge, such as "Ibiabánga ereniyó," were recorded on *Ibiono* (2001), track 6 (beginning at 2:05 minutes).

14. Ibiabánga is also known as Úbiabánga (El Chino Mokóngo, pers. comm.). Cf. Cabrera (1975: 360). Ibiabánga's sponsors were also known as Ítiá Bánga Pitinaróko Efí (Abelardo Empegó, pers. comm.).

15. Cf. Cabrera (1988a: 436).

16. Cf. Cabrera (1988a: 110). "Biabanga Pitinaroko: Èfik and Efor, 'Three different persons and only one true God' is what this phrase means" (Cabrera 1988a: 110, 472).

17. Cf. Nofuru (2002: 23).

18. Seven is an ideal number in Abakuá mythology (cf. Cabrera 1975: 187, 330).

19. Talbot (1923: 159). See also Cotton (1905: 302–303); Jones (1988b: vol. 3, 504); Messenger (1971: 208–209, 211); Simmons (1958: 123); Talbot (1912a: 422, 336–337). In spite of the anachronistic interpretations of contemporary born-again Christians in Calabar, there is no evidence of Christian influence in the symbolic importance of the number seven.

20. Essien (1993: 173). See also Nair (1972: 3).

21. Chief Nsan (2005, pers. comm.). In Calabar, *Mmọ̀nyọ́* is a long scepter, at the end of which is placed a basonko (plumed rod) to signify Ékpè. In Cuba, the plumed rod is called *munyón* after the

entire scepter; it also signifies spiritual authority and royalty. The Èkpè term *basonko* is the likely source for the Abakuá title Abasóngo, associated with a staff that represents the autonomy of Cuban lodges in the Èfìk lineage (cf. Cabrera 1988a: 21).

22. The title of Edidem has been used continuously to the present in Calabar, although in 1902 British colonists decreed that the title would officially become Obong; in Uruan the title was formerly Edidem Atakpor, but since the mid-twentieth century it has become Nsomm (cf. Hart 1964: para. 213–214; Nair 1972: 211; *Story of the Old Calabar* 1986: 144).

23. "The two common ancestors which feature in the traditional history of the Èfìks are Atai and Ekpo Ibanga Nkanta. From these two common ancestors the lineages branch . . . to embrace all the Èfìk families in Calabar" (Hart 1964: 40, para. 122; 77, para. 203; 184, para. 381). Confirmed by Engineer Bassey (2007, pers. comm.).

24. Chief Eyo (2005, pers. comm.). In the Cuban colony, this lodge was also known as "Itiabanga" (Cabrera 1988a: 258). In Cuba, the munyón of "Itiabanga" is named Sanga munyón, literally the "moving munyón" (see Èfìk interpretation of *asanga* in appendix of chants). Abakuá mythology speaks of the Orú (Uruan) ancestors who brought the munyón from their home to participate in the perfection of the Voice.

25. Cf. Hart (1964: 44, para. 128; 89, para. 223).

26. Hart (1964: 30, para. 81; 33, para. 98, para. 100). See also Asuquo (1978: 47); Aye (1991: 100); Urua et al. (2004: 95). For more perspectives on Efiom Ekpo Ibanga Nkanta's story, cf. Aye (2005: 18); Essien (1993: 79–81); Hart (1964: 35–36, para. 106–108; 40, para. 122).

27. Thanks to Ángel Guerrero (2007, pers. comm.). *Ntinya* is used in reference to the birth of Abakuá in Usagaré (cf. Cabrera 1975: 21).

28. Contemporary Uruan leaders claim an identity separate from the Ìbìbìò, although Uruan communities were considered part of Ìbìbìò by colonial anthropologists (Obong Nyong 2005, pers. comm.; cf. Essien 1993). In Cuba, the Bibí are known as "Oru-Bibí" (Cabrera 1988a: 111).

29. Cf. Hart (1964: 25, para. 65; 28, para. 71, 72; 30, para. 85); Jones (1970: xiii); Latham (1973: 9–10, 97); Nair (1972: 5).

30. The date 1871 is sculpted in iron at the front of Munyánga Efó's temple, in the barrio La Cuevita (reparto Nuñez), San Miguel de Padrón.

31. In 1863 in the barrio of Jesús María, members of Efóri Enkomón separated and formed their own lodge, calling it Aterenyón Kamá Nankúku, with the sponsorship of Efóri Enkomón. In 1871, Aterenyón, together with Efóri Enkomón, founded Munyánga Efó. Aterenyón did not last long; its members were reintegrated into Efóri Enkomón (Andrés Flores, pers. comm.).

32. The term *okambo* is used to mean "the skin of an old drum," meaning an ancient lodge, age being a sign of its authority. See this reference in chapter 7, in the lyrics for "Protesta Carabalí." *Mbóri* (goat) is discussed in chapter 1.

33. Cf. Ortiz (1954: 80). *Guajíro* is a term derived from the Guajíro Indians from Venezuela, who were enslaved and brought to Cuba. Over time, Cuban peasants of primarily Spanish descent became known as *guajíros*, as in the classic song "Guajíro Guantanamera."

34. The Spanish guards were the infamous Volunteers discussed in chapter 5. Another early member of Munyánga Efó was Francisco Rodríguez Lavín, whose title was Mbákara; he was a foreman in the wharves and a Freemason.

35. See discussion of the lodge Eklé Entáti Machecheré in chapter 3. Nchemiya is mentioned in the Cuban book *Los Ñáñigos* (1882: 17).

36. Cf. Cabrera (1988a: 386). In other words, the Nchemiyá Ibonkó lodge represents the "sound of the Èfìk fundament drum," making it parallel in meaning to the Efó lodge, Efóri Búma (thunder of Efut), as discussed in chapter 3.

37. In Calabar Ékpè practice, Èfìk speakers pronounce *Ebonkó*, whereas Qua (Ejagham) speakers pronounce *Ebongó* (Etubom B. E. Bassey, pers. comm.). These distnctions are maintained in Cuban Abakuá, who use both terms: *bonkó* for the Èfìk-derived fundamento and *bongó* for the Efut-derived fundamento (cf. Cabrera 1988a: 117, 125; Ortiz 1954: 431).

38. The nineteenth-century Havana lodge Efí Akana Bióngo no longer exists. "Akani obio" is an Èfìk phrase for "old town" (see discussion in chapter 3). According to the writing in iron on the door of their temple in Guanabacoa, "Efinanqueregua Icanfioro Nancuco" was born in 1873. Cf. López-Valdés (1985: 166). On 19 April 1998, I participated in the 125th anniversary party for the lodge.

39. The title of this lodge is Ikanfioró Nankúko, Makarará Nankáiro Efímeremo Awaná kerobia asuku anándiwára bénge. This means "The tribe of albinos living in the land of volcanoes" (*Makarará* is interpreted as "'albino"; Andrés Flores, pers. comm.). "The albinos were named Ikanfioro Makarará nankáiro" (El Chino Mokóngo, pers. comm.); cf. Cabrera (1958: 72). For albinos in Calabar, cf. Goldie (1901/1890: 43); Waddell (1863: 617).

40. Cf. Cabrera (1958: 127).

41. Cf. Hart (1964: 119, para. 273); Nair (1972: 290). In Èfìk naming practice, the first son is named after the father; therefore Ekeng Ewa would be son of Ewa Ekeng.

42. Cf. Goldie (1964/1862: 124, 358); Nair (1972: 290). Ikang Efiom Ékpè is a village in Akpabuyo (Archibong Eso, Iyámba of Obutong 2005, pers. comm.).

43. Archibong Eso (2005, pers. comm.). That is, Ikang is the House name, whereas Fioró is a personal name.

44. Cabrera (1988a: 376).

45. Urua et al. (2004: 107).

46. Chief Nsan (2005, pers. comm.). "Ikot Ata Uko (the brave ones)" (Hart 1964: 30, para. 84). Adak-uko (pronounced Adaukó) is the Èfìk community in Obioko that produced Eyo Honesty II. Eken Ewa, Ikang, and Adak-uko are all Èfìk people (Chief Eyo 2005, pers. comm.).

47. Archibong Eso (2005, pers. comm.).

48. Matute (1988: 63, 1990: 9). Also used were white sheep, white goat, white chickens, and white cloth.

49. Cf. Tablot (1912a: 161).

50. The chant would be "Nyámkpè Okarará" (Engineer Bassey 2005, pers. comm.).

51. Chief Iyámba (2005, pers. comm.).

52. Cf. Cabrera (1958: 70). See discussion in chapter 3.

53. Cf. Ardener et al. (1960: xxiv); Baikie (1966/1856: 25–26).

54. Cf. Forde (1956); Oku (1989: 82–84).

55. Cf. Cabrera (1988a: 217).

56. Cabrera (1988a: 412); Guanche (1983: 420).

57. The history of this lodge remains unclear. Several Obónes told me that "Bongó Taiba" refers to Ekório Efó Taiba, their godfathers. El Chino Mokóngo told me that Enyón Bakokó, the lodge of Andrés Petit, was the sponsor.

58. A document from the Ekório Efó Taiba lodge from 1884 states that "Ecoria Efor number one" founded "Eceniñén Efó" [Enseniyén Efó] in 188(?) (*Causa* 1884: 91). Either the oral history of this lodge is lost or remains private. The Obón responsible for this group, who at the time had been an initiate for fifty-two years, told me that he learned the history of his juego from Sosa-Rodríguez's book (1982: 143). Those who know him told me this story was a ploy.

59. Goldie (1964/1862: 357)

60. Connell (2002, pers. comm.).

61. Engineer Bassey (2004).

62. Orok Edem (2001, pers. comm.).

63. Goldie (1964/1862: 79).

64. I heard the term *Nseniyen* chanted during a libation at the Itiat Usé Uruan. It was interpreted as "we initiate our children" (*eyen* are children; Chief Eyo 2008, pers. comm.). In Èfìk and Ìbìbìò, *Mban nseniyen* means "I am initiated unto my sons," meaning "I have initiated myself and my offspring." This is a boast that the speaker's status is very high (Iberedem Essien 2008, pers. comm.).

65. According to the date written on its temple, this lodge was born on 25 December 1877. The "juego Uruá Abacuá" appears in the book *Los Ñáñigos* (1882: 16). This lodge is also popularly known as "Abakuá Orú," and its temple is in Guanabacoa. On 26 December 1999, I witnessed the initiation of an Iyámba, an Mbákara, two Íremes, and another title into this lodge.

66. "La nación Caravalí Induri sobre nombramiento de capatáz del cavildo del Santo Cristo de Buen Viaje." Archivo Nacional de Cuba, Havana, fondo Escribanía de Gobierno, file 125, no. 3 fol. (Childs 2006b: 242, n. 54).

67. In one example: "N-dür'-i—ën-yïng, *n*. A name ascribed to one, a title" (Goldie 1964/1862: 208).

68. Engineer Bassey (2007, pers. comm.).

69. Cf. Cabrera (1988a: 454).

70. The year 1878 was reported by Trujillo y Monagas (1882: 370). A nineteenth-century document written by a member of the Ekório Efó Taiba lodge says that "Ecoria Efor 1" was founded in 1874 and that "Ecoria Efor 2" was founded in 1880 (*Causa* 1884: 39, 91).

71. The document internal to "Ecoria Efó Taiba," written before 1884, states that "Ecoria Efó Ita" founded "Enlleguellé Efó" (*Causa* 1884: 91). Ecoria Efó Ita is another name for Ekório Efó First. Secondary sources have Enyegueyé Efó founded in 1878 in Regla (Guanche 1983: 420) or in 1882 (López-Valdés 1985: 170).

72. "Yambéke Enyegueyé was the name of a prince of Efó who became the Iyámba" (Andrés Flores, El Chino Mokóngo, pers. comm.). Martín (1946: 18) wrote that in the Duala language of coastal Cameroon, "Enyegueyé, prince. In Duala, nyegeyé, teacher." Martín did not mention his sources.

73. See the discussion of the composition "Criolla Carabalí" (1928) in chapter 7.

74. Eningheye is in Akamkpa L.G.A, in Cross River State. Originally an Ejagham settlement, there are presently many Ìbìbìò inhabitants (Charles Effiong 2005, pers. comm.).

75. Aningeje was originally located on a beachhead just below the Great Kwa Falls, being the last (or first) river port of the route between Calabar and Oban. After a paved road was built to Oban in the twentieth century, the village and its Ṁgbè shrine were moved from the beach up the hill. Thanks to Ntufam John Achot Okon for bringing me to Aningeje, his hometown, and its Ṁgbè shrine in December 2005. "Anengeje . . . a segment of the Ekoi [ejagham] people" are reported to have had a settlement near Mamfe, in present-day Cameroon, centuries ago (Aye 2000: 245).

76. Both Enyegueyé Efó First and Enyegueyé Second disintegrated in the late nineteenth century. Another lodge from the same lineage was named Inyiguiyí by its founders (cf. Cabrera 1975: 326–327, 1988a: 238). Because Inyiguiyí was popularly known as Enyegueyé, these three lodges are often confused (cf. Brown 2003a: 23; Palmié 2006: 105).

77. Cf. Roche y Monteagudo (1925/1908: 68). A document of the Ekório Efó Taiba lodge states that Akanarán Efó Munyón (Mukarará Efó) founded Ebion Efó on 18 June 1882 in Guanabacoa (*Causa* 1884: 91). Ebión Efó continues to function today in the barrio of Pogolotti.

78. Cf. Cabrera (1977: 1). Because Indarte was a hereditary family title, one finds various references to Indartes in Abakuá history.

79. José-Miguel Gómez (2003). Following Abakuá custom, the title ends with the name of the sponsor, in this case Okobio Mukurará. Kufón is temple in Abakuá; in Èfìk, "house" is *ufok* (Waddell 1863: 675).

80. Cf. Cabrera (1988a: 138).

81. See discussion in appendix of chants.

82. On its temple in Guanabacoa is written "Eron Entati Ibiono, 1888." Both Deschamps-Chappeaux (1968a: 44) and Castellanos García (1948: 599) wrote their foundation date as 1898. *Ntá*, like *Entáti*, is interpreted as a form of *itá*, "first."

83. "Sheep" is *eröng* in Èfìk and Ìbìbìò (Goldie 1964/1862: 89, 597; Talbot 1912a: 433; Urua et al. 2004: 21, 43).

84. Cf. Cabrera (1958: 70, 1975: 328, 1992/1954: 284). In Èfìk, *N'-tan* is "earth," "sand," "clay" (Goldie 1964/1862: 229).

85. See the appendix of chants for interpretations.

86. Andrés Flores said: "The founders of Eron Entá Ibióno meant to say with this title that they were 'kings of the music,' but this title was rejected by the Africans because, according to the tratado of Munandiaga, the skin of the ram was not effective for the fundamento" Cf. Cabrera (1992/1954: 284). In the Cross River region, Talbot (1912a: 67–70) documented an explanation of why sheep are not "an acceptable offering" for sacrifice, but instead goats are used, as in Abakuá practice.

87. The phrase "Sése bíbio kóndo Orú" was recorded by Abakuá masters on *Ibiono* (2001), track 6 (at 8:00 minutes). Regarding the Orú/Bibí distinction, one Abakuá leader told me: "The Orú are Bibí, but not all Bibí are Orú. The Erón are Bibí, but they are not Orú" (Ángel Guerrero 2004, pers. comm.). If *Orú* is derived from *Uruan* on the Cross River, and *Bibí* is *Ìbìbìò*, this makes sense in a Cross River context, because Uruan is a small region within a much larger Ìbìbìò zone, and contemporary Uruan and Ìbìbìò neighbors consider themselves to have distinct histories and customs.

88. Cf. Cabrera (1988a: 214).

89. Andrés Flores distinguished "Achacha úcho" as a phrase in the Suáma language and "kambo" as a Bríkamo term for "old."

90. Chief Eyo (2005, pers. comm.).

91. The temple of Odán Efí Nankúko is in the barrio of Pueblo Nuevo. On 22 January 2000 this lodge swore in six title-holders: Iyámba, Mosóngo, Enkóboro, Moní Bonkó, Moruá Yuansa, and Abasí. I was present the next day when seven obonékues were sworn in.

92. Cf. Miller (2005). See discussion in appendix of chants.

93. Cf. Cabrera (1958: 80, 1988a: 450, 1992/1954: 205, 207).

94. Thompson (1983: 241). See Reid (1989: 19, fig. 3) for a map of this river in Cameroon.

95. Cf. Cabrera (1958: 264). The foundation of the Efí Guéremo lodge in 1893 was directed by a man called "El niño," who received the title of Enkríkamo in the process. He was the grandson of Manuel Platanal and the brother of "Camarón."

96. Ángel Guerrero (2004, pers. comm.). Cf. Cabrera (1958: 137, 1988a: 147, 200).

97. Cf. Cabrera (1988a: 150).

98. Cf. Cabrera (1975: 269, 292, 1988a: 150–152). The phrase "Efí méremo obón Efí" was recorded on the *Ibiono* (2001), track 3 ("Apapa Efí"). In the 1940s, Harold Courlander (1949) recorded this chant: "Ooo Ekue, Kisóngo Kinyóngo Efí Méremo/Ndèm Efí Ubáne." This can be interpreted as "the Ékpè title-holder called Efí Méremo was consecrated through Èfìk spirituality."

99. Cf. Hart (1964, 55, para. 158). For a discussion of Eyamba, see the appendix of chants.

100. Eyamba (2005, pers. comm.). Cf. Hart (56, para 160).

101. Chief Eyo (2005, pers. comm.). "Efiem Ekpo was grandson of Ibanga Nkantá." (Etubom B. E. Bassey 2005, pers. comm.). See details about Ibanga in the footnotes of the lodge Ibiabánga Munyón in this appendix.

102. Connell (2002, pers. comm.); Goldie (1894: 7–8); Hart (1964: 69, para. 188, 153); Miller (2005: 38–39); Oku (1989: 13); *Story of the Old Calabar* (1986: 124).

103. Hallet (1964: 199).

104. Oku (1989: 13).

105. Latham (1973: 47–48). Cf. Asuquo (1978: 36); Crow (1830: 272); Noah (1980: 58).

106. Efí Kondó was born on 5 July 1903, sponsored by Efí Mbemoró First of Matanzas (Soto Rodrí-guez 2005, pers. comm.). Cf. Cabrera (1988a: 148).

107. In Cuba Efí Kóndó (mokondó), like *akanawán*, is a reference to the full-body masquerade cos-tumes of the Íreme.

108. Goldie (1964/1862: 7, 80); Miller (2005). See appendix of chants for details.

109. Cf. Roche y Monteagudo (1925/1908: 93). This treaty is known as Efí Kinyóngo Ubáne.

110. Cf. Cabrera (1975: 387; 1992/1954: 403). Abakuá leader Gómez (2003) wrote, "In Efor there was no music like we play today; they played the marímbula." This type of instrument has variant styles and names across sub-Saharan Africa. Kubik (2001: 171) has coined the umbrella term *lamel-lophone*, since its "sound is generated essentially by the vibration of thin lamellae or tongues of metal, wood or other material." See also Kubik (1964).

111. Crow (1830: 277). See also Talbot (1969/1926: vol. 3, 812–813).

112. *Èkòng*, masquerade; *Ikọng*, leaf; *Ukòm*, plantain. This mask, related to the ancient Èfìk grade Nyanyaku, is evoked in contemporary practice with the diminutive 'Aku. Its function in Ékpè is purely spiritual and features prominently in propitiations to ancestors (Etubom B. E. Bassey 2005, pers. comm.).

113. Etubom B. E. Bassey (2005, pers. comm.). See also Aye (1991: 30).

114. See discussion in chapter 1. Cubans understand "Ubáne" as an Èfìk territory.

115. "Efí Kondó sponsored Efí Kunákua Enyuao on 31 May 1908 in Matanzas." (Soto Rodríguez May 2005, pers. comm.). Cf. Cabrera (1975: 356).

116. *Enyuáo* is used in the initiatory phrase "what is written cannot be erased," meaning that one is consecrated for life.

117. Chief Archibong Eso (2005, pers. comm.); Effiong (2005). Ekong Anaku, in Akamkpa L.G.A., has a beachhead on a tributary of the Akwa Yaffe River, giving it access to Calabar (Okon 2005, pers. comm.). Talbot (1912a: 84) wrote that the town of "Ekkonnanakku" was built around 1904, but like many other Cross River villages, its name may derive from an earlier settlement.

118. Cf. Cabrera (1988a: 141, 522). Another version of this title is Efí Etéte ekómbre awanasita moréré (Andrés Flores, pers. comm.).

119. Chief Archibong Eso (2005, pers. comm.); Chief Eyo (2005, pers. comm.). Cf. Goldie (1964/1862: 93). In Cuba, Efí Etete's elevated status is expressed in terms of its age (cf. Cabrera 1988a: 141).

120. This particular practice is used by lodges from Efó lineages, I am told, who *rompe* (commence) a key segment of their ceremonies by lighting gunpowder.

121. Cf. Harris (1972: 125). A cannon represents authority; they were received from British mer-chants by their Cross River business associates in the early 1800s.

122. Cf. Goldie (1964/1862: xlv); Urua et al. (2004: 25). Thanks to Etim Ika (2005, pers. comm.), Creek Town, in the patio of whose home is a cannon.

123. Barbot (1744: 456, 459, 461).

124. Latham (1990: 73).

125. Simmons (1956: 68) referred to Antera Duke's diary entry of 25 January 1785.

126. Hallett (1964: 198).

127. Hutchinson (1970/1858: 132).

128. Etubom Essien E. Efiok (2008, pers. comm.)

129. As told to me by contemporary Abakuá leaders. Cf. Ortiz (1954: 55)

130. Cf. Cabrera (1958: 65). Sierón Nampóto is the "younger brother" of Efí Etéte; they performed plantes (ceremonies) consecutively for many years in Matanzas, before moving to Cárdenas (cf.

Cabrera 1975: 45). Cabrera (1988a: 56) found that "Odán Èfìk sponsored Sierón." The leaders of Odán Efí, however, negated this in our conversations.

131. Because its title ends with "Ekueri Tongó," several Abakuá in Havana thought that Sierón Nampóto was founded by Ekueri Tongó of Havana. My research in Cárdenas found their sponsors to be Efí Kunákwa.

132. Cabrera (1988a: 482).

133. The name Henshaw Town derives from an English interpretation of "Ansa."

134. Chief Eso Archibong Eso (2005, pers. comm.).

135. Talbot (1969/1926: vol. 2, 342).

136. Cf. Talbot (1969/1926: vol. 2, 347, vol. 3, 782).

137. Engineer Bassey (2001/1998: 101).

138. In this myth, the stone (orí) had contact with the divine Fish. The Cuban lodge Bongó Orí was named after it (founded in 1946). See also Cabrera (1988a: 458).

139. The earliest Abakuá temple that I learned about was a humble wooden Fambá being used in Los Pocitos, outside of Havana, by 1900.

140. Cabrera (1958: 92, n. 4).

141. "Efí Kondó sponsored Efi Irondó Tai Bekó, on September 15, 1917, in Matanzas" (Soto Rodríguez 2005, pers. comm.). Cf. Cabrera (1975: 367).

142. Cabrera (1988a: 247). The mines of Abakuá myth were used to extract the sacred chalk used to mark initiates and draw signatures of authorization. There are several ancient chalk quarries in the Calabar region (Ekpo 2005: 47). The red and yellow chalk also used in Ékpè ceremony is made by cooking the white chalk with plant materials (Chief Eyo 2008, pers. comm.).

143. Idundu is a Qua clan in Akpabuyo L.G.A. (Ekpo 2005: 16, 146). Nair (1972: 3) reported that Idundu was founded by Efut migrants from Cameroon. Idundu is an Efut name (Ekpo 2005: 72).

144. Anderson (1933: 19–20, para. 58).

Appendix 2. Comparing Ékpè and Abakuá Masks and Their Symbols

1. Benítez-Rojo (2000, pers. comm.).

2. Cf. Ortiz (1991b: 233). British colonists also referred to African maskers as "devils" (cf. Beatty 1915: illustrations facing pages 15, 21, 28, 34).

3. In Calabar, the Ebonko grade would have an Obong Ebonko and an Isung Ebonko (cf. Engineer Bassey 2001/1998: 49–50). In the Cross River region, there are variations in the names and numbers of grades according to the ethnic community. In Cuba, there are also variations in each ethnic lineage.

4. This issue requires further research, specifically in Efut and Usaghade in West Africa (cf. Connell 2004: 234–235).

5. Deschamps-Chappeaux (1968b: 51).

6. Cf. Miller (2008).

7. Engineer Bassey (2004, pers. comm.).

8. Engineer Bassey (2004, pers. comm.). See corresponding drawing in Bassey (2001/1998: 77).

9. Brown (2003a: 129–130); Roche y Monteagudo (1908: 16); Thompson (1983: 266).

10. The headpiece of the Ídèm in Talbot's photo hangs downward, indicating the Nyámkpè grade for Calabar Ékpè (cf. Engineer Basssey 2001/1998: 70, 118). Talbot (1912a: 42) identified this Ídèm as "Nkanda" in 1912, but in a later publication (1926: 786) called it simply an Ékpè "Image." Despite the otherwise striking visual similarities, these two masks seem to have had distinct functions (Engineer Bassey 2004, pers. comm.).

11. Cf. Brown (2003a: 122–123); Palmié (2003: 19, 2006: 110); Palmié and Pérez (2005: 291).

12. Cf. Engineer Bassey (2001/1998: 67–71, 77).

13. Thompson (1983: 233) identifies the checked pattern as "signifying leopard pelt."

14. Deschamps-Chappeaux (1972a: 40).

15. Pichardo (1985/1875: 228).

16. Waddell's (1863: 354) description dates from 1847.

17. Ortiz (1950a: 27). See also Cabrera (1958: 203, 231, 257, 1975: 22).

18. Engineer Bassey (2004, pers. comm.). See also Engineer Bassey (2001/1998: 71).

19. Deschamps-Chappeaux (1972a: 40).

20. Cabrera (1975: 22, 1988a: 427). Abakuá beckon an Íreme with the phrase: "akamanyére nyáya," meaning "come Íreme" (Ángel Guerrero 2007, pers. comm.).

21. Cf. Engineer Bassey (2001/1998: 71, 174). The Cuban chest piece is greatly reduced from the Calabar model, likely for convenience of transportation and evading authorities (e.g., compare Figures 24 and 31). The Cuban mask in Figure 6 (right) has a much larger raffia chest, indicating that the tradition was not lost, merely modified. Calabar Ékpè confirm that their large round raffia chest piece is not a recent invention, but an integral part of the Ídèm's apparatus.

22. In Cuba, cf. Cabrera (1988a: 397); Salillas (1901: 357). In Calabar, cf. Goldie (1964/1862: 214); Waddel (1863: 354).

23. Deschamps-Chappeaux (1972a: 39). Also in Cuba, Jameson (1821: 21–22) referred to African cabildos and their use of bells and masquerades. An early description from Calabar is found in Waddel (1863: 354).

24. The most commonly seen Ékpè masks in Calabar are the Ídèm Ikwo, also called Ékpè runners or messengers (cf. Engineer Bassey 2001/1998: 106–107). These have a knitted suit with a small tuft of raffia on the head.

25. Meza (1891; cited in Ortiz 1960: 12). Meza was apparently describing a procession held before the 1884 prohibition that ended this tradition.

26. See Eliot Elisofon's photographs of "Ejagham Ekpe society leopard dancers, Big Qua Town, Nigeria," from 1959, in the archives of the Smithsonian Institution, Local Numbers: EEPA EECL 3757 (-3762), E2 EJG 5 EE59.

27. Cf. Thompson (1983: 248, 253).

28. Cf. Engineer Bassey (2001/1998: 94, 96–97). *Isim* is tail in Èfìk and Ìbìbìò (Urua et al. 2004: 60). The Isim Ékpè costumed dance, then, represents the tail of the leopard, but it is also adorned with peacock feathers. While Isim Ékpè are part of the Ebongo grade, their use of peacock feathers refers to *Nkàndà*, which literally means "peacock" in Èfìk. In Ékpè Èfìk practice, the Nkàndà grade mask (ídèm Nkàndà) often wears peacock feathers upon its head. The ntang Nkàndà (feather of Nkàndà) is placed on the head of Ékpè members after their initiation. The Nkàndà grade uses exclusively Ukara cloth (Chief Ekenyong Eyo 2007, pers. comm.; Etubom Bassey 2007, pers. comm.; Urua et al. 2004: 99; cf. Aye 2000: 82).

29. Trujillo y Monagas (1882: 364).

30. Francisco Zamora "Minini" (2000, pers. comm.). Cf. Cabrera (1975: 35).

31. Cf. Engineer Bassey (2001/1998: 106–107).

32. Engineer Bassey (2001/1998: 39–40).

33. Engineer Bassey (2001/1998: 26–27); Thompson (1983: 260–262).

34. The five rhythms used in Ékpè ceremonial music are used for the titles of Ebongó, Nyámkpè, Okpoho, Oku Akama, and Nkàndà. The titles Iyámba and Mbàkàrà have no specific rhythms (Ika 2008, pers. comm.).

35. Etubom B. E. Bassey (2004, pers. comm.). This was in response to "Criolla Carabali" by Septeto Habanero, and *Ibiono* (2001) specifically, as well as other tracks in general.

36. Thompson (1983: 264–266).

37. Cf. Aye (1991: 39); Engineer Bassey (2001/1998: 27).

38. Calabar Ékpè leaders were of two opinions about the specific grade of the mask in the Ward (1911) photograph. Its outline is clearly that of Ebongo, while the projections on the back appear to be those of the Oku Akama mask. It nevertheless remains the earliest photograph known to the author of the Ebongo form from Calabar.

39. Akuaramína, spirit (Andrés Flores, pers. comm.). "Akuaramína ngo, a spirit that appeared to give faith when Efó was consecrating the baróko of Orú" (El Chino Mokóngo). "Akuaramína Orú" (Abelardo Empegó). "Akuaramina" (Cabrera 1958: frontispiece, 1988a: 42–43).

40. The earliest photo known to me of the *basonko* was taken in Calabar in the early 1900s (cf. Nicklin and Salmons 1988: fig. 1).

41. Cf. Onyile (2000); "Efik Dances" (1957).

42. "Jaw-Bone or House John Canoe," 1837–1838, *Sketches of Character*. Barbaro Martínez-Ruíz (2007: 112) confirmed this interpretation with Abakuá title-holder Felipe García Villamil of Matanzas.

43. Also referred to as Nyanyanga-yaku (Etubom B. E. Bassey 2004, pers. comm.; cf. Aye 2000: 70–72). The modernization of Ékpè occurred during the settlement of Creek Town.

44. Cf. Cabrera (1975: 22).

45. Ángel Guerrero (2007, pers. comm.)

46. Pronounced either "eri" or "edi" (Engineer Bassey 2004, pers. comm.).

47. Cf. Cabrera's description of the practice of an Efó lineage (Cabrera 1975: 39, 58).

48. Engineer Bassey (2004, pers. comm.)

49. Cf. Cabrera (1958: 206, 213, 1988a: 397).

50. Engineer Bassey (2004, pers. comm.).

Appendix 3. Abakuá Chants and Their Interpretations in Cross River Languages

1. Abímbọ́lá and Miller (1997: 140); Abímbọ́lá (1998).

2. Meek (1937: 73). See also Ruel (1969: 245).

3. Manfredi (1991: 265–173). See Anderson and Kreamer (1989: 73) for an example from Togo.

4. Akuetey (1998–1999: 83)

5. Thornton (1998b: 57).

6. Dennett (1887: 159).

7. Jones (1984: 63) observed that generally throughout eastern Nigeria each secret "society had its secret language and most societies had their own special forms of communication, either by signs or through voice disguisers."

8. Cf. Cabrera (1975: 36).

9. I have replaced the umlaut (two dots over a vowel) as used by Goldie in the old Èfik orthography with the subdot, as used in the current official orthography for Èfik, as well as Ìgbo and Yorùbá (cf. Essien c. 1982, 1985).

10. Narratives of conflicts between settlements where the victor takes an important drum and masks from the defeated are known Cross River region. For an example from Balondoland, see Nebengu (1990: 38).

11. Bekura (Bekora) is considered a Barombi settlement. It is a short drive from Ekondo Titi, a Balondo settlement. I thank the village head of Bekura Barombi, Chief Nyuja Ndengi George, whose title is Isong in the M̀gbè lodge, for receiving me in 2004.

12. Cf. Cabrera (1975: 90, 183, 189, 273, 388, 1992/1954: 285).

13. For examples, see Cabrera (1988a: 84, 1992/1954: 285).

14. Engineer Bassey (2004, pers. comm.).

15. For Cuba, cf. Ortiz (1954: vol. 4, 13).

16. The Nkàndà grade used four drums in a performance I witnessed by the Osam M̀gbè Big Qua Town, 31 December 2005.

17. Cabrera (1958: 89) documented a parallel interpretation.

18. Abiakpo Ikot Essien, a village community in Uyo Division (Lieber 1971: 48).

19. Cabrera (1988a: 144).

20. Irióngo has been interpreted in Èfìk as "idiongo," in this context, "the heart of Ékpè." Thus, "Atakpa is the center of Èfìk Ékpè."

21. In Èfìk, *Atakpa* means "real river" (or main river), as this was the Èfìk settlement on the Calabar River closest to the larger Cross River, before their merging with the Atlantic Ocean (Nair 1972: 5). See also Talbot (1969/1926: vol. 1, 185, 190); Waddell (1863: 309).

22. Connell (2007, pers. comm.) pointed out that in Èfìk, it would be "Èkòmò Efut."

23. Essien (1986: 9, 2005: 344) reported *ídẹm* as "masquerade" in Ìbìbìò with a falling tone over the "e." Depending upon the tones used, *ídém* is "body," but *ídèm* "is masquerade" (Etubom B. E. Bassey 2006, pers. comm.). After research in Calabar, I learned that the term as published earlier "ìdèm" was inaccurate (Miller 2005: 25), the correct tones being high, low.

24. Cabrera (1988a: 265, 495, 318). Consistent with the Cuban interpretations of *ékue* as a fish that emitted a sound like a leopard's roar, in Ìbìbìò *ékúè* is a large fish (Urau et al. 2004: 46).

25. Cf. Cabrera (1975: 20).

26. Cf. Cabrera (1988a: 20).

REFERENCES

■ ■ ■

Publications and Interviews

Abímbọ́lá, Wáńdé. 1973. The literature of the Ifá cult. In *Sources of Yorùbá History*. Ed. S. O. Biobaku. Oxford Studies in African Affairs. Oxford: Clarendon Press. Pp. 41–62.

Abímbọ́lá, Wáńdé. 1977. *Ifá Divination Poetry*. New York: NOK.

Abímbọ́lá, Wáńdé. 1998. Personal communication with the author. Cambridge, MA. 12 December.

Abímbọ́lá, Wáńdé, and Ivor Miller. 1997. *Ifá Will Mend Our Broken World: Thoughts on Yorùbá Culture in West Africa and the Diaspora*. Roxbury, MA: AIM Books.

Abraham, R. C. 1958. *Dictionary of Modern Yorùbá*. London: University of London Press.

Abreu, Richardo "Papín." 1999. One of four brothers in the rumba group Los Papines, Papín holds the title of Enkóboro in the Abakuá lodge Irongrí Efó. Interview on 20 April 1999, Havana.

Accounts and Papers. 1849. Contained in the Sessional Papers printed by order of the House of Lords, or presented by Royal Command. Vol. 19. London.

Achebe, Chinua. 1984/1959. *Things Fall Apart*. New York: Ballantine Books.

Acosta, Leonardo. 2003. *Cubano Be Cubano Bop: One Hundred Years of Jazz in Cuba*. Washington, DC: Smithsonian Books.

Acosta, Leonardo. 2004. *Otra vision de la música popular cubana*. Havana: Editorial letras cubanas.

Adams, Captain John. 1823/1822. *Remarks on the Country Extending from Cape Palmas to the River Congo; Including Observation on the Manners and Customs of the Inhabitants*. London.

Afigbo, Adiele E. 1981. *Ropes of Sand: Studies in Igbo History and Culture*. Ibadan, Nigeria: University Press Limited.

Agbor Esija, Okim. 2008. Conversations with H. H. Okim Agbor Esija, clan head of Ikom, village head of Abokim Ngbabor, Ikom Town, February.

Aimes, Hubert H. S. 1907. *A History of Slavery in Cuba, 1511–1868*. New York: G. P. Putnam's Sons.

Akak, Eyo Okon. 1982. *Efiks of Old Calabar*. Vol. 3, *Culture and Superstitions*. Calabar: Akak and Sons.

Akan, Chief Efiong D. Akan. 1992. When Nsomm Uruan Goes Home: Souvenir Programme for Final Traditional Burial Rites and Royal Obsequies of His Royal Highness Late Edidem Atakpor James Udo-Affia, the Nsomm of Uruan. Archives of Obong Nyong, Uyo.

Akanawán, Okpo. 2005. A priestess of the Ndèm diety. Conversations with the author in the home shrine of Okpo Akanawán. Ikot Esu town, Ikot Esu District, an Èfìk settlement part of Creek Town. February. Thanks to Mr. Etim Ika for facilitating this meeting.

Akpabot, Samuel Ekpe. 1971. Standard drum patterns in Nigeria. *African Music: Journal of the African Music Society* 5(1): 37–39.

Akpabot, Samuel Ekpe. 1975. *Ibibio Music in Nigerian Culture*. East Lansing: Michigan State University Press.

Akpabot, Samuel Ekpe. 1975–1976. The talking drums of Nigeria. *African Music: Journal of the African Msuic Society* 5(4): 36–40.

Akpanim, Chief Bassey O. 1998. Oron identity. In *The Oron Nation in Contemporary Nigeria*. Ed. O. E. Uya. Calabar, Nigeria. Pp. 19–39.

Akuetey, Caesar. 1998–1999. A preliminary study of Yevegbe: animist cult language in Eweland. *Journal of West African Languages* 27(1): 83–94.

Alagoa, E. J. 1971. Nineteenth-century revolutions in the eastern Delta States and Calabar. *Journal of the Historical Society of Nigeria* 5(4): 565–573.

Alagoa, E. J. 1998. Letter to the author. Department of History, Uniport, Nigeria, 13 April.

Alagoa, E. J. 1999/1980. The eastern Niger Delta and the Hinterland in the nineteenth century. In *Groundwork of Nigerian History*. Ed. Obaro Ikime. Ibandan, Nigeria: Heinemann Educational Books. Pp. 249–261.

Alfaro Echevarria, Luis. 1981. Elementos lexicales del español en los rituals afrocubanos. *Islas* 68: 179–209.

Alfonso Ballol, Berta, Mercedes Herrera Sorzano, Eudardo Moyano, Jesús Sanz Fernández, and Martín Socarras Matos. 1987. *El camino de hierro de la Habana a Güines: primer ferrocarril de Iberoamérica*. Madrid: Fundación de los Ferrocarriles Españoles.

Amankulor, Jas N. 1972. Ékpè festival as religious ritual and dance drama. *Ikenga: Journal of African Studies* 1.2(July): 37–47.

Amoah, F. E. K. 1992. Oral tradition and ethnicity in the creation of new states in Nigeria: the case of Akwa Ibom. *Research Review Institute of African Studies* n.s. 8(1–2): 76–89.

Andah, B. W. 1990. Prehistory of the upper Cross River people. In *History and Culture of the Upper Cross River*. Ed. S. O. Jaja, E. O. Erim, B. W. Andah. Enugu, Nigeria: Harris Publishers Ltd. Pp. 27–37.

Anderson, H. O. 1933. An Intelligence Report on the Isangeli Community of the Kumba Division, Cameroons Province. South West Provincial Archives, Buea.

Anderson, Martha G., and Christine Mullen Kreamer. 1989. *Wild Spirits, Strong Medicine: African Art and the Wilderness*. New York: Center for African Art.

Andrews, George Reid. 1980. *The Afro-Argentines of Buenos Aires, 1800–1900*. Madison: University of Wisconsin Press.

Andueza, José María de. 1841. *Isla de Cuba, pintoresca, histórica, literaria, mercantil é industrial*. Madrid.

Anene, J. C. 1966. *Southern Nigeria in Transition, 1885–1906*. London: Cambridge University Press.

Anene, J. C. 1970. *International Boundaries of Nigeria, 1885–1960: The Framework of an Emergent African Nation*. New York: Humanities Press.

Angarica, Mayito. 1993. Sr. Angarica is a babaláwo and grandson of Nicolás Angarica. Interview in the home of Idania Díaz, barrio de Colón, Habana, June.

Aniyom, Chief Onun D. A. 2005. Chief Aniyom is popularly known as "the encyclopedia of Umon"; he has been the Secretary of the Umon Clan since 1980, and holds the Mboko grade in Ékpè Umon. Conversations with the author in Calabar and Umon, January through March 2005.

Anoka, Kemjika, ed. 1979. *Pronouncing Dictionary of Igbo Place Names*. Oweri, Nigeria: Minstry of Information Cultural Division.

Anonymous. 1990s. Interviews by the author with Abakuá elders who did not want their names revealed. Havana and Matanzas, Cuba, from 1993 to 1999.

Anwana, Asuquo Okon. 2002. *Ekpe Imperium in South-Eastern Nigeria, 1600–1900*. Ph.D. diss., University of Calabar.

Archibong Eso, Chief Eso. 2004, 2005. Obong Iyámba of Efe Ékpè Asibong Ekondo of Obutong. Conversations with the author in Chief Archibong's home, Obutong, Calabar. Thanks to Asibong Eso Asibong, Chief Eso's son, for translations of Èfìk terms.

Ardener, Edwin. 1968. Documentary and linguistic evidence for the rise of the trading politics between Rio del Rey and Cameroons, 1500–1650. In *History and Social Anthropology*. Ed. I. M. Lewis. London: Tavistock. Pp. 81–126.

Ardener, Edwin. 1996. *Kingdom on Mount Cameroon: Studies in the History of the Cameroon Coast, 1500–1970*. Ed. Shirley Ardener. Providence, RI: Berghahn Books.

Ardener, Edwin, Shirley Ardener, and W. A. Warmington. 1960. *Plantation and Village in the Cameroons: Some Economic and Social Studies*. Nigerian Institute of Social and Economic Research. London: Oxford University Press.

Ardener, Shirley G. 1968. *Eye Witnesses to the Annexation of Cameroon (1883–1887)*. Ministry of Primary Education and West Cameroon Antiquities Commission. Buea: Government Press.

Armstrong, Robert G. 1954. Talking drums in the Benue–Cross River region of Nigeria. *Phylon* 15(4): 355–363.

Arrate, José Martín Félix de. 1949/1830. *Llave del Nuevo Mundo; antemural de las Indias occidentales. La Habana descripta: noticias de su fundación, aumentos y estado*. México: Fondo de cultura económica. [Written in 1761.]

Arrom, José Juan. 1983. Cimmarrón: apuntes sobre sus primeras documentaciones y su probable origin. *Revista española de antropología americana* (Madrid) 1: 47–57.

Asuquo, Chief Ukorebi U. 1978. The diary of Antera Duke of Old Calabar (1785–1788). *The Calabar Historical Journal* 2(1): 32–54.

Austen, Ralph A., and Jonathon Derrick. 1999. *Middlemen of the Cameroons Rivers: The Duala and Their Hinterland, c. 1600–1960*. Cambridge, UK: Cambridge University Press.

Àyándélé, E. A. 1966. *The Missionary Impact of Mondern Nigeria, 1842–1914: A Political and Social Analysis*. London: Longmans.

Aye, Efiong U. 1967. *Old Calabar through the Centuries*. Calabar: Hope Waddell Press.

Aye, Efiong U. 1991. *A Learner's Dictionary of the Èfìk Language*. Vol. 1, *Èfìk–English*. Ibadan, Nigeria: Evans Brothers Ltd.

Aye, Efiong U. 1994. *Akpabuyo in Transition*. Calabar: Appellac.

Aye, Efiong U. 2000. *The Èfìk People*. Calabar: Appellac.

Aye, Efiong U. 2005. Efik origins, migrations and settlement. In *The Efiks and Their Neighbours: Historical Perspecitives*. Ed. O. Uya, E. Aye, E. Nsan, E. Ndiyo. Calabar, Nigeria. Pp. 1–30.

Bacardí Moreau, Emilio. 1973. *De Cuba A Chafarinas: El denunciante de Pintó Epistolario (Obras completas de E.B.M reeditadas por Amalia Bacardí Cape)*. Madrid: Playor.

Bachiller y Morales, Antonio. 1883. *Cuba primitiva: Origen, lenguas, tradiciones e historia de los Indios de las Antillas Mayores y las Lucayas*. 2nd ed., corregida y aumentada. Havana: Miguel de Villa.

Baikie, William Balfour. 1966/1856. *Narrative of an Exploring Voyage up the Rivers Kwóra and Bínue (Commonly Known as the Niger and Tsádda) in 1854*. London: Frank Cass and Co.

Balmaseda, Francisco-Javier. 1869. *Los confinados a Fernando Póo e impresiónes de un viage a Guinea*. New York: Imprenta de la Revolución.

Barbot, Jean. 1744. An abstract of a voyage to New Calabar River, or Rio Real, in the year 1699. In *A Collection of Voyages and Travels, Some Now First Printed from Original Manuscripts, Others Now First Published in English*. 3rd ed., vol. 5. Ed. Awnsham Churchill. London. Pp. 455–466.

Barnet, Miguel. 1995. *Cultos afrocubanos: La Regla de Ocha; La Regla de Palo Monte*. Havana: Ediciones Unión.

Bascom, William R. 1952. Two forms of Afro-Cuban divination. In *Acculturation in the Americas: Proceedings and Selected Papers of the Twenty-ninth International Congress of Americanists*. Vol. 2. Ed. Sol Tax. Chicago: University of Chicago Press. Pp. 169–179.

Bassey, "Demmy." 2005. Mrs. Bassey (d. 2007) was a member of the Efe Ékpè Iyámba lodge of Atakpa and former highlife musician and composer who played in Ghana in the 1960s. Conversations with the author.

Bassey, Edang Yolanda Ekpo. 2008. Mrs. Bassey is a journalist and poet who hails from urban Ikom.

Bassey, Engineer Bassey Efiong. 2001/1998. *Ekpe Efik: A Theosophical Perspective*. Victoria, BC: Trafford.

Bassey, Engineer Bassey Efiong. 2004–2008. Bassey is an Ekpe title-holder. Conversations with the author in Chief Engineer Bassey's home, Calabar.

Bassey, Engineer Bassey Efiong. 2007. Letters to the author in response to questions about Ékpè history and interpreting Cuban phrases. 4 May, 8 June, 16 June.

Bassey, Etubom Bassey Ekpo. 2004–2005. Etubom Bassey is head of the King James Royal House of Cobham town (Ekoretonko). The House is in Calabar, Akpabuyo, Bakassi, and James Town in Akua Ibom State. He is chairman of the Cobhom Town Combined Council, that is, all the holdings and settlements of Cobham Town in the region. He is also Iyámba of Efe Ékpè Eyo Ema. In April 2008, as this study went to press, Bassey was capped as the Obong of Calabar. Conversations with the author, Calabar.

Bassey, P. O. E. 1999/1987. *A History of Oban, with Commentary*. 2nd ed. Port Harcourt: Riverside Communications.

Bassey, P. O. E. 2004. Bassey held the M̀gbè grade of Ntoe Okpoho in Big Qua Town until his death in February 2005. He was the first indigenous High Court Judge of Southeastern Nigeria. Interview with the author in Chief Honorable Bassey's home, Big Qua Town, Calabar.

Bassey Anating-Edem VI, Muri Joseph. 2004. Muri Bassey is the Clan Head of Efut Ekondo Clan, Calabar South L.G.A. He holds a title in the Efe Ékpè Atu Efut Ekondo. Conversations with the author, Calabar.

Bauza, Vanessa. 2003. Carnival runs in troupe director's blood. *South Florida Sun-Sentinel* 18 November.

Beatty, Kenneth James. 1915. *Human Leopards: An Account of the Trials of Human Leopards before the Special Commission Court; with a Note on Sierra Leone, Past and Present*. London: Hugh Rees, Ltd.

Becroft, Captain J. B. King. 1844. Details of explorations of the Old Calabar River, in 1841 and 1842. *Journal of the Royal Geographical Society of London* 14: 260–283.

Behrendt, Stephen, and Eric Graham. 2003. African merchants, notables and the slave trade at Old Calabar, 1720: evidence from the National Archives of Scotland. *History in Africa* 30: 37–61.

Ben-Amos, Paula. 1983. The power of kings: symbolism of a Benin ceremonial stool. In *The Art of Power/The Power of Art: Studies in Benin Iconography*. Eds. Paula Ben-Amos and Arnold Rubin. Los Angeles: UCLA Museum of Cultural History. Pp. 51–58.

Benítez-Rojo, Antonio. 1986. Power/sugar/literature: toward a reinterpretation of Cubaness. *Cuban Studies* 16: 9–31.

Benítez-Rojo, Antonio. 1996a. *The Repeating Island: The Caribbean and the Postmodern Perspective*. 2nd ed. Trans. James E. Maraniss. Durham, NC: Duke University Press.

Benítez-Rojo, Antonio. 1996b. The nineteenth-century Spanish American novel. In *The Cambridge History of Latin American Literature*. Vol. 1, *Discovery to Modernism*. Ed. Roberto González

Echevarría and Enrique Pupo-Walker. Cambridge, UK: Cambridge University Press. Pp. 417–489.

Benítez-Rojo, Antonio. 1996–2004. Conversations with the author, Amherst, MA.

Bergad, Laird W., Fe Iglesias García, and María del Carmen Barcia. 1995. *The Cuban Slave Market, 1790–1880*. Cambridge, UK: Cambridge University Press.

Berlin, Ira. 1998. *Many Thousands Gone: The First Two Centuries of Slavery in North America*. Cambridge, MA: The Belknap Press of Harvard University Press.

Bianchi Ross, Ciro. 2005. *Memoria oculta de la Habana*. Havana: Ediciones Union.

Bilby, Kenneth. 2006. *True-Born Maroons*. Gainesville: University Press of Florida.

Blanco, Domingo. 1900. Los Ñáñigos, cómo nacieron, su objeto, sus ceremonias. *Alrededor del Mundo* 2(37): 147–148.

Blanco-Aguilar, Jesús. 1992. *80 años de son y soneros en el Caribe, 1909–1989*. Caracas: Editorial Tropykos.

Blanco-Aguilar, Jesús. 2000. La fiesta cubana rumba. *Revista Salsa Cubana* 4(11): 13–16.

Blanco Fernández, Guillermo. 1998. Sr. Blanco is the Mokóngo of the group Muñánga Efó. Conversation at the temple of Muñánga Efó, San Miguel de Padrón, Havana, April.

Blier, Suzanne Preston. 1995. Path of the leopard: motherhood and majesty in early Danhomè. *Journal of African History* 36(3): 391–417.

Boccaccio, Giovanni. 1995. *The Decameron*. 2nd ed. Introduction, notes, and translation by G. H. McWilliam. New York: Penguin Books.

Bolívar Aróstegui, Natalia, and Carmen González. 1998. *Ta makuende yaya y las relgas de Palo Monte: mayombe, brillumba, kimbisa, shamalongo*. Havana: Ediciones Unión.

Bolster, W. Jeffrey. 1997. *Black Jacks: African American Seamen in the Age of Sail*. Cambridge, MA: Harvard University Press.

Bourdieu, Pierre. 1994. Rites of institution. In *Language and Symbolic Power*. Ed. John B. Thompson, trans. G. Raymond and M. Adamson. Cambridge, MA: Harvard University Press. Pp. 117–126.

Brain, R. 1981. The Fentem-Bangwa: a western Bamileke group. In *The Contribution of Ethnological Research to the History of Cameroon Cultures*. Vol. 2, no. 551. Ed. Claude Tardits. Paris: Éditions du centre national de la recherché scientifique. Pp. 355–360.

Brandon, George. 1993. *Santería from Africa to the New World: The Dead Sell Memories*. Bloomington: Indiana University Press.

Brandon, George. 2004. How Elegba was born: memory, death, and rebirth in Yoruba spirituality. *Contours: A Journal of the African Diaspora* 2(2): 157–173.

Brathwaite, Edward Kamau. 1971. *The Development of Creole Society in Jamaica, 1770–1820*. Oxford: Clarendon Press.

Brathwaite, Edward Kamau. 1985/1974. *Contradictory Omens: Cultural Diversity and Integration in the Caribbean*. Kingston, Jamaica: Savacou Publications.

Bremer, Fredrika. 1853. *The Homes of the New World: Impressions of America*. Vol. 2. Trans. Mary B. Howitt. New York: Harper and Bros.

Brown, David H. 2003a. *The Light Inside: Abakuá Society Arts and Cuban Cultural History*. Washington, DC: Smithsonian Institution Press.

Brown, David H. 2003b. *Santería Enthroned: Art, Ritual, and Innovation in an Afro-Cuban Religion*. Chicago: University of Chicago Press.

Bueno, Salvador. 1985. *Costumbristas cubanos del siglo XIX*. Caracas, Venezuela: Biblioteca Ayacucho.

Burrows, Edwin, and Mike Wallace. 1999. *Gotham: A History of New York City to 1898*. New York: Oxford University Press.

Burton, Richard F. 1969/1865. *Wit and Wisdom from West Africa*. New York: Negro University Press.

Caballero, Orlando. 2005. The Mokóngo of Efí Embemoró. Conversation in Sr. Caballero's home, Miami, FL, 7 November.

Cabrera, Lydia. 1950. La Ceiba y la sociedad secreta Abakuá. *Orígenes* 7(24): 16–47.

Cabrera, Lydia. 1958. *La Sociedad Secreta Abakuá: narrada por viejos adeptos*. Havana: Ediciones C.R.

Cabrera, Lydia. 1969. Ritual y símbolos de la iniciación en la Sociedad Secreta Abakuá. *Journal de la Société des Américanistes* (Paris) 58: 139–171.

Cabrera, Lydia. 1970. Refranes Abakuas. *Refranes de Negros Viejos: Recogidos por Lydia Cabrera*. Miami: Colección del Chicherekú.

Cabrera, Lydia. 1972. *Cuentos Negros de Cuba*. 2nd ed. Madrid: Colección del Chicherukú en el exilio.

Cabrera, Lydia. 1974. Refranes Abakuá; Folklore Infantil. In *La Enciclopedia de Cuba*. Vol. 6. San Juan-Madrid: Editorial Playor. Pp. 375–378, 401–408.

Cabrera, Lydia. 1975. *Anaforuana: Ritual y símbolos de la iniciación en la sociedad secreta Abakuá*. Madrid: Ediciones Madrid.

Cabrera, Lydia. 1976. *Francisco y Francisca: Chascarillos de negros viejos*. Miami: Colección del Chicherekú en el exilio.

Cabrera, Lydia. 1977. *La Regla Kimbisa del Santo Cristo del Buen Viaje*. Miami: Colección del Chicherekú en el exilio.

Cabrera, Lydia. 1979. *Relgas de Congo: Palo Monte Mayombe*. Miami: Peninsular.

Cabrera, Lydia. 1984. *Vocabulario Congo (El Bantú que se habla en Cuba)*. Miami: Colección del Chicherekú en el exilio.

Cabrera, Lydia. 1988a. *La Lengua Sagrada de los Ñáñigos*. Miami: Colección del Chicherekú en el exilio.

Cabrera, Lydia. 1988b. *Los animals en el folklore y la magia de Cuba*. Miami: Ediciones Universal.

Cabrera, Lydia. 1992/1954. *El Monte*. Miami: Colección del Chicherekú en el exilio.

Cabrera, Lydia. 1994. *Páginas Sueltas*. Ed., introduction, and notes by Isabel Castellanos. Miami: Ediciones Universal.

Cabrera, Lydia. 1996/1980. *Yemayá y Ochún: Kariocha, Iyalorichas y Olorichas*. Miami: Ediciones Universal.

Cabrera, Lydia. 2000/1969. Ritual y símbolos de la iniciación en la Sociedad Secreta Abakuá. *Catauro: Revista cubana de antropología* 1(1): 130–164.

Cabrera, Lydia. 2004. *Afro-Cuban Tales*. Trans. A. Hernández-Chiroldes and L. Yoder. Lincoln: University of Nebraska Press.

Cabrera, Raimundo. 1888. *Del parque a la luna*. Zarzuela. Revista comico-lirica sobre asuntos cubanos en un acto y en verso. Havana: Imprenta El retiro.

Cabrera, Raimundo. 1892. *Cartas a Govín: impresiones de viaje*. Havana: La Moderna.

Cabrera, Raimundo. 1896. *Cuba and the Cubans*. Trans. Laura Guiteras from the 8th Spanish ed. of *Cuba y sus jueces*. Philadelphia: The Levytype Co.

Cabrera-Peña, Miguel. 2007. Bárbara's son: the influence of Juan Gualberto Gómez on the political and journalistic trajectory of Lino D'Ou. *Islas* 2(7): 26–36.

Cairo, Ana. 2005. *Bembé para cimarrones*. Havana: Publicacions Acuario.

Calderón, Rebeca, Elsa Almaguer, and Milagros Villalón. 2000. Bantúes en la jurisdicción de Cuba: consideraciones tipológicas. *Del Caribe* (Santiago de Cuba) 31: 60–65.

Camejo P., José. 1910. Boceto historico del general Quintin Bandera, héroe de la Trocha de Mariel. In *Apuntes para la historia. Lacret y Banderas: dos heroes*. Havana: El Crisol. Pp. 28–59.

Camero, Candido. 2005. Mr. Camero is among the most influential Cuban percussionists in twentieth- century United States. Video-taped conversation with Román Díaz and the author, backstage before the "Noches Cubanas" concert at the World Music Institute, New York University, April.

Campos-Cárdenas, Juan "Chang." 2006. Chang is a title-holder in the Muñánga Efó lodge and founding member of the rumba group Yoruba Andabo. Conversations with the author in Havana, February.

Cantón-Navarro, José. 1998. *History of Cuba: The Challenge of the Yoke and the Star*. Havana: Editorial SI-MAR.

Carbonell, Luis. 2000. Luis Carbonell (b. 1923) is a performance artist whose recitals of poetry and short stories of Afro-Cuban and Afro-Antillian themes made him famous as "the water colorist of Antillian poetry." Interview with the author in his home, Havana.

Carney, Judith. 2001. *Black Rice: The African Origins of Rice Cultivation in the Americas*. Cambridge, MA: Harvard University Press.

Carpentier, Alejo. 1989/1946. *La música en Cuba*. 2nd ed. Havana: Editorial Pueblo y educación.

Castañeda, Digna. 1995. The female slave in Cuba during the first half of the nineteenth century. In *Engendering History: Caribbean Women in Historical Perspective*. Ed. Verene Shepherd, Bridget Brereton, Barbara Bailey. New York: St. Martin's Press. Pp. 141–154.

Castellanos García, Gerardo. 1948. *Relicario histórico: frutos coloniales y de la vieja Guanabacoa*. Havana: Editorial Libreria Selecta.

Castillo, Andrés. 198?. Alberto Zayas "El Melodioso." "Nuestros Artistas" section of a Guanabacoa bulletin. Cuba.

Causa criminal seguida de oficio contra Santiago Martín Llanelis y otros por asociación ilícita. 1884. 4 de noviembre, Archivo Nacional, Fondo Asuntos Políticos, Legajo 80, Exp. no. 10.

Centro de Estudios Militares. 2001–2005. *Diccionario enciclopédico de historia militar de Cuba: primera parte (1510–1898)*. 3 vols. Havana: Ediciones Verde Olivo.

Centro de investigación y desarrollo de la música cubana. 1997. *Instrumentos de la música folclórico-popular de Cuba*, vol 1. Havana: Editorial de ciencias sociales.

Chappottín, Miguel, Jr. 2006. Conversations with the author in Chappottín's (b. 1927, Habana) home, Old Havana. 15, 16, 25 February.

Childs, Matt. 2006a. *The 1812 Aponte Rebellion in Cuba*. Chapel Hill: University of North Carolina Press.

Childs, Matt. 2006b. The defects of being a black creole: the degrees of African identity in the Cuban Cabildos de Nación, 1790–1820. In *Slaves, Subjects, and Subversives: Blacks in Colonial Latin America*. Ed. Jane Landers and Barry Robinson. Albuquerque: University of New Mexico Press. Pp. 209–245.

Chilver, E. M. 1962. Nineteenth-century trade in the Bamenda Grassfields, Southern Cameroons. *Afrika und Übersee* 45(4): 233–257.

Chilver, E. M., and P. M. Kaberry. 1967. The Kingdom of Kom in West Cameroon. In *West African Kingdoms in the Nineteenth Century*. Ed. D. Forde and P. M. Kaberry. London: Oxford University Press. Pp. 123–151.

Clarkson, Thomas. 1789. *The Substance of the Evidence of Sundry Persons on the Slave-Trade, Collected in the Course of a Tour Made in the Autumn of the Year 1788*. London.

Clarkson, Thomas. 1968/1808. *The History of the Rise, Progress, and Accomplishment of the Abolition of the African Slave-Trade by the British Parliament*. Vol. 1. London: Frank Cass.

Clinton, J. V. 1961. King Eyo Honesty II of Creek Town. *Nigeria Magazine* 69: 182–188.

Cofiño, Manuel. 1977. *Cuando la sangre se parece al fuego*. Havana: Editorial de arte y literature.

Cohen, Peter F. 1999. Pierre Fatumbi Verger as social scientist. *Cahiers de Brésil Contemporain* 38/39: 127–151.

Cohen, Peter F. 2002. Orisha journeys: the role of travel in the birth of Yorùbá-Atlantic religions. *Archives de Sciences Sociales des Religions* 117(Jan–Mar): 17–36.

Cole, Herbert, M. Y. Chike, and C. Aniakor. 1984. *Igbo Arts: Community and Cosmos*. Los Angeles: University of California, Museum of Cultural History.

Connell, Bruce. 1997. *Mòkpè (Bakweri)–English Dictionary*. Materials collected by Edwin Ardener. Archiv Afrikanistischer Manuskripte. Köln: Rüdiger Köppe Verlag.

Connell, Bruce. 2001a. The role of language contact in the development of Usaghade. In *Historical Language Contact in Africa*. Ed. D. Nurse. SUGIA: Sprache und Geschichte in Afrika, vol. 16/17. Köln: Rüdiger Köppe Verlag. Pp. 51–81.

Connell, Bruce. 2001b. Letter to the author from the Department of Linguistics, York University, Canada, 20 November.

Connell, Bruce. 2002. Email to the author from the Department of Linguistics, York University, Canada, 11 September.

Connell, Bruce. 2004. Efik in Abakua: linguistic evidence for the formation of a diaspora identity. *Contours: A Journal of the African Diaspora* 2(2): 223–238.

Cornet, Joseph. 1982. *Art Royal Kuba*. Milano: Edizioni Sipiel.

Cosme-Baños, Pedro. 1998. *Los chinos en Regla, 1847–1997: documentos y comentarios*. Santiago de Cuba: Editorial Oriente.

Cotton, J. C. 1905. The people of Old Calabar. *Journal of the African Society* 4(15): 302–306.

Courlander, Harold. 1944. Abakwa meeting in Guanabacoa. *Journal of Negro History* 29(4): 461–470.

Courlander, Harold. 1949. Cult music of Cuba. Liner notes to a series of recordings. Ethnic Folkways Library. EFL-1410. Pp. 1–4.

Coyula, Mario. 2005. Sr. Coyula is an architect and planner and professor at the Faculty of Architecture of Havana. Email to the author, 13 August.

Crow, Hugh 1830. *Memoirs of the Late Captain Hugh Crow of Liverpool*. London: Longman, Rees, Orme, Brown, and Green.

Crowther, Rev. Samuel. 1860. *Isuama-Ibo Primer*. London: Church Missionary Society.

Crozier, D. H., and R. M. Blench, eds. 1992. *An Index of Nigerian Languages*. 2nd ed. Dallas, TX: Summer Institute of Languages.

Cuellar-Vizcaino, Manuel. 1956a. Mensaje secreto. Aire Libre column, *Tiempo*, 21 Diciembre. Havana.

Cuellar-Vizcaino, Manuel. 1956b. Más sobre los Ñáñigos. Aire Libre column, *Tiempo*, 23 Diciembre. Havana.

Cuellar-Vizcaino, Manuel. 1971. Un movimiento solidario con los 8 estudiantes del 71. *La Gaceta de Cuba*, no. 89, enero. Havana: UNEAC.

Cuervo, Armando. 2006. Mr. Cuervo is an obonékue of the Munandibá Efó lodge. He played percussion with Los Van Van from 1972 to 1978 and with Irakere from 1978 to 1981. Coversations with the author, Havana.

Daniell, W. F., Esq. 1848. On the natives of Old Callebar, west coast of Africa. *Journal of the Ethnographical Society of London* 1: 210–224.

Dawson, C. Daniel. 2000–2007. Conversations with the author, New York City.

Dayrell, Elphinstone. 1913. *Ikom Folk Stories from Southern Nigeria*. Occasional Papers, no. 3. London: Royal Anthropological Institute of Great Britain and Ireland.

Dayrell, Elphinstone. 1969/1910. *Folk Stories from Southern Nigeria*. New York: Negro University Press.

De Briñas, Felipe L. 1898. Mi tierra: leyendas de la Habana Antigua. Los Ñáñigos. *El Fígaro* 27 marzo, vol. 14, 1 p.

De la Fuente, Alejandro. 2001. *A Nation for All: Race, Inequality, and Politics in Twentieth-Century Cuba*. Chapel Hill: University of North Carolina Press.

De la Torre, José María. 1857. *Lo que fuimos y lo que somos, o La Habana Antigua y moderna*. Havana: Spencer and Co.

Delgado-Alfonso, Jorge. 2001. Conversation with the author about the painter's work "La fuerza del mambí," Havana, 4 July.

Dennett, R. E. 1887. *Seven Years among the Fjort, Being an English Trader's Experiences in the Congo District*. London: Sampson Low, Marston, Searle, and Rivington.

Deschamps-Chappeaux, Pedro. 1964. Margarito Blanco "Osongo de Ultán." *Boletin del Instituto de Historia y del Archivo Nacional* 65(Jul.–Dec.): 97–109.

Deschamps-Chappeaux, Pedro. 1968a. Potencias: secreto entre hombres. *Cuba revista mensual* (Havana) Año 7, no. 72. (April): 44–45.

Deschamps-Chappeaux, Pedro. 1968b. Cabildos: solo para esclavos. *Cuba revista mensual* (Havana) año 7, no. 69 (January): 50–51.

Deschamps-Chappeaux, Pedro. 1969a. Marcas Tribales de los Esclavos en Cuba. *Etnologia y folklore* (Havana) 8: 65–78.

Deschamps-Chappeaux, Pedro. 1969b. Cimarrones urbanos. *Revista de la Biblioteca Nacional "José Martí"* 11(2): 145–165.

Deschamps-Chappeaux, Pedro. 1971. *El negro en la economía habanera del siglo XIX*. Havana: UNEAC.

Deschamps-Chappeaux, Pedro. 1972a. Los Negros Curros del Manglar. In *Historia: Comisión de Activistas de Historia Regional 10 de Octubre*. Havana: Conferencia el 16 de octubre. Pp. 33–42.

Deschamps-Chappeaux, Pedro. 1972b. La Habana de intra y extramuros y los Cabildos de los negros de nación. In *Historia: Comisión de Activistas de Historia Regional 10 de Octubre*. Havana: Conferencia el 23 de octubre. Pp. 19–25.

Deschamps-Chappeaux, Pedro. 1974. Agustín Ceballos, capataz de muelle. *Contribución a la Historia de la gente sin historia*. Ed. Pedro Deschamps Chappeaux and Juan Pérez de la Riva. Havana: Editorial de ciencias sociales.

Deschamps-Chappeaux, Pedro. 1983. *Los cimarrones urbanos*. Havana: Editorial de ciencias sociales.

Deschamps-Chappeaux, Pedro. 1987. Rebeliones, cimarronaje y libertad en el Caribe. *Del Caribe* 8: 72–78.

Deschamps-Chappeaux, Pedro. 1990. Presencia religiosa en las sublevaciones de esclavos. *Del Caribe* 16–17: 101–105.

Díaz-Anaya, Ogduardo "Román." 2000–2007. Mr. Díaz is a professional percussionist from Havana. Personal communications with the author, New York City.

Díaz-Ayala, Cristóbal. 1993/1981. *Musica Cubana: Del Areyto a la Nueva Trova*. 3rd ed. Miami: Ediciones Universal.

Díaz-Ayala, Cristóbal. 1994. *Cuba canta y baila: discografía de la música cubana*. Vol. 1, *1898–1925*. San Juan, Puerto Rico: Fundación Musicalia.

Díaz-Ayala, Cristóbal. 1999–2004. Letters to the author.

Díaz-Ayala, Cristóbal. 2002. Cuba Canta y Baila: Encyclopedic Discography of Cuban Music, 1925–1960. Accessed 2007. http://gislab.fiu.edu/SMC/about.html.

Diccionario Enciclopédico de la Masonería. 1883. Havana: Editorial Gonzalez Porto.

Dike, K. Onwuka. 1956. *Trade and Politics in the Niger Delta, 1830–1885: An Introduction to the Economic and Political History of Nigeria*. Oxford: Clarendon Press.

Dike, K. Onwuko, and Felicia I. Ekejiuba. 1990. *The Aro of South-Eastern Nigeria, 1650–1980: A Study of Socio-Economic Formation and Transformation in Nigeria*. Ibadan, Nigeria: University Press of Ibadan.

Di Leo, Octavio. 2005. It all started in Madrid. In *Cuban Counterpoints: The Legacy of Fernando Ortiz*. Ed. M. Font and A. Quiroz. Lanham, MD: Lexington Books. Pp. 39–54.

Directorio de Artes, Comercio e Industrias de la Habana. 1859. Havana: Imprenta de Graupera.

Documentos: Constitución de un cabildo Carabali en 1814. 1924. *Archivos del Folklore Cubano* 1(3): 281–283.

Domingo del Monte: Centón Epistolario. 2002. Vol. 4. Biblioteca de Clásicos cubanos. Havana: Imagen contemporánea.

Donnan, Elizabeth. 1930–1935. *Documents Illustrative of the History of the Slave Trade to America.* 4 vols. Washington, DC: Carnegie Institution.

D'ou, Lino. 1977. *Papeles del TTE: Coronel Lino D'ou.* Havana: Unión de Escritores y Artistas de Cuba.

Dreke, Mario "Chabalonga." 2000. Chabalonga is the ekóbio (Abakuá brother) of Victor Herrera, as well as lifelong member of the comparsa Los Marqueses of Atarés. A transcript of this tape-recorded interview was revised by Chabalonga on 21 January 2000.

Drewal, H. J., J. Pemberton, and R. Abiodun. 1989. *Nine Centuries of African Art and Thought.* Ed. Allen Wardwell. New York: Center for African Art.

Duque, Matías. 1923. *Nuestra patria: lectura para niños.* Havana: Imprenta Montalvo, Cardenas and Co.

Dye, Ira. 1991. Physical and social profiles of early American seafarers, 1812–1815. In *Jack Tar in History: Essays in the History of Maritime Life and Labour.* Ed. Colin Howell and Richard J. Twomey. Fredericton, New Brunswick: Acadiensis Press. Pp. 220–235.

Ebot, Wilson Atem. 1978. *Witchcraft and Sorcery among the Ejagham (West Cameroon), with an Ethnographical Introduction.* Ph.D. diss., Institute of Dialect and Folklife Studies, School of English, University of Leeds.

Eco, Umberto. 1983/1980. *The Name of the Rose.* Trans. William Weaver. New York: Warner Books.

Edem, Orok. 2000. The Obong of Calabar saga: the political disintegration of the Efiks. www.nigerdeltacongress.com/oarticles/obong_of_calabar_saga.htm.

Edem, Orok. 2001. Email messages to the author, 9 January; 6 March.

Edet, Chief Hayford Solomon. 2007. Chief Edet is a M̀gbè title-holder, as well as village head of Mba Odoso Village Ikpai Ohom Clan. He is the honorable general secretary of the Qua Clans Constituted Assembly, Cross River State. Conversation with the author, Calabar, 31 December.

Effiong, Charles E. 2005. Prof. Effiong was the Vice Chancellor of the University of Calabar from 1988 to 1993; he holds the grade of Ntui Mboko in M̀gbè Oban. Conversations with the author, Calabar.

"Efik Dances." 1957. *Nigeria Magazine* (Lagos) 53: 150–169.

Efiok, Etubom Essien E. 2003, 2008. Etubom Efiok is a great-grandson of King Eyo VIII, the Obong Ebonkó of Efe Ékpè Iboku, and Etubom of King Eyo Nsa I, Efiom Ekpu dynasty of Adak-Uko (Creek Town). Conversations with the author in Michigan (2003) and Creek Town (2008).

Ekong, Ekong E. 1983. The concepts of metamorphosis and metempsychosis in Ibibio society. *Journal of Cultures and Ideas* (Ile-Ife, Nigeria) 1(1): 133–137.

Ekpo, Edet, et al. 2005. *The Quas: A Historical Perspective and Belief System.* Calabar: Bacon Publishers.

Ellis, Catherine J. 1983. When is a song not a song? A study from northern South Australia. *Bikmaus* 4(1): 136–144.

Ellis, Catherine J., and Linda M. Barwick. 1987. Musical syntax and the problem of meaning in a central Australian songline. *Musicology Australia* 10: 41–57.

Eltis, David, and David Richardson. 1997a. The "numbers game" and routes to slavery. *Slavery and Abolition* 18(1): 1–15.

Eltis, David, and David Richardson. 1997b. West Africa and the transatlantic slave trade: new evidence of long-run trends. *Slavery and Abolition* 18(1): 16–35.

Eltis, David, David Richardson, and Stephen D. Behrendt. 1999. Patterns in the transatlantic slave trade, 1662–1867: new indications of African origins of slaves arriving in the Americas. In *Black Imagination and the Middle Passage*. Ed. Maria Diedrich, Henry. L. Gates Jr., and Carl Pedersen. New York: Oxford University Press. Pp. 21–32.

Eltis, David, Stephen D. Behrendt, David Richardson, and Herbert S. Klein, eds. 2000. *The Trans-Atlantic Slave Trade: A Database on CD-ROM*. Cambridge: Cambridge University Press.

Ely, Dr. A. 1853. The island of Cuba: past and present. In *De Bow's Review*. Vol. 14, no. 2. New Orleans: J. D. B. De Bow. Pp. 93–122.

Entralgo, Elías José. 1953. *La liberación étnica cubana*. Havana.

Erim, E. O. 1990. Cross-cultural contacts between the Efik and the Upper-Cross River peoples, 1600–1900 A.D. In *Old Calabar Revisited*. Ed. S. O. Jaja, E. O. Erim, B. W. Andah. Enugu, Nigeria: Harris. Pp. 169–185.

Esen, Akpan J. A. 1982. *Ibibio Profile: A Psycho-Literary Projection*. Lagos and Calabar: Paico Press and Books.

Essien, Dominus. 1993. *Uruan People in Nigerian History*. Uyo, Nigeria: Modern Business Press.

Essien, Iberedem Fred Eno. 2008. Iberedem is an Uruan title meaning "one who is dependable." Essien holds the Nkàndà title in Ékpè. Conversations with the author in Mr. Essien's home, Uyo, Nigeria.

Essien, Okon E. n.d. (c. 1982). Efik orthography. In *Orthographies of Nigerian Languages*. Manual 1. Ed. A. Bamgboṣe. Lagos: National Language Centre, Federal Ministry of Education. Pp. 5–30.

Essien, Okon E. 1985. Ibibio orthography. In *Orthographies of Nigerian Languages*. Manual 3. Ed. A. Banjo. Lagos: National Language Centre, Federal Ministry of Education. Pp. 62–82.

Essien, Okon E. 1986. *Ibibio Names: Their Structure and Their Meanings*. Ibadan, Nigeria: Daystar Press.

Essien, Okon E. 1990. *A Grammar of the Ibibio Language*. Ibadan, Nigeria: University Press Limited.

Essien, Okon E. 2005. The so-called downstepped tone in Ibibio. In *Globalization and the Study of Languages in Africa*. Ed. Ozo-mekuri Ndimele. Port Harcourt, Nigeria: Grand Orbit Commumicationas and Emhai Press. Pp. 343–352.

Estrada, Stella. 2007. *Írimo*. Ourense, España: Ediciones Malberte.

Etim, Etubom Asuquo "Bambam." 2004. Etubom Etim is a masquerade maker in Calabar. Conversations with the author in Calabar, August and December.

Euba, Akin. 1988. *Essays on Music in Africa*. Vol. 1. Bayreuth, West Germany: IWALEWA, Haus, Universität Bayreuth.

Exquemelin, Alexandre Olivier. 1741. *The History of the Bucaniers, Free-Booters, and Pyrates of America*. Vol. 1. 4th ed. London. [Original in Dutch. 1678. *De americaensche zeerovers*. Amsterdam.]

Eyamba, Adam Efa. 2005. Chief Eyamba is a title-holder in the Efe Ékpè Iyámba Iboku Utan of Atakpa, Calabar. Conversations with the author, Calabar.

Eyo, Chief Effiom Ekpenyong. 2005. Chief Eyo is from Adak-Uko; being a descendant of Eyo Honesty II, he holds a chieftancy title in that House (Ibet Idem Ufok Eyo Honesty II). His Ékpè title is Mboko-mboko in Efe Ékpè Eyo Ema. Conversations with the author, Calabar.

Febles, Juan "Juanillo." 1996. Juanillo was born 1914 and died in 2004, Havana. Audio-cassette recorded conversations in Havana, December.

Federal Writers' Project of the Work Projects Administration for the State of Florida. 1940. *Florida: A Guide to the Southernmost State*. New York: Oxford University Press.

Fehderau, Harold W. 1992. *Dictionnaire Kituba (kikongo ya leta)–Anglais–français et Vocabulaire Français–Kituba*. Kinshasa: Editions Cedi.

Fermoselle, Rafael. 1974. *Política y color en Cuba: la guerrita de 1912*. Montevideo: Ediciones Géminis.

Fernández, Raul A. 2006. *From Afro-Cuban Rhythms to Latin Jazz*. Berkeley: University of California Press; Chicago: Center for Black Music Research, Columbia College.

Fernández-Carrillo, Enrique. 1881. El Ñáñigo. In *Tipos y Costumbres de la isla de Cuba*. Havana: Miguel de Villa. Pp. 141–145.

Fernández-Ferrer, Antonio. 1998. *La isla infinita de Fernando Ortiz*. Alicante: Instituto de Cultura Juan Gil-Albert.

Fernández-Mascaró, Guillermo. 1950. *Ecos de la manigua (el Maceo que yo conocí)*. Havana: P. Fernández. 24 pp.

Fernández-Pelon, Luis "el Pelon." 1994. Interview by Idania Diaz and Ivor Miller in his home, Miami, 23 September.

Fernández-Robaina, Tomás. 1985. *Bibliografía de Temas Afrocubanas*. Havana: Biblioteca Nacional.

Ferrer, Ada. 1999. *Insurgent Cuba: Race, Nation, and Revolution, 1868–1898*. Chapel Hill: University of North Carolina Press.

Fine, Michael L., and Friedrich Ladich. 2003. Sound production, spine locking, and related adaptations. In *Catfishes*. Vol. 1. Ed. G. Arratia, B. G. Kapoor, M. Chardon, R. Diogo. Enfield, NH: Science Publishers. Pp. 249–290.

Fitzgerald Marriott, H. P. 1899. The secret societies of West Africa. *Journal of the Royal Anthropological Institute* 29: 21–27.

Flint, Grover. 1898. *Marching with Gomez: A War Correspondent's Field Note-Book Kept During Four Months with the Cuban Army*. Boston: Lamson, Wolffe and Co.

Flores Casanova, Andrés. 1990s. Flores was a descendant of Calabar migrants. Interviews with the author in Havana, Cuba.

Foner, Philip S. 1962. *A History of Cuba and Its Relations with the United States*. Vol. 1, *1492–1845*. New York: International Publishers.

Foner, Philip S. 1977. *Antonio Maceo: The "Bronze Titan" of Cuba's Struggle for Independence*. New York: Monthly Review Press.

Forde, Daryll, ed. 1956. *Efik Traders of Old Calabar*. London: International African Institute.

Forde, Daryll. 1964. *Yakö Studies*. London: Oxford University Press.

Forde, Daryll, and G. I. Jones. 1950. *The Ibo and Ibibio-speaking Peoples of South-eastern Nigeria*. London: International African Institute.

Fox, William L. 1997. *Lodge of the Double-Headed Eagle: Two Centuries of Scottish Rite Freemasonry in America's Southern Jurisdiction*. Fayetteville: University of Arkansas Press.

Fox, William L., ed. 2001. *Valley of the Craftsmen: A Pictorial History—Scottish Rite Freemasonry in America's Southern Jurisdiction, 1801–2001*. Washington, D.C.: The Supreme Council, 33°, Ancient and Accepted Scottish Rite of Freemasonry, Southern Jurisdiction, U.S.A.

Franco, José Luciano. 1959. *Folklore Criollo y Afrocubano*. Havana: Publicaciones de la Junta Nacional de Arqueología y Etnología.

Franco, José Luciano. 1961. *Afroamérica*. Havana: Publicaciones de la Junta Nacional de Arqueología y Etnología.

Franco, José Luciano. 1967. Cuatro siglos de lucha por la libertad: Los palenques. *Revista de la Biblioteca nacional José Marti* 9(1): 5–44.

Franco, José Luciano. 1972. Surgimiento del Caserío de Jesús del Monte y sus estancias. In *Historia: Comisión de Activistas de Historia Regional 10 de Octubre*. Havana: Conferencia el 23 de octubre. Pp. 3–17.

Franco, José Luciano. 1973. *Los palenques de los negros cimarrones*. Havana: Colección historia.

Franco, José Luciano. 1974. La conspiración de Aponte, 1812. In *Ensayos historicos*. Ed. J. L. Franco. Havana: Editorial de ciencias sociales. Pp. 125–190.

Franco, José Luciano. 1975a. *Antonio Maceo: apuntes para una historia de su vida*. Vol. 1. Havana: Editorial de ciencias sociales.

Franco, José Luciano. 1975b. *La diáspora africana en el Nuevo Mundo*. Havana: Editorial de ciencias sociales.

Franco, José Luciano. 1980. *Comercio clandestino de esclavos*. Havana: Editorial de ciencias sociales.

Fuentes Guerra, Jesús, and Armin Schwegler. 2005. *Lengua y ritos del Palo Monte Mayombe: Dioses cubanos y sus fuentes africanas*. Madrid: Iberoamericana; Frankfurt: Vervuert.

Fyfe, Christopher. 1960. Peter Nicholls: Old Calabar and Freetown. *Journal of the Historical Society of Nigeria* 2(1): 105–114.

Fyfe, Christopher. 2005. Letter to the author in response to my query regarding the term *Kalabari* as used in Freetown, Sierra Leone, in the nineteenth century.

Gallenga, A. 1873. *The Pearl of the Antilles*. London: Chapman and Hall.

García-Chavez, Leonardo. 1930. *Historia de la Jurisdicción de Cárdenas*. Vol. 1. Havana: Cultural, S.A.

García del Pino, César. 1969. Diario de un deportado a Fernando Póo en 1869: Viaje de Fernando Poo a Mahon en el vapor *San Antonio*. *Revista de la Biblioteca Nacional José Martí* 11(1): 59–73.

Geary, Christraud M. 1988. *Images from Bamum: German Colonial Photography at the Court of King Njoya, Cameroon, West Africa, 1902–1915*. Washington, DC: Smithsonian Institution Press.

Gemelli Careri, Giovanni Francesco. 1699–1700. *Giro del mondo*. 6 vols. Napoli: Guiseppe Roselli.

Giro, Radamés, ed. 1995. Los motives del son. In *Panorama de la música popular cubana*. Havana: Editorial Letras Cubanas. Pp. 219–230.

Giro, Radamés. 2000–2006. Conversations with the author at the home of Sr. Giró, Havana.

Gladwin, Thomas. 1970. *East Is a Big Bird: Navigation and Logic on Puluwat Atoll*. Cambridge, MA: Harvard University Press.

Goldenberg, Robert. 1984. Talmud. In *Back to the Sources: Reading the Classic Jewish Texts*. Ed. Barry W. Holtz. New York: Summit Books. Pp. 129–175.

Goldie, Rev. Hugh. 1894. *Memoir of King Eyo VII of Old Calabar: A Christian King in Africa*. Old Calabar: United Presbyterian Mission Press.

Goldie, Rev. Hugh. 1901/1890. *Calabar and Its Mission*. New edition with additional chapters by Rev. J. T. Dean. Edinburgh: Oliphant.

Goldie, Rev. Hugh. 1960. *Efik Proverbs by Reverend Hugh Goldie*. Ed. Donald Simmons. American Association for African Research, no. 3. Calabar, Nigeria. 23 pp.

Goldie, Rev. Hugh. 1964/1862. *A Dictionary of the Efik Language, in Two Parts. 1. Efik and English. 2. English and Efik*. Westmead, England: Gregg Press.

Gómez, José-Miguel. 2003. A manuscript, signed by Mr. Gómez, was shared among his godchildren upon his death in 2003. Gómez was Mokóngo of Ebión Efó from 1926 to 2003; he lived to be the eldest Mokóngo of Cuba. He was a babaláwo; in Cuban-Kongo practice, he was Padre Enkiza Plaza Lirio Mama Chola, Templo 12, Santo Cristo del Buen Viaje (lineage of Andrés Petit).

Gomez, Michael A. 1998. *Exchanging Our Country Marks: The Transformation of African Identities in the Colonial and Antebellum South*. Chapel Hill: University of North Carolina Press.

Gómez, Zoila. 1977. *Amadeo Roldán*. Havana: Editorial Arte y Literatura.

Graeber, David. 2001. *Toward an Anthropological Theory of Value: The False Coin of Our Own Dreams*. New York: Palgrave.

Green, Margaret M. 1958. Sayings of the Ǫkǫnkǫ society of the Igbo-speaking people. *Bulletin of School of Oriental and African Studies* (London) 21: 157–173.

Greenbaum, Susan. 2003. Dr. Greenbaum is professor of anthropology at the University of South Florida. Email to the author, 3 March.

Greenfell, George. 1882. The Cameroons District, West Africa. *Proceedings of the Royal Geographical Society* 4(10): 585–595, with a map after p. 648.

Griffith, Tom, ed. 1997. *Travels of Marco Polo*. Hertfordshire, England: Wordsworth Classics of World Literature.

Grimes, Barbara F. 2000. *Ethnologue*. 14th ed. Dallas: SIL International. http://www.ethnologue.com.

Grzimek, Bernhard. 1972. *Grzimek's Animal Life Encyclopedia*. Vol. 2. New York: Van Nostrand.

Guanche, Jesús. 1983. *Procesos etnoculturales de Cuba*. Havana: Letras Cubanas.

Guerrero, Ángel. 2003–2007. Sr. Guerrero is a title-holder of the Itá Mukandá lodge and lead chanter in the *Ibiono* (2001) CD. Conversations with the author.

Guerrero, Rafael. 1896. *Crónica de la Guerra de Cuba y de la rebelión de Filipinas (1895–1896)*. Vol. 4. Barcelona: Editorial Maucci.

Guillén, Nicolás. 1984/1931. *Sóngoro Cosongo: poemas mulatos*. Buenos Aires: Editorial Losada.

Guirao, Ramón. 1938. *Orbita de la poesía afrocubana 1928–1937 (antologia)*. Havana: Ucar, García y Cía.

Gutierrez-Nuñez, Pablo Pasqual. 1995. Mbákara of Ikanfioró Nankuko. Interview with Ivor Miller and Luis Salinas in the home of Mr. Gutierrez (1906–1999), in the barrio of Belén, Havana, 13 March.

Hackett, Rosalind I. J. 1989. *Religion in Calabar: The Religious Life and History of a Nigerian Town*. Berlin: Mouton de Gruyter.

Hair, Paul Edward H. 1990. Antera Duke of Old Calabar: a little more about an African enterpreneur. *History in Africa* 17: 359–365.

Hair, Paul Edward H., ed. 1992. *Barbot's West African Vocabularies of c. 1680*. Liverpool: Center of African Studies, University of Liverpool.

Hale, Ken. 1998. On endangered languages and the importance of linguistic diversity. In *Endangered Languages: Language Loss and Community Response*. Ed. L. Grenoble and L. Whaley. Cambridge, UK: Cambridge University Press. Pp. 191–216.

Hall, Gwendolyn Midlo. 1992a. *Africans in Colonial Louisiana: The Development of Afro-Creole Culture in the Eighteenth Century*. Baton Rouge: Louisiana State University Press.

Hall, Gwendolyn Midlo. 1992b. The formation of Afro-Creole culture. In *Creole New Orleans: Race and Americanization*. Ed. Arnold R. Hirsch and Joseph Logsdon. Baton Rouge: Lousiana State University Press. Pp. 58–87.

Hallett, Robin, ed. 1964. Nicholls, 1804–1805. In *Records of the African Association, 1788–1831, of The Royal Geographical Society*. London: Thomas Nelson and Sons, Ltd. Pp. 191–210.

Hargreaves, Susan M. 1987. Political Economy of Nineteenth Century Bonny: A Study of Power, Authority, Legitimacy and Ideology in a Delta Trading Community from 1790–1914. Ph.D. diss., University of Birmingham.

Harris, Rosemary. 1972. The history of trade at Ikom, Eastern Nigeria. *Africa: Journal of the International African Institute* 42(2): 122–139.

Hart, A. Kalada. 1964. *Report of the Enquiry into the Dispute over the Obongship of Calabar*. Official Document no. 17. Enugu, Nigeria: Government Printer.

Hart, Mickey. 1991. *Planet Drum: A Celebration of Percussion and Rhythm*. New York: Harper San Francisco.

Hazard, Samuel. 1989/1871. *Cuba with Pen and Pencil*. Miami: Editorial Cubana.

Helg, Aline. 1995. *Our Rightful Share: The Afro-Cuban Struggle for Equality, 1886–1912*. Chapel Hill: University of North Carolina Press.

Helly, Denise. 1993. Introduction. In *The Cuba Commission Report: A Hidden History of the Chinese in Cuba—The Original English-Language Text of 1876*. Trans. Sidney W. Mintz. Baltimore, MD: Johns Hopkins University Press. Pp. 3–30.

Henderson, R. 1972. *The King in Every Man: Evolutionary Trends in Onitsha Ibo Society*. New Haven, CT: Yale University Press.

Henshaw, Chief Dr. James E. 2005. Dr. Henshaw is a medical doctor and a playwright. Conversations with the author in Dr. Henshaw's home, Calabar.

Hergesheimer, Joseph. 1920. *San Cristobal de la Habana*. New York: Knopf.

Hernández-Serrano, Luis. 2001. 27 de noviembre de 1871: También murieron Abakuá. *Juventud Rebelde* Dominical 25 November, 10.

Herrera, Dr. Mercedes. 2000. Daughter of Victor Herrera, as well as current director of the comparsa Los Marqueses de Atarés. Interview by the author. A transcript of this tape-recorded interview was revised by Dr. Herrera on 21 January 2000.

Herrera, Lázaro. 1999. Herrera, the first trumpeter of the Septeto Nacional, is considered the founder of the trumpet style in the Cuban son. Audio-recorded conversations in Mr. Herrera's home, Havana, February, March, April, and May.

Herrera Sorzano, Mercedes. 2006. Mr. Herrera is a historian of transportation. Conversations with the author in the Museo del Ferrocarril de Cuba, Havana, February.

Herskovits, Melville J. 1948. The contribution of Afroamerican studies to Africanist research. *American Anthropologist* 50 (1, Jan.–Mar.): 1–10.

Herskovits, Melville J. 1967. *Dahomey: An Ancient West African Kingdom*. 2 vols. Evanston, IL: Northwestern University Press.

Herskovits, Melville J. 1990/1941. *The myth of the Negro past*. 2nd ed. Introduction by Sidney W. Mintz. Boston: Beacon Press.

Hobbes, Thomas. 1991/1651. *Leviathan*. Ed. R. Tuck. Cambridge, UK: Cambridge University Press.

Hobsbawm, E. J. 1959. *Primitive Rebels: Studies in Archaic Forms of Social Movement in the Nineteenth and Twentieth Centuries*. New York: Norton and Co.

Hodges, Graham R., ed. 1993. *Black Itinerants of the Gospel: The Narratives of John Jea and George White*. Madison, WI: Madison House.

Holman, James. 1972/1827. *Travels in Madeira, Sierra Leone, Teneriffe, St. Jago, Cape Coast, Fernando Po, Prince Island, etc.* Freeport, NY: Books for Libraries.

Howard, Joseph H. 1967. *Drums in the Americas*. New York: Oak Publications.

Howard, Philip A. 1998. *Changing History: Afro-Cuban Cabildos and Societies of Color in the Nineteenth Century*. Baton Rouge: Louisiana State University.

Howard, Philip A. 1999. Creolization and integration: the development of a political culture among the Pan-Afro-Cuban benevolent societies, 1878–1985. In *Crossing Boundaries: Comparative History of Black People in Diaspora*. Ed. Darlene C. Hine and Jacqueline McLeod. Bloomington: Indiana University Press. Pp. 134–158.

Huet, Michel. 1996. *The Dances of Africa*. Text by Claude Savary. New York: Harry Abrams.

Hutchinson, Thomas J. 1861. On the social and domestic traits of the African tribes; with a glance at their superstitions, cannibalism, etc., etc. *Transactions of the Ethnological Society of London* 1: 327–340.

Hutchinson, Thomas J. 1970/1858. *Impressions of Western Africa, with Remarks on the Diseases of the Climate and a Report on the Peculiarities of Trade up the Rivers in the Bight of Biafra*. London: Frank Cass and Co.

Ibarra, Jorge. 1985. *Un análisis psicosocial del cubano: 1898–1925*. Havana: Editorial de ciencias sociales.

Ijoma, J. Oroko. 1998. The evolution of the Aro Kingdom. In *Building on the Debris of a Great Past: Proceedings of the First All-Aro National Conference, 1996*. Ed. Okoro Ijoma. Enugu. Nigeria: Fourth Dimension. Pp. 12–24.

Ika, Etim. 2005, 2008. Prince Ika, whose official name is Ekpeyong Cobham Antigha, is the son of the Muri Cobham Antigha Edet 4th of Efut Ifako Clan, Creek Town, Odukpani L.G.A. Conversations with the author, Calabar, December 2005, May 2008.

Iliad of Homer, The. 1961/1951. Translated and with an introduction by Richmond Lattimore. Chicago: University of Chicago Press.

Imbernó, Pedro José. 1891. *Guía geográfica y administrativa de la isla de Cuba*. Havana.

Imona, Chief (Prince) Francis Edim. 1996. *Know Your History: A Handbook of a Short History of Big Qua Town, Calabar*. Calabar: Anieson Printers.

Inglis, G. Douglas. 1985. The Spanish naval shipyard at Havana in the eighteenth century. In *New Aspects of Naval History: Selected Papers from the 5th Naval History Symposium*. Ed. Deptartment of History, U.S. Naval Academy. Baltimore, MD: The Nautical and Aviation Publishing Co. of America. Pp. 47–58.

Insuá-Brindis, Félix "Pupi." 2003–2005. "Pupi" is Tata Nkisi Malongo, a tradition he inherited from his Cuban Kongo ancestors. His grandfather, Catalino Brindis, was cousin of Claudio José Domingo Brindis de Salas (1852–1911), the famed nineteenth-century violinist. Converstations with the author, New York City.

Ishemo, Shubi L. 2002. From Africa to Cuba: a historical analysis of the Sociedad Secreta Abakuá (Ñañiguismo). *Review of African Political Economy* 92: 253–272.

Ita, Callixtus E. 2007. Retired pharmaceutical chemist and a full member of Ékpè through a Creek Town lodge. Email correspondence and telephone conversations with the author.

Itoh, Chief Esoh. 2004. Paramount ruler of the Balondo people of Cameroon. Conversations with the author in Ekondo Titi, southwestern Cameroon, August.

Iyanam, Chief Iyanam Uqua. 1998. Traditional rulership as symbols of Oron unity. In *The Oron Nation in Contemporary Nigeria*. Ed. O. E. Uya. Calabar, Nigeria. Pp. 40–60.

Jaja, E. A. 1977. *King Jaja of Opobo, 1821–1891: A Sketch History of the Development and Expansion of Opobo*. Lagos: Opobo Action Council.

James, Winston. 1998. *Holding Aloft the Banner of Ethiopia: Caribbean Radicalism in Early Twentieth-Century America*. London: Verso.

Jameson, Robert Francis. 1821. *Letters from the Havana, During the Year 1820, Containing an Account of the Present State of the Island of Cuba, and Observations on the Slave Trade*. London.

Jeffreys, M. D. W. 1935. *Old Calabar and Notes on the Ibibio Language*. Calabar, Nigeria: HWTI Press.

Jeffreys, M. D. W. 1956. The Nyama Society of the Ibibio women. *African Studies* (Johannesburg) 15(1): 15–28.

Johnson, Jerah. 1992. Colonial New Orleans: a fragment of the eighteenth-century French ethos. In *Creole New Orleans: Race and Americanization*. Ed. Arnold R. Hirsch and Joseph Logsdon. Baton Rouge: Louisiana State University Press. Pp. 12–57.

Johnston, Sir Harry Hamilton. 1888a. A journey up the Cross River, West Africa. *Proceedings of the Royal Geographical Society and Monthly Record of Geography* 10: 435–438.

Johnston, Sir Harry Hamilton. 1888b. The Bantu borderland in western Africa. *Proceedings of the Royal Geographical Society and Monthly Record of Geography* 10: 633–637.

Johnston, Sir Harry Hamilton. 1888c. The Niger Delta. *Proceedings of the Royal Geographical Society and Monthly Record of Geography* 10: 749–763.

Johnston, Sir Harry Hamilton. 1888d. Explorations in the Cameroons District of western equatorial Africa. *Scottish Geographical Magazine* 4: 513–536, map on p. 537.

Johnston, Sir Harry Hamilton. 1919–1922. *A Comparative Study of the Bantu and Semi-Bantu Languages.* 2 vols. Oxford: Claredon Press.

Jones, Gwilym Iwan. 1956. The political organization of Old Calabar. In *Efik Traders of Old Calabar.* Ed. Daryll Forde. London: International African Institute. Pp. 116–157.

Jones, Gwilym Iwan. 1963. *The Trading States of the Oil Rivers: A Study of Political Development in Eastern Nigeria.* London: Oxford University Press.

Jones, Gwilym Iwan. 1970. Introduction. In *Hope Masterton Waddell, Twenty-nine Years in the West Indies and Central Africa: A Review of Missionary Work and Adventure, 1829–1858.* 2d ed. London: F. Cass.

Jones, Gwilym Iwan. 1984. Secret societies and their masquerades. In *The Art of Eastern Nigeria.* Cambridge, UK: Cambridge University Press. Pp. 56–75.

Jones, Gwilym Iwan. 1988a. The Niger–Cross River hinterlands and their masks. In *West African Masks and Cultural Systems.* Vol. 126. Ed. Sidney Kasfir. Tervuren, België: Koninklijk Museum voor Midden-Africa. Pp. 109–122.

Jones, Gwilym Iwan. 1988b. *The Background of Eastern Nigerian History.* 3 vols. HRAFlex Books, FF1/3, Ethnography Series. New Haven, CT: Human Relations Areas Files.

Joseph, Richard A. 1974. The royal pretender: Prince Douala Manga Bell in Paris, 1919–1922. *Cahiers d'Etudes africaines* 14(54, 2): 339–358.

Kalu, Ogbu U. 1980/1978. Writing in precolonial Africa: a case study of Nsibidi. In *African Cultural Development.* Readings in African Humanities series. Ed. O. Kalu. Enugu, Nigeria: Fourth Dimension. Pp. 76–85.

Keay, R. W. J., C. F. A. Onochie, and D. P. Stanfield. 1964. *Nigerian Trees*, vol. 2. Ibadan, Nigeria: Federal Department of Forest Research.

Kennedy, Stetson. 1939. Testimony of Enrique: all he's living for (Enrique and Amanda). 3 January 1939. Adelpha Pollato (Cuban), 2315 12th Avenue, Ybor City, Tampa, Florida, cigar maker. Stetson Kennedy, writer. Reel 1, folder 130. Federal Writers' Project Papers, University of North Carolina Library, Chapell Hill. P. 21.

Kennedy, Stetson. 1940. Ñáñigos in Florida. *Southern Folklore Quarterly* 4(3): 153–156.

Kennedy, Stetson. 2002a. Letter to the author, 21 February.

Kennedy, Stetson. 2002b. Letter to the author, 16 March.

Kiddy, Elizabeth W. 2002. Who is the King of Congo? A new look at African and Afro-Brazilian kings in Brazil. In *Central Africans and Cultural Transformations in the American Diaspora.* Ed. Linda M. Heywood. Cambridge, UK: Cambridge University Press. Pp. 153–182.

Kimball, Richard B. 1850. *Cuba and the Cubans; Comprising a History of the Island of Cuba, Its Present Social, Political, and Domestic Condition; Also, Its Relation to England and the United States.* New York.

Kinni, Fongot. 2004. Interview with the author, University of Buea, southwestern Cameroon, August. Transcript was revised by Dr. Kinni by email, November 2004.

Kinni, Fongot. 2005. Email message to the author, 22 September.

Klein, Herbert S. 1966. The colored militia of Cuba: 1568–1868. *Caribbean Studies* 6(2): 17–27.

Klein, Herbert S. 1989/1967. *Slavery in the Americas: A Comparative Study of Virginia and Cuba*. Chicago: Elephant Paperback.

Knight, Franklin W. 1970. *Slave Society in Cuba during the Nineteenth Century*. Madison: University of Wisconsin Press.

Knight, Franklin W. 1988. *Slavery and the Transformation of Society in Cuba, 1511–1760: From Settler Society to Slave Society*. Kingston, Jamaica: Department of History, University of the West Indies, Mona.

Knight, Franklin W., with contributions by Y. Talib and P. D. Curtin. 1989. The African diaspora. In *UNESCO General History of Africa*. Vol. 6. *Africa in the Nineteenth Century until the 1880s*. Ed. J. F. Ade Ajayi. Paris: UNESCO. Pp. 749–772.

Koloss, Hans-Joachim. 1985. Obasinjom among the Ejagham. *African Arts* 18(2): 63–65, 98–101, 103.

Kopytoff, I. 1981. Aghem ethnogenesis and the Grassfields ecumene. In *Contribution de la recherché ethnologique a l'histoire des civilizations du Cameroun* [*The Contribution of Ethnological Research to the History of Cameroon Cultures*]. Vol. 2, no. 551. Paris: Éditions du centre national de la recherché scientifique. Pp. 371–381.

Kubik, Gerhard. 1962. *Yoruba Talking Instruments*. London: Transcription Feature Service. (Available at Schomburg Center Sc Audio C-21 [Side 2, no. 2]).

Kubik, Gerhard. 1964. Generic names for the Mbira. *African Music: Journal of the African Music Society* 3(3): 25–36.

Kubik, Gerhard. 1971. Music and dance education in Mukanda schools of Mbwela and Nkangela communities. *Proceedings of the Lusaka International Music Conference, 15–22 June 1971*. Lusaka: The Institute for African Studies. 35 pp.

Kubik, Gerhard. 1979. *Angolan Traits in Black Music, Games, and Dances of Brazil: A Study of African Cultural Extensions Overseas*. Estudos de Antropologia Cultural, no. 10. Lisboa: Junta de investigações científicas do ultramar.

Kubik, Gerhard. 1987. *Tuscona-Luchazi Ideographs: A Graphic Tradition Practiced by a People of West Central Africa*. Vienna: Föhrenau.

Kubik, Gerhard. 1999. *Africa and the Blues*. Jackson: University Press of Mississippi.

Kubik, Gerhard. 2001. Africa; Cameroon; lamellophone. In *The New Grove Dictionary of Music and Musicians*. 2nd ed. Ed. S. Sadie. New York: Grove. Pp. 190–210 (Vol. 1); 872–878 (Vol. 4); 171–181 (Vol. 14).

Kubik, Gerhard. 2003. Letter to the author from Chileka, Malawi, 18 September.

Kubik, Gerhard. 2005. Letter to the author from Chileka, Malawi, 21 July, regarding the geographical extent of drums in West and West-Central Africa whose sound is produced by friction.

Kubik, Gerhard. 2006. Converstation with the author, Center for Black Music Conference in Chicago, 15 March.

Kuethe, Allan J. 1986. *Cuba, 1753–1815: Crown, Military, and Society*. Knoxville: University of Tennessee Press.

Kuethe, Allan J. 1991. Havana in the eighteenth century. In *Atlantic Port Cities: Economy, Culture, and Society in the Atlantic World, 1650–1850*. Ed. Franklin W. Knight and Peggy K. Liss. Knoxville: University of Tennessee Press. Pp. 13–39.

Kunz, Hermann (el Mayor). 1909. *La guerra hispano-americana*. Traducción española del alemán por Manuel Martínez. Barcelona: Imprenta vda. D. Casanovas.

Laman, Karl E. 1962. *The Kongo*. Vol. 3. Studia Ethnographica Upsaliensia, no. 12. Upsala.

Lamb, Venice, and Alastair Lamb. 1981. *Au Cameroun: Weaving—Tissage*. Great Britain: Roxford Books.

Lamounier, Lucia. 1995. Between slavery and free labour: early experiments with free labour and paterns of slave emancipation in Brazil and Cuba. In *From Chattel Slaves to Wage Slaves: The*

Dynamics of Labour Bargaining in the Americas. Ed. Mary Turner. London: James Curey. Pp. 185–198.

Landaluze, Victor Patricio (illustrator). 1881. *Tipos y Costumbres de la Isla de Cuba*. Havana: Antonio Bachiller y Morales.

Landers, Jane. 1993. Black–Indian interaction in Spanish Florida. *Colonial Latin American Historical Review* 2(2): 141–162.

Landers, Jane. 1999. *Black society in Spanish Florida*. Urbana: University of Illinois Press.

Lane, Jane. 2005. *Blackface Cuba, 1840–1895*. Philadelphia: University of Pennsylvania Press.

Láoyè I, Timi of Ẹdẹ 1959. Yoruba drums. *Odu* 7(Mar.): 5–14.

Lapidus, Benjamin L. 2005. Changüí, son, and the Haitian connection. In *Cuban Counterpoints: The Legacy of Fernando Ortiz*. Ed. M. Font and A. Quiroz. Lanham, MD: Lexington Books. Pp. 237–246.

Lapidus, Benjamin L. 2007. ¡Este bongo que te llama!: El changüí guantanamero y las influencias extranjeras en el son cubano. Paper presented at the Second International Congress on Music, Identity, and Culture in the Caribbean. Santiago de los Caballeros, Dominican Republic, April.

Lapique-Becali, Zoila. 1979. *Música colonial cubana en las publicaciones periódicas (1812–1902)*. Vol. 1. Havana: Editorial Letras Cubanas.

Lapique-Becali, Zoila. 1995. Aportes Franco-Haitianos a la contradanza cubana: mitos y realidades. In *Panorama de la música popular cubana*. Ed. Radamés Giro. Havana: Editorial Letras Cubanas. Pp: 153–172.

Lapointe, Marie. 1997. *Los mayas rebeldes de Yucatán*. 2nd ed. Mérida, Yucatán, México: Maldonado.

Latham, A. J. H. 1972. Witchcraft accusations and economic tension in precolonial Old Calabar. *Journal of African History* 13(2): 249–260.

Latham, A. J. H. 1973. *Old Calabar, 1600–1891: The Impact of the International Economy upon a Traditional Society*. Oxford: Clarendon Press.

Latham, A. J. H. 1990. The precolonial economy: the lower Cross region. In *A History of the Cross River Region of Nigeria*. Ed. Monday B. Abasiattai. Enugu, Nigeria: University of Calabar Press and Harris. Pp. 70–89.

Lattimore, Richard. 1961/1951. Introduction. In *The Iliad of Homer*. Chicago: University of Chicago Press.

Leal, Rine. 1982. *La selva oscura: De los bufos a la neocolonia (Historia del teatro cubano de 1868 a 1902)*. Vol. 2. Havana: Editorial Arte y Literatura.

León, Argeliers. 1990. Para leer las firmas Abakuá. *Revista de la unión de escritores y artistas de Cuba* (Unión) 10: 2–13.

León, Julio A. 1976. *Poemas y cartas de los departados cubanos en la isla de Fernando Póo*. Self-published, Johnson C. Smith University, Charlotte, NC.

Le Roy y Gálvez, Luis Felipe. 1971. *A cien años del 71: El fusilamiento de los estudiantes*. Havana: Editorial de ciencias sociales.

Le Roy y Gálvez, Luis Felipe. 1973. El 27 de noviembre cien años después. In *Centenario del fusilamiento de los estudiantes de medicina*. Serie historica, no. 24. Ed. Luis Le Roy, Rafael O. Pedraza, Julio Le Riverend. Havana: Academia de Ciencias de Cuba. Pp. 4–8.

Levine, Robert M. 1990. *Cuba in the 1850s: Through the Lens of Charles DeForest Fredricks*. Tampa: University of South Florida Press.

Lewis, David. 1994. *We, the Navigators: The Ancient Art of Landfinding in the Pacific*. 2nd ed. Honolulu: University of Hawaii Press.

Lieber, J. W. 1971. *Efik and Ibibio Villages*. Vol. 2, *South East State*. Human Ecology and Education Series, Occasional Publication no. 13. Ibadan, Nigeria: Institute of Education. University of Ibadan.

Lináres Savio, Dra. María-Terésa. 1974. *La música y el pueblo.* Havana: Editorial Pueblo y Educación.

Lináres Savio, Dra. María-Terésa. 1996, 1997, 1998. Dra. Linares is the former director of El museo de la música, Havana. Tape-recorded interviews in the home of Dra. Linares, May 1996, 1997, and March of 1998.

Linebaugh, Peter, and Marcus Rediker. 2000. *The Many-Headed Hydra: Sailors, Slaves, Commoners, and the Hidden History of the Revolutionary Atlantic.* Boston: Beacon Press.

Lohse, Russel. 2002. Slave-trade nomenclature and African ethnicities in the Americas: evidence from early eighteenth-century Costa Rica. *Slavery and Abolition* 23(3): 73–92.

López-Valdés, Rafael. 1985. La sociedad secreta Abakuá en un grupo de trabajadores portuarios. In *Componentes Africanos en el etnos cubano.* Havana: Editorial de ciencias sociales. Pp. 151–185.

Los Ñáñigos: Su historia, sus prácticas, su lenguaje, con el facsímile de los sellos que usa cada uno de los juegos o agrupaciones. 1882. Havana: Imprenta La Correspondencia de Cuba.

Lovejoy, Paul. 1989. The impact of the Atlantic slave trade on Africa: a review of the literature. *Journal of African History* 30(3): 365–394.

Lovejoy, Paul E., and David Richardson. 1999. Trust, pawnship, and Atlantic history: the institutional foundations of the Old Calabar slave trade. *American Historical Review* 104(2): 333–355.

Lovejoy, Paul E., and David Richardson. 2001. Letters of the Old Calabar slave trade, 1760–1789. In *Genius in Bondage: Literature from the Early Black Atlantic.* Ed. V. Caretta and P. Gould. Lexington: University Press of Kentucky. Pp. 89–115.

Luis, William, and Julia Cuervo Hewitt. 1987. Santos y Santería: Conversación con Arcadio, santero de Guanabacoa. *Afro-Hispanic Review* 6 (Jan.): 9–17.

Maceo, Antonio. 1998/1952. *Antonio Maceo, Ideología política, cartas y otros documentos.* Vol. 1, *(1870–1894),* Vol. 2, *(1895–1896).* Havana: Editorial de ciencias sociales.

MacGaffey, Wyatt. 1977. Fetishism revisited: Kongo *Nkisi* in sociological perspective. *Africa* 47(2): 172–184.

Madden, Richard Robert. 1839. Deposition of Dr. Richard R. Madden, 20 November 1839, U.S. District Court, Connecticut. Madden, the British superintendent of liberated Africans in Havana in the late 1830s, made this statement for the Amistad trials. Microfilm Reel 98-4, National Archives, Washington, DC.

Mamonekene, Victor, and G. Teugels. 1993. *Faune des poissons d-eaux douces de la reserve de la Biosphere de Dimonika (Mayombe, Congo).* Annales Science Zoologiques, vol. 272. Tervuren, Belgique: Musee Royale de l'Afrique Centrale.

Manfredi, Victor. 1991. *Àgbọ̀ and Éhụgbọ̀: Ìgbo Linguistic Consciousness, Its Origins and Limits.* Ph.D. diss., Harvard University.

Manfredi, Victor. 2004. Philological perspectives on the southeastern Nigerian diaspora. *Contours: A Journal of the African Diaspora* 2(2): 239–287.

Mann, Kristin, and Edna Bay, eds. 2001. *Rethinking the African Diaspora: The Making of a Black Atlantic World in the Bight of Benin and Brazil.* London: Frank Cass.

Mansfeld, Alfred. 1908. *Urwald-dokumente: vier Jahre unter den Crossflussnegern Kameruns.* Berlin: Dietrich Reimer (Ernst Vohsen).

Mante, Thomas. 1772. *The History of the Late War in North America, and the Islands of the West Indies.* London.

María de la Torre, José. 1986/1857. *Lo que fuimos y lo que somos, o la Habana antigua y moderna.* Havana: Ediciones Históricas Cubanas.

Marino García, Justo. 2006. Mr. Marino holds the title of Moni Bonkó in the Efóri Enkomón lodge. He was a founding member of the rumba group Yoruba Andabo. Conversation with the author in Havana.

Marrero, Levi. 1956. *Historia económica de Cuba*. Havana: Universidad de La Habana.

Marrero, Levi. 1972–1987. *Cuba: Economía y sociedad*. 15 vols. Madrid: Editorial Playor.

Martí, José. 1977. *Our America: Writings on Latin America and the Struggle for Cuban Independence*. Ed. Philip Foner. New York: Monthly Review Press.

Martí, José. 1992. Una orden secreta de africanos. In *Obras Completas*. Vol. 5. Havana: Editorial de ciencias sociales. Pp. 324–325. [Originally published in *Patria*, 1 April 1983.]

Martín, Juan Luis. 1930. Los secretos de los ñáñigos. *Revista de la Habana* Feb.: 173–178.

Martín, Juan Luis. 1946. *Vocabularios de Ñáñigo y Lucumí*. Havana: Editorial Atalaya.

Martínez-Furé, Rogelio. 1968. Patakin. *Cuba revista mensual* (Havana) Pp. 62–69.

Martínez-Furé, Rogelio. 1976. *Palenque y mambisa*. Havana. [Text from performance by the Conjunto Folklórico Nacional, premiered in 1976 in Havana.]

Martínez-Furé, Rogelio. 1979. Los bríkamo. In *Diálogos imaginarios*. Havana: Arte y Literatura. Pp. 165–183.

Martínez-Furé, Rogelio. 1995, 1998–2006. Dr. Martínez-Furé was a founder of Cuba's National Folklore Ensemble and remains its artistic director. Conversations in the home of Dr. Martínez-Furé, Havana.

Martínez-Furé, Rogelio. 2001. Comentarios y debate. *Culturas encontradas: Cuba y los Estados Unidos*. Ed. Rafael Hernández y John H. Coatsworth. Havana: Centro de Investigación y Desarrollo de la Cultura Cubana Juan Marinello.

Martínez-Rodríguez, Raúl. 1978. *El General Enrique Loynaz del Castillo, autor del Himno Invasor Cubano*. Havana: Ministerio de cultura.

Martínez-Rodríguez, Raúl. 1995. La rumba en la provincia de Matnazas. In *Panorama de la música popular cubana*. Ed. Radamés Giro. Havana: Editorial Letras Cubanas. Pp. 139–151.

Martínez-Ruíz, Bárbaro. 2002. Speaking in action: processes of visual representation in the Bakongo world. In *Odantalan*. Ed. Victor Gama. Lisbon: PangeiArt and Prince Claus Fund. Pp. 89–117.

Martínez-Ruíz, Bárbaro. 2007. Sketches of memory: visual encounters with Africa in Jamaican culture. In *Art and Emancipation in Jamaica: Isaac Mendes Belisario and His Worlds*. Ed. T. Barringer, G. Forrester, and B. Martínez-Ruíz. New Haven, CT: Yale Center for British Art. Pp. 103–119.

Martínez-Vergne, Teresita. 1989. Politics and society in the Spanish Caribbean during the nineteenth century. In *The Modern Caribbean*. Ed. Franklin Knight and Colin Palmer. Chapel Hill: University of North Carolina Press. Pp. 185–202.

Martré, Gonzalo, and Silvestre Méndez. 1997. *Rumberos de ayer: músicos cubanos en México (1930–1950)*. Veracruz, México: Instituto Veracruzano de Cultura.

Marwick, William. 1897. *William and Louisa Anderson: A Record of Their Life and Work in Jamaica and Old Calabar*. Edinburgh, Scotland: Andrew Elliot.

Matory, J. Lorand. 2005. *Black Atlantic Religion: Tradition, Transnationalism, and Matriarchy in the Afro-Brazilian Candomblé*. Princeton, NJ: Princeton University Press.

Matute, Daniel Lyonga. 1988. *The Socio Cultural Legacies of the Bakweris of Cameroon*. Yaounde, Cameroon: CEPER.

McNeill, John Robert. 1985. *Atlantic Empires of France and Spain: Louisbourg and Havana, 1700–1763*. Chapel Hill: University of North Carolina Press.

Meek, C. K. 1937. *Law and Authority in a Nigerian Tribe: A Study in Indirect Rule*. Oxford: Oxford University Press.

Memorias de la Sociedad Patriótica de La Habana. 1842. Vol. 14. Havana: Imprenta del Gobierno y Capitania General por S.M.

Messenger, John C. 1959. The role of proverbs in a Nigerian judicial system. *Southwestern Journal of Anthropology* 15(1): 64–73.

Messenger, John C. 1967. The Christian concept of forgiveness and Anang morality. In *Readings in Missionary Anthropology*. Ed. W. A. Smalley. Tarrytown, NY: Practical Anthropology. Pp. 180–186.

Messenger, John C. 1971. Ibibio drama. *Africa: Journal of the International African Institute* 41(3): 208–222.

Meza, Ramón. 1891. El día de Reyes. *La Habana Elegante*, año 5, no. 2. Havana.

Miguel, Byron. 1990. *Seis Días de Noviembre: el fusilamiento de los estudiantes de medicina*. Miami, FL: Ediciones Universal.

Miller, Ivor. 1994. Celina González: queen of the Punto Cubano. *The Beat* 13. 2: 46–47.

Miller, Ivor. 1995a. The singer as priestess: interviews with two Cuban artists. In *Sounding Off! Music as Subversion/Resistance/Revolution*. Ed. Ron Sakolsky and Fred Wei-han Ho. New York: Autonomedia. Pp. 287–304.

Miller, Ivor. 1995b. *Belief and Power in Contemporary Cuba*. Ph.D. diss., Northwestern University, Department of Performance Studies.

Miller, Ivor. 2000a. Obras de fundación: la Sociedad Abakuá en los años 90. *Caminos: Revista Cubana de Pensamiento Socioteológico* (Havana) 13–14: 24–35.

Miller, Ivor. 2000b. A Secret society goes public: the relationship between Abakuá and Cuban popular culture. *African Studies Review* 43(1): 161–188.

Miller, Ivor. 2000c. Religious symbolism in Cuban political performance. *TDR: A Journal of Performance Studies* 44(2: T166): 30–55.

Miller, Ivor. 2002. *Aerosol Kingdom: Subway Painters of New York City*. Jackson: University Press of Mississippi.

Miller, Ivor. 2004a. The formation of African identities in the Americas: spiritual "ethnicity." *Contours: A Journal of the African Diaspora* 2(2): 193–222.

Miller, Ivor. 2004b. El tambor como madre en la sociedad Abakuá. *Madre África: conceptos maternos en escultura tradicional africana* (Madrid) April–June: 12–16.

Miller, Ivor. 2004c. Introduction. *Contours: A Journal of the African Diaspora* 2(2): 141–156.

Miller, Ivor. 2005. Cuban Abakuá chants: examining new evidence for the African Diaspora. *African Studies Review* 48(1): 23–58.

Miller, Ivor. 2009. Bongó Itá: Leopard Society music and language in West Africa, Western Cuba, and New York City. In *Bridging Diasporal Sacred Worlds: Black Music Scholarship and the Americas*. Ed. Samuel A. Floyd Jr. Berkeley: University of California Press.

Millet, José, and Rafael Brea. 1989. *Grupos folklóricos de Santiago de Cuba*. Santiago de Cuba: Editorial Oriente.

"Minini" (Francisco Zamora-Chirino). 2000. Minini is director of the folklore group AfroCuba of Matanzas. Conversations with the author in Matanzas, January.

Mintz, Sidney W. 1984. Africa *of* Latin America: an unguarded reflection. In *Africa in Latin America*. Ed. Manuel Moreno Fraginals, English translation. New York: Holmes and Meier. Pp. 286–305. [Original Spanish edition, 1977.]

Miró Argenter, José. 1942. *Cuba: crónicas de la guerra (la campaña de invasión)*. Vol. 1. 2nd ed. Havana: Editorial Lex.

Miró Argenter, José. 1945. *Cuba: crónicas de la guerra*. Vol. 2. 4th ed. Havana: Editorial Lex.

Molina, Lucía Dominga, and Mario Luis López. 2001. Afro-Argentineans: "forgotten" and "disappeared," yet still present. In *African Roots/American Cultures: Africa in the Creation of the Americas*. Ed. Sheila Walker, Lanham, MD: Rowman and Littlefield. Pp. 332–347.

Moliner-Casteñeda, Israel. 1988. Los Ñáñigos. *Del Caribe* 12: 13–18.

Moliner-Casteñeda, Israel. 1992. Los Cabildos de Africanos en al cuidad de Matanzas. Self-published, Matanzas. 65 pp.

Moliner-Casteñeda, Israel. 1998/1990. Los cultos zoolátricos. In *Estudios Afro-Cubanos*. Vol. 2. Ed. Lázara Menéndez. Havana: University of Havana. Pp. 381–402.

Moliner-Casteñeda, Israel, and Gladys Gutierrez-Rodríguez. 1987. La rumba. *Del Caribe* 9: 40–47.

Montaigne, Michel de. 1958. *The Complete Essays of Montaigne*. Trans. D. M. Frame. Stanford, CA: Stanford University Press.

Montejo-Arrechea, Carmen V. 2004. *Sociedades negras en Cuba: 1878–1960*. Havana: Editorial de ciencias sociales/Centro de investigación y desarrllo de la cultura cubana Juan Marinello.

Moore, Robin D. 1997. *Nationalizing Blackness: Afrocubanismo and Artistic Revolution in Havana, 1920–1940*. Pittsburgh: University of Pittsburgh Press.

Morales-Padrón, Francisco. 1972. Conspiraciones y masonería en Cuba (1810–1826). *Anuario de estudios americanos* 29: 343–377.

Moreno, Isidoro. 1997. *La antigua hermandad de los negros de Sevilla: Etnicidad, poder y sociedad en 600 años de historia*. Sevilla: Universidad de Sevilla.

Moreno-Fraginals, Manuel. 1986/1978. *El Ingenio: complejo económico social cubano del azúcar*. Vol. 2. Havana: Editorial de Ciencia Sociales.

Moreno-Fraginals, Manuel. 1996. *Cuba/España, España/Cuba: historia común*. 2nd ed. Barcelona: Crítica.

Moreno-Moreno, José Antonio. 1948. El "yangüe" fernandino. *África* (Madrid) 83–84: 411–412.

Moros y Morellón, José de, and Juan Miguel de los Ríos. 1844. *Memorias sobre las islas africanas de España, Fernando Póo y Annobón*. Madrid: Compañia Tipográfica.

Morúa-Delgado, Martín. 1975/1901. *La familia Unzúazu*. Havana: Editorial arte y literatura.

Mosongo, Prince Njong Effiong-Offiong. 1995. *An X-Ray on Bakassi Peninsular (Let's Save It)*. Self-published, Ekondo Titi, Cameroon.

Mosquera, Gerardo. 1996. Eleggúa at the (post?) modern crossroads: the presence of Africa in the visual art of Cuba. In *Santería Aesthetics in Contemporary Latin American Art*. Ed. Arturo Lindsay. Washington, DC: Smithsonian Institution Press. Pp. 225–258.

"Muerto Vivo", Ramon. 2004. Raised in Havana, where he was trained as a Tata Nkisi in the lineage of "Lemba kongo, kríyumba ngo," he was the lead voice in the recording *Lemba Kongo Muna Kongo* (2002). Recorded conversations with the author in Muerto Vivo's home in the Bronx, 7 April.

Mullin, Gerald W. 1972. *Flight and Rebellion Slave Resistance in Eighteenth-Century Virginia*. Oxford: Oxford University Press.

Mulvey, Patricia A. 1982. Slave confraternities in Brazil: their role in colonial society. *The Americas* 39(1): 39–68.

Muñoz y Gaviria, José (visconde de San Javier). n.d. *Tres años en Fernando Póo; viaje a África*. Madrid: Universario de Manini.

Murray, David R. 1980. *Odious Commerce: Britain, Spain and the Abolition of the Cuban Slave Trade*. Cambridge, UK: Cambridge University Press.

Muzio, María del Carmen. 1996. Andrés Petit: El hombre que vendió el secreto Abacuá. *Juventud Rebelde* (25 agosto): 11.

Muzio, María del Carmen. 2001. *Andrés Quimbisa*. Havana: Ediciones Union.

Mzeka, Paul N. 1980. *The Core Culture of Nso*. Introduction by Dan N. Latum. Agawam, MA: Jerome Radin Co.

Nair, Kannan K. 1972. *Politics and Society in South-eastern Nigeria, 1841–1906*. London: Frank Cass.

Navarro, Diego Joseph. 1929. Bando sobre prohibir el uso de armas y capas a negros y mulattos (Havana, 4 May 1779). *Boletín del Archivo Nacional* 28: 103–104.

Nebengu, Mgba Sama. 1990. *Origins and Settlement of the Balondo: A Historical Survey*. Ph.D. diss., Department of History, University of Yaounde, Cameroon.

Nicklin, Keith. 1984. Cross River Studies. *African Arts* 18(1): 24–27, 96.

Nicklin, Keith. 1991. Un emblème Ejagham de la société Ekpe [An Ejagham eblem of the Ekpe Society]. In *Art Tribal*. Geneva: Association des Amis du Musée Barbier-Muller. Pp. 3–18.

Nicklin, Keith. 1995. Emblem of the leopard spirit society: Ejagham, south-east Nigeria/south-west Cameroon. In *Africa: The Art of a Continent*. Ed. Tom Phillips. Munich: Prestel. Pp. 372–373.

Nicklin, Keith, and Jill Salmons. 1984. Cross River Art Styles. *African Arts* 18(1): 28–43, 93–94.

Nicklin, Keith, and Jill Salmons. 1988. Ikem: the history of a masquerade in southeast Nigeria. In *West African Masks and Cultural Systems*. Ed. Sidney Littlefield Kasfir. Tervuren, Belgique: Musée Royal d'Afrique Centrale. Pp. 123–149.

Nicol, Yves. 1929. *La Tribu des Bakoko. Etude monographique d'economie coloniale. Une stade de l'évoltion d'une tribu Noire au Cameroun*. Paris: Librairie coloniale orientaliste Larose.

Ñkaña, Esien Ekpe. 1984/1933. *Mutanda: The Search for Namondo*. Trans. Sam Eyo-Abidua. Calabar: Samson.

Ñkaña, Esien Ekpe. 2000/1933. *Mutanda Oyom Namondo*. Calabar: Wusen.

Noah, Monday Efiong. 1980. *Old Calabar: The City States and the Europeans, 1800–1885*. Uyo, Nigeria: Scholars Press.

Noah, Monday Efiong. 1990. Social and political developments: the lower Cross region, 1600–1900. In *A History of the Cross River Region of Nigeria*. Ed. Monday B. Abasiattai. Enugu, Nigeria: University of Calabar Press and Harris. Pp. 90–108.

Nofuru, Edmond. 2002. *Know the Oroko Ethnic Group*. Self-published, South West Province, Cameroon.

Northrup, David. 1978. *Trade without Rulers: Pre-Colonial Economic Development in South-Eastern Nigeria*. Oxford: Clarendon Press.

Northrup, David. 2000. Igbo and Igbo myth: culture and ethnicity in the Atlantic world, 1600–1850. *Slavery and Abolition* 21(3): 1–20.

Nowak, Ronald M. 1991. *Walker's Mammals of the World*. Vol. 2. 5th ed.. Baltimore, MD: Johns Hopkins University Press.

Nsan, Chief Emmanuel. 2005. From Ifundo, Akpabuyo, whose Ékpè is centered in Atakpa. Chief Nsan is a member of the Obong of Calabar's council. Conversations with the author.

Ntui Erim Onongha, Lt. Col. Ntufam Issac. 2005. Clan Head, Abijang-Ibunda, Etung L.G.A. Cross River State. Conversations with Chief Ntui in his village during three separate visits.

Nwaka, Geoffrey I. 1978. Secret societies and colonial change: a Nigerian example. *Cahiers d'études africaines* (Paris) 18(69–70): 187–200.

Nwokeji, G. Ugo. 2000. The Atlantic slave trade and population density: a historical demography of the Biafran hinterland. *Canadian Journal of African Studies* 34(3): 616–655.

Nyamnjoh, Francis B. 2005. Images of Nyongo amongst Bamenda Grassfielders in Whiteman Kontri. *Citizenship Studies* 9(3): 241–269.

Nyamnjoh, Francis B. 2006. *A Nose for Money*. Nairobi: East African Educational Publishers.

Nyong, Obong Bassey A. 2005. Obong Nyong is Iyámba of Obom Uruan from Mbiaya Uruan. Conversations with the author in Uyo, Akwa Ibom State.

Offiong, Daniel A. 1989. *Continuity and Change in Some Traditional Societies of Nigeria*. Zaria, Nigeria: Ahmadu Bello University Press.

O'Kelly, James J. 1874. *The Mambi-Land or Adventures of a Herald Correspondent in Cuba*. Philadelphia: J. B. Lippincott.

Okon, Ntufam John Achot. 2005. Ntufam Okon is the Clerk for the Cross River State House of Assembly. Ntufam is a title designating the Head of a House. He also holds the grade of Nkàndà in Aningeje M̀gbè. Conversation with the author, 9 March. Ntufam Okon brought me to his hometown of Aningeje and its M̀gbè shrine, 22 December.

Oku, Chief Essien Ekpenyong. 2005. Chief Oku is Obong Okpoho of Efe Esien Ékpè of Creek Town. Conversation with the author in Calabar, May.

Oku, Ekei Essien. 1989. *The Kings and Chiefs of Old Calabar (1795–1925)*. The Association for the Promotion of Efik Language, Literature and Culture, Calabar. Calabar: Glad Tidings Press.

Oku, Ekei Essien. 1990. Kings of Old Calabar. In *Old Calabar Revisited*. Ed. S. O. Jaja, E. O. Erim, B. W. Andah. Enugu, Nigeria: Harris. Pp. 20–45.

Olivera-Chirimini, Tomás. 2001. Candombe, African nations, and the Africanity of Uruguay. In *African Roots/American Cultures: Africa in the Creation of the Americas*. Ed. Sheila Walker. Lanham, MD: Rowman and Littlefield. Pp. 256–274.

Onyile, Onyile Bassey. 2000. Abang dance: radiance from the river and Efik ideal of femininity. *Ijele: Art eJournal of the African World*. Accessed 12 December 2006. http://www.africaresource.com/ijele/vol1.1/onyile.html.

Oqua III, Thomas Ika Ika. 2008. H.R.M. Ndidem (Dr.) Thomas Ika Ika Oqua III is Grand Patriarch/Ndidem of the Qua Nation and Paramount Ruler/President of the Traditional Rulers Council, Calabar Municipality, Cross River State. Conversations with the author, March.

Orejuela, Adriana. 2003. La Tropical: Bitácora de la música popular cubana del siglo XX. *Solar de la Timba*. Ed. 1. Año 1, junio–agosto. Accessed 8 September 2006. http://www.solardelatimba.com/main_art/esp_latropical.htm.

Oropesa, Frank. 1994–2006. Mr. Oropesa is the bongo player and manager of the Septeto Nacional de Ignacio Piñeiro, as well as an Abakuá title-holder. Conversations with the author in Havana.

Orovio, Helio. 1992. *Diccionario de la música cubana: Biográfico y técnico*. 2nd ed. Havana: Letras Cubanas.

Orovio, Helio. 2005. *El carnaval habanero: ensayo*. Havana: Ediciones extramuros.

Orozco, Román, and Natalia Bolivar-Aróstegui. 1998. *CubaSanta: Comunistas, santeros y cristianos en la isla de Fidel Castro*. Madrid: El Pais/Aguilar.

Ortiz, Fernando. 1906. *Hampa afrocubana: los negros brujos*. Madrid: Librería de Fernando Fe.

Ortiz, Fernando. 1924a. *Glosario de afronegrismos*. Havana: El siglo 20.

Ortiz, Fernando. 1924b. Personajes del folkore afrocubano. *Archivos del Folklore Cubano* 1(1): 62–75.

Ortiz, Fernando. 1927. Los Negros Curros: sus caracteres: la ostentación. *Archivos del Folklore Cubano* 2(4): 285–325.

Ortiz, Fernando. 1929. Los afrocubanos dientimellados. *Archivos del Folklore Cubano* 4(1): 16–29.

Ortiz, Fernando. 1939. Brujos o santeros. *Estudios Afrocubanos* (Havana) 3(1–4): 85–90.

Ortiz, Fernando. 1943. On the relations between blacks and whites. *Points of View* 7(Oct.): 1–12.

Ortiz, Fernando. 1950a. El origen de la tragedia y los ñáñigos. *Bohemia* 42(50): 26–28, 138–141.

Ortiz, Fernando. 1950b. ¿Dónde hay ñáñigos?" *Bohemia* 42(43): 4–5, 144–145, 156.

Ortiz, Fernando. 1950c. Los Espíritus o "diablitos" de los ñáñigos. *Bohemia* 42(39): 20–21, 114–115.

Ortiz, Fernando. 1952a. *Los instrumentos de la música afrocubana*. Vol. 1. Havana: Ministerio de Educación.

Ortiz, Fernando. 1952b. *Los instrumentos de la música afrocubana*. Vol. 2. Havana: Ministerio de Educación.

Ortiz, Fernando. 1952c. *Los instrumentos de la música afrocubana.* Vol. 3. Havana: Ministerio de Educación.

Ortiz, Fernando. 1954. *Los instrumentos de la música afrocubana.* Vol. 4. Havana: Cárdenas y Cía.

Ortiz, Fernando. 1955a. *Los instrumentos de la música afrocubana.* Vol. 5. Havana: Cárdenas y Cía.

Ortiz, Fernando. 1955b. Los negros "Matiabos" de Cuba." *Bohemia* 47(37): 8–9, 120–121, 130.

Ortiz, Fernando. 1956a. Letter from Ortiz to Dra. Vera Rubin at Columbia University, 23 March. Archives of the Research Institute for the Study of Man, New York City.

Ortiz, Fernando. 1956b. La secta conga de los "Matiabos" de Cuba. In *Libro Jubilar de Alfonso Reyes.* Mexico City: Universidad Nacional Autónoma de México, dirección general de diffusion cultural. Pp. 309–325.

Ortiz, Fernando. 1960. *La antigua fiesta afrocubana del "Día de Reyes."* Havana: Ministerio de Cultura. [Revised from the 1920 original: La fiesta afro-cubana del "Día de Reyes." *Revista Bimestre Cubana* 15(1): 5–26.]

Ortiz, Fernando. 1974. *Nuevo catauro de cubanismos.* Havana: Editorial de ciencias sociales.

Ortiz, Fernando. 1975a/1916. *Los negros esclavos.* Havana: Editorial de ciencias sociales.

Ortiz, Fernando. 1975b. Chano Pozo en Nueva York influye en el jazz. *Signos* (Santa Clara, Cuba) 17: 144–146.

Ortiz, Fernando. 1975c. *Historia de una pelea cubana contra los demonios.* Havana: Editorial de ciencias sociales.

Ortiz, Fernando. 1981/1951. *Los bailes y el teatro de los negros en el folklore de Cuba.* Havana: Letras Cubanas.

Ortiz, Fernando. 1984a. *Ensayos etnográficos.* Havana: Editorial de ciencias sociales.

Ortiz, Fernando. 1984b. Los cabildos afro-cubanos. In *Ensayos etnográficos.* Havana: Editorial de ciencias sociales. Pp. 11–40. [Originally published in *Revista Bimestre Cubana* 16(1), 1921.]

Ortiz, Fernando. 1986. *Los negros curros.* Havana: Editorial de ciencias sociales.

Ortiz, Fernando. 1991a/1924. *Glosario de afronegrismos.* Havana: Editorial de ciencias sociales.

Ortiz, Fernando. 1991b/1954. Los diablitos de Puerto Rico. In *Estudios etnosociológicos.* Comp. Isaac Barreal Fernández. Havana: Editorial de ciencias sociales. Pp. 232–239.

Ortiz, Fernando. 1991c/1940. *Contrapunteo cubano del tabaco y el azúcar.* Havana: Editorial de ciencias sociales.

Ortiz, Fernando. 1991d/1954. La tragedia de los ñáñigos. In *Estudios etnosociológicos.* Comp. Isaac Barreal Fernández. Havana: Editorial de Ciencias socials. Pp. 123–140.

Ortiz, Fernando. 1993a/1950. *La africania de la música folklórica de Cuba.* Havana: Letras Cubanas.

Ortiz, Fernando. 1993b/1950. *La "tragedia" de los ñáñigos.* Havana: Colección Raíces.

Ortiz, Fernando. 1995. *Los negros brujos.* Havana: Editorial de ciencias sociales. [Original 1906, *Hampa afrocubana: los negros brujos.*]

Ortiz, Fernando, Ramón Vasconcelos, and others. 1945–1946. Las Comparsas populares del carnaval habanero. *Estudios Afrocubanos* (Havana) 5: 129–147.

Ortiz Oderigo, Néstor. 1974. *Aspectos de la cultura africana en el Río de la Plata.* Buenos Aires: Edición Plus Ultra.

Ossorio, Amado. 1886. Á los expedicionarios en el Golfo de Guinea. *Revista de Geografía Comercial* (Madrid) 1(24): 337–363.

Ottenberg, Simon, and Linda Knudsen. 1985. Leopard Society masquerades: symbolism and diffusion. *African Arts* 18(2): 37–44, 93–95, 103–104.

Owen, William F. 1833. *Narrative of Voyages to Explore the Shores of Africa, Arabia and Madagascar, performed in H.M. Ships Leven and Barracouta, under the direction of Captain W. F. W. Owen, R.N. by command of the Lords Commissioners of the Admiralty.* London: Richard Bentley.

Padrón-Valdés, Abelardo. 1991. *General de tres guerras*. Havana: Editorial Letras Cubanas.

Palés Matos, Luis. 2000. Ñáñigo al cielo (Ñáñigo to heaven). *Selected Poems/Poesía selecta*. Trans. and introduction by Julio Marzán. Houston, Texas: Arte Público Press.

Paley, Ruth. 2002. After *Somerset*: Mansfield, slavery and the law in England, 1772–1830. In *Law, Crime and English Society, 1660–1830*. Ed. Norma Landau. Cambridge, UK: Cambridge University Press. Pp. 165–184.

"Palillo" (Roberto Pasqual Leal Sanz). 2006. Moní Bonkó of Mutága Efó; percussionist with the Mozambique group of Pello el Afrokan in the 1960s. Conversations with the author, February.

Palmer, Colin. 1976. *Slaves of the White God: Blacks in Mexico, 1570–1650*. Cambridge, MA: Harvard University Press.

Palmer, Colin. 1981. *Human Cargoes: The British Slave Trade to Spanish America, 1700–1739*. Urbana: University of Illinois Press.

Palmié, Stephan. 2003. Ekpe/Abakuá in Middle Passage: Time, Space and Units of Analysis in African American Historical Anthropology. Unpublished ms. Department of Anthropology, University of Chicago.

Palmié, Stephan. 2006. A view from itia ororó kande. *Social Anthropology* 14(1): 99–118.

Palmié, Stephan, and Elizabeth Pérez. 2005. An all too present absence: Fernando Ortiz's work on Abakuá in its sociocultural context. *New West Indian Guide* 79(3–4): 219–227.

Paquette, Robert L. 1988. *Sugar Is Made with Blood: The Conspiracy of La Escalera and the Conflict between Empires over Slavery in Cuba*. Middletown, CT: Wesleyan University Press.

Pascual Pons, Carmen. 1997. *Acercamiento a las Sociedades Secretas Abakuá en Guanabacoa*. Havana: Archivo del Museo de Guanabacoa.

Pazos, Gerardo "El Chino." 1998–2002. Mr. Pazos (1925–2002) was the Mokóngo of the Kamaroró Efó lodge. Conversations with the author in Havana.

Peel, J. D. Y. 1990. The pastor and the Babalawo: the interaction of religions in nineteenth-century Yorubaland. *Africa* 60 (3): 338–369.

Pérez, Louis A. 1983. *Cuba between Empires, 1878–1902*. Pittsburgh, PA: University of Pittsburgh Press.

Pérez, Louis A. 1988. *Cuba: Between Reform and Revolution*. New York: Oxford University Press.

Pérez, Louis A. 1999. *On Becoming Cuban*. Chapel Hill: University of North Carolina Press.

Pérez, Louis A. 2004. Professor Pérez is in the Department of History at the University of North Carolina. Letter to the author, 25 February.

Pérez, Louis A. 2006. Letter to the author, 19 April.

Pérez-Beato, Manuel. 1892. Curiosidades. Instrucciones y disposiciones reglamentarias para la sociedad de los ñánigos blancos. Part 1. *El curioso americano* 2(diciembre): 35–38.

Pérez-Beato, Manuel. 1893a. Curiosidades. Instrucciones y disposiciones reglamentarias para la sociedad de los ñánigos blancos. Part 2. *El curioso americano* 2(enero): 56–58.

Pérez-Beato, Manuel. 1893b. Respuestas. Negros cimarrones. *El curioso americano* 9(abril): 131.

Pérez de la Riva, Juan. 1963. Introducción. In *Correspondencia reservada del Capitán General Don Miguel Tacón con el Gobierno de Madrid, 1834–1836*. Havana: Consejo Nacional de la Cultura. Pp. 13–96.

Pérez de la Riva, Juan. 2000. *Los culíes chinos en Cuba (1847–1880)*. Contribución al estudio de la inmigración contratada en el Caribe. Havana: Editorial de ciencias sociales.

Pérez-Fernández, Rolando. 1986. Un caso de transculturación Bantú-Carabalí en Cuba. *Del Caribe* 6: 20–27.

Pérez-Rodríguez, Nancy, Clara Domínguez, Rosa Rodríguez, Orlando Silva, and Danubia Terry. 1982. *El cabildo carabalí isuama*. Santiago de Cuba: Editorial Oriente.

Pezuela, Jacobo de la. 1863. *Diccionario geografico, estadístico, histórico de la isla de Cuba*. Vol. 2. Madrid: Impressa del estab. de Mellado.

Philalethes, Demoticus. 1856. *Yankee Travels through the Island of Cuba; or, the Men and Government, the Laws and Customs of Cuba, Seen by American Eyes*. New York: D. Appleton and Co.

Pichardo, Esteban. 1985/1875. *Diccionario provincial casi razonado de vozes y frases cubanas*. 6th ed. Havana: Editorial de ciencias sociales.

Pike, Ruth. 1983. *Penal Servitude in Early Modern Spain*. Madison: University of Wisconsin Press.

Placencia-Romero, Miguel-Ángel. 2006. Miguel-Ángel is an "obonékue facultado" in the Ikanfioró lodge of Havana, as well as a babaláwo. Conversations with the author in Miguel-Ángel's home in the barrio of Jesús María, 24 May.

Ponte-Domínguez, Francisco J. 1944. *La Masonería en la independencia de Cuba (1809–1869)*. Conferencia dictada en la Gran Logia de la isla de Cuba. Havana.

Price, Richard. 1983. *First-Time: The Historical Vision of an Afro-American People*. Baltimore, MD: Johns Hopkins University Press.

Price, Richard, ed. 1996. *Maroon Societies: Rebel Slave Communities in the Americas*. 3rd ed. Baltimore, MD: Johns Hopkins University Press.

Price, Richard, and Sally Price. 1991. *Two Evenings in Saramaka*. Chicago: University of Chicago Press.

Proby, Kathryn Hall. 1981. *Mario Sanchez: Painter of Key West Memories*. Key West, FL: Southernmost Press.

Prussin, Labelle. 2005. Dr. Prussin is an art historian. Conversation in New York City.

Pujol, Jordi. 2001. *Chano Pozo: el tambor de Cuba, vida y música del legendario rumbero cubano*. Booklet and three-CD set. Barcelona: Tumbao Cuban Classics.

Qua Clans Constituted Assembly (QCCA). 2003. *The Position of the Qua People of Calabar in the Current Move by Government to Achieve Unity, Peace and Stability in Calabar*. Calabar, Nigeria.

Quiñones, Tato. 1994. *Ecorie Abakuá: cuatro ensayos sobre los ñáñigos cubanos*. Havana: Ediciones Unión.

Rama, Carlos M. 1967. *Los Afro-Uruguayos*. Montevideo: El siglo ilustrado, colección libros de bolsillo.

Reid, Gordon McGregor. 1989. *The Living Waters of the Korup Rainforest*. World Wildlife Federation report no. 3206/A8:1.

Reis, João José. 2001a. Quilombos and rebellions in Brazil. In *African Roots/American Cultures: Africa in the Creation of the Americas*. Ed. Sheila Walker. Lanham, MD: Rowman and Littlefield. Pp. 301–313.

Reis, João José. 2001b. Candomblé in nineteenth-century Bahia: priests, followers, clients. In *Rethinking the African Diaspora: The Making of a Black Atlantic World in the Bight of Benin and Brazil*. Ed. Kristin Mann and Edna G. Bay. London: Frank Cass. Pp. 116–134.

Richardson, David, ed. 1991–1996. *Bristol, Africa and the Eighteenth-century Slave Trade to America*. 4 vols. Bristol, UK: Bristol Records Society.

Rivero-Muñiz, José. 1961. *El movimiento obrero durante la primera intervención (1899–1902): Apuntes para la historia del proletariado en Cuba*. Las Villas, Cuba: Universidad de Las Villas.

Robertson, G. A. 1819. *Notes on Africa, Particularly Those Parts Which Are Situated between Cape Verd and the River Congo*. London.

Robreño, Gustavo. 1925. *La acera del Louvre: Novela histórica*. Havana: Imprenta y papeleria de Rambla, Bouza y Ca.

Roche y Monteagudo, Rafael. 1908. *La policía y sus misterios en Cuba; adicionada con "La policia judicial," procedimientos, formularios, leyes, reglamentos, ordenanzas y disposiciones que conciernen a los cuerpos de segurirad publica*. Havana: Imprenta La prueba.

Roche y Monteagudo, Rafael. 1914. *La policía y sus misterios en Cuba*. Segunda edición corredida, aumentada y adicionada con "La policia judicial," procedimientos, formularios, leyes, reglamentos, ordenanzas y disposiciones que conciernen a los cuerpos de segurirad publica. Havana: Imprenta y Papeleria de Ramba, Bouza y Ca.

Roche y Monteagudo, Rafael. 1925/1908. *La policía y sus misterios en Cuba*. 3a edición. Havana: La Moderna Poesía.

Rodríguez, Alejandro. 1881. *Reseña histórica de los ñáñigos de Cuba desde su creación a la fecha*. Unpublished ms. Archivo Nacional de Cuba, asuntos políticos, legajo 76, Exp. 56.

Rodríguez, Romero Jorge. 2001. The Afro populations of America's Southern Cone: organization, development, and culture in Argentina, Bolivia, Paraguay, and Uruguay. In *African Roots/American Cultures: Africa in the Creation of the Americas*. Ed. Sheila Walker. Lanham, MD: Rowman and Littlefield. Pp. 314–331.

Rodríguez-Domínguez, Ezequiel. 1967. *Iconografía del danzón*. Havana: Sub-Dirección Provincial de Música de La Habana.

Rodríguez-Fornaris, Abelardo. 2000–2002. Mr. Rodríguez was the Empegó of the Munyánga Efó lodge of Havana. Conversations with the author in Havana.

Rodríguez-Sarabia, Aída. 1957. *Mariana Grajales: Madre de Cuba*. Havana: Impresora Modelo.

Rodríguez-Solveira, Mariano. 1975. Prólogo a la segunda edición. In *Historia de una pelea cubana contra los demonios*. Fernando Ortiz. Havana: Editorial de ciencias sociales. Pp. 7–18.

Roig de Leuchsenring, Emilio. 1925. Recuerdos de antaño, "El día Reyes o de Diablitos." *Carteles* (Havana) 8(2): 6, 27, 30.

Roig de Leuchsenring, Emilio. 1945–1946. Las comparsas carnavalescas de La Habana en 1937. *Estudios Afrocubanos* (Havana) 5: 148–172.

Roig de Leuchsenring, Emilio. 1963. *La Habana: apuntes históricos*. Vol. 1. Havana: Editorial del Consejo Nacional de cultura.

Rojas, María Teresa de. 1947. *Indice y Extractos del Archivo de Protocolos de La Habana, 1578–1585*. Havana.

Roots of King Jaja: The Amiaigbo Born and Opobo Crowned Monarch. 1997. Dakar, Senegal: West African Museums Programme. Enugu, Nigeria: The British Council and National Commission for Museums and Monuments, Nigeria.

Röschenthaler, Ute M. 1998. Honoring Ejagham women. *African Arts* 31(2): 38–49, 92–93.

Rosevear, D. R. 1979. Oban revisited. *Nigerian Field* 44(2): 75–81.

Rout, Leslie B. Jr. 1976. *The African Experience in Spanish America: 1502 to the Present Day*. London: Oxford University Press.

Ruel, Malcolm. 1962. Banyang settlements. Part I, Pre-European settlement. *Man* 62(Jul.): 99–103.

Ruel, Malcolm. 1969. *Leopards and Leaders: Constitutional Politics among a Cross River People*. London: Tavistock.

Ruíz, Ernesto. 1986. *Máximo Gómez: Selección bibliográfica y documental*. Havana: Editorial Acaemia.

Russell, Nelson Vance. 1929. The reaction in England and America to the capture of Havana, 1762. *Hispanic American Historical Review* 9(3): 303–316.

Russell-Wood, A. J. R. 1974. Black and mulatto brotherhoods in colonial Brazil: a study in collective behavior. *Hispanic American Historical Review* 54: 567–602.

Salillas, Rafael. 1901. Los ñáñigos en Ceuta. *Revista General de Legislación y Jurisprudencia* 98: 337–360.

Salinas-Martínez, Luis. 1994. Ekueñón de Efí Abarako Nankabia. Interviews with author and Michel Díaz in the home of Sr. Salinas-Martínez (1919–1995), Havana Vieja, 21 October and 26 December.

Salinas-Martínez, Luis. 1995. Mr. Salinas held the title of Ekueñón in the Abarakó Sisi lodge. Interview with author in the barrio of Colón, 13 March. All Salinas material was revised by El Chino Mokóngo, friend of Salinas, in January 2002.

Santa-Cruz, Nicomedes. 1988. El negro en Iberoamérica. *Cuadernos Hispanoamericanos* 451–452: 7–46.

Sarracino, Rodolfo. 1988. *Los que volvieron a África*. Havana: Editorial de ciencias sociales.

Sarracino, Rodolfo. 1989. *Inglaterra: sus dos caras en la lucha cubana por la abolición*. Havana: Letras Cubanas.

Scarpaci, Joseph L., Roberto Segre, and Mario Coyula. 2002. *Havana: Two Faces of the Antillean Metropolis*. Rev. ed. Chapel Hill: University of North Carolina Press.

Scott, Julius S. 1991. Afro-American sailors and the international communication network: the case of Newport Bowers. In *Jack Tar in History: Essays in the History of Maritime Life and Labour*. Ed. Colin Howell and Richard J. Twomey. Fredericton, New Brunswick: Acadiensis Press. Pp. 37–52.

Scott, Rebecca J. 1985. *Slave Emancipation in Cuba: The Transition to Free Labor, 1860–1899*. Princeton, NJ: Princeton University Press.

Sentencia pronunciada por la Sección de la Comisión militar establecida en la cuidad de matanzas para conocer de la causa de conspiración de la gente de color. 1844. Cuba: Comisión militar ejecutiva y permanente.

Simmons, Donald C. 1956. An ethnographic sketch of the Efik people; notes on the diary [of Antera Duke]. In *Efik Traders of Old Calabar*. Ed. Daryll Forde. London: International African Institute. Pp. 1–26, 66–78.

Simmons, Donald C. 1958. Cultural functions of the Efik tone riddle. *Journal of American Folklore* 71(280): 123–138.

Skelton, Paul. 2004. Dr. Skelton is a marine-life specialist; email message to the author, 2 March.

Smith, Michael P. 1994. *Mardi Gras Indians*. Grenta, LA: Pelican.

Sociedad de los ñáñigos blancos. 1893. Instrucción y disposiciones reglamentarias para la Sociedad de los ñáñigos blancos. [Establecimiento Tipográfico de A. E., Habana, 1882.] *El Curioso Americano* 1(3): 35–38; 1(4): 56–58.

Sosa-Rodríguez, Enrique. 1982. *Los Ñáñigos*. Havana: Ediciones Casa de las Américas.

Sosa-Rodríguez, Enrique. 1984. *El Carabali*. Havana: Letras cubanas.

Sosa-Rodríguez, Enrique. 2001. Ñáñigos en Key West (1880?–1923?). *Catauro: revista cubana de antropología* 2(3): 159–171.

Sotonavarro, Arístides. 1980. Las secretas intenciones del Abakuá. In *Varios testimonios policiales*. Selección de texo y apéndice Juan Carlos Fernández; prólogo, Dirección del Ministerioe del Interior. Havana: Editorial Letras Cubanas. Pp. 271–278. [Originally published in *Revista Moncada*, Año 6, no. 6, enero 1972.]

Soto Rodríguez, Ernesto "El Sambo." 2005. Mr. Soto holds the title of Isunékue in the Itia Mukandá lodge of Havana; one of the leading ceremonial directors of contemporary Abakuá; participant in the 2001 recording *Ibiono*. Email message to the author, through Ángel Guerrero, in response to my inquiry.

Soto Rodríguez, Ernesto "El Sambo." 2006. Conversations with the author, Havana, February, March.

Soumonni, Elisée. 2001. Some reflections on the Brazilian legacy in Dahomey. In *Rethinking the African Disapora: The Making of a Black Atlantic World in the Bight of Benin and Brazil*. Ed. Kristin Mann and Edna G. Bay. London: Frank Cass. Pp. 61–71.

Sparks, Randy J. 2002. Two princes of Calabar: an Atlantic odyssey from slavery to freedom. *William and Mary Quarterly* 3rd ser. 59(3): 555–583.

Sparks, Randy J. 2003. *The Two Princes of Calabar: An Eighteenth-Century Atlantic Odyssey*. Cambridge, MA: Harvard University Press.

Spottswood, Richard K. 1990. *Ethnic Music on Records: A Discography of Ethnic Recordings Produced in the United States, 1893 to 1942*. Vol. 4. Urbana: University of Illinois Press.

Stewart, John. 1989. *African States and Rulers: An Encyclopedia of Native, Colonial, and Independent States and Rulers Past and Present*. Jefferson, NC: McFarland and Co.

Stewart, John. 1999. *African States and Rulers*. 2nd ed. Jefferson, NC: McFarland and Co.

Story of the Old Calabar: A Guide to the National Museum at The Old Residency, Calabar. 1986. Foreword by Ekpo O. Eyo. Lagos: National Commission for Museums and Monuments.

Stubbs, Jean. 1995. Social and political motherhood of Cuba: Mariana Grajales Cuello. In *Engendering History: Caribbean Women in Historical Perspective*. Ed. Verene Shepherd, Bridget Brereton, and Barbara Bailey. New York: St. Martin's Press. Pp. 296–315.

Stuckey, Sterling. 1994. *Going through the Storm: The Influence of African American Art in History*. New York: Oxford University Press.

Suarez Gonzáles, Pedro-Alberto "Pedrito el yuma." 2006. Holds the title of Moruá Eribó Engomo of the lodge Betongó Naróko Efó; one of the leading ceremonial directors of contemporary Abakuá; participant in the 2001 recording *Ibiono*. Conversations with the author, February, March.

Sublette, Ned. 2004. *Cuba and Its Music: From the First Drums to the Mambo*. Chicago: Chicago Review Press.

Sundiata, Ibrahim K. 1996. *From Slaving to Neoslavery: The Bight of Biafra and Fernando Po in the Era of Abolitioon, 1827–1930*. Madison: University of Wisconsin Press.

Svalesen, Leif. 2000. *The Slave Ship Fredensborg*. Trans. Pat Shaw and Selena Winsnes. Oslo: Aschehoug; Paris: UNESCO.

Swartenbroeckx, Pierre. 1973. *Dictionnarie Kikongo et Kutiuba–Francais*. Série 3, vol. 2. Bandundu, Democratic Republic of Congo: Ceeba.

Sweet, James H. 2003. *Recreating Africa: Culture, Kinship, and Religion in the African-Portuguese World, 1441–1770*. Chapel Hill: University of North Carolina Press.

Syme-Hastings, J. 1896. Cuba as it is: thrilling story of a newspaper correspondent, horrors of guerilla war. *Journal of the Knights of Labor* (Washington, DC) 5 November, 1, 4.

Talbot, Mrs. D. Amaury. 1915. *Women's Mysteries of a Primitive People: The Ibibios of Southern Nigeria*. London: Cassell and Co.

Talbot, Percy Amaury. 1910. The land of the Ekoi, southern Nigeria. *Geographical Journal* 36(6): 637–654.

Talbot, Percy Amaury. 1912a. *In the Shadow of the Bush*. London: William Heinemann.

Talbot, Percy Amaury. 1912b. Notes on the Ekoi. *National Geographic Magazine* 23(1): 32–38.

Talbot, Percy Amaury. 1923. *Life in Southern Nigeria: The Magic, Beliefs, and Customs of the Ibibio Tribe*. London: MacMillan and Co.

Talbot, Percy Amaury. 1969/1926. *The Peoples of Southern Nigeria: A Sketch of Their History, Ethnology, and Languages, with an Abstract of the 1921 Census*. 4 vols. London: Oxford University Press.

Tamuno, Tekena N. 1966. Before British police in Nigeria. *Nigeria Magazine* 89(June): 102–116.

Téllez, Tello. 1960. Apuntes sobre un congreso de Abacua. *El Avance revolucionario* (Havana) 1 abril, 2.

Teugels, G. G., G. M. Reid, and R. P. King. 1992. *Fishes of the Cross River basin (Cameroon-Nigeria): Taxonomy, Zoogeography, Ecology, and Conservation*. Annales Science Zoologiques, vol. 266. Tervuren, Belgique: Musee Royale de l'Afrique Centrale.

Thomas, Hugh. 1997. *The Slave Trade: The History of the Atlantic Slave Trade, 1440–1870*. New York: Simon and Schuster.

Thomas, Hugh. 1998/1971. *Cuba, or the Pursuit of Freedom.* 2nd ed. New York: Da Capo Press.

Thompson, Robert Farris. 1974. *African Art in Motion: Icon and Act.* Los Angeles: University of California Press.

Thompson, Robert Farris. 1983. *Flash of the Spirit: African and Afro-American Art and Philosophy.* New York: Vintage.

Thompson, Robert Farris. 1998. Tres flechas desde el monte: La influencia ejagham en el arte mundial. *Anales Museo de America* (Madrid) 6: 71–83.

Thornton, John K. 1998a. *Africa and Africans in the Making of the Atlantic World, 1400–1800.* 2nd ed. Cambridge, UK: Cambridge University Press.

Thornton, John K. 1998b. *The Kongolese Saint Anthony: Dona Beatriz Kimpa Vita and the Antonian Movement, 1684–1706.* Cambridge, UK: Cambridge University Press.

Thornton, John K. 1999. *Warfare in Atlantic Africa, 1500–1800.* London: University College of London Press.

Tone, John Lawrence. 2006. *War and Genocide in Cuba, 1895–1898.* Chapel Hill: University of North Carolina Press.

Torres-Cuevas, Eduardo. 2005. *Historia de la masonería cubana: seis ensayos.* Havana: Imagen Contemporanea.

"Totico" (Eugenio Arrango). 2005. Conversation with the author about compositions on the 1967 recording *Patato y Totico,* The Bronx, 13 August.

Trouillot, Michel-Rolph. 1982. Motion in the system: coffee, color, and slavery in eighteenth-century Saint-Domingue. *Review* 3(Winter): 331–388.

Trouillot, Michel-Rolph. 1995. *Silencing the Past: Power and the Production of History.* Boston: Beacon Press.

Trujillo y Monagas, D. José. 1882. *Los criminales de Cuba y D. José Trujillo: narración de los servicios prestados en el cuerpo de policía de La Habana.* Barcelona: Establecimiento Tipográfico de Fidel Giro.

Turnbull, David. 1969/1840. *Travels in the West. Cuba; with Notices of Porto Rico, and the Slave Trade.* New York: Negro University Press.

Udo-Ema, A. J. 1938. The Ekpe society. *Nigeria: A Quarterly Magazine of General Interest* 16: 314–316.

Udo-Ema, A. J. 1940. I consult a witch-doctor. *Nigeria: A Quarterly of General Interest* 20: 321–322.

Ukpong, Justin S. 1982. Sacrificial worship in Ibibio traditional religion. *Journal of Religion in Africa* 13(3): 161–188.

Unzueta y Yuste, Abelardo de. 1947. *História geografica de la isla de Fernando Póo.* Madrid: Instituto de Estudios Africanos.

Urfé, Odilio. 1977. La música y la danza en Cuba. Related by Manuel Moreno Fraginals. In *África en América Latina.* Paris: UNESCO. Pp. 215–237.

Urfé, Odilio. 1982. La música folkórica, popular y del teatro cubano. In *La cultura en Cuba socialista.* Havana: Editorial letras cubanas. Pp. 151–173.

Urfé, Odilio. 1992. Liner notes to *Arcaño y sus maravillas,* EGREM CD 0034.

Urrutia, Gustavo E. 1935. *Cuatro Charlas Radiofónicas.* Havana.

Urua, Eno-Abasi. 1998. Letter to the author sent from the Department of Linguistics and Nigerian Languages, University of Uyo, Nigeria, 12 January.

Urua, Eno-Abasi. 2005. Conversations at the University of Uyo, Nigeria.

Urua, Eno-Abasi. 2007. Email correspondence with the author regarding the interpretations of Cross River phrases.

Urua, Ẹnọ A., M. Ekpenyong, and Dafydd Gibbon. 2004. *Uyo Ibibio Dictionary*. Preprint draft V01 2004-06-13. ABUILD Language Documentation Curriculum Materials, no. 1. University of Uyo, Nigeria, and Universität Bielefeld, Germany.

U.S. War Department. 1900. *Report on the Census of Cuba, 1899*. Lt. Col. J. P. Sanger, Inspector-General, Director. Washington, DC: Government Printing Office.

Uwazie, Ernest E. 1994. Modes of indigenous disputing and legal interactions among the Igbos of southeastern Nigeria. *Journal of Legal Pluralism* 34: 87–103.

Uya, Okon Edet. 1984. *A History of Oron People of the Lower Cross River basin*. Oron, Nigeria: Manson.

Uya, Okon Edet. 1986. History, culture and unity in the Cross River region. In *The Role of the Arts in Nation Building*. Ed. M. B. Abasiattai. University of Calabar Faculty of Arts Occasional Publications, vol. 1. Calabar: Map Publishers. Pp. 27–48.

Uya, Okon Edet. 1990. Old Calabar Studies: An overview. In *Old Calabar Revisited*. Ed. S. O. Jaja, E. O. Erim, B. W. Andah. Enugu, Nigeria: Harris. Pp. 194–208.

Valdés-Infante, Emilio. 1898. *Los cubanos en Fernando Póo: Horrores de la dominación española, en 1897 a 1898*. Havana: Imprenta El Figaro.

Valentin, Peter. 1980. *Jujus in the Forest Area of West Cameroon*. Compiled, edited, and with an introduction by Peter Valentin. Basel: Basler Afrika Bibliographien.

Vansina, J. 1964. *Le Royaume Kuba*. Tervuren, België: Musée Royal de l'Afrique Centrale.

Vansina, Jan. 1990. *Paths in the Rainforest: Toward a History of Political Tradition in Equatorial Africa*. Madison: University of Wisconsin Press.

Vansina, Jan. 2007. Letter to the author regarding manuscript review, 2 September.

Vélez, María Teresa. 2000. *Drumming for the Gods: The Life and Times of Felipe García Villamil, Santero, Palero, and Abakuá*. Philadelphia: Temple University Press.

Verger, Pierre. 1957. *Notes sur le cult des orisa et vodun à Bahia, la Baie de tous les Saints, au Brésil et à l'ancienne Côte des Esclaves en Afrique*. Mémoires de l'institut Français d'Afrique Noire, no. 51. Dakar: l'institut Français d'Afrique Noire.

Verger, Pierre. 1976. *Trade Relations between the Bight of Benin and Bahia from the Seventeenth to Nineteenth Century*. Trans. Evelyn Crawford. Ibadan, Nigeria: Ibadan University Press.

Verger, Pierre. 1995. Letter to the author from Salvador, Bahia, 25 May.

Villaverde, Cirilo. 1992/1882. *Cecilia Valdés o La Loma del Ángel*. Madrid: Ediciones Cátedra.

Waddell, Rev. Hope Masterton. 1846–1855. *Journal of the Calabar Mission, Kept by the Rev. Hope M. Waddell*. MSS 7739-43, 6 vols. National Library of Scotland, Manuscripts Division.

Waddell, Rev. Hope Masterton. 1863. *Twenty-Nine Years in the West Indies and Central Africa: A Review of Missionary Work and Adventure, 1829–1858*. London: T. Nelson and Sons.

Walker, James Broom. 1871–1872. Note on the Old Calabar and Cross Rivers. *Proceedings of the Royal Geographical Society of London* 16(2): 135–137.

Walker, James Broom. 1877. Notes on the politics, religion and commerce of Old Calabar. *Journal of the Anthropological Institute of Great Britain and Ireland* 6(April): 119–124.

Ward, Rev. William James. 1911. *In and Around the Oron Country; or The Story of Primitive Methodism in Southern Nigeria*. London: W. A. Hammond.

Warner-Lewis, Maureen. 1991. *Guinea's Other Suns: The African Dynamic in Trinidad Culture*. Dover, MA: Majority Press.

Warnier, Jean-Pierre. 1985. *Échanges, développement et hiérarchies dans le Bamenda pré-colonial (Cameroun)*. Stuttgart: Franz Steiner Verlag Wiesbaden.

Watts, Pauline Moffitt. 1985. Prophecy and discovery: on the spiritual origins of Christopher Columbus's "Enterprise of the Indies." *American Historical Review* 90 (February): 73–102.

Weber, Max. 1968. *Economy and Society: An Outline of Interpretive Sociology*. Vol. 1. Ed. Guenther Roth and Claus Wittich, Trans. Ephraim Fischoff and others. Berkeley: University of California Press.

Weeks, John H. 1969/1914. *Among the Primitive Bakongo: A Record of Thrity Years' Close Intercourse with the Bakongo and Other Tribes of Equatorial Africa, with a Description of Their Habits, Customs and Religious Beliefs*. New York: Negro University Press.

Wells, Sharon. 1982. *Forgotten Legacy: Blacks in Nineteenth Century Key West*. Key West, FL: Historical Key West Preservation Board.

Williams, Gomer. 1897. *History of the Liverpool Privateers and Letters of Marque with an Account of the Liverpool Slave Trade*. London: William Heinemann.

Wood, Peter H. 1974. *Black Majority: Negroes in Colonial South Carolina from 1670 through the Stono Rebellion*. New York: Alfred Knopf.

Wurdeman, John G. 1844. *Notes on Cuba, Containing an Account of Its Discovery and Early History: A Description of the Face of the Country, Its Population, Resources, and Wealth; Its Institutions, and the Manners and Customs of Its Inhabitants, with Directions to Travelers Visiting the Island; by a Physician*. Boston: J. Munroe and Co.

Zanetti Lecuona, Oscar, and Alejandro García Alvarez. 1987. *Caminos para el azucar*. Havana: Editorial de ciencias sociales.

Zöller, Hugh. 1885. Batanga River, West Africa. *Scottish Geographical Magazine* 1: 387–388.

Audio Recordings

Álvarez, Adalberto. 1979. "Se quema la trocha." *A Bayamo en coche*. Grupo Son 14. Areito/Egrem LD-3834.

Barroso, Abelardo, con la Orquesta Sensación. 1996. "El guarjiro de Cunagua" (Guaguancó-Afro), by Juana González. *No hay como mi son: 1954–1956*. Carney.

Caignet, Félix B. 1993. "Carabalí." *Hot Music from Cuba 1907–1936*. Recorded by Ronda Lirica Oriental in 1928. Harlequin HQ CD 23.

Chano Pozo: el tambor de Cuba, vida y música del legendario rumbero cubano. 2001. Vols. 1–3. Tumbao Cuban Classics TCD 305.

Clave y Guaguancó. 1996. "Chévere," composed by Santos Ramírez. *Dejala en la puntica*. Recorded in Egrem Studios, Havana. Egrem CD 0211.

Conjunto de Percusión de Danza Nacional de Cuba. 1987. "Encame de Abakuá (Efó-Efí)." *Oba-Ilu. Homenaje: Jesús Pérez in Memoriam*. Egrem/Areito.

Conjunto Folklórico Nacional. 1964. "Cantos de Wemba," Goyo Hernández lead voice. *Conjunto Folklórico Nacional*. Areito LDA-3156. [Released as Grupo Folklórico de Cuba. "Canto de Wemba." *Toques y Cantos de Santos*, Vol. 2. Cubilandia C-CD 513.]

Conjunto Rumbavana. 1985. "A Belén le toca ahora," written by Arsenio Rodríguez, arranged by Joseíto González, recorded in Santiago de Cuba. *Cuban Gold 5*. Qbadisc QB 9027.

Coro Folklórico Cubano. 2001. "Marcha Abakuá." *En un solar habanero*. Recorded 1996 in Areito Studios, Havana. Egrem CD 0424.

Courlander, Harold. 1949. *Cult Music of Cuba*. Recorded in 1940. Ethnic Folkways Library Fe4410/Asch 78 rpm.

Ékpè Ita. 1975. "San Ikese Ekpabrukim," Ima Edi Obio Group. *"Ase"–Traditional*. Philips LP 6361-109. [Made in Nigeria.]

Ékpè Ita. 1976. "Ifot Ufok Etemi," Ima Edi Obio Group. *"Ase"–Traditional*. Vol. 2. Produced and directed by Chief Inyang Henshaw. Philips LP 6361-187.

Embale, Carlos. 1975. "Y a Matanzas," with Ines María. *Conjunto Guaguancó*. Egrem/Areito LDS-3428.

Embale, Carlos. 1992. "María la O," "Con su guaragura." *Rumbero Mayor*. Egrem CD NC 61-15.

Embale, Carlos. 1994. "Consuélate como yo," written by "Tío Tom." Recorded in 1950s, Havana. *Afro-Cuba: A Musical Anthology*. Rounder C 1088.

Festival in Havana. 2003. Arranged by Ignacio Piñiero. Recorded in Havana with the supervision of Odilio Urfé and the Instituto Musical de Investigaciones Folklóricas, spring 1955. Milestone Records MCD 9337-2. [See also Urfé, 1960s.]

Grupo AfroCuba. 1998. "Bríkamo," "Abakuá." *Raíces Africanas/African Roots*. Recorded February 1996, Egrem Studios, Havana. Shanachie 66009.

Grupo Afro-Cubano de Alberto Zayas. 1950s. "Acere," "Angoa." *Afro-Frenetic: Tambores de Cuba*. Panart Recording Corp. LP-3053.

Grupo Afro-Cubano de Alberto Zayas. 2001. "Que me critiquen" (Guaguancó), "El Yambú de los Barrios." *El Yambú de los Barrios*. Recorded in Havana 1955–1956. Tumbao Cuban Classics 708 D.L.B. 42350/2001.

Ibiono. 2001. Caribe Productions, produced by Dagoberto A. González Jr. Recorded in Havana, 2001. Caribe Productions CD 9607.

Kubik, Gerhard. 1962. *Yoruba Talking Instruments*. Transcription Feature Service [Schomburg Center, New York Public Library, Sc Audio C-21, side 2, no. 2].

La Música del pueblo de Cuba: Claves, rumbas y comparsas. 1972. "Canto Abakuá," "Marcha Abakuá," performed by Victor Herrera, guía, y su grupo. Recorded in situ in 1960 by Argeliers León. Arieto LP 3440, 3441. [Two LP set is a collection of recordings, in situ and in studio, recorded from 1950 to 1972.]

Lemba Kongo Muna Kongo. 2002. "Ngo saludando batalla," with musicians Ramon "Muerto Vivo," Felix "Pupy" Insua, Mario "Salsa" Insua, Román Díaz. Produced by Hector Delgado. Not released officially. Bronx, New York.

María Romeu, Antonio. 1996. "Chévere Macunchevere," composed by Estanislao Serviá. *Antonio María Romeu: Danzones*. Egrem CD0166.

Marquetti, Cheo. 1939. "Efí Embemoro" (Afro-Ñáñigo), written, lead vocals, and maracas by Cheo Marquetti. *Septeto Cauto: Congo se divierte*. Recorded in Havana. Tumbao TCD 113.

Méndez, Silvestre, y su tribu Afrocubana. 1957. *Bembé Araguá*. RCA Victor V-MKS-1361.

Mongo Santamaria. 1953. "Abacua Ecu Sagare," "Caumbia (rumba columbia)," "Consejo al vive bien." *Chango: Afrocuban Drums*. LP-1037. [Reissued in 2002 by Sonido.]

Mongo Santamaria. 2003. "Afro Blue." *Live at Jazz Alley*. Recorded in 1990. Rereleased by Concord Records SACD-1016-6.

Muñequitos de Matanzas, Los. 1977. "La viola," by Florencio Calle. Recorded in Havana. Egrem/Areito LD-3701.

Muñequitos de Matanzas, Los. 1983. "Lo que dice el Abacuá," "Abakuá #3." *Guaguancó/Columbia/Yambú*. Recorded at Estudio Siboney, Santiago de Cuba, 15–17 November 1983. Rereleased by Qbadisc QB9014.

Muñequitos de Matanzas, Los. 1995. "Wenva." *Vacunao*. Qbadisc QB 9017.

Muñequitos de Matanzas, Los. 1999. "Yumurí (Yamorí)." *Rumba Abierta*. Guaguancó matancero. Cuban Classics IV. Recorded in the late 1950s. Latino WSCD-4205.

Muñequitos de Matanzas, Los. 2001. "Ritmo Abacua," "La plegaria," by Florencio Calle. *Guaguancó Matancero*. Recorded in Havana 1956–1963. Tumbao TCD 707.

Muñequitos de Matanzas, Los. 2003. "La llave." *Rumberos de corazon: 50 aniversario*. Pimienta Records.

Musica afrocubana. 1993. "Encame," performed by Victor Herrera, guía, y su grupo. *Viejos cantos afrocubanos: antología de la música afrocubana*. Vol. 1. Recorded in situ in 1962 by Algiers León. Egrem C 3325.

Nka Asian Mkparawa Eburutu: Cultural Group Calabar. 1981. Director Etubom Asuquo Etim, Obong Nyamkpe of Efe Ékpè Eyo Ema. Ekondo Records ERLP 001.

Orquesta Antonio María Romeu. n.d. "Chévere Macumchevere," composed by Estanislao Serviá. *El Danzón*. Recorded 1960. Egrem LD 3037.

Patato y Totico. 1967. "Ya Yo E," "Rezo Abacua," "Nuestro barrio." Recorded 19 September 1967 in New York City. Original, Verve V6-5037; second release, MDC-10065.

Peña, Enrique. 1982. "El ñáñigo." *The Cuban Danzon: Its Ancestors and Descendants*. Ethnic Folkways Records FE 4066.

Piñeiro, Ignacio. c. 1925–1928. "Iyamba bero" (clave ñáñiga). Performed by Cruz, Bienvenido y Villalón. Columbia 2421-X (93950), 78 rpm.

Rodríguez, Arsenio. 1968. "Como se goze en el barrio." *Primitivo*. Recorded in New York City. Tico.

Rodríguez, Arsenio. 1995. "Canto Abacuá." *Leyendas/Legends: Quindembo–Afro Magic. La magia de Arsenio Rodríguez*. Recorded in 1963 in New York City. Sony Tropical DIC 81534/4-469742.

Rodríguez, Arsenio. 2003. *Los barrios de La Habana*. Orfeon CDL-16400.

Rodríguez, Arsenio, y su conjunto. 1957. "Adorenla como a Martí," composed by A. Rodríguez. *Sabroso y caliente*. Recorded in 1957 in New York City. Re-edited on Antilla CD-586.

Rodríguez, Arsenio, y su conjunto. 1992. "Como se goza en el barrio," composed by A. Rodríguez. Recorded in 1953 in New York City. Tumbao TCD 022.

Rodríguez, Arsenio, y su conjunto. 1993/1946–1950. "Juventud Amaliana," by Arsenio Rodríguez; "El Cerro tiene la llave," by Fernando Noa-Dominguez. Recorded in 1946 and 1948. *Montuneando con Arsenio Rodríguez*. Tumbao TCD 031. [The composer's names are listed on the *A todos los barrios*, BMG LP 3336-2-RL.]

Rodríguez, Arsenio, y su conjunto. 1994. "Los Sitios Hacere" (guaguancó), composed by Silvio A. Pino. *Dundunbanza: 1946–1951*. Recorded 6 September 1949. Tumbao TCD 043.

Rumboleros: La Protesta Carabalí. 2004. "Protesta Carabalí," by Pedro Vero Alfonso. Recorded in 1975 in Havana. Envidia B60 6325.

Sexteto Habanero. 1995. "Criolla Carabali," written by Guillermo Castillo. *Sexteto Habanero 1926–1931*. Recorded 29 May 1928, New York. Harlequin HQ CD 53.

Sierra Maestra. 1994. "Criolla Carabalí." *Con Sabor a Cuba*. Egrem 0084.

"Tumbando Caña." 2003. Santos Ramírez, composer. *Festival in Havana*. Recorded in 1955, arranged by Ignacio Piñeiro, supervised by OdilioUrfé. Remastered in 2003 by Fantasy Studios, Berkeley, CA. Milestone MCD 9337-2.

Urfé, Odilio. 1960s. "A Malanga," "La Chambelona," "Tumba la caña." *La Rumba y La Conga*. Recorded in 1955. ICIAC IC-508.

Van Van, Los. 1999. "Appapas del Calabar." *Llegó . . . Van Van*. Havana caliente–Atlantic 832227-2.

Vera, María Teresa. 1994. "En la alta sociedad," written by Ignacio Piñeiro. *Veinte Años*. Recorded in 1956. Egrem CD 0056.

Vera, María Teresa. 1998. "Los cantares del Abacuá," written by Ignacio Piñeiro. *María Teresa Vera y Rafael Zequeira: El legendario dúo de la trova cubana*. Recorded in 1923. Historical Recordings 1916–1924. Tumbao TCD 090.

"Wemba." 1994. Victor Herrera, lead voice. *Viejos cantos afrocubanos: antología de la música afrocubana*. Vol. 1. Recorded in Havana in situ in 1962 by Algiers León. Egrem C 3325. [Rereleased as *Afro-Cuba: A Musical Anthology*, Rounder C 1088.]

Yoruba Andabo: Del Yoruba al Son. 1997. "Enyenisón Enkama 2" (D.R.), arrangement and lead voice Ogduardo "Román" Díaz Anaya. *La isla de la música*, vol. 6. Magic Music/Universal CD FMD 75141.

Yoruba Andabo: el callejón de los rumberos. 1993. "Enyenisón Enkama *Africa habla*" (Abakuá), "Protesta Carabalí." Arrangement of traditional material and lead voice Ogduardo "Román" Díaz Anaya. Recorded in Egrem Studios, Havana, 1992. CDPm Records 2039.

Film and Video

"Afrique, je te plumerai" (Africa, I will fleece you). 1992. Jean-Marie Teno, director. Cameroon: California Newsreel. 88 minutes. In French with English subtitles.

"El Alacrán" (The Scorpion). 1999. Gloria Rolando, director. Havana: TV Latina/Imagenes del Caribe. 20 minutes.

"La Rumba: de donde viene la rumba" (The Rumba: Where does it come from?). 1978. Oscar Valdés, director. Written by Julio García Espinosa. Odilio Urfé, musical advisor. With Celeste Mendoza, Manuela Alonso, Carlos Embale, Muñequitos de Matanzas, et al. Havana: Instituto Cubano de Artes e Industrias Cinematograficos.

"Orígenes desde el Changuí" (Origins of the Changuí). 1986. Roberto Román and Danilo Orozco, producers and directors. Recorded in Guantanamo in the 1970s with Rafael Inciarte (1909–1991), investigador y músico. Havana: Instituto Cubano de radio y televisión Tele Turquino. Videocassette. 26 minutes.

INDEX

...

Àbàkpà (Qua Ejagham), 3, 6, 175, 215, 221n5, 234n10

Abakuá, xv, xvii, xix, xx, 3, 7, 8, 9, 14, 17, 70, 136
  aesthetic competition during rites, 113
  as alternative model for transmission of African ethnicity, 106–7, 116, 118, 171, 177
  "Anglo-Saxon" observer of, 116
  in anti-colonial movements, 34, 64, 82, 107, 121, 129, 150, 170, 171, 176
  attempt to found lodge in Miami, Fla., 133–34
  based upon Ékpè models, 3, 24, 28, 40, 51, 65, 68, 73, 82, 139, 175, 197, 204
  and *black curros*, 34, 70, 75, 79, 80–82, 87, 88, 113, 156, 251n115
  black members, 16, 18, 110, 112, 143
  branches of knowledge within, 21, 30
  in Calabar, 179–82
  and carnival groups, 89, 128, 161–63, 165, 173, 174
  ceremonies: follow planetary movement, 62–63; as theater, 4, 9, 116
  chants: in epic form, 194; language, 3, 7, 11, 12, 24, 30, 34, 39, 43, 54, 92, 110, 128, 138, 153, 161, 201–13, 280n3; used to map source regions, 9, 224n43, 261n133
  Chinese creoles, joining of, 117
  coded handshakes, 130, 249n51
  collective nature of rites, 134, 138
  as collective practice, 4, 20, 29, 43, 64, 82, 118, 137–39, 141
  compared to mafia, 25
  compared to Rastafarian elders and scholars of Judaic Talmud, 30
  as conduit for international communications, 85
  contemporary members reaction to Ékpè, xix, 33, 55, 178, 179–82
  as criminals, 24, 123, 136, 144, 160, 228n90
  "crossing staff" between lodges, 116, 125, 171, 268n43
  in Cuban National Army, 191
  and Cuban popular music, 7, 8, 14, 35, 36, 125, 153–74, 178
  cultural change engineered by Abakuá leaders, 104–5, 111, 115–16, 118
  debate over use of precious metals for ritual objects, 111–13, 265n55
  declared illegal, 1875, 24, 35, 122, 139, 140, 142, 151, 192
  as defended by non-initiates, 47
  as defense system for black communities, 70, 72, 73, 167, 173, 177, 287n123
  disguise practices, 144–45, 160, 210
  as dock workers, 16, 19, 22, 24, 70–71, 74, 83–85, 86, 88, 150, 165, 286n101, 292n36
  each lodge has distinct traditions, 112–13
  ekóbios, okóbios, brothers, 11, 44, 94, 99, 107, 120, 171, 184, 187, 202, 216, 233n156, 237n60, 288n131
  and Ékpè music, 197
  elders as scholars, 16, 24, 29–30, 31, 41, 43
  "embarking point," beachhead of, 58–59, 63, 93, 96, 183, 256n29, 262n141
  "encerronas," 64
  as enriched through cultural contact, 5
  executed during the Conspiracy of La Escalera (1844), 85
  expansion into Matanzas, 59, 85, 98–100, 282n34
  family traditions within, 165, 230n115